T&T CLARK COMPANION TO LITURGY

T&T CLARK COMPANION TO LITURGY

Edited by Alcuin Reid

t&t clark

LONDON · NEW YORK · OXFORD · NEW DELHI · SYDNEY

T&T CLARK
Bloomsbury Publishing Plc
50 Bedford Square, London, WC1B 3DP, UK
1385 Broadway, New York, NY 10018, USA
29 Earlsfort Terrace, Dublin 2, Ireland

BLOOMSBURY, T&T CLARK and the T&T Clark logo
are trademarks of Bloomsbury Publishing Plc

First published in Great Britain 2016
Paperback edition first published 2021

A catalogue record for this book is available from the British Library.

Library of Congress Cataloging-in-Publication Data
T&T Clark companion to liturgy: the western Catholic tradition / edited by Alcuin Reid.
pages cm
Includes bibliographical references and index.
ISBN 978-0-567-03442-7 (hardback)
1. Catholic Church–Liturgy–History. 2. Liturgics. I. Reid, Alcuin, editor. II. Title: T & T
Clark companion to liturgy.
BX1970.T25 2016
264'.02–dc23
2015018446

ISBN: HB: 978-0-56703-442-7
PB: 978-0-5677-0112-1
ePDF: 978-0-56766-577-5
eBook: 978-0-56766-578-2

Typeset by RefineCatch Limited, Bungay, Suffolk

*In profound gratitude for the liturgical example and
teaching of Pope Benedict XVI*

CONTENTS

Part V
A–Z OF THE STUDY OF CATHOLIC LITURGY

ABBREVIATIONS

AAS	*Acta Apostolicae Sedis* (Vatican City: Typis Polyglottis Vaticanis, 1909–).
BELS	Bibliotheca *Ephemerides Liturgicae: Subsidia* (Rome: Edizioni Liturgiche—Centro Liturgico Vincenziano, 1974–).
CCC	*Catechism of the Catholic Church* (rev. edn), (London: Burns & Oates, 1999).
CCCM	Corpus Christianorum Continuatio Mediaevalis (Turnhout: Brepols, 1966–).
CCL	Corpus Christianorum series Latina (Turnhout: Brepols, 1953–).
CSEL	Corpus Scriptorum Ecclesiasticorum Latinorum (Österreichischen Akademie der Wissenschaften: Vienna, 1866–).
CT	Görres-Gesellschaft Soc. (eds), *Concilium Tridentinum: Diarorum, Actorum, Epistolarum, Tractatuum nova collectio*, 16 vols., (Herder: Freiburg im Breisgau, 1901–80).
DACL	F. Cabrol, H. Leclercq & H.I. Marrou (eds), *Dictionnaire d'archéologie Chrétienne et de liturgie* (Paris: Letouzey et Ané, 1924–53).
DOL	ICEL, *Documents on the Liturgy: 1963–1979* (Collegeville: Liturgical Press, 1982).
DZ	Heinrich Denzinger, Peter Hünermann, Robert Fastiggi & Anne Nash (eds), *Enchiridion symbolorum definitionem et declarationem de rebus fidei et morum*, 43rd edn, Latin-English (San Francisco Ignatius Press, 2012).
ET	English translation.
HBS	Henry Bradshaw Society (London: Harrison & Sons, 1891–).
JRCW 11	*Joseph Ratzinger—Collected Works Vol. 11: Theology of the Liturgy* (San Francisco: Ignatius, 2014).
MLCT	Monumenta Liturgia Concilii Tridentina, M. Sodi & A.M. Triacca (eds), 6 vols (Vatican City: Libreria Editrice Vaticana, 1997–2005).
MLP	Monumenta Liturgica Piana, M. Sodi, A. Toniolo & P. Bruylants (eds), 5 vols (Vatican City: Libreria Editrice Vaticana, 2007–10).
MSIL	Monumenta Studia Instrumenta Liturgica, M. Sodi & A.M. Triacca (eds), (Vatican City: Libreria Editrice Vaticana, 2000–).
NL	Kevin Seasoltz, OSB (ed.), *The New Liturgy: A Documentation 1903–1965* (New York: Herder, 1966).
PL	Jacques Paul Migne (ed.), *Patrologia Latina* (Paris, 1841–55).
SC	*Sources Chrétiennes* (Paris: Éditions du Cerf, 1942–).
ST	*Studi e Testi* (Vatican City: Biblioteca Apostolica Vaticana, 1900–).

LIST OF CONTRIBUTORS

Anthony Chadwick was born in the north of England in an Anglican family and educated at St Peter's School in York. He read theology at Fribourg University in Switzerland, where he wrote his Licentiate thesis on the Roman liturgy at and after the Council of Trent under the tutorship of Fr Jakob Baumgartner. He is particularly interested in the Use of Sarum and the history of the liturgy in the late Middle Ages and the onset of the Renaissance. He serves as a priest in the Anglican Catholic Church and works as a freelance technical translator.

†**Anscar J. Chupungco OSB** (1939–2013), was a priest-monk of the Abbey of Our Lady of Montserrat in Manila. He held the position of President of the Pontifical Liturgical Institute in Rome where he taught history of the liturgy and liturgical inculturation. He established the Paul VI Institute of Liturgy in the Philippines for continuing liturgical formation and was its director. He served as Executive Secretary of the Philippine Episcopal Commission on Liturgy for eighteen years and was Secretary of the Asian Liturgy Forum. For fifteen years he served as consultant to the Congregation for Divine Worship. For ten years he was a member of the Advisory Committee of the International Commission on English in the Liturgy. He edited the *Handbook for Liturgical Studies* in five volumes (Collegeville, 1997–2000) and published numerous liturgical works, especially on inculturation.

† **Lázló Dobszay** (1935–2011) studied music at the Franz Liszt Academy of Music in Budapest. He also studied at the Lóránd Eötvös University in Budapest where he acquired a profound knowledge of literature and history. Dobszay was active as a young composer and involved in the movement concerned with reforms in Hungarian music education. He became part of the Folk Music Research Group at the Hungarian Academy of Sciences in 1966. In 1970 he joined the faculty at the Franz Liszt Academy and co-founded the *Schola Hungarica*. In 1976 he accepted the post of director of the early music department at the Hungarian Academy of Sciences' Institute for Musicology. He was one of the leading Hungarian conductors of chant and early Christian liturgical music and also one of the foremost Hungarian scholars in chant and modern liturgical music. His 2003 book *The Bugnini Liturgy and the Reform of the Reform* received wide attention in liturgical circles. This was followed by *The Restoration and Development of the Roman Rite* in 2010.

David W. Fagerberg is associate professor in the Department of Theology at the University of Notre Dame, and senior advisor to the Notre Dame Center for Liturgy after serving as director. He holds an MDiv from Luther Northwestern Seminary;

an MA from St John's University, Collegeville; an STM from Yale Divinity School; and a PhD from Yale University. He is a member of the Society for Catholic Liturgy, and the North American Academy for Liturgy. His work has explored how the Church's *lex credendi* (law of belief) is founded upon the Church's *lex orandi* (law of prayer). He has published articles on liturgical theology in various academic journals, and is the author of *Theologia Prima* (2003), *The Size of Chesterton's Catholicism* (1998), *What is Liturgical Theology?* (1992). Forthcoming is a collection of his essays on liturgical theology, a collection of his Chesterton essays from *Gilbert*. His monograph *On Liturgical Asceticism* was published in 2013.

Ben Gordon-Taylor, BA MA PhD (Dunelm), BA (Leeds), FRSA, is an Anglican priest. He teaches liturgy at the College of the Resurrection, Mirfield, and is Director of the Mirfield Liturgical Institute. He is Editorial Secretary of the Alcuin Club and Chair of the Society for Liturgical Study. He has co-edited, co-authored or contributed to a number of works on liturgical topics. He served in parishes in Cornwall and Northampton and then as Solway Fellow and chaplain of University College, Durham. He was educated at the universities of Durham and Leeds, gaining research degrees in history and in theology. His research interests include the concept of mystery in Western liturgy, liturgical theology and the properties and function of liturgical text. His publications include contributions to the Mirfield symposium *Priests in a People's Church* and *Companion to Common Worship* vols 1 & 2 (Alcuin Club/SPCK), as well as a number of journal articles and reviews. Since 2005, he has co-authored three Alcuin liturgy guides, and co-edited a book on the life and thought of Walter Frere for Canterbury Press.

Paul Gunter OSB, a priest-monk of Douai Abbey, England, gained a doctorate in Sacred Liturgy from the Pontifical Institute of Liturgy, Rome, in 2006 for a thesis entitled "Edmund Bishop and the Genius of the Roman Rite," after which he joined the faculty of the Institute where he is currently a Professor. From 2008–13 he was a consultant of the Office of Liturgical Celebrations of the Supreme Pontiff and from 2012 has been the Secretary of the Department for Christian Life and Worship of the Bishops' Conference of England and Wales.

Bruce Harbert was the Executive Director of the International Committee on English in the Liturgy (ICEL) from 2002–9. He gained a BA in English from Peterhouse, Cambridge, in 1966, with specialization in Medieval English and Medieval Latin and an MPhil in Medieval English from Merton College, Oxford, in 1968 with specialization in Medieval Latin. He received a BA in Philosophy from the Pontifical Gregorian University in 1975 and an STB from the Pontifical Gregorian University in 1978. In 1982 he received his STL from the Pontifical Institute of St Augustine. Monsignor Harbert has been Priest in Charge, Parish of St Anne, Streetly, West Midlands from 1996–2002, Catholic Chaplain at the University of Sussex from 1983–9 and Associate Pastor, Parish of Caterham, Surrey, 1981–83. His teaching experience includes terms as Paluch Lecturer, University of St Mary of the Lake/Mundelein Seminary, 2002; lecturer in Dogmatic Theology, St

Mary's College, Oscott, 1989–98; and lecturer in English Language and Medieval Literature, Mansfield, Merton, and Worcester Colleges, Oxford, 1968–74. He currently serves as a parish priest in the Archdiocese of Birmingham.

Robert Hayward is Professor of Hebrew in the Department of Theology and Religion, University of Durham, UK. His research focuses on Second Temple and Early Rabbinic Judaism, and ancient Jewish Bible Interpretation. He has contributed two essays to *The New Cambridge History of the Bible* edited by J. Carleton Paget and J. Schaper (Cambridge, 2013), "The Aramaic Targums" (pp. 218–41) and "Scripture in the Jerusalem Temple" (pp. 321–44). His most recent publication is "God as Father in the Pentateuchal Targumim: The Case of Abraham's Garden at Be'er Sheba", in (eds) T. Legrand and J. Joosten, *The Targums in the Light of Traditions of the Second Temple Period* (Brill: Leiden, 2014), pp. 97–119. He teaches Hebrew, Aramaic, and Syriac in the University of Durham.

Yitzhak Hen is Anna and Sam Lopin Professor of History at Ben-Gurion University of the Negev, Israel. He has published many books and articles on Merovingian and Carolingian history, the intellectual and religious culture of the post-Roman Barbarian kingdoms of Western Europe, early medieval liturgy, and early medieval manuscripts, including *Culture and Religion in Merovingian Gaul, 481–751* (1995), *The Sacramentary of Echternach* (1997), *The Royal Patronage of Liturgy in Frankish Gaul to the Death of Charles the Bald* (2001), *Roman Barbarians: The Royal Court and Culture in the Early Medieval West* (2007). He is Life Member of Clare Hall (University of Cambridge), and was Fellow in Residence at the Netherlands Institute for Advanced Study in the Humanities and Social Sciences (2000–1) and the Princeton Institute for Advanced Study (2012–13). Professor Hen is currently working on a study of Western Arianism, and he serves as General Editor of the series *Cultural Encounters in Late Antiquity and the Middle Ages* (Brepols).

Thomas M. Kocik (b. 1965) is a Catholic priest of the Diocese of Fall River, Massachusetts, where he has worked primarily in parish ministry. He is the author of *Apostolic Succession in an Ecumenical Context* (Alba House, 1996), *The Reform of the Reform? A Liturgical Debate* (Ignatius Press, 2003), *Loving and Living the Mass* (Zaccheus Press, 2007; 2nd edn, 2011), *The Fullness of Truth: Catholicism and the World's Major Religions* (Newman House Press, 2013), and many published articles, book reviews, and homilies. In addition, he has contributed several series of articles to his diocesan newspaper, *The Anchor*, including one on the Liturgical Movement and another on the Second Vatican Council. He is a member of the Society for Catholic Liturgy and former editor of its peer-reviewed journal *Antiphon*.

Uwe Michael Lang, born 1972 in Nuremberg, Germany, is a member of the Congregation of the Oratory of St Philip Neri in London, where he serves as Parish Priest. He holds a doctorate in theology from Oxford and is a Lecturer in Theology at Heythrop College in the University of London. He was a staff member of the Pontifical Commission for the Cultural Heritage of the Church (2007–8) and of the

Congregation for Divine Worship and the Discipline of the Sacraments (2008–12), as well as a Consultor to the Office for the Liturgical Celebrations of the Supreme Pontiff (2008–13). Since 2007 he has taught at the Master's course in "Architecture, Sacred Art and Liturgy" at the Università Europea di Roma/Ateneo Pontificio Regina Apostolorum. From 2008–11 he was Coordinator of the Master's programme. In the academic year 2011–12 he was *Professore incaricato* for the history of Christian worship and hagiography at the Pontifical Institute for Christian Archeology in Rome. He has published on Patristic and liturgical studies, including his book *Turning Towards the Lord: Orientation in Liturgical Prayer* (2nd edition, San Francisco, 2009), which came out first in German in 2003 with a preface by then-Cardinal Joseph Ratzinger and has since been translated into various languages. His most recent works are *The Voice of the Church at Prayer: Reflections on Liturgy and Language* (San Francisco: Ignatius, 2012) and *Signs of the Holy One* (San Francisco: Ignatius, 2015).

James Leachman is a priest-monk of St Benedict's Abbey, Ealing in London. After having been a monk of Nashdom Abbey, he entered the full communion of the Catholic Church and the novitiate of St Benedict's community in Ealing in 1985. He now teaches and writes in Rome and Great Britain. Dom James studied theology at Heythrop College in the University of London and then liturgy at the Pontifical Liturgical Institute, Rome. He returned to Rome in 2002 to teach and is now assistant tenured professor and assistant editor of *Ecclesia Orans*. He edited the volume *The Liturgical Subject: Subject, Subjectivity and the Human Person in Contemporary Liturgical Discussion And Critique* (2009) and has written articles in *Ecclesia Orans, Studia Liturgica, New Blackfriars, Sewanee Theological Review* and *Questions Liturgiques*. He serves also as visiting professor at the Catholic University of Leuven and on the editorial board of *Questions Liturgiques: Studies in Liturgy*. With Dom Daniel McCarthy, Dom James is co-founder and co-director of the *Appreciating the Liturgy* research and publishing project (2007) and more recently of the *Institutum Liturgicum in Anglia et Cambria* (2011), the latter of which is endorsed by the Catholic Bishops' Conference of England and Wales and offers a Summer Liturgy programme validated by the Catholic University of Leuven. He is co-editor, with Dom Daniel, of the corpus « Documenta Rerum Ecclesiasticarum Instaurata » series *Liturgiam Aestimare: Appreciating the Liturgy.*

James Monti graduated *Summa cum laude* from Saint Thomas Aquinas College in Sparkill, New York, USA with a BA degree in English (1982). As an author and a researcher in the fields of Catholic liturgy and hagiography, he has contributed numerous articles to Catholic publications. His books include *A Sense of the Sacred: Roman Catholic Worship in the Middle Ages* (Ignatius, 2012), *The King's Good Servant But God's First: The Life and Writings of St. Thomas More* (Ignatius, 1997) and *The Week of Salvation: History and Traditions of Holy Week* (Our Sunday Visitor, 1993). He is presently working toward the completion of a comprehensive work on the liturgical ceremonies of the Roman and other western rites as they were celebrated both universally and locally following the Council of Trent, during the "Baroque Era" (c. 1568–1799).

Timothy McDonnell is a musician living in Southwest Florida. Formerly on the faculty of music at Ave Maria University, he currently serves as the Artistic Director of the Symphonic Chorale of Southwest Florida. Before arriving in Florida, he served as master of the Music Chapel at the Pontifical North American College in the Vatican. He holds the Master of Music degree in choral conducting from Yale University, and the Doctor of Musical Arts degree in orchestral conducting from the University of South Carolina. Dr. McDonnell recently made his conducting debut with the Naples Philharmonic in three performances of Haydn's *The Creation* using a new translation of the German that he modeled on the Miltonian language of the original sources. Besides his American credits, has conducted in Italy, the Czech Republic and China and is very active as a composer and arranger.

Alcuin Reid is a monk of the Monastère Saint-Benoît in the Diocese of Fréjus-Toulon, France. After studies in Theology and in Education in Melbourne, Australia, he was awarded a PhD from King's College, University of London, for a thesis on twentieth-century liturgical reform (2002), which was subsequently published as *The Organic Development of the Liturgy* with a preface by Joseph Cardinal Ratzinger (Ignatius, 2005). He has lectured internationally and has published extensively on the Sacred Liturgy, including *Looking Again at the Question of the Liturgy with Cardinal Ratzinger* (2003), *The Monastic Diurnal* (2004), *The Ceremonies of the Roman Rite Described* (2009). His new edition of *A Bitter Trial: Evelyn Waugh and John Carmel Cardinal Heenan on the Liturgical Changes*, was published by Ignatius Press in 2011. Dom Alcuin was the principal organizer of Sacra Liturgia 2013, an international conference on the role of liturgical formation and celebration in the life and mission of the Church in Rome in June 2013 and edited its proceedings *Sacred Liturgy: The Source and Summit of the Life and Mission of the Church* (Ignatius, 2014). Dom Alcuin is the international coordinator of the ongoing *Sacra Liturgia* initiatives. He is working on *Continuity or Rupture? A Study of the Second Vatican Council's Reform of the Liturgy.*

Thomas Gordon Smith is a professor of architecture at the University of Notre Dame in Indiana and a practising architect. Mr Smith received the BA in art and the Master of Architecture from the University of California, Berkeley. He won the Rome Prize in Architecture at the American Academy in Rome in 1980. His publications include *Classical Architecture: Rule and Invention*, *Vitruvius on Architecture* (1988), and articles focused on nineteenth-century American architecture and furniture. Professional projects include Our Lady of the Annunciation Benedictine Abbey in Oklahoma and Our Lady of Guadalupe Seminary for the Priestly Fraternity of St Peter in Denton, Nebraska. At Notre Dame he designed the Cedar Grove Mausolea, the renovation of and addition to Bond Hall School of Architecture, and the Alliance for Catholic Education Building. Secular buildings include the Classical Galleries in the American Wing at the Metropolitan Museum of Art, New York; and the University Bookstore and the Student Recreation Complex at California State University, Stanislaus.

Susan Treacy, PhD, joined the faculty of Ave Maria University after having taught at Franciscan University of Steubenville, Luther College, and Emory University, where she was a Mellon Faculty Fellow in the Humanities. She has also been a visiting professor at The Liturgical Institute, University of St Mary of the Lake, Mundelein, Illinois. Dr Treacy holds the PhD in historical musicology from the University of North Texas; her BMus and MMus are from Oberlin Conservatory and the Manhattan School of Music. Her research interests are in Catholic liturgical music and in English devotional song of the sixteenth-eighteenth centuries. Recent articles include "Joseph Bonnet as a Catalyst in the Early Twentieth-Century Gregorian Chant Revival," in *Conference Proceedings from Gregorian Chant and Modern Composition for the Liturgy: Charles Tournemire's* L'Orgue Mystique *as Guide* (Richmond, VA: CMAA, forthcoming), and "A Chronicle of Attitudes towards Gregorian Chant in *Orate Fratres/Worship*, 1926–62," in Paul Collins, ed. *Renewal and Resistance: Catholic Church Music from the 1850s to Vatican II* (Oxford, 2010). Additionally, Dr Treacy is a regular contributor to the *Saint Austin Review*. She was on the editorial committee of *The Adoremus Hymnal* (1997) and is currently on the Board of Directors of the CMAA.

Daniel G. Van Slyke, STL, PhD is Associate Dean of Online Learning and Associate Professor of Theology at Holy Apostles College and Seminary in Cromwell, Connecticut. He has taught and lectured extensively on the graduate and undergraduate level, both in the classroom and online. With degrees in historical theology (PhD, St Louis University), systematic sacramental theology (STL, Mundelein Seminary), and moral theology (MA, University of Dallas), Dr Van Slyke has made numerous contributions to scholarship. His research focuses on ancient Christian worship, with special attention to blessings and exorcisms.

INTRODUCTION

In some ways this is a peculiar book—reflecting the particular state of liturgical scholarship at the beginning of the twenty-first century. Some scholars today retain the view which gained currency in the twentieth century that liturgical developments beyond a given point—roughly the late patristic age—are somehow inauthentic, and regard subsequent (particularly mediaeval) developments as corruptions or decadences of supposedly pristine liturgical forms.[1] Much twentieth-century liturgical writing, reform, innovation, and formation was predicated upon this assumption in the quest to restore supposedly earlier and allegedly purer forms. Combined with the desire, nay insistence, that the Sacred Liturgy be reformed so as to speak to, or reflect the values and interests of that indistinct and fluid entity "modern man," this principle submitted Western Catholic liturgy to what may only be called a crisis of identity in the life of the Church it has never before experienced.

More recent scholarship has reflected the fact that the liturgy has developed organically and in continuity throughout history, adopting new elements and shedding others over the course of generations in response to changing circumstances and particular needs, under the influence of God the Holy Spirit working in the Church. Certainly, liturgical history has seen ritual reform and growth, but nothing like that predicated on the mid-twentieth century "corruption theory." Accordingly, it is not possible to prune-back the supposed "overgrowth" of the liturgy to its primitive form or bare essentials without doing violence to legitimate later developments which have become an integral part of the organic whole. Rather, liturgical reform—and indeed, liturgical scholarship—must respect the organic development of the liturgy in the (equally) grace-filled centuries of the life of the Church. Whilst this in no way precludes proportionate pruning or development—as has been seen throughout the history of Western Catholic liturgy—it does proscribe radical de- and re-construction of a rite or of rites according to prevailing liturgical or theological scholarship, or according to the spirit of the age or the supposed needs of "contemporary man."

The call of the Second Vatican Council (1962–5) for true liturgical *instauratio* (renewal), which is based on sound liturgical theology, floundered somewhat in the ungodly haste to find means to facilitate as much external liturgical participation as could be realized as quickly as possible through the construction of new liturgical rites. Busy participation is not what the Council called for. Immersion in

---

1 Joseph A. Jungmann S.J. (1889–1975), was, perhaps, the most prominent proponent of this theory. For a synopsis of this view and further bibliography see: Alcuin Reid, *The Organic Development of the Liturgy*, 2nd edn (San Francisco: Ignatius Press, 2005), pp. 164–72.

and engagement with the action of Christ in the Sacred Liturgy is. For the former, vernacularization and ritual pedestrianization were essential means to the desired end. For the latter they are not, because Catholic liturgy is (as the Christian East has never forgotten) intrinsically latreutic—it is the worship of Almighty God, not a means of our own self-expression. It is inherently traditional—we receive its forms, we don't construct them. And its pastoral efficacy flows not from the measure it is adapted to our desires, but from the measure we adapt ourselves to its ritual, latreutic demands, and thereby enter into Christ's action in the public worship of His Church.

It is the view of this editor that, insofar as Western Catholic liturgy has deviated from its nature and tradition (and from the genuine reform called for by the Second Vatican Council),[2] remedial measures are urgently necessary. But there are Catholic scholars and liturgists who disagree with such a stance. From the outset it was hoped that this volume, as a guide to students of Western Catholic liturgy, would give voice to scholars of differing viewpoints. To that end Archbishop Piero Marini, John Baldovin SJ, Keith Pecklers SJ, Massimo Faggioli, and John O'Malley SJ were invited to contribute their reasoned perspectives. That they were unable to do so and that their voices are not heard in these pages is regrettable.

Dom Ansgar Chupungco (1939–2013) readily and generously accepted the invitation however, and although he has not lived to see his work appear in print, the editorial promise to respect the integrity of his contributions has been scrupulously observed. This policy necessitates stating clearly that the editor does not necessarily endorse the opinions of the contributors to this volume, just as he does not expect that they endorse his own. Our work stands on its merits and it is thus it should be judged. Therefore: read us critically! If this volume serves to expose uncritically accepted assumptions about the liturgy and facilitate sound liturgical scholarship in the future, it shall have done well. If our readers help to educate us, we shall be in their debt.

We are all in the debt of all the contributors who have so generously given of their time and expertise and who have waited for this volume finally to appear with much patience. Unfortunately another contributor, Professor Lázló Dobszay (1935–2011) died before his contribution was complete or published. With Professor Dobszay's chapter the notes and bibliography are substantially those of the editor, who must beg some indulgence in their regard. For both Dom Ansgar and Professor Dobszay: *Ut lux perpetua luceat eis!*

To so many friends who have assisted with bibliographical research, checked my own translations and contributions, proposed contributors and who generously gave of their advice and time, I am profoundly grateful. So too, I gratefully acknowledge the confidence of T&T Clark's commissioning editor Thomas Kraft,

2 See my discussion of the principles of the Council's Constitution on the Sacred Liturgy in: "Editor's Preface," A. Reid (ed.), *Sacred Liturgy: The Source and Summit of the Life and Mission of the Church* (San Francisco: Ignatius Press, 2014), pp. 7–12.

and of his successors at Bloomsbury who have so professionally seen this volume through to publication.

This volume is intended to be a companion to liturgical studies in the Western Catholic tradition at the beginning of the twenty-first century. As each chapter indicates, a vast body of literature and scholarship exists in this wide-ranging subject. It is my hope that students will find herein a means with which to approach aspects of the study of Western Catholic liturgy that will be academically instructive and practically informative for the good of liturgical scholarship and practice in the twenty-first century.

Dom Alcuin Reid
21 March 2015

Part I

WHAT IS THE LITURGY?

Chapter 1

LITURGICAL THEOLOGY

David W. Fagerberg

Every act of definition is a matter of deciding how broad or narrow to be: in other words, what to leave out. This is no less true when attempting to define the subject matter of liturgical theology, as we will try to do here. Does liturgical theology include sacramental theology, or does that belong to historians and systematicians? Does it include general theological reflection upon prayer, sacrifice, doxology, and acts of worship, or do these topics belong to biblical theology and comparative religious studies? If one makes the boundaries as wide as possible then liturgical theology would seem to include anything having to do with worship, however vaguely, but the field would be indiscernible from general theologies of worship. If one makes the boundaries as narrow as possible, then liturgical theology risks the isolation that comes with specialization, leaving the scholar puzzled about how liturgy relates to theology, and vice versa. Indeed, that puzzlement continues to surround the field of liturgical theology.

In resolving this dilemma, it seems agreed by all that special attention must be paid to the first term in the pair, "liturgy," and doing so has pitched the discussion in a certain direction. The term itself has only re-entered the academic world fairly recently. The Greek term *leitourgia* is ancient, of course, and the liturgical act itself is coextensive with the existence of the Church, but different vocabulary has been used to designate this activity. In classical Greek, *leitourgia* meant a public service undertaken on behalf of the people, and it was a only small stretch to apply this to religious cultic activity.

> As used originally in the Greek cities, "liturgy" could mean any "public service," but especially services that were accepted as done in the name of the city because they were linked to its most vital interests. In a culture permeated by religious values (as most of the traditional cultures were), "liturgy" thus understood was predicated first and foremost of actions expressing the city's relations to the world of divine powers on which it acknowledged itself to be dependent.[1]

However, the Latin vocabulary of the Middle Ages used a different nomenclature.

The Latin Church used terms like *officia divina, opus divinum,* and *sacri* or *ecclesiae ritus.* The use of the word *liturgia* [sic] in the context of the Mass did not appear in the Latin West until the 16th century, thanks to renaissance writers like G. Cassander, J. Pamelius, and J. Bona. For the other forms of worship the old Latin terms continued to be employed. The word appeared for the first time in official Latin documents during the pontificate of Gregory XVI (†1846).[2]

And dusting off the term *leitourgia* for use again left scholarship wondering in what cabinet drawer to file liturgy. Scholarship likes to create taxonomies, and its puzzlement over where liturgy belonged in the reigning taxonomy is seen in an amusing anecdote about Lambert Beauduin, whose speech in 1909 is conveniently called the beginning of the liturgical movement of the twentieth century.

> Cardinal Desire Mercier, president of the congress, wished that liturgy be among the themes treated, and Beauduin was found as a speaker on the topic. Beauduin experienced difficulty in finding a section under which to hold his speech, being rejected three times by the sections on doctrine, morality, and piety. He finally came to be listed under "art" with the subsection "liturgy and religious music."[3]

Answering what Athens has to do with Jerusalem seems easier than answering what theology has to do with liturgy *if* theology is defined as careful and critical thought done by trained minds in the academy, and *if* liturgy is defined as the emotional reaction by ordinary believers to stimuli coming from religious art and music, or defined as a branch of canon law concerned with rubrical infractions, or defined as the varying social patterns that emerge when people worship the Almighty, or defined as pious archeology, or poetic literary criticism, or private esthetics, or simple pastoral care. Is liturgy a theological science? A field called liturgiology emerged that could study liturgy's ritual and ceremonial development by a historical methodology that was acceptable to the academy, but the question how this relates to theology remained. Indeed, there still remains a slight tension between liturgical studies, on the one hand, and sacramental theology, on the other, with most schools wanting to accommodate both, but not necessarily knowing how to integrate them.

The second term of the pair, "theology," is generally assumed to come afterward—after the historian or ritual student has completed his work. This view is expressed by A.G. Martimort when he says, "Scientific liturgical history which was a seventeenth-century creation, showed the clergy and faithful the value and riches of the liturgy, its importance in the Church's tradition, the precise meaning of rites and prayers ..."[4] Then after that, he says, comes the theological step. "The results gained by historians must then become an object of theological study ..."[5] Liturgiology comes first, and theology comes second. This is the way their relationship has generally been framed, with the result that most scholars who identify their field as liturgical theology search for ways to move them closer together.

I submit that scholarship has tried two major methods to connect liturgy and theology: either liturgy is a special approach to theological matters, or else theology is done upon liturgical phenomena. The unlikely pairing of liturgy with theology has been attempted either by connecting liturgy with theology (by showing that it offers new perspectives on familiar theological topics), or by connecting theology with liturgy (by showing that liturgy is a worthy subject of theology's attention). In the first two sections of this chapter I will explore these two approaches and mention a few select authors as examples. I do not try to cover the whole field, but rather mention works illustratively so that readers see a hermeneutical key to the two predominant approaches, and so understand future studies when they appear. However, a different starting point was made by Alexander Schmemann, and so the third section of this chapter will explore a third hermeneutic which rejects the divide between liturgy and theology altogether.

Liturgy as subject matter for theology

It is common in the academy to couple words in order to mark off a certain area for exploration. Under this first hermeneutic, one begins with the latter word (theology) to name a familiar method and the former word (liturgical) names the subject to be studied. Academic theology is accustomed to studying numerous subjects: the bible, Christ, morality, the Church, sin and redemption, the Holy Spirit, angels, etc. and liturgical theology is thought to ensue when one slips the topic of liturgy into the mix. "Liturgical theology" talks about the Christian community's worship in the same way as "biblical theology" talks about the Bible. From the ivory tower, the academic lighthouse trains its spotlight of theology upon a hundred themes dotting the landscape below, and liturgical theology argues that the liturgy should be counted among them.

An argument is thus made to the theologian to include liturgy among his academic reflections, or even, perhaps, begin with liturgy. It is common for this approach to include a methodological apologetic. In *Context and Text*, Kevin Irwin includes the subtitle "Method in Liturgical Theology" to his book, and argues that "Liturgy is an *act of theology* in the sense that its statements and actions are addressed *to* God and are made *about* God." He calls such statements and actions "primary theology," and then claims that primary theology is the subject matter for the discipline he is defining: "*Secondary* theology is reflection on the act of liturgy as primary theology. Generally speaking for our purposes, liturgical theology is secondary theology."[6] In *Models of the Eucharist,* Irwin makes clear the value of liturgy for theology within a heading entitled "A Proposal: Principles for a Liturgical Theology of the Eucharist." The proposal asserts that the Eucharist is normative theologically, liturgically, and spiritually, so his principle says "I want to develop a theology derived from the liturgy (both rites and prayers) . . ."[7] He brings theology and liturgy closer together than they are frequently placed in the academy by claiming it is possible to derive a theology from liturgy, and by defining liturgical theology as reflection on the act of liturgy. In *Holy Things: a Liturgical Theology,* Gordon Lathrop begins with a series of questions that also point the reader straight toward the Church's ritual activities, questions such as: Why do people assemble to sometimes be washed and share a fragment of a meal? What does this gathering mean? And he locates our discipline by saying: "Liturgical theology asks these questions. It inquires into the meaning of the liturgy" and does so especially "by asking how the Christian meeting, in all its signs and words, says something authentic and reliable about God . . ."[8] His apologetic says that theologians who pay attention to liturgical activity will find their efforts rewarded. In *West Syrian Liturgical Theology,* Baby Varghese also starts with the question of meaning: "Christian theology is the search for meaning and the articulation of that meaning. As a theological discipline, liturgical theology aims at the elucidation of the meaning of the liturgy."[9] If theology deals with meaning, and if we are persuaded that liturgy is meaningful activity, then Varghese calls the thoughtful activity that elucidates the liturgy's meaning "liturgical theology." In *Celebrating Divine Mystery,* Catherine Vincie also focuses attention upon the assembly's celebration, which leads her to call the work "A Primer in Liturgical Theology."[10] The list of liturgical activities she places under secondary theological evaluation include the dialogic nature of liturgy, the symbolic nature of liturgy and sacrament, and the relationship between liturgy and culture.

In the above examples, theology takes notice of themes and activities done by a community at worship. That is the sense in which the liturgy is said to be primary: it is the event upon which theology reflects. And the academic's second order reflection is called liturgical theology. A defense of liturgical theology is offered by focusing theology's attention upon what happens in worship, and by proposing liturgy an apt subject for theological study, thus bringing theology and liturgy closer together.

Liturgy as contributing to theological study

There is a second strategy for connecting theology with liturgy, but it reverses the way the two words are connected, and thus reverses what is topic and what is method. Under this second hermeneutic, one begins with the first word (liturgical) to identify a method by which to approach the second word (theology). Thus liturgical theology uses the phenomenon of liturgy to approach theology anew, like narrative theology brings the practice of story-telling to approach theology anew. Adding the modifier "liturgical" to theology can be intended either to say the community should observe how its theology is preserved in ritual form, or to say ecclesiastical ingredients should be added to the academic stew, or even to describe the motivation that a scholar has for doing theology (this theology is doxological, spiritual, and prayerful). But it is especially concerned with seeing how theological subjects are expressed and embodied in a community's liturgical life, and hence a certain emphasis is given to ritual studies. If liturgy is thought to be a species in the genus of ritual, then "ritologists" (as they have taken to calling themselves) might help explain what liturgy adds, and how it works. This approach has proven equally adept at borrowing from earlier figures like Mary Douglas and Victor Turner, or from more recent figures like Catherine Bell and Ronald Grimes, because ritual theory seems somewhat flexible in the hands of its theological users. Theories of rite have proven equally able to explain high, stable, traditionalist liturgies, or explain low, evolving, creative liturgies.

The convergence of historical and ritual approaches has made liturgy a somewhat more neutral category, not confined only to high church traditions, and thus permitted Protestant theologians to pay new attention to liturgy. James Smith is an Evangelical who says that world views are born when our desires and hopes are shaped through participation in embodied rituals. "Liturgies – whether 'sacred' or 'secular' – shape and constitute our identities by forming our most fundamental desires and our most basic attunement to the world."[11] Although his readers must be warned, "Now, you may find yourself a bit skittish about the word sacramental …" they are eventually led to a series of theological truths proposed from an analysis of liturgy's fundamental ritual components. After considering how rituals shape people at the shopping mall, or in the military-entertainment complex, Smith surveys how people are shaped by rituals like the call to worship, confession, creed, sermon, prayer, Eucharist, and the sending forth. Simon Chan is a Pentecostal who tells evangelicals that if they are to overcome their "ecclesiological deficit" they will need to explore the ontology of the church as worshiping community. "It is through worship that the Church is decisively shaped *as* the ecclesial community. That is to say, the church that is the creation of the triune God is also formed by its action of corporate worship."[12] Discovering the theological nature of the Church therefore demands that we consider the shape of the liturgy, and that is what he means by liturgical theology. Chan thinks liturgy is an essential topic because it is the preeminent carrier of Christian theology.

This was a thesis Geoffrey Wainwright announced years ago in *Doxology*. He called his approach a "liturgical way of doing theology" because he was persuaded that the thread of worship must be woven into the fabric of the Church's life and thought. The list of topics in part I are reminiscent of a syllabus in systematic theology (anthropology, Christology, pneumatology, and ecclesiology) but Wainwright opens up new facets of them in part II by "a formal examination of the instruments of Christian tradition, the means by which the vision is transmitted through time."[13] Liturgy is a means of transmitting the vision, and the means should be taken into account while examining the contents. In *Primary Sources of Liturgical Theology*,[14] Dwight Vogel organizes his collection of articles around nine seminal questions with which he feels students of liturgical theology need to engage. After giving his own definition of liturgical theology, he asks how theology and liturgy are to be related, how liturgy can embody theological themes, what the theological function of liturgical language and ritual is, the role of the Word, and liturgy's relationship to cultural diversity, and to life itself. He thinks these theological concerns can be enhanced by paying attention to the liturgical rituals of various Church bodies.

In the above examples, liturgy conveys Christian identity or a doctrinal theme, and therefore merits our theological attention. The focus of liturgical theology, defined this way, is upon how liturgy expresses, and even forms, theological truths. Liturgy and theology are brought closer together by asking the theologian not to overlook the liturgical expressions of theology.

Liturgical theology

A different path was opened by the scholars who influenced my work. Alexander Schmemann says "Liturgical theology – and I cannot over-emphasize this – is *not* that part of theology, that 'discipline,' which deals with liturgy 'in itself,' has liturgy as its specific 'object,' but, first of all and above everything else, the attempt to grasp the 'theology' as revealed in and through liturgy."[15] And Aidan Kavanagh distinguishes liturgical theology from what is "done in academies out of books by elites with degrees producing theologies of this and that."

> To argue with minds accustomed to thinking of theology in such a manner that theology at its genesis is communitarian, even proletarian; that it is aboriginally liturgical in context, partly conscious and partly unconscious; that it stems from an experience of near chaos; that it is long term and dialectical; and that its agents are more likely to be charwomen and shopkeepers than pontiffs and professors – all this is to argue against the grain.... For what emerges most directly from an assembly's liturgical act is not a new species of theology among others. It is *theologia* itself.[16]

This hermeneutic does not start with the assumption that there are two things – the liturgical activity of the pious and the theological activity of the academic – and then puzzle over how to glue them together. Instead, this hermeneutic understands liturgical theology to mean that theology actually occurs in the liturgical matrix (Schmemann calls liturgy "the *locus theologicus par excellence*"[17]), that this theology takes liturgical form, that liturgy has theological content. This new starting point requires us to dilate our concept of liturgy, first, and our concept of theology, second. The remainder of this chapter will seek to appreciate the potential of this view.

First, our understanding of liturgy must be deeper than the ceremony the eye alone can see. Robert Taft directs us to Michelangelo's image on the ceiling of the Sistine chapel where the life-giving finger of God stretches out to almost, but not quite, touch the returning finger of Adam. He says metaphorically that liturgy is what jumps that gap. "Of course here I am using the term 'liturgy' in the broadest, Pauline sense, to include what the Fathers of the Church called the entire *oikonomia* or *commercium*, that ongoing, saving, give-and-take between God and us, the Jacob's ladder of salvation history."[18] Liturgy epiphanizes the mystery of God in sacramental form, a mystery that Jean Daniélou summarizes thus:

The Christian faith has only one object, the mystery of Christ dead and risen. But this unique mystery subsists under different modes: it is prefigured in the Old Testament, it is accomplished historically in the earthly life of Christ, it is contained in mystery in the sacraments, it is lived mystically in souls, it is accomplished socially in the Church, it is consummated eschatologically in the heavenly kingdom.[19]

God acts in the world with deeds that are His alone, Daniélou says in another place, creating, judging, making covenant, making holy. "There is, then, a fundamental analogy between these actions. The sacraments are simply the continuation in the era of the Church of God's acts in the Old Testament and the New. This is the proper significance of the relationship between the Bible and the liturgy. The Bible is a sacred history; the liturgy is a sacred history."[20] This thick definition sees liturgy as revelation, and revelation is not a pile of facts, it is rather an activity done by God. The liturgy of the Church is the earthly prolongation of his historical acts of salvation, recorded in Scripture and still life-giving, and the visibility of Christ's high priesthood in heaven. Henri de Lubac makes the same point: "For one and the same essential mystery permeates the whole of Scripture and liturgy, apart from which there is no participation in the mystery of God."[21] It is in that sense that we understand the phrase associated famously with de Lubac: the Eucharist makes the Church.[22] The Eucharist is not our production; and the Church is not our product. We do not make the Church through a thanksgiving ritual we have created; rather it is Christ making the Church (his mystical body) through the Eucharist (an ongoing, sacramental presence of himself in the Holy Spirit). To swim is a verb, swimmer is the noun; liturgy is a verb, Church (plural) or Christian (singular) is the noun. Liturgy is the verb form of "Church" and Church is the noun form of "liturgy."

In *Mediator Dei*, Pius XII warns about not penetrating any deeper than the ceremonial aspects or the prescriptive laws when defining liturgy. "It is an error, consequently, and a mistake to think of the sacred liturgy as merely the outward or visible part of divine worship or as an ornamental ceremonial. No less erroneous is the notion that it consists solely in a list of laws and prescriptions according to which the ecclesiastical hierarchy orders the sacred rites to be performed" (n. 25). He acknowledges the outward and visible ceremonial face of liturgy, of course, but seems to say that looking only at this fails to see the whole of the thing. It is like only seeing the visible part of the iceberg. A reality breaks surface in ritualized, sacramentalized, ceremonialized form, but it is connected to the mysterious work of God in our individual lives and in history. This is a point that Jean Corbon makes so beautifully in *The Wellspring of Worship*: "The liturgy, which is celebrated at certain moments but lived at every moment, is the one mystery of the Christ who gives life to human beings. . . . The Christ whom we celebrate is the identical Christ by whom we live; his mystery permeates both celebration and life."[23]

To fully comprehend the ritual liturgy we must appreciate the fullness of the reality it epiphanizes. The liturgy is our inclusion in a relationship between the Son and the Father. "The sacred liturgy is, consequently, the public worship which our

Redeemer as Head of the Church renders to the Father, as well as the worship which the community of the faithful renders to its Founder, and through Him to the heavenly Father. It is, in short, the worship rendered by the Mystical Body of Christ in the entirety of its Head and members" (*Mediator Dei*, 20). The Son worships the Father; the Church worships the Son, her founder; and through the Son, together with the Son, the Church worships the Father. All this occurs by the power of the Holy Spirit who is ushering the Church into a redeemed, eschatological, spiritual existence. Ingredient to Pius XII's definition of liturgy is the conviction that the liturgy is "nothing more nor less than the exercise of [Christ's] priestly function" (*Mediator Dei*, 22). The *Catechism of the Catholic Church* continues to affirm this.

> The word "liturgy" originally meant a "public work" or a "service in the name of/ on behalf of the people." In Christian tradition it means the participation of the People of God in "the work of God." Through the liturgy Christ, our redeemer and high priest, continues the work of our redemption in, with, and through his Church (n. 1069).
>
> In the New Testament the word "liturgy" refers not only to the celebration of divine worship but also to the proclamation of the Gospel and to active charity. In all of these situations it is a question of the service of God and neighbor. In a liturgical celebration the Church is servant in the image of her Lord, the one "*leitourgos*"; she shares in Christ's priesthood (worship), which is both prophetic (proclamation) and kingly (service of charity) (n. 1070).

And then the Catechism quotes *Sacrosanctum Concilium* n. 7: "The liturgy then is rightly seen as an exercise of the priestly office of Jesus Christ."

Beauduin begins his treatise *Liturgy, the Life of the Church* with a kind of syllogism that starts with the first cause.

> The superabundant source of all supernatural life is the sacerdotal power of the High Priest of the New Covenant.
>
> But this sanctifying power Jesus Christ does not exercise here below except through the ministry of a *visible sacerdotal hierarchy*.
>
> Hence close union with this hierarchy in the exercise of its priesthood is for *every* Christian and Catholic soul the authentic mode of union with the priesthood of Jesus Christ, and consequently the primary and indispensable source of supernatural life.[24]

There is an unfortunate tendency to understand hierarchy as if it is misspelled "higherarchy," as if it affirms a cold distance when it actually affirms an intimate connection. The word is a neologism by Dionysius the pseudo-Areopagite, and it only seems fair that the creator of the word gets first rights in defining the word.

> The goal of a hierarchy, then, is to enable beings to be as like as possible to God and to be one with him. A hierarchy has God as its leader of all understanding

and action. It is forever looking directly at the comeliness of God ... Hierarchy causes its members to be images of God in all respects, to be clear and spotless mirrors reflecting the glow of primordial light and indeed of God himself. It ensures that when its members have received this full and divine splendor they can then pass on this light generously and in accordance with God's will to beings further down the scale.[25]

To call the Church a hierarchy means that it has the power to bless, as Yves Congar points out when he defines hierarchy as "spiritual powers tending to salvation."[26] Under this definition, when someone asks me whether the Church is hierarchical I am inclined to answer, "I hope so." Let us hope it is not just the Jesus club getting together, but that it has the power to save. A more adequate mental image of hierarchy than a series of bureaucratic hurdles is the image of a vascular system of arteries and veins connecting every member of the body to its heart, Christ. The term means having a "sacred origin" (*hierus* + *arche*). To call the Church a hierarchy means that the Church does not originate in ourselves, and neither does her liturgy. Rather, we join a liturgy already in progress, so to speak. Virgil Michel, O.S.B., a pupil of Beauduin's (if only briefly), points to origin of liturgy in God Himself.

> The liturgy exercises the mediatorship of Christ; it reaches through Christ from God to man, connecting man with God.
> The liturgy, through Christ, comes from the Father, the eternal source of the divine life in the Trinity. It in turn addresses itself in a special way to the Father, rendering him the homage and the glory of which it is capable through the power of Christ. The flow of divine life between the eternal Father and the Church is achieved and completed through the operation of the Holy Ghost.
> The liturgy, reaching from God to man, and connecting man to the fullness of the Godhead, is the action of the Trinity in the Church. The Church in her liturgy partakes of the life of the divine society of the three persons in God.[27]

In the liturgy, the redeemed sinner tastes deification. In the liturgy, heaven descends upon earth to invite our entrance into the eschatological fulfillment of all creation. In the liturgy, all things pass through the hypostatic union to ascend to the Father's throne in heaven, becoming transfigured by the working of the Holy Spirit. That is why all the familiar religious accoutrements – temples, vestments, altars, the priesthood, sacrifices, sacred time, fasting, feasts, and more – look the same, yet different. Liturgy is not a species in the genus of religious ritual, because Christ is the new temple, Christ is the new priest, Christ is the altar and the victim, the head of a new hierarchy linking us to his Father in a new identity because Christ's indwelling makes us sons like him, and the Holy Spirit's indwelling makes us living temples.

This makes liturgy a unique activity among the religions of mankind because Christian liturgy is not one of the cults of Adam, it is the cult of the New Adam perpetuated in his body, the Church. First, Christ is a unique person, being the hypostatic union of divine and human natures; second, the Church is a unique entity, being the mystical body of Christ; and third, the liturgy is a unique activity for being the Church in motion. Christ is the hypostatic union of two natures in one person, without confusion, without separation, without change, without division. And liturgy is ritual in the way that Jesus was man: fully, but not only. We will not touch the real heart of liturgy by only examining what is available to the ritologist, as we will not touch the real identity of Jesus by only examining what is available to the historian.

All this has bearing on the question as to whether liturgy can change. In a facile way, yes; it is evident that there was a time before which an iconostasis existed, or a Latin sacramentary, or the feast of Corpus Christi. The Church has accepted the various gifts presented by the cultures she is evangelizing, and so expressed herself in new ways. But in the deeper sense, no, the liturgy cannot change. The priesthood which is exercised in the liturgy is Christ's eternal and unchanging priesthood. Schmemann understands *leitourgia* to be an action by which a group of people become something corporately they had not been as a mere collection of individuals, in order to perform a ministry on behalf of and in the interest of the whole community. The action in this case is Redemption won by Christ, and to that work a liturgist is joined when he or she is baptized into Christ and becomes his liturgical apprentice. The whole community on whose behalf the ministry is performed, in this case, is all the sons of Adam and daughters of Eve, i.e., everyone in the clan which Christ adopted as his own when he, himself, became a son of Adam at the Incarnation. Would we want Christ's work (*ergon*) of reconciliation to change? The work he came to do is bestow our deification and beatitude.

This thickened definition of liturgy begins with the Trinity's circulation of love that turns itself outward in creation. But creation is only the beginning of redemption, as redemption is the completion of creation. The work done by the Son and Spirit, in accomplishing the Father's good pleasure for all creation, is nothing less than to invite our ascent to participate in the very life of the Trinity. This cannot be forced, however, it must be done with our cooperation. So the fullest definition of liturgy I can propose is to say *it is the Trinity's perichoresis kenotically extended to invite our synergistic ascent into deification.* When we consider liturgical theology, this is the scope of the subject matter with which we are dealing.

Second, our understanding of theology must be dilated. We tend to think of theology as a mental activity because the person to whom we give the name "theologian" resides in the academy, alongside other scholars like sociologists and psychologists and biologists. A theologian might hold a faith-commitment, or serve the poor, or even engage in prayer, but the reason we tend to call that person a theologian is because of what he or she thinks about. The first hermeneutic identified earlier will bestow the title of liturgical theologian on the academic if the subject he thinks about is worship; the second hermeneutic will bestow the title if the academic takes account of worship rituals while thinking about his scholarly topic, but both hermeneutics share the same assumption that theology belongs in the academy, belongs to the academy. And if theology belongs only to the academy, then calling liturgy *theologia prima* is really only saying that liturgy provides straw for an academic Rumpelstiltskin to spin into theological gold.

Aidan Kavanagh opens a different understanding of *theologia prima*. In the liturgy we have an encounter that transforms us, like the sort of transforming encounter Moses experienced at the burning bush. God Almighty is as active on the altar as he was in the bush, and any who will bow down before God in the bush or on the altar is susceptible to the transfiguring experience.

> What results in the first instance from such an experience is deep change in the very lives of those who participate in the liturgical act. And deep change will affect their next liturgical act, however slightly. To detect that change in the subsequent liturgical act will be to discover where theology has passed, rather as physics detects atomic particles in tracks of their passage through a liquid medium ... The adjustment to change between acts on the part of the actors is both conscious and unconscious; it is always real. The results of this adjustment shows in the gradual evolution of the liturgical rites themselves ... It is the adjustment which is theological in all this. I hold that it is theology being born, theology in the first instance. It is what tradition has called *theologia prima*.[28]

Theology, Kavanagh suggests, is not located in our cognition, rather theology passes through our lives. After the tremor caused by the liturgical earthquake, hairline cracks are discovered in our mental constructs and social structures. Theology has passed by. Tomas Spidlik's digest of eastern spirituality notes that the Fathers "understood the practice of theology only as a personal communion with *Theos*, the Father, through the *Logos*, Christ, in the Holy Spirit – an experience lived in a state of prayer."[29] Archimandrite Vasileios echoes the point. "True theology is always living, a form of hierugy, something that changes our life and 'assumes' us into itself: we are to become theology. Understood in this way, theology is not a matter for specialists but a universal vocation; each is called to become a 'theologian soul.'"[30] God shapes the community in liturgical encounter, and the community makes adjustment to this encounter, becoming theologian souls. After this the historian can begin dusting the ritual for God's fingerprints.[31] Liturgical theology happens in the temple, not in the university office. Liturgical theology is not written with ink, it is written with incense and temples and feasts and icons and sacraments and relics. Its starting point is fasting and almsgiving, not the card catalog, and its telos is not a degree but sainthood.

Theologians are created over the course of their entire liturgical life: sacraments, sacramentals, daily prayer, observing the seasons of the year, and more, become the painter's brushes that make us into an icon of our prototype, or the sculptor's chisel working a block of marble. Within each person is an image of God that must be freed from stone-cold vices in order to create out of women and men a liturgical son who shares the Son's filial relationship with God the Father.

To liturgical theology must be added liturgical asceticism. Liturgy is a place of theological revelation by God, and grasping this theology requires a new mind: a *meta nous,* which is the root of *metanoia,* which means repentance. The stone must receive the carving, the patient must receive the healing, and the asceticism required to become liturgical theologians means the mortification begun in baptism must continue to soak into our minds, making them new. The liturgy creates the capacity for union with God, and union with God was called *theologia* in the ascetical tradition. Evagrius speaks of going through three stages. First, *praktike* begins by disciplining our sinful passions; and when the cataracts of sin are washed from our eyes, and we have attained a state of *apatheia,* then we can see creation properly, a second stage he calls *physike;* but third, we might rise to the supreme, calm, steady contemplation of God, which would be a union with God that he calls *theologia.* That is why he concludes, "If you are a theologian you truly pray. If you truly pray you are a theologian."[32]

This is the sense in which Kavanagh can call Mrs Murphy a liturgical theologian. She is the personified image of the corporate body of Christians which has been ascetically formed by traditional, sacramental, ritualized liturgical practices to become theologians. She is most assuredly neither a simple way to speak of the uneducated, nor representative of a public opinion poll, nor the laity in opposition to the hierarchy, nor the warm-hearted but simple-minded Christian. She represents the Church insofar as the Church has been trained to speak the language of primary theology. "The true primary theologian in the Church is the liturgical assembly,"[33] says Kavanagh, and:

> The language of the primary theologian ... more often consists in symbolic, metaphorical, sacramental words and actions which throw flashes of light upon chasms of rich ambiguity. As such, Mrs Murphy's language illuminates the chaotic landscape through which I must pick my professional way with the narrow laser-like beam of precise words and concepts – which is why what she does is primary and what I do is secondary; which is why, also, what she does is so much harder to do than what I do. My admiration for her and her colleagues is profound, and it deepens daily.[34]

To learn this grammar, one needs to be filled with the mind of Christ by becoming submissive to tradition – tradition here meaning "the mind of the Church." Becoming a Christian means learning to think with this mind, and act with this will, and love with this heart, because it is Christ's own self shared with his mystical body, the Church. Vladimir Lossky says that Tradition is the Holy Spirit in action. "The pure notion of Tradition can then be defined by saying that it is the life of the Holy Spirit in the Church, communicating to each member of the Body of Christ the faculty of hearing, of receiving, of knowing the Truth in the Light which belongs to it, and not according to the light of human reason."[35] Mrs Murphy is a traditional Christian.

Therefore, liturgical theology is received; it is not created. Liturgical theology receives the *lex orandi* of the Church; it does not create the *lex orandi* of our own desires. Much mischief has been caused by forgetting this fact (by overlooking the *lex* in *lex orandi,* if we may put it so). "When liturgy no longer serves as the constitutive foundation for secondary theology . . . [then] *Lex supplicandi legem statuat credendi* is effectively reversed,"[36] says Kavanagh. And "to reverse the maxim, subordinating the standard of worship to the standard of belief, makes a shambles of the dialectic of revelation."[37] The maxim that *lex orandi* establishes (*statuat*) the Church's *lex credendi* is a way of saying that God's activity establishes our belief. It does not mean, to the contrary, that worship reflects our theology; it does not mean that if we wish to produce a certain belief in the congregation we should begin by modifying their prayer. Our theology must be conformed to the revelation given by Christ to his apostles, and on whose apostolic foundation the Church stands. The apostolic faith is found working in the liturgy: "The mysteries of Christ's life are the foundations of what he would henceforth dispense in the sacraments, through the ministers of his Church, for 'what was visible in our Savior has passed over into his mysteries' " (*Catechism of the Catholic Church*, 115, quoting Pope Leo the Great). This is what makes liturgical theology primary, and by this theology the liturgical assembly works out the Church's *lex credendi*, something still different from what scholars work out in their office.

> This means that *lex credendi* is at root not merely something which is done exclusively by secondary theologians in their studies, as opposed to *lex supplicandi* done by non-theologians indulging in religious worship elsewhere. On the contrary, *lex credendi* is constantly being worked out, sustained and established as the faithful in assembly are constantly working out, sustaining, and establishing their *lex supplicandi* from one festive, ordered, aesthetic, canonical, and eschatological liturgical act to the next under grace.[38]

Kavanagh was fond of saying that liturgy is doing the world as the world was meant to be done. Schmemann said liturgical theology is not that discipline that has liturgy as its specific object; so what specific object does liturgical theology have? We suppose it is a new and transfigured world. Mrs Murphy does not look *at* the liturgy (as do people who possess master's degrees in liturgical studies), she looks *through* the liturgy at the world in the light of Mount Tabor. She sees the world as it was given by God (sacrament), and she sees the world as a gift to return to God (sacrifice). She has been capacitated to see all cosmic matter seeking its liturgical form. "The final destiny of water is to participate in the mystery of the Epiphany," writes Paul Evdokimov; "of wood, to become a cross; of the earth, to receive the body of the Lord during his rest on the Sabbath . . . Olive oil and water attain their fullness as conductor elements for grace on regenerated man. Wheat and wine achieve their ultimate *raison d'etre* in the eucharistic chalice."[39] Liturgical theology sees a three-dimensional world by looking binocularly through protological and eschatological lenses. At last the reason for creation is revealed (Maximus the Confessor said "Seek the reason why God created, for this is true knowledge"[40]); at last the end of creation is revealed (Nicholas Cabasilas said God created humanity in order to find a mother[41]). Thus liturgy becomes the basis of morality and social justice, for when our minds have been made new then the tired old patterns that sin has inflicted on us can be broken and right relationships (righteousness) can be reimagined. Virgil Michel therefore saw both the liturgical movement and Catholic Action to be expressions of spiritual renewal. Paul Marx, his biographer, comments, "It was no mere coincidence, Father Michel often said, that the restoration of the liturgy by St Pius X should be followed by 500 pages of pleas for Catholic Action written by Pius XI."[42] And it was the latter, Pius XI, who remarked, "In the final analysis all permanent Catholic social reform begins in the sanctuary."[43] Michel himself concocted a famous, short-hand syllogism.

> Pius X tells us that the liturgy is the indispensable source of the true Christian spirit; Pius XI says that the true Christian spirit is indispensable for social regeneration. Hence the conclusion: The liturgy is the indispensable basis of Christian social regeneration.[44]

Liturgy is no longer an isolated child playing in its own corner of the ritual sandbox.

Schmemann had an intuition for all this because of his capacious sense that Christianity exists "for the life of the world" (the title of one of his books[45]). Christianity exists to give the world a joy it cannot summon from within itself, on its own resources, by ushering the world into the joy of the Kingdom of God. In his posthumously published *Journals* he writes of an experience when he was a young man in Paris. He was simultaneously aware of the noisy, proletarian street on which he stood, and of a silent Mass being said nearby within the Church of St Charles of Monceau.

> This experience remains with me forever: a very strong sense of "life" in its physical, bodily reality, in the uniqueness of every minute and of its correlations with life's reality. At the same time, this interest has always been rooted solely in the correlation of all of this with what the silent Mass was a witness to and reminder of, the presence and the joy. What is that correlation? It seems to me that I am quite unable to explain and determine it, although it is actually the only thing that I talk and write about ("liturgical theology").[46]

By our regular pilgrimage from the profane into the sacred, we are renewed and returned again from the nave to the world, enabled to finally function in it a bit more like we were intended to function. Liturgy is participation by the body of Christ in the perichoresis of the Trinity; asceticism is the capacitation for that participation, called deification; theology is union with God, making the Church's liturgy a theological act. If liturgy means sharing the life of Christ (being washed in his resurrection, eating his body), and if askesis means discipline (in the sense of forming), then liturgical asceticism is the discipline required to become an icon of Christ and make his image visible in our faces. *Theologia* is knowing the Trinity, but in the Biblical sense of "knowing;" which, observes Paul Evdokimov, gives us "the patristic definition of theology: the experimental way of union with God."[47] (Experimental learning is the process of making meaning from experience.) This theology is a kind of knowing that requires a deep change in the mind (*nous*) of the knower, and such a change is ascetical, and it capacitates for liturgy.

Conclusion

How does this third hermeneutic commend itself? What value does it offer? It does not mean to suggest that academic theologians should give up their burgeoning interest in liturgy. To the contrary, we are glad to find scholars trying to bring liturgy and theology closer together, to occasionally pass each other in their orbits. We think it profitable for the academy to take liturgy more seriously. As Taft says, "To think that a homily of John Chrysostom or John Calvin, or a book by Karl Rahner or Karl Barth, is worthy of the theologian's attention, and fail to understand how the ways and the prayers by which these same gentlemen along with some other millions have worshiped God is worthy of the same, is the prejudice of those so locked into a narrow concept of expression as to think that only words communicate anything theological. Christian faith is not a set of verbal propositions."[48]

But Schmemann thinks that if the divide remains or if its bridging is artificial, then a problem still remains. It is the problem that occurred when liturgy, theology, and piety[49] were separated. The three components are supposed to bond to make a Christian, the way three atoms bond to make a molecule of water. Relax the bond, and although each atom might remain the same, the same molecule will not remain. He writes, "The goal of liturgical theology, as its very name indicates, is to overcome the fateful divorce between theology, liturgy and piety – a divorce which, as we have already tried to show elsewhere, has had disastrous consequences for theology as well as for liturgy and piety."[50] What were the results of letting these three atoms drift apart? Liturgy became ceremony, theology became an intellectual exercise, and piety lost its referent.

> It deprived *liturgy* of its proper understanding by the people, who began to see in it beautiful and mysterious ceremonies in which, while attending them, they take no real part. It deprived *theology* of its living source and made it into an intellectual exercise for intellectuals. It deprived *piety* of its living content and term of reference ... To understand liturgy from inside, to discover and experience that "epiphany" of God, world, and life which the liturgy contains and communicates, to relate this vision and this power to our own existence, to all our problems: such is the purpose of liturgical theology.[51]

Notes

1   I.H. Dalmais, "The Liturgy as a Celebration," in A.G. Martimort (ed.), *The Church at Prayer*, vol. 1 (Collegeville: The Liturgical Press, 1987), p. 233.
2   Anscar Chupungco, "A Definition of Liturgy," in A.J. Chupungco (ed.), *Handbook for Liturgical Studies*, vol. 1 (Collegeville: A Pueblo Book, Liturgical Press, 1977), p. 4.

Martimort names some texts in a footnote on page 7 of "Definitions and Methods," in
The Church at Prayer, vol. 1: "The expression *libri liturgici,* which quickly became
standard, occurs as early as 1832 in SCR [Decree of the Sacred Congregation for Rites]
2692; in 1897 *liturgia ambrosiana* occurs in SCR 3948, and in 1898 'de usu linguae
slavicae in sacra liturgia,' in SCR 3999. The 1917 Code of Canon Law definitively
accepts *liturgia* in can. 447."

3   Anthony Ruff, *Sacred Music and Liturgical Reform: Treasures and Transformations*
    (Chicago: Hillenbrand Books, 2007), p. 213.
4   A.G. Martimort, "Definitions and Methods," *The Church at Prayer,* vol. 1, p. 16. Bryan
    Spinks confesses that "when I read some attempts at studies described as Liturgical
    Theology, my response has been: this would have been so much better had the writer
    actually engaged with real liturgies and known a little history." "From Liturgical
    Theology to Liturgical Theologies: Schmemann's Legacy in Western Churches" *St.
    Vladimir's Theological Quarterly,* vol. 53, nos. 2–3, 2009 (pp. 231–249), p. 233.
5   Martimort, "Definitions and Methods," p. 17.
6   Kevin Irwin, *Context and Text: Method in Liturgical Theology* (Collegeville: Liturgical
    Press, 1994), pp. 44–5.
7   Kevin Irwin, *Models of the Eucharist* (Mahwah, NJ: Paulist Press, 2005), p. 18.
8   Gordon Lathrop, *Holy Things* (Minneapolis: Fortress Press, 1993), p. 3.
9   Baby Varghese, *West Syrian Liturgical Theology* (Cornwall: MPG Books, 2004), p. 10.
10 Catherine Vincie, *Celebrating Divine Mystery: A Primer in Liturgical Theology*
    (Collegeville: Liturgical Press, 2009).
11 James Smith, *Desiring the Kingdom* (Grand Rapids, MI: Baker Academic, 2009), p. 25.
12 Simon Chan, *Liturgical Theology: The Church as Worshiping Community* (Downer's
    Grove, IL: Intervarsity Press, 2006), p. 15.
13 Geoffrey Wainwright, *Doxology: The Praise of God in Worship, Doctrine, and Life* (New
    York: Oxford University Press, 1980), p. 5.
14 Dwight Vogel, *Primary Sources of Liturgical Theology: A Reader* (Collegeville: Liturgical
    Press, 2000).
15 Alexander Schmemann, "Liturgical Theology, Theology of Liturgy, and Liturgical
    Reform," in Thomas Fisch (ed.), *Liturgy and Tradition: Theological Reflections of
    Alexander Schmemann* (Crestwood, NY: St Vladimir's Seminary Press, 1990), p. 217.
16 Aidan Kavanagh, *On Liturgical Theology* (Collegeville: Liturgical Press, 1984), pp. 74–5.
17 Schmemann, "Liturgical Theology, Theology of Liturgy, and Liturgical Reform," p. 40.
18 Robert Taft, "What Does Liturgy Do?" in *Beyond East and West: Problems in Liturgical
    Understanding* (Rome: Pontifical Oriental Institute, 1997), p. 240.
19 Jean Daniélou, "Le symbolism des rites baptismaux," *Dieu vivant,* quoted in Robert Taft
    "Toward a Theology of the Christian Feast," in *Beyond East and West,* pp. 28–9.
20 Jean Daniélou, "The Sacraments and the History of Salvation," in *The Liturgy and the
    Word of God,* Proceedings of the Strasbourg Congress (Collegeville: Liturgical Press,
    1959).
21 Henri de Lubac, *Catholicism: Christ and the Common Destiny of Man* (San Francisco:
    Ignatius Press, 1988), p. 213.
22 Paul McPartlan's comparative study of Zizioulas and de Lubac notes that the double
    principle ("the Church makes the Eucharist" and "the Eucharist makes the Church")
    "appeared for the first time only in de Lubac's *Meditation sur l'Eglise,* in 1953. There,
    while he says that the Church and the Eucharist stand 'as cause to each other', it is
    clearly the second half of the principle that he regards as having been more
    neglected . . . De Lubac's *Corpus Mysticum* may be regarded as an extended defense of

the principle that 'the Eucharist makes the Church' and a weighty appeal for its restoration to the prominence it had before the full rise of scholasticism." *The Eucharist Makes the Church: Henri de Lubac and John Zizioulas in Dialogue* (Edinburgh, T&T Clark, 1993), pp. xv–xvi.

23 Jean Corbon, *The Wellspring of Worship* (New York: Paulist Press, 1988), p. 141.

24 Lambert Beauduin, *Liturgy, the Life of the Church* (Farnborough: Saint Michael's Abbey Press, 2002), p. 13.

25 Dionysius, *The Celestial Hierarchy*, chapter 3. This translation from *Pseudo-Dionysius: The Complete Works*, Classics of Western Spirituality (New York: Paulist Press, 1987), p. 154.

26 Yves Congar, *Lay People in the Church* (Westminster: The Newman Press, 1965), p. 353.

27 Virgil Michel, O.S.B., *The Liturgy of the Church* (New York: MacMillan Company, 1937), pp. 40.

28 Kavanagh, *On Liturgical Theology*, pp. 73–4

29 Thomas Spidlik, *The Spirituality of the Christian East* (Kalamazoo: Cistercian Press, 1986), p. 1.

30 Archimandrite Vasileios, *Hymn of Entry: Liturgy and Life in the Orthodox Church* (Crestwood: St Vladimir's Seminary Press, 1984), p. 27.

31 In an interesting way, this reverses Martimort's sequence. It's not that history comes first and then theology follows; Kavanagh is saying theology happens in the liturgical assembly, and then the liturgiologist can chart theology's passage.

32 Evagrius, Chapters on Prayer, #60. This translation in John Eudes Bamberger OCSO (trans.), *The Praktikos & Chapters on Prayer* (Kalamazoo, MI: Cistercian Publications, 1981), p. 65.

33 Kavanagh, *On Liturgical Theology*, p. 150.

34 Aidan Kavanagh, "Response: Primary Theology and Liturgical Act," *Worship* vol. 57 (July 1983), (pp. 321–4), p. 323.

35 Vladimir Lossky, "Tradition and Traditions," in *In the Image and Likeness of God* (Crestwood: St Vladimir's Seminary Press, 1985), pp. 151–2.

36 Kavanagh, *On Liturgical Theology*, p. 83

37 Ibid., p. 92

38 Ibid., p. 150.

39 Paul Evdokimov, *The Art of the Icon: A Theology of Beauty* (California: Oakwood Publications, 1990), pp. 117–18.

40 Maximus, "Four Hundred Chapters on Love," Fourth Century #5. This translation from *Maximus Confessor: Selected Writings*, The Classics of Western Spirituality (New York: Paulist Press, 1985), p. 76.

41 Olivier Clement, *The Roots of Christian Mysticism* (New York: New City Press, 1996), p. 293.

42 Paul Marx, *Virgil Michel and the Liturgical Movement* (Collegeville: Liturgical Press, 1957), p. 194.

43 The encyclical, *Mit Brennnender Sorge*, ("With Deep Anxiety"), quoted in Marx, *Virgil Michel*, p. 208.

44 Virgil Michel, "The Liturgy the Basis of Social Regeneration," *Orate Fratres* vol. 9 (1935), pp. 536–45; reprinted in Robert Spaeth (ed.), *The Social Question: Essays on Capitalism and Christianity by Fr. Virgil Michel, O.S.B.* (Collegeville: St John's University, 1987), p. 8.

45 Schmemann, *For the Life of the World* (Crestwood, NY: St Vladimir's Seminary Press, 1973).

46 Schmemann, *The Journals of Father Alexander Schmemann, 1973–1983* (Crestwood, NY: St Vladimir's Seminary Press, 2002), pp. 19–20.
47 Paul Evdokimov, *The Struggle with God* (New Jersey: Paulist Press, 1966), p. 108. (Republished as *Ages of the Spiritual Life* by St Vladimir's Seminary Press, 1998.)
48 Taft, "Liturgy as Theology," in *Beyond East and West*, p. 240.
49 This third element, that Schmemann calls piety, is what I mean when invoking the category of asceticism in my book, *On Liturgical Asceticism* (Washington DC: Catholic University of America Press, 2013).
50 Alexander Schmemann, *Of Water and the Spirit* (Crestwood: St Vladimir's Seminary Press, 1974), p. 12.
51 Ibid.

Bibliography

Beauduin, Lambert, *Liturgy, the Life of the Church* (Farnborough: Saint Michael's Abbey Press, 2002).
Corbon, Jean, *The Wellspring of Worship* (San Francisco: Ignatius Press, 2005).
Fagerberg, David W., *Theologia Prima: What is Liturgical Theology?* (Chicago: Hillenbrand Books, 2004).
—— *On Liturgical Asceticism* (Washington DC: Catholic University of America Press, 2013).
Irwin, Kevin, *Context and Text: Method in Liturgical Theology* (Collegeville: Liturgical Press, 1994).
Kavanagh, Aidan, O.S.B., *On Liturgical Theology* (Collegeville: Liturgical Press, 1984).
Lathrop, Gordon, *Holy Things: A Liturgical Theology* (Minneapolis: Fortress Press, 1993).
Michel, Virgil, O.S.B., *The Liturgy of the Church* (New York: MacMillan Publishing Co., 1937).
Schmemann, Alexander, *The Eucharist: Sacrament of the Kingdom* (Crestwood, NY: St Vladimir's Seminary Press, 1988).
Schmemann, Alexander, Thomas Fisch (ed.), *Liturgy and Tradition: Theological Reflections of Alexander Schmemann* (Crestwood, NY: St Vladimir's Seminary Press, 1990).
Taft, Robert, S.J., *Beyond East and West: Problems in Liturgical Understanding* (Rome: Pontifical Oriental Institute, 1997).
Vogel, Dwight, *Primary Sources of Liturgical Theology: a Reader* (Collegeville: Liturgical Press, 2000).
Wainwright, Geoffrey, *Doxology: The Praise of God in Worship, Doctrine, and Life* (New York: Oxford University Press, 1980).

Part II

THE LITURGY IN HISTORY

Chapter 2

THE JEWISH ROOTS OF CHRISTIAN LITURGY

Robert Hayward

This chapter sets out to explore aspects of the religious culture, thought, and practice of the Jewish people in their homeland during the period following the restoration of the Temple Service by Judah Maccabee in 164 BC until around 100 AD, that is, in the generation after the destruction of the Second Temple in 70 AD. The victories of the Maccabees over pagan attempts to destroy Judaism in the Holy Land went hand in hand with an intensified concern on the part of Jews for their religious traditions and observances, and a widespread desire to be wholly faithful to ancestral teachings.[1] Before the end of the second century BC, these concerns and desires had led to the emergence of different schools of thought within Judaism. Some of these are known to us today under the names Pharisees, Sadducees, and Essenes: there were others, too, who have left fainter traces in the historical record.[2] All these were united by a common goal: to love the Lord, the God of Israel, with a whole heart and soul. They differed when it came to deciding in detail how exactly the individual Jew should carry out this fundamental commandment. Members of these schools inevitably engaged in debate with one another, and with Jews who belonged to no particular group; and the Jewish documents surviving from the historical period which concerns us bear witness to a remarkably variegated religious situation. This variegation within Jewish religious culture sometimes expressed itself in distinctive types of discipline, piety, and heightened religious observance. As we shall see presently, from the second century BC onwards there existed particular ways of practising Judaism which require serious consideration in any account of the beginnings of Christian liturgy, for these ways were current in the time of Christ and the Apostles, and were familiar to the first generation of Christians.

All these variegated and differing ways of practising Judaism represented carefully conceived attempts to ensure that Israel behaved as a royal, priestly and holy nation, as God had commanded (Exod. 19:5–6). The reason for this is simple: the fundamental command to *love* the Lord cannot realistically be put into practice unless the Jewish people are in full accord with the God who commands them: "You shall *be holy*, as I, the Lord your God, am holy" (Lev. 19:2). They are to *be* holy, not simply to conduct themselves in a holy manner; and Scripture had shown how this could be possible, since the Holy God had commanded that Israel build Him a sanctuary, "so that I may dwell among them" (Exod. 25:8). By means of His Presence in that sanctuary, therefore, God's holiness, which properly belongs to Him alone, might be communicated to His people through the sacrifices, offerings, and formal ceremonies which He Himself had commanded.[3] We may anticipate a little at this point, and record that one of the most striking features of religious practice in the late Second Temple period was the appearance of groups of devout Jews who sought to extend and disseminate the holiness inherent in the Temple and its Service, far beyond the limits of the Temple building and Jerusalem, into the realm of everyday life. One distinguished student of Judaism has described this process as the "templization" of religious life.[4] By this means, the formal service of God prescribed for the Temple and its personnel might be applied to all Jews, enabling the building up of a holy nation carrying out the commands of its King and Lawgiver, the Holy One of Israel. In what follows we shall attempt to show that this deeply theological process, already well advanced in the first century AD, affords telling insights into the principles underlying the structure of the Catholic liturgy.

The Jewish texts considered here will generally be older than, or contemporary with, the earliest years of the Church.[5] Jesus Christ and the Apostles were Jews, and their formal, public approach to the worship of God was consonant with Judaism of their times. Thus we learn that they were familiar with the service of the Temple, about whose meaning contemporary Jewish sources are reasonably informative.

Indeed, the bond between the Jewish Temple and the nascent Church was both natural and profound; and common Jewish understandings of the Temple, and the determination of many Jews to live their daily lives in a manner informed by the ethos of the Temple—by careful observance of the laws relating to moral and ritual purity, by the pursuit of holiness, and by due reverence for the Divine Presence among the people Israel—were both known to the earliest Christians, and exerted a powerful influence on their ideas of how God should properly be worshipped. Furthermore, that unique act of Christian worship, the Eucharist, was from the beginning spoken of as a *sacrifice* (1 Cor. 10:14– 21), language which inevitably evokes the world of the Temple.[6]

Christ and His Apostles also frequented the Synagogue; but contemporary Jewish sources tell us very little about any "liturgy of the Synagogue" in the first two Christian centuries or in earlier times. There is direct evidence that the Torah was read and expounded in Synagogue on Sabbaths, and probably at other times.[7] By the first century, readings from the prophets on Sabbath also are attested.[8] By the time of the Mishnah, a system for regular reading of Torah portions, with special sections of Scripture allocated for particular sabbaths and festivals, was taken for granted; but we have no direct knowledge from the early third century or earlier of what this system entailed, beyond the overwhelming probability that the entire Torah was read in Babylonia once a year, whereas Jews in the Land of Israel took three years to complete the reading.[9] Our knowledge of formal, public prayer in the Synagogue is even more limited. Jews represented in some of the Dead Sea Scrolls offered formal prayers to God each day, and we are fortunate enough to possess documents, many of them quite fragmentary, giving the texts of their prayers.[10] The Therapeutae, an association of contemplative Jews described by Philo, also offered formal prayers, although no texts from this group have survived.[11] There is no literary trace, however, of formal, public prayer, or anything approximating to a "Synagogue liturgy", before 70 AD and for many years thereafter.[12]

Mention of Synagogue, however, properly directs our attention to the Law of Moses and the other Jewish Scriptures, and to the fundamental Christian dogma that in Jesus Christ those Scriptures are fulfilled (e.g., Matt. 1:22; Mk. 14:49; Lk. 4:21). At the head of them stand the books of Moses, the Torah; and beginning with Moses, Christ had instructed his Apostles about Himself (Lk. 24:27). Very extensive sections of the books of Moses prescribe commandments about the sanctuary; its sacred objects; the many sacrifices to be offered in it; the priests who are to serve in it; and the qualifications, both ritual and moral, of priests and Israelites who assist in its worship day by day, on the weekly sabbaths, and in the great festivals occurring each year. It is inconceivable that Christ, who explicitly states that He came to fulfil the Torah (Matt. 5:17–18), should fail to fulfil the laws about the Temple and its service, especially since these, unlike the other commandments, had been delivered to Moses in a very distinctive manner, according to a heavenly blue-print or pattern (Hebrew *tabnît*, Exod. 25:9) which Moses was to copy. The implication of this was clear: the sanctuary and its service were to be definitive earthly copies of the heavenly reality shown to Moses.[13] From this it would follow that the service offered by the priests and Israel in the earthly Temple was intended exactly to parallel and reflect the service of the angels and spiritual beings in the heavenly Temple, a matter which was to exercise mightily the author of the *Book of Jubilees*.[14] It should be carefully noted that the petition of the Lord's Prayer, "Thy will be done in earth, as it is in heaven" (Matt. 6:10), amongst many other things implies that formal service of the Almighty offered by His ministers and people on earth should be ordered in accordance with that willed in the high places of heaven.

The laws of the sanctuary, however, have a more direct reference to Christ Himself, since the earliest Christians remembered that Jesus had spoken of His body as a temple (John 2:21; 4:20–26), and affirmed that those who believed and were baptized into Him had become members of His body, the Church (Rom. 12:5; 1 Cor. 10:17; 12:20, 27; Col. 1:24). The Church itself constitutes a temple: this statement can be made by early Christian authors in a quite matter-of-fact manner, without elaboration, taking its sense for granted (2 Cor. 6:16; Eph. 2:21–22); and the language of the sanctuary is accordingly applied to the Church (1 Peter 2:5–9; Eph. 4:1–16). Now the notion that human beings could, in certain circumstances, constitute a temple for the Lord is one which was already familiar to Jews in later Second Temple times. Thus the writer(s) of the Dead Sea Scrolls document often designated a *Florilegium*, and sometimes called a "Midrash on the Last Days", declares that God "has issued command to build for Himself a sanctuary of men [*miqdash 'ādām*], to be offering up in it before Him deeds of thanksgiving."[15] The sanctuary, of course, is a house; and in Hebrew, as in English, this word may indicate both a building and an extended family. Philo, the Jewish philosopher of Alexandria and contemporary of Jesus, could describe the rational soul as God's temple; and perhaps related to such notions are later Rabbinic statements which expound aspects of the Temple Service as symbolizing groups of devout Jews.[16]

All this underlines the centrality of the Temple in Christian thought and practice from the beginning, and is affirmed by the continuing presence of Christ's followers in the Temple. The Gospel of St. Luke ends (24:53) with the declaration that they were *continually* in the Temple, praising and blessing God; and the early chapters of Acts reinforce this report (Acts 2:46; 5:12, 20, 42), noting also that a great number of Jewish priests were obedient to the faith (6:7).[17] As we have noted, a remarkable feature of late Second Temple Judaism was the growth of associations devoted to the practice of their ancestral religion, and expressing that commitment in *piety modelled on the Temple and its service*. Their goal was to "actualize" in some manner outside the Temple the purity and holiness which characterize the temple service; and one of the most important ways in which they achieved this was through eating and drinking in common. Their meals, eaten in carefully regulated purity, are central to their religious activity and identity; and thanks to evidence from the Dead Sea Scrolls we can discern their activities as early as the second century BC. The Scrolls include writings of a group described as *yahad*. This Hebrew word, often translated as "community" or "union," means "that which is one," and seems to have occupied the settlement at Qumran on the shores of the Dead Sea until the Romans captured the buildings in 68 A.D.[18] This *yahad* laid down rules for its daily meals:

> They shall eat as a *yahad* and they shall bless as a *yahad* and they shall take counsel as a *yahad*. And in every place where there shall be ten men of the council of the *yahad*, let there not be lacking from among them a priest. And they shall sit before him, each man according to his rank; and they shall be asked for their counsel in every matter. And when they shall prepare the table for eating and the *tirosh* for drinking, the priest shall stretch out his hand first to utter blessing over the first-fruits of the bread and the *tirosh*.[19]

Membership of the *yahad* was conditional upon a candidate's successful completion of a period of probation, one element of which was acquisition of knowledge of the *yahad*'s purity rules and the ritual ablutions they required, another the candidate's cultivating an awareness of his correct place in the group's strongly hierarchical structure. What were the reasons for these requirements? In brief, the *yahad* regarded itself as "the covenant of God" (1QS 5:8), whose members had solemnly undertaken to separate themselves from injustice and wickedness (1QS 5:10). Those who still adhered to such things are explicitly "not reckoned in His covenant" (1QS 5:11); and the *yahad* insists that such people "shall not come into the water so as to touch the pure food of the men of holiness"[20] (1QS 5:13). Thus the privilege of consuming the pure food of the *yahad* is insolubly linked to the group's self-understanding as a covenantal association; indeed, the opening paragraphs of the "Rule of the *Yahad*" indicate that people volunteered to join the group, and that those who were chosen for membership were said to "cross over into the covenant" (e.g., 1QS 1:15, 18, 20, 24; 2:10). This terminology is biblical, and carries particular connotations.[21] We find it used at Deut. 29:9–11, in a speech by Moses to Israel as the people are about to cross over the river Jordan to enter the Holy Land. To "cross over into the covenant" they must pass through the waters, and separate themselves from all wickedness. Indeed, this Scriptural narrative seems to determine much of what the *yahad* understood the covenant to involve.

As well as knowing the rules of purity, the candidate needed to know the hierarchical structure of the *yahad*, in which the priests ranked first, the Levites next, and then the lay-folk marshalled in ranks as an army of thousands, hundreds, fifties, and tens, "so that every man of Israel may each know his station (literally, 'the house of his standing') in the *yahad* of God" (1QS 2:22). Either within the *yahad*, or co-extensive with it, is a council of the *yahad*, which is explicitly spoken of as a temple.[22] It is described as "an everlasting plantation, a house of holiness (or: sanctuary) for Israel and a foundation of the holy of holies for Aaron ... to effect atonement for the Land" (1QS 8:5–6). The *yahad*-covenant group thus embodies an hierarchical order possessed of both military and priestly significance, the former inevitably recalling Israel's constitution as a military camp on its journey through the desert to the promised Land, the latter agreeing with the group's sense that it incorporates the Temple. It will be recalled that Israel as military encampment in the desert was accompanied by angels (see especially Exod. 23:20–25; 32:34; 33:2), and that the Temple is the meeting-place of heaven and earth, where the prophet Isaiah heard the heavenly beings chanting the Sanctus, hymning the Glory of the Lord of Hosts, the God of the armies of Israel (Isa. 6:3), and where an altar was also present (Isa. 6:6). The *yahad*-covenant thus includes a union between the heavenly angels and the earthly members; and the place of the pure meal in all this is evidently central, the legislator stating bluntly:

> And as for any individual of the men of the of the *yahad*, the covenant of the *yahad*, who shall turn aside from any commandment in any matter with a high hand, let him not touch the pure meal of the men of holiness (or: "the sanctuary") (1QS 8:17).

Given this, we must return to the regulations for the meal quoted earlier, and explore them more deeply. The members' participation in the meal is mentioned in the same breath as "blessing," that is, the recitation of formal prayer to the Almighty. A priest must be present at the meal and utter one or more such "blessings" before it. The Hebrew words translated "they shall prepare the table" represent technical language used of the table of the Bread of the Presence (Lev. 24:5–9), an offering in the ritual category "most holy", whose consumption is restricted to priests. The drink is designated "first-fruits": these belong to the priests, and are sacrificial in nature (Exod. 22:29; 23:19). The implications are clear: the meal is a religious event, described with the use of known sacrificial terminology. The drink is *tirosh*, which may signify "new wine" or "fruit juice": if the latter meaning is intended, yet another line of association with the Temple is suggested, for priests were forbidden to touch alcohol during the temple service (Lev. 10:8–11).[23] The same rules apply for the meal of the *yahad* when the Messiahs are present, except that the Priest Messiah utters the blessing first, and only then does the Messiah of Israel say the blessing, followed by the congregation of the *yahad*.[24] Sadly, no texts containing the words of blessing uttered over the bread and wine at *yahad* meals have survived to our day.

Besides documents that describe the practices of the *yahad*, however, we can derive further information from groups who appear to have behaved in a very similar fashion. Philo of Alexandria (ca. 30 BC–ca. AD 45) describes the well known Jewish group called Essenes, whom some scholars identify with the Qumran *yahad*; but accounts of the two societies differ to such a degree that it is more accurate to speak of two distinct, yet related organizations.[25] Philo reports that Essenes hold clothes and food in common, and emphasizes that they eat their meals together, but does not discuss the matter further.[26] He does, however, record the Essenes' overriding concern with holiness, order, ethical conduct, and purity.[27] The later writer Josephus (37–ca.100 AD) provides further details about them.[28] His description of Essene meals leaves no doubt about their religious character and their strongly sacrificial connotations. Thus before the meal, the Essenes don linen loin-cloths and bathe in cold water, a process described as *purification*.[29] They then gather in a building forbidden to those of different opinion, from there "as pure ones" entering the dining-room "as if it were some holy sacred space."[30] In silence, the baker sets forth bread, and the cook a dish for each person. No one eats until the priest offers a prayer; and when the meal is over the priest recites another prayer.[31] Thus both at the beginning and at the end of the meal they honor God as the provider of life.[32] Then they take off their garments, "as holy vestments," and return to work.[33] Josephus a little later records the stages by which a candidate is admitted to Essene society, and notes the purity requirements for membership, which include ritual bathing.[34] The vocabulary which Josephus uses to describe the Essene meals is strongly redolent of priesthood and Temple: the change of garments after the meal sets a clear boundary between the consecrated activity within the dining-room and the ordinary, unconsecrated world of work, and the priestly prayers likewise serve to distinguish between these two spheres, the one holy, the other unconsecrated.

Along with the *yahad* and the Essenes, we know of another ascetic Jewish group, living in the Egyptian diaspora, called Therapeutae, "worshippers" or "healers," whom Philo extols in his famous treatise *De Vita Contemplativa* (hereafter: *VC*). Their asceticism is very marked (*VC* 34–35); but the Sabbath they esteemed as holy and a festival, celebrating it with a simple meal of bread, salt, optional hyssop, and water (*VC* 37). Philo also describes what appears to be their principal common meal, which was most probably held at Pentecost. Then all members of the group, men on one side, women on another, met to pass the night in solemn vigil (*VC* 69). Their meal again consisted of pure water, bread, salt, and optional hyssop (*VC* 73). Philo comments on the sobriety of this event, comparing it directly with the sobriety of the priests offering sacrifice (*VC* 74). The meal was not eaten until the Scriptures had been expounded (*VC* 75–79) and a hymn had been sung: then was brought in the table:

On which is the completely pure food, leavened bread with a side-dish of salt with which hyssop has been mixed, on account of veneration for the holy table of the dedicated offering in the holy hall of the Temple. For on this are loaves and salt without any relishes, the loaves unleavened and the salt unmixed. For it is fitting that simplest and purest items be assigned to the best part of the priests as a prize for their service; and that others should emulate the same kind of things, but keep away from those that are (exactly) the same, so that their betters might possess a privilege (*VC* 81–82).

This meal was followed by hymns sung by two choirs, one of men, the other of women; these culminated in the formation of a single chorus, which Philo explicitly declares to be a copy of the choir which sang at the Red Sea after the Exodus (*VC* 83–86). Thus the Therapeutae celebrate the miracles performed at the Exodus, when the waters of the Red Sea became salvation for Israel, but destruction for their oppressors (*VC* 85–86).

The common meal of these Therapeutae was evidently modelled on the temple ritual of the Bread of the Presence (Lev. 24:5–9; Numb. 4:7; Exod. 25:23–30; 1 Chron. 9:32), and its participants strove to emulate the purity of the priests in the Temple service. Praise of God in particular for His redemption of Israel from Egypt completed the meal; and Philo ended his account of these matters by recording his sense of what the ritual signified: the choir of the Therapeutae imitates the choir at the Red Sea when Israel came out of Egypt, which saw God's redemptive miracles, was seized by the Divine Spirit and sang hymns of thanksgiving (*VC* 87–88). In truth, says Philo, "the goal of the thoughts and the words and the singers is reverence towards God" (*VC* 88). Philo has no doubt that these are ideal Jews, true contemplatives, "citizens of heaven and of the cosmos", who have acquired virtue and an anticipation of the height of happiness (*VC* 90).

Finally, we may include here, with due caution, societies of Jews mentioned in early Rabbinic texts who formed themselves into a *haburah* (company or association) and ate their food in common, while carefully observing rules of ritual purity which they deemed necessary.[35] All members of the *haburah* were required to be *ne'eman*, trustworthy or reliable, in matters of purity and in observing the correct procedures for separating priestly dues and tithe from produce before it was set forth as food. Those seeking admission to a *haburah* were examined as to their competence in all these matters, and were required to undergo instruction in them. It is probable, though not certain, that in the last century or so of the Temple's existence some Pharisees, at least, formed similar companies for the consumption of food; but it must be stressed that the evidence at our disposal does not warrant a simple one-to-one equivalence of Pharisees with people who formed such associations.[36]

The upshot of all this is fairly clear. We possess secure, direct evidence from later Second Temple times allowing us to describe a distinctive type of piety, found both in the Jewish homeland and in the diaspora, which sought to replicate in some measure the holiness and purity of the Temple and its service outside the Temple courts. For this type of piety, common meals consumed in purity, and in societies characterized by order and hierarchical structure, could be described in sacrificial terms. According to some of our sources, the ritual of the Bread of the Presence especially seems to have offered a model for these meals. Here, if we are not mistaken, the historical sources reveal to us a significant Jewish "root" of Christian liturgy. Such a nexus of purification (involving washing in clean water), leading to a religious meal consumed in a "templized" society characterized by a particular order, provided *a set of basic ritual principles* which would have been familiar to Our Lord Himself, the Jewish people of His time, and the Apostles. These principles were available for further theological development and transformation, *sometimes far-reaching*, as the implications of the Incarnation of the Second Person of the Holy Trinity who fulfils the Torah were made plain.[37] Their basic outlines remain in the Church to this day, however; and they are represented by the purification of baptism, which admits a person to the eucharistic sacrifice as a full member of the Church, a society properly characterized by hierarchical order.[38]

To this set of principles, a further Jewish dimension must be added. Christ suffered and endured His redemptive death at Passover time, when the consumption of a sacrificial meal in a state of ritual purity was *de rigueur* for all Jews who could attend the Temple. It was at this time that He formally instituted the Eucharist, thereby investing the rite with an obvious *redemptive* significance which, while present in some of the "templized" Jewish meals we have so far described, is not an invariable feature of them. The blood of the Passover victim, which saves the first-born of Israel from the destroyer and enables the people to go out from Egypt, redeemed from the bondage and shame of slavery, bears its own powerful and enduring theological significance which transfers itself to the eucharist without difficulty.[39] The consumption of wine at the Passover meal is not required by the biblical regulations for the feast; but it was evidently a Passover custom already taken for granted by the mid-second century BC, since *Jubilees* 49:6 makes mention of it. The association of wine with blood was well known to the Old Testament writers; and the custom of drinking it at Passover most likely originated as a graphic means of imprinting on the minds of the worshippers the redemptive effects of the blood of the Passover victim.[40] The Passover meal consumed in Jerusalem in Second Temple times was indeed a sacrificial meal, whose consumption in dwellings outside the Temple precincts effectively turned those houses into "mini-temples" for the occasion; and documents from the second century BC onwards give some idea of the momentous significance attributed to the Passover rites.[41] According to *Jubilees* 17:15–18, the prince of demons (there called Mastema), on the twelfth day of the first month, prompted God to test Abraham by commanding him to sacrifice his son Isaac. Abraham's obedience, on the fifteenth day of that month, which is the date of the feast of Passover, put Mastema to shame (*Jubilees* 18:1–13). We are told that Abraham observed this feast every year (*Jubilees* 18:18); and when its time came round in due course, as Israel were about to be redeemed from Egypt, *during the days of the Passover festival*, Mastema was "bound and shut up" from hurting Israel (*Jubilees* 48:15). Furthermore, devout observance of the day of Passover ensures that Israel will not suffer plague during the coming year (*Jubilees* 49:14). The *Book of Jubilees* was no obscure, sectarian volume, but enjoyed great prestige among the Jews of the Holy Land before the Temple was destroyed; and its interpretation of Passover and its rituals as a divinely granted effective means of binding and shutting up the demons is also encountered in the Dead Sea Scroll 4Q225, and elsewhere in texts of the Second Temple period.[42] These are instructive for another important reason, as we shall now see.

The association of Passover with the sacrifice of Isaac in the *Book of Jubilees*, and the consequent establishment of a firm link between Isaac's sacrifice and the events of the going forth from Egypt (in both events Mastema and the demonic powers under his control are put to shame and rendered powerless; in both events a lamb is offered as a sacrificial victim; in both events the future well-being of Israel is assured), permits the ancient Jewish exegetes to draw further theological conclusions, particularly about the lamb offered in sacrifice. Thus Philo, in his account of Abraham's life, tells how the Patriarch, if he had indeed been required to go ahead and sacrifice his son, would have carried out the law of sacrifice by offering up each one of his son's limbs separately.[43] In this way, Philo indicates that Isaac would have been sacrificed in the same manner as the two lambs offered every day in the Temple Service, the one in the morning, the other in the evening. The lamb offered in Isaac's place, therefore, could be construed as being in direct continuum with the lamb of the daily sacrifice, which constituted the essential part of the Temple liturgy. Later Rabbinic evidence confirms this by insisting that the lamb of the daily burnt offering should be bound in a particular manner: the Mishnah uses the Hebrew word 'āqad to express this requirement, and the one and only occurrence of this word in the Bible is found in the story of Isaac's sacrifice at Gen. 22:9. Thus the lambs of the daily burnt offering are to be tied up in exactly the same special way that Isaac was bound.[44] Offered day by day in the Temple Service, they evoked continually the sacrifice of Isaac long ago and, by extension, they called forth thoughts of the annually recurring feast of Passover, the festival of Israel's redemption.[45]

According to the biblical narrative, the lamb was the first animal explicitly to be named by species as a sacrificial offering;[46] and it was offered in place of Isaac, the beloved son of Abraham on a mountain in the land of Moriah (Gen. 22:2). Scripture tells us that on Mount Moriah in Jerusalem Solomon built the house of the Lord.[47] And it is in this place that lambs were daily offered, bound in the matter of Isaac. We thus return to where we began, to the Temple and its service; and to those pious Jews who, in the last centuries of the Temple's existence, sought to "templize" their lives by adopting a mode of life bound by rules of moral and ritual purity; religious meals described in sacrificial terms; and brought together into societies characterized by hierarchical order. The Passover-Isaac-daily offering dimension adds to this "templized" life the record of past redemption, and the hopes of redemption to come. Not for nothing does St Luke, at the start of his Gospel, state that the prophetess Anna did not depart from the Temple in speaking to all those who were awaiting the redemption of Jerusalem.[48]

It is time to draw together these observations and to offer, with due caution, some appraisal of their usefulness in discussions of the earliest beginnings of the

Catholic liturgy. We must begin by disposing of a misconception which is sometimes encountered in treatments of the Qumran *yahad* and other groups like them, that they rejected the Temple "cult" and its personnel as corrupt; and sought refuge in allegedly higher, so-called "spiritualized" forms of worship. Whatever criticisms ancient Jewish groups may have made of the Temple of their own times, there is no trace anywhere in the literature that they sought to *dispense with* the Temple as a divinely appointed institution, or to abandon what it represented theologically; rather, the very fact that so many groups sought to imitate its rituals and engage directly in its piety points quite in the opposite direction, that the Temple was so central to their understanding and devotion that Judaism could not be conceived of without it.[49] In the "templized" piety of Jewish groups briefly examined here, we encounter a concern for holiness, for moral and ritual purity, and for sacred order that betokens a longing for the Divine Presence, a desire to love and serve the Lord, and a willingness to live a simple, even ascetic life to attain those ends. In fine, the worship of the sanctuary had been commanded by God to Moses on Sinai: those commandments, therefore, set forth the basic principles for approaching God and serving Him as He had commanded; and certain Jews of Our Lord's time seem to have taken those principles very, very seriously indeed.

A survey of extant, dateable Jewish literature contemporary with, or earlier than, Our Lord and the Apostles reveals the following information that has unavoidable implications for the beginning of the Christian liturgy.

1. Several known groups of Jews formed themselves into voluntary, "templized" societies which sought to replicate the piety and holiness inherent in the Temple and its service. Some of these groups evidently regarded themselves as "human temples" of God.
2. Consequently, outside the Temple courts, principles deriving from the Torah commandments for the Temple Service could be, and were, applied to prayer and other kinds of religious activity. Pre-eminent among these is the principle that the service of God should be ordered, formal, and offered at regular times and seasons; it should be appropriate for the heavenly King, to whom it is directed. The orders of "fixed" prayer attested by texts from the Dead Sea Scrolls provide direct evidence for this development.
3. Those engaged in such religious duties should be, as far as possible, in a state of purity – certainly moral purity, and preferably in a state of ritual purity as well. The purity regulations, and their relative stringency, differed from group to group; but purification in water is a constant concern for the Jewish groups we have discussed.
4. Several Jewish groups known to us invested their common eating and drinking with special religious significance: known sacrificial terminology is commonly employed in the descriptions of these meals which have come down to us. In the case of the Qumran *yahad*, the solemn meals are directly related to the covenant which this group represents. Among the Therapeutae, their great annual meal was linked to Israel's redemption from Egypt. The

meals of both *yahad* and Therapeutae evoke the Temple ritual of the Bread of the Presence, which was understood as representing a thanksgiving for the creation.[50]

5. Hierarchical order is to the fore in the constitution of most of the groups considered here.

6. Any Jewish group whose piety and practice centred on the Temple service would have been aware that the lambs of the daily burnt offering "recalled" both the sacrifice of Isaac and the lambs of Passover, the festival which commemorated both Isaac's offering and the redemption from Egypt.

7. In the case of the *yahad*, the Essenes, and the Therapeutae, the heavenly world is never far away; and it may even be claimed that one of the goals of these groups is to gain access to, or at least knowledge of that world, such that they may do God's will on earth as it is done in heaven.

On this last matter there is more to be said. As we have noted, the *Book of Jubilees* emphasized the "synchronicity" of the worship of God in heaven by the highest angels, and service of the Temple on earth, where the angels are represented by the ministering priests (see especially Jubilees 31:14). Jews at Qumran claimed to have knowledge of the heavenly worship, and may also have believed that they themselves took part in it: the text called *Songs of the Sabbath Sacrifice* describes the worship offered by the animated parts of the heavenly Temple, and of the angels in their various orders: the climax of this worship is a heavenly sacrifice. These and other texts which witness to the close association between the Temple Service and angelic worship may cast light on the vexed question whether the *Sanctus* formed part of the earliest eucharistic rites. The textual evidence relating to this question remains patient of differing interpretations, inasmuch as scholars do not agree that there is certain, direct reference to the use of the *Sanctus* in the earliest liturgies; but the Church's perception of itself as a Temple; the known concern of Jews in Second Temple times for a worship which united the heavenly world with the earthly; and the fact that particular groups of Jews whose practices in respect of purification, religious meals, and hierarchical order are not dissimilar from those of the earliest Church claimed to have access to the heavenly worship, all suggest that the Sanctus might naturally have found a place in Christian liturgy from an early period.[51] Certainly New Testament writers were no strangers to the worship of heaven: it is, for example, described graphically and at length in St John's Apocalypse. Furthermore, the worship of the heavenly beings described by the Qumran *Songs of the Sabbath Sacrifice* in Song 13 centers on sacrificial offerings presented in the heavenly Temple; and in the second century AD St Irenaeus (*Adv. Haer.* IV. 21.5) would speak of the altar in the heavens to which our prayers and offerings are directed. In tune with this, the *sursum corda* of the Mass echoes the words of the Apostle, that those risen with Christ should seek those things that are above, where Christ is at God's right hand.[52] What is above is the heavenly world, where archangels and celestial powers continually serve God and chant His praises. The Jews who wrote and preserved the texts we have all too briefly surveyed, in setting their religious goals and aspirations so firmly on the Temple and its service, were looking not only to this world, but to the heavenly realms. The ramifications of their insights for the Church should not be difficult to determine.

Notes

1 The crisis involving the Seleucid monarch Antiochus IV Epiphanes (175–164 BC), which reached its climax in his desecration of the Temple and his attempt to abolish Judaism, is told in the First and Second Books of Maccabees. For a critical analysis of these events and of the restoration of the Temple service under Judah Maccabee, see the classic study of E. Bickerman, *The God of the Maccabees* (Leiden: Brill, 1979). A clear example from this period of a clarion call for Jews to be faithful to their ancestral religion is represented by the *Book of Jubilees*, which reached its final form around 150 BC. For English translation, see: O.S. Wintermute, "Jubilees," in J.H. Charlesworth (ed.), *The Old Testament Pseuepigrapha*, vol. 2 (London: Darton, Longman & Todd, 1985), pp. 35–142. For an informative treatment of this text and its attitudes to priesthood and purity, see: M Himmelfarb, *A Kingdom of Priests. Ancestry and Merit in Ancient Judaism* (Philadelphia: University of Philadelphia Press, 2006), pp. 53–84.

2 For the relationship of some, or all of these groups to the traditional Jews named "Hasideans" by 1 Macc. 2:42; 7:13; 2 Macc.14:6, see: J. Kampen, *The Hasideans and the Origins of Pharisaism: A Study in 1 and 2 Maccabees* (Atlanta: Scholars Press, 1988).

3 The Scriptural foundations of all this, and developments in the Second Temple period, are critically examined by Jacob Milgrom, *Leviticus*, 3 vols., Anchor Bible 3, 3A, 3B (New York: Doubleday, 1991, 2000, 2000). A summary of this indispensible work is available as J. Milgrom, *Leviticus: A Continental Commentary* (Minneapolis: Fortress Press, 2004). See also J. Naudé, "Holiness in the Dead Sea Scrolls," in P.W. Flint & J.C. VanderKam (eds), *The Dead Sea Scrolls After Fifty Years: A Comprehensive Assessment*, vol. 2 (Leiden: Brill, 1999), pp. 171–99.

4 See: S. Fine, *This Holy Place: On the Sanctity of the Synagogue During the Greco-Roman Period* (Notre Dame: University of Notre Dame Press, 1997), pp. 32, 35, 41–55, 79–94.

5 The evidence of the Rabbinic literature will therefore be used sparingly, and for two reasons. First, with the exception of the short document *Megillat Ta'anith* (The Scroll of Fasts), which may date from the first century, the oldest compilation of Rabbinic texts, the Mishnah, did not receive its final form until around 200 AD. While the Mishnah undoubtedly contains information originating in earlier times, the precise dating of that information is always difficult, often controversial, and sometimes speculative. See: H.L. Strack & G. Stemberger, *Introduction to the Talmud and Midrash* (Minneapolis: Fortress Press, 1992), pp. 119–66. Second, recent researches have pointed to the somewhat limited authority enjoyed by the Rabbis, themselves members of an élite scholarly group, in the Jewish homeland before the later fourth century. See especially: Hayim Lapin, "The Origins and Development of the Rabbinic Movement in the Land of Israel," in Katz (ed.), *The Cambridge History of Judaism: Volume 4 The Late Roman-Rabbinic Period* (Cambridge: Cambridge University Press, 2006), pp. 206–29 and bibliography cited there. This recent assessment of the scope of Rabbinic authority has, however, been challenged. See: Ben Zion Rosenfeld, "The Title 'Rabbi' in Third- to Seventh Century-Inscriptions in Palestine: Revisited," *Journal of Jewish Studies* 61 (2010), pp. 234–56. Even so, Rabbinic information about the Temple Service and Synagogue (see further below) is often less concerned with the historical realities of those institutions than with the expression of Rabbinic ideals for them.

6 The expression "the blood of the covenant" used by Christ at the institution of the Eucharist (Matt. 26:28; Mk. 14:24; Lk. 22:20; compare 1 Cor. 11:25) is overtly sacrificial in character. See: Exod. 24:8. The sacrificial nature of the Eucharist is simply taken for granted by early writers such as Ignatius of Antioch (e.g., *Ad Smyrn.* 8:1; *Ad Phil.* 4:1); Irenaeus (e.g., *Adv. Haer.* IV. 17.5; 18:2); and Tertullian (*De Oratione* 6:2). *Didache* 14:1–3 speaks of the Eucharist as a sacrifice: most students of this text seem now to date it to around 100 AD, although its provenance, theology, and relationship to the New Testament and early Patristic writings remain contested and the subject of intense scholarly debate. See: J.A. Draper (ed.), *The Didache in Modern Research* (Leiden: Brill, 1996); and M. del Verme, *Didache and Judaism: Jewish Roots of an Ancient Christian-Jewish Work* (London & New York: T&T Clark, 2008).

7 See: Philo, *Legatio ad Gaium* 156; *Hypothetica* 7:12; *De Somniis* II. 127 speaking of Jews in general; *Quod Omnis* 81–82 of the Essenes; Josephus, *Contra Apionem* II. 175; and the pre-70 Theodotos Inscription from Jerusalem, which reads: "Theodotos ... built the synagogue for reading the Law and studying the commandments," J.-B. Frey, *Corpus Inscriptionum Judaicarum* II (reprinted New York: Ktav, 1975), number 1404.

8 See: Luke 4:17–19; Acts 13:14–15.

9 See: *m.Meg.* 3:4; *t.Meg* 3:1–10; and discussion in L.I. Levene, *The Ancient Synagogue. The First Thousand Years* (New Haven: Yale University Press, 2000), pp. 506–10.

10 See: B. Nitzan, *Qumran Prayer and Religious Poetry* (Leiden: Brill, 1994); D.K. Falk, *Daily, Sabbath, and Festival Prayers in the Dead Sea Scrolls* (Leiden: Brill, 1998). There is, indeed, considerable documentary evidence for fixed orders of prayer associated with designated days and times among the Dead Sea texts: these prayers praise God as Creator, and celebrate His uniqueness, kingship, and His mercy to Israel, and His glory. There are also prayers beseeching God for forgiveness and pardon, for understanding and knowledge in the Torah, for peace, and for final redemption, which resonate clearly with the themes of prayers known to us from the Synagogue service today. There are, however, important differences between the contents of these prayers preserved by the Dead Sea Jews and the Synagogue prayers given in later documents: see Nitzan, *Qumran Prayer*, pp. 47–87.

11 On the prayer of the Therapeutae and its relationship to the ascetic life, see: Joan E. Taylor, *Jewish Women Philosophers of First Century Alexandria. Philo's 'Therapeutae' Reconsidered* (Oxford: Oxford University Press, 2003), pp. 126–53.

12 For what can be known of the origins of the Synagogue liturgy, see: Levine, *Ancient Synagogue*, pp. 501–60, and the magisterial article of S.C. Reif, "Prayer and Liturgy" in C. Hezser (ed.), *The Oxford Handbook of Jewish Daily Life in Roman Palestine* (Oxford: Oxford University Press, 2010), pp. 545–65.

13 As early as the third century BC, the Jewish translators of the Bible into Greek indicate that the Hebrew word *tabnît* was understood in this sense: they rendered it with the Greek term *paradeigma*, a word deeply associated with Plato's philosophy. The Jewish thinker Philo was to develop this insight much further: for further references to the understanding of the earthly sanctuary as a representation of the heavenly reality, see the discussion in A. le Boulluec & P. Sandevoir, *La Bible d'Alexandrie 2 L'Exode* (Paris: Cerf, 1989), pp. 252–3.

14 On this "synchronicity" between the heavenly and earthly worship in *Jubilees*, see: C.T.R. Hayward, *The Jewish Temple: A Non-Biblical Sourcebook* (London: Routledge, 1996), pp. 85–107

15 For discussion of the notion that Jews of the Dead Sea perceived themselves as a "human temple," see: Devorah Dimant, '4QFlorilegium and the Idea of the Community

as Temple', in A. Caquot, M. Hadas-Level & J. Riaud (eds), *Hellenica et Judaica: Hommage à Valentin Nikiprowetzky* (Leuven-Paris: Peeters, 1986), pp. 165–89; F. Schmidt, *How the Temple Thinks: Identity and Social Cohesion in Ancient Judaism* (Sheffield: Sheffield Academic Press, 2001), pp. 152, 162–4; Hannah K. Harrington, *The Purity Texts*, Companion to the Qumran Scrolls 5 (London: T&T Clark, 2004), pp. 28–38; J. Klawans, *Purity, Sacrifice, and the Temple. Symbolism and Supersessionism in the Study of Ancient Judaism* (Oxford: Oxford University Press, 2006), pp. 162–8. The word translated above as "thanksgiving," Hebrew *tôdāh*, is not entirely clear in the manuscript: it might be read as *tôrāh*, in which case the text would refer to "deeds of the Law." Unfortunately space forbids discussion of this important matter.

16 For Philo, see: *De Somniis* I.215; and for Rabbinic understandings of the Temple's structure and furnishings as symbolic of pious groups and individuals, see the Aramaic Targum Pseudo-Jonathan of Exod. 40:1–11, an English version of which is available in Michael Maher, *Targum Pseudo-Jonathan: Exodus*, The Aramaic Bible 2 (Collegeville: Liturgical Press, 1994), pp. 272–3. This symbolism can easily be reversed, such that the pious persons represent, or effectively constitute structures of the Temple. The Targum lies outside our time-frame; but *The Songs of the Sabbath Sacrifice* from the Dead Sea Scrolls do not, and their description of the heavenly Temple, whose walls and structures function as animate items uttering praise to the Almighty is striking and suggestive. See James R. Davila, "Exploring the Mystical Background of the Dead Sea Scrolls," in T.H. Lim & J.J. Collins (eds), *The Oxford Handbook of the Dead Sea Scrolls* (Oxford: Oxford University Press, 2010), pp. 44–5.

17 They also go to the Temple at the hour of prayer (Acts 3:1), that is, at the time of the daily sacrifice of the lamb and the incense, the *Tamid*. According to Rabbinic tradition (*m. Tamid* 3:2–3), this service began at dawn, the time when the Apostles are said to have been present (5:21).

18 For most recent discussion of differing scholarly views regarding the identity of the group at Qumran, and the relationship of the Qumran settlement to the documents discovered in the Dead Sea Caves, see: John J. Collins, *Beyond the Qumran Community. The Sectarian Movement of the Dead Sea Scrolls* (Grand Rapids: Eerdmans, 2010), pp. 166–208, who emphasizes that members of the *yahad* almost certainly lived in places other than Qumran, an important observation which is increasingly recognized in Dead Sea Scrolls scholarship. Translations of Dead Sea Scrolls offered here are mine, made from the texts printed in F. García Martinez & E.J.C. Tigchelaar, *The Dead Sea Scrolls Study Edition*, 2 vols (Leiden: Brill, 1997, 1998).

19 1QS 6:2–5. While most students of these texts agree that the meals of the Qumran *yahad* were religious events with strong sacral connotations, some dispute such an assessment of them: see, most recently, B. Eckhardt, "Meals and Politics in the *Yahad*: A Reconsideration," *Dead Sea Discoveries* 17 (2010), pp. 180–209. Against such assessments, see the compelling arguments of R. Kugler, "Making All Experience Religious: The Hegemony of Ritual at Qumran," *Journal for the Study of Judaism* 33 (2002), pp. 131–52, particularly pp. 137–8, and J. Magness, *Stone and Dung, Oil and Spit. Jewish Daily Life in the Time of Jesus* (Grand Rapids: Eerdmans, 2011), pp. 77–84.

20 An equally valid translation of the final phrase would be: "the men of the sanctuary," since the Hebrew noun *qōdesh* may signify both the abstract noun "holiness" and the proper noun "sanctuary, holy place."

21 See especially: Annie Jaubert, *La Notion d'Alliance dans le Judaïsme aux abords de l'ère chrétienne* (Paris: Seuil, 1963), pp. 212–14.

22 There is some scholarly discussion about the relationship of this council to the *yahad*; but the evidence strongly suggests that the council is an integral part of the *yahad*, not a splinter-group deriving from it. See further: Collins, *Beyond the Qumran Community*, pp. 69–74.

23 Scripture here records the duty of priests to distinguish between what is holy and what is unconsecrated: indulgence in wine can easily impair this, and Nadab and Abihu, who are condemned in Lev. 10:1–5, are reputed in a number of Rabbinic sources to have been drunk. See: *Sifra Shemini* Parashah 1.7; *Lev. Rab.* 12:1; *Tanhuma Buber Ahare Mot* 7.

24 See: 1QSᵃ 2:17–22.

25 See: A. Baumgarten, "Who Cares and Why Does It Matter? Qumran and the Essenes, Once Again!" *Dead Sea Discoveries* 11 (2004), pp.174–90. Collins, *Beyond the Qumran Community*, pp. 122–56 is inclined on balance to accept the identity of the *yahad* with Eseenes, although he scrupulously records the views of scholars who do not accept this identity, and notes that the *yahad* itself apparently allowed for a variety of practice.

26 Philo, *Quod Omnis Probus Liber Sit* 86; *Apologia Pro Iudaeis (Hypothetica)* 5, 11.

27 For holiness, see *Quod Omnis* 75, 91; *Apologia* 1: the very name "Essene" Philo explains with reference to this quality; and note how Philo stresses their concern for the holy Sabbath, when they meet in holy places called synagogues, sitting in order of rank (*Quod Omnis* 81–82). For their ethical concerns, see *Quod Omnis* 80; and on purity, which is strongly linked to love of God, *Quod Omnis* 84. Essene frugality is a feature of both accounts of the group; in *Apologia* 3, 7 Philo notes their mature years and (*Apologia* 13) their care for the aged.

28 See Josephus, *War* I.78–80; II. 113, 119–61 (the longest Jewish account of the Essenes), 267; III.11; V. 145; *Antiquities* XIII. 171–171; XV.371–379; XVIII.18–22; *Life* 10–11.

29 *War* II. 129. The Greek term for purification is *hagneia*: note that in LXX this word is used for the level of purity required for a Nazirite vow (Numb. 6:20, 21): see comments by G. Dorival, *La Bible d'Alexandrie 4 Les Nombres* (Paris: Cerf, 1994), pp. 243–4. The same word is used to speak of the purity of the Jerusalem Temple at 1 Macc. 14:36.

30 *War* II.129. "Pure ones" represents Greek *katharoi*, an adjective that in LXX may refer both to ritual purity (e.g., Lev. 7:19) and moral purity (e.g, Numb. 8:7; Prv. 20:9). The "sacred space" which Josephus mentions is Greek *temenos*, which frequently refers to a sacred precinct of a temple or shrine.

31 *War* II.130–31.

32 The "provider" translates Greek *chorēgos*, signifying one who defrays the expenses of the chorus in the performance of a tragic drama and, by extension, comes to mean one who provides a public service for the benefit of others. At the end of a meal at which bread has been eaten, modern Jews, following an invitation to bless "Him of whose bounty (literally, 'of what belongs to Him') we have eaten," reply: "Blessed be He of whose bounty (literally, 'of what belongs to Him') we have eaten, and *by whose goodness we live.*"

33 *War* II.131.

34 *War* II. 138.

35 See: *m.Demai* 2:2–3; *Tosefta Demai* 2:2, 10–12; and S. Lieberman, "The Discipline in the So-Called Dead Sea Manual of Discipline," *JBL* 71 (1952), pp. 199–206; Ch. Rabin, *Qumran Studies* (Oxford: Oxford University Press, 1957), pp. 12–21; A. Oppenheimer, "Haverim," in L.H. Schiffman & J.C. Vanderkam (eds), *Encyclopedia of the Dead Sea Scrolls*, vol. 2 (New York: Oxford University Press, 2000), pp. 333–6.

36 On the *haburah* and the Pharisees, consult the judicious remarks of J. Klawans, *Impurity and Sin in Ancient Judaism* (Oxford: Oxford University Press, 2000),

pp. 108–10, where he convincingly challenges the opinions of E.P. Sanders, "Did the Pharisees Eat Ordinary Food in Purity?" in Sanders's book *Jewish Law from Jesus to the Mishnah: Five Studies* (London: SCM Press, 1990), pp. 131–254.

37 It should be emphasized that the Jewish traditions we have noted, and many others not mentioned here, were not transferred into Christianity in any simplistic fashion. The Jewish rules of purity, for example, were set aside in respect of the food laws (see Mk. 7:1–16; Acts 10:9–16; note, however, the remarks and qualifications of St Paul on this subject at Rom. 14:1–8, where continuing observance of these laws is at least permitted for some Christians). The purity laws regarding sexual conduct, however, were retained in force (see: 1 Cor. 5:1–15; 6:12–16). Similarly, the Christian priesthood ceased to be a hereditary affair, as it is among the Jews; nonetheless, very early Christian authorities continued to speak of Christian ministers explicitly in terms of the priests and Levites of the Old Testament: see 1 Clement 41:1–13.

38 See especially: 1 Cor. 14:40, where the Apostle commands that *everything* in the Church be done in order: the last word translates Greek *taxis*, the very word used by Philo of the order prevailing among the Essenes (*Quod Omnis* 81, where they sit in orders or ranks in their synagogues on sabbath) and the Therapeuatae (*VC* 75, 80, in respect of their meals and sacred chants), and by Josephus of the Essenes at their meals (*War* II.130, 132). The principal rule book of the Qumran *yahad* is called *serekh ha-yahad*, "the order of the *yahad*": the term *serekh* is found also in Aramaic, and features in the *Aramaic Testament of Levi* discovered among the Dead Sea Scrolls. We are fortunate to possess a Greek version of parts of this document, in which it is clear that the Greek word *taxis* has been used to represent an original *serekh*.

39 Thus St Paul can state baldly, without having to explain himself, that "our Passover is sacrificed for us, Christ" (1 Cor. 5:7), and can refer to the unleavened bread accompanying the Paschal sacrifice and its symbolic significance as known to addressees, many of whom may not have been of Jewish birth. The Apostle's earlier command to "purge out the old leaven" refers to a requirement, not mentioned in the Bible, to remove all traces of leaven from dwellings. This ruling is attested as early as the fifth century BC in the famous "Passover Papyrus" from Elephantine in Egypt. See: A.E. Cowley, *Aramaic Papyri of the Fifth Century B.C.* (Oxford: Clarendon Press, 1923), pp. 62–3.

40 For the co-relation of grapes, wine, and blood in Scripture, see: Gen. 49:11; Deut. 32:14; 1 Macc. 6:34; Isa. 63:3; and (with reference specifically to the Temple service) Ecclus. 50:16 (Vulgate).

41 The Passover *Seder* meal of modern times, with its four cups of wine and accompanying narrative (*Haggadah*) of the events at the going forth from Egypt; the questions posed by the children and the corresponding answers; the symbolic meanings attached to the components of the meal; and the exposition of sections of Scripture, have often been invoked in discussions about the origins of Christian worship. The earliest accounts of the *Seder* may be found in *m.Pesahim* 10. It cannot, however, properly be employed to explain aspects of the Gospel accounts of the institution of the Eucharist; and its value as a source for the study of later Christian liturgical developments is uncertain, and hedged about with myriad qualifications. The evidence at our disposal supports most strongly the conclusion that the *Haggadah* originated after the destruction of the Temple in 70. See: B.M. Bokser, *The Origins of the Seder: The Passover Rite and Early Rabbinic Judaism* (Berkeley: University of California Press, 1984); I.J. Yuval, "Easter and Passover as Early Jewish-Christian Dialogue," in P.F. Bradshaw & L.A. Hoffman (eds), *Passover and Easter: Origin and*

History to Modern Times (Notre Dame: University of Notre Dame Pres, 1999), pp. 98–214. For the contrary view, that even in the days before 70 the Passover meal was followed by a commemoration of some kind, see: J. Tabory, "Towards a History of the Paschal Meal," in Bradshaw & Hoffman (eds), *Passover and Easter*, pp. 62–80; idem, "Jewish Festivals in Late Antiquity," in Katz (ed.), *Cambridge History of Judaism*, pp. 556–72; but it must be stressed that no texts surviving from the pre-70 period unambiguously and directly attest to such a commemoration.

42 For concise, up-to-date information on *Jubilees*, see now: M. Segal, article "Jubilees, Book of," in J.J. Collins & D.C. Harlow (eds), *The Eerdmans Dictionary of Early Judaism* (Grand Rapids: Eerdmans, 2010), pp. 843–6. It is almost certain that this book (or at the very least the traditions which inform it) was known to several New Testament writers: see the still invaluable observations of R.H. Charles, "The Book of Jubilees," in R.H. Charles (ed.), *The Apocrypha and Pseudepigrapha of the Old Testament*, vol. 2 (Oxford: Clarendon Press, 1913), pp. 9–10. On the Dead Sea text which expounds Isaac's sacrifice as a willing victim, see J. Kugel, "Exegetical Notes on 4Q225 'Pseudo-Jubilees,'" *Dead Sea Discoveries* 13 (2006), pp. 61–98.

43 Philo, *De Abrahamo* 198.

44 See *m. Tamid* 4:1, where the anonymous Mishnah states the rule: "They do not tie the lamb (of the daily sacrifice), but bind it, *me'aqîdin 'ôtô*": for Hebrew text and notes see P. Blackman, *Mishnayoth, volume 5 Order Kodashim* (New York: The Judaica Press, 1964), pp. 482–3, where he remarks that what the Mishnah forbids here is the tying of fore-legs together and hind-legs together as in idolatrous sacrifice; rather, the text orders the binding of each fore-leg to its corresponding hind-leg.

45 From the outset, the Eucharist was offered at least once a week, sometimes daily when circumstances permitted. It was never confined to an annual celebration, whereas Passover to this day is celebrated but once a year, in the springtime. The "extension" (as it were) of Isaac's sacrifice and of the Passover offering to the daily offering of the lamb in the service of the Temple is highly instructive here, as indicating how, within ancient Judaism, single significant theological events could be regularly re-presented, as it were, in the Temple Service.

46 The accounts of the earlier sacrifices of Abel and Cain (Gen. 4:3–5) and of Noah (Gen. 8:20–22) do not specify the victims; and the offering of Melchizedek consisted of bread and wine (Gen. 14:18–20). Jewish tradition concerning the latter is to the fore in the Canon of the Mass in the prayer *Supra quae*, where Melchizedek is designated *summus sacerdos*. He is never accorded this title in Scripture; but post-biblical Jewish tradition does so refer to him as, for example, in the Aramaic Bible translations (Targums) of Gen. 14:18 represented in Targum Neofiti and the Fragment Targum (Paris Manuscript). See R. le Déaut, "Le titre *Summus Sacerdos* donné à Melchisédech est-il d'origine juive?" *Recherches de Science Religieuse* 50 (1962), pp. 222–9.

47 See: 2 Chronicles 3:1, where St. Jerome translates: *Et coepit Salomon aedificare domum Domini in Hierusalem in monte Moria.*

48 See: Luke 2:36–38; and 2:25–35 for Symeon, *justus et timoratus expectans consolationem Israhel*, who is also in the Temple when he sees the Christ. Both Symeon and Anna represent the frugal, ascetic type of piety centred on the Temple which recalls in some manner the simplicity of living prescribed in the rules of the *yahad* and among the Therapeutae; both Anna and Symeon may, indeed, point to the existence of much larger groups of Jewish people sharing their opinions than extant sources mention. It is, nonetheless, among these particular representatives of Judaism that the Gospel states, without sensing the need for explanation, that Christ was unambiguously

acknowledged; and the note that a number of Jewish priests accepted the faith (Acts 6:7) should not be forgotten in this regard.

49 For a penetrating critique of negative and sometimes ill-informed representations in scholarly literature of the Jewish priesthood, Temple service, and formal rituals required by the Torah, see Klawans, *Purity, Sacrifice, and Temple,* which demonstrates the enduring centrality of the sanctuary and its sacrificial service in Jewish religious life. The fall of the Temple presented Jews with a major problem, on which see R. Goldenberg, 'The Destruction of the Jerusalem Temple: its Meaning and its Consequences,' in Katz (ed.), *Cambridge History of Judaism,* 191–205. In modern Orthodox Judaism, the reading of the portions of Scripture commanding the various sacrifices takes place in the Synagogue service; and this solemn reciting of the commandments and reflection upon them is offered in place of the sacrifices themselves.

50 So Philo, *De Spec. Legibus* I.172–173; *De Vita Mosis* II.104; *Quis Rerum Divinarum Heres Sit* 226, who speaks of the twelve loaves set out on the pure table in the holy place as both testifying to and representing thanksgiving for the order of creation and the Lord's provision of food for His creatures.

51 For the texts of *Songs of the Sabbath Sacrifice,* where angelic worship culminates in a celestial sacrifice, see: García Martinez & Tigchelaar, *The Dead Sea Scrolls Study Edition,* vol. 2, pp. 811–37, and the remarks of Klawans, *Purity, Sacrifice, and the Temple,* pp. 134–8, and P. Schäfer, *The Origins of Jewish Mysticism* (Princeton-Oxford: Princeton University Press, 2009), pp. 144–9. The complex problem of the place of the Sanctus in the eucharistic rites of antiquity has been thoroughly examined by Bryan Spinks: see particularly his "The Jewish Sources for the Sanctus," *The Heythrop Journal* 21 (1980), pp. 168–79, and *The Sanctus in the Eucharistic Prayer* (Cambridge: Cambridge University Press, 2002). The several forms of the Jewish prayer *Qedushah* (which quotes Isa. 6:3), and its formal adoption into the Synagogue service, present many interesting points of comparison with the Sanctus as we have here discussed it: see Levene, *The Ancient Synagogue,* pp. 540–5.

52 See: Col. 3:1–2, *igitur si conresurrexistis Christo quae sursum sunt quaerite ubi Christus est in dextera Dei sedens. quae sursum sunt sapite.* See also: Eph. 1:20. Note also the prayer *Supplices te* of the Roman Canon, in which Christ, spoken of as *angelus,* is petitioned to take the sacrifice offered on earth *in sublime altare tuum, in conspectu divinae majestatis tuae.*

Bibliography

Baumgarten, A., "Who Cares and Why Does It Matter? Qumran and the Essenes, Once Again!" *Dead Sea Discoveries,* 11 (2004), pp. 174–90.

Bickerman, E., *The God of the Maccabees* (Leiden: Brill, 1979).

Blackman, P., *Mishnayoth Volume 5 Order Kodashim* (New York: The Judaica Press, 1964).

Bokser, B.M., *The Origins of the Seder: The Passover Rite and Early Rabbinic Judaism* (Berkeley: University of California Press, 1984).

Bradshaw, P.F., *Eucharistic Origins* (Oxford: Oxford University Press, 2004).

Charles, R.H., "The Book of Jubilees" in R.H. Charles (ed.), *The Apocrypha and Pseudepigrapha of the Old Testament,* vol. 2 (Oxford: Clarendon Press, 1913), pp. 1–82.

Collins, J.J., *Beyond the Qumran Community: The Sectarian Movement of the Dead Sea Scrolls* (Grand Rapids: Eerdmans 2010).

Cowley, A.E., *Aramaic Papyri of the Fifth Century B.C.* (Oxford: Clarendon Press, 1923).

Davila, J.R., "Exploring the Mystical Background of the Dead Sea Scrolls," in T.H. Lim & J.J. Collins (eds), *The Oxford Handbook of the Dead Sea Scrolls* (Oxford: Oxford University Press, 2010), pp. 433–54.

Del Verme, M., *Didache and Judaism: Jewish Roots of an Ancient Christian-Jewish Work* (London-New York: T&T Clark, 2008).

Dimant, D., "*4QFlorilegium* and the Idea of the Community as Temple," in A. Caquot, M. Hadas-Level, & J. Riaud (eds), *Hellenica et Judaica: Hommage à Valentin Nikiprowetzky* (Leuven & Paris: Peeters, 1986), pp. 165–89.

Dorival, G., *La Bible d'Alexandrie 4 Les Nombres* (Paris: Cerf, 1994).

Draper, J.A. (ed.), *The Didache in Modern Research* (Leiden: Brill, 1996).

Eckhardt, B., "Meals and Politics in the *Yahad*: A Reconsideration," *Dead Sea Discoveries*, 17 (2010), pp. 180–209.

Falk, D.K., *Daily, Sabbath, and Festival Prayers in the Dead Sea Scrolls* (Leiden: Brill, 1998).

Fine, S., *This Holy Place: On the Sanctity of the Synagogue during the Greco-Roman Period* (Notre Dame: University of Notre Dame Press, 1997).

Frey, J.-B., *Corpus Inscriptionum Judaicarum II* (repr., New York: Ktav, 1975).

García Martinez, F. & E.J.C. Tigchelaar, *The Dead Sea Scrolls Study Edition*, 2 vols (Leiden: Brill, 1997, 1998).

Goldenberg, R., "The Destruction of the Jerusalem Temple: its Meaning and its Consequences," in S. Katz (ed.), *The Cambridge History of Judaism. Volume 4 The Late Roman-Rabbinic Period* (Cambridge: Cambridge University Press, 2006), pp. 191–205.

Harrington, H.K., *The Purity Texts* (London: T&T Clark, 2004).

Hayward, C.T.R., *The Jewish Temple: A Non-Biblical Sourcebook* (London: Routledge, 1996).

Himmelfarb, M., *A Kingdom of Priests. Ancestry and Merit in Ancient Judaism* (Philadelphia: University of Philadelphia Press, 2006).

Jaubert, A., *La Notion d'Alliance dans le Judaïsme aux abords de l'ère chrétienne* (Paris: Seuil, 1963).

Kampen, J., *The Hasideans and the Origins of Pharisaism: A Study in 1 and 2 Maccabees* (Atlanta: Scholars Press, 1988).

Klawans, J., *Impurity and Sin in Ancient Judaism* (Oxford: Oxford University Press, 2000).

—— *Purity, Sacrifice, and the Temple. Symbolism and Supersessionism in the Study of Ancient Judaism* (Oxford: Oxford University Press, 2006).

Kugel, J., "Exegetical Notes on 4Q225 'Pseudo-Jubilees,'" *Dead Sea Discoveries* 13 (2006), pp. 61–98.

Kugler, R., "Making All Experience Religious: The Hegemony of Ritual at Qumran," *Journal for the Study of Judaism*, 33 (2002), pp. 131–52.

Lapin, H., "The Origins and Development of the Rabbinic Movement in the Land of Israel," in Katz (ed.), *The Cambridge History of Judaism. Volume 4 The Late-Roman Rabbinic Period* (Cambridge: Cambridge University Press, 2006), pp. 206–29.

Le Boulluec, A. & P. Sandevoir, *La Bible d'Alexandrie 2 L'Exode* (Paris: Cerf, 1989).

Le Déaut, R., "Le titre Summus Sacerdos donné à Melchisédech est-il d'origine juive?" *Recherches de Science Religieuse*, 50 (1962), pp. 222–9.

Levene, L.I., *The Ancient Synagogue: The First Thousand Years* (New Haven: Yale University Press, 2000).

Lieberman, S., "The Discipline in the So-Called Dead Sea Manual of Discipline," *Journal of Biblical Literature* 71 (1952), pp. 199–306.

Magness, J., *Stone and Dung, Oil and Spit. Jewish Daily Life in the Time of Jesus* (Grand Rapids: Eerdmans, 2011).

Maher, M., *Targum Pseudo-Jonathan: Exodus* (Collegeville: Liturgical Press, 1994).

Milgrom, J., *Leviticus*, 3 vols (New York: Doubleday, 1991, 2000, 2000).

—— *Leviticus. A Continental Commentary* (Minneapolis: Fortress Press, 2004).

Naudé, J., "Holiness in the Dead Sea Scrolls," in P.W. Flint & J.C. VanderKam, *The Dead Sea Scrolls after Fifty Years: A Comprehensive Assessment*, vol. 2 (Leiden: Brill, 1999), pp. 171–99.

Nitzan, B., *Qumran Prayer and Religious Poetry* (Ledien: Brill, 1994).

Oppenheimer, A., "Haverim," in L.H. Schiffman & J.C. VanderKam, *Encyclopedia of the Dead Sea Scrolls*, vol. 2 (New York: Oxford University Press, 2000), pp. 333–6.

Rabin, Ch., *Qumran Studies* (Oxford: Oxford University Press, 1957).

Reif, S.C., "Prayer and Liturgy," in C. Hezser (ed.), *The Oxford Handbook of Jewish Daily Life in Roman Palestine* (Oxford: Oxford University Press, 2010), pp. 545–65.

Rosenfeld, Ben Zion, "The Title 'Rabbi' in Third- to Seventh-Century Inscriptions in Palestine: Revisited," *Journal of Jewish Studies* 61 (2010), pp. 234–56.

Sanders, E.P., *Jewish Law from Jesus to the Mishnah: Five Studies* (London: SCM Press, 1990).

Schäfer, P., *The Origins of Jewish Mysticism* (Princeton & Oxford: Princeton University Press, 2009).

Schmidt, F., *How the Temple Thinks: Identity and Social Cohesion in Ancient Judaism* (Sheffield: Sheffield Academic Press, 2001).

Segal, M., "Jubilees, Book of," in J.J. Collins & D.C. Harlow (eds), *The Eerdmans Dictionary of Early Judaism* (Grand Rapids: Eerdmans, (2010), pp. 843–6.

Spinks, B.D., "The Jewish Sources for the Sanctus," *The Heythrop Journal*, 21 (1980), pp. 168–79.

—— *The Sanctus in the Eucharistic Prayer* (Cambridge: Cambridge University Press, 2002).

Strack, H.L. & G. Stemberger, *Introduction to the Talmud and Midrash* (Minneapolis: Fortress Press, 1992).

Tabory, J., "Towards a History of the Paschal Meal," in P.F. Bradshaw & L.A. Hoffman (eds), *Passover and Easter: Origin and History to Modern Times* (Notre Dame: University of Notre Dame Press, 1999), pp. 62–80.

—— "Festivals in Late Antiquity" in Katz (ed.), *The Cambridge History of Judaism. Volume 4: The Late Roman-Rabbinic Period* (Cambridge: Cambridge University Press, 2006), pp. 556–72.

Taylor, J., *Jewish Women Philosophers of First Century Alexandria. Philo's 'Therapeutae' Reconsidered* (Oxford: Oxford University Press, 2003).

Wintermute, O.S., "Jubilees," in J.H. Charlesworth (ed.), *The Old Testament Pseudepigrapha*, vol. 2 (London: Darton, Longman & Todd, 1985) pp. 35–142.

Yuval, I.J. (1999), "Easter and Passover as Early Jewish-Christian Dialogue," in P.F. Bradshaw & L.A. Hoffman (eds), *Passover and Easter: Origin and History to Modern Times* (Notre Dame: University of Notre Dame Press, 1999), pp. 98–214.

Chapter 3

THE STUDY OF EARLY CHRISTIAN WORSHIP

Daniel G. Van Slyke

The study of early Christian worship is no mere matter of historical interest; it has directly and dramatically transformed the manner in which hundreds of thousands of Christians worship every day. Therefore, this chapter will begin by outlining the practical impact that mid-twentieth century scholarship on early Christian worship exerted on the liturgical revisions among Catholics as well as many Protestants which followed the Second Vatican Council. Special attention will be given to the theory that Hippolytus wrote a document known as the *Apostolic Tradition* that witnesses Roman liturgical practice in the early-third century. In the second section, the recent shifts in methodology that have marked the field of early Christian studies in general, and of the study of early Christian worship in particular, will be outlined. Having appropriated the radical reorientation of the field, the third and final section goes beyond the limitations of contemporary methodology in order to appreciate the significance of early Christian worship from the perspective of early Christians themselves.

This chapter focuses on the study of early Christian worship rather than on early Christian worship itself. Several sophisticated but accessible overviews and summaries on early Christian worship have recently been published in English,[1] and collections of the major source texts are readily available.[2] No overview or collection, however, could do justice to the sheer volume of scholarship on ancient Christian worship that has been produced since the mid-twentieth century. Therefore, this study aims at two more modest goals. First, it will illustrate, with particular examples from the post-conciliar revisions of Roman liturgical books, the influence of the study of early Christian worship on contemporary liturgical practice. Second, it will outline wider trends in the academic field of ancient Christian worship as a whole with a view to suggesting a rationale for such study that will ensure it a future.

I. Practical impact of the study of early Christian worship in the liturgical revisions of the twentieth century

A. Impact of early Christian studies on revised liturgical books

The scholars who constructed liturgical history, as it is widely known and accepted today, made their most extensive contributions in the twentieth century. That is also when historical scholarship had the most impact on the actual practice of liturgy, especially through its influence on the revision of liturgical books, which affected their very shape and content. Therefore, it is apropos to begin the study of early Christian worship by stressing its practical consequences in the twentieth and twenty-first centuries.

This influence was especially mediated through a number of consultors or experts who worked on the production of liturgical books following the Second Vatican Council. The Council's Constitution on the Sacred Liturgy *Sacrosanctum Concilium* (4 December 1963) insisted upon the role of history in the *instauratio*—renewal or restoration—of Roman liturgical books:

> In order that healthy tradition (*sana traditio*) can be preserved while yet allowing room for legitimate development, thorough investigation—theological, historical and pastoral—of the individual parts of the liturgy up for revision is always to be the first step ... Finally, changes should not be made unless a real and proven need of the church requires them, and care should be taken to see that new forms grow in some way organically out of the forms already existing (n. 23).[3]

The Council Fathers further mandated that: "As soon as possible, the books used in the liturgy are to be revised, with experts brought in (*peritis adhibitis*), and bishops from various parts of the world consulted" (n. 25). In these brief passages, *Sacrosanctum Concilium* marks historical investigation as a cornerstone in the foundation of the restored liturgical books, thereby heightening the influence of scholars deemed as experts or *periti* in Christian history.

Pope Paul VI sought to implement the Council's mandates in part by forming a special commission to carry out the revisions in his motu proprio *Sacram Liturgiam* of January 25, 1964.[4] It was entitled the *Consilium for the Implementation of the Constitution on the Sacred Liturgy* (*Consilium ad Exsequendam Constitutionem de Sacra Liturgia*). The forty members of the *Consilium* were cardinals and bishops who oversaw the process of revision. A group of consultors, most of whom were highly educated priest-scholars, carried out the actual work of revision, that is, the production of revised texts.[5] A number of the most prominent experts in the history of Christian worship at the time served as consultors, including Bernard Botte, Louis Bouyer, Pierre-Marie Gy, Pierre Jounel, Josef Jungmann, Aimé-Georges Martimort, Adrien Nocent, and Rembert Weakland.[6] As was expected, in their work of revising liturgical books, these consultors drew from the theories and presuppositions regarding early Christian liturgy that were current during their time.

B. The heyday of Hippolytus

Of all the historical theories relating to early Christian liturgy current in the mid-twentieth century, the one regarding Hippolytus of Rome and a document known as the *Apostolic Tradition* had by far the most overwhelming practical impact. The theory in question posits that Hippolytus, a priest and later an anti-pope in Rome, wrote a document titled the *Apostolic Tradition*, which represents Roman liturgical practices in the early third century. Most histories of early Christian worship assumed this as fact, and the *Apostolic Tradition* remains staple piece of evidence for many studies. Considering this theory, then, will demonstrate several points. First, the agendas of scholars hankering for liturgical reform have prejudiced the study of early Christian liturgy. Second, the study of early Christian liturgy has had a practical impact, illustrated here in the revision of Roman liturgical books in the twentieth century. Third, scholarship on liturgical history is limited and imperfect; theories and methods once widely accepted may prove untenable later.

Before illustrating these three points, a more detailed introduction to the source and the genre to which it belongs is in order. The *Apostolic Tradition* belongs to a genre of literature from the first centuries of Christianity known as "ancient church orders." Examples of this genre include the *Didache*, the *Didascalia Apostolorum*, and the *Testamentum Domini*. Ancient church orders read like manuals intended for the leaders of early Christian communities, "purporting to offer authoritative 'apostolic' prescriptions on matters of moral conduct, liturgical practice, and ecclesiastical organization and discipline."[7] The ancient church orders contain material dating from the second through the fourth centuries, although attempts to establish their exact provenance are largely inconclusive. Similarly inconclusive are the myriad attempts that have been made to determine the relationships among the various ancient church orders, many of which have similar or related material. Most of the ancient church orders were discovered or re-discovered in the late-nineteenth century, and therefore attracted much attention from scholars throughout the twentieth century. When the eminent German scholar Georg Kretschmar summarized research on early Christian liturgy up to the 1980s, he devoted much of his attention to various theories regarding the inter-relationships among the ancient church orders, beginning with the *Apostolic Tradition*.[8] Although ancient church orders have fascinated scholars, the attention placed upon the genre is out of proportion with its actual influence in the development of living liturgical rites throughout the centuries.

The *Apostolic Tradition* survives in more or less complete versions in several languages: Latin, Sahidic, Arabic, Ethiopic, and some Greek fragments. Among liturgical rites briefly indicated in the *Apostolic Tradition* one finds ordination rites for bishops, presbyters, and deacons, a eucharistic prayer in the context of the ordination of a bishop, prescriptions regarding Christian initiation, blessings for oil and cheese, and various jumbled directions for such matters as fasting, almsgiving, and the manner of treating and receiving the Eucharist. John F. Baldovin summarizes the commonly-held theory regarding the authorship of the *Apostolic Tradition* that was widely accepted until the 1990s:

Here we have a church order that gives us data on important ecclesiastical practices from the early-third century. The writer was a presbyter/theologian, named Hippolytus, who opposed Bishop Callistus of Rome over the latter's laxity in readmitting sinners to church fellowship. He thus became a schismatic anti-pope, but was reconciled before his death as a martyr. A conservative, he advocated ancient usages of the Church. A crusty old parish priest unwilling to abide by his bishop's liturgical innovations, he set down in a single document these rather antiquarian rules for liturgy and church conduct.[9]

This synthesis was championed by, among others, Josef Jungmann. Jungmann was a member of the *Consilium* and the single most influential historian of ancient Christian liturgy in the mid-twentieth century.[10] His two-volume *Missarum Solemnia*, translated as *Mass of the Roman Rite*, was practically a handbook for the consultors who worked on revising the Roman liturgy after the Second Vatican Council. The work remains widely read and influential. Jungmann holds that Hippolytus wrote the *Apostolic Tradition* around the year 215. For Jungmann, the *Apostolic Tradition* provides a "type" or "model formulary" of the anaphora or eucharistic prayer as it was said in early third-century Rome.[11] Hence Jungmann employs its anaphora as a constant point of reference throughout his study.

Complications arise when the anaphora of the *Apostolic Tradition* is compared with the Roman canon, which was the only eucharistic prayer used in the Roman Rite for at least fourteen centuries.[12] Quoted at length by St Ambrose in the late fourth century,[13] the Roman canon differs radically from the eucharistic prayer contained in the *Apostolic Tradition*. For Jungmann, the assumption that the *Apostolic Tradition* records the eucharistic prayer of early third-century Rome justifies criticism of the Roman canon as a corruption of the primitive Roman usage: "In contrast to the smooth-flowing eucharistic prayer recorded by Hippolytus, the Roman canon, with its separate members and steps, and its broken-up lists of saints, presents a picture of great complexity."[14] This statement hints that an agenda in favor of reforming the liturgy prejudices interpretation of the sources. Moreover, Jungmann was not the only consultor of the *Consilium* to compare unfavorably the Roman canon with the prayer attributed to Hippolytus. Bernard Botte likewise was keenly interested in the *Apostolic Tradition*. He put great effort into reconstructing the text from its surviving manuscripts in Latin, Sahidic, Arabic, Bohairic, and Ethiopic, along with the few extant fragments in Greek.[15] Like Jungmann, Botte held that Hippolytus authored the work and that it provided an anaphora composed in third-century Rome.[16] Adrien Nocent, in an article written during the period in which he served on the *Consilium*, also moves from praising Hippolytus to enumerating "the problems raised by our canon."[17]

This agenda or prejudice against the Roman canon, bolstered in part by the study of early Christian worship, had a practical influence on the liturgical reform of the twentieth century. Jungmann, Botte and Nocent worked on *Consilium* study groups dedicated to revising various parts of the Mass. Thus the members of the *Consilium* considered the *Apostolic Tradition*'s anaphora to be representative of "sound" Roman tradition, and regarded it as a viable and even preferable alternative to the Roman canon. In fact, despite a number of dissimilarities,[18] the Hippolytan anaphora is frequently cited as the main source for eucharistic Prayer II of the post-Vatican II Roman missal.[19] Eucharistic Prayer II is now used more frequently than any of the others, including the ancient Roman canon. Brevity appears to be the primary reason for its popularity, although its pretensions to representing the ancient prayer of the Roman Church greatly bolster its prestige. The Hippolytan anaphora also served as the basis for revised eucharistic rites in the Church of England's *Book of Common Worship* and among United Methodists.

Yet the widely accepted synthesis regarding the *Apostolic Tradition* rested on shaky grounds. Thus the third point of this section arises: scholarship on liturgical history is limited and imperfect. Louis Bouyer incisively criticized the hypothesis that Hippolytus wrote the *Apostolic Tradition*, and that it includes the eucharistic prayer of early-third-century Rome:

> As we have seen, the intrinsic reasons that are present for so thinking—we mean those that can result from a knowledge of [Hippolytus'] work and personality— are so flimsy, not to say non-existent, that it seems that this alone ought to be enough to dispel the curious illusion to which the majority of modern scholars have succumbed. To explain the evolution that might have produced the canon of the Roman Mass of St Gregory with Hippolytus' liturgy as a starting point, is to set a task for ourselves that has no chance of success. Without sufficient reason, even without any probability of success we should be committing ourselves to an impossible route. By continuing to follow this course, we will be fated to end up with the idea that the canon of the Roman Mass is inexplicable, unjustifiable and unacceptable, merely because we have wished at all costs to impose upon it an explanation that does not stand up.[20]

Jungmann must have been aware of the criticisms articulated by Bouyer, since they served on the very same study group,[21] while Botte and Nocent likely knew Bouyer's work as well. Hence these consultors had good reason to suspect that the *Apostolic Tradition* was not quite central to the history of the Roman Mass. Why, then, did they use it as the very cornerstone in that history?

Further investigation again points to a pre-conceived agenda that, as Bouyer suggested, concerned the Roman canon all along. A number of the scholars destined for the *Consilium* targeted the Roman canon as a "problem" as early as 1951.[22] In that year, the Trier Liturgical Institute organized a meeting at the Abbey of Maria Laach in Germany.[23] According to Botte's report, Jungmann proposed making changes to the Roman canon. Other scholars in attendance thought it too difficult to change the present text, but apparently proposed composing alternative eucharistic prayers instead.[24] When these same scholars became consultors of the *Consilium*, they continued to view the Roman canon as a problem but could not change it much on account of its venerable antiquity and continuous use. Hence they proceeded to compose alternative eucharistic prayers, and pre-eminent among the new anaphoras was one purportedly based upon the *Apostolic Tradition*.[25] It appears that commitment to the agenda to alter or eliminate the

Roman canon drove many scholars of the *Consilium*—whether consciously or not—to accept an ultimately unsustainable hypothesis regarding the *Apostolic Tradition*.

Bouyer's doubts about the "curious illusion" fostered by Botte and Jungmann have been vindicated by subsequent historical research.[26] Paul Bradshaw, a foremost expert on ancient church orders, argues that "the very existence of a work entitled *Apostolic Tradition* by Hippolytus of Rome is not above suspicion."[27] Detailed analyses of the *Apostolic Tradition* in recent years suggest that it is "an aggregation of material from different sources, quite possibly arising from different geographical regions and probably from different historical periods, from perhaps as early as the mid-second century to as late as the mid-fourth."[28] In short, the *Apostolic Tradition* simply does not represent the eucharistic prayer of third-century Rome, and may not represent a prayer actually used by any ancient community. Recent research, then, has shattered the historical hypothesis behind the use of the *Apostolic Tradition* by twentieth-century liturgists.

What is the practical impact on the liturgy of the now-defunct theory regarding Hippolytus and the *Apostolic Tradition*? Through eucharistic prayer II, the anaphora formerly attributed to Hippolytus remains at the heart of the Missal of Pope Paul VI. The *Consilium* directly drew from the *Apostolic Tradition* when revising several other liturgical rites as well. The Rite of Christian Initiation of Adults is an obvious example: "the Roman Catholic adult catechumenate would never have taken its present shape without the framework provided by Hippolytus."[29] Less well-known is the direct influence of the *Apostolic Tradition* upon the consecratory prayers in the revised rites of ordination.[30] Other uses of the *Apostolic Tradition* are still more dubious. For example, the terminology regarding consecration to the offices of acolyte and lector has shifted from "ordination" to "institution" on the basis of an appeal to the so-called *Apostolic Tradition*.[31] On the theoretical level, the assumption that the *Apostolic Tradition* represents practices from the third-century or earlier underlies numerous opinions that remain common in surveys of the history of liturgy and practical proposals for reform. One example is the notion that Gallican religious culture introduced bewildering complexity to an essentially simple Roman celebration.[32]

In short, an outdated historical theory directly impacted the revision of numerous liturgical rites. This consideration does not invalidate the revised rites approved by the Church, although it does draw into question the process by which they were produced. Nonetheless, rather than face the problem squarely, liturgical scholars have tended to ignore it. Therefore, the faulty hypothesis that Hippolyus wrote the *Apostolic Tradition* remains widely accepted in the field of liturgical studies.[33] As a result, the fields of early Christian studies and liturgy, once closely connected for the pragmatic purpose of reforming the liturgy, have begun to drift apart. This drift has been exacerbated by the conclusion of the practical work of revising contemporary liturgical rites—work that proceeded feverishly in the 1960s and 1970s, but dissipated and largely drew to conclusion in the 1980s and 1990s.

C. Archeologism: the antiquity of any agenda

The theory that Hippolytus recorded the Roman liturgy of the early third century has been examined above to demonstrate the influence and limits of scholarship on early Christian worship, as well as the extent to which agendas for reform color such scholarship. The influence stems from a methodological presupposition that the most ancient demonstrable example of Christian worship is or should be the most authoritative, and therefore the one to be restored and enacted. This presupposition has been called "archeologism" or "antiquarianism." Joseph Ratzinger commented on the influence of antiquarianism over liturgical studies in the twentieth century:

> As I see it, the problem with a large part of modern liturgiology is that it tends to recognize only antiquity as a source, and therefore normative, and to regard everything developed later, in the Middle Ages and through the Council of Trent, as decadent. And so one ends up with dubious reconstructions of the most ancient practice, fluctuating criteria, and never-ending suggestions for reform, which lead ultimately to the disintegration of the liturgy that has evolved in a living way. On the other hand, it is important and necessary to see that we cannot take as our norm the ancient in itself and as such, nor must we automatically write off later developments as alien to the original form of the liturgy. There can be a thoroughly living kind of development in which a seed at the origin of something ripens and bears fruit.[34]

Baldovin takes issue with Ratzinger's "serious indictment of the kind of work that many liturgical historians do." Baldovin asks, "Does the work of modern liturgiology really romanticize the early church in a way that treats all subsequent development as mistaken?"[35] The answer depends in part upon what is meant by "modern." If the word designates the early- and mid-twentieth century, as Ratzinger uses it, then even Baldovin admits that such romanticization is evident among the most prominent scholars in the field at that time, including Jungmann. In 1947, Pope Pius XII warned noted tendencies toward archeologism in come circles, and warned against it:

> The liturgy of the early ages is most certainly worthy of all veneration. But ancient usage must not be esteemed more suitable and proper, either in its own right or in its significance for later times and new situations, on the simple ground that it carries the savor and aroma of antiquity. The more recent liturgical rites likewise deserve reverence and respect. They, too, owe their inspiration to the Holy Spirit, who assists the Church in every age ... it is neither wise nor laudable to reduce everything to antiquity by every possible device.[36]

Pius XII's admonition rests upon faith in the Holy Spirit's perennial guidance of the Church, which assures the worthiness of recent, living rites, as well as ancient ones. An historical theory or demonstrable conclusion that an ancient Christian community observed a given rite does not entail that that practice should be employed today. Why not, for example, reintroduce daily catechumenal exorcisms conducted with breathing gestures, in the manner witnessed by Cyril of Jerusalem?[37] Endowing with undue authority an ancient rite—or a scholar's theory about an ancient rite—is fundamentally problematic.

In a sense, however, both Ratzinger and Baldovin tactfully sidestep a deeper problem with archeologism. Very few liturgists wish, for strictly romantic reasons, to reestablish the worship of antiquity. Calls to return to ancient practice typically mask attempts to institute a personal agenda. The previous section demonstrated this: many scholars who called for a return to the pristine primitive Roman anaphora of Hippolytus were driven by an agenda to reform the Roman canon. They followed a "method of argument" which Robert Taft characterizes as justifying "startling liturgical innovation" with an "appeal to ancient tradition":

> That the facts may not justify this appeal to the past is irrelevant . . . the facts are beside the point. The dynamics involved have nothing to do with conclusions from liturgical history. Rather, it is a question of seeking precedents in earlier tradition for what one has already decided to do. We are dealing, in short, with the strategies reformers employ to claim authority for their views.[38]

Whenever the line between historian of early Christian worship and liturgical reformer is blurred, this method of argument may come into play. Archeologism manifests itself when past precedents are invoked for the sake of implementing present liturgical agendas. Such agendas often underlie commitment to historical theories; the perceived veracity of a theory depends upon the extent to which it conforms to the scholar's views. The question of the orientation of the priest during the eucharistic prayer provides an example: those who advocate praying the eucharistic prayer "facing the people" argue on the basis of historical theories as readily as those who advocate Mass "facing liturgical East."[39] The classic example, which will be considered below, is the attempt, driven by confessional or theological presuppositions, to find one single apostolic origin or "shape" of Christian eucharistic worship.

Nonetheless, such archeologism is strongly evident in contemporary liturgical scholarship and in the revision of liturgical books conducted by the *Consilium* for Implementing the Constitution on the Sacred Liturgy following the Second Vatican Council. Archeologism is far less evident, however, in the field of early Christian studies properly speaking. Before going on to consider that field, two common forms of archeologism merit brief consideration: the appeal to a primitive age for which little or no evidence exists; and the appeal to a 'golden age' of ancient Christian liturgy for which abundant evidence does exist.

Reformers seeking change in or justification for contemporary practice are not always content with ancient forms of worship for which evidence exists; they often appeal to a primitive practice witnessed by little or no evidence. Given the scarcity or ambiguity of evidence for liturgical rites in the pre-Nicene period, reformers can make a multitude of claims about them. Some Protestants, for example, claim or assume that their worship reflects the word-based services of pristine apostolic times before the development of elaborate liturgies was spurred on by the Christianization of the Roman Empire in the fourth century. Indeed, any sermon that bores someone into slumber can claim apostolic precedence on the basis of the story of Paul and Eutyches (Acts 20:7–9). Yet Scripture does not reveal what sort of worship might have taken place when Paul stopped speaking. Attempts to discern primitive Christian liturgical rites on the basis of evidence from Scripture have proven thoroughly inconclusive.[40]

A second application of antiquarianism appeals to a "golden age" of ancient Christian liturgy for which abundant evidence exists.[41] This golden age is typically associated with the fourth and fifth centuries. Surviving catechetical sermons of Cyril of Jerusalem, Ambrose of Milan, John Chrysostom, and Theodore of Mopsuestia,[42] along with other sources including the voluminous writings of Augustine, provide a considerable body of evidence for rites of initiation and their interpretation during this period. Yet the liturgies witnessed by these sources are so elaborate and difficult to sustain that their disappearance after the fifth century is entirely understandable. Nonetheless, the members of the *Consilium* appealed to this golden age, and patterned the Rite of Christian Initiation of Adults after the system reflected in these sources.[43] As the furor of liturgical revision that immediately followed the Second Vatican Council dissipated, more sophisticated scholars recognized the problem with the search for a golden age. Baldovin, for example, admits to having idolized a given period: "I used to labor under the conviction that the fourth century represented a kind of pinnacle of liturgical development, after which everything went downhill."[44]

D. The end of historical hegemony

Obviously Baldovin has since reconsidered this conviction. He came to define "antiquarianism" as "the search for the past in a (vain) effort to repeat it," and rightly assert that such a project "cannot be the task of the liturgical historian."[45] To illustrate a more legitimate approach to the field, Baldovin approvingly quotes Robert Taft: "The purpose of this history is not to recover the past (which is impossible), much less to imitate it (which would be fatuous), but to understand liturgy which, because it has a history, can only be understood in motion, just as the way to understand a top is to spin it."[46] In place of "antiquarianism," Baldovin advocates a "non-classicist approach," that is, "a history which does not idolize frozen moment in the tradition but rather … tries to understand how this important monument of the way we worship came about and how it relates to other aspects of belief and practice."[47]

Before the passage just quoted, Taft claimed that "history is a science not of past happenings, but of present understanding … history is not events, but events that have become ideas—and ideas are of the present."[48] This salutary observation draws attention to the subjectivity of the contemporary student of ancient worship, who often is not content merely to understand and to relate. Such students are drawn to apply what they have learned, and thereby double as reformers with ideas about manipulating worship in the present. Baldovin, for example, is committed to a contemporary notion of incluturation; he emphasizes the historical or socio-cultural context of the development of rites to encourage an ongoing project of continuous inculturation and reform.[49] So long as reform remains the scholar's goal, research into ancient liturgy is as likely to be influenced by the agenda for reform as the reform is likely to be influenced by the research. Given the intrinsic relation between the two, it is not surprising that the interest of liturgists in liturgical history has waned during the past two decades, in keeping with the winding down of the project of liturgical renewal.

Having been disabused of the notion of a golden age, Baldovin pronounces, "the dominance that liturgical history once held in the field of liturgical studies is long gone."[50] In doing so, he sounds a theme that resonates not only in the field of liturgical studies, but also in the broader fields of theology and early Christian studies: antiquity is no longer considered normative. The next section of this essay will explore recent shifts in early Christian studies that challenge any attempt to approach ancient Christian liturgy as normative.

II. Methodological shifts in the study of ancient Christian worship

A. Normative no more: from confessional patristics to secular early Christian studies

Baldovin's announcement that the authority of liturgical history has waned reflects an eclipse of authority within the broader field that encompasses the study of ancient Christian worship, that is, patristics or early Christian studies. This field has undergone two major shifts in the past century.

The eminent scholar Charles Kannengiesser signaled the first shift in 1989. Kannengiesser reported a secularization of the field following World War II. As a scholarly discipline, patristics left behind "its theological, scholastic, non-historical context,"[51] and "emigrated ... from the theologates to the state universities."[52] Kannengiesser especially emphasized "a broad social dimension" of the discipline: "patristics has undergone both a methodological and a social metamorphosis, out of which it had been reborn as nothing less than a hermeneutic of the historical foundations of European culture."[53]

Consciously writing from a postwar European perspective, Kannengiesser happily noted the demise of the theological, apologetic, and confessional motivations of earlier patristics scholars and hailed the vast and "fruitful" expansion of the field in secular, "professional academia."[54] The gathering and editing of ancient Christian manuscripts, which began in the nineteenth century and continued throughout the twentieth, made possible the rise of patristics as an academic discipline.[55] The number of books, articles, and conferences dedicated to patristics increased exponentially in the second half of the twentieth century.

In the late-twentieth and early-twenty-first century, polemics based upon confessional alliances became more muted, although they continued. On the other hand, an anti-confessional and even anti-Christian approach of the modern period—of which Edward Gibbon's (d. 1794) *Decline and Fall of the Roman Empire* is an early and monumental example—has risen to prominence. The non-confessional or non-Christian turn of early Christian studies followed a shift in its institutional placement away from departments of theology: the field "is now conceptualized less often as a branch of 'church history' than as an aspect of late ancient history and literature," according to Elizabeth Clark. "Neither denominationally oriented institutions *nor* religious studies departments ... can now claim a monopoly on the field. Institutional arrangements, it is clear, have been central to the development of 'early Christian studies', especially in North America."[56] Early Christian studies, then, have become increasingly less theological as the influence grows of anthropological, sociological, psychological, philosophical, literary, legal, political, economic, feminist, and sex- or body-focused approaches and methodologies. The secularization that Kannengiesser noted is all but complete.

Kannengiesser foresaw a second shift, driven in part by feminist claims and hinted at above, in the very name of the field "patristics."[57] Especially in North America, what was known as "patristics" fifty years ago is today identified as "early Christian studies." Since "patristics" is derived from *pater* or "father," a desire for gender inclusivity drives the name change. Nonetheless, the chief rationale for the new name is a shift in the function and purpose of the now-secularized field. "The Fathers" are no longer considered as authoritative or normative sources in liturgy, theology, or anything else. In the apologetic and confessional contexts that Kannengiesser correctly identified as waning, the "Fathers of the Church" bore theological, moral, and ritual authority.[58] Such confessional theologians and apologists—who today are few in number and disregarded in most academic circles—indentified four criteria that determined whether or not a particular Christian author should be numbered among the "Fathers": antiquity, holiness of life, orthodox teaching, and ecclesiastical approval.[59] From the perspective of the secularized discipline of early Christian studies, the final three criteria are irrelevant. All that remains to define the field is "antiquity," that is, the time period of "early Christianity." Hence the designation of the field as "early Christian studies" is entirely apt. Authors once labeled "Fathers of the Church" are no longer considered authoritative sources within the secularized academy (including many institutions with ecclesiastical affiliation), within liturgical studies, or even within many theological circles.

This is not to say that the title "patristics" has entirely disappeared. Even where the word might be retained, as for example among Italian scholars, a representative of the field as illustrious as Manlio Simonetti can assert that there is no difference between patristics and classical studies, since scholars in both fields proceed on the basis of the same methodologies.[60] Detailed studies of singularly unedifying disputes about dating and philological issues present one manifestation among many of methodologies purified of faith claims.[61] Whether one calls the field patristics or early Christian studies, two factors remain: the methodologies and presuppositions of the discipline are predominantly secular; and the figures studied are no longer considered as authorities.

B. Loss of linear development and rise of the comparative method

The shifts in the field of early Christian studies necessarily have impacted the study of early Christian worship. Perhaps nowhere is this more evident than in the rejection of the claim that the earliest liturgical practice is the most pristine, simple, and authoritative, and that later rites linearly developed from that pristine norm.

At the dawn of the twentieth century, scholars—tainted, Kannengiesser would note, by apologetic and confessional theological concerns—attempted to trace liturgical practices in a linear line back to Christ or the apostles. The notion of a linear development of liturgy has been thoroughly discredited. Paul Bradshaw might be called the reigning "master of method" in the study of early Christian worship. His *Search for the Origins of Christian Worship*,[62] now in its second edition, offers a thorough explanation of the radical shift of perspective that took place in late-twentieth century scholarship on early Christian worship.[63]

Bradshaw argues that, up to the twentieth century, modern scholars "began from the usually unspoken presupposition that in a matter as important as [worship], Jesus himself—or at least the apostles—would have left clear directives which all Christian communities would have followed."[64] Scholars therefore attempted to explain the multiplicity in liturgical rites as derivations of an original apostolic model, which they attempted to unearth. Bradshaw briefly describes several methods or models that sought to achieve this end. The "Philological Model" argued that the development of the liturgy moved from "brevity to prolixity" in the course of time. Gregory Dix's *The Shape of the Liturgy* articulates what Bradshaw calls the "Structural Approach." This approach eschewed the attempt to find a single original apostolic eucharistic rite, but did not altogether abandon the notion.[65] For Dix, the common origin of liturgical rites rests in the structure or the shape of the liturgy, not in any particular details.[66] Bradshaw argues that the evidence tends in another direction: from the very start there was a great variety in the forms of worship. Liturgical rites progressed, therefore, from variety to a conscious and forced unification.[67] The "Organic Approach" of Anton Baumstark[68] adopted evolutionary theory from biological sciences and claimed that the development of the liturgy was like that of a living organism: "the method was systematic comparison and subsequent clarification on the basis of a supposed line of descent from the origin of the species."[69] Baumstark posited several laws of development "that he believed governed the process of the historical evolution of the liturgy."[70]

Developed by scholars influenced by Baumstark, the "Comparative Method" has emerged as the most influential model today. While retaining Baumstrak's basic principles, they distance themselves from his "laws," which are sometimes useful guidelines not to be applied absolutely. These scholars closely compare similarities and differences in liturgical practices among geographical locales, time periods, and ecclesiastical traditions.[71] The focus of this method is on diversity. An early and influential example of the comparative method is Gabriele Winkler's "The Original Meaning of the Prebaptismal Anointing and Its Implications," which demonstrates that liturgical diversity in early Christian initiation practice was normative.[72] As Maxwell E. Johnson puts it, "a focus precisely on the *diversity* and distinct *variety* ... has been the great contribution of comparative liturgical scholarship over the past 30 years."[73] The comparative method not only has made a great contribution; it dominates the study of ancient worship.

C. Delighting in diversity

In view of the inadequacy of any method aiming at uncovering a coherent or unitive history of interrelations among ancient ritual practices, scholars are left with the diversity of rites reflected in evidence from distinct times and geographical locations, and even distinct communities within the same time and place. Researchers scrutinize the evidence from the first few centuries of Christianity, apply the comparative method, and emphasize the diversity they find.

Consensus regarding the diversity of early Christian liturgical rites emerged in the 1970s. Georg Kretschmar noted it in a bibliographical article on recent research in 1977: "the present state of scholarly concern with the early history of Christian baptism makes it hard to go on speaking of a single original and therefore normative form of baptism."[74] Kretschmar's article is seen as "a major turning point in the history of initiation scholarship. Instead of repeating previous attempts at harmonizing the diverse patterns discerned in Christian antiquity into a single normative or classic shape, Kretschmar challenges this traditional approach altogether by taking this ancient diversity seriously."[75] Aptly surmising that the same principle will hold true of the Eucharist and other ancient Christian rites, Kretschmar asserted that the "plurality of possibilities is itself apostolic."[76] As Taft bluntly phrased the point in a study of the origins of the Christian calendar and feast days, "any attempt to look back in order to 'recover the original tradition' is futile, because it does not exist."[77]

Kretschmar's principle has become a working presupposition among scholars, articulated aptly by Johnson: "We should not ... expect to find only one 'apostolic' liturgical practice or theology, surviving in this period of the church's history before the Council of Nicaea (325) but, rather, great diversity both within the rites themselves and in their theological interpretations."[78] Shorter studies in the field now tend to narrowly focus on the worship of one location or tradition, while more lengthy monographs tend to be organized geographically.[79] In both cases, the method of focus and organization highlights differences in ritual patterns and theological interpretations from various locations. The comparative method has engendered a broad consensus: diversity, plurality, and complexity were not products of liturgical development over the centuries; they existed from the very beginning of Christian worship. Scholars are left to embrace diversity and to content themselves with ambiguity.

D. We do not know what we thought we knew: the hermeneutic of suspicion

In addition to emphasizing diversity, recent studies in ancient worship also emphasize the uncertainty and ambiguity of what can be known about their subject.

When the fragmentary nature of the evidence and the problems of interpreting it are adequately taken into account, scholars assert that rather little can be known about Christian worship in the first several centuries. Typical is the following statement: "Since there is a relative dearth of evidence from before the fourth century, and materials once thought primitive have been found to contain later strata... reconstructions of the earlier eucharist have to be informed conjectures."[80] On the one hand, any given explanation or account of the liturgy, such as Ambrose's homilies on the rites of initiation, cannot be presumed to mention everything that was said or done. On the other hand, one "cannot assume that just because something is not mentioned it was not being practiced."[81] This makes reconstruction of ancient rites an exceedingly tricky endeavor.

Furthermore, the available evidence must be approached with the "hermeneutics of suspicion" akin to the method that marks contemporary biblical studies. Illustrating a few givens of such hermeneutics, Bradshaw warns that the researcher "need to be aware of being too ready to draw the following conclusions": (a) that authoritative-sounding statements are always genuinely authoritative; (b) that liturgical legislation is evidence of actual practice; (c) that when a variety of explanations exist for the origin of a practice, one of them must be genuine.[82] Bradshaw's warnings again highlight the limits of historical science.

Yet one can become enamored of critical hermeneutics and take them too far. Robert J. Daly, for example, appears so dumbstruck as to place a sort of naive faith in the "inexorable progress" of "a series of ever more sophisticated refinements in the historical-critical method."[83] Daly's all-but-professed faith in the historical-critical method quickly translates into the practical two-fold agenda of a liturgical reformer: to challenge "official Roman Catholic magisterial teaching" on the one hand, and to enable ecumenical, interreligious, and inculturated worship, on the other.[84] For example, Daly advocates disabusing the Catholic faithful of their "traditional belief in the transformation of the eucharistic gifts" by emphasizing in preaching and catechesis a subjective or phenomenological interpretation "that the most important transformation is the one that is taking place in the Christian faithful as they celebrate and go forth to life the Eucharist."[85] More circumspect scholars refrain from proffering such reformist prescriptions, leaving to others the task of working out the practical results of their research—if indeed there are any.

III. Toward a renewal of the study of ancient Christian worship

Thus far, this essay has addressed the major shifts in the field of early Christian studies and developments in the methods of the study of ancient Christian worship. The comparative method, with its commitment to diversity, and the hermeneutics of suspicion have deconstructed earlier theories and have fragmented perceptions of unity and linearity in the development of liturgical rites. These shifts, along with the slackening of the pace of contemporary liturgical reform, have contributed to the alienation of faith-based liturgical studies from the secularized study of early Christian worship. How can this gap be bridged?

This final section sketches a positive approach to early Christian worship, an approach that involves something of a paradigm shift. The goal of this paradigm shift is to revisit evidence left by ancient Christians in order to understand worship to the greatest possible extent from their perspective. Concrete prescriptions for liturgical rites must not to be sought in theories about ancient practices. Principles or attitudes and approaches to worship, on the other hand, clearly arise from a careful reading of ancient sources. These transcend (although not absolutely) the critical details of discrete rites that can absorb practitioners of the comparative method. When appropriated with empathy and deference, these principles can serve to free us from the concerns, the demands, and the agendas affecting contemporary worship.

To this end, I propose by way of example three authentic principles that are articulated by ancient Christian authors: a basic attitude of conservativism; the necessity of translation from the kingdom of darkness to the kingdom of light; and the centrality of the praise of God. Before addressing these examples, however, the distraction posed by the very word "liturgy" itself must be exposed in order that it might be avoided.

A. Early Christian 'liturgy'?

The noun "liturgy" and its adjective "liturgical" can mislead discussions about the ancient Latin Church. Greek Christians of the past and the present use "liturgy" primarily to indicate the eucharistic service. A transliteration from a Greek term, *liturgia* appears only twice in Latin patristic writings. In the first instance, Pope Julius I (337–352), writing to a Greek-speaking eastern community, apparently uses *liturgia* to designate the Mass.[86] In the second instance, Augustine notes that Greek Christians call the "ministry or service" which is due to God alone *liturgia* or *latria*.[87] This is the sole surviving instance in which Augustine employs the word *liturgia*. By contrast, in a revealing passage of the *City of God*, he discusses the various words used to indicate the worship due to God alone. There Augustine argues that the best term for describing it is the Greek *latreia*. This word, he testifies, is usually translated as *servitus* (service), but in reality there is no adequate equivalent in the Latin language. Other possible contenders include *cultus* (cult), *religio* (religion), and *pietas* (piety), but none of these has the precise content of the Greek *latreia* or the Latin *servitus*.[88]

In addition to *servitus* and *cultus*, ancient Latin Christians also indicated divine worship in general with such words as *officium*, *munus*, and *ministerium*. They did not speak about *liturgia*. What is today called a study "on liturgy" in ancient times was entitled "on ecclesiastical offices" (*De ecclesiasticis officiis*).[89] *Liturgia* makes one of its first appearances in the West in the titles of Protestant liturgical books, including the Latin translation of Calvin's Strasbourg rite (*Liturgia sacra*),[90] and the Anglican Book of Common Prayer (*Liturgia, seu Liber precum communium*).[91] *Liturgia* also appears from the sixteenth century in studies on and collections of rites of worship, especially eastern rites.[92] Having been thus introduced, the word was adapted into Latin discourse on divine worship, and it gradually acquired theological content.[93]

The point here is that "liturgy" delineates a modern category of thought or field of study that does not exist among ancient Christians as such. Contemporary presuppositions about "liturgy," therefore, may distract from the manner in which ancient Christians both worshipped and understood their worship and its role in their lives. From the perspective of seeing worship through the eyes of early Christians, Cyprian Vagaggini observes that "the Fathers" regard liturgy "from the point of view of its spiritual or theological value," which is "intimately connected" with catechesis, asceticism, morality, and spirituality: "In this we have a characteristic trait of the relations between liturgy and theology in the Fathers."[94] Vagaggini makes a second observation:

> The method of presentation pursued by the Fathers in treating the liturgy is predominantly expositive, irenic, and even contemplative; they sought above all to address the faithful and explain to them the theological significance which the liturgy has for the believer who practices it, as well as its ascetical-moral value.[95]

Vagaggini's learned comments highlight a two-fold theological concern with which ancient Christian commentators approached their worship services: a contemplative or expositive concern focused on knowing, loving, and worshipping God; and a pastoral concern focused on significance of worship in the lives of the Christian faithful.

Three demonstrable principles or themes among many exemplify this two-fold theological concern. These notions are articulated by ancient Christian authors and ensconced in their worship: conservativism; apotropaic deliverance; and the centrality of the praise of God.

B. Conservativism

The first theme that arises as a concern of ancient Christian themselves is conservativism in worship. In the minds of early Christians, the rites and symbols of Christian worship are authoritative and salutary in part because they are ancient, having been handed down by Christians of the previous generations. Their antiquity assures their value as the subject of contemplation and their pastoral efficacy. Three debates among early Christians witness the application of this conservativism: the controversy over the date of Easter in the second century; the baptismal controversy of the third century; and the semi-Pelagian or Augustinian controversy[96] of the fifth century.

In the late second century, Victor I of Rome (189–98) attempted to enforce the Roman practice of celebrating Easter on the Sunday following the fourteenth of the Jewish month Nisan. Polycrates of Ephesus wrote a letter to Victor defending the practice of Christians in Asia Minor of observing Easter on the Quartodeciman, that is, the fourteenth of Nisan itself. In the letter, which is preserved by Eusebius, Polycrates enumerates the "great luminaries" of Asia who followed the practice before him all the way back to John the Apostle, and concludes that he will continue to observe the tradition handed down to him.[97] Victor also prompted the bishops in Palestine to discuss and defend "at great length the tradition concerning the Passover which had come down to them from the succession of the Apostles."[98] Both sides of the dispute claimed to be conserving the tradition that was handed down to them by their predecessors in the faith, all the way back to the apostles.[99]

Both sides also claimed to be following received tradition in the mid-third-century controversy between Stephen of Rome (254–57) and Cyprian of Carthage (248–58) over the question of baptisms administered by heretics. Stephen argued that the application of water along with invocation of the Trinity, in accordance with Christ's command (Mt. 28:19), ensured the validity of baptism, even among heretics. Thus a former heretic who wished to enter the Catholic Church did not need baptism (or rebaptism). Cyprian, on the other hand, insisted that those outside the Church have no power to baptize, and so former heretics entering the Catholic fold must be baptized. Stephen explicitly claimed to be preserving the ancient practice of the Church. To this argument, Cyprian replied: "There are some who bring up custom as an objection against us when they are defeated by reason, as if custom were more important than truth …" But Cyprian did not appeal to truth without also appealing to ancient tradition: "There is no such evidence of the apostles having approved heretical baptism."[100]

In his debate with Julian of Eclanum over questions associated with the Pelagian controversy, Augustine repeatedly draws attention to rites of exsufflating and exorcising infant catechumens. Exsufflation was a breathing, spitting, or blowing gesture intended to insult and expel the Devil. Augustine cites these widespread practices as theological proofs that infants suffer from the effects of original sin and need redemption from slavery to the Devil.[101] Augustine insists that the practice of exsufflating and exorcising infant catechumens is inherited from his predecessors. He cites not only the Milanese baptismal rites under Ambrose at the time of his baptism in the spring of 387,[102] but also the earlier practice of Hilary, Gregory, and Cyprian.[103] This, Augustine argues, was the universal practice of the primitive Church, against which Julian declares war if he contends that infants about to be baptized need not be exsufflated.[104] Augustine's opponents never appear to challenge the weight of his appeal to ancient practice or his insistence on the necessity of exorcising even infant catechumens. Therefore he makes this argument with increasing boldness and frequency in his final work against the Pelagians, the *Opus imperfectum*.

These three examples illustrate a general rule: in early Christian controversies over rites of worship, all sides claimed to be following the practices inherited from their predecessors. These observations are not intended to deny that liturgical innovation occurred among early Christians; it certainly did. Nonetheless, the basic principle remains: ancient Christians highly regarded the liturgical rites and customs inherited from previous generations, considered them to be endowed with authority and effect, and fought to preserve them to the greatest extent possible.

C. From the kingdom of darkness to the kingdom of light

Many themes dear to early Christians have been sidelined by researchers of the past century pursing very different agendas and concerns. Perhaps the most striking of these is the prominence of attention to the role of demons and the struggle against them in the life of the individual believer and in salvation history. Early Christians were convinced of a need to be delivered from the power of the Devil, and of the power of their rites of worship to effect such deliverance. Scholars have tended to dismiss the apotropaic or anti-demonic themes of ancient worship as latter ritual additions (starting in the third century) that first arose among suspect communities associated with Gnosticism.[105] Yet the student seeking to understand worship from the perspective of surviving early Christians evidence cannot ignore the prominence of apotropaic elements.

The so-called *Apostolic Tradition* offers a first example. At the consecration of the bread, the document's eucharistic prayer emphasizes Christ's mission to end the devil's dominion:

> When he was being handed over to voluntary suffering, that he might destroy death and break the bonds of the devil, and tread down hell and illuminate the righteous, and fix a limit and manifest the resurrection, taking bread [and] giving thanks to you, he said: "Take, eat, this is my body that will be broken for you."[106]

This significant apotropaic phrase, occurring as it does in the narrative of institution, has attracted little attention and is not reflected in eucharistic prayer II.

Apotropaic content is above all evident in the rites of initiation. In many regions and over many centuries catechumens were subjected to rites that included exorcistic gestures such as exsufflation in order to insult the devil, repel him, and, together with exorcism, effect the removal of the catechumen from the possession of the evil one or from the power of darkness. In the debate with Julian already cited, Augustine writes of exsufflation and exorcism as delivering one from the power of darkness, thereby enabling the rebirth that transfers one from Adam to Christ.[107] Julian, Augustine argues, attacks the universal Church insofar as his theology contradicts the rite of exsufflation:

> Along with the Pelagians this fellow abandons this apostolic and Catholic faith which is absolutely true and most solidly founded. For he does not want the newborn to be under the power of the devil so that little ones are brought to Christ to be rescued from the power of darkness and transferred into his kingdom (Col. 1:13). And so, he accuses the Church spread throughout the whole world, because everywhere in the Church all the little infants to be baptized undergo exsufflation only so that the prince of this world might be driven out of them (Jn. 12:31). As vessels of anger (Rom. 9:22) they are necessarily held in his power, when they are born of Adam, if they are not reborn in Christ and transferred into his kingdom (Col. 1:13), after having been made vessels of mercy (Rom. 9:23) by his grace.[108]

By citing Colossians 1:13, Augustine suggests that the apotropaic effects of Christian initiation, and perhaps also exorcistic gestures, originated in apostolic times. With the word "vessels" (*uasa*), Augustine connects the exorcistic context of Matthew 12:29, where Jesus speaks of binding the strong one to seize his *uasa*, with Paul's discussion of *uasa irae* and *uasa misericordiae* in Romans 9:22–23. When speaking of casting out the devil Augustine consistently uses the word *foras*, drawn from John 12:31. Augustine weaves these scriptural citations and allusions together with the Church's practice of exorcizing and exsufflating infant catechumens into a tapestry illustrating that all are vessels of wrath born in darkness, under the power of the prince of the world. This power must be cast out before the infant can be transferred into the kingdom of God. Exorcism and exsufflation, then, accomplish the expulsion of the devil's power which is necessary before one is baptized in Christ.[109]

Although Augustine may explain it more clearly than other early Christian authors, the principles he articulates regarding the apotropaic effects of Christian initiation were widely assumed by early Christians and are ensconced in much of the evidence for worship during the period. It is a principle of ancient Christian worship, then, that one must be transferred out of the kingdom of darkness in order to be oriented towards the praise of God; in other words, one function of Christian ritual is to break the power of the Devil. Augustine also articulates the final principle of early Christian worship to be considered here: the transfer or deliverance from evil is not an end in itself; rather, it serves the purpose of the praise of God.

D. The praise and glory of God

Augustine expresses the centrality of the praise of God most completely and poetically in his *Confessions*. The striking address to God with which the work begins, unique among the genres of literature known at the time, demonstrates that praising God is the purpose not only of the *Confessions*, but of human life itself.[110] The *Confessions* is an extended expression of praise elaborating what is articulated in these first sentences:

> "You are great, Lord, and highly to be praised" (Ps. 47:2): "great is your power and your wisdom is immeasurable" (Ps. 146:5). Man, a small part of your creation, desires to praise you—man, "carrying around his mortality" (2 Cor. 4:10), carrying around evidence of his sin and evidence that you "resist the proud" (1 Pet. 5:5). Nevertheless man, a small part of your creation, desires to praise you. You excite him such that he delights to praise you, because you have made us for yourself, and our heart is restless until it rests in you.[111]

With these words Augustine illustrates that the rational creature is both created by God and called to the final end of being with God; nothing other than God will satisfy the restless yearnings of the human heart. More to the point, the passage roots the end of the creature in the praise of God: "You excite him such that he delights to praise you." Augustine closely ties the rational creature's vocation to rest in God with the delight of praising God.

In the first eight books of the *Confessions*, Augustine recounts the removal of personal obstacles of sin and pride that prevented him from praising God. For Augustine, the confession of sins necessarily entails a confession of praise.[112] Hence he writes, "Let silence about your praises be for the person who does not consider your mercies (Ps. 77: 4)."[113] Augustine can only confess the praise of God after he confesses his sins with contrition and seeks forgiveness of them through baptism. Thus only after his conversion does Augustine experience the delight of praising God. In book IX of the *Confessions*, drawing heavily from the text of the Psalms, Augustine repeatedly expresses the sheer delight he experienced in praising God immediately following his conversion.

Praise is the highest form of prayer; unique among all the forms of prayer insofar as it is for God's own sake, without reference to what God does for the one praying. Augustine distinguishes praise or *laus* from the other kinds of prayers he labels as *oratio*.[114] *Oratio* is based on the necessities under which we labor in this mortal life. So long as we are on this earth, our *laus* or praise must necessarily be mixed with *oratio*. In heaven, however, God meets all the needs of the saints.[115] The utility of petitionary prayer falls away while only praise, the sheer expression of love for God, remains.[116] All prayer, then, will ultimately be resolved in praise. In this sense praise is the end of prayer; praise is the eternal prayer expressed by the saints whose hearts find rest in the heavenly Jerusalem.[117] This is best summarized in the words of Psalm 83, words that express Augustine's notion of heavenly beatitude: "Blessed are they who dwell in your house; they will praise you forever and ever." The significance of praise among other ancient Christians could be elaborated at greater length. For here once again Augustine discusses and articulates a principle of worship that is widely presumed without explanation by early Christians.

In conclusion, this section first demonstrated that students of early Christian worship misleadingly impose the notion of "liturgy" upon ancient texts that lack such a distinct category of thought. Then sample debates and writings from the period were briefly examined to posit three authentic principles regarding worship actually articulated by ancient Christian authors: conservativism; the necessity of deliverance from evil; and the centrality of the praise of God. These examples are set forth in order to sketch an approach to early Christian worship that takes diversity into account while still finding coherence, and that attempts to understand ancient worship from the perspective of those who engaged in it, insofar as possible without succumbing to the pitfalls of practical agendas for liturgy in the present.

Conclusion[118]

The first part of this essay demonstrated the practical impact of the study of early Christian worship on liturgical revisions following the Second Vatican Council. The question was raised, via a discussion of archeologism, of the extent to which agendas for liturgical reform in the present color the study of worship in the past. In some cases, mistaken historical theories and insufficiently nuanced approaches to the history of Christian worship had immense practical impact. This is above all evident in the use made of the theory that Hippolytus of Rome wrote a document known as the *Apostolic Tradition*.

The second part related dramatic shifts in the field of early Christian studies in general, and the field of ancient Christian worship in particular, as the twentieth century drew to a close. The fields became more secular and the methodology more sophisticated, while the normative value of ancient worship was drawn into question. The predominance of the comparative method has resulted in a fragmentation of the knowledge of early Christian worship marked by the presumption of primitive diversity, the questioning of early theories and methods, and the hermeneutics-of-suspicion emphasis on the limits of attempts at reconstructing early ritual practices.

Confessional liturgical studies have drifted from the field of early Christian worship for several reasons. First, the momentum for liturgical reform has dissipated. Second, the secularization of the study of early Christian worship tends towards deconstruction and fragmentation without leaving much of substance for faith-based reflection and pastoral care. Finally, archeologism has been abandoned such that even within worshipping Christian communities primitive practices are no longer deemed normative.

The final part provided a suggestion for bridging the gap between liturgical studies and the study of ancient worship, and thereby for ensuring the ongoing relevance of the latter field. Once the limitations and potential distractions of the modern term "liturgy" are set aside, actual principles of ancient Christian worship can be sought through a serious and empathetic engagement of the sources. Three central principles were discussed by way of example: the centrality of the praise of God; the ritual power of deliverance from the Devil; and a basic conservativism with regard to received rites. The presupposition of these principles is widespread among early Christians. Appropriating such principles potentially enables the student of liturgical studies to transcend the dangers posed by contemporary agendas for liturgical reform and the fragmentation of the study of early Christian worship that can result from the currently dominant methodologies.

Notes

1   Especially noteworthy is Paul Bradshaw's 104-page monograph, *Early Christian Worship: A Basic Introduction to Ideas and Practice*, 2nd edn (London: SPCK, 2010). For essay-length summaries of the major areas of research, see: Maxwell E. Johnson, "Christian Initiation," in Susan Ashbrook Harvey & David G. Hunter (eds), *The Oxford Handbook of Early Christian Studies* (New York: Oxford University Press, 2008), pp. 693–710; Daniel Sheerin, "Eucharistic Liturgy," in *The Oxford Handbook of Early Christian Studies*, pp. 711–43; Maxwell E. Johnson, "The Apostolic Tradition," in Geoffrey Wainwright & Karen B. Westerfield Tucker (eds), *The Oxford History of Christian Worship* (Oxford: Oxford University Press, 2006), pp. 33–75.

2   Lawrence J. Johnson, *Worship in the Early Church: An Anthology of Historical Sources*, 4 vols (Collegeville: Liturgical Press, 2009), which includes a massive collection of

sources from the first to the sixth century in English translation, is readily accessible in hard-copy and electronic formats.

3   Second Vatican Council, Constitution on the Sacred Liturgy *Sacrosanctum Concilium*, §23 (4 December 1963), Norman P. Tanner et al. (eds and trans), *Decrees of the Ecumenical Councils*, vol. 2, *Trent – Vatican II* (Washington DC: Georgetown University Press, 1990), p. 826.

4   Paul VI, Motu proprio *Sacram Liturgiam* (January 25, 1964); International Commission on English in the Liturgy (ed.), *Documents on the Liturgy 1963–1979: Conciliar, Papal, and Curial Texts* (Collegeville: Liturgical Press, 1982), §280, no. 20, p. 85.

5   While the conciliar directives are given first and foremost to the bishops themselves, *Sacrosanctum Concilium* §25 enjoins the employment of experts (*periti*) in carrying them out. Some commentators have pointed out how extensive the influence of experts became in carrying out the revision: see, e.g., Joseph Cardinal Ratzinger, "Assessment and Future Prospects," in Alcuin Reid (ed.), *Looking Again at the Question of the Liturgy with Cardinal Ratzinger: Proceedings of the July 2001 Fontgombault Liturgical Conference* (Farnborough: St Michael's Abbey Press, 2003), p. 147.

6   The consultors are listed in *Consilium ad Exsequendam Constitutionem de Sacra Liturgia, Elenchus membrorum – consultorum consiliariorum coetuum a studiis* (Vatican City, 1967), pp. 19–36.

7   Paul F. Bradshaw, *The Search for the Origins of Christian Worship: Sources and Methods for the Study of Early Liturgy*, 2nd edn (Oxford: Oxford University Press, 2002), p. 73.

8   Georg Kretschmar, "Early Christian Liturgy in the Light of Contemporary Historical Research," *Studia Liturgica* 16 (1986–87), pp. 31–53.

9   John F. Baldovin, "Hippolytus and the *Apostolic Tradition*: Recent Research and Commentary," *Theological Studies* 64 (2003), pp. 520–42 (p. 521).

10 A Festschrift in honor of Jungmann claims without exaggeration: "It is impossible to overestimate the contribution of Josef Jungmann to the Second Vatican Council, above all, to the pastoral renewal of the liturgy – to the momentum for reform which had been gathering energy for decades, to the climate within which it unfolded, to its preparations, inner workings, implementation and reception around the world. By the time the Council was announced Jungmann was already the elder statesman of the liturgical movement whose writing, teaching and preaching had formed a generation of scholars and pastors." Kathleen Hughes, "Jungmann's Influence on Vatican II: Meticulous Scholarship at the Service of a Living Liturgy," in Joanne M. Pierce & Michael Downey (eds), *Source and Summit: Commemorating Josef A. Jungmann, S.J.*, (Collegeville: Liturgical Press, 1999), p. 21. For an illuminating discussion of Jungmann's influence and biases see Alcuin Reid, *The Organic Development of the Liturgy: The Principles of Liturgical Reform and Their Relation to the Twentieth Century Liturgical Movement Prior to the Second Vatican Council*, 2nd edn (San Francisco: Ignatius Press, 2005), pp. 164–72.

11 Josef A. Jungmann, Francis A. Brunner, trans., Charles K. Riepe, rev., *The Mass of the Roman Rite: Its Origins and Development* (*Missarum Sollemnia*), abridged edn (New York: Benziger, 1961), pp. 18–20 (p. 20). The first German edition was printed in 1949.

12 Dominic E. Serra, "The Roman Canon: The Theological Significance of Its Structure and Syntax," *Ecclesia Orans* 20 (2003), pp. 99–128 (p. 102): following a concise overview of the history of the canon, Serra writes, "Some sixteen centuries of uninterrupted and exclusive use by Roman rite Christians make the Canon one of the most time-honored of current liturgical texts."

13 For a comparison of Ambrose's citations with the Roman canon's more definitive later form, see Guy Nicholls, "The History of the Prayers of the Roman Canon," in *Theological and Historical Aspects of the Roman Missal: The Proceedings of the Fifth International Colloquium of Historical, Canonical and Theological Studies on the Roman Catholic Liturgy* (Kingston & Surbiton: CIEL UK, 2000), pp. 39–40.

14 Jungmann, *Mass of the Roman Rite,* p. 37. For an example of the influence of this line of criticism, see National Conference of Catholic Bishops, Bishops' Committee on the Liturgy, *The New Eucharistic Prayers and Prefaces* (Washington DC: Bishops' Committee on the Liturgy, 1968), p. 13.

15 Bernard Botte, *La tradition apostolique de saint Hippolyte: essai de reconstitution,* Liturgiewissenschaftliche Quellen und Forschungen 39 (Münster Westfalen: Aschendorff, 1963), and *Hippolyte de Rome: La tradition apostolique,* Sources Chrétiennes 11bis (Paris: Cerf, 1984, with previous editions published in 1946 and 1968).

16 See Botte, *Essai de reconstitution,* pp. xiv–xv.

17 Adrien Nocent, "The Parts of the Mass," in William Baraúna & Jovian Lang (eds), *The Liturgy of Vatican II: A Symposium in Two Volumes,* vol. 2 (Chicago: Franciscan Herald Press, 1966), pp. 28–61 (p. 50). Consider also the following citations from the same source: "No longer should anyone be surprised by the statement that our Roman canon of the Mass is theologically rather poor" (p. 44); "There is no doubt that, in the 4th century, no one in Rome was scandalized at the proclamation of a eucharistic prayer which certainly was not a Latin translation of the Greek anaphora used in the preceding centuries and which was, if we can judge by its plan as given to us by Hippolytus, more respectful of the ancient tradition of the Jewish blessing" (p. 45).

18 See the discussion and detailed comparison of the second eucharistic prayer with "Hippolytus" in Enrico Mazza, Matthew J. O'Connell (trans.), *The Eucharistic Prayers of the Roman Rite* (New York: Pueblo, 1986), pp. 90–100.

19 *Consilium,* Guidelines *Au cours des derniers mois* to assist catechesis on the anaphoras of the Mass (June 2, 1968), in *Documents on the Liturgy 1963–1979,* §1957, p. 618: "Anaphora II is intentionally short, made up of simple ideas. The anaphora of Hippolytus (from the beginning of the 3rd century) is the inspiration of its style and much of its phrasing." See also Bishops' Committee on the Liturgy, *New Eucharistic Prayers,* p. 36.

20 Louis Bouyer, Charles Underhilll Quinn (trans.), *Eucharist: Theology and Spirituality of the Eucharistic Prayer* (Notre Dame: University of Notre Dame Press, 1968), pp. 189–90; originally published in Paris, 1966.

21 *Elenchus membrorum – consultorum,* p. 47.

22 For an extended example, see Cipriano Vagaggini, Peter Coughlan (trans.), *The Canon of the Mass and Liturgical Reform* (Staten Island, NY: Alba House, 1967), p. 17: "The Roman canon presents those engaged in liturgical reform with problems both in the text and in the actions that accompany the text."

23 Bernard Botte, John Sullivan (trans.), *From Silence to Participation: An Insider's View of Liturgical Renewal* (Washington DC: Pastoral Press, 1988), p. 145. On the significance of this conference as "a critical moment" in the twentieth-century liturgical reform, see Reid, *Organic Development of the Liturgy,* pp. 186–94.

24 Botte, *From Silence to Participation,* pp. 146–47.

25 Cassian Folsom, "From One Eucharistic Prayer to Many: How it Happened and Why;"; this study, which originally appeared as a series of articles in the *Adoremus Bulletin* 2.4–6 (1996), is available (as of 18 December 2004) at: http://www.adoremus. org/9-11-96-FolsomEuch.html

26 For a review of the development in scholarship on the *Apostolic Tradition*, see Baldovin, "Hippolytus and the *Apostolic Tradition*," pp. 520–42.

27 Bradshaw, *Search for the Origins,* p. 82; cf. Botte, *Essai de reconstitution*, p. xi.

28 Paul F. Bradshaw, Maxwell E. Johnson, L. Edward Phillips, and Harold W. Attridge, *The Apostolic Tradition* (Minneapolis: Fortress, 2002), p. 14.

29 Baldovin, "Hippolytus and the *Apostolic Tradition*," p. 521.

30 Susan K. Wood, *Sacramental Orders*, Lex Orandi Series (Collegeville: Liturgical Press, 2000), p. 45: "One of the most significant changes in the 1968 rite, retained in the 1990 rite, was to replace the consecratory prayer of the bishop with the prayer from the *Apostolic Tradition* of Hippolytus."

31 For example, Annibale Bugnini, Matthew J. O'Connell (trans.), *The Reform of the Liturgy 1948–1975* (Collegeville: Liturgical Press, 1990), p. 745: "This change of terminology for 'minor orders' is a return to the usage of the early Church: a lector is not ordained, 'but is instated when the bishop gives him the book; for he does not receive the laying on of hands' (Hippolytus, *Traditio Apostolica* 10–13)."

32 For an argument that the reverse is true and that the simple Gallic celebration was infused with complexity upon the introduction of Roman influence, see Matthieu Smyth, *La liturgie oubliée: la prière eucharistique en Gaule antique et dans l'Occident non romain* (Paris: Cerf, 2003), p. 574 and passim.

33 See, for example, the most popular textbook used in courses on liturgy and sacraments in North America today: Joseph Martos, *Doors to the Sacred: A Historical Introduction to Sacraments in the Catholic Church*, revised and updated edn (Ligouri, MO: Liguori/Triumph, 2001), p. 219: "The most complete description of early eucharistic worship in the western empire was set down by Hippolytus of Rome around the year 215 in his liturgical book, *The Apostolic Tradition*." For a more nuanced example, see Robert Cabié, Matthew J. O'Connell (trans.), *The Church at Prayer: An Introduction to the Liturgy vol. 2: The Eucharist* (Collegeville: Liturgical Press, 1986), p. 26: Cabié hedges when he refers to "a document that scholars have identified with the *Apostolic Tradition* of Hippolytus" without questioning the attribution; but he goes on to provide the document with its usual privileged place in the history of the Eucharist.

34 Joseph Ratzinger, John Saward (trans.), *The Spirit of the Liturgy* (San Francisco: Ignatius Press, 2000), p. 82.

35 John F. Baldovin, "The Uses of Liturgical History," *Worship* 82 (2008), pp. 2–18 (p. 2).

36 Note the pointed admonition of Pius XII in *Mediator Dei*, *Acta apostolicae sedis* 39 (1947), §§61–62, pp. 545–46.

37 Cyril of Jerusalem, *Protocatechesis*, 9, F.L. Cross (ed.), *St. Cyril of Jerusalem's Lectures on the Christian Sacraments* (Crestwood, NY: St Vladimir's Seminary Press, 1986), pp. 45–6.

38 Robert Taft, " 'Eastern Presuppositions' and Western Liturgical Renewal," *Antiphon* 5 (2000), pp. 10–22 (p. 10).

39 See the exchange on this question between Pierre-Marie Gy and Cardinal Ratzinger in the pages of *La Maison-Dieu*: Pierre-Marie Gy, "*L'Esprit de la liturgie* du cardinal Ratzinger: est-il fidèle au concile, ou en réaction contre?" *La Maison-Dieu* 229 (2002), pp. 171–8; and Joseph Cardinal Ratzinger, "Réponse du cardinal Ratzinger au père Gy," *La Maison-Dieu* 230 (2002), pp. 113–20. The exchange was translated by Stephen Maddux for *Antiphon* 11 (2007), pp. 90–102. I do not deny that one of these positions better corresponds to the available evidence than the other.

40 See Bradshaw, *Search for the Origins*, pp. 47–72.

41 See, e.g., Marcel Metzger, Madeleine M. Beaumont (trans.), *History of the Liturgy: The Major Stages* (Collegeville: Liturgical Press, 1997), p. 111.

42 Edward Yarnold, *The Awe-Inspiring Rites of Initiation: The Origins of the R.C.I.A.* (Collegeville: Liturgical Press, 1994), provides extensive selections from these sermons.

43 Ibid., p. 2.

44 Yarnold, ibid., provides English translations of much of these sources.

45 Baldovin, "Uses of Liturgical History," p. 6.

46 Robert Taft, *Beyond East and West: Problems in Liturgical Understanding*, 2nd edn (Rome: Edizioni Orientalia Christiana, Pontifical Oriental Institute, 1997), p. 192.

47 Baldovin, "Uses of Liturgical History," p. 8.

48 Taft, *Beyond East and West*, p. 191.

49 Baldovin, "Uses of Liturgical History," p. 7: "I also want to agree with Anscar Chupungco who understood the first generation of liturgies produced after the Council as a kind of bare-bones reform that still required quite a bit of inculturation." Baldovin cites Anscar Chupungco, *Liturgies of the Future: The Process and Methods of Inculturation* (New York: Paulist Press, 1989).

50 Baldovin, ibid., p. 8.

51 Charles Kannengiesser, "The Future of Patristics," *Theological Studies* 52 (1991), pp. 128–39 (p. 138).

52 Charles Kannengiesser, "Fifty Years of Patristics," *Theological Studies* 50 (1989), pp. 633–56 (p. 640).

53 Kannengiesser, "Future of Patristics," p. 132.

54 Kannengiesser, ibid., p. 131.

55 See Elizabeth A. Clark, "From Patristics to Early Christian Studies," in *The Oxford Handbook of Early Christian Studies*, pp. 8–9.

56 Clark, "From Patristics to Early Christian Studies," p. 16.

57 Kannengiesser, "Future of Patristics," p. 138.

58 Clark, "From Patristics to Early Christian Studies," p. 14: in the late twentieth century, the "term 'patristics' fell increasingly into disuse, taken as a sign of ecclesiasticism, maleness, and 'orthodoxy', from which some scholars wished to dissociate themselves." Elizabeth Clark herself is prominent among this group of "some scholars."

59 For example, Boniface Ramsey, *Beginning to Read the Fathers* (New York: Paulist Press, 1985), pp. 4–7; Jimmy Akin, *The Fathers Know Best: Your Essential Guide to the Teachings of the Early Church* (San Diego: Catholic Answers, 2010), pp. 24–25.

60 Manlio Simonetti, "Le scienze patristiche oggi: Questioni fondamentali di contenuti e di metodo," *Vetera Christianorum* 46 (2009), pp. 5–15.

61 Consider, for example, the debate over dating key documents of the baptismal controversy of the mid-third century, the most recent contribution to which is Karl Shuve, "Cyprian of Carthage's Writings from the Rebaptism Controversy: Two Revisionary Proposals Reconsidered," *The Journal of Theological Studies* 61 (2010), pp. 627–43.

62 Bryan Spinks, "Liturgical Laxative," *Expository Times* 104 (1992–93), p. 60: "Liturgical study is one of those disciplines which suffers from having too few standard textbooks, and they are prone to reproduce previous 'assured facts' of scholarship. Paul Bradshaw's book … is a much needed liturgical laxative which should effectively clear out a much silted discipline. He brings together the evidence to show just how unassured most of the facts are relating to early liturgical origins … This book signals that a new era in liturgical study has not commenced."

63 Andrew Gregory, "Liturgical Laxative: A Repeat Prescription," *The Expository Times* 116 (2004–5), pp. 142–43: "Widely acclaimed both as an authoritative overview of recent scholarship and as a model of a new and methodologically more secure approach to liturgical scholarship, Bradshaw's readable text has proven itself both as an indispensable summary of a wide range of scholarship and as a useful took for further work. Not only has it made abundantly clear that we know much less about early Jewish and Christian worship than we once claimed to do, but also it has helped to show how best we may assess such evidence that we have."

64 Bradshaw, *Search for the Origins*, p. 1.

65 Gregory Dix, *The Shape of the Liturgy* (New York: Seabury Press, 1982, c. 1945).

66 Bradshaw, *Search for the Origins*, p. 7.

67 See Robert Taft, "How Liturgies Grow: The Evolution of the Byzantine Divine Liturgy," *Orientalia Christiana Periodica* 43 (1977), pp. 355–78.

68 Anton Baumstark, *Liturgie comparée; principes et méthodes pour l'étude historique des liturgies chrétiennes,* 3rd edn (Chevetogne: Éditions de Chevetogne, 1953). ET: F.L Cross (ed.), B. Botte (rev.), *Comparative Liturgy* (A.R. Mowbray: London, 1958).

69 Bradshaw, *Search for the Origins*, p. 9.

70 Ibid., p. 11.

71 Ibid., p. 14.

72 Gabriele Winkler, "The Original Meaning of the Prebaptismal Anointing and Its Implications," *Worship* 52 (1978), pp. 24–45; reprinted in *Living Water, Sealing Spirit: Readings on Christian Initiation* (Collegeville: Liturgical Press, 1995), pp. 58–81.

73 Maxwell E. Johnson, "Christian Initiation," in *The Oxford Handbook of Early Christian Studies,* p. 694.

74 Georg Kretschmar, "Recent Research on Christian Initiation," *Studia Liturgica* 12 (1977), pp. 87–106 (p. 102).

75 Maxwell E. Johnson, 'Introduction,' in *Living Water, Sealing Spirit: Readings on Christian Initiation,* p. xiii.

76 Kretschmar, "Recent Research on Christian Initiation," p. 103.

77 Taft, *Beyond East and West,* p. 48.

78 Maxwell E. Johnson, "Apostolic Tradition" in *The Oxford History of Christian Worship,* pp. 34–5.

79 For example, Bryan D. Spinks, *Early and Medieval Rituals and Theologies of Baptism: From the New Testament to the Council of Trent* (Aldershot: Ashgate Publishing Company, 2006).

80 Daniel Sheerin, "Eucharistic Liturgy," in *The Oxford Handbook of Early Christian Studies,* p. 712.

81 Bradshaw, *Search for the Origins*, pp. 17–20.

82 Ibid., p. 19.

83 Robert J. Daly, "Eucharistic Origins: From the New Testament to the Liturgies of the Golden Age," *Theological Studies* 66 (2005), pp. 3–22 (p. 14).

84 Ibid., pp. 18, 20.

85 Ibid., p. 21.

86 "Ex hujus autem dictis hoc nos consequenter observamus: qui fieri potuit ut is, qui pone januam aeger decumberet, tunc stererit, liturgiam celebrarit, ac oblationem fecerit?" *Epistula Julii ad Antiochenus* XII, in PL 8:896.

87 "Si ergo nusquam [sic] in eloquis divinis reperitur sanctos Angelos appellatos deos, ea mihi causa potissimum occurrit, ne isto nomine homines ad hoc adificarentur, ut ministerium vel servitium religionis, quae graece liturgia, vel latria dicitur, sanctis

Angelis exhiberent; quod nec ipsi exhiberi ab hominibus volunt, nisi illi Deo qui et ipsorum et hominum Deus est." Augustine, *Enarratio In Psalmum CXXXV*, in PL 37:1757.

88 Augustine, *De civitate Dei* X.1, Bernardus Dombart and Alfonsus Kalb (eds), *Sancti Aurelii Augustini episcopi De civitate Dei libri XXII*, 4th edn, vol. 1, Bibliotheca Scriptorum Graecorum et Romanorum Teubneriana (Stutgardiae: Teubner, 1993), pp. 402–4. For more on this passage, see F. Van Der Meer, Brian Battershaw and G. R. Lamb (trans.), *Augustine the Bishop: The Life and Work of a Father of the Church*, (New York: Sheed and Ward, 1961), pp. 277–78.

89 Isidore of Seville, *De ecclesiasticis officiis*, in CCSL 113.

90 V. Poullain, A. C. Honders (ed.), *Liturgia sacra* (1551–5), (Leiden, 1970); see Geoffrey J. Cuming, *A History of Anglican Liturgy*, 2nd edn (London: Macmillan, 1982), p. 75.

91 *Liturgia seu Liber precum communium, et administrationis sacramentorum aliorumque rituum atque ceremoniarum ecclesiæ: juxta usum Ecclesiæ Anglicanæ : una cum Psalterio seu Psalmis Davidis* (London: Mearne, 1670).

92 For example, *Missa apostolica, sive, He theia leitourgia tou hagiou aposotolou Petrou: Divinvm sacrificivm Sancti Apostoli Petri: cvm Wilhelmi Lindani . . . Apologia pro eadem D. Petri Apostoli liturgia: item vetustissimus in S. Apostolicae Missae Latine canone commentarius* (Antverpiae: Plantini, 1589); Victor Scialach, *Liturgiae s. Basilii magni, s. Gregorii Theologi, s. Cyrilli Alexandrini, ex Arabico conversae* (Augustae Vindelicolum: C. Mangum, 1604); Jean Mabillon, *De liturgia gallicana: libri III in quibus veteris missae* (Luteciae Parisiorum: E. Martin et J. Boudot, 1685); Eusebe Renaudot, *Liturgiarum orientalium collectio. Accedunt dissertationes quatuor: I. De liturgiarum orientalium origine et authoritate. II. De liturgiis Alexandrinis. III. De lingua Coptica. IV. De patriarcha Alexandrino cum officio ordinatinis ejusdem*, 2 vols. (Paris: Coignard, 1715–16); Giuseppe A. Assemani, *Codex liturgicus ecclesiae universae in XV libros distributus, in quo continentur libri rituales, missales, pontificales, officia, dyptica, etc. ecclesiarum occidentis & orientis*, 13 vols (Rome 1749–66); Prosper Guéranger, *Institutions liturgiques*, 3 vols (Paris: Julien & Lanier, 1840–51); see J. H. Miller et al., "Liturgy," in *New Catholic Encyclopedia*, vol. 8, 2nd edn (Detroit: Thomson Gale, 2003), p. 727.

93 For example, F. A. Zaccaria, *Bibliotheca ritualis*, vol. 1 (Rome: Monaldini, 1776), lv–lxxxviii, as discussed in Geoffrey Wainwright, *Doxology: The Praise of God in Worship, Doctrine, and Life* (New York: Oxford University Press, 1980), p. 220. Réginald Grégoire, *Dictionnaire de spiritualité ascétique et mystique*, vol. 9 (Paris: Beauchesne, 1976), p. 932: "L'entrée dans la langue ecclésiastique latine du grec λειτοργία (*liturgia*), à partir du 16ᵉ siècle, et son emploi de plus en plus généralisé depuis la fin du 19e siècle auraient pu fournir occasion à l'élaboration d'une théologie de la liturgie."

94 Cyprian Vagaggini, Leonard J. Doyle & W.A. Jurgens (trans.), *Theological Dimensions of the Liturgy: A General Treatise on the Theology of the Liturgy* (Collegeville: Liturgical Press, 1976), p. 596.

95 Ibid., pp. 596–97.

96 On the designation of this controversy, see Alexander Y. Hwang, *Intrepid Lover of Perfect Grace: The Life and Thought of Prosper of Aquitaine* (Washington, DC: Catholic University of America Press, 2009), pp. 2–6.

97 Eusebius, *Ecclesiastical History*, V, 24, in Roy J. Deferrari (trans.), *Eusebius Pamphili Ecclesiastical History, Books 1–5*, The Fathers of the Church: A New Translation, vol. 19 (Washington, DC: Catholic University of America Press, 1953), p. 335.

98 Eusebius, *Ecclesiastical History*, V, 25, 339.

99 C.F.E. Brightman, "The Quartodeciman Question," in Everett Ferguson, David M. Scholer & Paul Corby Finney (eds), *Worship in Early Christianity*, Studies in Early Christianity, vol. 15 (New York: Garland Publishing, 1993), pp. 322–38; Jonathan Joseph Armstrong, "The Paschal Controversy and the Emergence of the Fourfold Gospel Canon," *Studia Patristica* 45 (2010), pp. 115–23; see also A. Stewart-Sykes, *The Lamb's High Feast. Melito, Peri Pascha and the Quartodeciman Paschal Liturgy at Sardis*, Supplements to *Vigiliae Christianae*, vol. 42 (Leiden/Boston/Köln: Brill 1998).

100 Cyprian, *Letter 73*, 13, in S.L. Greenslade (trans. and ed.), *Early Latin Theology*, Library of Christian Classics (Philadelphia: Westminster, 1956), p. 164.

101 Daniel Van Slyke, "Augustine and Catechumenal *exsufflatio*: An Integral Element of Christian Initiation," *Ephemerides Liturgicae* 118 (2004), pp. 175–208 (pp. 197–98).

102 Augustine provides a first-hand witness that Ambrose presided over such rites in *Contra Iulianum (opus imperfectum), IV.*120, in PL 45, 1414 and IV.108, in PL 45, 1404.

103 Augustine, *Contra Iulianum (opus imperfectum), I.*117, p. 134.

104 Augustine, *Contra Iulianum (opus imperfectum), III.*144, pp. 450–51.

105 For example, Henry Ansgar Kelly, *The Devil at Baptism: Ritual, Theology, and Drama* (Ithaca, NY: Cornell University Press, 1985); Elizabeth A. Leeper, "From Alexandria to Rome: The Valentinian Connection to the Incorporation of Exorcism as a Pre-baptismal Rite," *Vigiliae Christianae* 44 (1990), pp. 6–24.

106 Translation from the Latin version, in *The Apostolic Tradition*, Paul F. Bradshaw, Maxwell E. Johnson, and L. Edward Phillips (Minneapolis: Augsburg, 2002), pp. 38–40.

107 *Contra Iulianum (opus imperfectum), III.*182, in CSEL 85.1, 482; *Contra Iulianum (opus imperfectum), I.*60, in CSEL 85.1, 57–58.

108 *De nuptiis et concupiscentia* II.18.33, in CSEL 42, 286–87, in Roland J. Teske (trans.), *Answer to the Pelagians II*, The Works of St Augustine: A Translation for the 21st Century I.24 (Hyde Park, NY: New City Press, 1998), p. 74.

109 See Germán Mártil, *La tradición en san Agustín: a través de la controversia pelagiana* (Madrid: Espasa-Calpe 1943), p. 106; Anthony Dupont, "La presencia de los temas antipelagianos *baptismus paruulorum* y *peccatum originale* en los *sermones ad populum* de Agustín, ¿Una perspectiva pastoral sobre asuntos doctrinales y polémicos?" *Augustinus* 55 (2010), pp. 109–27; for a discussion of how Augustine uses the baptismal practices of the Church to articulate a theology of original sin before his debate with Julian, see Vittorino Grossi, *La liturgia battesimale in S. Agostino: studio sulla catechesi del peccato originale negli anni 393–412* (Rome: Institutum Patristicum Augustinianum, 1970), pp. 94–101.

110 The thesis that the *Confessions* are an act of worship modeled on the psalms is argued by John Sylvester-Johnson, "The Psalms in the Confessions of Augustine," Ph.D. diss., Southern Baptist Theological Seminary, 1981.

111 Augustinus, *Confessiones* 1.1.1, James J. O'Donnell (ed.), *Confessions*, vol. 1, *Introduction and Text* (Oxford: Clarendon Press, 1992), p. 3, my translation.

112 Jean Gaillard, "Louange," in M. Viller et al. (eds), *Dictionnaire de spiritualité ascétique et mystique*, vol. 9 (Paris: Beauchesne, 1976), p. 1025.

113 *Confessiones* 6.7.12, in O'Donnell, *Confessions*, p. 65; Henry Chadwick (trans.), in Augustine, *Confessions* (New York: Oxford University Press, 1991), p. 100.

114 Augustine's thought on prayer is more fully elaborated in the *Enarrationes*, which "prolong the [prayer] of the *Confessions* and manifest the spiritual and mystical experience of Augustine," and most concisely in *Ep.* 130 to Proba. A. Hamman,

"Prayer III: The Latin West in the 4th and 5th Centuries," in Angelo Di Berardino (ed.), Adrian Walford (trans.), *Encyclopedia of the Early Church* (New York: Oxford University Press, 1992), p. 708.

115 Augustine, *Epistula* 130.14.27, in CSEL 44, 72.

116 Monique Vincent, *Saint Augustin maître de prière d'après les* Enarrationes in psalmos (Paris: Beauchesne, 1990), p. 389; Rebecca H. Weaver, "Prayer," in *Augustine Through The Ages: An Encyclopedia*, ed. Allan D. Fitzgerald et al. (Grand Rapids: William B. Eerdmans), p. 671.

117 Weaver, "Prayer," p. 674; Gaillard, "Louange," p. 1025.

118 I gratefully acknowledge my indebtedness to Fadi Auro, who provided invaluable assistance in the production of this chapter.

Bibliography

Baldovin, John F. "The Uses of Liturgical History." *Worship* 82 (2008): 2–18.

Botte, Bernard. John Sullivan (trans.). *From Silence to Participation: An Insider's View of Liturgical Renewal.* Washington DC: Pastoral Press, 1988.

Bradshaw, Paul F., Maxwell E. Johnson, L. Edward Phillips, and Harold W. Attridge. *The Apostolic Tradition.* Minneapolis: Fortress, 2002.

Bradshaw, Paul F. *The Search for the Origins of Christian Worship: Sources and Methods for the Study of Early Liturgy.* 2nd edn. Oxford: Oxford University Press, 2002.

Johnson, Lawrence J. *Worship in the Early Church: An Anthology of Historical Sources*, 4 vols. Collegeville: Liturgical Press, 2009.

Reid, Alcuin. *The Organic Development of the Liturgy: The Principles of Liturgical Reform and their Relation to the Twentieth Century Liturgical Movement Prior to the Second Vatican Council*, 2nd edn. San Francisco: Ignatius Press, 2005.

Chapter 4

KEY THEMES IN THE STUDY OF MEDIEVAL LITURGY

Yitzhak Hen

The way in which the study of liturgy was perceived by historians, theologians, and literary critics is accurately reflected in these words, written more than three decades ago:

> Liturgical history is pure scholarship: painstakingly detailed, extremely technical, highly esoteric, and compulsively fascinating. Its practitioners, like the initiates of an ancient mystery cult, pour the fruits of their research into learned journals with splendidly arcane titles like *Ephemerides Liturgicae* and *Sacris Erudiri*. It is hard for a mere layman to penetrate these mysteries . . .[1]

The reasons for that dim view are complex. In part, the study of liturgy had fared badly because it became extremely technical and rigid, following strictly the guidelines and methods put forward by the seventeenth-century founders of the field. But it was also the peculiar nature of liturgical studies, as developed in the last three centuries, that has set liturgy apart from the general trends of theological and historical research. Scholars who submerged themselves in the study of liturgy too often tend to ignore the context in which the liturgy evolved, as if liturgical texts were produced in a political and cultural vacuum. This resulted in a frustrating segregation and detachment of liturgical studies, which gradually became less and less accessible to historians and theologians.[2] Moreover, like the study of hagiography in the eighteenth and nineteenth centuries, the study of liturgy was dominated by a selective and highly educated group of monks and clerics, and hence was straightforwardly associated with religious piety and observance.

Luckily, things have moved forward, and the study of medieval liturgy has witnessed a dramatic resurgence of interest in recent decades. From an obscure domain for a chosen few, the study of liturgy became part and parcel of any historical, religious, artistic, and literary analysis of medieval society and culture. Liturgy, it appears, was gradually recognized by scholars as an important indicator of cultural creativity and social development, and the great potential that lies within the study of liturgy was acknowledged by historians, theologians, and literary critics. As the anthropologist Clifford Geertz has pointed out, "it is, primarily at least, out of the context of concrete acts of religious observance that religious conviction emerges on the human plane."[3] In other words, liturgy is a unique and indispensable tool for the study of any Christian society in its historical, cultural, and spiritual context. It gives us a rare glimpse of the actual rites people performed, but it also provides a great deal of information about the perceptions, ideas, and preoccupations of the society in question.

In what follows, I should like to explore some of the most important and exciting recent developments in the study of liturgy. But first, let us consider the ways in which liturgy was studied in the past, before it became an instructive analytical tool in recent years.

The study of liturgy from Mabillon onwards

Although the origins of liturgical studies can be sought and found in the liturgical commentaries of the early Middle Ages,[4] the beginning of modern interest in the liturgy as a subject of study is intimately associated with the development of the general interest in medieval history which characterized sixteenth- and seventeenth-century Europe.[5] It is, then, not at all surprising that the man who best epitomizes seventeenth-century scholarship in the West, Jean Mabillon (d. 1707), is also the most outstanding precursor of modern liturgical studies.

Born of a peasant family, Mabillon entered the Benedictine order immediately after completing his education. He spent several years in the monasteries of Nogent, Corbie, and Soissons, before joining the congregation of Saint Maur at the abbey of Saint-Germain-des-Prés in Paris, which was already renowned for its scholarly erudition.[6] In 1681, Mabillon published his most famous and ground-breaking work, *De re diplomatica*,[7] and four years later he published his pioneer work on the Gallican liturgy, which was inspired by the discovery of early liturgical texts, such as the Lectionary of Luxeuil (Paris, BnF lat. 9427) and the Bobbio Missal (Paris, BnF lat. 13246).[8] Subsequent liturgical studies, which benefited from Mabillon's journeys throughout Europe in quest of manuscripts and rare books, were published in two volumes of collected essays.[9]

It is true that even before Mabillon, scholars in France, Germany, and Italy published material related to the study of medieval liturgy.[10] Yet, it was the liturgical work of Mabillon and his disciples that set the Maurists of Saint-Germain-des-Prés in the very front rank of modern liturgists.[11] Furthermore, the guidelines set by Mabillon in his liturgical research dominated liturgical studies for many a generation to come. Following Mabillon's model, liturgists in the past concentrated on texts, classified them, looked for their origins, illustrated their development, and edited them. This was the core of liturgical studies, and very little has changed since the time of Mabillon regarding the questions liturgists ask and the answers they seek. What has changed is, on the one hand, our knowledge of the auxiliary disciplines, such as codicology and palaeography, which enable scholars to date and locate manuscripts more accurately and to produce better editions; and, on the other hand, the widening knowledge of liturgical practices, sources, and traditions, which permits scholars to draw more precise conclusions. An outstanding example of such a progress is the work that has been done in recent years on the *Gothic Missal*.

The so-called *Gothic Missal* (Vatican City, Biblioteca Apostolica Vaticana, Reg. lat. 317) is one of the most important representatives of the pre-Carolingian liturgical tradition of Merovingian Gaul, commonly known as the Gallican liturgy. Copied around the year 700 by at least three different scribes, and colorfully decorated by three different artists, this *de luxe* Merovingian sacramentary originated from a centre where the script of Luxeuil was used, and was copied for a church in Burgundy, possibly Autun or Besançon. In its present form, the *Gothic Missal* contains 543 formulae, arranged in seventy-seven Mass formularies, of which thirty-two are for the temporal cycle, thirty-six for the sanctoral cycle, two for baptism, six Sunday Masses, and one daily Mass. At least one formulary at the beginning of the sacramentary, and an unknown number of formularies at the end, are missing. Although incomplete, this outstanding liturgical manuscript received numerous editions since the end of the seventeenth century: the most notable ones are by Henry M. Bannister for the Henry Bradshaw Society,[12] and by Leo C. Mohlberg for the series Rerum ecclesiasticarum documenta.[13] Whereas Bannister followed the manuscript very closely (but alas, without any punctuation and with minimal references to linguistic issues), Mohlberg's edition suffers from many transcription and printing errors, as well as from his uneven treatment of grammatical and orthographical peculiarities.

In 2005, almost half a century after Mohlberg's edition became the standard text of the *Gothic Missal*, Els Rose has published a new, meticulous, and flawless edition of this fascinating sacramentary,[14] to which she added a lengthy and most informative introduction.[15] The core of her introduction is a careful analysis of the *Gothic Missal*'s Latin,[16] and as Rose clearly demonstrates, the *Gothic Missal* is a remarkable evidence for the vitality and creativity of Merovingian Latin, which, in the past, was unjustly and anachronistically dismissed as dull, vulgar, or corrupt. The rest of Rose's introduction is a detailed study of the liturgical commemoration of the saints in the *Gothic Missal*,[17] in an attempt to trace the various traditions that influenced the Gallican liturgy, to which the *Gothic Missal* belongs. Rose's edition of the *Gothic Missal*, I would submit, is the latest and most erudite liturgical enterprise in the philological-textual tradition established by Mabillon.

A different aspect of Mabillon's scholarly heritage is the study of liturgical traditions and the local developments of peculiar rites. It is customary to divide the liturgical traditions of Late Antiquity and the early Middle Ages into two groups, following historically determined geo-political and geo-cultural divisions, that is, Eastern liturgies (which include the liturgy of Jerusalem, the Nestorian or East Syrian liturgy, the Antiochean or West Syrian liturgy, the Alexandrian tradition, the Ethiopian liturgy, and the Byzantine or Constantinopolitan liturgy),[18] and Western traditions, amongst which the most important and influential was the liturgical rite of Rome.[19] Yet, throughout Late Antiquity and the early Middle Ages other liturgical practices emerged in the Latin West, such as the North African liturgy, the Mozarabic liturgy of Spain, the Gallican liturgy, which evolved in Merovingian Gaul, and the liturgies which emerged in Ireland and Anglo-Saxon England.[20]

Ever since the publication of Mabillon's *De liturgia gallicana* in 1685, scholars were busy identifying the various liturgical traditions, their sources, as well as the pace and nature of their evolvement. Although in the past scholars were accustomed to evaluate the various western liturgical traditions as mere derivatives of the Roman rite, modern scholarship tends to acknowledge greater creativity and individuality in each of these sub-divisions of the western rite. An interesting case in point is the study of the liturgy of early medieval Ireland.

To outline the nature and character of the early Irish liturgy is an extremely difficult task. Not only is the evidence relatively fragmentary and disparate, it is also extremely ambiguous. This fundamental disadvantage, coupled with a strong sense of local patriotism, as well as a certain notion of romanticism, led in the past to the building of vast but fragile theories on the origins, development and nature of the early Irish liturgy, highlighting its uniqueness and impact on the liturgy of the early medieval West. Frederick E. Warren's monumental analysis of the early Irish liturgical sources, which was published in 1881,[21] had clearly set the tone for subsequent studies of the early Irish liturgy.[22] According to him, a separate and unique liturgical tradition – the so-called Celtic Rite – was practised in early medieval Ireland, and this tradition can be reconstructed from the various bits and pieces of liturgical books that survive.

Over the last thirty years or so, there has been an immense proliferation of scholarly interest in issues related to the early history of Ireland, which resulted in a better understanding of the period.[23] It is a commonplace nowadays that early medieval Ireland was not "a Dark Age Hippy colony inhabited by gentle gurus doing their own Christian thing far removed from the stultifying influence of sub-Roman bishops and their dioceses."[24] In more than one respect, early medieval Ireland was integrated into the history of Western Europe, and the notion of an independent "Celtic Church" was justly put into question. The time, then, was ripe for a major reassessment of the early Irish liturgy.

Breaking free of Warren's shade, and shedding off the romanticism and prejudice that characterized most studies of the early Irish liturgy, Neil X. O'Donoghue has risen to the challenge, and systematically re-examined the early Irish liturgical sources (both written, archeological and iconographic) in light of modern research.[25] Surprisingly, but not unexpectedly, his conclusions point to the fact that the liturgy celebrated in early medieval Ireland was much more mainstream than is often proposed. According to him, there is no hard evidence to imply that a separate Irish rite had ever existed, and it is highly probable that the early Irish used a form of the Gallican liturgy that was common to most of the West.[26] These conclusions, one should stress, accord extremely well with the general developments in the study of early Irish history, and they shed a fresh new light on the contacts between the Irish Church and the Continent.

Tattered manuscripts under the spotlight

The core of liturgical studies rests on close analysis of the manuscript evidence. Thus, it is essential to examine the surviving liturgical manuscripts and fragments of manuscripts, in order to form a more accurate notion of the type of liturgy used, as well as its social and cultural implications. Various catalogues of liturgical manuscripts were produced in the past, the most comprehensive and widespread of which is Klaus Gamber's *Codices liturgici latini antiquiores*, which was published in the early 1960s and supplemented with a subsidia volume in the late 1980s.[27] These volumes are still the starting point for any investigation of medieval liturgical manuscripts, albeit the fact that Gamber's analysis and typology are in many cases out of date and in need of a serious revision according to modern scholarship.

Attempts to revise Gamber's survey and analysis were constantly made in the past decades, but on a very limited scale. These revisions tend to group the liturgical manuscripts according to geo-political and geo-cultural divisions, focus on a single group, and hence provide a reassessment of only a restricted selection of liturgical manuscripts. Most prominent examples of such enterprises are the recent re-evaluations of the liturgical sources from medieval England. In 1995, Richard W. Pfaff edited an annotated catalogue of the liturgical manuscripts from Anglo-Saxon England,[28] and in 2009 he published his monumental study on the liturgy of medieval England,[29] which is guided almost exclusively by the examination of liturgical manuscripts and by focusing on the textual transmission of liturgical texts. Pfaff's book, in this respect, is indeed a major achievement, and although one does not have to agree with everything he says, *The Liturgy in Medieval England* provides a solid basis for future analyses of the English liturgy.

Producing catalogs of liturgical manuscripts is a daunting task. The alternative is to study a single liturgical manuscript in its religious, cultural, social, and even political context. In the past, whenever a liturgist or an historian wished to examine the liturgical developments and characteristics of a certain period or a certain region, she or he turned directly to the lavishly-produced liturgical manuscripts. This, however, is one of the most misleading biases prevailing in liturgical studies, for it forces the liturgist to concentrate on a select group of *de luxe* or well-prepared volumes, which were produced for rich and well-established ecclesiastical institutions, such as monasteries or cathedral churches. But this situation can only be a circumstantial anomaly. Luxurious liturgical codices could not have been the bulk of the liturgical productivity of medieval *scriptoria*. It is only reasonable to assume that a vast number of liturgical manuscripts of a lesser artistic or codicological quality, but not necessarily of inferior liturgical importance, were also copied and distributed, despite the fact that very few of them survive intact.[30]

In recent years, increasing numbers of studies of smaller, simpler and much cheaper liturgical manuscripts that were produced for the use of missionaries, priests of small churches and itinerant preachers, have contributed much to our understanding of early medieval liturgy, and of what pastoral care really consisted of in the Middle Ages.[31] The so-called Bobbio Missal (Paris, BnF lat. 13246) is one of the most illustrious examples of such a book. Copied in south-eastern France in the last decades of Merovingian rule, the Bobbio Missal is, to cite Elias A. Lowe, "the work of a private individual – a cleric who made a copy of the service book of which he stood in need, and which, to judge from its size, he probably carried about with him in his travels."[32] Thus, judging from the script, the manuscript layout, and its content, the Bobbio Missal can justifiably be described as a *vade mecum* of a Merovingian priest.[33] When compared with the splendid Merovingian sacramentaries of the late seventh and eighth century,[34] the Bobbio Missal seems poor and unpretentious. But should these *de luxe* sacramentaries be the yardstick by which the Bobbio Missal, or any other small liturgical compilations are to be measured?

In an important paper titled "Célébration épiscopale et célébration prebyteriale: une essai de typologie," the liturgist Niels Rasmussen suggested a new way to arrange the typology of early medieval liturgical manuscripts. According to him, both the material aspects and layout of a manuscript, as well as its liturgical content can help us to determine the manuscript's destination and function. Sacramentaries, for example, were produced for monastic, episcopal, and presbyterial use, and only by examining their external form and liturgical content can one determine to which of the above mentioned categories a certain manuscript belongs.[35] A good example which elucidates Rasmussen's observations is a small liturgical manuscript from Brussels (Brussels, BR 10127–10144).[36] The modesty in the preparation of this volume, its small and handy form (similar to a Penguin paperback), and the peculiar character of the short sacramentary which it accommodates, containing the prayers for only eleven major feasts of the liturgical year, all suggest that it was produced for a priest of some small rural church.[37]

Following Rasmussen, I have suggested two more criteria that can be added to Rasmussen's double yardstick. First, the content of the entire manuscript, and not just its liturgical section, can disclose the manuscript's functional destination. Second, the combination of two or more types of liturgical book in one manuscript indicates a destination far from an ecclesiastical or a monastic centre. Indeed, the Brussels manuscript just mentioned can help us to illustrate this point as well, for its liturgical section is juxtaposed with a plethora of canonical and doctrinal material, which is usually absent from *de luxe* liturgical manuscripts. The liturgical section itself, furthermore, is composed from a selection of different liturgical pieces, and contains a unique combination of a sacramentary, a lectionary, an antiphonary, several *ordines*, and various other ceremonial instructions. These peculiarities imply that the manuscript was composed with a view to assisting an itinerant or rural priest in a remote area, providing him with a selection of liturgical and doctrinal material he might need in order to execute his job.[38]

Similar studies have yielded similar conclusions. For example, Helen Gittos' analysis of the so-called Red Book of Darley (Cambridge, Corpus Christi College 422) and Victoria Thompson's discussion of Oxford, Bodleian Library, Laud. Misc. 482, clearly demonstrate that both eleventh-century books were compiled with a local priest in mind, and both were designed to assist this priest in executing his pastoral duties.[39] The Red Book of Darley, as pointed out by Gittos, "seems to contain almost everything that the putative parish priest required."[40] Whether these texts were selected and copied by the original owner of the book for his personal use, as suggested by Christopher Hohler,[41] or whether the compilation was prepared in a well-established centre for the use of local priests, is, unfortunately, impossible to gauge. Similarly, the carefully selected texts in Oxford, Bodleian Library, MS Laud. Misc. 482, suggest that it was designed to help the clergy in administering their ministry to the sick and dying.[42] This focus on modest liturgical manuscripts, rather than on *de luxe* and lavishly produced ones, is proving to be seminal for our understanding of medieval liturgy and its religious as well as cultural significance.[43]

Liturgy and society

Whereas the study of liturgical manuscripts forms the basis for any liturgical investigation, focusing on thematic issues within the liturgy led scholars into a completely different line of inquiry. In recent years scholars, such as Arnold Angenendt,[44] Rosamond McKitterick,[45] Janet Nelson,[46] or Frederick Paxton,[47] to name only a few of the most outstanding, have tried to shift the emphasis of liturgical research, after realizing that the importance of the study of liturgy goes far beyond the simple fact that it elucidates the way people celebrated their solemn rites and festivals. Consequently, scholars began to use liturgical sources as an analytical tool for the study of political ideology,[48] marriage practices,[49] perceptions of death and penance,[50] various rites of passage,[51] the formation of communal memory,[52] and many other topics, which were not normally on the agenda of liturgists. Hence, alongside the more traditional lines of inquiry, a new and different appreciation of liturgy evolved, whose objectives were to set liturgy fully into its cultural, historical and even theological context.

In his book *Liturgie et société au Moyen Age*,[53] Éric Palazzo gives a panoramic view of the functions and manifestations of liturgy in medieval society, from its role in punctuating the Christian calendar, through the place of various rites in the life of the individual, and up to the multi-layered interaction between liturgy and the arts.[54] Palazzo is, of course, not the first one to touch upon these issues, but he was certainly the first one to integrate them into a coherent argument about the crucial role of liturgy in medieval society as a whole. Liturgy, according to Palazzo, was part and parcel of medieval society, not only because it was practised by medieval people, but also because it helped shape their social and cultural world, and it had a crucial role in disseminating ideals and values that later became part of these people's world view. It is this line of interpretation of medieval liturgy that enabled scholars to ask new questions, and use liturgy both as an historical goldmine of information, and as a gateway for the study of social, cultural, and religious practices. Let us give just three examples that stemmed from this new trend of liturgical studies, namely the interaction between liturgy and politics, liturgy and drama, and the formation of communal memory.

Liturgy and politics

The royal patronage of liturgy was a common practice in Frankish Gaul. At the beginning of the seventh century, after heaping on Saint-Denis a huge amount of treasure and landed property, King Dagobert I (d. 639) made an attempt to institute at the abbey the singing of psalms in shifts (*per turmas*),[55] following the model of Saint-Maurice of Agaune.[56] By instituting and enforcing religious practices – in this case the so-called *laus perennis* – Dagobert exercised control over the monks of Saint-Denis, securing their prayers, and consequently increasing his chances for salvation. Given the fact that Dagobert was about to entrust his bones to the abbey of Saint-Denis, these matters were not to be taken lightly.

Although unsuccessful in the long term, Dagobert's endeavor to institute a perpetual chant in Saint-Denis is an important turning point in the history of the royal patronage of liturgy in Frankish Gaul.[57] Dagobert, it seems, realized the political power within the patronage of liturgy, and for the first time in Frankish history, we hear of a king who clearly linked the endowment of riches to ecclesiastical institutions with prayers. Subsequently, in seventh-century Francia, acts of liturgical patronage became an instrument by which heavenly protection could be sought for the benefit of the kingdom and its ruler.

It is, then, not at all surprising that several of the liturgical books from early medieval Francia contain prayers *pro rege, pro regibus,* or *in pace.*[58] Not only were these prayers an emotional appeal, asking God to protect the kingdom's peace, to secure its stability, and to grant victory to the ruler, they also disseminate what appears to be an utterly Christian political ideology. For example, the Old Gelasian Sacramentary (Vatican City, Biblioteca Apostolica Vaticana, Reg. lat. 316 + Paris BnF lat. 7193), which was copied at the mid-eighth century in either Chelles or Jouarre includes a Mass urging God to "...let your servants N., our kings, adorn the triumph of your virtue skilfully, so that they, who are *principes* by your command, may always be powerful in their duty."[59] Later on in the same Mass, God is asked to give the guidance of his wisdom to the rulers, "...so that drinking from your fountain for their assemblies they may please you and may rise above all the kingdoms."[60] Similarly, the prayer *infra actionem* of the very same Mass beseeches God to accept the oblation "...just as you regarded it worthy to bestow upon him the power of ruling, gracious and generous [as you are] receive [him under your protection]; and implored grant our entreaty, so that confident in the protection of your majesty, he may be blessed with age and kingdom."[61] Finally, the Mass concludes with a wish for peace, "O God, who prepared the eternal Roman empire by evangelical predicting, present the celestial arms to your servants N., our *principes*, so that the peace of the churches may not be troubled by the storm of wars."[62] Although the formula *rex Dei gratia* was not yet used by the Merovingian kings and their advisors, its notion was already embedded in the *missa pro regibus* of the Old Gelasian Sacramentary.

Thus, the prayers for the king, as well as those for time of war and for peace, express a genuine concern for the general well-being of the kingdom, but they also transmit a clear and well-developed Christian perception of rulership. The idea of such services was, no doubt, an inheritance of late antique and Byzantine traditions.[63] Yet, the Merovingians harnessed those traditions and anchored them in a complex network of patronage, endowments, and liturgical practice. It seems, therefore, that the later Merovingians and their advisers used the patronage of liturgy as a political machinery of royal propaganda. Through the prayers on behalf of the king and the kingdom, the Frankish kings disseminated political messages of consensus, solidarity, peace, and victory to their subjects, and through these prayers the king made his presence felt throughout the kingdom. Moreover, the prayers for the king and the kingdom in times of crisis made each and every subject personally involved and responsible for the welfare of the ruler and of the kingdom as a whole. Hence, these prayers helped to sustain "Frankish unity" by creating what Janet Nelson would term "Frankish self-identification."[64] In other words, the Merovingian prayers *pro regibus* reflect Merovingian realities of consensus politics, and ideas of peace and solidarity within the kingdom that were to become the prevailing characteristics of the Carolingian political ideology under Pippin III (d. 751), Charlemagne (d. 814), and their successors.[65] But as they did in so many matters, the Carolingians operated on a much more grandiose scale. It will suffice to mention here the immense effort taken by the Carolingians to organize coronations, large scale liturgical processions in times of crisis, lavish acts of patronage, and, of course, the *laudes regiae*,[66] to demonstrate how the Carolingians adopted and endorsed the Merovingian tradition of patronizing liturgy for political purposes.

Similarly, to give just one more example, the liturgical reaction of Christian Europe to the demise of the Crusader kingdom of Jerusalem had a crucial role in keeping the Crusader idea alive, and in disseminating an urgent call to liberate Jerusalem by means of new Holy Land crusades.[67] As argued by Amnon Linder, the dynamic developments in the liturgy for the liberation of Jerusalem from the thirteenth century onwards should be understood against the desperate papal efforts to revive the idea of crusade. Liturgy, it appears, became a means by which the Pope and his curia had hoped to encourage Christian rulers to take part in the effort to salvage the Holy Land. Through the peculiar types of liturgical rite that evolved in Western Europe throughout the later Middle Ages (i.e. the Clamor, the three principal Mass prayers, the dedicated war Mass, the English Trental of St Gregory, and the bidding prayers) this message was disseminated throughout Europe, and consequently it propagated the notion that each and every Christian is responsible for the success of the crusades.

Liturgy and drama

The idea that the Christian rite is a form of theatrical performance goes back at least to the ninth-century controversial scholar Amalarius of Metz,[68] who was the first to interpret the liturgy as "drama."[69] Modern scholars followed suit,[70] and soon the Christian eucharistic rite was even dubbed as "the drama of the Middle Ages."[71] This is not the place to rehearse the various observations made by scholars throughout the years on either the interrelationship between liturgy and drama in the Middle Ages,[72] or the emergence of liturgical drama.[73] However, I would like to mention two recent studies that approach the study of liturgical drama from a different angle. The first is the use of vernacular sermons as part of the effort to analyse the dramatic liturgy of Anglo-Saxon England; the other is a fascinating study of the performance of a single liturgical drama in a particular context.

The tenth century was a significant turning point in the history of the Anglo-Saxon Church. The so-called Benedictine reform movement set new standards and led the Anglo-Saxon Church on a new path.[74] It was also a crucial stage in the formation of the Anglo-Saxon liturgy, and, according to M. Bradford Bedingfield, it was then that the liturgy of the late Anglo-Saxon Church became "dramatic," in an attempt to establish a connection between its audience and biblical models.[75] Hence, the late Anglo-Saxon liturgy was formed in a way that encouraged identification with biblical figures, and this relationship between the participant and the biblical model was highlighted and elaborated by both the rituals and the vernacular preaching. This, Bradford Bedingfield suggests, is the dramatic quality of the late Anglo-Saxon liturgical rites. Whereas one can argue with the somewhat superficial hypothesis that lies behind this study, its extensive use of vernacular homilies and sermons alongside other liturgical sources is to be congratulated as a new model for pursuing liturgical studies.

One of the dramatic liturgical acts analysed by Bradford Bedingfield in his book is the so-called *Visitatio sepulchri* (also known as *Quem quaeritis?*),[76] which was performed throughout Western Europe on the morning of Easter day. This short liturgical drama, which relates the visit of the three Marys to the empty tomb of Christ, was introduced into the liturgy in the tenth century,[77] and as Peter Dronke has mordantly pointed out, it "received an almost inordinate amount of scholarly attention – and controversy – in the last half-century."[78] And yet, Iris Shagrir's study of the performance of the *Visitatio sepulchri* at the Crusader Church of the Holy Sepulchre in Jerusalem offers some fresh insights on the dissemination of this liturgical piece.[79]

The so-called Breviary of Barletta (Barletta, Santo Sepulcro, no shelf-mark), which was produced for the Augustinian canons of the Holy Sepulchre, provides some unique information on the liturgical cycle of the twelfth-century Latin Church of the Holy Sepulchre in Jerusalem.[80] Tucked between various prayers and formulae, Shagrir has found a distinctive version of the *Visitatio sepulchri*, which, according to the breviary itself, was performed at dawn of Easter morning (*In die sancto pasche ad matutinas*). This version, however, was not a straightforward copy or a simple transplant of a Western rite into the liturgical cycle of Jerusalem. The use of space in the Barletta version of the *Visitatio sepulchri* is well adapted to the specific floor plan of the newly built complex of the Holy Sepulchre, so as to orchestrate the movement from the high altar in the east, to the tomb itself, and back to the middle of the choir. Then the patriarch, who was sitting next to the high altar, begun chanting the *Te Deum*, and thus completed an imaginary circle. Moreover, from the various instruction added to the text, one can also discern a particular use of light – candles, bright garments that glowed in the darkness at the crack of dawn, and the *Te Deum* that marked daybreak. These and other variations in the text reflect "the adjustments of the celebration of a Western Latin rite to a space consecrated by time-honoured local tradition, and in front of a varied audience of non-Catholic and even non-Christian denominations."[81] Such interactions and adjustments are, perhaps, the most eloquent evidence for the sheer vitality and creativity of liturgists in the Middle Ages, and Shagrir's study is exemplary in the way it combines manuscript studies with various aspects of liturgical studies in an attempt to portray the actual atmosphere and the impression of the liturgical act on the participants.

Liturgy and memory

Liturgy in the Middle Ages had a crucial role in creating and disseminating communal memory. The Eucharist itself is, perhaps, the first and most basic attempt to form a specific Christian memory of past events,[82] and the practice of reciting the names of the dead during Mass is one of the earliest examples of an attempt to shape communal memory on a smaller, and more local, scale.[83] The various local sanctoral cycles functioned in similar ways.[84] Let us take, for example, the sanctoral cycle of Auxerre in Burgundy. Very few saints were venerated in Auxerre before the fifth century, and none of them can be identified as a local saint. This situation was changed dramatically by Bishop Germanus (d. 437/448), whose dynamic personality manifested itself not only in building churches, collecting relics and instituting new saints' feasts in the city, but also in the fact that he was the first saint from Auxerre in a long line of local saints. After Germanus' episcopacy, the number of saints venerated in Auxerre continuously multiplied, and by the time of Bishop Aunarius (d. 605) the sanctoral cycle of Auxerre was composed of feasts in honor of more than thirty saints, the vast majority of which were bishops, clerics, abbots, and monks in and around the city.[85]

Although the exact date of the saint's death was not always known, the day of the relics' translation and deposition in the church, which eventually became the day in which the saint was venerated, could have been planned carefully, and the sanctoral cycle of Auxerre seems to have been a well-planned case. Twelve feasts in honor of local saints were assigned in Auxerre to the month of May, and this attempt to turn the month of May into a prolonged period of liturgical celebrations is enough to demonstrate how the Christian authorities used and manipulated the commemorative festivals of local saints in order to model the communal memory and strengthen the Christian identity of the local community.[86]

An interesting aspect of the very same phenomenon can be found in the use of the Apocryphal Acts in the liturgical commemoration of the Apostles. In what is commonly accepted as the earliest reference to the Apocryphal Acts of the Apostles, Eusebius of Caesarea (d. 339) recorded a series of spurious and dubious Acts, which he condemned as unorthodox and unauthorized.[87] Eusebius' succinct and astute report on the Apocryphal Acts is extremely revealing. Not only does it document the proliferation of such treatises at a fairly early stage of Christian history, it also points to the fact that these unorthodox and unauthorized compositions, although condemned by Christian authorities, were known to everyone and read by many, not the least by churchmen. This attraction-rejection tension is one of the most prevailing characteristics of the transmission and dissemination of the Apocryphal Acts from the time of Eusebius to the present day. Although questioned, denounced and dismissed as heretical, these treatises were copied, translated, and re-written time and again throughout Late Antiquity and the Middle Ages, hence becoming an integral part of what may be termed the Christian heritage of the medieval world.

In her recent book, Els Rose examines the complicated and multi-layered relations between the liturgical commemoration of the Apostles and the Apocryphal literature that recorded their lives and activities.[88] According to her, the various practices of ritual commemoration had a crucial role in the transmission and dissemination of Apocryphal Acts, as well as in the transformation of these narrative traditions as a result of their incorporation into the ritual context. For example, in the case of Matthew, a gradual process of acquaintance with Apocryphal traditions can be traced. Whereas the earliest Gallican Mass in honor of Matthew (to be found in a seventh-century Palimpsest Sacramentary, Munich, Bayerische Staatsbibliothek, Clm 14429), as well as the Masses for Matthew in the eighth-century Gelasian Sacramentaries rely almost exclusively on canonical Scripture, the Mass for Matthew in the Spanish *Liber Mozarabicus* is imbued with thematic and literary borrowings from the Apocryphal *Passio Matthaei*, as transmitted by the Latin Collection of Pseudo-Abdias. However, both liturgical traditions – the Frankish and the Mozarabic – made ample use of doctrinal material that echoes some of the Christological debates of the fourth and the fifth century in order to counterbalance Matthew's endorsement of Christ's humanity. Moreover, the Apocryphal theme of Matthew's martyrdom, which is central to the commemoration of Matthew in the Spanish liturgy, was later adopted and elaborated in various hymns, most notably by Alfanus of Salerno (d. 1085), as a relevant model for political and ecclesiastical change.[89]

This liturgical use of the Apocryphal Acts determined the ways in which the Apostles were portrayed and remembered. Not only did the various liturgical traditions propagate a new image of the Apostles as founders of local churches, stressing their role in the battle against demons and their qualities as persuasive preachers, these liturgical commemorations also endorsed the notion of the Apostles as martyrs, thus turning the eyewitnesses of Christ's life and work into blood-witnesses, the ultimate *imitatores Christi*. Moreover, a brief look at the companions, with whom the Apostles were associated, reveals that unlike the Apocryphal Acts, the various liturgies that relied heavily on Apocryphal narratives were reluctant to attribute a major role to women in the foundation of Christian communities. On the other hand, the very same liturgies emphasized the special bond between the Apostles and local rulers, maybe as a wishful reflection on the political situation of their time. Once again, the role of liturgy in propagating ideas and shaping the Christian memory is revealed.

The foregoing survey is by no means exhaustive. It is extremely selective and, I should stress, impressionistic. I am well aware of the fact that other historians, art historians, musicologists, theologians, or literary critics, would have chosen different themes in the study of liturgy and other instructive examples. It is impossible in such a short survey to encompass all the recent developments in liturgical studies. Choices had to be made, and important themes and studies had to be left out. Still, I hope, the various case studies surveyed above elucidate some of the new trends in liturgical studies, and clarify the great potential that lies within the study of liturgy. These new trends brought liturgy back to the attention of scholars working on medieval culture and society, and consequently they turned the study of liturgy into less intimidating and aloof a discipline.

Although the focus of liturgical studies has been changed in recent decades, this shift of interest must not be taken to imply that liturgical studies, in the textual-philological tradition established by Mabillon, are not necessary anymore. Such studies of the texts, their formulation and their dissemination are the basis for any liturgical investigation. Without them no further research into the cultural aspects of the liturgy can be carried out. Notwithstanding their fundamental differences, these two approaches are not irreconcilable. They simply give different highlights and tonalities to the study of liturgy.

Notes

1 Jeffrey Richards, *Consul of God. The Life and Times of Gregory the Great* (London & Boston: Routledge & Kegan Paul, 1980), p. 119.

2 This detachment is exactly the reason that led Cyrille Vogel to publish his most important and learned introduction to the liturgical sources of the Middle Ages. See: Cyrille Vogel; *Medieval Liturgy: An Introduction to the Sources,* William Storey & Niels K. Rasmussen (trans. & rev.) (Washington DC: Pastoral Press, 1986), p. 1.

3 Cliford Geertz, "Religion as a cultural system," in *The Interpretation of Cultures* (New York: Basic Books, 1973), pp. 87–125 (pp. 112–13).

4 See: Vogel, *Medieval Liturgy*, pp. 10–13; Yitzhak Hen, *The Royal Patronage of Liturgy in Frankish Gaul to the Death of Charles the Bald (877)*, Henry Bradshaw Society, subsidia 3 (London: Boydell & Brewer, 2001), pp. 4–10.

5 On the development of medieval studies in the sixteenth and seventeenth century, see: Rosamond McKitterick, "The study of Frankish history in France and Germany in the sixteenth and seventeenth centuries," *Francia* 8 (1991), pp. 556–72 [reprinted in eadem, *The Frankish Kings and Culture* (Aldershot: Ashgate, 1995), chapter XIV]; Jurgen Voss, *Das Mittelalter im historischen Denken Frankreichs. Untersuchung zur Geschichte des Mittelalterbegriffes und der Mittelalterbewertung von der zweiten Hälfte des 16. bis zur Mitte des 19. Jahrhunderts* (Munich: Wilhelm Fink, 1972).

6 On Mabillon and the Maurists, see: David Knowles, "Jean Mabillon," *Journal of Ecclesiastical History* 10 (1959), pp. 153–73; idem, *Great Historical Enterprises: Problems in Monastic History* (London: Thomas Nelson, 1963), pp. 35–62; Henri Leclercq, "Mabillon, Jean," DACL X.1, cols 427–724; Blandine Barret-Kriegel, *Jean Mabillon* (Paris: PUF, 1988).

7 Jean Mabillon, *De re diplomatica* (Paris: J.B.Coignard, 1681). A supplement was published by Mabillon in 1704, and a second edition was prepared after his death by Thierry Ruinart.

8 Jean Mabillon, *De liturgia gallicana libri tres* (Paris: Martin et Boudot, 1685); reprinted in PL 72, cols. 99–447.

9 Jean Mabillon, *Museum Italicum*, 2 vols (Paris: Edmund Martin et al., 1687–9); the second volume was reprinted in PL 72, cols 851–1408.

10 For a list of the major early works, see: Vogel, *Medieval Liturgy*, pp. 17–20.

11 Mabillon's devoted pupil and companion, Thierry Ruinart (d. 1709), was not particularly interested in liturgy, so it was basically Edmond Martène (d. 1739) who succeeded Mabillon as the leading liturgist among the Maurists. Martène is best known for his *De antiquis ecclesiae ritibus*, 3 vols (Rouen: Behourt, 1700–2; reprinted Antwerp, 1736–8).

12 Henry M. Bannister (ed.), *Missale Gothicum: A Gallican Sacramentary*, Henry Bradshaw Society 52 & 54 (London: Harrison, 1917 & 1919).

13 Leo C. Mohlberg (ed.), *Missale Gothicum: Das das gallikanische sakramentar (Cod. Vatican. Regin. Lat. 317) des VII–VIII. Jahrhunderts. Facsimile und kommentar* (Augsburg: Benno Filser Verlag, 1929); idem, *Missale Gothicum (Vat. Reg. Lat. 317)*, Rerum ecclesiasticarum documenta, series maior 5 (Rome: Herder, 1961).

14 Els Rose, (ed.), *Missale Gothicum e codice Vaticano Reginensi latino 317*, CCSL 159D (Turnhout: Brepols, 2005).

15 Ibid., pp. 12–348.

16 Ibid., pp. 23–187.

17 Ibid., pp. 189–328.

18 For a general survey of eastern liturgies, see: Archdale A. King, *The Rites of Eastern Christendom*, 2 vols. (Rome, Catholic Book Agency & Tipografia Polyglotta Vaticana, 1947–8); Irénée H. Dalmais, *Liturgies d'orient*, Rites et symboles 10 (Paris: Cerf, 1980); Irénée H. Dalmais, "The eastern liturgical families," in Aime G. Martimort (ed.), *The Church at Prayer*, 4 vols, M.J. O'Connell (trans.) (London, Geoffrey Chapman, 1986–7), vol. I, pp. 27–43.

19 On the liturgy of Rome, see: Geoffrey G. Willis, *A History of Early Roman Liturgy to the Death of Pope Gregory the Great*, Henry Bradshaw Society, subsidia 1 (London: Boydell & Brewer, 1994); Archdale A. King, *The Liturgy of the Roman Church* (London: Longmans, 1957).

20 For a general survey on western liturgies, see: Archdale A. King, *Liturgies of the Past* (London: Longmans, 1959); idem, *Liturgies of the Primatial Sees* (London: Longmans, 1957); Pierre-Marie Gy, "History of the Liturgy in the West to the Council of Trent," in Martimort, *The Church at Prayer*, vol. I, pp. 45–61.

21 See: Frederick E. Warren, *The Liturgy and Ritual of the Early Irish Church* (Oxford: Oxford University Press, 1881); reprinted with a lengthy new introduction by Jane Stevenson (Woodbridge: Boydell Press, 1987); reprinted again with a short preface and updated bibliography by Neil X. O'Donoghue (Piscataway NJ: Gorgias Press, 2010).

22 See also: Louis Gougard, *Christianity in Celtic Lands. A History of the Churches of the Celts, their Origin, their Development, Influence and Mutual Relations*, M. Joynt (trans.) (London: Sheed & Ward, 1932); reprinted with an introduction by Jean-Michel Picard (Dublin: Four Courts Press, 1992), pp. 313–38; King, *Liturgies of the Past*, pp. 186–275; Mark Schneiders, "The origins of the early Irish liturgy," in Próinséas Ní Chatháin & Michael Richter (eds.), *Ireland and Europe in the Early Middle Ages: Learning and Literature* (Stuttgart: Klett-Cotta, 1996), pp. 76–98; Matthieu Smyth, *La liturgie oubliée: la prière eucharistique en Gaule antique et dans l'Occident non romain* (Paris: Cerf, 2003), pp. 114–24.

23 For an up-to-date survey of early medieval Ireland, see: Thomas M. Charles-Edwards, *Early Christian Ireland* (Cambridge University Press: Cambridge, 2007). See also: Dáibhí Ó Cróinín, *Early Medieval Ireland, 400–1000* (London & New York: Longman,

1995), and the various papers in Dáibhí Ó Cróinín (ed.), *A New History of Ireland, I – Prehistoric and Early Ireland* (Oxford: Clarendon Press, 2005).

24 Alfred J. Smyth, "The Golden Age of early Irish monasticism: myth or historical reality?" in Brendan Bradshaw & Dáire Keogh (eds), *Christianity in Ireland: Revisiting the Story* (Dublin: Columba Press, 2002), pp. 21–9 (p. 21).

25 Neil X. O'Donoghue, *The Eucharist in Pre-Norman Ireland* (Notre Dame: University of Notre Dame Press, 2011).

26 Ibid., especially pp. 199–200. Although written independently, I have reached similar conclusions in my "The nature and character of the early Irish liturgy," in *L'Irlanda e gli Irlandesi nell'alto medioevo*, Settimane di studio del Centro italiano di studi sull'alto medioevo 57 (Spoleto: Presso la sede della Fondazione, 2010), pp. 353–80.

27 Klaus Gamber (ed.), *Codices liturgici latini antiquiores*, 2 vols., Spicilegii Friburgensis subsidia 1 (Freiburg: Universitatsverlag, 1963; 2nd ed. 1968); supplemented by Bonifacio Baroffio et al., Spicilegii Friburgensis subsidia 1A (Freiburg: Universitatsverlag, 1988).

28 Richard W. Pfaff (ed.), *The Liturgical Books of Anglo-Saxon England*, Old English Newsletter, subsidia 23 (Kalamazoo: Medieval Institute, Western Michigan University, 1995).

29 Richard W. Pfaff, *The Liturgy in Medieval England: A History* (Cambridge: Cambridge University Press, 2009).

30 On the institutional bias in the preservation of liturgical manuscripts, see: Yitzhak Hen, "A liturgical handbook for the use of a rural priest (Brussels, B R 10127–10144)," in Marco Mostert (ed.), *Organising the Written Word: Scripts, Manuscripts, and Texts* (Turnhout: Brepols, forthcoming).

31 See, for example, Yitzhak Hen, "The knowledge of canon law among rural priests: the evidence of two manuscripts from around 800," *Journal of Theological Studies* 50 (1999), pp. 117–34; idem, "Educating the clergy: canon law and liturgy in a Carolingian handbook from the time of Charles the Bald," in Yitzhak Hen (ed.), *De Sion Exibit Lex et Verbum Domini from Hierusalem: Studies on Medieval Law, Liturgy and Literature in Honour of Amnon Linder*, Cultural encounters in Late Antiquity and the Middle Ages 1 (Turnhout: Brepols, 2001); idem, "A liturgical handbook;" Sven Meeder, "The early Irish Stowe Missal's destination and function," *Early Medieval Europe* 13 (2005), pp. 179–94.

32 Elias A. Lowe, "The palaeography of the Bobbio Missal," in André Wilmart, Elias A. Lowe & H.A. Wilson (eds). *The Bobbio Missal: Notes and Studies*, Henry Bradshaw Society 61 (London: Harrison, 1924), pp. 59–106 (pp. 67–68); reprinted in idem, Ludwig Bieler (ed.), *Palaeographical Papers*, 2 vols. (Oxford: Oxford University Press, 1972), I, pp. 142–81.

33 See the various papers in Yitzhak Hen & Rob Meens (eds), *The Bobbio Missal: Liturgy and Religious Culture in Merovingian Gaul* (Cambridge: Cambridge University Press, 2004).

34 On these manuscripts, see: Vogel, *Medieval Liturgy*. See also: Philipe Bernard, *Du chant romain au chant grégorien (VIe-XIIIe siècle)* (Paris: Cerf, 1996); Hen, *The Royal Patronage of Liturgy*; Smyth, *La liturgie oubliée*, and see the references cited there.

35 Niels K. Rasmussen, "Célébration épiscopale et célébration prebyteriale: une essai de typologie," in *Segni e riti nella chiesa altomedievale occidentale*, Settimane di studio del Centro italiano di studi sull'alto medioevo 33 (Spoleto: Presso la sede della Fondazione, 1987), pp. 581–603.

36 On this manuscript, see: Hen, "The knowledge of canon law"; "A liturgical handbook" and see the further bibliography listed there. The sacramentary of this manuscript was

published as Carl Coebergh & Pierre de Puniet (eds), *Liber sacramentorum excarpsus*, CCCM 47 (Turnhout: Brepols, 1977), pp. 81–110.

37 Hen, "A liturgical handbook." See also: Rasmussen, *Les pontificaux*, pp. 436–; Donald A. Bullough, "The Carolingian liturgical experience," in Robert N. Swanson (ed.), *Community and Change in Christian Worship*, Studies in Church History 35 (Woodbridge: Boydell & Brewer, 1999), pp. 29–64 (pp. 48–9).

38 Hen, "A liturgical handbook."

39 Helen Gittos, "Is there any evidence for the liturgy of parish churches in late Anglo-Saxon England? The Red Book of Darley and the status of Old English," in Francesca Tinti (ed.), *Pastoral Care in Late Anglo-Saxon England*, Anglo-Saxon Studies 6 (Woodbridge: Boydell & Brewer, 2005), pp. 63–82; Victoria Thompson, "The pastoral contact in late Anglo-Saxon England: priest and parishioner in Oxford, Bodleian Library, MS Laud. Miscellaneous 482," in ibid., pp. 106–120.

40 Gittos, "Is there any evidence for the liturgy," p. 69.

41 Christopher Hohler, "The Red Book of Darley," in *Nordiskt Kollokvium II I latinsk liturgiformforskning* (Stockholm: Institutionen för klassiska språk vid Stockholms Universitet, 1972), pp. 39–47.

42 Thompson, "The pastoral contact in late Anglo-Saxon England."

43 See also: the comments by Éric Palazzo, "L'avenir des recherches sur les livres liturgiques du Moyen Age occidental," in Daniel Saulnier, Katarina Livjanic & Christelle Cazaux-Kowalski (eds), *Lingua mea calamus scribae: Mélanges offerts à madame Marie-Noël Colette par ses collègues, étudients et amis* (Solesmes: Éditions du Solesmes, 2009), pp. 295–304.

44 See, for example, Arnold Angenendt, "Missa specialis. Zugleich ein Beitrag zur Entstehung der Privatmessen," *Frühmittelalterliche Studien* 17 (1983), pp. 153–221; idem, "Theologie und Liturgie der mittelalterlichen Toten-Memoria," in Karl Schmid and Joachim Wollasch (eds), *Memoria. Der geschichtliche Zeugniswert des liturgischen Gedenkens im Mittelalter* (MunichL Fink, 1984), pp. 79–199; idem, "Liturgiewissenschaft und Kirchengeschichte am Beispiel der frühmittelalterlichen Taufgeschichte," in Klemens Richter (ed.), *Liturgie: ein vergessenes Thema der Theologie?* (Freiburg: Herder, 1986), pp. 99–112.

45 Rosamond McKitterick, *The Frankish Church and the Carolingian Reforms, 789–895* (London: Royal Historical Society, 1977), especially pp. 115–54. See also: eadem, "Unity and diversity in the Carolingian Church," in Robert N. Swanson (ed.), *Unity and Diversity in the Church*, Studies in Church History 32 (Oxford: Blackwell, 1996), pp. 59–82.

46 See the various papers collected in Janet L. Nelson, *Politics and Ritual in Early Medieval Europe* (London: Hambledon Press, 1986).

47 Frederick S. Paxton, *Christianizing Death. The Creation of a Ritual Process in Early Medieval Europe* (Ithaca and London: Cornell University Press, 1990).

48 On liturgy and political ideology, see below pp. 80–81.

49 See, for example: Yitzhak Hen, *Culture and Religion in Merovingian Gaul, A.D. 481–751* (Leiden, New York and Cologne: Brill, 1995), pp. 122–37; David d'Avrey, *Medieval Marriage: Symbolism and Society* (Oxford: Oxford University Press, 2004).

50 On death, see: Paxton, *Christianizing Death*; Éric Rebillard, *The Care of the Death in Late Antiquity*, Elizabeth Trapnell-Rawlings (trans.) (Ithaca and London: Cornell University Press, 2009). On the liturgy of penance, see: Sarah Hamilton, *The Practice of Penance, 900–1050* (Woodbridge: Boydell & Brewer, 2001).

51 See, for example, Yitzhak Hen, "The early medieval *Barbatoria*," in Miri Rubin (ed.), *Medieval Christianity in Practice* (Princeton and Oxford: Princeton University Press, 2009), pp. 21–4, and see the bibliography cited there.

52 See below, pp. 83–84.
53 Éric Palazzo, *Liturgie et société au Moyen Age* (Paris: Aubier, 2000).
54 On this aspect, see: Éric Palazzo, "Art and liturgy in the Middle Ages: survey of research (1980–2003)," *Journal of English and Germanic Philology* 105 (2006), pp. 170–84; idem, "Art, liturgy, and the five senses in the early Middle Ages," *Viator* 41 (2010), pp. 25–56.
55 On Dagobert and his patronage of liturgy, see: Yitzhak Hen, "Flirtant avec la liturgie: rois et liturgie en Gaule franque," *Cahiers de civilization medieval* 50 (2007), pp. 33–42.
56 Barbara Rosenwein, "Perennial prayer at Agaune," in Sharon Farmer and Barbara Rosenwein (eds), *Monks and Nuns, Saints and Outcasts: Religion in Medieval Society. Essays in Honor of Lester K. Little* (Ithaca & London: Cornell University Press, 2000), pp. 37–56.
57 See, for example: Eugen Ewig, "La prière pour le roi et le royaume dans les privilèges épiscopaux de l'époque mérovingienne," in *Mélanges offerts à Jean Dauvillier* (Toulouse: Centre d'histoire juridique méridionale, 1979), pp. 255–67.
58 Some of these Masses were analysed by Michael McCormick, *Eternal Victory. Triumphal Rulership in Late Antiquity, Byzantium and the Early Medieval West* (Cambridge: Cambridge University Press, 1986), pp. 344–47; Yitzhak Hen, "The uses of the Bible and the perception of kingship in Merovingian Gaul," *Early Medieval Europe* 7 (1998), pp. 277–89; Mary Garrison, "The *missa pro principe* in the Bobbio Missal," in Hen & Meens (eds), *The Bobbio Missal*, pp. 187–205.
59 Leo C. Mohlberg et al. (eds), *Liber sacramentorum Romanae aecclesiae ordinis anni circuli (Sacramentarium Gelasianum)*, Rerum Ecclesiasticarum Documenta. Series maior 4 (Rome: Herder, 1960), III.62.1505.
60 Ibid., III.62.1506.
61 Ibid., III.62.1508.
62 Ibid., III.62.1509.
63 See, for example: McCormick, *Eternal Victory*, especially pp. 238–52. See also: Philippe Bernard, "La 'liturgie de la victoire'. Mise en scène du pouvoir, *ordo missae* et psalmodie responsoriale dans l'Antiquité tardive et le haut Moyen Age. Réflexions à partir de l'*Expositio* du Pseudo-Germain de Paris," *Ecclesia orans* 13 (1996), pp. 349–406.
64 See: Janet L. Nelson, "The Lord's anointed and the people's choice: Carolingian royal ritual," in David Cannadine & Simon Price (eds), *Rituals of Royalty. Power and Ceremonials in Traditional Societies* (Cambridge: Cambridge University Press, 1987), pp. 137–80 (pp. 147–9). See also: Mary Garrison, "The Franks as the new Israel? Education for an identity from Pippin to Charlemagne," in Yitzhak Hen & Matthew Innes (eds), *The Uses of the Past in the Early Middle Ages* (Cambridge: Cambridge University Press, 2000), pp. 114–61 (pp. 140–6).
65 See, for example, Janet L. Nelson, "Kingship, law and liturgy in the political thought of Hincmar of Rheims," *English Historical Review* 92 (1977), pp. 241–79 [reprinted in eadem, *Politics and Ritual*, pp. 133–71]; eadem, "Legislation and consensus in the reign of Charles the Bald," in Patrick Wormald et al. (eds), *Ideal and Reality. Studies in Frankish and Anglo-Saxon Society Presented to J.M. Wallace-Hadrill* (Oxford: Blackwell, 1983), pp. 202–27 [reprinted in eadem, *Politics and Ritual*, pp. 91–116]; Karl F. Morrison, *The Mimetic Tradition of Reform in the West* (Princeton: Princeton University Press, 1982), pp. 136–61; idem, "'Unum ex multis': Hincmar of Rheims' medical and aesthetic rationales of unification," in *Nascita dell'Europa ed Europa Carolingia: un'equazione de verificale*, Settimane di studio del Centro italiano di studi sull'alto medioevo 27 (Spoleto: Presso la sede della Fondazione, 1981), pp. 583–712.

66 On all these, see: Hen, *The Royal Patronage of Liturgy*, pp. 42–130 and see there for further references.

67 See: Amnon Linder, *Raising Arms: Liturgy in the Struggle to Liberate Jerusalem in the Late Middle Ages*, Cultural Encounters in Late Antiquity and the Middle Ages 2 (Turnhout: Brepols, 2003).

68 On the ways in which Amalarius of Metz is perceived by modern scholars, see my review of Christopher A. Jones, *A Lost Work by Amalarius of Metz* (London: Boydell & Brewer, 2001), in *Early Medieval Europe* 11 (2003), pp. 401–2.

69 See: Christine C. Schnusenberg, *The Relationship between the Church and the Theatre* (New York: University Press of America, 1988), especially pp. 163–369.

70 The starting point on this issue is Karl Young, *The Drama of the Medieval Church*, 2 vols (Oxford: Clarendon Press, 1933).

71 O.B. Hardison, *Christian Rite and Christian Drama in the Middle Ages* (Baltimore: Johns Hopkins Press, 1965), p. viii.

72 For a general survey, see: Friedrich Rainer, "Drama and ritual," *Themes in Drama* 5 (1983), pp. 159–223; Herman Reifenberg, "Gottesdienst und das dramatischen Perspektiven zum Verhältnis Liturgie – Darstellungkinst – Theater," in Hansjakob Becker and Reiner Kaczynski (eds), *Liturgie und Dichtung*, 2 vols (St Ottilien: EOS Verlag, 1983), II, pp. 227–55.

73 For a superb survey of the emergence of early medieval liturgical drama, see: Susan Rankin, "Liturgical drama," in Richard Crocker & David Hiley (eds), *The New Oxford History of Music*, II – *The Early Middle Ages to 1300* (Oxford: Oxford University Press, 1990), pp. 310–56.

74 The amount of literature on the Benedictine Reform is enormous and cannot be listed here. For a short survey, see: John Blair, *The Church in Anglo-Saxon Society* (Oxford: Oxford University Press, 2005), pp. 346–54. See also: Catherine Cubitt, "Review article: The tenth-century Benedictine Reform in England," *Early Medieval Europe* 6 (1997), pp. 77–94; Nicola Robertson, "The Benedictine Reform: current and future scholarship," *Literature Compass* 3 (2006), pp. 282–99.

75 See: M. Bradford Bedingfield, *The Dramatic Liturgy of Anglo-Saxon England*, Anglo-Saxon Studies 1 (Woodbridge: Boydell Press, 2002).

76 Bedingfield, *The Dramatic Liturgy of Anglo-Saxon England*, pp. 156–70.

77 Nils Holger Petersen, "Les textes polyvalents du *Quem quaeritis* à Winchester au Xe siècle," *Revue de musicology* 86 (2000), pp. 105–18.

78 Peter Dronke, *Nine Medieval Latin Plays* (Cambridge: Cambridge University Press, 1994), p. xvii.

79 Iris Shagrir, "The *Visitatio Sepulchri* in the Latin Church of the Holy Sepulchre in Jerusalem," *Al-Masāq* 22 (2010), pp. 57–77.

80 The manuscript was analysed by Shagrir, ibid., pp. 58–60, and see there for further references.

81 Ibid., p. 60.

82 The starting point on that issue, is Gregory Dix, *The Shape of Liturgy*, 2nd ed. (London: Dacre Press, 1945), pp. 243–47.

83 See: Megan McLaughlin, *Consorting with the Saints: Prayer for the Dead in Early Medieval France* (Ithaca and London: Cornell University Press, 1994), pp. 90–101.

84 See, for example: Hen, *Culture and Religion*, pp. 82–120; Brigitte Beaujard, *Le culte de saints en Gaule* (Paris: Cerf, 2000), especially pp. 455–510.

85 *Gesta Pontificum Autissiodorensium*, c. 19, Michel Sot et al. (eds), *Les gestes des évêques d'Auxerre*, 2 vols (Paris: Belles Lettres, 2002), I, pp. 70–7.

86 On the sanctoral cycle of Auxerre, see: Jean-Charles Picard, "Espace urbain et
    sépultures épiscopales à Auxerre," *Revue d'histoire de l'Église de France* 168 (1976),
    pp. 205–22 [reprinted in Pierre Riché (ed.), *La christianisation des pays entre Loire et
    Rhin (IVe-VIIe siècle)*, (Paris: Cerf, 1993), pp. 205–22, with an updated bibliography
    on pp. 264–5]; Hen, *Culture and Religion*, pp. 97–100.
87 Eusebius of Caesarea, G.A. Williamson (trans.), *History of the Church*
    (Harmondsworth: Penguin Books, 1965), III.25, pp. 134–5.
88 Els Rose, *Ritual Memory: The Apocryphal Acts and Liturgical Commemoration in the
    Early Medieval West (c. 500–1215)*, Mittellateinische Studien und Texte 40 (Leiden and
    Boston: Brill, 2009).
89 Rose, *Ritual Memory*, pp. 163–212.

Select Bibliograpy

Bediengfield, M. Bradford, *The Dramatic Liturgy of Anglo-Saxon England*, Anglo-Saxon
    Studies 1 (Wooddbridge: Boydell Press, 2002).
Bernard, Philipe, *Du chant romain au chant grégorien (VIe-XIIIe siècle)*, (Paris: Cerf, 1996).
Dalmais, Irénée H., *Liturgies d'orient*, Rites et symboles 10 (Paris: Cerf, 1980).
Dix, Gregory, *The Shape of Liturgy*, 2nd ed. (London: Dacre Press, 1945).
Gamber, Klaus (ed.), *Codices liturgici latini antiquiores*, 2 vols, Spicilegii Friburgensis
    subsidia 1 (Freiburg: Universitatsverlag, 1963; 2nd ed. 1968); supplemented by
    Bonifacio Baroffio et al., Spicilegii Friburgensis subsidia 1A (Freiburg:
    Universitatsverlag, 1988).
Hamilton, Sarah, *The Practice of Penance, 900–1050* (Woodbridge: Boydell & Brewer, 2001).
Hardison, O.B., *Christian Rite and Christian Drama in the Middle Ages* (Baltimore: Johns
    Hopkins Press, 1965).
Hen, Yitzhak, *Culture and Religion in Merovingian Gaul, A.D. 481–751* (Leiden, New York
    and Cologne: Brill, 1995).
—*The Royal Patronage of Liturgy in Frankish Gaul to the Death of Charles the Bald (877)*,
    Henry Bradshaw Society, subsidia 3 (London: Boydell & Brewer, 2001).
—& Rob Meens (eds), *The Bobbio Missal: Liturgy and Religious Culture in Merovingian
    Gaul*, (Cambridge: Cambridge University Press, 2004).
Jones, Christopher A., *A Lost Work by Amalarius of Metz*, Henry Bradshaw Society,
    subsidia 2 (London: Boydell & Brewer, 2001).
Jungmann, Josef A., Francis A. Brunner (trans.), *The Early Liturgy to the Time of Gregory
    the Great* (Notre Dame: Notre Dame University Press, 1959).
King, Archdale A., *Liturgies of the Past* (London: Longmans, 1959).
—*Liturgies of the Primatial Sees* (London: Longmans, 1957).
—*The Liturgy of the Roman Church* (London: Longmans, 1957).
—*The Rites of Eastern Christendom*, 2 vols (Rome: Catholic Book Agency & Tipografia
    Polyglotta Vaticana, 1947–8).
Linder, Amnon, *Raising Arms: Liturgy in the Struggle to Liberate Jerusalem in the Late
    Middle Ages*, Cultural Encounters in Late Antiquity and the Middle Ages 2 (Turnhout:
    Brepols, 2003).
Martimort A.-G. (ed.), *The Church at Prayer*, 4 vols, M.J. O'Connell (trans.) (London,
    Geoffrey Chapman, 1986–7).
McCormick, Michael, *Eternal Victory: Triumphal Rulership in Late Antiquity, Byzantium
    and the Early Medieval West* (Cambridge: Cambridge University Press, 1986).

McKitterick, Rosamond, *The Frankish Church and the Carolingian Reforms, 789–895* (London: Royal Historical Society, 1977).

McLaughlin, Megan, *Consorting with the Saints: Prayer for the Dead in Early Medieval France* (Ithaca & London: Cornell University Press, 1994).

Morrison, Karl F., *The Mimetic Tradition of Reform in the West* (Princeton: Princeton University Press, 1982).

Nelson, Janet L., *Politics and Ritual in Early Medieval Europe* (London: Hambledon Press, 1986).

O'Donoghue, Neil X., *The Eucharist in Pre-Norman Ireland* (Notre Dame: University of Notre Dame Press, 2011).

Palazzo, Éric, *A History of Liturgical Books from the Beginning to the Thirteenth Century*, Madeleine Beaumont (trans.) (Collegeville: Liturgical Press, 1998).

—*Liturgie et société au Moyen Age* (Paris: Aubier, 2000).

Paxton, Frederick S., *Christianizing Death: The Creation of a Ritual Process in Early Medieval Europe* (Ithaca and London: Cornell University Press, 1990).

Pfaff, Richard W., *The Liturgy in Medieval England: A History* (Cambridge: Cambridge University Press, 2009).

—(ed.), *The Liturgical Books of Anglo-Saxon England*, Old English Newsletter, subsidia 23 (Kalamazoo: Medieval Institute, Western Michigan University, 1995).

Rankin, Susan, "Liturgical drama," in Richard Crocker & David Hiley (eds), *The New Oxford History of Music*, II – *The Early Middle Ages to 1300* (Oxford: Oxford University Press, 1990), pp. 310–56.

Rebillard, Éric, *The Care of the Death in Late Antiquity*, Elizabeth Trapnell-Rawlings (trans.) (Ithaca and London: Cornell University Press, 2009).

Robertson, Nicola, "The Benedictine Reform: current and future scholarship," *Literature Compass* 3 (2006), pp. 282–99.

Rose, Els, *Ritual Memory: The Apocryphal Acts and Liturgical Commemoration in the Early Medieval West (c. 500–1215)*, Mittellateinische Studien und Texte 40 (Leiden & Boston: Brill, 2009).

Schnusenberg, Christine C., *The Relationship between the Church and the Theatre* (New York: University Press of America, 1988).

Smyth, Matthieu, *La liturgie oubliée: la priére eucharistique en Gaule antique et dans l'Occident non romain* (Paris: Cerf, 2003).

Spinks, Bryan D., *Early and Medieval Rituals and Theologies of Baptism* (Aldershot: Asgate, 2006).

Tinti, Francesca (ed.), *Pastoral Care in Late Anglo-Saxon England*, Anglo-Saxon Studies 6 (Woodbridge: Boydell & Brewer, 2005).

Vogel, Cyrille, *Medieval Liturgy: An Introduction to the Sources*, William Storey & Niels K. Rasmussen (trans. & rev.) (Washington DC: Pastoral Press, 1986).

Warren, Frederick E., *The Liturgy and Ritual of the Early Irish Church* (Oxford: Oxford University Press, 1881), reprinted with a lengthy new introduction by Jane Stevenson (Woodbridge: Boydell Press, 1987), reprinted again with a short preface and updated bibliography by Neil X. O'Donoghue (Piscataway NJ: Gorgias Press, 2010).

Willis, Geoffrey G., *A History of Early Roman Liturgy to the Death of Pope Gregory the Great*, Henry Bradshaw Society, subsidia 1 (London: Boydell & Brewer, 1994).

Young, Karl, *The Drama of the Medieval Church*, 2 vols (Oxford: Clarendon Press, 1933).

Chapter 5

LATE MEDIEVAL LITURGY: A CELEBRATION OF EMMANUEL—"GOD WITH US"

James Monti

In the constitutions that the Spanish Counter-Reformation prelate Saint Juan de Ribera (1532–1611) composed for the chapel of Corpus Christi College, the house of ecclesiastical learning that he founded in Valencia, he enjoins that the chapel's liturgical rites be celebrated in a manner "which perceives that those who sing them take into account that they are in the presence of our Lord God, speaking with His supreme and infinite Majesty; and that they should thus move those listening to the same devotion and veneration of this Lord, and of his holy Temple."[1] This timeless understanding of the liturgy as an encounter between the creature, conscious of his human frailty and sinfulness, with the Creator who infinitely transcends him, profoundly shaped the era of late medieval liturgy, defined here as opening with the thirteenth century and concluding with the issuance of the *Missale Romanum* of 1570, a period that witnessed the introduction of new feasts, prayers, rites, and processions of a more overtly devotional nature. The increasingly explicit representations of events from the life, death, and resurrection of Christ in late medieval liturgical rites, calculated to stir the faithful to greater religious devotion and affective piety, can be seen as the centuries-old equivalent to the project of "New Evangelization" in our own time, which seeks new means of engaging the human heart in the message of the Gospel.

As the Church embarked upon the thirteenth century, she was governed by a profoundly liturgical pontiff, Innocent III (c. 1160; 1198–1216), who, prior to ascending the Chair of Peter, had composed one of the greatest medieval commentaries on the rites of the Mass, *De sacro altaris mysterio*.[2] During the thirteenth century, the development of the Western liturgy was shaped in large part by liturgical exchanges between the Roman curia and the newly founded Franciscan Order. After embracing as its own both a missal and a breviary of the Roman curia, the Franciscans introduced adapted versions of these liturgical books that were in turn embraced by the Papal Court.[3] Toward the close of the 1200s, detailed instructions for the celebration of Mass were compiled by two prelates of the Roman curia, Latino Cardinal Malabranca (†1294) and William Durandus (c. 1230–96), providing well-ordered directions that facilitated a more reverential celebration of the Eucharist and established to a considerable extent the corpus of rubrics that entered the *Missale Romanum* of 1570.[4] Durandus, who following his years in Rome governed as bishop the French see of Mende, also compiled a pontifical comprising rites for celebrating holy orders, confirmation, and other episcopal ceremonies that with relatively few changes entered the *Pontificale Romanum* of 1595–96.[5] Moreover, he authored what proved to be the most influential liturgical commentary of the later Middle Ages, the *Rationale divinorum officiorum*, a work of encyclopedic scope offering mystical, allegorical explanations of a wide range of liturgical rites and practices.[6]

From the pontificate of Blessed Gregory X (1210; 1271–76) onward, ceremonials were compiled to provide rubrics specifically for papal liturgical celebrations. These important texts not only charted the course of the papal liturgy over the fourteenth and fifteenth centuries, but also shaped to a considerable extent the organic development of the liturgy throughout the west.[7] In the mid-fifteenth century, the codification of liturgical rites was revolutionized by the introduction of printing, with the first printed edition of the *Missale Romanum* appearing in 1474. Toward the close of the 1400s, two papal masters of ceremonies, Agostino Patrizio Piccolomini (c. 1435–95) and John Burchard (c. 1450–1506), perfected the corpus of Roman rite rubrics, with Piccolomini compiling the definitive edition of the papal ceremonial (the *Caeremoniale Romanum*, c. 1488) and Burchard composing an authoritative instructional manual for the fitting celebration of Mass, his 1498 *Ordo servandus per sacerdotem in celebratione misse* (*Order to be Observed by a Priest in the Celebration of Mass*),[8] the text that formed the basis for the Mass instructions of the 1570 *Missale Romanum*.[9] Another papal master of ceremonies, Paride de Grassis (c. 1470–1528), in the early 1520s wrote a liturgical manual for cardinals and bishops that also contributed to the rubrics of the 1570 *Missale Romanum*.[10]

Paralleling developments in Rome, religious communities sought to define in writing their own liturgical traditions, an effort exemplified by the Franciscans' *Ordo missalis* (c. 1244) of their superior general Haymo of Faversham (†1244),[11] the Dominicans' *Ordinarium juxta ritum sacri ordinis Fratrum Praedicatorum* and *Missale minorum altarium* (1256),[12] and the Carmelites' *Ordinarium* (c. 1312) compiled by their German provincial Sibert de Beka (c. 1265–1332).[13] The communities of canons regular played a major role in developing liturgical ceremonies and practices of a more devotional and representational nature that became a hallmark of late medieval worship. The *ars celebrandi* ("art of celebrating") of late medieval worship was fostered by liturgical commentators ranging from Sicard of Cremona (†1215), Pope Innocent III (†1216), and William Durandus at the outset of this era to Radulph of Rivo (†1403), Denis the Carthusian (1402–71), Gabriel Biel (c. 1425–95) and John Bechoffen (†c. after 1505) later in the period.

The late medieval era opened with a pivotal event at the dawn of the thirteenth century that set the course of liturgical development for centuries to come: the introduction of the elevation of the Eucharist following the consecration during the Roman Canon of the Mass, a bold, visually powerful affirmation of the Church's belief in the real presence of Christ in this sacrament.[14] The effulgence of the Gregorian chant tradition, the birth of polyphonic chant, and the construction of gothic cathedrals across Western Europe were the artistic offspring of a late medieval liturgy nurtured by an ever-deepening consciousness of this mystery in the hearts of the clergy and the laity alike. In 1264, the Church established a new feast devoted specifically to the Eucharist, Corpus Christi. The custom of celebrating this solemnity with a procession, a practice that began in Cologne, Germany, around 1270 and spread far and wide over the century that followed, brought the consolation of the Lord's continuing presence in this Sacrament into the byways of daily life. This procession, as well as the elevation of the Eucharist at the consecration, both intended to inspire those gazing upon the Sacrament to respond with external acts of adoration, fostered greater reverence for the Savior's divinity.

Yet as late medieval Christendom was deepening its perception of Christ as the Son of God through these eucharistic celebrations, it was simultaneously deepening its perception of the Lord's humanity through flourishing devotions to the mysteries of his birth and Passion, as well as to the Blessed Virgin Mary through whom he assumed his human nature. Thus the preoccupation of the late medieval Church with both the Eucharist and the Passion established a refined theological balance, nurturing a healthy and harmonious Christology.

The culture of late medieval Christendom was profoundly centered upon the liturgy and the Mass in particular. As the historian Eamon Duffy has observed, "The liturgy was in fact the principal reservoir from which the religious paradigms and beliefs of the people were drawn."[15] The Mass was seen as a cosmic event in which the celebrant, *in persona Christi*, goes forth to do battle with Satan.[16] The allegorical interpretation of the Mass and other liturgical ceremonies constituted a medieval response to the Lord's command that the Eucharist be celebrated in remembrance of him (1 Cor. 11:25), casting each action of the liturgical rite as an opportunity to remember the Lord by recalling the various events of his life, death, resurrection, and ascension into heaven. These allegorical interpretations of the liturgy were fully biblical and Christocentric in their content, envisioning the Mass as an epitome of the history of salvation. Building upon the foundational perception of the entire Old Testament as prophetic of Christ, medieval liturgists saw the Mass as bathed in the light of the patriarchs, the prophets, and the Levitical worship in the Temple of Solomon. Thus Durandus as well as other medieval liturgists explained the words and actions of the priest during the Roman Canon as representing the sacrifice that the high priest's entry into the Holy of Holies prefigured and which Christ accomplished on Calvary and offered in the sanctuary of Heaven:

> Truly, long ago the Temple was divided in two parts, with the veil interposed. The first part was called the Holy, but the inner, the Holy of Holies. Whatever therefore in the office of the Mass is done before the Secret [i.e., the Roman Canon] is as it were in the first habitation; but what is done in the Secret is within the Holy of Holies.[17]

The introduction of the elevation of the Host following the consecration necessitated a fitting response of worship in the form of liturgical actions expressing the adoration of the people and clergy alike. There already existed, probably by the end of the eighth century, the kneeling of the assisting clergy and the congregation for the entire Roman canon.[18] But it was only after the addition of the elevation to the rubrics of the consecration that there began to appear, from the fourteenth century onward, references to the practice of the celebrant himself offering an act of worship to the newly consecrated Eucharist. Many late medieval missals describe this act of adoration as simply a bow. But already in the fourteenth century, some priests upon completing the words of consecration were dropping to their knees to express their worship of the Sacrament. By the late fifteenth century this practice had spread to the point of entering the liturgy of Rome, where it appears for the first time in the 1485 *Pontificalis liber*, the earliest printed edition of the *Pontificale Romanum*, compiled by two papal masters of ceremonies, Patrizio Piccolomini and John Burchard: "... [the celebrant] ... should bring forth the words of consecration distinctly and reverently, and having genuflected afterward should devoutly adore the consecrated host. Then he should modestly elevate it with both his hands, and show it to the people to be adored."[19] Evidence that in many cases priests celebrating Mass were genuflecting to the Sacrament following the consecration even when the missals they were using called only for a bow is provided by a Mass commentary of the Augustinian theologian John Bechoffen published in 1505:

> And thus where it is prescribed to bow reverently, it is well of the celebrant of the Mass to supplicate his Creator and Savior on his knees with the utmost devotion, reverence, and honor, to glorify Him on his knees. And this for recognizing himself to be earth and dust in consideration of so great a God with all possible humility and reverence, by which means these outward things are signs of interior things; and the Creator Himself ought to be honored and praised by His creature for the benefit of having been able to have known Him ... Therefore, they are to be put to shame if perchance they should turn lukewarm, or more so, haughty and arrogant, who on this occasion do not fear with an erect neck scarcely to bend one knee to their Creator, Savior, and awesome Judge ...[20]

Beyond the Mass, other rites of the Church underwent healthy, theologically cogent and pastorally opportune development during the later centuries of the Middle Ages. Thus, late medieval marriage rites were endowed with evocative symbolic actions, such as the binding together of the couple with a priest's stole, a colored ribbon or a veil, and the prostration of the couple before the altar, impressing upon those receiving this sacrament the indissolubility of their union and the sacredness of their vocation as a commitment to God as well as to each other. The words and gestures surrounding the Good Friday unveiling of the cross presented the Passion of Christ as a theophany, an awesome revelation of the Lord's divinity wrought by his loving sacrifice.[21] William Durandus left a lasting and positive imprint upon the rites of holy orders with new ritual gestures and prayers, including the oration he composed for the imposition of the miter upon the head of a newly ordained bishop, endowing this head vesture with a rich symbolism drawn from the miter worn by the high priest Aaron (Ex 29: 9; 39: 26) while casting the miter as a symbol of the bishop's role as a champion of truth:

> We place, O Lord, upon the head of this bishop and champion the helmet of your fortification and salvation, that with an honored countenance and a head armed with the horns of each Testament he may appear fearsome to the adversaries of truth and appear their mighty enemy, you bestowing upon him your grace, who adorned the face of your servant Moses, endowed by the company of your discourse with the horns of your most clear light and truth, and who ordered a tiara to be placed + upon the head of Aaron your high priest ...[22]

It was during the late medieval period that a lavish liturgical rite was developed for the solemn canonization of new saints, celebrated at St. Peter's Basilica in an amazing blaze of candlelight with a papal Mass that included a richly symbolic Offertory presentation of live birds representing the heaven-oriented virtues of the saints. The rite of placing a new shepherd on the chair of St Peter was likewise enriched during this period with increasingly elaborate ceremonies for the election and installation of a Roman pontiff that for all their festive splendor did not fail to remind the new pope of his own mortality with a ritual burning and extinction of a bit of tow before his eyes, accompanied by the admonition, "Holy Father, thus passes the glory of the world."[23]

Across late medieval Europe, many dioceses and religious congregations observed their own local adaptations of the Roman rite, variants that combined a remarkable fidelity to the prayers and actions of the ancient Roman liturgy, inherited especially from the *Gregorian Sacramentary*, with newer ceremonies that arose organically as liturgical expressions of heightened devotion to the Eucharist, and the nativity, Passion, death and resurrection of Christ, as well as the Blessed Virgin Mary and the saints. A detailed picture of these local observances can be obtained from the liturgical books that various dioceses published in the late fifteenth and sixteenth centuries up until the issuance of the *Missale Romanum* of 1570 that in most cases supplanted the diocesan rites. A particularly fine example of the diocesan liturgies of late medieval Christendom is provided by the *Missale Pallantinum* of 1567, a missal of over 800 pages published for the Spanish see of Palencia. Several ceremonies described by the missal as "from the custom of the Church of Palencia" are given in an appendix at the end of the book, including the following Holy Thursday observance of keeping a solemnized watch of psalmody chanted in a plaintive monotone before the Blessed Sacrament reserved on this day in the repository (here referred to as the "*monumento,*" i.e., the "tomb" of Christ – see: A–Z):

> On Holy Thursday, after the Eucharist shall have been reserved in a fitting place, which the public calls the *monumento,* from the custom of the Church of Palencia several canons with clerics of the choir should assist before the

monumento, divided into the customary two choirs, clothed in choir vestments, singing the Psalms of David, morosely, devoutly, in a lowered voice, which they do until the Friday following [Good Friday], as long as the Body of Christ is reserved in the *monumento*. But when the canonical hours are sung in the choir, or Mass is celebrated, or a sermon is done for the people, or the washing of the feet is celebrated, the Psalms of this kind are not sung. And at the end of the Psalms the *Glory be to the Father* is not said, but they are somewhat silent, saying the Lord's Prayer. Neither the canticles nor the Athanasian Creed are sung, but only the Psalms of David, beginning from the first . . .[24]

Among the other ceremonies in the appendix of the missal is the following Lenten practice evidently unique to Spain (due to the close dependency of medieval liturgical texts upon the Latin Vulgate Bible, all scriptural citations to follow are from the Douay-Rheims translation of the Vulgate):

On the Saturday before Passion Sunday, from the custom of the Church of Palencia, the Psalms of Vespers having been completed in the choir, while the responsory is sung, the prelate, without other pontifical gear, but with a choir cloak, his head covered, and without a *caudatarius* [i.e., a porter to carry the train of his vestment], or, he [the prelate] being absent, a deacon, or another from the foremost [members] of the choir, having taken with him twelve canons divided into two choirs, they go forth processionally to the sacristy with black cloaks and with their heads covered. And coming to a stop there before the door, the responsory having been completed in the choir, the prelate takes a black silk standard marked with a red cross, and gradually elevating it, he begins the hymn, *Vexilla regis prodeunt* [*The standards of the King go forth*], etc. The twelve canons respond kneeling, *The mystery of the Cross shines*, etc., who in kneeling remain before the standard of the cross. And the verse having been finished, the twelve canons rise, and the choir sings the second verse [*His flesh*] *pierced* [*with nails*], etc.; and proceeding the twelve canons come to a stop before the choir and the altar, and standing they sing the third verse, *Who wounded*, proceeding again. Afterwards the choir [sings] the fourth [verse]: *Those things have been accomplished*. Meanwhile the twelve canons proceed with the standard to the step of the altar. There kneeling they sing the verse, *Beauteous* [*and shining*] *tree*. The prelate with the standard halts on the highest step of the altar, kneeling. Afterward the choir sings the verse, *Blessed* [*tree*], *upon whose* [*branches*]. Which having been finished, the twelve canons, prostrate upon the step, lie silently meditating with him [the prelate] upon the divine mysteries, and the singers sing the verse, *O cross*. Meanwhile he who carries the standard waves it to the right and the left of the altar morosely. Which having been finished, the choir sings the verse, *To you,* [*O God,*] *supreme* [*Trinity*]. Afterward the boys in the choir say the verse [Ps. 139:2], *Deliver me, O Lord,* [*from the evil man*]. And in the choir one from the canons begins the antiphon [Jn. 8:20], *No man laid hands* [*on him*], and the choir sings the *Magnificat*. Then the twelve canons who have thus far lain prostrate rise with the prelate and return processionally two by two to the choir.

The standard, nevertheless, having been erected, remains until when Vespers should be finished. Meanwhile they who are in the choir ought also to be kneeling. It is fitting, however, that all the particular churches should imitate their mother, each according to its own manner and ability. This, however, ought to be done five times: this Saturday and the following Sunday [Passion Sunday], and the [following] Saturday and Palm Sunday, and Wednesday of Tenebrae [Wednesday of Holy Week].[25]

The present era is ripe for significant new findings in the study of late medieval liturgy as computer technology makes an ever-widening range of primary sources increasingly accessible via the Internet. Yet even with the new electronic resources the foundational works of late medieval liturgical study remain as important as ever. Many of these are cited in our endnotes, with a bibliography of further important references at the end of this chapter. Liturgical research has been revolutionized by digitization projects underway at Europe's major libraries, allowing a scholar anywhere in the world to examine, page by page, countless early printed missals, rituals, ceremonials, processionals, and breviaries. To demonstrate the potential in this regard, we shall devote the remainder of this chapter to a new finding regarding the history of Good Friday rites in late medieval Portugal, a finding facilitated by the 2011 digitization of a hitherto overlooked liturgical text of Coimbra.

One particularly striking example of what the local rites of late medieval western Christendom had to offer has been preserved to the present day in the Portuguese city of Braga: the Good Friday "Theophoric procession" ("the transporting of God"), formerly called the "*enterro*" ("burial"), a solemn eucharistic procession symbolizing the burial of Christ during which the Blessed Sacrament is carried on a bier, covered with a black veil, as two boy choristers sing a lament in honor of the slain Redeemer — the chant *Heu, heu Domine* ("Alas, alas, Lord"), known as the *Planctus* — at the conclusion of which the Eucharist is placed in an urn-shaped tabernacle draped in black.[26] This ceremony, which formerly flourished across much of Portugal from the fifteenth to the seventeenth centuries, is a distinctly Portuguese variant of the Good Friday rite known as the *Depositio,* in which a crucifix, an image of Christ resting in death, or the Blessed Sacrament would be carried to a representation of the Savior's tomb and be symbolically "buried" there. Traceable in Europe to tenth century Germany and England,[27] this ceremony may be a descendant of a rite of "washing the cross" in the Good Friday liturgy of fifth to eighth century Jerusalem.[28] Although there is no record of this practice entering the papal liturgy, the fifteenth century English pilgrim and Augustinian friar John Capgrave (†1464), visiting Rome around 1450, states that on Holy Saturday at the Basilica of St John Lateran he saw laid "an image of Christ in a grave."[29]

As one of several dioceses permitted by St Pius V (1504; 1566–72) to retain their own rites, the see of Braga continued to celebrate the liturgy according to its missal of 1558 up until the publication of a new missal in 1924. The latter, essentially a reprint of the 1558 missal, preserved the late medieval form of the Braga liturgy until the 1970s, when some post-Vatican II modifications were introduced. This post-conciliar reform nonetheless left the Theophoric procession of Good Friday intact.

The origin and development of this ceremony as it existed in Portugal was intensively investigated by two eminent liturgical scholars, Archdale King (1890–1972) and Solange Corbin (1903–73).[30] According to the latter, the history of the *Depositio* rite in Portugal begins in 1385 with the arrival of the English princess Philippa of Lancaster (1359–1415), who left her native land to become the bride of Portugal's King John I (c. 1357; 1385–1433). Among Philippa's retinue were English clerics who continued to celebrate the liturgy according to the Sarum Rite of England.[31] Hence on Good Friday these clerics would have observed a fairly simple form of the *Depositio* in which the celebrant would place both a crucifix and the Eucharist within a representation of the Holy Sepulchre which he would then incense and close as two responsories and three antiphons were recited.[32] It is in a letter of the Portuguese abbot and former royal secretary João Álvares dating from 1467 that we find the first mention of the chanting of the aforesaid *Planctus* during the Good Friday *Depositio* at his monastery of Paço de Sousa, a reference indicating that by the mid-fifteenth century the Sarum *Depositio* had been supplanted in Portugal by a significantly more dramatic and elaborate form of this ceremony,[33] a rite most probably descended from similar observances in Padua and Venice, Italy.[34]

The earliest full description of the Portuguese *Depositio* appears in Braga's *Missale Bracarense* of 1558.[35] Neither Archdale King nor Solange Corbin was able to find any other pre-seventeenth century account of the procession with as much information regarding the rite as the 1558 Braga missal provides. Yet there is a liturgical text nearly contemporaneous with the Braga missal that does describe the ceremony at considerable length as it was celebrated by the Augustinian Canons Regular of the Monastery of the Holy Cross in Coimbra. This text, a 1563 customary, unmentioned by either King or Corbin,[36] may have been overlooked by these scholars because the ceremony appears neither in the Good Friday chapter of the book nor in an appendix, but rather, unexpectedly, at the outset of the chapter regarding Easter Sunday.[37]

The Coimbra ceremony differs in several respects from its Braga counterpart. It does not appear to be derived from the Braga observance, but rather seems to constitute an independent variant of an earlier tradition out of which both the Braga and Coimbra versions of the rite arose. The Coimbra procession corresponds in many ways to the form of this Good Friday rite that existed at the royal chapel of the Portuguese monarchy as described by the royal chaplain Father Lucas de Andrade in his 1653 work, *Manual das ceremonias do Officio solemne da Semana Sancta*,[38] and the version of this procession prescribed in a Carmelite processional published at Lisbon in 1610 for the order's Portuguese province.[39] The background of Baltasar Limpo (1478; 1550–58), the Braga archbishop who issued the 1558 missal in which this city's version of the rite first appears, who had served as a Carmelite theology professor in Lisbon and had founded a Carmelite academic institute in Coimbra, raises the possibility that he was the originator of the Braga ceremony, inspired perhaps by his own experiences of this custom in Lisbon and Coimbra. However the Braga version of this rite arose, it bears the imprint of Spanish influence, for unlike the Carmelite and Coimbra texts, it contains several rubrical details clearly borrowed from Spanish forms of the Holy Thursday eucharistic procession.[40]

The rite as it was celebrated at the Monastery of the Holy Cross in Coimbra is a testament to the liturgical vocation of the canons, who in the preface to their 1563 customary describe their religious community as "applied and directed to the worship of the Lord God and the perfection of the Divine Offices, by which it greatly shines in the devout ceremonies which are kept within it" (author's translation).[41] The ceremony has a deeply biblical orientation, with the chants mostly drawn from the Scriptures. The covering of the participants' heads is a biblical sign of mourning (see: 2 Kgs 15:30), and the carrying of the Eucharist on a bier by four priests evokes the imagery of the Levites who bore the Ark of the Covenant (1 Chron 15:15: "And the sons of Levi took the ark of God as Moses had commanded, according to the word of the Lord, upon their shoulders, with the staves"):

> ... on the fifth day of the Supper [Holy Thursday] the priest puts away two Hosts, and on that day the Most Holy Sacrament is not put in the Sepulchre [i.e., it is not put in the same repository as that which will be used to represent the Tomb of Christ at the end of the Good Friday *Depositio* rite], but is placed into a *custodia* [monstrance] and is carried to a most suitable altar, which is called the Garden, where it shall be with all pomp and veneration, and with all the torches and lamps lit. And on the sixth day [Good Friday], after all the above-said [ceremonies of Good Friday] have been done, the entire convent, unshod and with their heads covered with the sleeves of their surplices, goes to the chapel, where lit torches should be given to all. And straightaway a sarcophagus covered with a black cloth, made in such a way that it can be carried by four [bearers], shall be brought to a table which shall be next to the first step of the altar and covered in mourning; and the interior of the bier shall hold a stone with corporals also spread [over it], upon which the *custodia* with the Most Holy Sacrament is to be placed in such a way that it should not be able to be shifted to one side within. And the priest, having incensed on his knees and having taken into his hands the Most Holy Sacrament, which remains in the *custodia*, covered with a black veil, turning himself to the people, begins the Psalm [66], *May God have mercy on us,* intoning it, saying the entire verse, and with the choir or cantors responding with another [verse]. And as this is being said, they place the Most Holy Sacrament in the sarcophagus, and he [the priest] closes it. Having finished the psalm with *Have mercy on us, O Lord* at the end, the sarcophagus is taken onto the shoulders of four priests, vested in black copes, and with their heads covered with the sleeves of their surplices; and a procession is made through the cloister or the church, the priest going last with a chasuble, and the ministers in completely black dalmatics with their heads covered with amices, and unshod; and in front of those around the sarcophagus two brothers vested in short capes,

having also covered their heads with their hoods, singing in the manner of a lamentation the verse, *Alas, alas, Lord; alas, alas, our Savior.* To which the choir or cantors reply in the same manner, who say the following verses: *We are become orphans without a father: our mothers are as widows* [Lam 5:3]. *The crown is fallen from our head: woe to us, for we have sinned* [Lam 5:16]. *Behold, O Lord, my affliction, because the enemy is lifted up* [Lam 1:9]. *My people, what have I done to thee, or in what have I saddened thee? Answer me* [Mic 6:3]. *Shall evil be rendered for good, because they have digged a pit for my soul?* [Jer 18:20]. *See, O Lord, their iniquity, and judge the cause of my soul* [cf. Lam. 3:58–59]. *Let them be confounded that persecute me, and let not me be confounded* [Jer. 17:18]. *Deliver me, O Lord, from the evil man: rescue me from the unjust man* [Ps. 139:1]. *O all ye that pass by the way, attend, and see if there be any sorrow like to my sorrow* [Lam. 1:12]. *Lament him, like [a virgin], my people; wail, O shepherds, in ashes and sackcloth. Wail, O shepherds, and cry out; for the great and exceedingly bitter day has come. Take heed, all peoples, and see my sorrow. Weep for him as for a firstborn son, for the innocent Lord has been slain. Let us mourn for the Lord Jesus Christ, whom we now deliver to the sepulchre.* And all or [as much as] shall be necessary shall be said for a second time, always finishing at the last verse. And arriving at the place where the Sepulchre shall be arranged (inside of which the sacristan shall already have the altar stone with the corporals, and a cross with the cloth of wounds [presumably a banner of the Five Wounds of Christ]), the responsory *The Lord having been buried* [*Sepulto Domino*] is sung, with its verse and repeated portion. And meanwhile the *custodia* with the Most Holy Sacrament is taken out from the sarcophagus, and put in the Sepulchre, and placed on the corporals over the altar stone. And after having incensed it, the priest and the ministers go down on their knees before it, keeping open the door of the Sepulchre, and singing the responsory. He [the priest] alone says the following verses, [with] the choir or the cantors responding. Verse [Ps. 75: 3]: *His place is in peace.* Response: *And his abode in Sion.* Verse [Ps. 87: 5–6]: *I am counted among them that go down to the pit.* Response: *I am become as a man without help, free among the dead.* Verse [Ps. 4:9]: *In peace in the selfsame* (here he shall close the door of the Sepulchre). Response [Ps. 15: 9]: *I will sleep, and I will rest.* Verse: *My flesh.* Response: *Shall rest in hope.*

He [the priest] by himself says this prayer.

Prayer:

Lord Jesus Christ, who in the last hour of the day, having been taken down from the Cross, were reclined in the arms of your most holy Mother (as it is piously believed), whose soul the sword of your death pierced, and who after her maternal and bitter embraces, and her tearful weeping, rested for three days in the Sepulchre: grant that we who contemplate your Passion, the demons having been conquered by it, may be delivered from present evils, and from eternal death. Who live and reign with God the Father, in the unity of the Holy Spirit, God, unto ages of ages. Response: *Amen.*

Having ended this, all retire to the sacristy to remove their vestments, keeping all the torches, flambeaux and large candles lit at the Sepulcher.[42]

The above Collect at the close of the Coimbra rite (*Domine Jesu Christe qui hora diei ultima . . .*) appears in almost every extant text of the Portuguese *Depositio* rite, with the notable exception of the Braga version of the ceremony. The latter utilizes a Collect found in medieval English versions of the *Depositio* ceremony, and may thus be an artifact of the earliest observances of the *Depositio* in Portugal celebrated by the English clergy in the retinue of Princess Philippa of Lancaster. By contrast, the Collect used in the Coimbra ceremony is evidently of Portuguese origin; the Coimbra text constitutes the earliest extant text in which this prayer can be found.[43]

One of the hallmarks of the pontificate of Pope Francis has been his insistence that the Church in our time must increasingly manifest herself as a "Church of the poor," and that in the pursuit of this objective her priests and people must be willing to go out into the streets to proclaim the Gospel in a more direct and intelligible manner to those who do not yet know Christ or who have forgotten or marginalized him. The affective piety of late medieval worship shows us one potentially fruitful path toward the achievement of this goal.

Notes

1   Spanish text in St Juan de Ribera, *Constituciones de la Capilla del Colegio y Seminario de Corpus Christi* (Valencia: Juan Bautista Marçal, 1625); digitized text, Biblioteca Virtual del Patrimonio Bibliografico, Madrid, n.d., chap. 1, pp. 3–4 (author's translation).

2   Pope Innocent III, *De sacro altaris mysterio*, PL 217, cols 763–916.

3   Stephen J.P. Van Dijk, OFM & Joan Hazelden Walker, *The Origins of the Modern Roman Liturgy: The Liturgy of the Papal Court and the Franciscan Order in the Thirteenth Century* (Westminster, MD & London: Newman Press & Darton, Longman and Todd, 1960), pp. 91–253.

4   Text of Cardinal Malabranca's *Ceremonial of a Cardinal Bishop* (c. 1280) in Marc Dykmans, SJ (ed.), *Le cérémonial papal de la fin du Moyen âge à la Renaissance*, vol. 1, BIHBR 24 (Bruxelles & Rome: Institut Historique Belge de Rome, 1977), pp. 220–63; text of Durandus' Instructions (c. 1294) in J. Berthelé, "Les Instructions et constitutions de Guillaume Durand le Spéculateur," in *Académie des Sciences et Lettres de Montpellier: Mémoires de la Section des Lettres*, 2nd series, vol. 3 (1900–7), pp. 1–148 (pp. 54–77, 79–80) (sections regarding the Mass).

5   Pontifical of Durandus in Michel Andrieu (ed.), *Le pontifical romain au moyen-âge: Tome III: Le Pontifical de Guillaume Durand*, ST 88 (Vatican City: Biblioteca Apostolica Vaticana, 1940).

6   Text in A. Davril, OSB & T.M. Thibodeau (eds.), *Guillelmi Duranti: Rationale divinorum officiorum*, CCCM, vols. 140, 140a, 140b (Turnhout: Brepols, 1995–2000).

7   Texts in Marc Dykmans, SJ (ed.), *Le cérémonial papal de la fin du Moyen âge à la Renaissance*, BIHBR 24–27 (Bruxelles & Rome: Institut Historique Belge de Rome, 1977–85); idem (ed.), *L'oeuvre de Patrizi Piccolomini, ou Le cérémonial papal de la première Renaissance*, vol. 1, ST 293 (Vatican City: Biblioteca Apostolica Vaticana, 1980).

8   *Ordo misse secundum consuetudinem sancte Romane ecclesie* (alternate title) (Rome: Stefano Planck,1498); digitized text (Vatican City: Biblioteca Apostolica Vaticana, Digitized incunabula, n.d.).

9 Text in Manlio Sodi & Achille Maria Triacca (eds.), *Missale Romanum: Editio Princeps (1570)*, facsimile edition, MLCT 2 (Vatican City: Libreria Editrice Vaticana, 1998), pp. 9–22 (new pagination).

10 Paride de Grassis, *De caeremoniis cardinalium et episcoporum in eorum dioecesibus* (Rome: Bernardinus Donangelus, 1587); digitized text, Bayerische Staatsbibliothek, Munich, 2009.

11 Stephen J.P. Van Dijk, OFM, *Sources of the Modern Roman Liturgy: The Ordinals by Haymo of Faversham and Related Documents (1243–1307)*, Studia et Documenta Franciscana (Leiden: Brill, 1963), vol. 2, pp. 242–3.

12 Texts in Francis Guerrini, OP (ed.) (with the authorization of Louis Theissling, OP), *Ordinarium juxta ritum sacri ordinis Fratrum Praedicatorum* (Rome: Collegium Angelicum, 1921).

13 Text in Benedict Zimmerman (ed.), *Ordinaire de l'ordre de Notre-Dame du Mont-Carmel*, Bibliothèque liturgique, vol. 13 (Paris: Alphonse Picard et Fils, 1910).

14 This elevation is first mentioned in a synodal decree of Paris dated to before 1215 and attributed, at least formerly, to Bishop Odo of Sully (1196–1208); see: V.L. Kennedy, CSB, "The Date of the Parisian Decree on the Elevation of the Host," *Mediaeval Studies* 8 (1948), pp. 87–96. For the original decree, see: *Synodicae constitutiones*, chap. 8, no. 28, in J.D. Mansi (ed.), *Sacrorum conciliorum nova et amplissima collectio,* vol. 22 (Venice: Antonius Zatta, 1778; repr. Paris and Leipzig: Huberto Welter, 1903), col. 682.

15 Eamon Duffy, *The Stripping of the Altars: Traditional Religion in England, c. 1400–c. 1580* (New Haven & London: Yale University Press, 1992), p. 2.

16 See, for example: Sicard of Cremona, *Mitrale*, bk 3, chap. 9, PL 213, col. 144.

17 Latin text in Durandus, *Rationale* (CCCM 140), bk 4, chap. 1, no. 13, p. 243, translated in James Monti, *A Sense of the Sacred: Roman Catholic Worship in the Middle Ages* (San Francisco: Ignatius Press, 2012), p. 55.

18 The evidence in this regard is provided by the Frankish text *Roman Ordo 17* (c. 790), with further evidence given by a ninth century Gaelic-language treatise on the Mass accompanying the text of Ireland's *Stowe Missal*; see: Monti, ibid., pp. 66–7.

19 Latin text in Manlio Sodi (ed.), *Il "Pontificalis liber" di Agostino Patrizi Piccolomini e Giovanni Burcardo (1485)*, facsimile edition, MSIL 43 (Vatican City: Libreria Editrice Vaticana, 2006), p. 567 (new pagination), (author's translation).

20 Latin text in John Bechoffen, *Quadruplex missalis expositio* (Basel: Michael Furter, 1505); digitized text (Munich: Bayerische Staatsbibliothek, 2007), sig. D2v–D3r; translated in Monti, *A Sense of the Sacred*, p. 65.

21 See: Monti, *A Sense of the Sacred*, pp. 413–14, 431–2.

22 Andrieu, *Le Pontifical Romain . . . de Guillaume Durand*, p. 389, translated in Monti, ibid., p. 198.

23 *Caeremoniale Romanum*, c. 1488 (Latin text), in Dykmans, *L'oeuvre de Patrizi Piccolomini,* vol. 1, p. 70, translated in Monti, ibid., p. 552.

24 Latin text in *Missale Pallantinum* (Palencia: Sebastian Martinez, 1567); digitized text (Madrid: Biblioteca Digital Hispanica, Biblioteca Nacional de Espana, 2012), fols 399v–400r (author's translation).

25 Ibid., fol. 399v (author's translation).

26 See the websites diocese-braga.pt and semanasantabraga.com for contemporary descriptions of this rite.

27 For tenth century Germany, see: *Vita s. Udalrici Augustani episcopi*, chap. 4, PL 135, cols 1020–21; for tenth century England, see: Thomas Symons (trans.), *Regularis*

Concordia: The Monastic Agreement of the Monks and Nuns of the English Nation, Medieval Classics (New York: Oxford University Press, 1953), chap. 4, no. 46, pp. 44–5.

28 Monti, *A Sense of the Sacred*, pp. 409, 444.

29 John Capgrave, *Ye Solace of Pilgrimes*, chap. 53, in C.A. Mills (ed.), *Ye Solsace of Pilgrimes: A Description of Rome, circa A.D. 1450, by John Capgrave, am Ausin Friar of Kings Lynn* (London and New York: Henry Frowde, 1911), p. 154 (spelling modernized).

30 Archdale King, *Liturgies of the Primatial Sees*, Rites of Western Christendom, vol. 3 (London: Longmans, 1957), pp. 278–81; Solange Corbin, *La déposition liturgique du Christ au Vendredi saint: Sa place dans l'histoire des rites et du théâtre religieux* (Paris & Lisbon: Les belles lettres & Livraria Bertrand, 1960), especially pp. 131–59.

31 Corbin, *La déposition liturgique du Christ*, pp. 132–4.

32 Rubrics of the late thirteenth century *Sarum Missal* in John Wickham Legg (ed.), *The Sarum Missal, edited from Three Early Manuscripts* (Oxford: Clarendon Press, 1916), p. 115.

33 Corbin, *La déposition liturgique du Christ*, pp. 136–7.

34 The earliest known rite of this nature is found in a processional of fourteenth to fifteenth century Padua. See: Monti, *A Sense of the Sacred*, pp. 445–8, 454–6. Regarding Venice, see: King, *Liturgies of the Primatial Sees*, pp. 279–80.

35 *Missale iuxta usum & ordinem almae Bracarensis ecclesiae Hispaniarum primatis* (Lyon: Pierre Fradin, 1558), fols 95r–96r.

36 Corbin (*La déposition liturgique du Christ*, p. 138, footnote) lists four sixteenth century liturgical books of Coimbra that she consulted, noting that none of them contained the *Depositio* rite. She makes no mention of the 1563 customary.

37 Portuguese and Latin text in *Ordinario e ceremonial da Ordem dos Conegos regulares da ordem do bemaventurado nosso Padre sancto Augustinho, & da congregacam de sancta Cruz de Coimbra* (Coimbra: Canonicos regulares de Moesteyro de sancta Cruz, 1563); digitized text (Lisbon: Biblioteca Nacional Digital, Biblioteca Nacional de Portugal, 2011), pt 1, chap.18, fols 23r–24v.

38 Lucas de Andrade, *Manual das ceremonias do Officio solemne da Semana Sancta* (Lisbon: Antonio Alvarez, 1653); digitized text (Lisbon: Biblioteca Nacional Digital, Biblioteca Nacional de Portugal, 2009), chap. 7, nos 86–92, pp. 111–24.

39 Gaspar Campello, *Processionarium Fratrum Ordinis Virginis Mariae de Monte Carmelo* (Lisbon: Peter Crasbeeck, 1610); digitized text (Lisbon: Biblioteca Nacional Digital, Biblioteca Nacional de Portugal, 2010), fols 67r–70r.

40 The placement of an altar stone (ara), corporals, a Bible or missal, a small cross, a small bell, empty cruets and the keys to the church in the bier enclosing the Blessed Sacrament specified in the Braga missal corresponds to the placement of all these objects within the *monumento* for the Holy Thursday reposition of the Eucharist specified in the 1533 missal of Salamanca and the 1567 missal of Palencia. See respectively: *Missale ad usum alme ecclesie Salmanticensis* (Salamanca: Juan de Junta, 1533); digitized text (Salamanca: Universidad de Salamanca, Gredos Repositorio Documental, 2010), fol. 63r; *Missale Pallantinum*, fol. 106v.

41 *Ordinario e ceremonial . . . de Coimbra*, preface, fol. 1v.

42 Ibid., pt 1, chap. 18, fols. 23r–24v (author's translation).

43 A misprint in the index of Corbin's work (*La déposition liturgique du Christ*, p. 323, citing p. 249) gives the impression that this prayer is traceable to an early fourteenth century ritual of Breslau, Germany (Adolph Franz, *Das Rituale des Bischofs Heinrich I. von Breslau*, Freiburg im Breisgau, Germany: Herder, 1912, p. 32); the prayer in the latter, however, in no way corresponds to the Portuguese Collect.

Bibliography

Amberg, Gottfried (ed.), *Ceremoniale Coloniense.* Studien zur Kölner Kirchengeschichte, 17 (Siegburg: Franz Schmitt, 1982).

Browe, Peter, SJ (ed.), *Textus antiqui de festo Corporis Christi.* Opuscula et textus historiam ecclesiae eiusque vitam atque doctrinam illustrantia, Series liturgica, fasc. 4 (Münster: Aschendorff, 1934).

Dobszay, László (ed.), *Liber ordinarius Agriensis (1509).* Musicalia Danubiana, subsidia, 1 (Budapest: Magyar Tudományos Akadémia Zenetudományi Intézet, 2000).

Franz, Adolph (ed.), *Die kirchlichen Benediktionen im Mittelalter,* 2 vols (Freiburg im Breisgau: Herder, 1909; repr. Graz: Akademische Druck – U. Verlagsanstalt, 1960).

Jungmann, Josef A., SJ, *The Mass of the Roman Rite: Its Origins and Development,* 2 vols (New York: Benziger Bros., 1951–55).

Lippe, Robert (ed.), *Missale Romanum: Mediolani, 1474.* Henry Bradshaw Society, vols. 17 & 33 (London: Henry Bradshaw Society, 1899, 1907).

Martène, Edmond, *De antiquis ecclesiae ritibus,* 4 vols (Venice: Johannes Baptista Novelli, 1763–4).

Martimort, Aimé-Georges, *La documentation liturgique de Dom Edmond Martène,* Studi e testi, 279 (Vatican City: Biblioteca Apostolica Vaticana, 1978).

Vogel, Cyrille, William Storey & Niels Krogh Rasmussen, OP (trans. & rev.), *Medieval Liturgy: An Introduction to the Sources* (Washington, DC: Pastoral Press, 1986).

Young, Karl, *The Drama of the Medieval Church,* 2 vols (Oxford: Clarendon Press, 1933).

Chapter 6

THE ROMAN MISSAL OF THE COUNCIL OF TRENT

Anthony J. Chadwick

The time of the Council of Trent is a decisive stage in the history of the liturgy. Most published works on the history of the liturgy written more than twenty or thirty years ago tend to reflect a partial view of liturgical renewal or development. It would seem that the motivation for reforming the Roman liturgy was a part of the general reaction by the Church to the religious crisis in Europe at the time, and an effort to restore the credibility of the clergy and parish life.

The 'corrected' liturgical books of 1568 and 1570 are also monuments of the humanist spirit of the Church during the Renaissance period. There was a tendency towards rationalism and a desire for sobriety in Catholic worship. This work was not simply that of a pope, but a constant effort to seek order and reverence in the liturgy over the previous three hundred years. We find the influence of the mendicant orders of the thirteenth century and a tremendous amount of work done in the early Renaissance period by rubricists and specialists in ceremonies eager to avoid the danger of the most authentic liturgical tradition being lost.

Some of our sources give the impression of extreme decadence in the Church during the early sixteenth century being a cause of a popular reformation and revolt from religion depending on a clerical and priestly caste. More recent authors give a counterweight to an excessively severe historical evaluation of the late mediaeval period. It would seem most realistic to consider that the situation of the late mediaeval Church was not uniform.

I. Work on the Latin liturgy before the Council of Trent

The main question about the reform of the Roman liturgy in the sixteenth century is why it was considered necessary. It is generally believed that the Council of Trent was a reaction to the crisis caused by the Reformation and an effort to recover the institutional Church's credibility. It is important to avoid an excessively simplistic view. The quality of religious life and the existence of abuses in different places were not uniform. In those places where the Roman rite was increasingly used, centralization and codification were a gradual process with its beginning more or less in the thirteenth century, colluding with the increasing centralization of authority in the Church. One of the first historians to draw a more positive image of pre-Reformation English religion is Eamon Duffy.[1] Another important work, touching this period briefly, is Alcuin Reid's *The Organic Development of the Liturgy*.[2] Earlier authors, like Jungmann,[3] sought theological reasons behind the liturgical shifts. The French liturgical scholar, A.-G. Martimort,[4] also sought to contrast the liturgical neo-Platonist theology of the age of the Fathers with the devotional writings of later times.[5]

Our subject is a period during which codes of directions and rubrics were written to ensure the correct celebration of Mass. The most likely reason for this would be a gradual shift from *oral* to *written* tradition, a desire to preserve records for posterity lest they be lost. This tendency might also have been provoked by cases of priests unable to celebrate correctly through lack of training.

The first written books of liturgical rites, the *Ordines Romani*, marked the beginning of such records. During the period with which we are dealing, a major event of the thirteenth century was the *Missale plenum* to replace a collection of books corresponding with the roles of the priest, cantors and readers. This marks the beginning of the possibility for a priest to celebrate alone, a turning point in the development of the Roman liturgy.[6]

The process of correcting the Roman rite of Mass from the thirteenth century is a complex question owing to the multiplicity of its regional variations. In the Latin West, since the disappearance of the Gallican and Celtic rites, the parent rite of nearly all the local diocesan usages is that of the Roman Church.[7] During this period, we find both the spread of a uniform Roman rite and the diversification of local variations of this rite.

Until the appearance of the *Missale plenum* in the thirteenth century,[8] Mass was celebrated from three types of books: the sacramentary containing the texts for the priest at the altar; the lectionaries with the biblical reading and Gospels for the deacon, subdeacon, and readers; and the chant books.[9] One can make a parallel between the formation of the missal on one hand and the breviary on the other.[10] Thus, the first collection of liturgical texts in a single book became known as the *Missale plenum* or *plenarium*,[11] containing the sacramentary, lectionary, and chant books.[12] A single book made it easier to celebrate privately.[13] The private Mass was, to a point, a consequence of the evolution of the *Missale plenum*.[14] When a private Mass had been said using only the sacramentary, the Bible readings and sung parts were simply left out,[15] unless some of these were included in the priest's sacramentary, or if a lectionary was available and placed elsewhere on the altar.[16]

The *Missale plenum* was a clerical book, like the breviary, and was intended for celebration at the altar. It was convenient for priests who had to travel and for small parishes.[17] It is thus in the thirteenth century that the *Missale plenum* replaced the sacramentary.[18] From this moment, we find the priest reading all the texts of the Mass, including the reader's part. This later became a rule, even at solemn Mass where readers, subdeacon, deacon, and singers were available.[19] This would seem to be the origin of the ceremonies being based on low Mass rather than low Mass being a reduction of the normative pontifical Mass, from which the solemn form with deacon and subdeacon is also a reduction.[20]

The origin of the missal that was to become the primary source for the 1570 missal was the liturgy of the Papal Court from the first half of the thirteenth century.[21] Innocent III (1161; 1198–1216) initiated a liturgical reform that was to have increasing influence in the whole of the Latin Church. His successors began to dream of spreading this liturgy in the whole western world; this wish was finally realized by Pius V in 1570. The Bishop of Assisi, Guido II, adopted the liturgy of the Roman court in his cathedral. He and Francis of Assisi (c. 1181–1226) were on intimate terms, and this liturgy was adopted by the Franciscan Order.[22]

The Franciscans adopted this rite of the Roman curia and spread it far and wide in the Catholic world. One of their number, Haymo of Faversham (c. 1239–44),[23] wrote out the first complete order for Mass in its private form for the use of Franciscan itinerant priests.[24] It began with the words *Indutus planeta*.[25] This *Ordo* was an early attempt at fixing the priest's ceremonies at Mass. Such attempts had already been made in large monasteries, such as Mainz and St Gallen.[26]

Haymo presented the *Indutus planeta* to the Chapter in Bologna in 1243. Its purpose was to describe the ceremonies according to the custom of the Roman Church, but only those of the celebrant priest.[27] It was not concerned with the roles of the assistants, the choir or the people. Its source was the Court Ceremonial for Mass quoted in the Pontifical of Innocent III.[28] As the Franciscans thus spread the use of the Roman liturgy wherever they went, the *Indutus* became the only complete ceremonial for the private Mass.[29] After the Pontificate of Innocent IV (1195; 1243–54), more religious Orders adopted the use of the Roman liturgy. By 1295, the papal library possessed three Franciscan ordinals, and their codified ceremonials were adopted in the Papal Court.[30] Thus was born the uniform tendency of the Western liturgy, paving the way for the reform of 1570.[31]

This Franciscan-Roman liturgy formed the basis for the first printed Roman missal (*Ordo Missalis secundum consuetudinem Romanæ Curiæ*) which was published at Milan in 1474.[32] The invention of the printing press revolutionized the development of the Roman liturgy, eliminating copyists' errors. The text therefore became more or less fixed, but there were more than 320 editions between 1474 and 1570, mainly from Italian and French publishers.[33] These editions of the missal of the Roman curia were by no means standard or uniform. The point that varies the most is the final blessing.[34]

The work of John Burchard (c. 1450–1506) is most significant before the Council of Trent. This was to be the most important single source for the 1570 missal. The rubrics needed more work than the body of liturgical texts. John Burchard was born at Strasbourg towards 1450 and became Pontifical Master of Ceremonies in 1483. Having served Sixtus IV, Innocent VIII, and Alexander VI in this function, he became Bishop of Città del Castello and Orta in 1503. Burchard played an important role in the elaboration of the Roman Pontifical of Augustine Patrizi, published in 1485.[35] Burchard participated also in the production of the *Cæremoniale Romanum* of Patrizi, published in 1516.[36] This work includes the *Ordo Missæ*.[37] The *Ordo servandus per sacerdotem in celebratione Missæ sine cantu et sine ministris secundum ritum sanctæ Romanæ Ecclesiæ* appeared in 1498.[38] Approved by Alexander VI in 1501, it was edited a number of times: in 1523 it appeared in the *Liber Sacerdotalis* of Castellani and was translated into Italian in 1534. From 1541, it is to be found in some editions of the Roman missal.[39]

In his preface, Burchard indicates the reason for his work. It was necessary for the Church to offer all priests a firm and universal rule, especially for the newly ordained.[40] It was a collation of rubrics from earlier sources of authority. On examination of the text of Burchard's *Ordo*, it is easy to see the origins of the development of the *Ritus Servandus* of 1570. However, many elements of this *Ordo* are richer and directly inherited from a number of medieval diocesan missals. The Gloria is *farced* with Marian interpolations, as may be found in the northern French and English uses.[41] A feature of particular interest in Burchard's *Ordo* is the offertory procession, abolished in the 1570 missal. When the gifts were brought to the altar, the celebrant was directed to go to the Epistle corner, to take off his maniple and to accept the offerings. Each of the faithful kissed the priest's hand and made his offering. The celebrant would say: *Acceptabile sit sacrificium tuum omnipotenti Deo* or *Centuplum accipias: et vitam æternam possideas*.[42] Having accepted the oblations, the priest put on his maniple and went to the middle of the altar. He then proceeded with the offering of the host. The rest of this offertory rite was exactly reproduced in the 1570 missal. For the canon, all the rubrics are as in the Tridentine missal, though differently worded. There are already genuflections before and after the elevation of the host and the chalice.[43] Another curious aspect of the old *Ordo* is the usage of the *Missa Sicca*.[44]

Burchard's successor as Papal Master of Ceremonies was Paris of Grassi (†1528), who was opposed to the humanist-inspired reform attempts, and collaborated with Patrizi in his work on the pontifical ceremonial. Paris left a manuscript of the last *Ordo Romanus*, which served as a Roman ceremonial.

The Theatines, as an Order, were interested in questions of liturgy, as their libraries show by their phenomenal collections of liturgical sources. Gianpietro Caraffa, the future Pope Paul IV (1476; 1555–59), competed against Francisco Cardinal de Quiñones (c. 1482–1540) who wanted to produce a shorter and simpler office for private recitation. Permission to try a new breviary in the Theatine Order was granted by dispensation of Clement VII. Caraffa provided clearer rubrics and recast the system of readings at Matins. Caraffa's method of work was ruthless.[45] After his election as Paul IV in 1555, Caraffa enlisted the help of Bernardine Cardinal Schotto and William Sirleto, both of whom later worked on the post-Tridentine commission.[46] Much of Caraffa's work was adopted in the Roman breviary of 1568.

II. The Council of Trent on liturgical abuses

For the Tridentine Fathers, as for men like Burchard and Caraffa, and Haymo of Faversham before them, the problem of the liturgy was to be considered as part of a wider movement of reform in the Catholic Church. Putting it simply, the Council of Trent was concerned about two things: halting the spread of the Protestant Reformation and restoring the credibility of the Church. Reflections on the liturgy spanned the gap between scholastic sacramental theology and the practical reform of abuses in the clergy, notably those arising from ignorance as well as delinquency.

The primary source for the Council of Trent is the sixteen-volume set of books containing the *Acta* and a vast volume of documents reproduced in their original languages (CT). One of the most detailed works for studying the liturgy at the Council of Trent is a fine doctoral thesis by Reinold Theisen.[47] For the history of the Council in general, nothing equals the work of Hubert Jedin.[48] The Council was rigorous in its protocol and methods for debating and defining its teaching. Its approach to the liturgy was apologetic, theological, and surprisingly psychological. The fathers labored at length to consider the usefulness of keeping a formal liturgy with its ceremonies and symbols. Liturgy is good for the worshipping human being and favors his or her spiritual life and union with God. Without it, such a spiritual life would be made more difficult. This is a humanist and pastoral element that gives us cause to respect and esteem the Council of Trent.

Over and above sacramental theology, both the real presence of Christ in the Eucharist and the sacrifice of the Mass, various aspects of the liturgy had to be dealt with in detail, such as the Roman canon, not saying the whole Mass in an audible voice and, of course, the liturgical use of Latin versus the vernacular. The Acts of the Council show a certain number of Fathers open to the vernacular, in view of the fact that non-Latin languages were used in some parts of Europe from about the time of the Council of Constance. In this study, what seems the most important is the way the Council dealt with abuses in the liturgy—some were quite serious.

The Council had already brought up the question of the missal in the first period (1546–47).[49] Before the beginning of the twenty-second Session, in 1562, the subject of the celebration of Mass was taken up in earnest. A general congregation of 20 July of that year appointed a commission of seven prelates[50] to look into the problem of liturgical abuses.[51] It met in six sessions,[52] and on 8 August that year, presented to the Cardinal Legate Hercules of Gonzaga a long memoir that was later abridged.[53] The abuses they listed were in six categories: the Mass, the celebrant and ministers, the vestments and material requisites, the place of worship, the time of Mass, and connected with the lay assistance (*auditoribus*).

Concerning abuses in the Mass itself, the commission reported that many apocryphal texts had crept into the introits, prefaces[54] and prayers of the Mass.[55] The prelates found confusion in the rubrics, and desired uniformity in the question of rites.[56] Significantly, they observed that, at the offertory, the non-consecrated bread and wine were respectively called *a holy and immaculate host* and the *chalice of salvation*.[57] The Roman offertory resulted from the fusion of the French and German traditions. They objected to the multiplied signs of the cross over the consecrated elements,[58] which are not in fact an abusive practice, but long established in liturgical tradition. The practice of farcing was considered an abuse.[59] They warned of the custom of deploying a specified numbers of candles for certain feasts.[60]

There were also more pecuniary abuses. Some priests took several stipends for one Mass,[61] or simply grabbed the money and failed to celebrate the Mass. The precept of the parish curate's *missa pro populo* was often not taken very seriously, for they were celebrating votive or requiem Masses elsewhere.[62] The prelates reported on the problem of *missæ siccæ* and Mass celebrated several times a day. The commission disapproved of the practice of celebrating several Masses successively[63] or of celebrating private Masses while a solemn Mass was being sung in the same church.[64]

Other abuses arose more from carelessness, such as leaving the bodies of the deceased in a state of advanced putrefaction to lie in chapels of repose under the church, causing the kind of stench one can imagine. Many suggestions were made to offences against Christian modesty and decency, such as licentiousness and drunkenness on the occasion of processions and first Masses of newly ordained priests.[65] The seven prelates recommended that priests were to celebrate Mass with devotion and due preparation, in order that the Sacrifice is fruitful and that scandal is avoided, lest religion be brought into disrepute.

Priests were not following the rubrics.[66] The prelates reported what they had seen in the parishes. Some priests made up the rite as they went along, adding improvised prayers to the official texts of the Mass. Some problems arose from exuberant piety, like bowing the head when elevating the host, and ran the risk of spilling the chalice when holding it over their heads as they genuflected or bowed. Priests were found licking the paten after communion. The practice of elevating the host during the *Pater noster* was not unknown.[67] Other priests left the altar during Mass without just cause. There is a (probably apocryphal) story told about a bishop visiting a parish and finding a very dirty host on the paten. The priest had been using the same host for fifty years, consecrating it over and over again, but not consuming it.

The prelates were shocked by what they perceived as irreverence or inappropriate piety. Priests were celebrating barefooted.[68] The commission recommended that chalices should be made only of precious metal. Masses were being celebrated in profane places. Churches were turned to profane use and parodies of the Mass were performed on occasions.[69] It had been a long tradition in the Church that Mass was not to be celebrated before dawn or in the afternoon or evening, which was often not observed. Priests were marrying couples during Advent and Lent.[70]

Lay people lacked reverence, conversing in church and walking around during the ceremonies.[71] Vagrants begged in churches, and the prelates suggested that they should be made to remain outside the doors of the church. Some people came to church indecently dressed and allowed animals to wander into the sanctuary. The prelates wished to restore the ancient discipline of dismissing the unbaptized and excommunicated before the Mass of the Faithful. They also wanted people to attend services in their own parish churches and cathedrals.[72]

From this long list of abuses, the prelates drew up a *Compendium abusuum circa sacrificium missæ*.[73] They called for a reform of the Roman missal and uniformity of rites. All that was abusive was to be abolished. The rest was to be continued and propagated by all priests, regular and secular.[74] The Compendium summarized the previously mentioned abuses and gave proposals for reform.

On 10 September 1562, nine canons on abuses in the Mass were submitted to the Fathers for examination.[75] The first of these proposed to abolish *profani lucri et sordida cupiditas* and to root out fraudulent practices in regard to stipends.[76] The second called for an end to *missæ siccæ*.[77] Canon three laid down that priests should not binate without pastoral necessity, on pain of suspension.[78] The fourth called for a restricted use of votive Masses, and that these were not to be celebrated on Sundays and feast days.[79] The fifth concerned the Mass of the Dead and the right occasions for its celebration.[80] Canon six expressed a desire, out of respect for the Holy Mysteries, to abolish the celebration of Mass anywhere but in a consecrated building. In cases of necessity, priests would have to consult their ordinary.[81] Canons seven and eight concerned the care of liturgical material and the way of saying and singing the Mass.[82] The final canon (9) recommended the exclusion from churches of the excommunicated and public sinners.[83]

The Fathers discussed these canons, and the drafts were shortened. The minutes of these discussions are lengthy and meticulous,[84] and it is out of our scope to elaborate on them. The *Decretum de observandis et evitandis in celebratione missæ*,[85] was passed on 17 September 1562. This was the final result of the commission's work. Most of the text was merely a resume; it had to be in order for all the Council Fathers to be in agreement.

The Council was particularly concerned about pecuniary abuses and the risk of fraud being committed by false or irregular priests. Inappropriate and secular music had crept into the liturgy, as had questionable customs of popular religion. There was concern for extreme liturgical diversity, not only from diocese to diocese but also between parishes, and in some cases within one parish. In some places there were apocryphal elements and corruptions such as questionable breviary readings and liturgical parodies.

What did they find wrong? In some missals, they found too many prefaces or unusual texts in the propers. Some prefaces were newly composed rather than recovered from ancient sources.[86] Irrationalism abounded. The prelates reporting the abuses did not say precisely which missals should be discarded and which ones should be retained.

Some Fathers wished for slight amendments to the decree on doctrinal grounds. One Father, Lavellinus, desired to abolish the use of portable altars.[87] Nevertheless, the decree was promulgated. The commission prescribed a reform, a unification of the missal.[88] We know that the missal was already under consideration, for material was brought from Rome to Trent.[89] Charles Borromeo wrote again to the Legates on 20 October 1563, advising that a Gregorian Sacramentary had been brought from the Vatican library for the Tridentine Fathers to examine while working on the contemporary Roman missal.[90]

The question of working on the liturgical books was discussed at the General Congregation of 26–27 October 1563, as the Bishop of Salamanca, Pietro Gongales de Mendoga, records in his diary.[91] This deliberation is recorded in a letter of the Bishop of Fænza, Giovanni Battista Sighiselli, to Sirleto, thanking the latter for his observations.[92] It was, however, impossible to consider undertaking a reform of the missal at the Council itself, for risk of an undue delay in bringing all the proceedings to a close. At the end of the twenty-fifth and ultimate session, held on 4 December 1563, the Fathers decided to refer the whole question to the Roman Pontiff.[93]

III. The missal of 1570

After Paul IV, Giovanni Angelo di Medici was elected Pope and took the name of Pius IV (1499; 1559–65). Pius IV took a great interest in the progress of the Council of Trent. The Council having resumed in 1562, he sent to the Fathers the liturgical work of Paul IV, which mainly concerned the breviary. It was to avoid further delays in closing the Council that the Legates finally confided the liturgical reform to Pius IV, this resolution having been approved in the twenty-fifth session. The manuscripts of Paul IV were taken back to Rome, and Pius IV instituted a commission to undertake the work of codifying the missal and breviary. Pius IV had barely instituted his commission when he died in 1565.

We know little about this commission or its work.[94] To the frustration of historians, it left no minutes of its deliberations.[95] Indeed, despite the assiduous research of liturgical historians such as Jedin, Bäumer, Batiffol, Frutaz, Jungmann, and Schmid, if there are still any records of the commission's deliberations, they have yet to come to light. There are two major documents on the Tridentine reform of the missal which give us some idea of the commission's working methods discovered in the Vatican Library by Amato Pietro Frutaz.[96] The other document that provides some insights is the Bull *Quo primum* of St Pius V. There is also a facsimile edition of the 1570 missal published in 1998.[97]

The only other available document is a missal printed at Venice on 8 October 1497 by Giovanni Battista di Sessa.[98] In this missal, a considerable quantity of handwritten notes by William Cardinal Sirleto (1514–85) are to be found.[99] Their authenticity is verifiable by comparison with Sirleto's other autograph manuscripts.[100] Though we have already seen evidence of his interest in this matter at the Council of Trent in the form of letters to the Legates, these notes give valuable indications on Sirleto's work. This missal is divided into five parts: the calendar, temporal, sanctoral, common of saints, and votive Masses. The content, except the calendar, is substantially identical to the *Princeps* edition of the *Missale Romanum* published by Antonio Zarotto at Milan in 1474. Sirleto's annotations are mostly in the margins, but sometimes between the printed lines. In the calendar, many saints' feasts are deleted and notes inserted.[101] Interestingly, not all the corrections he proposed were included in the definitive rite of 1570.[102] Sirleto proposed no change in the *Ordo Missæ* except for a simplification of the *fractio panis*.[103]

The task of the commission was simply to correct the books of the Roman liturgy on the basis of existing usage.[104] What methods did they use? Given the paucity of primary sources, we can only make conjectures on the commission's working methods based on their work on the breviary. This does tell us something about the commission itself.

When Pius IV died on 10 December 1565, Michæl Ghislieri succeeded him, taking the name of Pius V (1504; 1566–72). Pius V confirmed the institution of the commission and augmented its numbers. Pius IV had chosen four members, and this number was increased to eight[105]: Cardinal Bernardine Schotto (Sciotto or Scotti) (†1568),[106] William Sirleto, Julius Poggiani (Giulio Poggi),[107] Curtio di Franchi,[108] Vincenzo Masso,[109] Messer Accursio,[110] Antonio Cardinal Caraffa (†1591),[111] and Pedro Ponce de Leon de Plasencia (1559–73).[112] It is very possible that other scholars or advisors belonged to the commission, under Pius IV and Pius V, and worked on the missal and breviary.

As we know little about the commission's deliberations about the Mass, it is reasonable to compare what is known about its work on the breviary.[113] Indeed, one of the documents discovered by Frutaz, *Information for the correction of the missal*, suggests that the commission linked the missal and breviary closely. It would logically follow that the principle governing the reform of the breviary would also apply to that of the missal, which Jungmann asserts was based on the *Missale secundum consuetudinem Romanæ Curiæ*.[114]

What are the differences between the 1570 missal and the commission's known sources?[115] The two primary sources were the missal of the Roman curia and the *Ordo* of John Burchard.[116] There are very few differences in the order of Mass. For the feast of the Transfiguration, Sirleto proposed the Preface of the Epiphany, which was turned down.[117] He deleted prefaces for the feasts of Francis of Assisi and Augustine, and corrected the text of the final blessing from *In unitate Sancti Spiritus, benedicat vos Pater et Filius* to the version in the 1570 missal: *Benedicat vos omnipotens Deus, Pater et Filius et Spiritus Sanctus.*[118]

We know of no other deliberations or propositions concerning the ordinary. The priest's preparatory prayers were to be said at the altar instead of the psalm *Iudica me* being said on the way to the altar in the older medieval rites.[119] The introit texts are no longer troped.[120] The practice of farcing the *Kyrie* and *Gloria*, for the sake of simplicity, was swept away, leaving the ninefold *Kyrie* and the primitive text of the *Gloria*.[121] Farcing was numbered by the Tridentine commission among the abuses, and this rubric was still found in nineteenth century missals: "Thus shall be said the *Gloria in excelsis,* even at Masses of Blessed Mary, when it is to be said."[122] The greatest loss in the 1570 missal is the elimination of all but five of the sequences: the *Lauda Sion*, the *Veni Sancte Spiritus*, the *Victimæ Paschali laudes*, the *Dies Iræ*, and the *Stabat Mater*, which were undoubtedly among the best. The *Victimæ Paschali laudes* was slightly retouched, leaving out the fifth strophe and improving the Latin of the fourth. The reason given for this is that the sequence, occupying a space between the *Alleluia* and the Gospel, was not typical of the ancient Roman liturgy, or the humanist tradition.[123]

Unfortunately, the commission, probably for fear of pecuniary abuses on the part of the clergy, abolished the offertory procession that had somehow survived in Burchard's *Ordo*. Still on the subject of the offertory, a very slight change can be detected in the *Suscipe, Sancta Trinitas*. Attention is drawn to the ablative case of "in honore beatæ Mariæ" that was rendered in the accusative case in the 1570 missal.[124] Sirleto recommended an improvement to the chant of the Prefaces.[125]

The text of the canon was left untouched, but the rubrics were slightly modified. The rubrics concerning the elevations and genuflections were fixed. However, both genuflections and elevations appeared in the 1498 Roman missal.[126]

The three private communion prayers were fixed.[127] The ablutions were tidied up. Neither Burchard nor Pius V entirely settled the blessing at the end of Mass. It was still permissible for a simple priest to give a triple blessing at solemn Mass as a bishop does today.[128] In the various editions of the Roman missal of 1474, 1530, and 1540, the blessing was sometimes given before the *Placeat*, a later innovation than the blessing. In the 1570 missal, the blessing is given after the *Placeat* and the kissing of the altar.[129] It is also possible to say that the blessing follows the *Ite missa est* and the *Placeat* because it is an add-on. Some Roman missals before 1570 gave the possibility of a special form of blessing at Masses of the Dead, but the commission decided that there should be no blessing of the living in these Masses. Before the 1570 missal, the so-called "Last Gospel" (Jn. 1:1–14) was recited by memory as the priest left the altar. The 1570 missal has it read at the altar, immediately after the blessing and with an introduction similar to the Gospel of the day.[130]

We have substantial information on the commission's work on the calendar, mainly from Frutaz, Bäumer, and Klauser.[131] Most of Sirleto's annotations concern the calendar and more especially the sanctoral. By the end of the Middle Ages, the calendar had become so full of saints' feasts that the temporal cycle was almost totally obscured. The calendar of 1568 and 1570 halted the trend of increasing numbers of saints' feasts.[132] The commission reduced the number of feasts in the sanctoral to allow the temporal cycle to manifest itself on some 150 days of the year, not counting octaves.[133] Indeed, the prelates introduced no new feasts. This reduction was achieved by keeping only those feasts that were kept in Rome up to the eleventh century.[134] A few of the later feasts introduced under the influence of the Franciscans were retained, and few of those were non-Italian saints.[135] Eighty-five per cent of the saints retained belong to the first four centuries of the Church's history, and half of these are martyrs. The remainder of the feasts fall into groups of doctors, founders of religious orders, confessors, and virgins. All the feasts of Our Lord and of the Blessed Virgin Mary were retained, with the exception of the Presentation of Our Lady (21 November).[136] Of the saints retained, more than a third of the number are Romans, and twelve per cent are Italians. All the New Testament saints are included, and Spain, France and England each contributed two saints. Germany is represented by St Ursula.[137] Thus the calendar was carefully pruned and then sparingly embellished with a few more recent feasts of universal interest. This quite drastic pruning of the sanctoral is proof of the commission's severity and desire for sobriety in the Roman rite. A study of the history of the calendar reveals that the commission's ideal was the liturgy of the time of St Gregory VII (c. 1020; 1073–85).[138]

In the temporal cycle we find no changes in the calendar common to the missal and the breviary.[139] The breviary commission's work on the liturgical year demonstrates the aim of restoring the Roman rite,[140] as Sirleto insisted,[141] that the temporal cycle was to be given greater importance by the pruning of saints' feasts. Focke and Heinrichs[142] concluded that the 1570 calendar reflects the *Ordo officiorum Ecclesiæ Lateranensis* composed by Prior Bernard about 1145.[143] It is in this light that Sirleto modified the calendar of the Venetian missal of Sesso, which was of a Franciscan type.[144] A number of Franciscan saints were deleted from the universal calendar, which then became a combination of the twelfth century Lateran *Ordo* and the Franciscan sanctoral with some feasts removed and others added.[145] Sirleto was particularly concerned to free the ferias of Lent.[146] His work goes into minute detail, correcting the Latin text, deleting feasts, and amending priorities of those retained.[147] Many of these corrections were accepted by the commission and adopted in the calendar of 1568 and 1570. As the 1570 missal was issued under the Julian calendar, there were errors in its method of computing the date of Easter. Gregory XIII corrected these in 1582 at the same time as issuing the Gregorian calendar.[148]

Octaves were also dramatically simplified. The Common of Saints was tidied up.[149] Votive Masses were also regulated with thirty-seven complete votive Masses in the 1570 missal.[150] Rubrics were formulated to restrict severely the use of votive Masses.[151] Under these rubrics, a votive Mass may be celebrated on any feria of the week.

The *Ordo Missæ* of John Burchard was the main source for the rubrics.[152] The *Liber Sacerdotalis* published in Venice in 1523 contains Burchard's *Ordo*,[153] and it began to be printed as a preface to the missal from 1534. Whilst Le Brun attests, not very accurately, that Burchard's *Ordo* is copied almost word for word,[154] it can be said that the two texts are closely related.[155]

The first few pages of Burchard's *Ordo* are used in the first section of the *Ritus servandus in celebratione Missæ* of the 1570 missal. The text, except for the vesting prayers and the *Summe sacerdos* prayer, is entirely remodelled. In the Pianine missal, this extremely long prayer is divided up into the days of the week, to be recited with the other prayers of preparation for Mass. Page 133 of the *Ordo* corresponds with section two of the *Ritus: De Ingressu Sacerdotis ad Altare*.[156] Again, the wording is considerably modified and the directions recast. Pages 134–7 of the *Ordo* correspond with section 3: *De Principio Missæ* ... but only a few rubrics of the latter indicate its source.[157] The section of the *Ordo* beginning *Dicto Simbolo* corresponds with section VII of the *Ritus servandus: De Offertorio*. There was provision for an offertory procession in Burchard's *Ordo*, but this was not adopted in the 1570 missal.[158]

The similarity between Burchard's treatment of the canon to the end of the Mass and that of the Tridentine missal is marked. The reference to the consecration candle being lit at the *Hanc igitur* is not found in any missal until 1605.[159] Burchard's rubric on what is to be omitted at Masses of the Dead is greatly expanded in the 1570 missal, but the rubric on celebrating two or three Masses in one day is omitted. References to "dry Masses" are omitted in the 1570 missal in accordance with their abolition.

The lectionary adopted was that of Murbach, as in the missal of 1474.[160] The version used for the Scripture readings is the Vulgate, which was revised under Clement VIII in 1592. For the psalter, the sung parts of the Mass are from the Old Roman version.[161]

What is obvious from the Roman lectionary is that provision is generally made only for Sundays, and for these readings to be repeated in ferial weekday Masses. It had been suggested at the Council of Trent that unused Pauline and Gospel passages be used for these ferial weekday Masses, inserting them into the proper of the previous Sunday.[162] This plan was not considered, and nothing came of it.

Although the Bull *Quo primum*, by means of which Pius V promulgated the 1570 missal, is of more interest to canonists than to a study of liturgical history,[163] questions of a hermeneutic of continuity and of organic development are of interest. Whether Pius V's legislation arrested organic development, or whether the rite had already grown to full maturity and was no longer developing is a question worthy of further study. Certainly Pius V's legislation became an institution through the establishment of the Sacred Congregation of Rites in 1588.[164]

Interestingly, Pius V did not intend to impose absolute liturgical uniformity, and allowed local and particular rites of more than 200 years' standing to continue by virtue of immemorial custom. Inevitably, as Roman centralism was a key feature of the Counter-Reformation, most particular rites were laid aside or forgotten in favor of the 1570 missal. Happily, some local uses survived or even revived, for example that of Lyon.

The word that most adequately describes the commission's work is *restoration*, not compilation or fabrication. By this means, the continuity of tradition is assured in the liturgy.[165] Cardinal Sirleto objected to the idea that the commission wished to create a new rite: it set out to improve the liturgy as received in tradition, adapting a few details to the needs of the times, without substantially altering it.[166] The principle outlined by Pius V in the Bull *Quo primum* comes to mind: the idea of restoring *the pristine purity of the Roman liturgy*.[167] This is a conservative approach of *moderate archeologism*.

The commission's reference was a fully developed Roman liturgical rite characterized by sobriety, simplicity, uniformity and clarity.[168] It worked to restore the liturgy to its pristine state at the time of the reformer Pope Gregory VII, and to retain a few contemporary elements of universal significance or pastoral value.[169] Gregory VII—the champion and defender of Roman tradition in the commission's eyes—was a most significant figure in the movement of ecclesiastical reform and the formation of medieval Church politics. We are led to believe that the commission saw themselves as renewing the same work of reform and Roman centralism.

In their view, one of the means to this end was liturgical uniformity. In some places, different rites could be found in a single church, in which each priest did as he pleased.[170] Henceforth the regulation of rites was no longer to be under the jurisdiction of diocesan bishops but the Holy See. A rite that was sober in character (polyphonic church music came within an inch of being abolished, and it was Palestrina who saved it through his *Missa Papa Marcelli*), with clear rubrics and regulated by the Holy See, was less liable to be abused. Whilst liturgical uniformity in the whole Church was never absolute, it seemed reasonable that the liturgy within a single rite should be substantially uniform and its celebration disciplined.[171]

We have to study this reform through the eyes of men of the Church faced with a situation of crisis and the need to restore the Church's credibility in an emerging

Renaissance culture. In the end, the work of producing the new liturgical books moved remarkably quickly. The missal was promulgated 14 July 1570; the breviary had already been published two years before, in 1568.

IV. The missal of 1570 and what it meant

In the context of current debate Nathan Mitchell has opined that "the liturgical reforms prompted by the Council of Trent were far more unprecedented and untraditional than those which followed Vatican II."[172] Whilst it is tempting to be critical of any reform of the liturgy "from above" as opposed to leaving it to its own devices in a "natural" process of development and inculturation, what history teaches us is that the Council of Trent went ahead with an unprecedented *codification* of the Roman liturgy because printing made it possible and that there were serious pragmatic reasons for it. A sound historian would be very wary of interpolating anachronic academic or pastoral considerations from our own time here. The conservative character of the 1570 missal is certainly clear—very little was changed in the ordinary of the Mass compared with the missal of 1474.

It perhaps should not be forgotten that the Tridentine liturgical reform was less concerned with the liturgical rites themselves than with the general credibility of the Church in a situation of crisis. The influences of humanism and realism were also determining factors.

The reform did not find a solution that would protect the liturgical life of the Church from future abuse and negligence. Indeed, in time, the stiffness and rigidity of the Tridentine liturgy and the rubricism that often accompanied it would become a subject of criticism by twentieth-century authors such as Louis Bouyer and Annibale Bugnini.[173] Rubrical exactitude and concern for ritual integrity and uniformity remained an overriding influence in those places where the Roman liturgy was accepted and implemented until the period after World War II.

Many questions for further study arise from this movement towards Roman centralism and authoritarianism and its consequences for later periods.[174] In particular, how well was the 1570 missal received in dioceses and parishes? Indeed, the Archdiocese of Paris did not completely move over to the Roman rite until the late nineteenth century. It is important to note that this liturgical reform was not perfect in every way, and left a number of pastoral questions open; for example the use of the vernacular was admitted in theory by many of the fathers of Trent, but Latin was kept in practice. Indeed, some of the issues of the mid sixteenth century would arise again later.

Notes

1   Eamon Duffy, *The Stripping of the Altars, Traditional Religion in England 1400–1580* (New Haven: Yale University Press, 1992).

2 Alcuin Reid, *The Organic Development of the Liturgy*, 2nd edn (San Francisco: Ignatius Press, 2005).
3 J.A. Jungmann, *The Mass of the Roman Rite (Missarum Sollemnia)*, (Westminster: Christian Classics, 1986).
4 A.G. Martimort (ed.), *L'Eglise en Prière: 2 – L'Eucharistie* (Paris: Desclée, 1983); ET: *The Church at Prayer: Vol. II – The Eucharist* (Collegeville: Liturgical Press, 1986).
5 See: A. Wilmart, "Primum in ordine," *Ephemerides Liturgicæ*, 50 (1936), pp. 133–9; T. Simmons, *The Lay Folk's Mass Book* (London: Early English Text Society, 1879); Langford's *Meditations on the Mass* in J. Wickham Legg (ed.), *Tracts on the Mass* (London: Harrison, 1904), pp. 19ff. Until the invention of the printing press, these works were confined to manuscript copies. They, however, formed the basis of popular preaching.
6 Jungmann, *The Mass of the Roman rite,* vol. I, pp. 103–4; A. Fortescue, *The Mass: A Study of the Roman Liturgy* (London: Longmans, Green & Co., 1917), p. 184; F. Cabrol, "Missel Romain," in DACL, vol. XI, col. 1483; G. Duret, "Les Livres Liturgiques," in R. Aigrain (ed.), *Liturgia* (Paris: Bloud & Gay, 1930), p. 412; Martimort, *L'Eglise en Prière: L'Eucharistie*, p. 154.
7 Fortescue, *The Mass*, pp. 199–205.
8 Ibid., p 190.
9 S. Van Dijk, & J. Hazelden Walker, *The Origins of the Modern Roman Liturgy: The Liturgy of the Papal Court and the Franciscan Order in the Thirteenth Century* (London: Darton, Longman & Todd, 1960), pp. 57–8.
10 Ibid., p. 58. This parallel development of the missal and breviary is only coincidental.
11 Ibid., p. 59.
12 Jungmann, *The Mass of the Roman Rite*, vol. I, p. 105.
13 Ibid., p 107; cf. Van Dijk & Hazelden Walker, *The Origins of the Modern Roman Liturgy*, p. 61.
14 Van Dijk & Hazelden Walker, ibid., p 61. Fortescue (*The Mass,* p. 189) affirms the contrary, that the low Mass was the *raison d'être* of the *Missale plenum*. Van Dijk & Hazelden Walker produce arguments from modern scholars to state which caused what.
15 Jungmann, *The Mass of the Roman Rite*, vol. I, p. 105.
16 Van Dijk & Hazelden Walker, *The Origins of the Modern Roman Liturgy,* p. 62.
17 Ibid., pp. 64–5.
18 Jungmann, *The Mass of the Roman Rite*, vol. I, p. 104.
19 Ibid., p. 106.
20 See: R. Winch, *The Canonical Mass of the English Orthodox* (Oxford: Gregorian Club, 1988), p. 47: "The Tridentine book ... maintains the notion that a 'low' celebration is somehow the most primitive."
21 Martimort, *L'Eglise en Prière: L'Eucharistie*, p. 187; see: M. Andrieu, "L'Ordinaire de la Chapelle papale et le Cardinal Jacques Gætani Stefaneschi," *Ephemerides Liturgicæ* 49 (1935), pp. 230–60.
22 Van Dijk & Hazelden Walker, *The Origins of the Modern Roman Liturgy,* pp. 398–99.
23 Hymo of Faversham was the fourth minister general of the Franciscan Order. He joined the Order as a priest and a man of erudition in 1224. In 1230 he developed the Franciscan Rule and took part in a delegation to have it approved by the Pope. He had considerable influence in his Order and the academic world.
24 Martimort, *L'Eglise en Prière: L'Eucharistie,* p. 160; see: Van Dijk & Hazelden Walker, *The Origins of the Modern Roman Liturgy*, pp. 292–301.

25 The text of *Indutus planeta* is reproduced in Wickham Legg, *Tracts on the Mass*, pp. 179–89.

26 Theodor Klauser, *A Short History of the Western Liturgy* (Oxford: Oxford University Press, 1979), pp. 104–5.

27 Van Dijk & Hazelden Walker, *The Origins of the Modern Roman Liturgy*, pp. 292–3.

28 Ibid., p. 294; see: M. Andrieu, *Le pontifical romain au moyen age*, ST vol. 87 (1940).

29 Van Dijk & Hazelden Walker, *The Origins of the Modern Roman Liturgy*, p. 297; cf. Jungmann, *The Mass of the Roman Rite*, vol. I, pp. 412, 441, 455; vol. II, pp. 292, 349, 351 & 443.

30 Van Dijk & Hazelden Walker, *The Origins of the Modern Roman Liturgy*, pp. 297; 411.

31 Jungmann, *The Mass of the Roman Rite*, vol. I, pp. 101–2.

32 An edition of this missal can be found in volume XVII of the Henry Bradshaw Society: R. Lippe (ed.), *Missale Romanum Mediolani 1474*, vol. I (London: Harrison, 1899).

33 Jungmann, *The Mass of the Roman Rite*, vol. I, p. 102; see: R. Menthe, "Ein Missale Romanum von 1481," in: *Franziskan Studien*, 20 (1933), pp. 89–129.

34 Jungmann, *The Mass of the Roman Rite*, vol. II, pp. 446–7.

35 Pierre de Puniet, OSB, *The Roman Pontifical* (London: Longmans, Green & Co., 1932), p. 47; see: *Pontificalis ordinis liber*, published in 1485, in A. Patrizi, *Cæremoniale Romanum*, (Farnborough: Gregg, 1965). The original preface is an appendix in the facsimile edition. Patrizi declares: "Horum laborum socium mihi adiunxi Iohannem Burchardum."

36 J. Burchard & A. Patrizi, J Catalani (ed.), *Sacrarum cæremoniarum sive Rituum ecclesiasticorum Sanctæ Romanæ Ecclesiæ libri tres* (Rome: Antonii de Rubeis, 1750).

37 Pierre Jounel, *Les rites de la Messe: ritus servandus in celebratione Missæ* (Tournai: Desclée, 1963), p. 9. In this work treating the rubrics of the 1962 edition of the Roman missal, Jounel traces a general history of the *Ritus Servandus*.

38 Wickham Legg, *Tracts on the Mass*, pp. 124–74. Wickham Legg is wrong in saying that Burchard's *Ordo Missæ* appeared in 1502, for a copy from 1498 is to be found in the Vatican Library (Incunables, IV, 528): cf. Jounel, *Les rites de la Messe*, p. 10.

39 Jounel, ibid.

40 Wickham Legg, *Tracts on the Mass*, p. 126.

41 Ibid., p. 249.

42 Ibid., p. 149.

43 Ibid., pp. 156–7.

44 Ibid., p. 173. The term *missa sicca* was originally derived from a form of rite customary for the Communion of the Sick. The priest read the fore-mass in the sick-room and proceeded to the *Pater noster*, having skipped the canon, and gave communion under the form of bread. Hence the *dry Mass* was so-called, for it involved the use of no liquid. The nearest equivalent to this celebration allowed in the Tridentine missal is the ancient Mass of the Presanctified on Good Friday, when no Mass is celebrated, or the Blessing of Palms on Palm Sunday. The *missa sicca* was a commemorative rite, used in such places where a real Mass would not be prudent, for example on a ship at sea. However, the *dry Mass* became abusive.

45 S. Bäumer, *Histoire du Bréviaire*, vol. II, (Herder: Rome, 1967), p. 154; see: J. Tufo, *Historia della religione de' padri cherici regolari* (Rome: Guglielmo Faciotto & Stefano Paolini, 1609–16), vol. II, C. XCVI, pp. 8–13.

46 Bäumer, ibid., p. 155.

47 Reinold Theisen, *Mass liturgy and the Council of Trent* (Collegeville: St John's University Press, 1965).

48 H. Jedin, *Geschichte des Konzils von Trient*, 4 vols (Freiburg im Breisgau: Herder, 1949–75). Only two volumes have been published in English: E. Graf (trans.), *A History of the Council of Trent*, vols I & II (London & Edinburgh: Thomas Nelson, 1957 & 1961).

49 Jungmann, *The Mass of the Roman Rite*, vol. I, p. 133.

50 The Latin names of the members of the commission were: Ludovicus Beccatellus, Iulius Pavesius, Urbanus de Ruere, Hercules Rettinger, Bernardus de Bene, Martinus de Corduba, and Andreas Dutitius Sbardellatus.

51 J. Riviere, *La Messe durant la période de la Reforme et du Concile de Trente*, in: A. Vacant, E. Mangenot & E. Amann (eds), *Dictionnaire de Theologie Catholique*, vol. X (Paris: Letouzey et Ané, 1929), col. 1085–1142; col. 1126; see: CT VIII, 719–20: "Item quod deputentur aliqui patres ad colligendos abusus super dicto sacrificio missæ."

52 July 24, 25, 26 and 31, and August 5 and 8, 1562.

53 See: CT VIII, 916–24, 9.

54 Ibid., 917, 11–15 and note 3. Such prefaces were those of Sts Jerome, Augustine, Roch, and Christopher.

55 Ibid., 6: ". . . ut missalia omnia a superstitiosis et apocryphis orationibus repurgata."

56 Ibid., 9–10: "Ut certæ quædam cæremoniarum rubricæ præscribantur, quas celebrantes uniformiter servent, ne novis aut diversis ritibus populus offendatur et scandalizetur."

57 Ibid., 16–18. These formulæ were not changed in the missal of 1570. See also: Paul Tirot, *Histoire des prières d'offertoire dans la liturgie romaine du VIIe au XVIe siècle* (Rome: Edizione Liturgiche, 1985). This difficulty only occurs in the Roman rite, taking its offertory prayers from the Rhenan tradition.

58 Ibid., 19–20. This practice also continued in the Pianine missal.

59 Ibid., 27–30. Farcing was the practice of introducing apocryphal texts into the *Kyrie* and *Gloria*. The commission give the example of "gubernans Mariam, coronans," etc., which figured in the Roman missal of 1474.

60 Ibid., 31–8; see: A. Franz, *Die Messe im deutschen Mittelalter* (Freiburg im Breisgau: Herder, 1902), p 115. For example, the Mass of Saint Sophia required seven candles, as did that of the Holy Spirit. That of the twelve Apostles required twelve candles. The determining factor was allegory. The variation in the number of candles in the Tridentine missal is governed by the solemnity of the Feast: two are used for low Mass, and four, six or ten are used for sung Mass.

61 Ibid., 39–42; see: Franz, *Die Messe im deutschen Mittelalter*, p 84.

62 Ibid., 918, 1–5.

63 Ibid., 6–7. This practice was continued in the missal of 1570 at Christmas and All Souls.

64 Ibid., 7–8. This was not abolished in 1570.

65 Ibid., 16–40.

66 Ibid., 42–919, 9.

67 At the Mass of the Presanctified on Good Friday in the Pianine missal the Host is elevated with the right hand after the *Pater*. In some local uses, the paten was likewise elevated during the Embolism following the *Pater*. This rite evolved from bringing the paten to the altar with the *Sancta* upon it in the old Roman *ordines*.

68 CT VIII, 919, 39 – 920, 27. This is common in some of the oriental rites. Religious priests were often distinguished by not wearing shoes.

69 Cf. E. Lodi, *Enchiridion Euchologicum Fontium Liturgicorum* (Rome: Edizioni Liturgiche, 1979), pp. 1712–17. These pages contain two parody-mass rites in barbaric Latin: the *Missa contra Hussitas* and the *Missa potatorum et lusorum*.

70 CT VIII, 920, 28 – 921, 16.

71 Cf. L. Bouyer, *Liturgy and Architecture* (Notre Dame: University of Notre Dame Press, 1967), p. 80.

72 CT VIII, 921, 17–35.

73 Ibid., 40 – 924,9.

74 Ibid., 921, 40–46: "Ut sancta Dei ecclesia, quoad fieri potest, unius labii sit, utque uniformitas celebrandi missas inter eos servetur, qui instituto et ritu S.R.E. celebrant, abusque, qui hominum incuria et superstitione fortasse in venerandum missæ sacrificium irrepsere, tollantur: missalia secundum usum et veteram consuetudinem S.R.E. reformentur, omnibus iis, quæ clanculum irrepserunt, repurgatis, ut omni ex parte eadem Pura, nitida et integra proponantur, quibus de cetero celebrantes omnes uti teneantur, tam regulares quam seculares, salvis tamen consuetudinibus legitimis et non abusivibus regnorum."

75 Ibid., 926, 25–928, 5.

76 Ibid., 926, 25–32.

77 Ibid., 33–39; see: Jungmann, *The Mass of the Roman Rite*, vol. I, p. 385.

78 Ibid., 40–927, 3.

79 Ibid., 927, 4–8.

80 Ibid., 9–14.

81 Ibid., 15–22.

82 Ibid., 23–46.

83 Ibid., 928, 1–5.

84 Ibid., 6 – 942, 50.

85 Ibid., 962, 23 – 963, 31.

86 Jungmann, *The Mass of the Roman Rite*, vol. II, p. 121; see: A. Zak, "Über die Präfationen," *Theol. prakt. Ouartelschrift* 58 (1905), pp. 307–25.

87 CT VIII, 964, 47–8.

88 Ibid., 916–21.

89 P. Frutaz, "Contributo alla storia della riforma del Messale promulgato da san Pio V nel 1570," in: *Problemi di vita religiosa in Italia nel Cinquecento* (Padova, Ed. Antenore, 1960), pp. 187–214. (p. 188). On July 6, 1563, St Charles Borromeo wrote to the Legates: "Mons. Rev.mo di Trani (card. Giov. Bernardino Scotti) mette insieme le annotationi che si fecero al tempo di Paulo IIII, sopra il breuiario et il messale, et dice che le manderà quanto prima potra a le SS.rie VV. Ill.me insieme con alcune considerationi che papa Paulo medesimo haueua fatte sopra questa materia." G. Mercati, *Opere minori*, III 1907–16, ST vol. 78 (1937), pp. 370–1.

90 Ibid., pp. 188–9: "Hauendo il S.or Car.le di loreno ueduto in questa libraria vaticana un Messale antico che chiamano di san Gregorio; sua Sig.ria Ill.ma hà guidicato molto a proposito che si mandi costà, acciò sia uisto da li Deputati a riformar il Messale moderno. Così di ordine di N. S.re io lo mando con questo ordinario a le SS. VV. Ill.me in una tela cerata, et ben conditionato. Prego quelle a farmi dar auuiso a parte de la riceuuta per satisfattione, et chiarezza di questi custodi de la libraria, et sopra tutto faranno hauergli buona cura, acciò non si perda, ma si restituisca in man loro, et si riporti insieme con gli altri a Roma." See: Archivio Segreto Vaticano, *Conc.* 68, f. 139 (304). We also know that the Tridentine Fathers also had recourse to a contemporary missal edited at Venice in 1558.

91 Ibid., p. 189; see: CT II, 706.

92 Ibid., pp. 189–90; see: Biblioteca Ap. Vaticana: cod. Vat. lat. 6189, f. 198.

93 CT IX, 1106 (*De indice librorum, et catechismo, breviario et missali*).

94 P. Frutaz, "Contributo alla storia Messale promulgato da san Pio V nel 1570," p. 191; Klauser, *A Short History of the Western Liturgy*, pp. 124–9.

95 Jungmann, *The Mass of the Roman Rite*, vol. I, p. 135. Cf. J. Schmid, "Studien über die Reform des römischen Breviers und Missale unter Pius V," *Theologische Ouartalschrift*, 66 (1884), pp. 451–83, 621–64; P. Batiffol, *Histoire du Bréviaire romain* (Paris: Picard 1911), pp. 294–314; Jedin, "Das Konzil von Trient und die Reform der liturgischen Bücher," *Ephemerides Liturgicæ*, LIX (1945), pp. 5–38; idem, "Das Konzil von Trient und die Reform des Römischen Messbuches," *Liturgisches Leben* VI (1939), pp. 52–4.

96 These documents are conserved at the Vatican Library: cod. Vat. lat. 6171, f. 67r–v (twelve questions treated by the commission); cod. Vat. lat. 12607, ff. 8r–11v (information for the correction of the missal). The latter document bears the signature of Leonardo Marini, a member of the commission and Archbishop of Lanciano (1560–66) and Bishop of Alba (1566–72).

97 M. Sodi & A.M. Triacca (eds), *Missale Romanum: Editio Princeps 1570*, MLCT vol. 2 (1998). It is surprising to see an allusion to conflicts in the Church in the editors' introduction to this purely historical and scholarly edition—as if an edition of this missal has to be justified. Sodi's extensive references confirm much of our own choice of sources. In respect of Trent and the post-conciliar commission, Sodi draws our attention to the divergence of opinion between those members who wanted absolute liturgical uniformity in the Church and those who supported the rights of local custom and usage. The work of comparing the 1474 and 1570 missals is thorough and impressive, though a similar comparison between the 1570 missal and that of 1962 seems a little less germane in this context. In the conclusion we find attempts to debunk the idea of a rupture between the 1570 missal and all its editions up to 1962 on one hand, and the rite promulgated by Paul VI on the other. This mars the quality of this otherwise excellent introduction.

98 Bibl. Ap. Vat., Inc. IV, 29; see: V. Masséna, *Les Missels imprimés à Venise de 1481 à 1600: Description, illustration, bibliographie* (Paris: Rothschild, 1896); M. Sander, *Le livre à figures italiens depuis 1467 jusqu'à 1530. Essai de sa bibliographie et de son histoire*, vol. II (Milan: U. Hoepli, 1942).

99 Frutaz, "Contributo alla storia della riforma del Messale promulgato da san Pio V nel 1570," pp. 193–4. Sirleto took an important part in the work of the commission, particularly on the Roman Catechism, the missal, breviary and the Vulgate of Sixtus V. During Schotto's absences, Sirleto took over the presidency of the commission.

100 See: G. Mercati, *Opere minori*, ST vols. 76–9 (1937); Pio Paschini, "La Riforma Gregoriana del Martirologio Romano," *Schola Cattolica* 51 (1923) pp. 198–211; idem. *Guglielmo Sirleto ed il Decreto Tridentino sull'edizione critica della Bibbia* (Lecco: La Grafica, 1935); idem. "Guglielmo Sirleto prima del cardinalato," in P. Paschini, *Tre ricerche sulla storia della Chiesa nel Cinquecento* (Rome: Edizioni Liturghe, 1945), pp. 155–281; idem. "Il cardinale Guglielmo Sirleto in Calabria," *Rivista di storia della Chiesa in Italia*, I (1947), pp. 22–37.

101 Frutaz, "Contributo alla storia della riforma del Messale promulgato da san Pio V nel 1570," pp. 196–7.

102 Ibid., p. 197.

103 Ibid., p. 198. The change proposed was to remove the *little elevation* at the *Per ipsum* (end of the Canon), which was not adopted in the 1570 missal. Another proposition was a rewording of the prayer for when the priest drops a small part of the broken Host into the chalice before the *Agnus Dei*.

104 Bäumer, *Histoire du Bréviaire*, vol. II, p. 167.

105 Ibid., pp. 168–74.

106 Cardinal Bernardine Schotto presided over the deliberative meetings of the commission, apart from a few months he spent away from Rome in his episcopal residence at Piacenza.

107 Julius Poggiani (Giulio Poggi), an esteemed latinist worked closely with Sirleto, above all in the literary composition of the breviary lessons, and the adaption of those taken from the breviary of Quiñones.

108 Curtio di Franchi took an important advisory role in the reform work of the commission. He became Canon of St. Peter's in 1568 and was proposed to Pius V as canonical visitor of several Italian dioceses.

109 Vincenzo Masso was a Theatine regular cleric, reputed for his knowledge of ecclesiastical history.

110 Messer Accursio is mentioned in a note of Cardinal Sirleto as having collaborated in the work of the commission, but we know nothing precise about him.

111 According to a text in the Vatican Library (Codex Urbinas, Cod. Vatic. 1666, fol. 119), Cardinal Antonio Caraffa belonged to the commission. From his short biography by Moroni ("Fu nominato prefetto della Congregazione del concilio e della stabilità da Sisto V per la correzione della Biblia, del Breviario e del Messale romano"), we know something of his work on the Vulgate, the breviary and the missal. See: G. Moroni (ed.), *Dizionario di erudizione storico-ecclesiastica*, vol. IX (Venice: Emiliana, 1841), p. 245, col. a.

112 Pedro Ponce de Leon de Plasencia was a foreign bishop who did not take a direct part in the work of the commission. He corresponded with Cardinal Sirleto and was very useful for their work. We can quote a proposition he made concerning the Mass: the saints named in the canon of the Mass should be taken into account when working on the calendar. However, this would concern the sanctoral of the breviary more than the rite of Mass.

113 Bäumer, *Histoire du Bréviaire*, vol. II, pp 175–76.

114 Jungmann, *The Mass of the Roman Rite*, vol. I, p. 135.

115 Klauser, *A Short History of the Western Liturgy*, p. 124.

116 See: Wickham Legg, *Tracts on the Mass*, pp 119–78.

117 Frutaz, "Contributo alla storia della riforma del Messale promulgato da san Pio V nel 1570," p. 200.

118 Ibid, p. 201.

119 Jungmann, *The Mass of the Roman Rite*, vol. I, p. 294. The reason for this was that if these prayers were recited in procession, they were likely to be said without attention or devotion. For the Pianine commission, all the prayers of the Mass had to have a true meaning.

120 Ibid., p. 327. Troping had been the practice of extending the length of the introit by adding texts, not always of biblical origin. However, in later reforms of the missal of 1570, a whole psalm could be sung at the introit, as was done at the coronation of Pius XI in 1922.

121 Ibid., pp. 345 & 359; see: Fortescue, *The Mass*, p. 238. A vestige of this farcing was kept in the Tridentine missal, or more precisely in the gradual: the names *Kyrie Rex Genitor, Lux et origo, Orbis factor*, etc. are preserved as titles for the different Gregorian musical settings of the Masses found in the *Graduale Romanum*.

122 Jungmann, *The Mass of the Roman Rite*, p. 359: "Sic dicitur Gloria in excelsis, etiam in missis beatæ Mariæ, quando dicendum est."

123 Ibid., p. 437; see: Fortescue, *The Mass*, p. 275. It can be argued that the prudence of the commission was a little excessive.

124 Pierre Lebrun, *Explication des prières et cérémonies de la Messe*, vol. I (Paris: Gauthier, 1828), pp. 285–6. Jungmann, *The Mass of the Roman Rite*, vol. II, p. 50. The expression of this word in the accusative case was not standardized absolutely until a decree of the Sacred Congregation of Rites on May 25, 1877. Many medieval versions of this prayer read "in commemorationem," as did a number of French missals in the seventeenth century.

125 Frutaz, "Contributo alla storia della riforma del Messale promulgato da san Pio V nel 1570," p. 213: "Il canto delli prefatij si è detto correggerlo secondo la capella di S. S.ta e quando si potesse mettere il canto disteso ad ogni prefatio si farria cosa molto commoda ad ognuno." (Informatione per la correttione del Missale.)

126 Jungmann, *The Mass of the Roman Rite*, vol. II, p. 213; see: Fortescue, *The Mass*, p. 341. A kind of "half genuflection" was known in some of the medieval rites. This action was accomplished by touching the calf of the left leg with the right knee, a sort of curtsy. Up to the fifteenth century in most places the simple bow prevailed.

127 Fortescue, *The Mass*, p. 382.

128 Jungmann, *The Mass of the Roman Rite*, vol. II, pp. 444–5. This triple blessing followed the versicles and responses as at a pontifical Mass: "V. Sit nomen Domini benedictum. R. Ex hoc nunc et usque in sæculum. V. Adiutorium nostrum in nomine Domini. R. Qui fecit cælum et terram." See: *Missale Romanum* (Antwerp: Plantin, 1572), Ritus servandus, XII, 7. This was abolished by Clement VIII in 1604. Following this directive, a simple priest could no longer sing the blessing or make the triple sign of the cross.

129 Ibid., p. 446. Another reason has been advanced for the reversal of 1570, which seems not very convincing, that the Mass that has begun with the kissing of the altar should end likewise.

130 Some proper Last Gospels were instituted by Pius V as a relic from the days of the *Missa sicca*, but were rare until a decree of the S. Congregation of Rites of March 29, 1922.

131 Klauser, *A Short History of the Western Liturgy*, p. 124.

132 Ibid., p. 125.

133 Jungmann, *The Mass of the Roman Rite*, vol. I, pp. 135–6.

134 Klauser, *A Short History of the Western Liturgy*, p. 125; cf. Jungmann, *The Mass of the Roman Rite*, p. 136; see: E. Focke & H. Heinrichs, "Das Kalendar des Missale Pianum und seine Tendenzen," *Theol. Quartalschrift*, CXX (1939), pp. 383–400, 461–9.

135 Jungmann, *The Mass of the Roman Rite*, vol. I, p. 136; cf. Focke & Heinrichs, ibid., p. 466.

136 Klauser, *A Short History of the Western Liturgy*, p. 126. The feast of the Presentation of the Blessed Virgin Mary was reintroduced under Gregory XIII at the behest of Sirleto. The feast of St Anne (July 26) was also reinstated.

137 Ibid., p. 126.

138 Ibid; see: Focke & Heinrichs, "Das Kalendar des Missale Pianum und seine Tendenzen," pp. 461–9.

139 Frutaz, "Contributo alla storia della riforma del Messale promulgato da san Pio V nel 1570;" Bäumer, *Histoire du Bréviaire*, vol. II, pp 175–220. Apart from the Vatican documents mentioned for the missal, mostly concerning the calendar, there are three documents for the reform of the breviary: the breviary itself and the Bull of promulgation of Pius V. We have parallels of these two for the missal. The third

document giving information of the commission's work is a report in Italian or *Promemoria* in the form of a letter. It was composed by a member of the commission, probably Archbishop Leonardo Marini of Lanciano, and addressed to one of his cardinal friends. It begins: "Perchè si comprendra bene in che consiste la corettione del Breviario qual'si e fatta . . ." and ends: "Occorrono delle altre cosette . . . quelle nel scorrere del Breviario si potranno un altra volta dire." Vatican Archives, codex 47 (*Concil. Trident.*, fol. 312 sq.).

140 Frutaz, ibid., p. 201. Before the missal of 1570, there was diversity, not only between the calendars of the missal and breviary, but between those of different editions of the missal. See: G. Low, "Calendario della Chiesa universale," in *Enciclopedia Cattolica*, vol. III (Vatican City: Città del Vaticano, 1949), pp. 364–72.

141 Bäumer, *Histoire du Bréviaire*, vol. II, p. 176.

142 Focke & Heinrichs, "Das Kalendar des Missale Pianum und seine Tendenzen."

143 See: L. Fischer (ed.), *Bernhardi cardinalis et Lateranensis Ecclesiæ Prioris Ordo officiorum Ecclesiæ Lateranensis* (Munich: Datterer, 1916).

144 Frutaz, "Contributo alla storia della riforma del Messale promulgato da san Pio V nel 1570," p. 204.

145 Ibid., p. 205.

146 Sirleto was familiar with the canon from the Decretals of Gratian (Causa 33, q. IV, c. VIII et c. IX): "Non oportet in quadragesima aut nuptias vel quælibet natalitia celebrari." 33 q IIIJ; "Non oportet ex concilio laodicensi; Non licet in XLma natales martyrum celebrare." 33 q IIIJ. See: "Decretum Magistri Gratiani," in Emil Friedberg (ed.), *Corpus Iuris Canonici* (Leipzig: Bernhardi Tauchnitz, 1879), p. 1249.

147 Cf. Frutaz, "Contributo alla storia della riforma del Messale promulgato da san Pio V nel 1570," pp. 206–7. The annotations of Sirleto for the month of January are given as an example.

148 Bäumer, *Histoire du Bréviaire*, vol. II, p. 194. The problem was the question of calculating the lunar cycle by means of the Golden Numbers. Pius V's correction of this was erroneous, and did not take into account the fact that the Julian calendar was ten days late.

149 Jungmann, *The Mass of the Roman Rite*, vol. I, p. 136. A Common of Saints is to be found in some of the ancient sacramentaries, lectionaries, and antiphoners.

150 Ibid., p 136.

151 *Rubricæ generales*, IV, 3.

152 Wickham Legg, *Tracts on the Mass*, pp. 124–74. These pages contain an edition of John Burchard's *Ordo Missæ*. Wickham Legg erroneously gives 1502 as the date of publication.

153 Ibid., pp. 25–22 (in Roman numerals for the introduction)."

154 Lebrun, *Explication des prières et cérémonies de la Messe*, vol. I, p. 423: "L'Ordo Missæ de Burcard (sic), imprimé vers l'an 1500, et copié presque de mot à mot par le saint Pape Pie V."

155 Wickham Legg, *Tracts on the Mass*, p. xxvii. Wickham Legg makes it clear in a note on p. 249 that the Pianine missal he uses for comparison with Burchard's *Ordo* is one printed at Venice in 1571 by John Variscus.

156 This page number refers to the edition found in Wickham Legg's Tracts on the Mass.

157 Wickham Legg, *Tracts on the Mass*, p. 249.

158 Jungmann, *The Mass of the Roman Rite*, vol. I, p 136. The wording of this rubric in Burchard's *Ordo* was: "Si sint qui volentes offere: celebrans accedit ad cornu Epistole: ubi stans detecto capite latere suo sinistro altari verso deponit manipulum de brachio

sinistro: et accipiens illud in manum dextram porrigit summitatem eius: singulis offerentibus osculandum dicens singulis. Acceptabile sit sacrificium tuum omnipotenti Deo. Vel Centuplum accipias: et vitam eternam possideas. Accepta omnium oblatione celebrans reponit manipulum in brachium sinistrum, etc."

159 Wickham Legg, *Tracts on the Mass*, p. 250.

160 A. Nocent, *La célébration eucharistique avant et après Saint Pie V* (Paris: Beauchesne, 1977), p. 45. The Lectionary of Murbach dated from the end of the eighth century. See: A. Wilmart, "Le Comes de Murbach," *Revue Benedictine* 30 (1913), pp. 25–69.

161 Henri Rabotin, "*Les textes liturgiques*," in Aigrain, *Liturgia*, p. 354. The Old Roman Psalter is not used for the psalmody in the Office, but the Vulgate Psalter.

162 Jungmann, *The Mass of the Roman Rite*, vol. I, p. 403; see: Jedin, *Das Konzil von Trient und die Reform des Römischen Messbuches*, p. 55. A ferial weekday lectionary similar to some of the mediaeval diocesan missals was authorized in 1964.

163 Neri Capponi, *Some Juridical Considerations on the Reform of the Liturgy* (Edinburgh: Una Voce, 1979); Raymond Dulac, "La Bulle Quo primum," *Itinéraires*, 162 (1972), pp. 13–47. On the customary character of liturgical legislation concerning the Mass before 1570, see: C. Vogel, *Medieval Liturgy: An Introduction to the Sources* (Washington: Pastoral Press, 1986), pp. 1–20; Noirot, *Liturgie* (droit) in R. Naz (ed.), *Dictionnaire de droit canonique*, VI (Paris: Letouzey et Ané, 1957), pp. 535–94; F. Cimitier, "La liturgie et le Droit canonique," in Aigrain, *Liturgia*, pp. 29–58. Some of these studies contributed to Benedict XVI's *Summorum Pontificum* of July 2007 and to the conclusion that Paul VI had not abrogated the 1962 missal.

164 See: Klauser, *A Short History of the Western Liturgy*, pp. 129–35, chapter IV, iii: The Congregation of Rites and its working methods.

165 Bäumer, *Histoire du Bréviaire*, vol. II, p. 176: "Par ce moyen seul on pourrait conserver la continuité de la tradition chrétienne dans la liturgie et montrer que, de même que la foi et l'organisation de l'Eglise sont toujours restées les mêmes, de même sa liturgie ne s'est pas modifiée essentiellement, encore que chacun des membres de ce corps organique se soit développé dans le courant des siècles a la façon de tout corps vivant."

166 In one of his writings, Sirleto protests against the expression "compilare" which appears in the Bull of promulgation of the breviary. For the president of the commission, the breviary was not "compilatum" but corrected and reformed: "Fu riformato co'li Breviarii antichi quanto alle cose essentiali e important" (cod. Vat. 6171, fol. 15).

167 Pius V, Bull, "Quo primum," quoted in Frutaz, "Contributo alla storia della riforma del Messale promulgato da san Pio V nel 1570," pp. 192–3.

168 Klauser, *A Short History of the Western Liturgy*, p. 127. See: H. Jedin, "Concilio tridentino e riforma dei libri liturgici," in H. Jedin, *Chiesa della fede: chiesa della storia* (Brescia: Morcelliana, 1972), p. 416.

169 See: Klauser, ibid., p 127; Jedin, ibid.

170 Cf. Jungmann, *The Mass of the Roman Rite*, vol. I, p. 134; Jedin, *Das Konzil von Trient und die Reform des Römischen Messbuches*, pp. 34–5. Jedin observed that the confusion of rites was confounded by the onset of the Reformation. At this time, some priests started their own reforms, in some cases even leaving out the canon.

171 Fortescue, *The Mass*, p. 208.

172 Nathan Mitchell, "The Amen Corner: Rereading Reform," *Worship* 80 (2006), pp. 453–66 (p. 465).

173 See: Louis Bouyer, *The Decomposition of Catholicism* (Chicago: Franciscan Herald Press, 1969); Annibale Bugnini, *The Reform of the Liturgy 1948–1975*, (Collegeville: Liturgical Press, 1982).

174 See: Geoffrey Hull, *The Banished Heart: Origins of Heteropraxis in the Catholic Church* (London: T&T Clark, 2010).

Bibliography

Aigrain R., (ed.), *Liturgia* (Paris: Bloud & Gay, 1930).

Andrieu, M., "L'Ordinaire de la Chapelle papale et le Cardinal Jacques Gætani Stefaneschi," *Ephemerides Liturgicæ* 49 (1935), pp. 230–60.

—— *Les Ordines Romani du Haut Moyen Age*, 5 vols (Louvain: Spicilegium Sacrum Lovaniense, 1931–65).

—— *Le Pontifical romain au moyen âge*, 4 vols (Vatican City: Biblioteca Apostolica Vaticana, 1938–41).

Battifol, P., *Histoire du Bréviaire romain*, 3rd edn (Paris: Picard 1911); ET: A. Baylay (trans), *History of the Roman Breviary* (New York: Longmans, Green & Co, 1912).

—— *Leçons sur La Messe* (Paris: J. Gabalda, 1927).

Bäumer, S., *Histoire du Bréviaire*, 2 vols (Rome: Herder, 1967).

Botte, B., *L Ordinaire de la Messe: texte critique, traduction et études* (Paris & Louvain: Cerf & Abbaye du Mont César, 1953).

Bouyer, L., *Life and Liturgy* (London: Sheed & Ward, 1956).

—— *Liturgy and Architecture* (Notre Dame: University of Notre Dame Press, 1967).

Burchard, J. & A Patrizi, J. Catalani (ed.), *Sacrarum cæremoniarum sive Rituum ecclesiasticorum Sanctæ Romanæ Ecclesiæ libri tres* (Rome: Antonii de Rubeis, 1750).

Cabrol, F., "Missel Romain" DACL vol. XI cols 1468–94.

—— "La Messe Romaine" in Aigrain, *Liturgia*, pp. 509–53.

Clark A., "The Origin and Development of the Offertory Rite," *Ephemerides Liturgicæ* LXIV (1950), pp. 309–44.

Clark, F., *Eucharistic Sacrifice and the Reformation* (Oxford: Blackwell, 1967).

De Marco, A., *The Church of Rome and the Problem of the Vernacular versus the Liturgical Language* (Washington DC: Catholic University of America Press, 1960).

De Puniet, P. *The Roman Pontifical* (London: Longmans, Green & Co., 1932).

Dix, G., *The Shape of the Liturgy* (London: Dacre Press, 1945).

Duffy, E., *The Stripping of the Altars, Traditional Religion in England 1400–1580* (New Haven: Yale University Press, 1992).

Dumoutet, E., *Le Désir de voir l'Hostie* (Paris: Beauchesne, 1926).

Duret, G., "Les Livres Liturgiques," in Aigrain, *Liturgia*, pp. 397–435.

Duval, A., *Des Sacrements au Concile de Trente* (Paris: Cerf, 1985).

Ferreres, J.B., *Historia del Misal Romano* (Barcelona: Subirana, 1929).

Focke, E. & H. Heinrichs, "Das Kalendar des Missale Pianum vom Jahre 1570 und seine Tendenzen," *Theol. Quartalschrift* 120 (1939), pp. 383–400; 461–9.

Fortescue, A., *The Mass a Study of the Roman Liturgy* (London: Longmans, Green & Co., 1917).

Fransen, P., "Reflexions sur l'anathème au Concile de Trente (Bologne 10–14 Sept. 1547)," *Ephemerides Theologicæ Lovanienses* 29 (1953), pp. 657–72.

Frutaz, A.P., "Contributo alla storia della riforma del Messale promulgato da san Pio V nel 1570," in *Problemi di vita religiosa in Italia nel Cinquecento* (Padova: Ed. Antenore, 1960), pp. 187–214.

Görres-Gesellschaft Soc. (eds), *Concilium Tridentinum: Diarorum, Actorum, Epistolarum, Tractatuum nova collectio*, 16 vols (Herder: Freiburg im Breisgau, 1901–80).

Guéranger, P., *Institutions liturgiques*, 3 vols (Le Mans & Paris: Fleuriot & Débecourt, 1840–51).

Gy, P.M., *La Liturgie dans l'Histoire* (Paris: Cerf, 1990).

Hull, G., *The Banished Heart: Origins of Heteropraxis in the Catholic Church* (London: T&T Clark, 2010).

Jedin, H., "Das Konzil von Trient und die Reform des römischen Messbuches," *Liturgisches Leben* VI (1939), pp. 30–66.

—— *Geschichte des Konzils von Trient, Band II: Erste Trienter Tagungsperiode (1545–1547)*, (Freiburg: Herder, 1957).

—— "Das Konzil von Trient und die Reform der liturgischen Bücher," *Ephemerides Liturgicæ* LIX (1945), pp. 5–38. Italian translation: "Concilio tridentino e riforma dei libri liturgici," in H. Jedin, *Chiesa della fede: chiesa della storia* (Brescia: Morcelliana, 1972), pp. 391–425.

—— *Girolamo Seripando: Sein Leben und Denken im Geisteskampf des 16. Jahrhunderts*, vol. II (Würzburg: Rita-Verlag, 1937).

Jounel, P., *Les rites de la Messe: ritus servandus in celebratione Missæ* (Tournai: Desclée, 1963).

Jungmann, J.A., *The Mass of the Roman Rite (Missarum Sollemnia)*, 2 vols (Westminster: Christian Classics, 1986).

King, A.A., *Liturgy of the Roman Church* (London: Longmans, 1959).

—— *Liturgies of the Past* (London: Longmans, 1959).

—— *Liturgies of the Religious Orders* (London: Longmans, 1955).

Klauser, T., *A Short History of the Western Liturgy* (Oxford: Oxford University Press, 1979).

Le Plat, J., *Monumentorum ad Historiam Tridentini*, vol. 4 (Louvain: Typographia Academica, 1784).

Lennerz, H., "Notulæ Tridentinæ," *Gregorianum* 27 (1946), pp. 136–42.

Lewis, C.A., *The Silent Recitation of the Canon of the Mass* (Bay St Louis: Divine Word Missionaries, 1962).

Lippe, R., (ed.), *Missale Romanum: Mediolani 1474*, 2 vols (London: Henry Bradshaw Society, 1899 & 1907).

Lodi, E., *Enchiridion Euchologicum Fontium Liturgicorum* (Rome: Edizioni Liturgiche, 1979).

Löw, G., "Calendario della Chiesa universale," in *Enciclopedia Cattolica*, vol. III (Vatican City: Città del Vaticano, 1949), pp. 364–72.

Martimort, A.G. (ed.), *L'Eglise en Prière: 2 - L'Eucharistie* (Paris: Desclée, 1983); ET: *The Church at Prayer: Vol. II - The Eucharist* (Collegeville: Liturgical Press, 1986).

Masséna, V., *Les missels imprimés à Venise de 1481 a 1600: description, illustration, bibliographie* (Paris: Rothschild, 1896).

Menthe, R., "Ein Missale Romanum von 1481," *Franziskan Studien*, 20 (1933), pp. 89–129.

Messenger, E.C., *The Reformation, the Mass and the Priesthood: A Documented History with special reference to Anglican Orders*, 2 vols (London: Longmans, Green & Co., 1936–7).

Nocent, A., *La célébration eucharistique avant et après Saint Pie V* (Paris: Beauchesne, 1977).

Paschini, P., *Guglielmo Sirleto ed il Decreto Tridentino sull'edizione critica della Bibbia* (Lecco: La Grafica, 1935).

—— "Guglielmo Sirleto prima del cardinalato," in P. Paschini, *Tre ricerche sulla storia della Chiesa nel Cinquecento* (Rome: Edizioni Liturghe, 1945), pp. 155–281.

—— "Il cardinale Guglielmo Sirleto in Calabria," *Rivista di storia della Chiesa in Italia*, I (1947), pp. 22–37.

Patrizi, A., *Cæremoniale Romanum* (Farnborough: Gregg, 1965).

Rabotin, H., "Les Textes liturgiques," in Aigrain, *Liturgia*, pp. 343–70.

Reid, A., *The Organic Development of the Liturgy*, 2nd edn (San Francisco: Ignatius Press, 2005).

Riviere, J., "La Messe durant la période de la Réforme et du Concile de Trente," in A. Vacant, E. Mangenot & E. Amann (eds), *Dictionnaire de Theologie Catholique*, vol. X (Paris: Letouzey et Ané, 1929), cols 1085–1142.

Sander, M., *Le livre à figures italien depuis 1467 jusqu'à 1530: essai de sa bibliographie et de son histoire*, vol. II (Milan: U. Hoepli, 1942).

Schmidt, H., *Liturgie en langue vulgaire: le problème de la langue liturgique chez les premiers réformateurs et au Concile de Trente* (Rome: Gregorian University, 1950).

Scoppola, P., *Ricerche per la storia religiosa di Roma*, vol. 8 (Rome: Edizioni di Storia e di Letteratura, 1990).

Simmons, T.F., *The Lay Folks' Mass Book* (London: Early English Text Society, 1879).

Sodi, M. & A.M. Triacca (eds), *Missale Romanum: Editio Princeps 1570* (Vatican City: Libreria Editrice Vaticana, 1998).

Theisen, R., *Mass liturgy and the Council of Trent* (Collegeville: St John's University Press, 1965).

Tirot, P., *Histoire des prières de l'offertoire dans la liturgie romaine du VIIe au XVIe siècle* (Rome: Edizioni Liturgiche, 1985).

Van Dijk, S., & J. Hazelden Walker, *The Origins of the Modern Roman Liturgy: The Liturgy of the Papal Court and the Franciscan Order in the Thirteenth Century* (London: Darton, Longman & Todd, 1960).

—— *The Ordinal of the Papal Court from Innocent III to Boniface VIII and Related Documents* (Fribourg: University Press, 1975).

Vogel, C., *Medieval Liturgy: An Introduction to the Sources* (Washington: Pastoral Press, 1986).

Wickham Legg, J.W., *Tracts on the Mass* (London: Harrison, 1904).

Wilmart, A., "Primum in Ordine," *Ephemerides Liturgicæ*, 50 (1936), pp. 133–9.

—— "Le Comes de Murbach," *Revue Bénédictine*, 30 (1913), pp. 25–69.

Zak, A., *Über die Præfationen*, *Theol. prakt Quartelschrift*, 58 (1905), pp. 307–25.

Chapter 7

IN PURSUIT OF PARTICIPATION—LITURGY AND LITURGISTS IN EARLY MODERN AND POST-ENLIGHTENMENT CATHOLICISM

Alcuin Reid

The late medieval period

It is widely held that on the eve of the Council of Trent, in the words of Theodor Klauser (1894–1984), the liturgy in the West was a "somewhat sorry picture."[1] Prominent late twentieth-century liturgists such as Anscar Chupungco OSB (1939–2013), emeritus President of the Pontifical Institute of Sacred Liturgy, went so far as to say that "there was something insidious about this period," and that it included a "dangerous malaise that announced the total collapse of the Church's life of worship."[2] "External vitality hid the malaise of clericalism, exaggerated allegorism, misplaced devotion to the Mass, a form of spirituality that dispensed with the liturgy as its source, and most of all the loss of an ecclesial sense caused by individualism," Chupungco asserted.[3] According to this view, which grounds the widely accepted scholarship of Joseph Jungmann SJ (1889–1975),[4] in the Middle Ages the liturgical life of the Church became nothing less than corrupt.

Corrupt, that is, if one views the period from the more "enlightened" perspective of twentieth-century liturgical scholarship. There was little if any authentic participation in the liturgy according to this view—it was no longer fit for purpose and itself required radical reform.

Historians of the period, however, present a more nuanced if not a rather different picture. There are many studies of extant medieval liturgical books (i.e. the books for ministerial use in celebrating the rites) which provide evidence of a rich liturgical life in cathedral, collegiate, and monastic churches.[5] Are these, however, themselves not monuments to precisely that corrupt and "clerical" liturgy from participation in which, some liturgists insist, the laity were excluded? Perhaps not: scholarship which examines sources beyond the official liturgical books—Books of Hours and other literature intended for the laity, as well as liturgical art and architecture and links between the liturgy and popular culture, etc.—demonstrates that the laity, lettered and unlettered, did in fact ordinarily participate in the liturgical life of the Church.

In her study, "Liturgy and the Laity in Late Medieval France,"[6] Virginia Reinburg, Associate Professor of History, Boston College, argues that "the clergy expected lay people to participate in the liturgy in a distinctive way—a way distinguishable from the clergy's more doctrinally instructed participation, but possessing its own integrity."[7] This, she asserts, "is a notion of lay participation in the Mass quite different from that on which the Protestant and Catholic reformers later insisted," which was "less concerned with intellectual grasp of eucharistic doctrine or scriptural teachings, than with assuming a proper role in the drama of the Mass."[8] In this, Reinburg argues, "the laity shared as a body, despite differences in age, social status, gender, level of literacy, and devotional interest." The Mass was "a sacred rite uniting them with God, the Church, and each other."[9] "Late medieval liturgy," she asserts, "can be viewed as the establishment of social and spiritual solidarity among God, the Church, and the lay community."[10]

The participation of which Reinburg speaks is not necessarily what would be demanded by a post-enlightenment or a postmodern full, conscious, and active participation in the liturgical rites and prayers, but it is nevertheless a real connection with the action of Christ in the Sacred Liturgy. It is a genuine liturgical participation of its era.

The integral role of the liturgy in everyday medieval lay life and peoples' connection with it is further underlined by the work of Professor Eamon Duffy of the University of Cambridge who has more than ably demonstrated the role of the liturgy in the cultural synthesis that was pre-Reformation England.[11] That "the worshipping life of English people c. 1450–1550 [is] characterised by an intense and widespread emotional and intellectual investment," is now accepted by scholars of the period as "hard to dispute."[12]

What can be disputed are the simplistic and somewhat revisionist assertions accepted by late twentieth-century liturgists and repeated by the Professor of Liturgy at the Pontifical Gregorian University, Keith Pecklers SJ (1958–), who hold that the liturgical life of the Church was bleak on the eve of the Council of Trent and that "the liturgy's relationship to the daily life of Christians was lost."[13] His older and profoundly influential confrere, Jungmann, went so far as to say that the liturgy had become "a lifeless civil act."[14] No; there was indeed a relationship, a most profound one, involving a real, living and fruitful participation in the liturgy which was itself an integral part of daily life and culture.

We should note, also, that in unfragmented medieval Christian culture, formation in the meaning and role of the liturgy and in the manner in which one participated in it occurred naturally, intuitively as it were, and was not a matter of extraneous instruction. The Sacred Liturgy was a natural and fundamental reality in the world in which one grew up—not something in which one had to be didactically catechized or take a course of studies in order to understand. Students of this period do well to take account of this cultural reality, so profoundly different to our own.

The Council of Trent and its aftermath

This medieval cultural synthesis was not likely long to survive the influence of Renaissance Humanism. As Reinburg observes, "Humanists, Protestants, and Catholic reformers alike seem to find problematic a strict identification between the physical or secular and the spiritual." Thus, "by insisting that lay congregants aspire to a reasonable level of informed participation, both Reformations together [Protestant and Catholic] created a definitive rupture with the late medieval drama of the Mass, in which everyone had distinct but equally valuable and necessary parts to play."[15]

The intellectual climate of the sixteenth century, together with the ecclesiastical turmoil of the Protestant Reformation in its various manifestations, and the Catholic response culminating in the Council of Trent (1545–63), ushered in the period aptly termed by Georgetown University's John W. O'Malley SJ as "early modern Catholicism."[16] Contemporary liturgical understanding and scholarship is profoundly influenced by this period, and the modern concern to facilitate a literate, rational participation in the liturgy finds it origins at this time and needs to be understood in its light.

There is no doubt that the Council of Trent wanted more than the liturgical participation of late medieval times. In response to the Protestant complaint that "Saying that we should have devotion, whether in prayer or in ceremony, whilst understanding nothing, is a great mockery ... The heart requires understanding,"[17] Trent's twenty-second session (17 September 1562), whilst not judging it expedient that the Mass be celebrated in the vernacular,[18] nevertheless insisted that:

> Lest the children beg for food but no one gives to them [cf. Lam. 4:4] pastors and all who have the care of souls must frequently, either by themselves or through others, explain during the celebration of Masses some of the readings of the Mass and, among other things, give some instruction about the mystery of this most holy sacrifice, especially on Sundays and feast days.[19]

This call for the intellectual formation of the laity by the pastoral clergy goes hand in hand with the Council's desire for "the faithful present at every Mass to communicate in it not only by spiritual devotion but also by sacramental reception of the Eucharist, so that the fruits of this most holy sacrifice could be theirs more fully,"[20] even though the possibility of the wider reception of Holy Communion under both species was not adopted—due to doctrinal, not liturgical, reasons.[21]

Yet whilst desiring sacramental participation Trent, in response to Protestant errors, approved and commended Masses in which only the priest communicated sacramentally and at which the faithful participated devotionally.[22] Thus the Council did not deprecate the devotional participation of the late medieval Church, whilst at the same time calling for further education and formation in the sacred rites and for more frequent sacramental participation in them.[23]

This nuanced approach to liturgical participation is the basis of Western Catholic practice in the early modern era. Two significant features of the

Renaissance—greater literacy and the growth of printing—meant that devotional books containing liturgical texts, increasingly including vernacular translations, were no longer the sole preserve of the wealthy: an intellectual grasp of the meaning of the liturgical rites, and therefore a more conscious participation in them, was facilitated further.

The German lay scholar Anton Baumstark (1872–1948) makes an important observation about the liturgy of the Roman rite after Trent:

> The Church now enlisted into its service the late humanism of the Renaissance, whose culture emphasised the individual and delighted in the senses. The baroque created its rich spaces, inundated by the dazzling light of white stucco and the intensity of resplendent colours. To further its own brilliant rise, the young Society of Jesus fostered both aspects of Renaissance culture. In contrast to the centrifugal forces unleashed by the Protestant Reformation ... a spirit of ecclesiastical centralisation—with a discipline as strict as can be imagined— came fully into play in the sixteenth century. This spirit also found in the Jesuits its most trustworthy custodians and self-sacrificing standard-bearers.[24]

The liturgical manifestation of this centralism was the Congregation of Sacred Rites established as part of the general reform of the Roman curia carried out by Pope Sixtus V in 1588. The Congregation was charged with responsibility for "vigilance for the observance of sacred rites, restoration and reformation of ceremonies, reform and correction of liturgical books ... the celebration of feast days ... [and] solution of controversies over precedence and other liturgical matters."[25]

The Australian scholar Geoffrey Hull describes this period as a transition "from Tradition to obedience" in the Church, where centralism gradually gives rise to uncritical obedience and eventually ultramontanism, almost rendering ecclesiastical authority, most specifically the papacy, the *arbiter* of Tradition rather than its custodian.[26] Whilst "the content and forms of the traditional faith remained the same ... the spontaneous religiosity of the Middle Ages was giving way to the regimented and self-conscious Catholicism of the Counter Reformation," Hull argues.[27]

Liturgically, there can be no doubt that the Congregation of Sacred Rites ensured that local bishops retained few if any of the prerogatives over liturgical books and rites enjoyed by their predecessors before Trent—save Gallican France, whose complete liturgical submission to Rome was not accomplished until the nineteenth century.[28] Similarly, it was Roman Congregations whose authority determined liturgical discipline in distant mission lands, such as China, not without difficulties and to the possible detriment of the Church's mission in these places.[29]

This centralism certainly ensured the doctrinal orthodoxy deemed necessary by Trent, but quite possibly the uniformity so often insisted upon in the name of ensuring greater liturgical discipline may have been at the expense of the possibility of a legitimate diversity and a truly organic inculturation—one that respected substantial unity. In this period of history the ritual permissions requested (usually involving some use of the vernacular, particularly in singing), were often motivated by a desire that indigenous people for whom the Latin tongue and European culture were foreign might find means by which more easily to participate in the Roman liturgy. The rigidity with which some permissions were refused meant that for missions in non-Western cultures participation in the liturgy was far less straightforward and the work of explicit liturgical formation was therefore more onerous.

The *Devotio Moderna*

So, too, the spirituality of early modern Catholicism impacted on participation and formation in the Sacred Liturgy *as liturgy*. The late medieval *devotio moderna*, stressing personal meditation and internal prayer as opposed to external liturgical ritual, was a strong influence on many of the new religious orders of the period. In the Society of Jesus (founded 1534) and the Spiritual Exercises of St Ignatius of Loyola (1491-1556) the *devotio moderna* found fertile soil and gained its most fervent promoters.

A significant feature of many sixteenth-century orders, including the Jesuits, was their exclusion of the choral celebration of the Divine Office. Robert Taft SJ (1932-) insists that this exclusion was not of anti-liturgical intent, but was rather a freeing from the obligation of communal prayer in order that nothing "would hinder the mobility and freedom Ignatius wished for the apostolic endeavours he envisaged as the vocation of his men."[30] The Jesuit *Constitutions*, Taft continues, "explicitly state that Jesuits who 'experience devotion in them' [the Hours of the Office] . . . will find plenty of opportunity to assist at them."[31]

The question here, however, is not one of the legitimacy of prioritizing apostolic endeavor: it is of the relegation of the liturgical celebration of the Divine Office to the status of merely one devotion amongst others. Even those new orders for whom choir obligation was retained—the Capuchin Franciscans (founded 1528) and the Discalced Carmelites (founded 1593)—the *recto tono* recitation of the Divine Office was the norm. The *liturgical* celebration of the Office was an official duty to be accomplished efficiently so as to leave time for mediation and prayer after the manner of the *devotio moderna* according to the charism of the order. It is easy to see how, with such liturgical reductionism, the *public* celebration of low Mass could so easily became an accepted practice, if not the norm, pastorally and even conventually. It should also be clear that, with the ascendancy of this approach, the truth that the Sacred Liturgy is the "primary and indispensible source from which the faithful are to derive the true Christian spirit"[32] could easily be obscured.[33]

In liturgically minimalist celebrations, the possibility of actual participation is likely to be reduced proportionally. If liturgical formation is more a matter of immersion in the living and ongoing celebration of the *ecclesia* than one of positive instruction, liturgical minimalism stunts liturgical formation. And indeed, if the prevailing spiritual trend is in favor of private meditation or other devotional exercises—even at the liturgy—the very possibility of participation in the liturgy (howsoever minimalized) and of being formed by the liturgy is further obstructed.

In his famous essay "The Genius of the Roman Rite," the lay English liturgical historian Edmund Bishop (1846–1917) asserted that the liturgical centralism following Trent and its rigid enforcement by the Congregation of Sacred Rites which ended the pre-Reformation elasticity of the liturgical books "is the explanation of the rapid growth, the wonderful variety, and great development . . . of what we call 'devotions.'"[34] However, another explanation is possible. The primary cause of the rapid growth of such parallel practices, rather than simply the liturgical rigidity maintained by the Congregation of Sacred Rites, may well be attributable to the a-liturgical spirituality of the *devotio moderna*. For in this we find a relegation of the Sacred Liturgy from the primacy in the spiritual life which is its by right, not because the liturgical rites are fixed or supervised—or indeed because they retain the use of a sacred language or do not permit the reception of the Chalice to laity, etc.—but because Renaissance man, Protestant and Catholic, was first and foremost an individual. In this cultural milieu the *devotio moderna* found fertile soil indeed. As these practices took root and grew, successive generations developed a spiritual life more distant still from the Church's liturgical life. The significance of this historical phenomenon ought not to be underestimated.

Survivals of the liturgical spirit

Nevertheless the ensuing centuries did see the promotion of the liturgy and participation in it. Standing tall amongst Counter-Reformation figures is the reforming archbishop of Milan, St Charles Borromeo (1538–84), who expended an extraordinary amount of energy ensuring correct liturgical observance, regulating even the small details of the arrangement of churches—including the placement of the tabernacle on the high altar and the installation of altar rails so as to promote piety when receiving Holy Communion—and promoting catechesis and instruction (of the clergy also), thus facilitating intelligent participation in the liturgy—which for Borromeo was most certainly the source and summit of the life and mission of the Church. "That such a cardinal, such a Saint, thought the vast labour expanded on the reformation of ceremonial of his province worthwhile is, for us, a much needed lesson in value judgement."[35]

So too, as recent scholarship has underlined, "liturgical music was of significant interest and a source of intense spiritual meaning for Borromeo."[36] That is to say, it formed an integral part of his liturgical vision and reform. Whilst still in Rome, Borromeo was influential in promoting the music of Giovanni Pierluigi da Palestrina (c. 1525–94), whose polyphony Borromeo found beautiful and intelligible and, given the Council of Trent's proscription of "music in which a base and suggestive element is introduced into the organ playing or singing"[37] and its discussion of the need for "singing in musical modes . . . not to afford vain delight to the ear" but to allow the words to be comprehensible,[38] he nevertheless judged suitable for liturgical use.[39] In Milan, Borromeo is also found encouraging the work of Tomás Luis de Victoria (1548–1611).[40]

This was the dawn of the age of the Baroque, with its confident if not triumphal celebration of absolute and eternal values in a majestic and courtly style and its "assembling of all possible sensuous creation in the service of high ideals."[41] Its liturgical architecture—the prototype of which was the Jesuit church of the Gesù in Rome, consecrated in 1584 and not built for the choral celebration of the Divine Office—music and rhetoric were at times somewhat over-confident and, in the hands of those influenced by the *devotio moderna* and widely propagated by them, tended to promote pious practices and ideas rather than giving priority to connecting with the action of the liturgical rites themselves. The tendency for the liturgy to be regarded as an impressive and edifying, even devotional, spectacle apart from—or during which one got on with—one's "true" spiritual practices was real. If it is indeed the case that the liturgy became "part of the legal ordinance which had to be observed, but not something that people really live,"[42] this was not a felicitous state of affairs.[43]

It has to be said that (then, as today) when architecture, music, and other arts become the mistress rather than the servant of the liturgical rites, or are seen as ends in themselves to be "performed on a liturgical stage" and subject the liturgy to their own fashions and demands, participation in the Church's liturgy is set at least at one remove. That is not to deny either the possibility of legitimate development in these fields or indeed to assert that the Baroque is intrinsically inimical to the liturgy or liturgical participation: Baroque churches, music, vessels, and vestments, etc., can and do serve to facilitate people's connection with Christ's action in the Sacred Liturgy to this day. They were and are, very often, works of considerable artistic skill and beauty offered to the Church out of love of God and a desire to put the best of man's creativity at the service of the Church's worship. However, one needs perhaps the discernment of a Borromeo, who could distinguish the liturgical integrity of Palestrina's works from those of other composers, in order to ensure that it is indeed the liturgy and not simply art, or even devotionalism, that is being advanced at the expense of the authentic celebration of the Church's liturgical rites.

Yet who can deny that Baroque architecture with its large open spaces promoted a visual participation in the liturgy which twentieth-century church architects would simply take for granted? And who can say that the growth of the worship of the Blessed Sacrament and the popularity of the Corpus Christi procession found in this period was to the detriment of the Church or an inauthentic development? With highly operatic arrangements of liturgical texts involving elaborate solo performances, or arrangements that fail to respect the textual integrity of the liturgy, or which occlude it, certainly, it is difficult to say that the liturgy—the Church's official public worship of Almighty God—and not the art, is being placed first.[44] Nevertheless, they can be profoundly beautiful in themselves and evoke genuine religious sentiment.[45]

In studying this period, one may make a rightful distinction between religious art which may find a legitimate home in many and varied contexts, and religious art for which the Sacred Liturgy is its proper domicile: the door to the latter is much narrower than the first. It is also important to avoid the assumption that any use of "Baroque" in a sentence containing the word "liturgy" can only be pejorative. Even Jungmann admits that whilst "the Baroque period itself preferred to draw from secondary channels ... yet from these it nourished an amazingly rich life."[46] It is, perhaps for future scholars further to consider this apparent dilemma.[47]

Indeed, the Baroque period saw attempts to facilitate participation in the liturgy through comprehension. A *Missel romain selon le règlement du Concile de Trente: Traduit en François* [sic], prepared by Joseph de Voisin (c. 1610–85), chaplain to the Prince of Conti, and a Doctor at the Sorbonne, was published in five volumes in Paris in 1660 by Frederic Leonard. It enjoyed a Royal warrant and the approbation of the Vicars General of Paris and of the Chancellor of the University. This very early peoples' missal contains the complete vernacular translations of the Ordinary of the Mass—including the Roman canon—as well as of the propers of the seasons and the sanctoral.

An audacious venture for its time, it is not surprising that it attracted controversy: the Assembly of the Clergy, alarmed to see the liturgical texts entirely in the vernacular, condemned it in 1660 and referred the matter to Rome. By the Brief *Ad aures nostras* of January 12, 1661, Pope Alexander VII (1599; 1655–67), placed the missal on the Index and ordered that all copies be burnt. Roman relations with the Court of the young Louis XIV (1638; 1643–1715) being strained, the French ignored the Pope's strictures.[48] The missal proved popular, went through several editions over the coming century, and was increasingly imitated.

De Voisin was not alone. The writings of his younger compatriot Nicholas le Tourneaux (1640–86) reflected his conviction "that the celebration of the Liturgy should be an exercise of the mind and heart,"[49] as his work published in 1680, *De la meilleure manière d'entendre la sainte Messe,* makes clear in its insistence on the faithful's connection to the liturgical rites according to the "spirit of the Church."[50] So too, the Italian Ludovico Antonio Muratori (1672–1750)[51] combined liturgical scholarship with promotion of liturgical piety, though his most famous work *Della Regolata Devozione dei Cristiani,* published in 1747,[52] moves beyond simply the promotion of liturgical participation and eschewed anything that seemed to have a hint of superstition or magic about it, preferring what would come to be called "noble simplicity."[53]

Perhaps the most famous promoter of liturgical participation in this period was the scholarly and zealous Theatine, St Giuseppe Tommasi (1649–1713), a consulter to the Congregation of Sacred Rites who worked for the foundation of a Roman academic Institute for the Liturgy (the development of critical liturgical scholarship was another significant feature of the period, which included the scholarly industry of the French Benedictine congregation of St Maur).[54] Tommasi advocated ritual reform,[55] as well as promoting good liturgical practice, including the introduction of Gregorian chant into his titular church of S. Martino ai Monti during his fewer than six months in the sacred purple.

In his fourteen-page *Breve istruzione del modo di assistere fruttuosamente al santo sacrificio della Messa, secondo lo spirito della Chiesa per le persone che non intendono la lingua latina,* first published in 1710,[56] Tommasi set out for the simple faithful the rudiments of liturgical participation, giving a simplified vernacular version of the *Ordo Missæ* to be followed at the corresponding part of the Mass. He intended "to facilitate the most fruitful manner of assisting at Holy Mass," and even encouraged responding verbally to the priest (in Latin) where this was possible.[57]

Unlike de Voisin, Tommasi was in Rome. Far from being censured by the Congregation of Sacred Rites or any other authority, his efforts were at least indirectly rewarded by his elevation to the cardinalate.[58] The liturgical spirit had not been completely stifled by elaborate Baroque display, devotional practices of the heirs to the *devotio moderna,* or by the centralized control of the liturgical rites. Certainly, the efforts related above were exceptions and at times drew criticism, but they are also witnesses to the ability of the spirit of the liturgy to impart the conviction that the riches of the Church's liturgical rites are not the concern merely of those with a particular "liturgical" devotion, but should be the staple spiritual nourishment of the whole Church, cleric or lay, lettered or not, and that enabling participation in them is vital.

Other spirits visited upon the Sacred Liturgy

The rise of what came to be known as "Jansenism" in the seventeenth century is, perhaps, one of the most significant spiritual and theological phenomena following Trent. Jansenism's desire to restore primitive Christian doctrine and practice and its progress towards an ascetical Puritanism could not but impact on the Sacred Liturgy. Jansenism emerged in a France which was strongly Gallican and witnessed the dawn of the Enlightenment. Liturgically, Jansenism's severe antiquarianism, Gallicanism's anti-Roman independence and the self-conscious modernity of the Enlightenment proved to be a potent cocktail indeed.[59]

No longer was the question one of what one ought to do in order to facilitate participation in the liturgy; rather, the issue became one of how the liturgy should be simplified in order to facilitate participation. Any respect due to the developed rites themselves is laid to one side (regardless of any objective value) in the haste to achieve immediate, rational participation by means of ritual reform.

Thus, participation facilitated by liturgical reform (for which read "radical simplification") is the hallmark of the Enlightenment liturgies, of which the most famous are the reforms enacted by the Abbé Jacques Jubé of Asnières (1674–1745), in his church outside of Paris, and of the 1786 diocesan synod called by the bishop of Pistoia, Tuscany, Scipio Ricci (1741–1810). Their simplification of church architecture, disdain of flowers and relics, promotion of vocal participation of the people including in the vernacular, praying of hitherto silent prayers aloud, etc. are described as "curiously modern" by some late twentieth-century liturgists who regarded this period as a prophetic anticipation of modern reforms.[60] This is a phenomenon which most certainly merits further study.

At the time, the Curé d'Asnières was banished and the efforts of Bishop Ricci provoked a popular revolt and formal condemnation in 1794 by the Bull *Auctorem fidei* of Pope Pius VI. Pius VI did not enter into dialogue about the merit or otherwise of the specific reforms in themselves, nor did he simply condemn the rank disobedience to liturgical law they showed. Instead he condemned them for being rash, "injurious to the pious and approved custom of the Church" and even "favourable to the charges of heretics against" the Church.[61] In so doing, he rejected the "short-cut" to liturgical participation advocated by the Enlightenment liturgists, insisting that the Sacred Liturgy as developed in tradition was not to be manipulated to that end. Immersion in the riches of that tradition, not quick ritual change, was what was in fact necessary to achieve fruitful participation.

The nineteenth century

Whether or not by way of reaction to Enlightenment excesses, the nineteenth century saw something of a revival in interest in the liturgy, albeit tinged with romanticism and ultramontanism. The Industrial Revolution furnished the means for rapid advances in manufacturing, and liturgical art and architecture benefitted in their turn. The revival of gothic architecture led in France by Eugène Viollet-le-Duc (1814–79) and promoted in England and beyond by Augustus Welby Pugin (1812–52), was but one beneficiary.

Viollet-le-Duc came to prominence for his work on the cathedral of Notre-Dame in Paris, and worked principally on the restoration of existing buildings, ecclesiastical and secular. Pugin, a convert to Catholicism in 1834 and thereafter a zealous apostle of the synthesis of liturgical art, architecture, and ornament of the Middle Ages, "to the edification of the faithful and as lively illustrations of the Sacred Mysteries," as he wrote in the preface to his famous *Glossary of Ecclesiastical Ornament*,[62] frequently worked on new commissions in an England experiencing a Catholic resurgence, and in many ways had more opportunities freely to exercise his creative genius. For Pugin, immersion into a liturgical space in which all elements were in harmony (ritual elements also—though it would never have occurred to him to question this) led to participation. Pugin designed *everything* for his churches (vessels, vestments, furniture, etc.) so as to ensure that integrity. Thus the liturgical habitat could form the person and unlock the riches of the mysteries celebrated through the consonance of each element of the liturgical environment (and act).

Pugin's age enjoyed greater literacy than the Middle Ages, and the use of bilingual missals which facilitated participation in the textual content of the liturgy was increasingly common. Yet Pugin's emphasis on the visual if not the sensual constituent of Catholic worship serves to remind us still that the cerebral is but one, albeit important, element of participation in the whole complex that is Catholic worship.[63]

Antonio Rosmini (1797–1855), whose works were controversial in their day, developed a theology of the Church as the Mystical Body of Christ and of the common priesthood of all the baptized. Upon this theological basis he promoted active and conscious participation in the Liturgy whilst *rejecting* the use of the vernacular as a blanket solution. Participation in the liturgy was clearly not, for Rosmini, a matter of facile comprehension or rote recitation of words—rather it was a conscious taking of one's rightful place in the celebration of the *ecclesia*.[64] Rosmini is discussed further in the appendix to this chapter together with Edmund Bishop.

The English secular priest Daniel Rock (1799–1871) published works promoting a greater understanding of the liturgy. His small work, *The Liturgy of the Mass and Common Vespers for Sundays* (London: Booker, 1832) was followed by his widely known two-volume *Hierurgia or the Holy Sacrifice of the Mass* (London: Booker, 1833), explaining the ceremonies and doctrines of the Mass. At the time it was as much an apologetic work as one aimed at the formation of Catholics. Rock's four-volume *The Church of Our Fathers as seen in St Osmund's Rite for the Cathedral of Salisbury* (London: C. Dolman, 1849–53) was an extensive and influential scholarly endeavor in its day.[65]

The liturgical celebrity of the nineteenth century is, without doubt, Dom Prosper Guéranger (1805–75), whose restoration of monastic life in France and the resultant Benedictine Congregation of Solesmes was, and is to this day, of importance to the Sacred Liturgy in the West. He was most certainly a romantic and an energetic ultramontanist—almost singlehandedly bringing about the capitulation of the Gallican rites in use throughout France to those of Rome.[66]

Guéranger's many writings demonstrate his concern for the liturgy well beyond the cloister. Amongst them his popular fifteen-volume *L'Année Liturgique*, first published in 1841 and by no means perfect in the scholarship it contains,[67] may be described as nothing less than a popular manual of liturgical formation structured on the liturgical year in order to promote liturgical piety, as its preface indicates: "Liturgical prayer would soon become powerless, were the faithful not to take a real share in it, or, at least not to associate themselves to it in [the] heart. It can heal and save the world, but only on the condition that it be understood."[68] The young Abbot of Solesmes appealed: "Open your hearts, children of the Catholic Church, and come and pray the prayer of your Mother."[69]

Guéranger's initiative spread widely. Its impact was to immerse ordinary people into the riches of the Sacred Liturgy—not only the Mass—and thereby to enable them to participate in it. Guéranger took no shortcuts: his dream—rather, his conviction—that the ordinary faithful should and could be connected to the riches and wealth of the Church's liturgical life, supported by his practical efforts and spread throughout Europe by his monastic children,[70] make it possible to say that the somewhat isolated efforts to promote liturgical participation in previous centuries certainly coalesced in the nineteenth century into efforts to promote liturgical piety—the cornerstone of the twentieth-century liturgical movement.

Conclusion

From the Council of Trent until the dawn of the twentieth century, the liturgy in the West was, on paper (i.e. in the liturgical books), relatively fixed. Late nineteenth-century man, however, living in a more literate, post-Enlightenment world, changed forever by the Industrial Revolution, was by no means the same as his fifteenth- or sixteenth-century ancestors. The quiet, affective participation in the multivalent rites of the Church's liturgy of his fifteenth- or early sixteenth-century forebears was long since gone. More rational pious exercises dominated the spiritual life of Western Catholicism, and the sensual appetites of nineteenth-century man had been thoroughly indulged with the Baroque and its progeny. Whether he participated more fully in the Church's liturgy itself is a most pertinent question indeed.

Yet efforts to reassert the Sacred Liturgy's centrality as the source and summit of all Christian life and work surfaced in different ways throughout this period, and scholarly research into the liturgy increased. The temptation to refashion the liturgy according to the tastes of "modern man" also arose. The liturgical movement of the twentieth century inherited these efforts and also this temptation. Similarly, it would have to do battle with the propagators of the pious exercises. A study of how it dealt with these tributaries pertains to the following chapter.

In moving forward to this study, the reflections on the early modern and post-Enlightenment periods by one of the zealous apostles (and perhaps also a prophetic critic) of the liturgical movement, the French Oratorian Louis Bouyer (1913–2004), serve to encapsulate the issues at hand:

> The men of the seventeenth century were sure that the short-cut formulae of their theological and controversial handbooks were enough to hold all the pith and marrow of Christian tradition concerning the Eucharist. Therefore so long as they retained somewhere in the background of a ceremony the substance of the rites and the texts of the traditional liturgy, they believed themselves to be perfectly Catholic, and felt quite entitled to dress up these rites and texts to resemble as closely as possible the profane performances of the culture of that period, paying no attention at all to the ways in which the eucharistic doctrine had traditionally been expressed in the rites and texts themselves. But do not many people today do exactly the same kind of thing when they try to disguise a rubrically correct low Mass by reading and singing in the vernacular, to make it resemble as closely as possible the style of public meeting now popular, endeavoring also to give to the performance of the sacred rite itself a setting resembling that of the stadium, of the factory, or of the movie-theatre? Is it not of the very essence of the Baroque spirit to transpose into a worldly setting a liturgy envisioned merely as an external formality?
>
> The great lesson, then, that we should learn from... the Baroque mentality and its influence on the liturgy, is that a real understanding of the nature of the liturgy as it is in itself, and the will to follow out the implications of that nature is the primary necessity for any living use and practice of it. And, as a consequence, the second lesson is that, to do this, it is necessary not to force upon the liturgy a culture or tendencies foreign to it, but rather to try to put ourselves into its own spiritual world and to attune ourselves to its own modes of thought, feeling and outward expression.[71]

Notes

1 T. Klauser, *A Short History of the Western Liturgy: An account and some reflections*, 2nd edn (Oxford: Oxford University Press, 1979) p. 97.
2 A. Chupungco, "History of the Roman Liturgy until the Fifteenth Century," A. Chupungco (ed.), *Handbook for Liturgical Studies*, vol. I (Collegeville: Liturgical Press, 1997), pp. 131–52 (p. 150).
3 Ibid., p. 151.
4 See: A. Reid, *The Organic Development of the Liturgy: The Principles of Liturgical Reform and Their Relation to the Twentieth Century Liturgical Movement Prior to the Second Vatican Council*, 2nd edn (San Francisco: Ignatius Press, 2005) pp. 164–72.
5 For an example of recent scholarship see: R. Pfaff, *The Liturgy in Medieval England: A History* (Cambridge: Cambridge University Press, 2009).
6 Virginia Reinburg, "Liturgy and the Laity in Late Medieval and Reformation France," *The Sixteenth Century Journal* 23 (1992), pp. 526–47.
7 Ibid., p. 529.
8 Ibid., pp. 529–30.
9 Ibid., p. 541.
10 Ibid., p. 542.
11 See: E. Duffy, *Marking the Hours: English People and their Prayers 1240–1570* (New Haven: Yale University Press, 2006); *The Voices of Morebath: Reformation and Rebellion in an English Village* (New Haven: Yale University Press, 2001); *The Stripping of the Altars* (New Haven: Yale University Press, 1992).
12 Pfaff, *The Liturgy in Medieval England*, pp. 552, 553.
13 K. Pecklers, "History of the Roman Liturgy from the Sixteenth until the Twentieth Centuries" Chupungco, *Handbook for Liturgical Studies*, vol. I, pp. 153–78 (p. 154).
14 J. Jungmann, *Pastoral Liturgy* (London: Challoner Publications, 1962), p. 69.
15 Reinburg, "Liturgy and the Laity in Late Medieval and Reformation France," p. 546.
16 See: J.W. O'Malley, *Trent and All That: Renaming Catholicism in the Early Modern Era* (Cambridge, MA: Harvard University Press, 2002).
17 John Calvin, Preface to *Pseaumes octantetrois de David* (1551), cited in Reinburg, "Liturgy and the Laity in Late Medieval and Reformation France," p. 545.
18 See: C. Korolevsky, *Living Languages in Catholic Worship: An Historical Enquiry* (London, New York & Toronto: Longman Green & Co., 1957), pp. 96–9. Korolevsky's bibliographical references are valuable.
19 DZ 1749.
20 DZ 1747. See also Session 13 (October 11, 1551), chapter 8, which expressed the desire that the faithful "will be able to receive frequently their super-substantial bread [cf. Mt 6:11]. May it truly be the life of their souls and continual health for their minds;" DZ 1649.
21 See: Session 21 (July 16, 1562); DZ 1725–34.
22 Session 22, chapter 6; DZ 1747.
23 See further: Reinold Theisen, *Mass Liturgy and the Council of Trent* (Collegeville: St John's University Press, 1965).
24 A. Baumstark, *On the Historical Development of Liturgy* (Collegeville: Liturgical Press, 2011), p. 233.
25 Frederick R. McManus, *The Congregation of Sacred Rites* (Washington DC: Catholic University of America Press, 1954), p. 27.
26 See: Geoffrey Hull, *The Banished Heart: Origins of Heteropraxis in the Catholic Church* (London: T&T Clark, 2010), chapter 9.

27 Ibid., p. 140.
28 See: Reid, *The Organic Development of the Liturgy,* pp. 56–60.
29 See: Korolevsky, *Living Languages in Catholic Worship,* pp. 102–4.
30 Robert Taft SJ, *The Liturgy of the Hours in East and West* (Collegeville: Liturgical Press, 1986) p. 301.
31 Ibid., pp. 301–2.
32 *Sacrosanctum Concilium,* § 14. See also: Pius X, motu proprio, *Tra le sollecitudine,* November 22, 1903.
33 I first encountered this phenomenon well after the Second Vatican Council: in 1983 Fr Cornelius P. Finn SJ (1910–93), moderator of my year group at Corpus Christi Seminary in the Archdiocese of Melbourne, Australia, insisted to us on the priority of a daily half hour of mental prayer over the celebration of the liturgy, including that of a priest offering a daily Mass privately or completing his praying of the Divine Office.
34 Edmund Bishop, *Liturgica Historica* (Oxford: Clarendon Press, 1918) p. 18.
35 M.A. Chapman, "The Liturgical Directions of Saint Charles Borromeo: Terminal Essay," *Liturgical Arts* 7 (1939), pp. 10–13 (p. 13). Other essays in this series may be found in *Liturgical Arts* 3 (1934), pp. 142–8; 4 (1935), pp. 109–18; 5 (1936), pp. 60–3, pp. 105–9; 6 (1938), pp. 91–4. See also: Edward Schaefer, "A Reexamination of Palestrina's Role in the Catholic Reformation," *The Choral Journal* 35 (1994), pp. 19–25.
36 Daniele V. Filippi, "Carlo Borromeo and Tomás Luis de Victoria: a gift, two letters and a recruiting campaign," *Early Music* 43 (2015), pp. 37–51 (p. 47); idem., "*Carlo Borromeo e la musica, "a lui naturalmente grata,"* Antonio Addamiano & Francesco Luisi (eds), *Atti del Congresso Internazionale di Musica Sacra (Roma, 26 maggi–1 giugno 2011),* 3 vols (Città del Vaticano: Libreria Editrice Vaticana, 2013), vol. 2, pp. 665–76.
37 Session 22, September 17, 1562, "Decree on things to be observed and avoided in celebrating Mass," N. Tanner (ed.), *Decrees of the Ecumenical Councils,* vol. II (London & Washington DC: Sheed & Ward & Georgetown University Press, 1990), pp. 736–7 (p. 737). DZ does not include this decree.
38 Craig Monson, "The Council of Trent Revisited," James Haar (ed.) *European Music 1520–1640* (London: Boydell & Brewer, 2006), pp. 401–21 (p. 402). Monson is citing a draft canon in the end not adopted by the Council.
39 See: E.L. Taunton, "St Charles and Palestrina" Letter, *The Tablet,* October 18, 1884, pp. 23–4. Taunton repeats the myth that the *Missa Papae Marcelli* was composed specifically at Borromeo's request—something held as not credible by modern scholars. Nevertheless, that Borromeo was an important patron of Palestrina and considered his compositions most suitable for liturgical use is not disputed.
40 See: Filippi, "Carlo Borromeo and Tomás Luis de Victoria: a gift, two letters and a recruiting campaign." Worthy of note in respect of contemporary liturgical music— although composed in utterly different circumstances—are the Catholic compositions of the English composer William Byrd (†1623).
41 Jungmann, *Pastoral Liturgy,* p. 81.
42 Ibid., p. 87.
43 For a (characteristically) trenchant critique of the Baroque period see: Louis Bouyer, *Life and Liturgy* (London: Sheed & Ward, 1956), pp. 1–9. Interestingly Bouyer concedes: "the rigid and unintelligent traditionalism, which is so prominent a feature of the true Baroque mentality, was the providential means whereby the Church managed to keep her liturgical treasures safe throughout a long period when scarcely anyone was capable of understanding their true worth . . . the treasures of the liturgy have at least

been preserved,—while we may well wonder occasionally what would remain for future generations of the faithful if some modern promoters of a 'living' liturgy were allowed complete freedom to remodel the Church's liturgy according to their own ideas" (p. 9).

44 Perhaps the apotheosis of sublime art with little regard for the integrity of the liturgy is the 1775 "Little organ Mass" of Joseph Haydn (1732–1809), where subsequent phrases of the liturgical text are sung by different singers simultaneously—so as to save time! It is, of course, a *missa brevis*. R.R. Terry (1865–1938) would argue that "from Bach onwards ... musical expression and musical completeness had become primary objects. In vain do we look for the ecclesiastical spirit, that thing so subtle in itself and so difficult of definition, but so real to the artist who has ears to hear and a soul to feel," R.R. Terry, *The Music of the Roman Rite* (London: Burns, Oates & Washbourne, 1931) pp. 27–8.

45 It is certainly possible for literate twenty-first-century man, liturgically well-formed, to participate fully, consciously, and actively in the Sacred Liturgy through many of these compositions. But that does require a thorough liturgical formation and—given that is rare—a liturgical discretion in the use of such pieces, so that a choir, soloists, instrumentalists, etc. are not "seen" to be on stage or performing—as they would be at a concert—but are clearly placing—and are seen to be placing—their expertise at the service of the Sacred Liturgy (themselves, as members of the *ecclesia* at worship). A choir loft can serve well here. It must be said that when anything sung or played in the liturgy evokes applause it is a clear sign of the lack of liturgical formation of those applauding and of the necessary discretion on the part of those responsible for the preparation of the celebration of the Sacred Liturgy. So too, when singers or instrumentalists are seen to be disinterested in the rite other than when they themselves are "performing," their presence can become a counter-sign to all that the Sacred Liturgy is.

46 Jungmann, *Pastoral Liturgy*, p. 89.

47 See: Jesus A. Ramos-Kittrell, "Music, Liturgy, and Devotional Piety in New Spain: Baroque Religious Culture and the Re-evaluation of Religious Reform during the 18th Century," *Latin American Music Review / Revista de Música Latinoamericana* 31 (2010), pp. 79–100.

48 See: Prosper Guéranger OSB, *Institutions Liturgiques*, 2nd edn, vol. II (Paris et Bruxelles: Société Générale de Librarie Catholique, 1880), pp. 11–17, 118.

49 J.D. Crichton, *Lights in the Darkness: Forerunners of the Liturgical Movement* (Dublin: Columba Press, 1996), p. 57.

50 Nicholas le Tourneuax, *De la meilleure manière d'entendre la sainte Messe* (Paris: Lambert Roulland, 1680); see chapter VII, pp. 291ff.

51 See: Annunciata Parati, *Pionieri del Movimento Liturgico: Cenni storici* (Vatican City: Libreria Editrice Vaticana, 2004), pp. 15–21.

52 Ludovico Muratori, *Della Regolata Devozione dei Cristiani* (Venice: Giambattista Albrizzi, 1747).

53 See: Alcuin Reid, "Noble Simplicity Revisited," D.V. Twomey SVD & Janet E. Rutherford (eds), *Benedict XVI and Beauty in Sacred Art and Architecture* (Dublin & New York: Four Courts & Scepter, 2011), pp. 94–111 (p. 94).

54 See: J. Fenwick & B. Spinks, *Worship and Transition: The Twentieth Century Liturgical Movement* (Edinburgh: T&T Clark, 1995), pp. 13–14; E. Cattaneo, *Il culto cristiano in occidente: note e storiche*, BELS 13 (2003), pp. 326–8. Cattaneo also devotes a chapter to the "pastoral" liturgical scholarship of the eighteenth century (pp. 354–431).

55 His principles were antiquarian and his proposals were never adopted; see: Reid, *The Organic Development of the Liturgy,* pp. 48–9. See also: Giovanni Mercati, *Opuscoli Inediti del Beato Card. Giuseppe Tommasi Tratti in Luce,* ST 15 (1905).

56 See: Antonius Franciscus Vezzozi, *Venerabilis Viri Josephi Mariæ Thomasii: Opera Omnia,* vol. VII, (Rome: Typographia Paladis, 1754), pp. 337–50. The bibliographical references given by Cattaneo, *Il culto cristiano in occidente,* p. 369 fn. 19, and by Crichton, *Lights in Darkness,* p. 13, are erroneous.

57 See: ibid., pp. 338–9.

58 Tommasi was created cardinal at the age of 62 in 1712, but was never consecrated to the episcopate. This was not an extraordinary practice at the time.

59 See: Reid, *The Organic Development of the Liturgy,* pp. 49ff.

60 See: ibid., pp. 51ff, including an extensive bibliography referring to discussions of the import of these reforms.

61 DZ 2631–3.

62 Augustus Welby Pugin, *Glossary of Ecclesiastical Ornament,* 2nd edn (London: Henry Bohn, 1846) p. vii.

63 Whilst Pugin was a gothic exclusivist and would argue that medieval forms were the perfection of Christian art to the exclusion of others, especially of the Baroque, it can be argued that his principle of integral harmony is equally applicable. The chapel of St John the Baptist commissioned by King John of Portugal (1689-1750) for the Jesuit church of St Roch, Lisbon, with its integral furnishings and ornaments, etc., is a salient example. Pugin's reaction to the arrival of the Oratorian Frederick William Faber (1814–63) and five companions in London in 1849 and their establishment of a temporary and utterly Baroque chapel was characteristically strong, as a letter he wrote to the Lord Shrewsbury indicates: "Has your Lordship heard that the Oratorians have opened the Lowther Rooms as a chapel,—a place for the vilest debauchery, masquerades etc.—one night a MASKED BALL, next BENEDICTUS [sic (Benediction)]. This appears to me perfectly monstrous, and I give the whole order up for ever. What a degradation for religion. Why, it is worse than the Socialists. What a place to celebrate the mysteries of religion in! I cannot conceive how it is allowed . . . Well may they cry out against [rood] screens or anything else. I always said they wanted rooms, not churches, and now they have got them. Sad times! I cannot imagine what the world will come to, if it goes on much longer." Cited in: Peter F. Anson, *Fashions in Church Furnishings 1840-1940* (London: The Faith Press, 1960), pp. 39–40.

64 See: Crichton, *Lights in the Darkness,* p. 25–9. See also: Parati, *Pionieri del Movimento Liturgico,* pp. 51–5.

65 See: Crichton, *Lights in the Darkness,* pp. 82–6. Crichton acknowledges that Rock "would have liked the people to *understand* the liturgy and to respond to its mysterious beauty," but laments that "in his writings there is no indication that he ever thought of them singing the liturgy or responding to it vocally." Crichton notes that, "In his *Church of Our Fathers* Rock rather pathetically expresses his desire for the restoration of the Bidding Prayers as known in the Middle Ages" (p. 86).

66 See: Reid, *The Organic Development of the Liturgy,* pp. 56ff.

67 See: L. Bouyer, *Life and Liturgy,* p. 14.

68 Prosper Guéranger, Laurence Shepherd, trans., *The Liturgical Year: Advent,* 2nd edn (Dublin: Duffy, 1870), pp. 6–7.

69 Translation from: Cuthbert Johnson OSB, *Prosper Guéranger (1805–1875): A Liturgical Theologian: An Introduction to his liturgical writings and work* (Rome: Pontificio Ateneo

S. Anselmo, 1984), p. 350; French: "Dilatez donc vos cœurs, enfants de l'Eglise catholique, et venez prier de la prière de votre Mère."
70 See: Reid, *The Organic Development of the Liturgy,* p. 66.
71 L. Bouyer, *Life and Liturgy,* pp. 8–9.

Bibliography

Bouyer, Louis, *Life and Liturgy* (London: Sheed & Ward, 1956).
Cattaneo, Enrico, *Il culto cristiano in occidente: note e storiche*, BELS 13 (2003).
Crichton, J.D., *Lights in the Darkness: Forerunners of the Liturgical Movement* (Dublin: Columba Press, 1996).
Klauser, Theodor, *A Short History of the Western Liturgy*, 2nd edn (Oxford: Oxford University Press, 1979).
Parati, Annunciata, *Pionieri del Movimento Liturgico: Cenni storici* (Vatican City: Libreria Editrice Vaticana, 2004).
Reid, Alcuin, *The Organic Development of the Liturgy: The Principles of Liturgical Reform and Their Relation to the Twentieth Century Liturgical Movement Prior to the Second Vatican Council*, 2nd edn (San Francisco: Ignatius Press, 2005).
Reinburg, Virginia, "Liturgy and the Laity in Late Medieval and Reformation France," *The Sixteenth Century Journal*, 23 (1992), pp. 526–47.
White, James F., *Roman Catholic Worship: Trent to Today* (New York & Mahwah, NJ: Paulist Press, 1995).

Appendix—Two nineteenth-century liturgists

Paul Gunter OSB

Antonio Rosmini (1797–1855)

The Italian priest Antonio Rosmini, founder of the Institute of Charity, is best known in intellectual circles as a philosopher as his substantial works testify, but it was his short tract "Delle Cinque Piaghe della Santa Chiesa" (On the Five Wounds of Holy Church) that spoke prophetically on the ecclesial life of the Church that provoked as much controversy as hope. The first two "wounds" invoked the importance of the liturgical life of the Church. Though written in 1832, he did not publish it until 1848 in the wake of the election of Pius IX (1792; 1846–78). Against his wishes, however, it was issued in many editions, even in English at the hands of an Anglican canon, and was placed on the Index of Forbidden Books.

The first wound, "the wound in the left hand of holy Church: the division between people and clergy at public worship," identified the laity as separated from the Church at worship through lack of comprehension. Rosmini posited as a reason, not only absence of vitalizing instruction, but also that Latin had ceased to be the language of the people. Nonetheless, contrary to some expectations, Rosmini did not opine the abolition of Latin or even the introduction of the vernacular into the liturgy. Instead, listing five advantages of keeping the Latin language in worship, he wrote that Latin reflects the immutability of the faith; that Latin unites in a single rite many Christians from different backgrounds; that Latin presents the unity and greatness of the Church visibly and encourages common fraternity; that Latin avoids the temptation for the liturgy to become over familiar or "an over-worldly, super-human atmosphere"; and that Latin provides links of posterity with the saints of old who prayed in the same way.

Rosmini also identified disadvantages of the vernacular, citing complexities of misunderstandings within modern languages that divide communities. He raised the frustrations brought by constant changes in words at the liturgy and the problems of the precise translation of important theological concepts in modern languages.

Logically, he listed as the second wound: "The insufficient education of the clergy," while looking to the episcopate to heal it. Opening this wound, he stated that preaching and the liturgy were the two great schools open to the Christian people in the early Christian centuries, adding that priests in the Early Church had come from such fervent Christian communities that participated fully in the liturgy. Rosmini lamented that neglect of the faithful by clergy meant that liturgies were not understood, that knowledge of the Word of God was scarce and that the people were ill-equipped because of ignorance to participate in liturgical celebrations.

Rosmini suffered the polarizing effects his insights had brought to the Austrian Empire of 1848 and the Church, but lit a torch of hope for those projecting beyond that time towards a Church wherein these wounds would be recognized honestly and mended by a desire for liturgical life as the source of incentive, moral principles, style and method. He was beatified in 2007.

Edmund Bishop (1846–1917)

The English lay scholar Edmund Bishop is ably chronicled by the biography of Nigel Abercrombie. Since that work was published in 1959, huge changes have influenced types of reflection and ecclesial enquiry that, in the light of Bishop's contribution, merit considerable study. However, Bishop's own work is his best advertisement. A sample of Bishop's work, embracing a vast corpus of liturgical interest is collected in *Liturgica Historica*, which was edited posthumously in 1918 for the Clarendon Press by his disciple and scribe, Hugh Connelly, a monk of Downside Abbey, where Bishop's papers and library continue to be cherished and protected.

Bishop's most famous paper, "The Genius of the Roman Rite," was delivered in 1899. This paper has proved pivotal to an understanding of the genesis of Western liturgy and has been an inspiration to the studies that have followed in its train of thought. Whilst it imbued, to no mean extent, the mentality of the Constitution on the Sacred Liturgy promulgated during the Second Vatican Council, it continues, no less, to influence the official Vatican documents of the twenty-first century.

From an historical perspective, the various contributions of Edmund Bishop to the Church, both during his life and subsequently, need placing in the wider liturgical contexts of the period beyond their immediate bookish appeal. The Catholic liturgical identity of England and Wales, yet alone the contribution of Edmund Bishop, could not be presented separately from other events, social and political. The Reformation had caused institutional discontinuity to English Catholics and such liturgy as survived did so in very few places. The nineteenth century saw a renewed Catholic life with attendant liturgical and devotional expressions manifesting the "geniuses" of different lands that could work in opposition to each other. Bishop showed what these "geniuses" were. Since Bishop had spent some of his early years at school in Belgium, he had been exposed to European Catholic life. This wider grasp of culture penetrated the mind of Bishop, who was of disposition a natural and insatiable autodidact. That cultural awareness expanded Bishop's mind continually.

Bishop articulated ground-breaking discoveries in his paper on the "genius" contained in the Roman rite. He perceived the liturgy of the Church to be its life-force since he understood the Sacred Liturgy as the purest form of worship, which, without the Church, would lack context. Described by J. Wickham Legg (1843–1921) as "the foremost of living liturgists," Bishop looked for purity in liturgical forms that he was no more likely to find in the Mass, as celebrated at the time of his death in 1917, than in the Mass of Paul VI, albeit for different reasons. His tastes identified the coherence of a liturgiologist, his research the pursuits of a liturgist. Whilst he named the essential characteristics of the Roman rite as "soberness and sense," he was aware that his diligence for the liturgy rendered him out of step with much of the popular devotion that appealed to many Catholics during the final third of the nineteenth century.

Bibliography

AaVv, *Witness: A Journal for the Members and Friends of the Institute of Charity*, special edition, n. 23 (July 2008).

Abercrombie, Nigel, *The Life and Work of Edmund Bishop* (London: Longmans, 1959).

Bishop, E., *Liturgica Historica* (Oxford: Clarendon Press, 1918).

Belsito, A.A., *Rosmini Today: The Five Wounds of Holy Church: A Presentation* (Carlton, Nottingham: Rosminian Publications, 2014).

Gunter, Paul, *Edmund Bishop and the Genius of the Roman Rite*, Excerptum (Pontificum Athaneum S. Anselmi de Urbe, Pontificum Institutum Liturgicum: Rome, 2006).

Hill, John Michael, *Antonio Rosmini: Persecuted Prophet* (Leominster: Gracewing, 2014).

Leetham, Claude, *Rosmini: Priest, Philosopher and Patriot* (London: Longmans, Green & Co., 1957).

Chapter 8

THE TWENTIETH-CENTURY LITURGICAL MOVEMENT

Alcuin Reid

The origins of the liturgical movement

Any study of the liturgical movement in twentieth-century Western Catholicism must be grounded in the nineteenth-century liturgical revivals out of which it grew.

These revivals were multifaceted, ranging from the somewhat romantic revival of gothic liturgical architecture led in France by Eugène Viollet-le-Duc (1814–79) and promoted in England and beyond by Augustus Welby Pugin (1812–52), the facilitation of greater understanding of the liturgical rites through the increasing publication of books containing the liturgical texts in Latin and vernacular translation, and the equally romantic and highly successful restoration of monastic life in France by Dom Prosper Guéranger (1805–75), resulting in the Benedictine Congregation of Solesmes which grew rapidly in continental Europe, arriving in England at the beginning of the twentieth century, and which has had a lasting impact on the Sacred Liturgy in the West to this day. The liturgical sensibility that formed an integral component of the Anglican Oxford Movement ought to be noted also.

The essence of Catholic nineteenth-century liturgical revival was what we may call "liturgical piety," i.e., that Christ's faithful would ordinarily find the necessary nourishment for Christian life through conscious connection with and contemplation of the faith of the Church as it is celebrated in the liturgical rites and prayers throughout the annual round of seasons and feasts of the liturgical year, taking due priority over the practice of an unrelated, however worthy, devotional exercise.

This assertion of the primacy of the Sacred Liturgy in the spiritual life was necessary due to the post-Reformation ascendency of the *devotio moderna* with its individualistic spiritual practices—so congenial for Renaissance man—with their somewhat a-liturgical foci. The liturgy had in some ways been relegated to the status of simply one devotion amongst others. Sometimes it was seen as a duty to be accomplished before one could attend more properly to one's spiritual life through mental prayer.

Dom Guéranger's popular fifteen-volume *L'Année Liturgique* demonstrates the intentions of the proponents of liturgical piety. The Preface to this work, first published in French in 1841 and widely translated (English 1867; German 1875; Italian 1884),[1] which may be described as nothing less than a popular manual of liturgical formation structured on the Church's seasons and feasts, including the liturgical texts, translations, and commentary, asserts: "Liturgical prayer would soon become powerless, were the faithful not to take a real share in it, or, at least not to associate themselves to it in [the] heart. It can heal and save the world, but only on the condition that it be understood."[2] He then appealed: "Open your hearts, children of the Catholic Church, and come and pray the prayer of your Mother,"[3] giving voice to the spirit of the somewhat disparate efforts of nineteenth-century liturgical revival—and articulating what would become the fundamental principle of the subsequent liturgical movement.

It is important to note the fundamentally pastoral nature of this revival. Some twentieth-century scholars have dismissed the efforts of Pugin, Guéranger, et al., as 'tainted' by romanticism for past ages. Such criticism is disingenuous. Is love for what is true, beautiful and good—even of an idealized past—an intrinsically pejorative reality? Howsoever inspired by the past, these men asserted the efficacy of the liturgy (and its architecture, music, etc.) to raise ordinary hearts and minds to God in the age in which they lived, to the true worship of God and thereby facilitate evangelical witness in the world. They would not have described their efforts as "pastoral" in the somewhat self-conscious way this term would be employed in the late twentieth century; nevertheless, pastoral they indeed were.

It is also important to acknowledge the theology—more specifically the ecclesiology—initially implicit and gradually more explicit, in the efforts to reconnect people with the liturgical life of the Church. This was articulated by Antonio Rosmini (1797–1855), in his theology of the Church as the Mystical Body of Christ and of the common priesthood of all the baptized: upon this basis he promoted active and conscious participation of all in the liturgy.

So too, the growth of and interest in historical liturgical scholarship is significant. The English autodidact and Catholic layman, Edmund Bishop (1846–1917), stands out, as does the Henry Bradshaw Society (predominantly, though not exclusively, of Anglican origin), founded in 1890 for the purpose of editing and publishing rare liturgical texts. The growth of academic interest in and work on the history of the liturgy, by no means an exclusively Anglophone phenomenon, served to increase an appreciation of the breadth and riches of the Western liturgical tradition. Whilst this work, somewhat "neutral" in respect of questions of reform that would arise in the twentieth century, was at one remove from the popular level at which the likes of Guéranger directed his efforts, the corpus of material it produced and the historical awareness it generated laid foundations upon which later generations would build.

The beginning of the liturgical movement

The election to the papacy of Giuseppe Melchiore Cardinal Sarto as Pope Pius X (1835; 1903–14), whose ministry as a priest and bishop had been largely pastoral and who had promoted initiatives inspired by Solesmes, lent to the hitherto somewhat disparate efforts at liturgical revival the support of papal authority. In one of his first acts, the new pope addressed what he saw as the problem of sacred music in the liturgy. His motu proprio *Tra le sollecutidine* of November 22, 1903 articulated the conviction that:

> It being our ardent desire to see the true Christian spirit restored in every respect and preserved by all the faithful, we deem it necessary to provide before everything else for the sanctity and dignity of the temple, in which the faithful assemble for the object of acquiring this spirit from its indispensable fount, which is the active participation in the holy mysteries and in the public and solemn prayer of the Church.[4]

The articulation of this principle—that the "true Christian spirit" is acquired from the "indispensible fount" of the "active participation in the holy mysteries and in the public and solemn prayer of the Church"—was the cornerstone upon which the twentieth-century liturgical movement would be built.

Its architect was a "spiritual grandson" of Dom Guéranger, Dom Lambert Beauduin (1873–1960), a Belgian priest who entered the young Benedictine Abbey of Mont-César in 1906 and who, in the course of his formation, underwent a transformation which showed him the primary place of the Sacred Liturgy in the spiritual life and which set him 'on fire' within.

This flamed into a zeal in Beauduin to the extent that, whilst yet a junior monk and a young priest, he sought to enlist the support of the abbots at the General Chapter of the Solesmes Congregation in July 1909 in the promotion of liturgical piety as the Church's primary spirituality—not necessarily a difficult task if one remembers Dom Guéranger's principles—but also in its widespread promotion at the popular level. Following Pius X, he argued that all, not just monks, should live from this "indispensible fount," and proposed that monasteries should initiate a revival in their own liturgical formation and life (including the relegation of non-liturgical devotions to a secondary place, outside of choir), by facilitating the participation of people in the monastic liturgy, and through their publications and other apostolic activities.

Beauduin followed this with an appeal *ad extra* at the September 1909 Catholic Congress at Malines, calling for practical measures aimed at widespread comprehension of and participation in the liturgical rites of the Church. His observation that "thus all the faithful will be required to give up the recitation of private prayers during the different liturgical rites,"[5] is perhaps a telling indictment of the prevailing disconnection between liturgy and the spiritual life of his day. It is worth underlining that Beauduin's vision was by no means limited to the rite of Mass: the promotion of the praying of some of the Divine Office by the faithful, as well as the liturgical celebration of at least Sunday vespers, were seen as integral.

Aided by a sympathetic monastic infrastructure, Beauduin's initiative rapidly became a movement which organized "Liturgical Weeks" designed to initiate and form secular clergy and others in liturgical principles, and share methods for their pastoral application, published further Latin-vernacular editions of liturgical rites as well as writings on the meaning and nature of the Sacred Liturgy, and occasioned the appearance of new journals in various languages.

Opposition to the liturgical movement

The nascent liturgical movement was not without its critics. Writing in the renowned French journal *Études* at the end of 1913, Fr Jean-Joseph Navatel SJ (1853–1935) mounted a lengthy and spirited defence not only of the validity, but also of the normative place in the spiritual life, of ordered individual meditation according to the methods developed in the early modern period.[6] According to Navatel, personal piety held historical priority and was of primary pastoral value.[7] Those who proposed liturgical piety as normative were guilty of supporting something with little more than "a very relative efficacy."[8] "The word "liturgy" presents to the mind a vague, indefinite perspective, rendering it capable of receiving practically everything that one wants to put into it,"[9] he asserted. He held that the work of formation to bring about the necessary conditions in which participation in solemn Mass is a more spiritually nourishing experience than participation in a low Mass was simply too difficult to attempt.[10]

Earlier in 1913, Dom Maurice Festugière (1870–1950), a monk of Maredsous, Belguim, had observed:

> The sons of St. Ignatius—as they are the first to recognise—draw their spiritual life from their meditation, and the object of this is very often (we do not say always and necessarily) without relation to the liturgy. For them the breviary is nothing more than a religious duty. In their eyes solemn Mass and sung vespers are no more than exceptions; they do not engage themselves in promoting these communal forms of prayer, which are so necessary for parish life.[11]

As Festugière makes clear, the liturgical movement asserted the *pastoral* priority of liturgical participation in the fullest possible celebration of the liturgy—it is this which is "so necessary for parish life." It is important to be clear that in its origins the reform promoted by the liturgical movement was of people's manner of approaching, and of the clergy's celebration of, the liturgical rites, and— significantly—not the reform of the rites themselves.[12] Though never translated, Festugière's *La Liturgie Catholique: Essai de Synthèse*, remains a valuable testament to the foundational principles of the liturgical movement and a significant exposition of liturgical theology and piety.

Beauduin replied to Navatel's critique in *Les Questions Liturgiques*, a newly-established journal intended for the liturgical formation of the clergy.[13] His article is worthy of close study, for its careful rebuttal of Navatel's claims with the assertion that "liturgical piety ... is the authentic and official piety of holy Church," as opposed to simply one of many approved forms of spirituality, and also for the autobiographical account Beauduin gives of his own conversion to liturgical piety.

The article also provided Beauduin with the occasion once again to assert the essence of the liturgical movement:

> To live the work of the redemption fully each day to the glory of the Heavenly Father in the concrete and authentic form that the holy Church has given ... through her eucharistic liturgy; to identify ourselves with our Mother, the Roman Church, and to accomplish our adoration and our prayers by her and for her; to sanctify and to offer to God the acts of each day and of each hour, enveloping them in the daily liturgy of the Mass and the breviary; in brief, to live with our Mother and thereby with Jesus Christ and with God, this interior life that the Church has organised for her children of which her rites, formulas and the liturgical cycle are the authentic vehicle; this is the fundamental activity of liturgical piety.[14]

One of Navatel's criticisms of the liturgical movement was that it promoted a specifically "Benedictine" spirituality just as the practice of ordered mental prayer as promoted by the Jesuits was "Ignatian." It is true—as the passage above illustrates—that the liturgical piety being promoted was thoroughly in harmony with classical Benedictine life, which is no doubt why it found so many monastic apostles. But Beauduin countered this attempt to relativize liturgical piety with the observation that "it is not Benedictine, but Catholic."[15] This claim to objectivity for liturgical piety, and its ecclesiological implications, ought not to go unnoticed.

Although this controversy was certainly not dispassionate—Beauduin concluded his reply to Navatel with the provocative request that the latter, when preaching the spirituality of his order in his retreats, also "consecrate one hour to the spiritual method of the holy Church"[16]—it served to clarify the fundamental aims of the liturgical movement and occasioned Beauduin's 1914 booklet *La Piété de L'Église*, which effectively become its theological and practical charter.

La Piété de L'Église—The charter of the liturgical movement

No study of the twentieth-century liturgical movement can be said to be complete without reference to Beauduin's *La Piété de L'Église*, first published in English in 1926 as *Liturgy: the Life of the Church*. This seminal text, firmly grounded in the principles of Guéranger and Pius X, articulates the theological bases of liturgical piety, discusses the factors mitigating against it (which are not altogether that different over a century later), and then turns to a proposal of practical means of implementing the liturgical movement. This text is indispensible reading for any serious student of the liturgy and of twentieth-century liturgical reform. It may also be said to furnish some fundamental criteria necessary for any assessment of the latter.

It is appropriate to allow the text to speak for itself. Beauduin writes:

> It is impossible, therefore, to overemphasise the fact that souls seeking God must associate themselves as intimately and as frequently as possible with all the manifestations of the hierarchical priestly life [the Liturgy] ... and which places them directly under the influence of the priesthood of Jesus Christ Himself.
>
> That is the primary law of the sanctity of souls. For all alike, wise and ignorant, infants and adults, lay and religious, Christians of the first and Christians of the twentieth century, leaders of an active or of a contemplative life, for *all the faithful of the Church without exception,* the greatest possible active and frequent participation in the priestly life of the visible hierarchy, according to the manner prescribed in the liturgical canons, is the *normal and infallible path* to a solid piety that is sane, abundant, and truly Catholic, that makes them children of their holy mother the Church in the fullest sense of this ancient and Christian phrase.[17]

Beauduin underlines the tangible—if not the incarnational—nature of the Sacred Liturgy, insisting that:

> The whole priestly influence is exercised on the members of the Church *only* by means of sensible, *authentic* forms, which are its vehicle. Formulas, readings, chants, rites, material elements, in short, all the externals of the Liturgy, are *indispensable* for sharing in the thoughts, the teachings, the acts of adoration, the sentiments, the graces which Christ and His visible priesthood destine for us. Hence, to minimise this visible contact under the pretext that the soul can then better achieve something interior, or that invisible communion suffices, is at the same time to diminish the priestly influence of the hierarchy and consequently the action of Christ in our souls.[18]

Thus, he asserts the vital importance of:

> The parish solemn Mass and of all collective manifestations of the Christian life; a faith, full of confidence and respect, in the rites of the sacraments and the sacramentals; the sanctification of the day of the Lord; the pious and collective celebration of the great events of the liturgical cycle; the life of our Lord, of the Virgin Mother, of the Saints, lived by *the whole Christian people* through the liturgical feasts; the spirit of penitence inculcated by Lent; knowledge of the Psalms, the Gospels, the Acts of the Apostles, the Epistles, the Sacred Scriptures in general, which form the fabric of the liturgical books; the cult of the dead, to which the Liturgy of the Church has given so Christian a character; the many wholesome practices which formerly transmitted to family and social life the

echo of the piety of the Church, and conserved in human society, now secularised, a deeply religious character; in a word, this constant affirmation of supernatural realities, which created a collective Catholic mentality and proclaimed here below the rights of the Most Holy Trinity ...[19]

For Beauduin the Liturgy has both an objectivity in tradition whilst being a living reality capable of development:

Above all the Liturgy is: 1. *One.* Unity of belief, of discipline, of common fellowship, must necessarily show itself in worship; and despite certain divergences the Liturgy is fundamentally, profoundly *one.* 2. *Traditional.* This unity must be realised also in point of time. The Church of today is the Church of all times and of all peoples; hence her Liturgy is traditional. This characteristic is so important that it receives precedence over that of uniformity, as is seen in the preservation of the Oriental rites. 3. *Living.* The former characteristic does not make of the Liturgy a fossilised antique, a museum curiosity. The Liturgy *lives* and unfolds itself also today and, because universal, is of the twentieth century as well as of the first. It lives and follows the dogmatic and organic developments of the Church herself.[20]

Beauduin presents a detailed "plan of action" for the implementation of these principles:

The central idea to be realised by the liturgical movement is the following: To have the Christian people all live the same spiritual life, to have them all nourished by the official worship of holy mother Church.

The means to be employed towards this end are of two kinds. The first have reference to the acts of worship itself; the others to the liturgical activity exercised outside these acts.

The Acts of Worship. In this field, the members of the liturgical movement desire to contribute with all their strength to the attainment of the following aims:

1. The active participation of the Christian people in the Holy Sacrifice of the Mass by means of understanding and following the liturgical rites and texts.
2. Emphasis of the importance of solemn Mass and of Sunday parish services, and assistance at the restoration of collective liturgical singing in the official gatherings of the faithful.
3. Seconding of all efforts to preserve or to re-establish the Vespers and Compline of the Sunday, and to give those services a place second only to that of the Holy Sacrifice of the Mass.
4. Acquaintance, and active association, with the rites and sacraments received or assisted at, and the spread of this knowledge among others.
5. Fostering a great respect for, and confidence in, the blessings of our Mother Church.

6. Restoration of the Liturgy of the Dead to a place of honour, observance of the custom of Vigils and Lauds, giving greater solemnity to the funeral services, and getting the faithful to assist thereat, thus efficaciously combating the dechristianising of the rite of the dead.

Liturgical Activity outside of cultural acts.[21] In this field there are four ways in which the members can assist at the furtherance of the liturgical movement:

A. *Piety*

1. Restoration to a place of honour among Christians of the traditional liturgical seasons: Advent, Christmas Time, Lent, Easter Time, octaves of feasts, feasts of the Blessed Virgin, the Apostles, and the great missionary saints of our religion.
2. The basing of our daily private devotions, meditation, reading, etc., on the daily instructions of the Liturgy, the Psalms, the other liturgical books, and the fundamental dogmas of Catholic worship.
3. Reanimation and sublimation of the devotions dear to the people by nourishing them at the source of the Liturgy.

B. *Study*

1. Promotion of the scientific study of the Catholic Liturgy.
2. Popularisation of the scientific knowledge in special reviews and publications.
3. Promotion of the study and, above all, the practice of liturgical prayers in educational institutions.
4. Aiming to give regular liturgical education to circles, associations, etc., and to employ all the customary methods of popularisation to this end.

C. *Arts*

1. Promoting the application of all the instructions of Pius X in his *Motu proprio* on Church music.
2. Aiming to have the artists that are called to exercise a sacred art, architecture, painting, sculpture, etc., receive an education that will give them an understanding of the spirit and the rules of the Church's Liturgy.
3. Making known to artists and writers the fruitful inspiration to art that the Church offers in her Liturgy.

D. *Propaganda*

1. Using all means to spread popular liturgical publications that show the import of the principal part of the Liturgy: Sunday Mass, Vespers, Sacraments, Liturgy of the Dead, etc.

2. Reawakening the old liturgical traditions in the home, that link domestic joys with the calendar of the Church, and using for this end especially the musical works composed for such purposes.

To all Catholics we address a burning appeal in favour of the activities that aim to realise as far as possible the program of liturgical restoration we have here outlined."[22]

This practical charter of the liturgical movement speaks eloquently, today as then.

Hermeneutical approaches to the texts of the early liturgical movement

It is apposite to consider the question of the hermeneutic to be applied to texts such as those of Beauduin and other pioneers of the liturgical movement. This is a particularly important issue given that often these works are read with a vision filtered by the light of the liturgical Constitution of the Second Vatican Council and even dazzled by the glare of the liturgical watershed which followed it.

In an admittedly popular work—but no less important for so being—*Keys to the Council: Unlocking the Teaching of Vatican II*, we read: "The many ideas advanced by Beauduin prior to the First World War were embraced by many others in the liturgical renewal movement and they were received as the guiding principles of the liturgical reform undertaken by the Second Vatican Council."[23] If by this the authors meant the ideas advanced in *Liturgy: The Life of the Church*, they would be correct. However the sentence quoted comes after a litany of unreferenced assertions that Beauduin was proposing numerous ritual and architectural reforms including the reception of Holy Communion in the hand whilst standing and under both species. A thorough review of these assertions belongs elsewhere,[24] however they serve to illustrate the problem frequently arising in both popular and scholarly works.[25]

This tendency to assert that the efforts of these pioneers implicitly or even explicitly justify almost any liturgical reform from the latter part of the twentieth century is tenuous scholarship indeed and such a hermeneutic must be rejected. These texts must be read in their context. We must be good historians and stand in the shoes of those who wrote them in the hope of reconnecting the spiritual life of the Church of their day with the Sacred Liturgy, not of reforming its rites. One of Beauduin's contemporaries, Dom Bernard Botte (1883–1980), underlines this reality:

We should note that the liturgical movement, at its beginning, was not a reformist movement. Dom Beauduin knew very well that there were some cobwebs on that venerable monument called Liturgy. One day or another these would have to be dusted away. But he did not consider this as essential and, at any rate, it was not his business . . . He regarded the Liturgy as a traditional given which we first of all had to try to understand.[26]

The hermeneutic proposed when approaching the earlier writings of the liturgical movement (up to the 1940s), is one of allowing the texts to stand as they were written and to understand them as efforts to reform people and practice, not rites. To see them as strategic attempts to lay the foundations for later ritual change is to read into them that which is simply not there—an error made by scholars of differing outlooks.[27]

Scholars and other writers who wish to use these early works to justify or to criticize later developments must make the necessary distinctions between the author's intentions and the use made of the work, always asking whether such uses are in accord with the author's principles. Such critical reading will furnish much insight into the nature of the liturgy, liturgical piety and true liturgical development.

To read these texts thus is to allow their vision further to shed light today. Certainly their ideas and principles had influence as the twentieth century progressed and the liturgical movement did indeed begin to speak of and work towards ritual reform—Pius X foresaw the need for reform of the missal and breviary as early as 1911. However, we can neither understand nor critically study these later phenomena if we do not approach the foundations of the liturgical movement with the correct hermeneutic.

Seminal texts in the study of the liturgical movement

There are immense riches in the literature generated by the early liturgical movement. Many writings remain in their original languages, principally French and German as well as Italian, though a number are available in English translation. The serious student is wise not to ignore the large corpus of untranslated material.

In particular, the fifteen volumes of the *Cours et Conferences des Semaines Liturgiques* generated by the "Liturgical Weeks" held in 1912 and 1913, and then from 1924 until 1937 and in 1948, merit attention.[28] In them one finds contributions by Beauduin, Botte, Blessed Columba Marmion (1858–1923), Dom Fernand Cabrol (1855–1937), Dom Pierre de Puniet (1877–1941), Désiré-Joseph Cardinal Mercier (1851–1926), the young Father Joseph Cardjin (1882–1967; created cardinal in 1965), Dom Bernard Capelle (1884–1961), Dom Olivier Rousseau (1898–1984), Msgr Camille Callewaert (1866–1943), Dom Gaspar Lefèbvre (1880–1966), and numerous other scholars and pastoral clergy addressing historical and practical questions. The topics addressed—all grounded in the principle of active participation articulated by Pius X—range from how to form secondary school students in the liturgy to how to teach a working class parish to sing Gregorian chant. These volumes are a testament to the vision and widespread efforts of many clergy and religious in seeking to form others in liturgical piety and have much to teach us about the liturgical movement, certainly, but also about the nature of the Sacred Liturgy, active participation, and what is truly pastoral liturgy.

The published proceedings from the North American National Liturgical Weeks, which commenced in 1940 and continued until 1969,[29] are a similar though later witness to the efforts of the liturgical movement, demonstrating widespread efforts in promoting liturgical piety and the emergence of questions of liturgical reform, though the latter is clearly a secondary matter. Contributors include Msgr Martin Hellriegel (1890–1981), Gerald Ellard SJ (1894–1963), Hans Anscar Reinhold (1897–1968), Msgr Reynold Hillenbrand (1904–79), and a number of religious women and laity—all addressing practical ways of bringing about active participation in the Sacred Liturgy through formation and various pastoral initiatives as well as exploring related theological and historical questions. That the latter volumes are contemporaneous with the liturgical reforms promulgated from the 1950s onward renders them important historical sources for understanding these reforms, particularly in their grass-roots application. The final volumes witness to the divergence of some activists from the original ideals of the liturgical movement.

But we must return to earlier texts. One cannot ignore the writings of Idelfons Herwegen (1874–1946), Blessed Alfredo Idelfonso Schuster (1880–1954), Emmanuel Caronti (1882–1966), Pius Parsch (1884–1954), Romano Guardini (1885–1968), and Dom Virgil Michel (1888–1938). It is these, together with those of Beauduin, to which we must turn if we are to comprehend the liturgical movement.

Amongst these, Guardini's *The Spirit of the Liturgy*—originally published in 1918 by Herwegen—looms large as a profound treatise on the fundamental place of the Sacred Liturgy in the spiritual life. Its conclusion is indicative of its beauty and depth:

> In the liturgy the Logos has been assigned its fitting precedence over the will. Hence the wonderful power of relaxation proper to the liturgy, and its deep reposefulness. Hence its apparent consummation entirely in the contemplation, adoration and glorification of Divine Truth. This is also the explanation of the fact that the liturgy is apparently so little disturbed by the petty troubles and needs of everyday life. It also accounts for the comparative rareness of its attempts at direct teaching and direct inculcation of virtue. The liturgy has something in itself reminiscent of the stars, of their eternally fixed and even course, of their inflexible order, of their profound silence, and of the infinite space in which they are poised. It is only in appearance, however, that the liturgy is so detached and untroubled by the actions and strivings and moral position of men. For in reality it knows that those who live by it will be true and spiritually sound, and at peace to the depths of their being; and that when they leave its sacred confines to enter life they will be men of courage.[30]

Guardini's less well-known, but no less beautiful work, *Sacred Signs*, illustrates the simple, humble, and practical applications of this vision. Of the simple act of kneeling he writes:

> When you bend the knee, let it not be a mere hasty gesture. Give it a soul! But the soul of kneeling, of a genuflection, is the bowing down of the innermost heart in

reverence and awe before God. When you come into the church and before you leave, or when you pass the altar or the Blessed Sacrament, then kneel; let your knee really rest on the ground. Do it slowly, and let your heart respond, so that the outward and inward act may proclaim the greatness of God.

That is humility, and it is truth; and every time you do it, it will do your soul good.[31]

Here we glimpse the true spirit of the liturgical movement: the promotion of conscious unity of heart, mind, and body in the liturgical worship of Almighty God—in as simple an act as a genuflection. As a lecture given by Herwegen in 1912 makes clear, the nature and purpose of this connection is that transformation of the person in Christ upon which all of Christian life and mission is based: "Whosoever lives the liturgical life of the Church according to her venerable and hallowed ordering, will find therein all the grades of perfection; his life will become a work of beauty, and will attain its everlasting value in its progressive transfiguration."[32]

The periodicals to which the movement gave rise are another important resource for study. These chronicle the movement's ideals and practical efforts across the globe. They include: *Questions liturgiques et paroissiales* (French, 1911), *La Vie et Les Arts Liturgiques* (French, 1913), *Rivista Liturgica* (Italian, 1914), *Ons Liturgisch Tidschrift* (Dutch, 1916), *Ecclesia Orans* (German, 1918), *Bollettino Liturgico* (Italian, 1923), *Orate Fratres* (English, 1926), *Opus Dei* (Portuguese, 1926), *Bibel und Liturgie* (German, 1926), *L'Artisan Liturgique* (French, 1927), *Liturgische Zeitschrift* (German, 1929), *Mysterium Christi* (Polish, 1929), *Liturgy* (English, 1929), *Liturgical Arts Quarterly* (English, 1932); *Liturgia* (Italian, 1933), *Liturgisches Leben* (German, 1934), *Living Parish* (English, 1941), *Liturgia* (Spanish, 1944), *La Maison-Dieu* (French, 1945), and *Ora et Labora* (Portuguese, 1953). One must also include the earlier *Ephemerides Liturgicae* (Italian, 1887). The unexplored material amassed in these volumes demands further scholarly attention.

Amongst these *Orate Fratres* (entitled *Worship* from December 1951) is of singular importance for English-speakers, not only because it chronicles the activity of the liturgical movement in the USA and the wider Anglophone world, but also because it presented ongoing reports of activities beyond these bounds and at times published important articles appearing in other journals in English translation. To read through its volumes from the beginning is instructive and will give a student an accurate perspective when considering the ideals and initiatives they chronicle. As with the National Liturgical Weeks, later volumes are indicative of a change in priorities if not direction—which itself invites critical study.

The periodicals are perhaps the best testament of what an American Jesuit described in the 1930s as the movement's desire to bring about widespread formation in "the nature of corporate worship in general" and "the nature and rite of each office in particular,"[33] requiring "no small amount of far-reaching and detailed instruction in season and out of season."[34] This formation encompassed liturgical history and theology, art, architecture, music, and more. As but a taste of this material, students would do well to ponder the brief article "Winged

Words" of Justine Ward (1879–1975), published in the first volume of *Orate Fratres* in 1926.[35]

A passage from an autobiography indicates another important source for the study of the liturgical movement:

> Every new step into the Liturgy was a great event for me. Each new book I was given was something precious to me, and I could not dream of anything more beautiful. It was a riveting adventure to move by degrees into the mysterious world of the Liturgy which was being enacted before us and for us there on the altar. It was becoming more and more clear to me that here I was encountering a reality that no one had simply thought up, a reality that no official authority or great individual had created. This mysterious fabric of texts and actions had grown from the faith of the Church over the centuries. It bore the whole weight of history within itself, and yet, at the same time, it was much more than the product of human history. Every century had left its mark upon it ... Not everything was logical. Things sometimes got complicated and it was not always easy to find one's way. But precisely this is what made the whole edifice wonderful, like one's own home. Naturally, the child I then was did not grasp every aspect of this, but I started down the road of the Liturgy, and this became a continuous process of growth into a grand reality transcending all particular individuals and generations, a reality that became an occasion for me of ever-new amazement and discovery. The inexhaustible reality of the Catholic Liturgy has accompanied me though all phases of life, and so I shall have to speak of it time and time again.[36]

The author is, of course, Joseph Cardinal Ratzinger (1927–; Pope Benedict XVI 2005–13), recalling the gift of his first bi-lingual missal. Such missals and other booklets containing the liturgical texts, vernacular translations, and introductions to and explanations of the rites were the successors of Guéranger's *L'Année Liturgique*, and were widely promoted by the liturgical movement. Much energy and scholarship, as well as love, care, and attention was expended in producing volumes whose contents and craftsmanship were instruments of widespread liturgical formation, as Ratzinger testifies. They too warrant scholarly consideration.

The liturgical movement and theology

In its origins, the liturgical movement was not self-consciously theological in that it was not primarily advocating a new theology. Rather, it was recalling people to the fundamental and necessary connection with the living and ongoing celebration of the *ecclesia*—of Christ's saving mysteries *in actu*—that is the Sacred Liturgy and out of which theological reflection arises. In this the movement was implicitly fostering a new theological outlook, of the liturgy as *theologia prima*. The claim to the liturgy's primacy and objectivity in the spiritual life naturally asserted its theological primacy.

As noted above, the nineteenth-century Italian Antonio Rosmini based his efforts to promote liturgical piety on the theology of the Church as the Mystical Body of Christ and of the common priesthood of all the baptized. Both took root in the twentieth century, the former culminating in the 1943 encyclical letter of Pope Pius XII (1876; 1939–1958), *Mystici Corporis Christi*. The latter was underlined in Pius XII's 1947 encyclical *Mediator Dei* and took its rightful place in the 1964 Dogmatic Constitution *Lumen Gentium* of the Second Vatican Council. The theology of the Church as "the People of God" may be said to share these origins.

These theologies and their ecclesiology informed and grounded the ongoing efforts of the liturgical movement to promote liturgical piety. In this we see that these efforts are not distinct from what has become known as the twentieth-century theological *Ressourcement* movement—in reality belonging to the early and middle decades of that century—with its emphasis on a return to biblical and patristic texts as sources for renewal. Much study remains to be done on the influence of each movement on the other, particularly in respect of liturgical reform, and some studies which have appeared take positions utterly foreign to the leaders of either movement.[37]

Two specific theological developments of the liturgical movement are noteworthy. The first is the mystery theology, the *Mysterienlehre,* of Dom Odo Casel (1886–1948). In the 1930s (published in English in 1962 as *The Mystery of Christian Worship*), Casel asserted:

> What is necessary is a living, active sharing in the redeeming deed of Christ … For this purpose the Lord has given us the mysteries of worship: the sacred actions which we perform, but which, at the same time, the Lord performs upon us by his priests' service in the Church. Through these actions it becomes possible for us to share most intensively and concretely in a kind of immediate contact, yet most spiritually too, in God's saving acts.[38]

Accordingly Christ acts today ordinarily through the mystery of the Sacred Liturgy, through the celebration of the sacraments and the unfolding of the entire liturgical year. The objectivity Casel thus gave to the liturgy appeared stark at the time and it provoked controversy which continued well after *Mediator Dei*. His theology—one of the tributaries to that of the Second Vatican Council—deserves revisiting in any twenty-first century liturgical *ressourcement*.[39]

Out of this, and indebted also to *Mystici Corporis Christi* and *Mediator Dei*, emerged the theology of the liturgy as the "Paschal Mystery" of the death and resurrection of Christ. This theological approach was new and exciting to many, and quite different from the prevailing neo-scholastic approach. *Le Mystère Paschal* of Louis Bouyer (1913–2004), published in French in 1947 and in English in 1951, stands as its fundamental text, augmented by his 1955 *Liturgical Piety* (published in England in 1956 as *Life and Liturgy*).

Certainly, this theology may be seen as a sound development that enhances the understanding of the liturgy as the ongoing communal, or better, the *ecclesial* celebration and immersion of all the baptized into the entire mystery of Christ's life *and* saving death *and* resurrection. Whilst some have regarded it as a de-emphasis or even a denial of the theology of the Mass as a propitiatory sacrifice, the unbloody re-enactment of the Sacrifice of Calvary,[40] of itself and at the time this development can be said to be a legitimate theological enrichment. It was enthusiastically adopted in the drafting of the Council's schema on the Sacred Liturgy. Some of the liturgical uses to which it and other theological developments were later put, however, raise questions for study elsewhere.

The liturgical movement and ritual reform

The liturgical movement is perhaps best known—and sometimes deprecated—for the liturgical reforms enacted during the 1950s, 1960s, and beyond. However, we must not allow the tail to wag the dog: the liturgical movement was primarily about the establishment of a strong and vital liturgical life throughout the Church where the fullest possible celebration of the Church's liturgy as handed on in tradition, and liturgical piety, would be the norm. Only secondarily and in that context did questions of liturgical reform arise—as its history makes clear.

Furthermore, the liturgical movement properly so called was rightly cautious about liturgical reform. It knew well the issue of whether "modern man" could connect with liturgical tradition or not. As Guardini would ask in his famous 1964 letter: is modern man "capable of a liturgical act?"[41] Thus the movement considered whether people could be formed so as to profit from participation in the Sacred Liturgy—a long path to travel requiring much sustained effort—or whether the liturgy itself should be adapted to the exigencies of modern man—a shorter and easier route to take by far. The critical question is: do both paths lead to the same destination, to that end desired by Guéranger, Pius X, Beauduin, et al.? As one writer asserted in 1938, "'before doing something,' before 'acting,' we should concern ourselves about *being* . . . before you think of the liturgical movement, *be fully liturgical yourself* . . ."[42]

The second and third chapters of my work *The Organic Development of the Liturgy* deal extensively with these questions, and it is impossible to reproduce its content or bibliography here: what follows assumes access to that documentation. However, it is necessary for any student of this period to be aware of at least the key moments in the history of twentieth-century liturgical reform up to the Second Vatican Council.

Pius X is the first, if not the fundamental liturgical reformer of the twentieth century.[43] His substantial 1911 reform of the Roman Breviary, based on longstanding pastoral considerations, was also a "root and branch reform,"[44] which, as Robert Taft SJ (1932–) has argued, "for anyone with a sense of the history of the office . . . was a shocking departure from almost universal Christian Tradition."[45] In short, elements of this reform were based on somewhat antiquarian and pastorally expedient principles which were imposed by a papal authority that had grown somewhat positivist: whatever was ordered was to be accepted as correct regardless of any considerations arising from liturgical tradition.

This is a crucial moment in twentieth-century liturgical reform, indeed in liturgical history, and it too merits further study. As the Roman breviary was at the time primarily a clerical book, and as the Holy See's anti-Modernist strictures were in full-flight, Pius X's actions passed largely—though not entirely—without criticism. Yet in this reform the principle that the Roman Pontiff could do what he wished in respect of liturgical tradition saw the light of day.

As noted above, Pius X foresaw that liturgical reform would continue and embrace the missal also, speaking of the formation of a commission to be entrusted with this work. The First World War and his own death in 1914 forestalled that eventuality. The literature of the following decades does not suggest that either Rome or liturgical movement activists were particularly anxious about realizing such a programme in the short term, though the Holy See continued its promotion of liturgical piety and authorized various minor reforms as well as increasingly granting permission for the use of the vernacular.[46]

What the liturgical movement did do was increasingly to discuss the possibility of liturgical reform, and the principles upon which it should be based. One such discussion took place in the pages of *Orate Fratres* between 1936–40 and illustrates differing and even one questionable approach to liturgical reform.[47] Their perspectives are instructive. So too are the "Normes practiques pour les réformes liturgiques" articulated by Beauduin in 1945 for the inaugural issue of *La Maison-Dieu*, which, far from being a call for and radical recasting of rites, sought to recognize the possibility of liturgical development and articulate bases upon which it could proceed.[48]

In an attempt to facilitate participation in the liturgy, some, including Guardini, Herwegen, and Parsch, adopted and promoted a reformed *manner of celebrating* the rites—bold steps for the early twentieth century. These changes often included dialogue between priest and people at low Mass, the priest celebrating *versus populum*, a use of the vernacular beyond that currently permitted, etc. In these initiatives, which gained attention and popularity, it is important to note that the individuals respected the structure and content of the liturgical rites (the missal, its lectionary, the calendar, the breviary, etc.) as a given. They did not reform the liturgical rites themselves, but sought appropriate means of connecting people with it—means which invite critical examination and which demonstrate some of the insights and errors of the period.

It was in this context that the Sacred Congregation of Rites formally resumed consideration of liturgical reform in 1946 and that Pius XII established a commission for liturgical reform, whose members were appointed in 1948. The same year "a bold move . . . a free—and risky—undertaking by the young editor-in-chief" of *Ephemerides Liturgicæ* was undertaken. He addressed a questionnaire on liturgical reform to the journal's collaborators, summarizing the responses in an article the following year, "Per una riforma liturgica generale," publicly asserting that the time had come to revise the liturgical books. The editor was Annibale Bugnini CM (1912–82), the most prominent of the younger liturgical movement activists for whom ritual reform increasingly became imperative.[49]

Bugnini was appointed secretary of Pius XII's commission in 1948, the work of which commission was *sub secreto*. Yet his editorial role for a prominent if not semi-official liturgical journal gave him a public forum in which to raise and promote ideas.[50] This dynamic—of ongoing official consideration of reform in secret with some of the same people engaging in 'consciousness-raising' through journals, national and international congresses and study days (and in due course themselves being influenced by the *desiderata* raised in these public forums)—is a key feature of the liturgical movement's engagement with liturgical reform from 1948 onward. To study one aspect without taking into account its relation with the other is insufficient, and the literature of the latter is vast.

In a study of the work of Pius XII's commission,[51] there are two fundamental sources. The first, *La riforma liturgica di Pio XII*, published its secret documentation. The second, *The Development of the Liturgical Reform*, chronicles the involvement of Ferdinando Antonelli OFM (1896–1993; created Cardinal in 1983)—a member of the commission from its inception—and includes a substantial appendix containing the minutes of the commission's meetings in English translation. Bugnini's own work, *The Reform of the Liturgy: 1948–1975*, devotes but few pages to this commission.

The reforms prepared by the commission, amongst which the 1955 reform of Holy Week looms large—though those to the calendar (1955) and the code of rubrics (1960) are also significant—require careful study. Aspects, such as returning the time of the celebration of the paschal vigil to the night before Easter Sunday, or the increasing insistence that the celebrant listen to readings sung by the deacon or subdeacon rather than also reciting them himself, arise from sound principles. In others, particularly in the radical recasting of the Good Friday liturgy, it is possible to identify the influence of pastoral expediency, antiquarian enthusiasms, and something of an itch for innovation in an attempt to bring about active participation in rites somewhat hastily simplified in order to achieve that end.

The 1958 Instruction of the Congregation of Rites on Sacred Music and Liturgy, *De musica sacra*, stands out amongst the reforms and enthusiasms of these years as a monument to the ideals of the liturgical movement and its principles. It was seen as an official summary and recapitulation of them addressed in the manner of a legislative document in order to bring about a measure of uniformity in liturgical initiatives throughout the Western Church. Key figures emphasized its importance, almost acclaiming it as the consummation of the movement's aims.[52] Antonelli, in an early commentary originally published in *L'Osservatore Romano*, asserted:

> If [what is set forth in this Instruction] is accomplished, the true, sound liturgical movement will take on a new life, some less praiseworthy exaggerations will be eliminated, and all the faithful—this is the most important point—will be brought ever nearer to the fountains of grace which the Liturgy opens up to them, while the Liturgy itself will become for the Christian people, as it was for centuries, the great school of supernatural life and holiness.[53]

Pius XII's commission for liturgical reform continued its work under St. John XXIII (1881; 1958–63), but was overtaken by the work of the Liturgical Preparatory

Commission for the Second Vatican Council, which included many of the same personnel. A study of their activity belongs elsewhere.[54]

Conclusion

Perhaps the most crucial question in the study of the twentieth-century liturgical movement is whether, in pursuing ritual reform, it outran itself and lost sight of its original, moderate pastoral goals. Too many studies treat it as a mere forerunner of the reforms effected after the Second Vatican Council. The historical reality, however, is that those engaged in the movement never expected a Council or an ensuing radical liturgical reform, but worked for modest reform of the liturgy as received in tradition.

When John XXIII announced the Council in January 1959, the changes that would in fact be effected in little more than a decade were beyond the wildest fantasies of even Bugnini. Yet, as Archbishop Bugnini recalled many years later of his 1948–9 questionnaire and article on liturgical reform: "fortune favours the brave."[55] The opportunity that arose through the Council to push liturgical reform further is thus another historical factor for consideration.

In 1968 Bouyer raised this question starkly:

> We must speak plainly: there is practically no liturgy worthy of the name today in the Catholic Church. Yesterday's liturgy was hardly more than an embalmed cadaver. What people call liturgy today is little more than this same cadaver decomposed … Perhaps in no other area is there a greater distance (and even formal opposition) between what the Council worked out and what we actually have. Under the pretext of "adapting" the liturgy, people have simply forgotten that it can only be the traditional expression of the Christian mystery in all its spring-like fullness. I have perhaps spent the greater part of my priestly life in attempting to explain it. But now I have the impression, and I am not alone, that those who took it upon themselves to apply (?) the Council's directives on this point have turned their backs deliberately on what Beauduin, Casel and Pius Parsch had set out to do, and to which I had tried vainly to add some small contribution of my own.[56]

It is a question which serious students of the twentieth-century liturgical movement must consider. In doing so they would do well to accept the challenge Bouyer issued on the same page as his lament: "When one has thrown everything out, people will have to return to these sources."[57]

Notes

1 Cf. Cuthbert Johnson OSB, *Prosper Guéranger (1805–1875): A Liturgical Theologian: An Introduction to his liturgical writings and work,* Studia Anselmiana 89 (Rome: Pontificio Ateneo S. Anselmo, 1984), p. 429.

2 Prosper Guéranger, Laurence Shepherd (trans.), *The Liturgical Year: Advent,* 2nd edn (Dublin: Duffy, 1870), pp. 6–7.

3 Translation from Johnson, *Prosper Guéranger,* p. 350.

4 NL, p. 4.

5 "Ainsi, tous les fidèles seront amenés à renoncer pendant les offices divers à la récitation des prières privées." André Haquin, *Dom Lambert Beauduin et le Renouveau Liturgique* (Gembloux: Éditions Duclot, 1970), p. 241.

6 Jean-Joseph Navatel SJ, "L'Apostolat Liturgique et La Piété Personnelle," *Études* 20 (1913), pp. 449–76.

7 See: ibid., pp. 462, 465–6.

8 "... qu'une efficacité très relative," ibid., p. 451.

9 "... le mot de liturgie ouvre devant l'esprit une perspective vague, indéfinie, susceptible de recevoir presque tout ce que l'on veut y mettre," ibid., p. 452.

10 See: ibid., p. 455. n. 1.

11 "Les fils de saint Ignace—ils sont les premiers à le reconnaitre—tirent leur vie spirituelle de leur médiation; el l'objet de celle-ci est très souvent (Nous ne disons-pas: toujours et nécessairement.) sans relation avec la liturgie. Le bréviaire ne représente pour eux qu'*un devoir* de religion. La grand'messe et les vêpres chantées ne sont à leurs yeux qu'actes tout à fait exceptionnels: ils ne s'emploieront donc pas à favoriser ces formes sociales de la prière, pourtant nécessaires à la vie paroissiale." Maurice Festugière, *La Liturgie Catholique: Essai de Synthèse* (Maredsous: Abbaye de Maredsous, 1913), p. 41.

12 Keith Pecklers' assertion in "*Ressourcement* and the Renewal of Catholic Liturgy: On Celebrating the New Rite" in Gabriel Flynn & Paul D. Murray, eds, *Ressourcement: A Movement for Renewal in Twentieth Century Catholic Theology* (Oxford: Oxford University Press, 2012), pp. 318–32 (p. 323), that Dom Beauduin "lamented the fact that the liturgy of the day deprived the faithful of drinking from that deeper source as nourishment for the Christian mission" is groundless, most particularly in the light of the source upon which he draws (see: "La Vraie Prière de l'Église" – Communication de Dom L. Beauduin au Congrès des Œuvres Catholiques de Malines – 23 Septembre 1909 in Haquin, *Dom Lambert Beauduin et le Renouveau Liturgique,* pp. 238–41). Beauduin is criticizing the lack of connection of the faithful with the liturgy, not the liturgy itself.

13 Lambert Beauduin, "Mise au point nécessaire: Réponse au R. P. Navatel," *Les Questions Liturgiques,* t. 4 (1913–14), pp. 7, 84–104.

14 "Vivre chaque jour pleinement l'œuvre de la Rédemption, à la gloire du Père céleste, dans la forme concrète et authentique que la sainte Église lui a donnée par sa liturgie eucharistique; nous identifier avec notre Mère l'Église romaine et accomplir par elle et pour elle nos adorations et nos prières ; sanctifier et offrir à Dieu les actes de chaque jour et de chaque heure, en les enveloppant dans la liturgie quotidienne de la messe et du Bréviaire ; bref, vivre avec notre Mère et dès lors avec Jésus-Christ et avec Dieu, cette vie intérieure que l'Église a organisée pour ses enfants et dont les rites, les formules et le cycle de la liturgie sont le véhicule authentique, voilà l'activité fondamentale de la piété liturgique," ibid., p. 95.

15 "elle n'est pas bénédictine mais catholique," ibid., p. 98.

16 "il consacrera une heure à la méthode spirituelle de la sainte Église," ibid., p. 104.

17 Lambert Beauduin OSB, *Liturgy: the Life of the Church* 3rd edn (Farnborough: St Michael's Abbey Press, 2002), pp. 15–16.

18 Ibid., p. 17.

19 Ibid., p. 19.
20 Ibid., p. 34.
21 Sic. Better translated "outside acts of worship."
22 Ibid., pp. 52–3.
23 Richard R. Gaillardetz & Catherine E. Clifford, *Keys to the Council: Unlocking the Teaching of Vatican II* (Collegeville: Liturgical Press, 2012), p. 24.
24 In correspondence with the authors it has emerged that they have relied on a secondary source biography (Jacques Mortiau & Raymond Loonbeek, *Dom Lambert Beauduin: Visionnaire et précurseur* (Paris: Éditions du Cerf & Éditions du Chevetogne, 2005)), without careful research of Beauduin's writings on the liturgy from that period—a research which is as rewarding as it is revealing.
25 As in Pecklers, "*Ressourcement* and the Renewal of Catholic Liturgy," noted above.
26 Bernard Botte OSB, *From Silence to Participation: An Insider's View of Liturgical Renewal* (Washington DC: Pastoral Press, 1988), pp. 22–3.
27 See: Roberto de Mattei, *The Second Vatican Council: An Unwritten Story* (Fitzwilliam NH: Loreto Publications, 2012), pp. 24–33. De Mattei seeks to place the "new" liturgical movement (from Beauduin onward) within an overall framework of the continuation of modernism from its inception. See also: Didier Bonneterre, *The Liturgical Movement or the Trojan Horse in the City of God* (Kansas City: Angelus Press, 2002). This work is not a study that reaches a conclusion, but a conclusion which seeks the support of a study.
28 *Cours et Conferences des Semaines Liturgiques*, Tomes I–XV (Louvain: Abbaye du Mont-César, 1913–48). Tome VIII « Tables: 1912–1928 » published in 1937 is particularly useful.
29 In the late 1960s the Liturgical Weeks caused controversy and no longer attracted sufficient numbers; see "Chronicle," *Worship* 42 (1968) p. 502; 43 (1969) p. 375; 44 (1970) pp. 188–9.
30 Romano Guardini, *The Spirit of the Liturgy* (London: Sheed & Ward, 1930), pp. 148–9.
31 Romano Guardini, *Sacred Signs* (London: Sheed & Ward, 1930), p. 10.
32 Idelfons Herwegen, *Liturgy's Inner Beauty* (Collegeville: Liturgical Press, 1955), p. 44.
33 Gerald Ellard SJ, "Liturgical Formation: the Means and the Ends," *Worship*, 7 (1932/3), pp. 255–60 (p. 256).
34 Ibid., p. 260.
35 Justine Ward, "Winged Words," *Worship* 1 (1926/7), pp. 109–12.
36 Joseph Ratzinger, *Milestones: Memoirs 1927–1977* (San Francisco: Ignatius Press, 1997) pp. 19–20.
37 For example, Keith Pecklers would have that these led to the liturgy rightly becoming a self conscious expression of any and practically all ecclesial activity: "Unlike its Tridentine form, Vatican II worship was to reach out widely to embrace all of God's world. Liturgy, then, was necessarily concerned about life outside of the sanctuary walls: human liberation, justice and mercy for the poor and oppressed, dialogue with other Christians and with non-Christian believers," "*Ressourcement* and the Renewal of Catholic Liturgy," p. 331. Subjecting the liturgy to aspects of the Church's mission thus risks rendering the *culmen et fons* of the life and mission of the Church an intentional and subjective reflection of those endeavours. It ignores the fact that the Sacred Liturgy is the indispensible and objective encounter of Christ in His Church gathered first and foremost to worship Almighty God, and that it is through this holy encounter that the Church finds her identity and mission. The Church does not impose an identity upon the liturgy, as Pecklers' description of "Vatican II worship" suggests. Rather it is Christ in and through the liturgical encounter who gives the Church her identity and mission.

38 Odo Casel, *The Mystery of Christian Worship and other writings* (London: Darton, Longman and Todd, 1962), pp. 14–15.
39 See: Aidan Nichols OP, "Odo Casel Revisited," *Antiphon* III (1998), pp. 12–20.
40 See: The Society of St Pius X, *The Problem of the Liturgical Reform* (Kansas City: Angelus Press, 2001).
41 See: "A Letter from Romano Guardini" *Herder Correspondence,* Special Issue, 1964, pp. 24–6.
42 Theodore Wesseling OSB, *Liturgy and Life* (London, New York & Toronto: Longmans, Green & Co, 1938), p. 119.
43 See: Alcuin Reid, *The Organic Development of the Liturgy: The Principles of Liturgical Reform and Their Relation to the Twentieth Century Liturgical Movement Prior to the Second Vatican Council,* 2nd edn (San Francisco: Ignatius Press, 2005), pp. 75–8.
44 See: ibid., p. 75.
45 Citied in: ibid., p. 76.
46 See: ibid., pp. 126–35.
47 See: ibid., pp. 100–10.
48 See: ibid., pp. 135–7.
49 See: ibid., pp. 147–50.
50 Bugnini explicitly acknowledges this in his autobiographical memoir. See: Annibale Bugnini CM, *Liturgiae Cultor et Amator: Servì La Chiesa* (Rome: Edizioni Liturgiche, 2012), p. 48.
51 See: Reid, *The Organic Development of the Liturgy,* pp. 150–64.
52 See: ibid., pp. 258–62.
53 Citied in: ibid., p. 262.
54 I hope to do this in my forthcoming work: *Continuity or Rupture? A Study of the Liturgical Reform of the Second Vatican Council.*
55 Annibale Bugnini CM, *The Reform of the Liturgy 1948–1975* (Collegeville: Liturgical Press, 1990), p. 11.
56 Louis Bouyer, *The Decomposition of Catholicism* (Chicago: Franciscan Herald Press, 1969), p. 105.
57 Ibid.

Bibliography

(A more comprehensive bibliography may be found in my work *The Organic Development of the Liturgy,* listed below.)

Documents of the Holy See

Braga, Carlo, CM & Annibale, Bugnini CM (eds), *Documenta ad Instaurationem Liturgicam Spectantia* (Rome: Centro Liturgico Vincenziano, 2000).
Braga, Carlo, CM (ed.), *La riforma liturgica di Pio XII* (Rome: Centro Liturgico Vincenziano, 2003).

Classical writings

Beauduin, Lambert, OSB, *Liturgy: The Life of the Church*, 1st & 2nd edns (Collegeville: Liturgical Press, 1926 & 1929); 3rd edn (Farnborough: St Michael's Abbey Press, 2002).

Bouyer, Louis, *Liturgical Piety* (Notre Dame: University of Notre Dame Press, 1955); also published as *Life and Liturgy* (London: Sheed & Ward, 1956).
—— *The Paschal Mystery: Meditations on the Last Three Days of Holy Week* (London: George Allen & Unwin, 1951).
Caronti, Emmanuale, OSB, *The Spirit of the Liturgy* (Collegeville: Liturgical Press, 1926).
Casel, Odo, OSB, *The Mystery of Christian Worship and Other Writings* (Westminster, Maryland, & London: Newman Press & Darton, Longman & Todd, 1962).
Guardini, Romano, *Sacred Signs* (London: Sheed & Ward, 1930).
—— *The Spirit of the Liturgy* (London: Sheed & Ward, 1930).
Herwegen, Ildefons, OSB, *The Art-Principle of the Liturgy* (Collegeville: Liturgical Press, 1931); 2nd edn, *Liturgy's Inner Beauty* (Collegeville: Liturgical Press, 1953).
The Liturgical Conference, *What is the Liturgical Movement?* 2nd edn (Elsberry: The Liturgical Conference, 1956).
Michel, Virgil, OSB, *The Liturgy of the Church* (New York: Macmillan, 1938).
Parsch, Pius, *The Liturgy of the Mass,* 3rd edn (London & St Louis: Herder, 1957).
Shuster, Alfredo Idelfonso, A. Levelis-Marke (trans.), *The Sacramentary (Liber Sacramentorum): Historical and Liturgical Notes on the Roman Missal,* 5 vols (Burns, Oates & Washbourne: London, 1924–30).
—— Inos Biffi (ed.), *La Sacra Liturgia "Il cuore della Chiesa orante"* (Piemme: Casale Monferrato, 1996).
Wesseling, Theodore, OSB, *Liturgy and Life* (London, New York & Toronto: Longmans, Green & Co, 1938).

Other sources

Bugnini, Annibale, CM, *The Reform of the Liturgy 1948–1975* (Collegeville: Liturgical Press, 1990).
Botte, Bernard, OSB, *From Silence to Participation: An Insider's View of Liturgical Renewal* (Washington DC: Pastoral Press, 1988).
Giampietro, Nicola, *The Development of the Liturgical Reform: As Seen by Cardinal Ferdinando Antonelli from 1948–1970* (Fort Collins: Roman Catholic Books, 2009).
Reid, Alcuin, *The Organic Development of the Liturgy: The Principles of the Liturgical Reform and their Relation to the Twentieth-Century Liturgical Movement Prior to the Second Vatican Council,* 2nd edn (San Francisco: Ignatius Press, 2005).
Rousseau, Olivier, OSB, *The Progress of the Liturgy: An Historical Sketch from the Beginning of the Nineteenth Century to the Pontificate of Pius X* (Maryland: Newman Press, 1951).

Chapter 9

THE LITURGY OF THE SACRAMENTS

James G. Leachman OSB

Introduction

This chapter is designed to lead the reader through the major periods of cultural change in the West in order to indicate clearly that the changes in the liturgical forms of the sacraments occurred in the context of the cultural changes in each period. The work which I have consulted throughout the preparation of this chapter is that of Dom Burkhart Neunheuser (1903–2003), *Storia della Liturgia attraverso le epoche culturali.*[1] I have included some accessible studies in English which, even though they are not very recent publications, give a reliable guide to the study of the material. Since the most recent books in English on the subject are at least ten years old, I have endeavoured to add more recent studies.

I have limited myself to an historical and cultural study and do not treat the sacraments from the perspective of the human sciences (psychology, anthropology, linguistics, arts) and refer only rarely to the theology of the sacraments limiting myself, rather, to the liturgical forms and the ecclesial and cultural milieux in which the sacraments evolved. We can see the periodical emergence of church and liturgical reformers, notably Gregory the Great, Charlemagne, Hildebrand, Innocent III, Pius V, and Pius XII. Yet their work of liturgical reform could not be addressed satisfactorily until liturgical scientists had recovered the ancient liturgical sources. Only after the Council of Trent, with these liturgical sources and a more centralized authority and better communications, could the classical liturgical movement begin and only under these circumstances would the liturgical renewal initiated by Pius XII be able to bear fruit.

In his classic work, Neunheuser, one of the founders of the Pontifical Institute of Liturgy in 1961, affirms three principal points. First, that the Church in itself cannot fall into error in essentials. At the same time, however, the Church exists in human form and is therefore always partial, lacking, and wanting. As the Son of God in his incarnation was abased to our lowliness, so the Church carries the whole weight of our humanity in her nature. This is concretely expressed in article 21 of the Constitution *Sacrosanctum Concilium* of the Second Vatican Council, "the liturgy is made up of unchangeable elements divinely instituted, and of elements subject to change."

Second, the historical facts evidence this continuity and change: the continual development of the bare liturgical forms of the New Testament period; and the changes leading to increasingly rich liturgical forms and abundant, even ceaseless, reforms and adaptations. The task in this chapter is to simply outline the principal facts which illustrate liturgical development across the centuries.

Third, we should pose questions to ourselves while considering this process of liturgical change. Does liturgical development always proceed from the less to the more perfect? Do we find any degeneration or regression at all in the history of the liturgy? Are these latter seen more clearly after efforts of reform? How do we judge the liturgical changes? Are they always the result of the inspiration of the Holy Spirit and are they thus always to be retained as ideal expressions? Do changes occur spontaneously or even randomly or are they expressions of a slow maturation down the centuries? How do the various expressions of the liturgy both reach out in evangelization to embrace the people of each time and place? How does liturgy challenge the secular with eternal values?[2]

The sacraments in apostolic times

In apostolic times we see simple, even meagre, liturgical forms for the sacraments, or "mysteries" in Greek. The sacraments were instituted by Jesus Christ who, by taking basic elements and forms from Jewish worship, gave a new content to these Jewish forms: his own self. The content of the sacraments is always the living presence of Jesus Christ, Word of God incarnate of the Virgin Mary, our flesh assumed by the divine. Thus, always, in the celebration and reception of the sacraments, our human nature participates in the divine, just as the Word of God participated in our lowliness.

Baptisma

Jesus Christ was baptized and instructed others to baptize, reflecting Jewish forms of proselyte baptism and John the Baptist's baptism of repentance. The apostles practised baptism, Pauline doctrine interpreting baptism as being baptized into the body of Christ. The evidence of sub-apostolic times in the *Didache* (c. 90–110 AD) gives us the first liturgical forms for the ceremony: threefold immersion or aspersion in the name of the Holy Trinity.[3]

Oratio – Euchè

Jesus Christ prayed frequently, and often also during the night. He prayed in the presence of his disciples and alone. He joined the prayer of the synagogue assembly and we presume that he prayed at home in the family.

The apostles faithfully continued the practice of Jesus and the evidence of sub-apostolic times suggests that these practices were handed down to later generations. We find evidence of the first liturgical bases of reconciliation (Jn 8:10; Eph. 4:32) and anointing (Jas 5:14–16), but not explicitly of matrimony.

Fractio panis – ta klasmata tou artou

At the Last Supper, the Lord Jesus gathered the twelve in order to eat a meal with them following Jewish sacred ritual, instructing them to continue to celebrate afterwards in memory of his death.

Academic discussion continues about whether the Last Supper was a fellowship meal or a Passover celebration, but it is more important here to note that it was in the context of the recitation of prayers recited over cups and bread a meal was celebrated, in the course of which are recited the "blessings" (*berakoth*) over the broken bread and over the "third cup," at the end of the meal.

In Jesus' celebration a new purpose, "a new and peculiar meaning" for the meal is announced. Gregory Dix reminds us that the repetition of the Supper was quite normal for the Jewish apostles. The novelty was that it was to be done "for the recalling of Me," of Jesus after his death.[4]

Diakonia–episkope–taxus/ordo

In the Apostolic Church ministries were, of course, essential, yet this period is one of transition in the sense that there were still charismatic as well as institutional ministries. In the *Didache*, for example, prophets, apostles, and *episkopoi* (overseers or bishops) were allowed to preside at the eucharist,[5] though the document gives no forms of prayer for the insitution of these ministries.

The sacraments in Greek and Latin cultures (110–399)

In this period of history the Gospel passes from the Hebrew-Aramaic speaking to the Syriac, Greek, and Latin-speaking populations of the Roman Empire by means of the Syriac, Greek (*koiné*), and Latin languages. Christian Apologists such as Justin Martyr and Irenaeus of Lyons write in Greek and give us information of the celebration of the sacraments.[6]

Although Christian authors in northern Africa (Tertullian, Cyprian of Carthage, Augustine of Hippo), Spain (Himerius of Tarragona), and in northern Italy (Ambrose of Milan, Chromatius of Aquileia, Zeno of Verona) now tended to write in Latin, the liturgy in Rome was still celebrated in Greek. The passage of the Christian liturgy in Rome from the Greek to the Latin language occurred at the hand of Pope Damasus (366–84).[7] As a result of these changes, the sacraments were radically remodelled to reflect a public rather than a clandestine celebration. By the beginning of the fifth century the Roman language and culture would come to colour the liturgy of the Roman church in such a decisive way as to give rise to a new liturgical language, ecclesiastical Latin. This is a period of creativity, heroism and the continuous development of Christianity and of the *Christian* liturgy.

Baptisma and sphragis

The baptismal bath given in the name of Jesus develops in the third and fourth centuries into a complex of solemn rites, which include the preparation and steps of the catechumenate, the solemn act of baptism with solemn blessing of the water and profession of faith and a complementary rite of anointing (*confirmatio*).[8] The *Apostolic Tradition*, commonly ascribed to Hippolytus, may represent the practice of a Greek-speaking community in early third-century Rome.[9] The related Latin practice of the see of Milan in the fourth century is described by its bishop, Ambrose.[10]

Fractio panis – eucharistia

The *fractio panis* or *klasmata*, that is the supper which recalls and proclaims the death of the Lord, comes clearly to express the foundational elements of thanksgiving, invocation, active remembrance, and intercession, and comes to be known by the technical term *eucharistia*.[11] The *Apostolic Tradition* gives a third-century Greek eucharistic rite.

Diakonia–Episkope–Ordo

In the *Apostolic Tradition* we find already the texts of the ordination of bishop, presbyter, and deacon.[12] Eusebius of Caesarea refers to a letter of Pope Cornelius to Fabius of Antioch in 251 recording seven orders of clergy in Rome. As well as bishop, he names presbyters, deacons, sub-deacons, acolytes, exorcists, readers, and porters.[13]

Anointing of the sick and reconciliation of the excommunicated

No Roman texts of anointing from the third and fourth centuries have survived, though *Apostolic Tradition* gives a prayer for the blessing of oil.[14] The practice of penance, or, more accurately, the possibility of a second, post-baptismal forgiveness of sins because of a serious fall, begins to appear towards the middle of the second century: *The Shepherd*, written in Greek by Hermas, a Roman, is devoted entirely to the subject of penance.[15]

Matrimony

According to the Roman law of the Imperial Age, marriage consisted essentially in a *consensus*, a mutual self-gift of the spouses. Betrothal, clearly distinct from marriage in the third century, was celebrated at a family meal: after the exchange of promises the fiancé gave the young girl an iron ring and some presents (*arrhae sponsaliciae*) as a pledge of their future union. The marriage ceremony itself had three stages. The first was the dressing of the bride, who wore a crown and a yellow veil with red highlights (*flammeum*), the distinctive mark of married women. The second stage, in the bride's home, involved the presentation of the bride by a married woman (the *pronuba*), the consultation of the soothsayers, and the reading of the contract (*tabulae nuptiales*) in the presence of witnesses. After the exchange of consents, the *pronuba* delivered the young girl to her husband by having them join hands (*dextrarum iunctio*). A sacrifice to the family gods preceded the wedding feast. The third stage was an evening procession with the bride to her husband's house; the latter led her into the house, offered her water and fire; the pair were conducted to the bridal chamber, where the husband removed the bride's cloak, and everyone else withdrew.

Until the peace of Constantine, the only liturgical celebration of marriage that Christians experienced were these pagan rites performed in the family, but avoiding idolatrous elements, such as consulting soothsayers and the sacrifice, and the licentious aspects of the wedding feast and procession. There is no evidence until the fourth century of a liturgical blessing or the participation of a priest.[16]

The classical Roman form of the sacraments (400–799)

The Christian faith had been proclaimed *religio licita* in the Roman Empire by Constantine in 312, and the abolition of paganism by Theodosius in 390 effectively established Catholicism as the religion of the Empire. Yet the invader Alaric the King of the Visigoths sacked Rome on 24 August 410.

In 474, Theodoric, the greatest of the Ostrogothic kings, was elected to the throne of his nation to the north and east of Italy. After various periods of warfare and alliance with Zeno, the Byzantine emperor, Theodoric invaded Italy in 488 (with the consent and advice of the emperor), slew Odoacer, the first barbarian ruler of Italy, and became ruler himself. He held the power although not the title of the Western Roman emperors.[17]

The Catholic and Roman Christians used their creative genius, the Latin language, and their Roman culture, in this most difficult period to express a new ecclesial and liturgical identity in new liturgical texts and books (*Sacramentaria, Lectionaria, Antiphonalia, Ordines*), buildings (*basilicae, baptisteria*), vesture, ornament and ceremonial over and against the Arian Gothic invaders.[18] It is in this period that the Merovingian Dynasty (500–751) was established in what is now France and Germany. The baptism of Clovis I, first king of the Salian Franks by Remigius at Rheims in 496 or 498 marked the beginning of a new period of greater stability for the Catholic Church on the Continent.

In the 590s, when the long struggle between the Lombards and Constantinople for the domination of Italy was nearing its climax, Pope Gregory sent forty missionary monks to bring the faith to England.

Baptism, "*confirmatio*" and Eucharist in the *Sacramentarium Veronense, Ordo Romanus 11* and the *Sacramentarium Gelasianum*

At the beginning of this period, Roman liturgical sources referring to initiation are rare. The Verona Sacramentary, a compilation of Mass booklets reflecting the papal liturgy between 400–560 and compiled between 561–74 lacks the booklets for Christmas to Pentecost, therefore also, we presume, the rites of initiation.[19] *Ordo Romanus* 11, reflecting the practice of the fifth and sixth centuries, informs us of the extended Lenten preparation of catechumens for baptism, which occured in the Easter vigil.[20]

With the passage of the Roman liturgical books north of the Alps and the acceptance of Catholic Christianity by the peoples in those lands, the solemn public rites of preparation for the sacraments during the catechumenate were gradually reduced. The pastoral need to "sacramentalize" the pagans and Arians of those lands was judged to be more important than a full catechetical preparation. The missionary efforts of Bishop Birinus in England give a clear example. Sent by Pope Honorius I (625–38) to convert the Mercians in Britain, Birinus on his journey encountered the pagan Saxons of the Thames Valley, where King Cynegils of Wessex allowed Birinus to preach and to baptize him. Many of the royal courtiers also expressed a desire to become Christian, so at the "Brightwell" (Berkshire) crossing of the Thames near Dorchester, Birinus arranged for a large proportion of the Court to be baptized.[21] Thus the complex of solemn rites developed in the third and fourth centuries in the Roman Empire, and which flowered in the fifth and sixth centuries, was soon abbreviated and adapted for the new mission territories north of the Alps, and then, over the next centuries, also in Rome.

Ordinations: the Old Roman Tradition and the Carolingian Tradition

We find that the seven orders which are listed in *Traditio apostolica* (c. 215) are retained in the *Statuta Ecclesiae antiqua*, a document of around 500.

Pierre Jounel, like many who follow him, is of the opinion that there are two strata in the Roman tradition of ordinations, the Old Roman Tradition which had reached its full maturity by the time of Gregory I, and a set of Frankish additions mostly dating from the Carolingian period.

Two ancient sacramentaries, which give the text of the prayers for the consecrations of a bishop and the ordination of priests and deacon, and several *Ordines*, which describe the rites, help us to identify the characteristics of the Old Roman Tradition. These are the Leonine sacramentary (*Sacramentarium Veronense*), the *Hadrianum*, and "Ordo romanus 34" dated about 750. The ordination liturgy familiar to St Leo or St Gregory showed a sobriety and only the minimum number of clear signs that St Augustine saw as the mark of the Christian liturgy.[22] The rites are very adequately described by Jounel in 1988,[23] though little work has been done in this area in the past thirty years.

Matrimony: *Velatio et porrectio manuum*[24] in the *Sacramentarium Veronense*, the *Sacramentarium Gelasianum*, and the *Sacramentarium Hadrianum*

Although the *Sacramentarium Veronese* provides a Mass for spouses with the *velatio nuptialis* and a prayer for the fertility of the bride,[25] we find no structured ritual for this sacrament before the eleventh century. The *Sacramentarium Gelasianum* adds a prayer after communion which mentions both spouses, a new prayer over the gifts, a preface that is found in no other book, and also a second *Hanc Igitur*.[26] The *Hadrianum ex authentico* changes the texts once again, not always felicitously.[27]

Anointing in the *Sacramentarium Gelasianum* and the *Sacramentarium Hadrianum*

The Old Roman Tradition, evidenced by a letter from Pope Innocent I to Decentius of Gubbio, attests to this sacrament already in 416, but only with the *Hadrianum* and the *Sacramentarium Gelasianum* do we find liturgical formulae for the blessing of the oil on Holy Thursday.[28] The Carolingian tradition in the *Sacramentarium Hadrianum* gives what seems to be an adaption of the older prayer; references to the body are made more spiritual; "corporis" is expanded by the phrase "spiritus et ..." and "tutamentum mentis et corporis" becomes "tutamentum corporis, animae et spiritus".[29]

The *Hadrianum ex authentico* (*Sacramentarium Hadrianum*) also had two prayers: *Ad visitandum infirmum* before an *Oratio super paenitentem*.[30] The Old Gelasian Sacramentary had four prayer formularies and a set of Mass orations for visiting the sick.[31]

Reconciliation: solemn public penance in the *Sacramentarium Gelasianum* and the *Sacramentarium Hadrianum*

The Old Roman Tradition of public penance is first evidenced in the papacy of Gregory I (†604) when solemn public penance is begun on "feria secunda post caput Quadragesimae," a Monday. The *Hadrianum*, the papal Sacramentary given by Pope Hadrian I to Charlemagne in 785–6, gives a prayer over the people[32] and prayers "pro peccatis."[33]

The Gelasian tradition of sacramentaries places the beginning of public penance on the Wednesday (*feria IV*) after the Sunday, "in capite quadragesimae."[34] On Holy Thursday (*feria V*) the penitents were reconciled by the bishop,[35] and the *Supplementum* to the *Hadrianum* composed by Benedict of Aniane (747–821) gives corresponding rites.[36]

After the sixth century, solemn public penance became ever rarer, for it was substituted by private or "tariffed" penance, a practice introduced to the Continent by Irish monks.

The Franco-Germanic and medieval Roman forms (800–1199)

Even before the year 800, some of the Roman liturgical books had travelled north and encountered the Gallican liturgy. The first to do so was the Old Gelasian Sacramentary (*Sacramentarium Gelasianum*), composed between 627–715 for the presbyteral lituries of the titular churches in Rome. The manuscript had already been copied in the Abbey of Chelles in northern France around the year 750. A little later, Pope Hadrian I had given the *Hadrianum*, the papal Sacramentary, to Charlemagne in 785–6.

Now the *Ordines Romani* and other liturgical books are copied and carried north of the Alps where they too are developed to express the genius of the Franco-Germanic and other cultures. These revised liturgical books and ceremonies of the Roman rite thus began to express the local cultures in the different lands; the Franco-Germanic Empire, Britain and Scandinavia.

Three great Germanic dynasties would control large tracts of Western Europe over this lengthy period of 400 years. Emperor Charles the Great (Charlemagne), the first of the Carolingian emperors, was crowned in St Peter's Rome, Christmas Day 800, and his successors ruled until about 911. Charles' influence over the Western Church was such that he could use the unity and authority of the church to strengthen his authority in the Empire.[37]

At Charles' bidding, for example, Theodulph, Bishop of Orléans, wrote two important capitularies (cartularies) the first of which was a reminder to the priests of his diocese of the importance of manual labour, study, prayer, and chastity, and referring also to the discipline of baptism, anointing, reconciliation, and matrimony.[38] Norsemen (Vikings) settled in the land between the Seine and the Loire (Neustria), and Charles the Simple, by the Treaty of Saint-Clair-sur-Epte in 911, granted the Viking leader Rollo the county of Rouen, the basis of the future Duchy of Normandy.

The Saxon dynasty lasted from 919–1024; Otto I, the Great, was crowned as third Saxon emperor in Rome in 962. It was under Otto I that the Mainz Pontifical (the Romano-Germanic Pontifical) was established in Rome in the mid-tenth century. Other revised liturgical books were also brought back to the papal chapels in Rome, where the imprint of Franco-Germanic culture comes to be seen in the papal liturgy, the "new Roman" liturgy of the Middle Ages. In 966, Mieszko, duke of Poland, accepted Latin Christianity and with it the literate Latin civilization of which the Church was guardian, protector and advocate.

The Franconian dynasty lasted from 1024–1137 and it was in this period that the Normans gradually expanded their territory and incorporated much of Neustria into it. (When the margrave of Neustria became king in 987, the history of the march ended, to be replaced by the history of the various comital fiefs which were to rise in power within it.) They extended their territory to England, Ireland, Spain, Italy, Sicily, and even Byzantium and Palestine. Their architectural, artistic, and cultural heritage deeply affected the life of the Church in those lands.[39] Pope Gregory VII (Hildebrand) attempted a reform of the Church, suppressing the Mozarabic rite, attempting liturgical centralization, and setting a precedent that the Roman rite would be normative for Latin Christianity.[40]

Baptism, confirmation, and Eucharist in the *Sacramentarium Gellonensis*, tenth- and twelfth-century pontificals and the *Ordines Romani*

The Carolingian Tradition. The Roman liturgy was introduced and gradually imposed upon the church of Gaul; a Capitulary of 789 ordered bishops "ut secundum morem romanum baptizent".[41] Benedict of Aniane's *Supplement* to the *Hadrianum* was prepared and the Emperor launched an inquiry among the metropolitans of his territory about the way baptisms were being celebrated. The answers were often influenced by a little work whose opening words were "Primo paganus,"[42] referred to by Alcuin. It was a very short list of the various rites of initiation and the new practices were organized into a ritual compilation known as *Ordo antiquus romanus* (*Ordo* L in Andrieu), which incorporates the old *Ordo* XI as enriched with some Gallicanisms; this *Ordo* L is part of the *PRG* which originated in Mainz around 950. The Ottonian emperors then introduced this Rhenish book to Rome, where it was revised, then appearing as the twelfth-century Roman pontifical. The Roman liturgical books of the eighth century show that the rites of the catechumenate have become mere vestiges as the practice of baptizing infants becomes common practice.[43]

Ordinatio in tenth- and twelfth-century pontificals

The Carolingian Tradition, the Romano-Frankish usage replaced the Old Roman liturgy that combined simplicity and depth with a set of rites whose purpose was "to show the effects of grace and sacramental power on the recipients. The sacramental sign has developed into a profusion of symbols that bring the liturgy to the threshold of sacred drama."[44]

This revised Romano-Frankish liturgy, incorporated into the Romano-Germanic pontifical, was introduced into Rome in the tenth century, where like other rites it was revised, then appearing as the twelfth-century Roman pontifical. Between the twelfth century and the 1968 recasting of the ritual of ordinations, this rite would undergo only minor developments.[45]

Matrimony

Unlike other sacraments, the Old Roman Tradition of matrimony was not ousted or suppressed by a Carolingian adaptation containing Gallican elements. The most widespread form of marriage liturgy in Gaul and the Celtic countries consisted in a blessing of the spouses in the bridal chamber.[46] This blessing *in thalamo* was eliminated in Gaul when the Old Roman rite was received, but it persisted in England.[47]

Anointing in the *Sacramentarium Gellonensis* and the supplement to the *Hadrianum*

The eighth-century Gelasian sacramentary incorporated the ritual of the Old (Roman) Gelasian into a larger collection of prayers, preceding the *Reconcilatio paenitentis ad mortem,* the *Commendatio animae,* and rituals of burial.[48] From here the ritual passed into the Carolingian *Supplementum* to the *Hadrianum,* where it was located after the reconciliation of penitents on Holy Thursday.[49]

Reconciliation in the *Sacramentarium Gelasianum*

The ritual of tarrif-penance which displaced canonical penance is evidenced in the Old Gelasian Sacramentary.[50] The ritual almost always took place in the church, with only the priest and penitent involved.[51]

"Secundum usum Romanae Ecclesiae" and the autumn of the Middle Ages (1200–1499)

Enormous social and political movements affected Europe and influenced the life of the Church in this period. In the four centuries between 900 and 1300, the medieval Papacy had gained enormous influence and wealth. The growing strength of the French monarchy between 1000 and 1300 and the increasing power of Anglo-Norman England after 1066 shifted the centre of political and economic power in Europe towards the North and West. The Crusades, involving all European countries, had begun in 1095 and would last until 1291, reducing both population and prosperity.

Pope Innocent III convoked the Fourth Lateran Council in 1215 to crown the work of his pontificate; and its canons express his ideas. The Council established the requirements of confession at least once a year and communion at Easter time as the minimum requirement for church membership, called the Easter duty.

The fourteenth and fifteenth centuries brought even greater disaster for Christians in the west. The Black Death between 1300 and 1450 reduced the population of Europe by about one third and the growing power of monarchs led to intense rivalries and wars. The Hundred Years War between France and England (1337–1453) and the schisms and heresies between 1347 and 1450 were portents of ecclesial and national divisions to come. Culturally and religiously the period was very rich, but rich and beautiful like the Autumn ... and like the Autumn it was a preparation for a death.

The Catholic Church was a constant presence in the life of almost every woman, man and child in Western Europe. It unified, while political and economic forces divided nations and people. In the fifteenth century the invention of the printing press by Gutenberg in 1445 gave an impulse to the centralization of control over liturgy. The first edition of the *Missale Romanum* appeared in 1474, and the *Pontificalis ordinis liber* (*Pontificale Romanum*) in 1485. We could say that this period closes with the European excursion to the Americas in 1492.

Baptism, confirmation, and Eucharist (1200–1499)

In the course of the twelfth century it became common practice to celebrate baptism in the first few days after birth.[52] The catechumenate was abolished, though many of its elements were incorporated into a clumsily constructed continuous rite. Adult converts to the Christian faith were baptized using the same form as were infants.

The thirteenth-century pontifical of the Roman curia does not give a rite of baptism, only an *Ordo ad consignandos pueros sive infantes*.[53] The bishop's role is limited to confirming children already baptized by a priest. The same is true of the Pontifical of William Durandus, Bishop of Mende dating from 1292–5. William Durandus replaced the kiss of peace at the end of the ceremony with a slap (*alapa*) to which he ascribed a rather questionable symbolism,[54] and replaced the laying on of the hand of each confirmand with an extension of both hands over all the confirmandi, "super confirmandi extensis manibus dicit."[55]

Ordination in the thirteenth-century pontifical of the Roman curia, the pontifical of Durandus and the *Pontificalis ordinis liber* (1200–1499)

The ordination rites pass, little changed, into the thirteenth-century pontifical of the Roman curia and the pontifical of Durandus. The first printed edition of the Roman pontifical (1485) simply put its seal of approval on the additions that William Durandus of Mende had made to the previous ritual.[56]

Matrimony

The understanding of Christian marriage shifted from being the gift of a daughter to the groom's family to a contract between the spouses.[57] Local customs were added to the rite and many of these survived well into the sixteenth century and later; the joining of hands, a veiling of the couple, the exchange of rings, a gift of money to the bride's family, a kiss, a meal, the blessing of the chamber, gloves for the bride,[58] lighted candles sometimes accompanied by a prayer such as "Per oblationem huius presentis luminis accendat Deus ignem sui amoris in cordibus vestris."[59]

Of all this abundant symbolism only the exchange of rings would find a place in the *Rituale Romanum* of 1614; and the mutual consent, already common doctrine in the thirteenth century and described as the "form" of the sacrament in the *Commentary on the Sentences* by St Thomas becomes the central act of the celebration.[60]

Anointing

While the diocesan clergy were still using the lengthy ordo in the Romano-Germanic Pontifical (tenth-century *Romano-germanique* pontifical), Cluniac monks had produced a much-shortened rite in the *Consuetudines Cluniacenses* in the eleventh and twelfth centuries.[61] This Cluniac ritual exerted an influence on the thirteenth-century pontifical of the Roman curia.[62] It was the long version of this that Franciscans took and shortened still further,[63] and this version in turn has been used down the centuries.

Reconciliation (1200–1499)

This sacrament was stripped of a liturgy in the mind of scholastic theologians when they claimed, following the Doctor Angelicus, that the Gospel injunction "Whatever you loose on earth shall be loosed on heaven," necessarily implied that the form of the sacrament must be the words in the indicative mood: "Ego te absolvo." The Church made this view its own at the Council of Florence (1441–5),[64] and later at Trent,[65] and thus the juridical and the sacramental roles of the liturgy of reconciliation were combined.

The Council of Trent (1500–99) and the Baroque (1600–99)

After the desperate spiritual situation left by Pope Alexander VI (1492–1503), Pope Julius II (1503–13) did little better, though he did encourage the celebration of the canonical hours of prayer.[66] The fifth Lateran Council (1512–17) saw both the death of Julius II and a request to Leo X in 1514 for the reform of the Church that would include the education of the clergy and some vernacular liturgy.[67] Castellani published new editions both of the *Pontificale Romanum* in 1520, where for the first time the word "*confirmatio*" appears in an officially approved Roman liturgical text,[68] and of the the first *Rituale Romanum* (a *Liber Sacerdotalis*) in 1523. Yet the reform was too tardy and tepid for some. The publication of Martin Luther's *Disputatio* in 1517, Henry VIII's *First Act of Supremacy* in 1534, and John Calvin's *Institutes of the Christian Religion* in 1536 marked the formal beginnings of the Protestant Reformation. The wars of religion and the secession of large portions of the Church in Scandinavia, Britain, Germany, and France left the Catholic Church as a "rump" in the Mediterranean.

Only by a rapid and decisive reform movement would the Catholic Church be able to respond to this most dangerous situation. The Council of Trent (1545–63) was the firm response, and from the new papal printing presses there rolled the revised missals, rituals, pontificals, and other books mandated by the Council. In the Bulls promulgating the renewed liturgical books we see expressed the intentions of the Council and of the Supreme Pontiffs: "Quae divini Officii formula . . . necessaria visa res est, quae ad pristinam orandi regulam revocaretur,"[69] and ". . . ad pristinam Missale ipsum sanctorum Patrum normam ac ritum restituerunt."[70] All the good will notwithstanding, due to the lack of ancient liturgical sources, the reform was only able to purge aberrations and restore the medieval Franco-Germanic Roman rite, much as it had been left by Hildebrand (1020–84).

The Baroque was a period formed by a confident Catholic spirit renewed and strengthened by the Council of Trent and its faithful propagandists, the Roman Pontiffs, and great bishops like Carlo and Federico Borromeo. It is still the Middle Ages, but reformed and purified. Every aspect of Catholic Europe's society, music, architecture, art, and sculpture finds itself for the last time influenced and dominated by religion and the transcendent. As a result, the sacraments are celebrated sumptuously, confidently, and with a sense of theatre, as in an imperial court. One question to ask is whether, beyond the European heartland of Catholicism, this confident liturgy impressed either Protestants in Northern Europe, or the indigenous peoples in the Orient and the Americas to whom Catholicism would be presented by Franciscan, Dominican and Jesuit missionaries.

Some corrections to Pius V's *Missale Romanum* proved necessary, and Pope Clement VIII replaced it with a new typical edition on 7 July 1604. A further revised typical edition was promulgated by Pope Urban VIII on 2 September 1634.

Baptism, confirmation and Eucharist in *Missale Romanum* 1570 and the rituals of 1523, 1584 and 1614

The *Liber Sacerdotalis* of Alberto Castellani had two *ordines* for baptism, both organized as a continuous rite as did the earlier pontifical of Durandus.

After the Council of Trent, among the preparatory studies done for a new book of rituals, Cardinal Santori's draft (*RSR 1584*) provided for the restoration of the ancient discipline of the scrutinies, especially in mission countries, but this suggestion was not maintained in the Roman Ritual promulgated by Paul V in 1614. This later ritual book was never imposed on the diocese of the Roman Church, only "proposed." It contained an *Ordo baptismi adultorum*[71] and an *Ordo baptismi parvulorum.*[72] In both cases baptism was a single continuous rite whose stages were marked only by bringing the catechumen into the church after the penultimate exorcism and by the priest changing from violet to white after the prebaptismal anointing.[73]

Ordination in the *Pontificale Romanum* of 1595 and 1596

Research on the changes between the *Pontificalis ordinis liber* and the *Pontificale Romanum* of 1596 is difficult to discover. It seems, at first glance, that "except for the addition made to the ritual of the subdiaconate in the fifteenth century, the Roman Church until 1968 followed the Pontifical of William Durandus almost word for word,"[74] and only that change was made in the preparation of the 1596 *Pontificale Romanum.*

Matrimony in the *Rituale Romanum* of 1614[75]

The Council of Trent in 1563, in the decree *Tametsi,*[76] was the first to require canonical form for validity of marriage. There were in fact two stages of revision of the rite; first the preparation of the new rite in the 1570 *Missale Romanum,*[77] and then the 1614 *Rituale Romanum.*[78] The Council did not intend to suppress local rituals, and in fact diocesan rituals, at least in France and in England and Wales included customs and prayers different from those in the 1614 *Rituale.*[79]

Anointing in the Rituals of 1523, 1584, and 1614

The version of the rite that the Franciscans took was accepted into the sixteenth-century Rituals of Alberto Castellani (*Liber Sacerdotalis*) and Cardinal J.S. Santori

(*Rituale sacramentorum*), then entering the 1614 *Rituale* as "De Sacramento extremo Vnctionis".[80]

Reconciliation in the *Rituale Romanum* of 1614

The Ritual of 1614 on the one hand was the first to prescribe a grille between penitent and priest, on the other it intended to add a degree of public presence to the rite. The priest was to wear a surplice and stole if possible, and the rite should preferably be in church and in a confessional. The new rite began with an exhortation. At the strictly priestly prayer, the *Indulgentiam*, the priest was to raise his right hand towards the penitent. There was an absolution from censures and the rite ended with the prayer *Passio Domini*.[81]

The sacraments during the Enlightenment (1700–99)

Although this period is short and little researched, it is important since it shows an important aspect of the relationship between Church and State. Under the influence of the secular Enlightenment, the growth of science and of democracy, local rulers in Europe began to assert the need and the right of local churches to begin church, and therefore liturgical, reform. The resulting local Synods of Pistoia and Ems were vain attempts to reform the Church and the liturgical books, and deserve further study.

Benedict XIV (1740–58) decided to restore the ancient gesture at the moment of anointing in Confirmation: he ordered ministers to lay the hand flat on the head of the one being anointed.[82] In the eighteenth century the *Pontificale Romanum* of 1596 continued to be used for ordinations until the publication of the *Pontificale Romanum* of 1752. The 1614 *Rituale* continued to be used for these sacraments until the publication of the 1752 edition.

The sacraments during the Romantic restoration (1800–1909)

In the first decades of the nineteenth century the influence and vigour of many European ecclesiastical centers, Paris, Milan, and Vienna in the Catholic Church, the Church of England centred upon Canterbury, Calvinists, Lutherans, Presbyterians in Geneva, Berlin, and Edinburgh, was waning. The Industrial Revolution all over Europe was gradually substituting economic laws for the traditional ethical standards and connections with the land, and subsuming spiritual values to the idols of industry and wealth.[83]

Then, unexpectedly, there began in 1833 three movements of reform, which were to have profound consequences for the Church. On 11 July 1833, Prosper Guéranger refounded Benedictine life at Solesmes. Three days later, on 14 July 1833, John Keble gave the Assize Sermon at St Mary's Church, Oxford, thus establishing the Oxford Movement in the Church of England. Two months later in

Germany, J.A. Möhler was fiercely attacked over his book, *Symbolism*, and this marked the beginning of the new school of Catholic theology at the University of Tübingen.[84]

All three movements were working to renew the Church as one, holy and catholic based upon traditionally religious and human values, a sacramental vision of the Church as a divine community and the recovery of much that had been lost in the Reformation and Counter-reformation. The new ideal was the glorious Church of the late Middle Ages. The three "prophetic" ecclesial movements had to confront a general disregard for the monastic life, a very low appreciation of the liturgy, and an ossified scholastic theology. The result was an astounding revival of study and the arts. The creative ferment produced beautifully illustrated missals, rituals, and pontificals, and many beautiful new church buildings.

Pope Pius IX (1846–78) faced enormous difficulties: the secular power of the papacy was ended by the revolution in 1848, French troops occupied the papal states from 1850 to 1870 when troops of Victor Emmanuel took Rome. Popular Catholic sentiment rallied behind "papa Mastai" and he was able to centralize the government of the Church and promote missions. Pope Leo XIII (1878–1903) then led the church into the twentieth century.

Yet all during the nineteenth century, the liturgical books of the Roman rite had remained almost totally unaltered. The missal (1570), pontifical (1752), and *Rituale* (1752) were all reprinted many times,[85] yet with very few changes indeed. The intellectual renewal of Catholicism, including protests against abuses and dreams of what might be possible, gave an impetus to the study of liturgical sources which would one day make the liturgical reforms of Vatican II possible.

Pope Pius X (1903–14), in response to these hopes, referring to the extraordinary state of liturgical music in some countries, published the motu proprio, *Tra le Sollecitudini* on 22 November 1903.

Nor should one overlook the initial signs of the influence which would be exerted upon the churches in Europe by the newly established dioceses in the Belgian, Dutch, French, German, Portuguese, and British colonies, and possessions abroad. The need for new attitudes and practices to evangelize and catechize in African and Asian territories showed the pastoral need there for restoring the catechumenate and, at least on occasion, for the vernacular.

The sacraments during the liturgical movement (1909–59)

It is convenient to see the history of the liturgy in the twentieth century in four periods which relate directly not only to the secular history of Europe but also to the spread of the Roman rite in Africa and Asia.

The first period (1909–14) marks the beginning of the classical liturgical movement in Europe and its spread to other continents. The motu proprio of Pio X *Tra le sollecitudini* of 22 November 1903 presents the celebrated phrase concerning "partecipatio active" in the liturgical rites. The movement's spread is certainly linked with the initiative of the Belgian monk, Dom L. Beauduin (1873–1960) and a layman, Georg Kurth (1847–1916), with the protection of Cardinal D. Mercier (1851–1926) of Malines, Belgium. In 1909, during the *Congrès National des Oeuvres Catholiques* at Malines, Beauduin gave his lecture *La vraie prière de l'église*.[86] In it, he underlined the importance of full active participation of all Christians in the life and ministry of the Church, particularly in the liturgy.

The second period (1914–43) marks the rapid spread of the movement with associated conferences and publications in Europe and North America and of rapid growth of the Church outside Europe and the Americas.

The third period (1943–55) sees Pope Pius XII naming seven members of the Roman curia as members of a Commission for the Liturgical Reform on 28 May 1947. It was later enlarged somewhat but remained limited to members of the Curia. Little is still known of the Commission's work, but we know the titles of the "*Memoria*" which guided its work. The Acts of the session between 1948–60 have been published only relatively recently.[87]

The fourth period (1955–61) saw the arrival of many requests to the commission from liturgical centres in France and Germany. The main accomplishments of the Pian Commission were: the restoration of the Easter Vigil (February 1, 1951), the new edition of *Rituale Romanum* (January 25, 1952), the reform of Holy Week (November 16, 1955), the simplification of rubrics (March 23, 1955), the new *Codex rubricarum* (July 26, 1960), and the new edition of *Pontificalum Romanum, partes prima et tertia* (February 28, 1962), *pars secunda* (April 13, 1961).

In this period many former European colonies began to win their independence. On January 25, 1959, Pope John XXIII had already announced that an Ecumenical Council was to be held in Rome.[88]

Little study has been done on the liturgical books of the early twentieth century. The *Pontificale Romanum* of 1888 was republished when necessary and the Pian Reform issued a new editio typica in 1961–2. The *Rituale Romanum 1614* was slightly revised in 1913, 1925 and the Pian Reform issued the sixth editio typica in 1952. The 1925 rite of anointing is briefly described by P. Rouillard.[89]

The sacraments and the Second Vatican Council (1960–2009)

On January 25, 1959, Pope John XXIII announced an Ecumenical Council in Rome. On 5 June 1960, a Preparatory Commission on the Liturgy was created under the presidency of Cardinal Cicognani, and one month later Annibale Bugnini, a Vincentian (†1982) was named secretary. The most recent edition of the Missal of Trent was promulgated by a decree of 23 June 1962, fewer than four months before the Council opened. The Constitution on the Liturgy, *Sacrosanctum Concilium*, was promulgated on 4 December 1963.[90]

The twenty-nine ritual books, sacramentaries, and pontificals, mandated by the Second Vatican Council, emerged in their Latin *editiones typicae* over the following forty years, the last being the *Martyrologium Romanum* in 2001. The books of the *Pontificale Romanum* which concern us are the following, with their dates of promulgation: *De Ordinatione diaconi, presbyteri et episcopi* (18 June 1968) and *De*

Ordinatione episcopi, presbyterorum et diaconorum (18 June 1989); *Ordo Confirmationis* (15 August 1971). Those of the *Rituale Romanum* are seven in all, including: *Ordo Baptismi parvulorum* (15 May 1969); *Ordo Initiationis Christianae Adultorum* (January 6, 1972); *Ordo Celebrandi Matrimonium* (March 19, 1969; editio typica altera March 19, 1990); *Ordo Paenitentiae* (December 2, 1971); *Ordo Unctionis infirmorum eorumque pastoralis curae* (November 3, 1972).

Baptism, confirmation, and Eucharist

The three revised rites of infant and adult baptism and of confirmation, promulgated between 1969 and 1973, have received a great deal of study, because of which there is a considerable bibliography.[91]

Ordination and ordinary ministries

The revised rites of ordination were promulgated by Paul VI in the Apostolic Constitution *Pontificali Romanis* of June 18 1968,[92] recasting the ritual of ordinations.[93] The rite was revised in 1990, changing the order of presenting the ordinations in the ritual book.

Matrimony

Despite great freedom given to episcopal conferences to adaptation of the renewed post-conciliar ritual, very few countries have used this, or have submitted proposals that were acceptable to the Congregation for Divine Worship and the Discipline of the Sacraments. Six points characterize the proposed renewal: the rite takes place after the Liturgy of the Word and before the presentation of the gifts, a greatly enlarged selection of readings is proposed, the formula for the promises is more explicit, the ancient preface for marriage has been restored from the *Sacramentarium Gelasianum*, the blessing of the bride is now a blessing of bride and groom, and in the 1991 edition an epiclesis has been added to the nuptial blessing. Only two rather out-of-date studies, dating from 1987 and 1997 are available in English.[94]

Anointing

A lengthy, if now incomplete, bibliography on the sacrament of anointing the sick is available in the periodical *Ephemerides Liturgicae*,[95] and a reliable study of the rite is also available.[96]

Reconciliation

The story of the revised rite of penance is particularly interesting. On 8 May 1969 the *Consilium* was dissolved and the Congregation of Rites was divided into the Congregation for Divine Worship and the Congregation for the Causes of the

Saints. The discussion on the rite of penance was presented to a special committee of the new Congregation of Divine Worship. The committee finished its work at the end of 1969, but it was never approved. A second committee was convened with, among others, P. Jounel of Paris, P. Visentin OSB of Padua, H.B. Meier SJ of Innsbruck and K. Donovan SJ of London. The final text was promulgated only on 2 December 1973.[97] A lengthy, if now incomplete, bibliography on the sacrament of reconcilation is available in J. Dallen's volume.[98]

Unlike the liturgical provisions of previous Councils and papacies, because of the pastoral concession that liturgy might also be celebrated in the vernacular, two further stages of implementation, translation and implementation, had to occur before the renewed rites could be celebrated in the vernacular. Whereas the *Liturgia Horarum, Missale Romanum, Ordo Baptismi Parvulorum*, and rites of ordination may be celebrated, at least occasionally in the Latin tongue, without difficulty, it makes no sense to celebrate the *Ordo* using the Latin text

More than fifty years after the promulgation of the Constitution *Sacrosanctum Concilium*, we are in a better position to judge the work of the Council and the impact of the documents.[99] Already on the occasion of the twentieth anniversary of the Constitution, the Congregation for Divine Worship held a Congress of the presidents and secretaries of National Liturgical Commissions in Rome from 23–28 October 1984. The acts of the Congress include the testimonies of pastors who affirm the benefit of the reform for their local churches.[100]

Conclusion

After this brief consideration of cultural periods, the liturgical books, and the growth of liturgical science, we can see both the periodical emergence of secular and church liturgical reformers, and that liturgical reform was much frustrated until liturgical scientists could recover ancient sources.

Nor should one forget the influence recently exerted upon the local churches in Europe by the Churches in the former European colonies. Evangelization and catechesis in Africa and Asia had proved the need for new attitudes and practices, especially the pastoral needs in the missions for the vernacular and for restoring the catechumenate. This mission experience would later impact upon the European churches in a process we might call "reverse mission", whereby the newer churches would bring a re-revitalization of the older in their need for a renewed proclamation of the gospel in the industrial and technological worlds of the twentieth century. The renewed forms of liturgical celebrations of the sacraments, promulgated by the Second Vatican Council, were needed to assist the growth of the Church worldwide.

Only after the rediscovery of the ancient sources of the liturgy could the classical liturgical movement begin; only then could the liturgical renewal initiated by Pius XII bear fruit. One wonders whether, had the decision to concede the general vernacular celebration of all the liturgical rites not been made, would the course of the Pian and Vatican II reform and its implementation have run more smoothly? One wonders too, will the face of the Latin Roman rite church and her liturgies in the twenty-first century remain European and American or become more Asian and African, thus bringing to the fore again, as at the first Pentecost, the universal aspect of the Church.

May the prayers of St. John XXIII assist this New Pentecost:

> Renova aetate hac nostra per novam veluti Pentecosten mirabilia tua, atque Ecclesiae Sanctae concede, ut cum Maria, Matre Iesu, unanimiter et instanter in oratione perseverans, itemque a Beato Petro ducta, divini Salvatoris regnum amplificet, regnum veritatis et iustitiae, regnum amoris et pacis. Amen.[101]

Notes

1 B. Neunheuser, *Storia della Liturgia attraverso le epoche culturali*, BELS 11 (1999).

2 Ibid. pp. 26–7.

3 W. Rordorf & A. Tuillier (eds), *La Doctrine des Douze Apôtres (Didache)*, SC 248 bis (1998), ch. 7 "Le baptême," pp. 170–3.

4 G. Dix, *Shape of the Liturgy* (London: Dacre Press, 1945), p. 56.

5 Rordorf & Tuillier, *La Doctrine des Douze Apôtres*, ch. 11 "Les apôtres, Les prophètes," pp. 184–7; ch. 15 "La hiérarchie locale," pp. 192–5.

6 C. Munier (ed.), *Apologies pour les Chrétiens*, SC 507 (2006), Justinus Martyr, *Apologia* I, 61, 3–13, pp. 288–93. O. Rousseau (ed.), *Demonstration de la Prédication Apostolique*, SC 406 (1995), Irenaeus Lugdunensis, *Demonstrations* 3, 7, 42, pp. 140–2.

7 J. Pinell, "Origini e primi sviluppi del Rito Romano," in D. Sartore & A.M. Triacca (eds), *Nuovo Dizionario di Liturgia* (Cinisello Balsamo: Paoline, 1984), pp. 779–82 (p. 779).
   C. Mohrmann, "Les origines de la latinité chrétienne à Rome," *Vigiliae Christianae* 3 (1949), pp. 67–106, 163–83; "Quelques observations sur l'evolution stylistique du canon de la messe romaine," *Vigiliae Christianae* 4 (1950), pp. 1–19.

8 R. Refoulé (ed.), Tertullianus, Quintus Septimus Florus, *De Baptismo*, VII, 1, SC 35 (1952), p. 76.

9 B. Botte (ed.), *La Tradition Apostolique de Saint Hippolyte: Essai de reconstruction*, Liturgiewissenschaftliche Quellen und Forschungen 39 (Münster: Aschendorff, 1989), chs 15–21, pp. 32–59.

10 B. Botte (ed.), Ambrosius Mediolensis, *De Mysteriis, De Sacramentis*, SC 25 bis (1961).

11 *La Tradition Apostolique de Saint Hippolyte*, ch 4, "De oblatione", 10–17.

12 Ibid, ch. 3, "Oratio consecrationis episcopi," pp. 6–7; ch. 7 "De presbyteris", pp. 20–3; ch. 7 "De diaconis," pp. 22–7.

13 G. Bardy (ed.), Eusebius Caesariensis, *Historia Ecclesiastica*, Liber VI, c. 43, para 11, SC 41 (1955), p. 156.

14 *La Tradition Apostolique de Saint Hippolyte*, ch 5, "De oblatio olei," pp. 18–19.

15 Hermas, *Visiones, Mandata, Similitudines* in H. Karpp & D. Devoti (eds), *La penitenza: Fonti sull'origine della penitenza nella Chiesa antica* (Turin: Società Editrice Internazionale, 1973), pp. 36–95.

16 J. Evenou, "The First Three Centuries" in A.-G. Martimort (ed.), M.J. O'Connell (trans.), *The Church at Prayer: An Introduction to the Liturgy – Vol. 3 The Sacraments* (London & Collegeville: Geoffrey Chapman & Liturgical Press, 1988), pp. 186–9.

17 J.M. Wallace-Hadrill, *The Barbarian West 400-800* (Oxford: Blackwells, 1997), pp. 33–4.

18 E. Bishop, "The Genius of the Roman Rite," in *Liturgica Historica* (Oxford: Clarendon Press, 1918), pp. 1–19.

19 L.C. Mohlberg, L. Eizenhöfer & P. Siffrin (eds.), *Sacramentarium Veronense* (olim dictum Leonianum) (*Cod. Bibl. Capit. Veron. LXXXV [80]*), (Rome: Herder, 1978).

20 M. Andrieu (ed.), "Ordo Romanus 11," in *Les Ordines Romani du haut moyen age*, Études et documents 23 (Louvain: Spicilegium Sacrum Lovaniense, 1971), 2, pp. 415–47 (*Ordo Romanus 11*); pp. 363–447, esp. ch 2: "L'Ordo XI et les sacramentaires romains," pp. 380–408 and the text, pp. 417–17.

21 A. Crépin & M. Lapidge (eds), Beda venerabilis, *Historia ecclesiastica gentis Anglorum*, SC 489 (2005), book 1, ch.7, pp. 132–40.

22 Augustinus Hipponensis, *De doctrina Christiana* 3, 9, 13 (CCL 32: 86).

23 P. Jounel, "The Ancient Roman Rituals of Ordinations," in Martimort, *The Sacraments*, pp. 151–62.

24 A. Nocent, "Christian Marriage from the Fourth to the Tenth Century," in A.J. Chupungco (ed.), E. Hagman, D. Cotter, M. Beaumont & M.J. O'Connell (trans.), *Handbook for Liturgical Studies - Vol. 4: Sacraments and Sacramentals* (Collegeville: Liturgical Press, 2000), pp. 285–91; J. Evenou, "The Fourth to the Seventh Centuries," Martimort, *The Sacraments*, pp. 189–92, esp. p. 89.

25 Mohlberg, *Sacramentarium Veronense*, xxxi. incipit uelatio nuptialis, nn. 1105–10, pp. 139–40.

26 L.C. Mohlberg, L.Eizenhöfer & P. Siffrin (eds), *Liber sacramentorum romanae aeclesiae ordinis anni circuli*, no. 382–3 (*Cod. Vat. Reg. Lat. 316/Paris Bibl. Nat. 7193, 41/56*) (*Sacramentarium Gelasianum*), (Rome: Herder, 1981), L. incipit accio nuptialis, nn. 1443–55, pp. 208–10.

27 J. Deshusses (ed.), *Le Sacramentaire Grégorien: Ses principales formes d'après les plus anciens manuscrits*, Spicilegium Friburgense 16 (Fribourg: Éditions universitaires, 1992) 1, p. 200. oratn. ad sponsas velandas, nn. 833–9, pp. 308–11.

28 "Hadrianum ex authentico, ad fidem codicis Cameracensis 164, cum pluribus *collatis* codicibus saeculo IX exaratis," n. 334 in ibid, 1, p. 172; Mohlberg, *Liber sacramentorum romanae aeclesiae ordinis anni circuli*, p. 61.

29 A.G. Martimort, "The Prayer of the Sick and Anointing During the First Seven Centuries: Latin Formularies," in Martimort, *The Sacraments*, p. 121.

30 Deshusses, *Le Sacramentaire Grégorien*, 208. orat. ad uisitandum infirmum, nn. 987–8, p. 338; 209. ortn. super paenitentem, n. 989, p. 338.

31 Mohlberg, *Liber sacramentorum romanae aeclesiae ordinis anni circuli*, lxviiii. oratio super infirmum in domo, nn. 1535–8, pp. 221–2; lxx. item orationes ad missam pro infirmum, nn. 1539–42, p. 222; followed by lxxi. oratio pro reddita sanitatem n. 1543, p. 222, and lxii. oratio Intrantibus in domo sive benedictio, nn 1544–7, p. 223; lxxiii. item orationes ad missas, nn. 1548–53, pp. 223–4.

32 Deshusses, *Le Sacramentaire Grégorien*, p. 39. feria ii ad sanctum petrum as uincula, n. 174, p. 135.

33 Ibid, p. 201; orationes pro peccatis, nn. 840–75, pp. 311–17.

34 Mohlberg, *Liber sacramentorum romanae aeclesiae ordinis anni circuli*,, xvi. ordo agentes publicam paenitentiam, n. 83, p. 18.

35 Mohlberg, *Liber sacramentorum romanae aeclesiae ordinis anni circuli*,, xxxviii. orationes in quinta feria, nn. 349–51, pp. 55–6; ordo agentibus publicam paenitentiam, nn. 352–9, pp. 56–7; item ad reconciliandum penitentem, nn. 360–3, pp. 57–8.

36 Supplement to the *Hadrianum*, xcxvii. orationes ad reconciliandum penitentem feria v in cena domini, nn. 1383–5, pp. 452–3.

37 R. McKitterick, *Charlemagne: The Formation of a European Identity* (Cambridge: Cambridge University Press, 2008), p. 313.

38 G.D. Mansi (ed.), Theodulphus Aurelianensis, *Ab anno 855 usque ad annum 868,* Sacrorum Conciliorum nova et amplissima collectio 13 (Paris: H. Welter, 1908), pp. 933 sqq; A. Boretius (ed.), *Capitularia regum francorum,* vol. 1 (Hannover: Impensis Biblipolii Hahniani, 1881), nn. 123, 242–4; n. 177, pp. 362–6.

39 E. Van Houts, *The Normans in Europe* (Manchester: Manchester University Press, 2000), *passim.*

40 E. Foley & N. Mitchell, "The Drive Towards Liturgical Uniformity in the Latin West," in E. Foley, N. Mitchell, J.M. Pierce & D.W. Trautman (eds), *A Commentary on the General Instruction of the Roman Missal* (Collegeville: Liturgical Press, 2008), pp. 11–17.

41 *Duplex legislationis edictum 23*; Boretius, *Capitularia regum francorum,* p. 64.

42 Alcuinus, Ep. 134 and 137; E. Dümmler (ed.), *Epistolae karolini aevi,* vol. 2, (Berlin: Weiderman, 1895), pp. 202–3, 214–15.

43 R. Cabié, "The Evolution of Initiation in the West from the Twelfth and Thirteenth Centuries On," in Martimort, *The Sacraments,* pp. 70–7, esp p. 71.

44 *Sacramentarium Gellonensis* nn. 2878–87.

45 P. Jounel, "The Ordination Ritual at Rome in about the year One Thousand," in Martimort, *The Sacraments,* pp. 164–9.

46 J. Evenou, "Gaul, Spain and the Celtic Countries: The 'Benedictio in Thalamo'," in ibid, pp. 191–2; J. Evenou, "Marriage at the Door of the Church in the Middle Age," in Martimort, ibid, pp. 198–200.

47 See, for example, G. Greenwell (ed.), *The Pontifical of Egbert, Archbishop of York, A.D. 732–766. Now first printed from a manuscript of the tenth century in the Imperial Library, Paris* (Paris, BN lat. 10575), (London: Surtees Society 1853), pp. 125–6; H.M.J. Banting (ed.), *Two Anglo-Saxon Pontificals: The Egbert and Sidney Sussex Pontificals,* HBS 104 (1989).

48 Mohlberg, *Liber sacramentorum romanae aeclesiae ordinis anni circuli,* lxviiii. oratio super infirmum in domo, nn. 1535–8, pp. 221–2; lxx. item orationes ad missam pro infirmum, no 1539–42, p. 222; followed by lxxi. oratio pro reddita sanitatem n. 1543, p. 222, and lxii. oratio Intrantibus in domo sive benedictio, nn. 1544–7, p. 223; lxxiii. item orationes ad missas, nn. 1548–53, pp. 223–4.

49 Mohlberg, *Liber sacramentorum romanae aeclesiae ordinis anni circuli,,* lxviiii. oratio super infirmum in domo, nn. 1535–8, pp. 221–2.

50 Supplement to the *Hadrianum,* xcviiii. orationes ad uisitandum infirmum, nn. 1386–91, pp. 453–5; idem., c. missa pro infirmum, nn 1392–4, pp. 455–6.

51 P.M. Gy, "The Ritual in Tariff-Penance," in Martimort, *The Sacraments,* pp. 109–110.

52 R. Cabié, "The Evolution of Initiation in the West from the Twelfth and Thirteenth Centuries On," in ibid, pp. 70–7, esp pp. 72–3.

53 M. Andrieu (ed.), *Le pontifical de la Curie Romaine au XIIIe siècle,* ST 87 (1940), 34, *Ordo ad consignandos pueros sive infantes,* pp. 452–3.

54 A. Cellier (ed.), Guillelmus Durandus (William Durandus), *Rationale divinorum officiorum* (Lyons: Cellier, 1672), V I, 84 de confirmatione, 6–8, 368; A. Davril & T.M. Thibomeau (eds), *Rationale divinorum officiorum Guillelmi Duranti: libri V et VI,* CCM 140 A (1998), pp. 433–4.

55 M. Andrieu (ed.), *Le pontifical romain du XIIe siècle,* ST 86 (1938), 32, 31; p. 247; *Le pontifical de la Curie Romaine au XIIIe siècle,* 34, 1, p. 452; *Le pontifical de Guillaume Durand,* ST 88 (1940), I, 1, 2, p. 333.

56 P. Jounel, "The Ritual of Ordination from the Thirteenth to the Twentieth Century," in Martimort, *The Sacraments*, pp. 170-2.

57 J.B. Molin & P. Mutembe, *Le rituel du mariage en France du XIIe au XVIe siècle* (Paris: Beauchesne, 1974), p. 108.

58 W.G. Henderson (ed.), *Manuale et processionale ad usum insignis ecclesiae Eboracensis,* (London & Durham: Surtees Society, 1875), Ordines V, VI, X; *Missale Salisburgensis* 1555; Molin-Mutembe, *Le Rituel du mariage*, p. 110.

59 J.B. Molin, "Un rituel italien du mariage au XVIe siècle," *Ecclesia Orans* 2 (1985), pp. 163-71.

60 *In 4 Sent.,* d. 26, q. 1, art. 1 ad 2. Cf. also q.2. art 3 ad 2; Molin-Mutembe, *Le Rituel,* p. 125, n. 25.

61 P. Dinter (ed.), *Liber tramitis aevi Odilonis abbatis,* (Sieberg: Schmitt, 1980), nn. 193-4, pp. 269-72.

62 Described in Martimort, *The Sacraments*, p. 132.

63 *Ordo Romanus XLVIII, Ordo ad visitandum infirmum; Ordo Romanus XLIX, Ordo « compendiosus et consequens » ad unguendum infirmum,* Andrieu, *Le pontifical de la Curie Romaine au XIIIe siècle,* pp. 486-90, 490-6.

64 DZ 1323.

65 DZ 1673; P.M. Gy, "The Ritual Down to Vatican II," in Martimort, *The Sacraments*, pp. 112-13.

66 Julius II, *Bull,* February 19, 1513; *Collectiones Bullarum Brevium aliorumque diplomatum sacrosanctae Basilicae Vaticanae,* vol. II (Rome: Typographus Pontificius Vaticanus, 1750), pp. 348-51.

67 J.B. Mittarelli & A. Costadoni (eds), V. Quirini & T. Giustiniani, *Libellus supplex ad Leonem X* (Venice: Annales Camaldulenises, 1773), pp. 612-719; liturgical part: pp. 668-714.

68 K.B. Osborne, *The Christian Sacraments of Initiation: Baptism, Confirmation, Eucharist* (New York/Mahwah: Paulist Press, 1987), p. 138.

69 Bull of Pius V, *Quod ad nobis* for the *Breviarium Romanum* 1568.

70 Bull of Pius V, *Quo primum* for the *Missale Romanum* 1570.

71 "De Sacram. Baptis. De Baptismo Adultorum," M. Sodi & J.J. Flores Arcas (eds), *Rituale Romanum: editio princeps 1614,* MLCT 5 (2004), pp. 19-36.

72 "De Sacramento Baptismi rite admnistrando," ibid, pp. 13-26.

73 R. Cabié, "The Evolution of Initiation in the West from the Twelfth and Thirteenth Centuries On," in Martimort, *The Sacraments*, p. 73.

74 P. Jounel, "The Ritual of Ordination from the Thirteenth to the Twentieth Century," in Martimort, *The Sacraments*, p. 171, and n. 83, citing E. Dekkers, *Clavis patrum latinorum* (Steenbrugge: St. Pietersabdij, 1961), n. 1222.

75 A. Nocent, "Christian Marriage from the Eleventh Century to Vatican II," in Chupungco, *Sacraments and Sacramentals*, pp. 291-7.

76 DZ 1813-1816. See A. Duval, "La formule 'Ego vos in matrimonium coniugo' au concile de Trente," La Maison Dieu 99 (1969), pp. 144-53.

77 Missa votiva "Pro sponso et sponsa," M. Sodi & A.M. Triacca (eds), *Missale Romanum: editio princeps 1570,* MLCT 2 (1998), pp. 636-8.

78 "De Sacramento Matrimonii," Sodi & Flores Arcas, *Rituale Romanum: editio princeps 1614,* pp. 136-40.

79 J. Evenou, "Marriage in the West After the Council of Trent," in Martimort, *The Sacraments*, pp. 200-1.

80 Sodi & Flores Arcas, *Rituale Romanum: editio princeps 1614,* "De Sacramento extremo Vnctionis," pp. 56–63. For a more detailed treatment see Martimort, *The Sacraments,* pp. 132–3.

81 Ibid, "De sacramento poenitentiae", pp. 40–7; P.M. Gy, "The Ritual Down to Vatican II," Martimort, *The Sacraments,* p. 113.

82 The correction was made only in the *ordo* for confirmation that was put in an appendix of the Pontifical and intended for cases when there was to be only one confirmand. In the main text of the *Pontificale Romanum* 1752 we find the formula, "*Tunc extensis versus confirmandos manibus, dicit:*" url: *http://www.liturgialatina.org/pontificale/008. htm* (accessed: 6 February 2011).

83 One remarkable publication in England was P. Gandolphy (ed.), *Liturgy or a Book of Common Prayer, and administration of Sacraments, with other Rites and Ceremonies of the Church. For the use of all Christians in the United Kingdom, of Great Britain and Ireland* (London: Keating, Brown & Keating,1812), described in J.D. Crichton, *Worship in a Hidden Church* (Blackrock: Columba Press, 1988), p. 95.

84 R.W. Franklin, *Nineteenth-century Churches: The History of the new Catholicism in Württemberg, England and France* (New York & London: Garland Publishing, 1987), p. 1.

85 Let one example of each liturgical book of the sacraments suffice: *Missale romanum, ex decreto sacrosancti Concilii Tridentini restitutum S. Pii V pontificis maximi jussu editum Clementis VIII et Urbani VIII auctoritate recognitum cum aditamentis novissiimis* (Turin: Petri Marietti, 1880); *Pontificale Romanum Benedicto Clementis VIII ac Urbani VIII jussu editum, postremo a SS. Domini nostro Benedicto XIV. Recognitum et castigatum* (Venice: Balleoni, 1823); *Rituale romanum Pauli V pontificis maximi jussu editum et a Benedicto XIV auctum et castigatum, cui ad usum missionariorum apostolicorum nova nunc primum accedit benedictionum et instructionum appendix* (Rome: Typis s. Congregationis de Propaganda Fide, 1864).

86 Beauduin, L., "La Vraie Prière de l'Église," developed and later published as *La Pieté de l'Église: Principes et Faits* (Louvain: Mont César & Maredsous, 1914). ET: *Liturgy: The Life of the Church,* 3rd edn (Farnborough: St Michael's Abbey Press, 2002).

87 A. Bugnini, *The Reform of the Liturgy: 1948–1975* (Collegeville: Liturgical Press, 1990), pp. 5–10; C. Braga, *La Riforma Liturgica di Pio XII*: BELS 128 (2003), document 1: *La "Memoria sulla Riforma liturgica."*

88 John XXIII, Apostolic Constitution, *Humanae Salutis,* AAS 51 (1959), p. 832.

89 P. Rouillard, "The Sacrament of Extreme Unction: Twelfth to Twentieth Century," in Chupungco, *Sacraments and Sacramentals,* pp. 175–8.

90 Second Vatican Council, "Sacrosanctum Concilium," AAS 54 (1964), pp. 97–138.

91 A. Kavanagh, *The Shape of Baptism: The Rite of Christian Initiation* (New York: Pueblo Books, 1978; Collegeville: Liturgical Press, 1991); G. Austin, *Anointing with the Spirit: The Rite of Confirmation/The Use of Oil and Chrism* (New York: Pueblo Books, 1985; Collegeville: Liturgical Press, 2000); A. Nocent, "L'Ordo Confirmationis: Un rituel qui exige de profonds remaniements," *Studia Liturgica* 8 (1991), pp. 277–91; P. Turner, *Confirmation: The Baby in Solomon's Court* (New York: Paulist Press, 1993).

92 Paul VI, Apostolic Constitution *Pontificalis Romani* (June 18 1968) AAS 60 (1968) pp. 369–73.

93 P. Jounel, "The New Ritual for Ordinations," in Martimort, *The Sacraments,* pp. 172–9.

94 K.W. Stevenson, *To Join Together: The Rite of Marriage* (New York: Pueblo Books, 1987; Collegeville: Liturgical Press, 1994), pp. 245–55; A. Nocent, "The Rite of Marriage after Vatican II," in Chupungco, *Sacraments and Sacramentals,* pp. 297–301.

95 A.-M. Triacca, "Per una rassegna sul sacramento dell'unzione degli infermi",
    Ephemerides Liturgicae 89 (1975), pp. 397–467.

96 C.W. Gusmer, *And You Visited Me: Sacramental Ministry to the Sick and Dying* (New
    York: Pueblo Books, 1984; Collegeville: The Liturgical Press, 1990).

97 J. Dallen, *Reconciling Community: The Rite of Penance* (New York: Pueblo Books, 1986;
    Collegeville: The Liturgical Press, 1991), pp. 213–14; K. Donovan, "History of Penance
    in the West," *Music and Liturgy* 1 (1974), pp. 8–13; idem, "The New Ordo
    Paenitentiae," *Clergy Review* 59 (1974), pp. 660–71.

98 Dallen, *Reconciling Community,* pp. 408–32.

99 A.J. Chupungco, "Sacrosanctum Concilium: Its Vision and Achievements," *Ecclesia
    Orans* 13 (1996), pp. 495–14.

100 Congregazione per il Culto Divino: *Atti del Convegno dei presidenti e segretari delle
    Commissioni nazionali di Liturgia* (Padua: Edizioni Messaggero, 1986).

101 Renew Your wonders in our time, as though for [by] a new Pentecost and grant that
    the holy Church, persevering singlemindedly and continuously in prayer, together
    with Mary, the mother of Jesus, and also under the guidance of St. Peter, may increase
    the reign of the Divine Saviour, the reign of truth and justice, the reign of love and
    peace. Amen. John XXIII, Apostolic Constitution *Humanae Salutis,* AAS 51 (1959),
    p. 832.

102 Vogel writes: "By the XVI century, the process of liturgical codification was over . . .
    (and) the documents liturgical scholars collected were to prove helpful for the (later)
    study of medieval liturgy," *Medieval Liturgy,* p. 17. Thus many first editions of key
    texts were published within one hundred years after the end of the Council of
    Trent.

103 Ibid, pp. 38–9.

104 I. Scicolone, *Il Cardinale Giuseppe Tomasi di Lampedusa e gli inizi della scienza
    liturgica* Studia Anselmiana 82 [Analecta Liturgica 5], (Rome: Pontificium Athenaeum
    S. Anselmi de Urbe, 1981) p. 79 n. 44.

105 Ibid, pp. 79 n. 45.

106 Ibid, pp. 79 n. 46; A. Gruys & J.P. Gumbert (eds), *Codicologica: Towards a Science of
    Handwritten Books* (*Litterae textuales*), (Leiden: Brill, 1976), p. 44, names the codex as
    the *Sacramentaire de Corbie*; F.S. Paxton, *Christianizing Death: Creation of a Ritual
    Process in Early Medieval Europe* (Ithaca & London: Cornell University Press 1996),
    p. 149 n. 78, calls it the St Eligius sacramentary; K. Gamber, *Codices liturgici latini
    antiquiores,* Spicilegii Friburgensis Subsidia 1 (Freiburg: Universitätsverlag Freiburg
    Schweiz Freiburg, 1968), p. 901.

107 J. Crichton, "The First liturgical Saint, Giuseppe Tommasi (1649–1713)," in *Lights in
    the Darkness: Forerunners of the Liturgical Movement* (Blackrock: Columba Press,
    1996), pp. 11–13; Scicolone, *Il Cardinale Giuseppe Tomasi, passim.*

108 Scicolone, ibid. pp. 70–5.

109 Ibid. pp. 75–6.

110 Ibid. pp. 76–7.

111 Ibid. pp. 77–8.

112 G. O'Connor, *The sources of the Orations of the* Missale Parisiense *of 1738: A study
    of the Concordances* (Rome: Pontificium Athenaeum S. Anselmi de Urbe, 2004),
    pp. 1–2.

113 J. Crichton, "Lodovico Antonio Muratori (1627–1750)," in *Lights in the Darkness,*
    pp. 14–24.

Bibliography

The sacraments in apostolic times

Neunheuser, B., *Storia della Liturgia attraverso le epoche culturali,* BELS 11 (1999),
pp. 29–43 "L'epoca del nuovo testamento: le forme apostoliche fondamentali."
Beckwith, R.T., "The Jewish Background to Christian Worship" in C. Jones, G. Wainwright,
E. Yarnold & P. Bradshaw (eds), *The Study of Liturgy* (London: SPCK, 1992), pp. 68–80.
Brown, R.E., *The Church the Apostles Left Behind* (Mahwah: Paulist Press, 1984).
Cattaneo, E., *Il culto cristiano in occidente* (Rome: CLV, 1984), pp. 16–17 "Alle origini del
culto cristiano; dall'ebraismo al cristianesimo."
Chupungco, A.J., "The Jewish Roots" in A.J. Chupungco (ed.), E. Hagman, D. Cotter,
M. Beaumont (trans.), *Sacramenti e sacramentali* (Casale Monferrato: Piemme, 1997),
pp. 98–102.
—— *Worship: Beyond Inculturation* (Washington DC: Pastoral Press, 1994), pp. 1–18
"Baptism in the Early Church and its Cultural Settings."
Dix, G., *The Shape of the Liturgy* (London: Dacre Press, 1945).
Grelot, P., *La liturgie dans le Nouveau Testament* (Paris: Desclée, 1991).
Gy, P.M., "Les anciennes prières d'ordination" *La Maison-Dieu* n. 138 (1979), pp. 93–122.
Fisher, E.J., (ed.) *The Jewish Roots to Christian Liturgy* (New York: Paulist Press, 1990),
pp. 39–51.
Klauser, T., J. Halliburton (trans.), *A Short History of the Western Liturgy: An Account and
Some Reflections* (Oxford: Oxford University Press, 1979).
Marsili, S., "Continuità ebraica e novità cristiano" in S. Marsili, J. Pinell, A.M. Triacca,
T. Federici, A. Nocent & B. Neunheuser (eds), *La liturgia: panorama storico generale*
(Casale Monferrato: Marietti, 1978), pp. 13–39.
Oesterley, W.O.E., *The Jewish Background to the Christian Liturgy* (Oxford: Oxford
University Press, 1925).

Liturgical sources

*The Holy Bible Containing the Old and New Testaments with the Apocryphal /
Deuterocanonical Books, New Revised Standard Version* (Oxford University Press: New
York & Oxford, 1989).
*Nova Vulgata Bibliorum Sacrorum editio: Sacrosancti Oecumenici Concilii Vaticani II
ratione habita iussu Pauli PP. VI recognita auctoritate Pauli PP. II promulgata, editio
typica altera* (Vatican City: LEV, 1998).
Rordorf, W. & A. Tuillier (eds), *La Doctrine des Douze Apôtres (Didache),* (SC 248: 1998).

The sacraments in Greek and Latin cultures (110–399)

Neunheuser, *Storia della Liturgia attraverso le epoche culturali,* pp. 45–64 "L'ingresso
definitivo nel mondo Greco-latino."
Andrieu, M., *Les ordines romani du haute Moyen Age,* vol. 3 (Louvain: Spicilegium sacrum
Lovaniense, 1961), notes 541–3 "Origine Romaine de l'Ordo XXXIV: Le rituel des
ordinations, date, son influence en Pays Franc."
Dix, G., *Jew and Greek: A Study in the Primitive Church* (Westminster: Dacre Press, 1953),
pp. 76–112 "The Gospel for the Greeks."

Liturgical sources

Botte, B. (ed.), *La Tradition Apostolique de Saint Hippolyte: Essai de reconstruction* (Münster: Aschendorff, 1989).

Karpp, H. & D. Devoti Hermas (eds), *Visiones, Mandata, Similitudines, La penitenza: Fonti sull'origine della penitenza nella Chiesa antica* (Torino: Società Editrice Internazionale, 1973), pp. 36–95.

Munier, C. (ed.), Justinus Martyr, *Apologia I, Apologies pour les Chrétiens*, SC 507 (2006), pp. 126–318.

Rousseau, O. (ed.), Irenaeus Lugdunensis, *Demonstration de la Prédication Apostolique*, SC 406 (1995).

Simonetti, M. & C. Moreschini (eds), Cyprianus Carthaginensis (Thascius Caecilius), *De dominica oratione*, CCL 3A (1976), pp. 90–113.

—— Cyprianus Carthaginensis, *De mortalitate*, CCL 3A (1976), pp. 17–32.

Tertullianus, Quintus Septimus Florus, *De Baptismo (Traité du Baptême)*, R. Refoulé (ed.) SC 35 (1952).

The classical Roman form of the sacraments (400–799)

Neunheuser, *Storia della Liturgia attraverso le epoche culturali*, pp. 79–94, "L'epoca della liturgia romana pura."

Beda venerabilis, D. Hurst (trans.), *The Commentary on the Seven Catholic Epistles* (Cistercian Studies 28), (Kalamazoo: Cistercian Publications, 1985), pp. 61–2.

Bishop, E., *Liturgica Historica* (Oxford: Clarendon Press, 1918), pp. 1–19 "The Genius of the Roman Rite."

Crépin A. & M. Lapidge (eds), Beda venerabilis, *Historia ecclesiastica gentis Anglorum*, vols 1–3, SC (2005), pp. 489–91.

Vogel, C., W.G. Storey & N.K. Rasmussen (trans. & rev.), *Medieval Liturgy: An Introduction to the Sources* (Washington DC: Pastoral Press, 1986).

Wallace-Hadrill, J.M., *The Barbarian West 400–800* (Oxford: Blackwells, 1997).

Liturgical sources

Andrieu, M. (ed.), *Les Ordines Romani du haut moyen âge: Tome 2: Les textes (Ordines I–XIII)*, Études et documents 23 (Louvain: Spicilegium Sacrum Lovaniense, 1948).

—— *Les Ordines Romani du haut moyen age*, Études et documents 23 (Louvain: Spicilegium Sacrum Lovaniense, 1971), vol. 2, pp. 1–108 "Ordo Romanus Primus", pp. 415–47 "Ordo Romanus 11".

—— *Les Ordines Romani du haut moyen age*, Études et documents 24 (Louvain: Spicilegium Sacrum Lovaniense, 1974), vol. 3, pp. 601–19 "Ordo Romanus 34."

—— *Les Ordines Romani du haute Moyen Age*, Études et Documents, 24 (Louvain: Spicilegium sacrum Lovaniense, 1961), vol. 3, pp. 616–19 "Statuta Ecclesiae antiqua", nn. 541–3.

Deshusses, J. (ed.), *Le Sacramentaire Grégorien: Ses principales formes d'après les plus anciens manuscrits*, 3 vols, Spicilegium Friburgense 16 (Fribourg: Éditions universitaires, 1992), "Hadrianum ex authentico, ad fidem codicis Cameracensis 164, cum pluribus collatis codicibus saeculo IX exaratis", vol. 1, nn. 1–1018, 83–348.

L. Duchesne, *Étude sur le Liber pontificalis* (Paris: Thorin, 1877).

—— *Le Liber pontificalis: texte, introduction et commentaire*, 2 vols (Paris: Thorin, 1884–92).

—— *Le Liber Pontificalis: texte, introduction et commentaire* vol. I (Paris: Boccard, 1981).

Mohlberg, L.C., l. Eizenhöfer & P. Siffrin (eds), *Liber sacramentorum romanae aeclesiae ordinis anni circuli: Cod. Vat. Reg. Lat. 316/Paris Bibl. Nat. 7193, 41/56* (*Sacramentarium Gelasianum*), (Rome: Herder, 1981).

—— *Sacramentarium Veronense* (olim dictum Leonianum) *Cod. Bibl. Capit. Veron. LXXXV [80]*, (Rome: Herder, 1978).

The Franco-Germanic and medieval Roman forms (800–1199)

Neunheuser, *Storia della Liturgia attraverso le epoche culturali*, pp. 95–108 "Passaggio della liturgia romana pura al mondo Franco-germanico", pp. 109–21 "Formazione della liturgia 'romana' del Medioevo."

Cowdrey, H.E.J., *Pope Gregory VII, 1073–1085* (Oxford: Oxford University Press, 1998).

—— "Pope Gregory VII (1073–85) and the Liturgy," *Journal of Theological Studies* 55 (2004), pp. 55–83.

Foley, E. & N. Mitchell, "The Drive Towards Liturgical Uniformity in the Latin West," in E. Foley, N. Mitchell, J.M. Pierce & D.W. Trautman (eds), *A Commentary on the General Instruction of the Roman Missal* (Collegeville: Liturgical Press, 2008), pp. 11–17.

McKitterick, R., *Charlemagne: The Formation of a European Identity* (Cambridge: Cambridge University Press, 2008).

Van Houts, E., *The Normans in Europe* (Manchester: Manchester University Press, 2000).

Liturgical sources

Andrieu, M. (ed.), *Le pontifical romain du XIIe siècle*, ST 86 (1938).

Dümmler, E. (ed.), *Epistolae karolini aevi*, vol. 2 (Berlin: Weiderman, 1895), pp. 202–3, 214–15 Alcuinus, Epistulae 134 & 137.

Mohlberg et al. (eds), *Liber sacramentorum romanae aeclesiae ordinis anni circuli.*

Vogel, C. & R. Elze (eds), *Le pontifical Romano-germanique du dixième siècle*, 3 vols ST 226–7, 269 (1963–72).

"Secundum usum Romanae Ecclesiae" and the Autumn of the Middle Ages (1200–1499)

Neunheuser, *Storia della Liturgia attraverso le epoche culturali*, pp. 123–31 "L'epoca della Liturgia 'Secundum Usum Romanae Curiae.'"

Huizinga, J., R.J. Payton & U. Mammitzsch (trans.), *The Autumn of the Middle Ages* (Chicago: University of Chicago Press, 1996).

—— F.J. Hopman (trans.), *The Waning of the Middle Ages: A study of the forms of life, thought and art in France and the Netherlands in the XIVth and XVth centuries* (London: Edward Arnold & Co., 1924) and subsequent editions.

Jungmann, J.A., W. Naberhaus (trans.), "Liturgy on the Eve of the Reformation," *Worship* 33 (1959), pp. 505–15.

—— R. Walls (trans.) *Pastoral Liturgy* (New York & London: Herder & Challoner, 1962), pp. 64–80.

Molin, J.B. & P. Mutembe, *Le rituel du mariage en France du XIIe au XVIe siècle* (Paris: Beauchesne, 1974).

Liturgical sources

Andrieu, *Le pontifical romain du XIIe siècle.*
—— *Le pontifical de Guillaume Durand,* ST 88 (1940).
Lippe, R. (ed.), *Missale Romanum: Mediolani 1474,* 2 vols, HBS 17, 33 (1899, 1907).
Patrizi Piccolomini, A. (ed.), *Pontificalis ordinis liber* (Rome: Impressus, 1485).

The Council of Trent (1500–99) and the Baroque (1600–99)

Neunheuser, *Storia della Liturgia attraverso le epoche culturali,* pp. 133–9 "La Riforma e il Concilio di Trento," pp. 141–5 "Il Barocco."
Cattaneo, *Il culto cristiano in occidente,* pp. 281–305 "Le riforme promosse dal Concilio Lateranense V e da Lutero."
Löwenberg, B., *Das Rituale des Kardinals Julius Antonius Sanctorius. Ein Beitrag zur Entstehungsgeschichte des Rituale Romanum* (Munich: Druk des Salesianischen Offizin, 1937).

Liturgical sources

Castellani, A. (ed), *Liber sacerdotalis auctoritate sanctissimi d. dni viri Leonis decimi approbatus* (Venice: Nachdr. d. Ausg, 1523).
—— *Pontificale secundum ritum Sacrosancte Romane Ecclesie cum multis additionibus opportunis ex apostolica bibliotheca sumptis & alias non impressis: opus sane laudabile atque diuinum* (Venice: Giunta, 1510, 1520, 1543, 1561).
Santori, G.A. Cardinale (comp.), *Rituale sacramentorum Romanum Gregorii papæ XIII p. m. iussu editum* (Rome: n.p., 1584 [sic])
Sodi, M. & A.M. Triacca (eds), *Missale Romanum: editio princeps 1570,* MLCT 2 (1998), with the Bull of Pius V *Quo primum tempore.*
—— *Pontificale Romanum: editio princeps 1596,* MLCT 1 (1997), with the Bull of Clement VIII *Ex quo in Ecclesia Dei.*
Sodi, M. & J.J. Flores Arcas, (eds), *Rituale Romanum: editio princeps 1614,* MLCT 5 (2004), with the Bull of Clement VIII *Cum novissime.*

Liturgical Resources recovered[102]

Bianchini, F., *Verona Sacramentary,* (Rome: n.p., 1735).[103]
Pamelius, J. (Jacques de Joigny de Pamèle), *Liturgicon Ecclesiae latinae,* 2 vols (Cologne: Agrippinae, 1571), containing the Codex *Capit. Metrop. n. 137* of the Gregorian Sacramentary.[104]
Rocca, Angelo, *S. Gregorii M. Liber Sacramentorum,* (Rome: n.p., 1593), containing *Cod. Vat. Lat 3806.*[105]
Ménard, N.H., *Divi Gregori papae I Liber sacramentorum* (Paris: n.p., 1642) containing the Codex *Paris, B.N. ms. Lat. 12051,* a mixed Gelasiano-Gregorian sacramentary.[106]
Mabillon, J., *De liturgia gallicana libri tres* (Paris: Martin & Boudot, 1685).
—— & M. Germain, *Museum italicum seu collectio veterum scriptorum ex bibliothecis italicis eruti,* 2 vols (Paris: Martin & Boudot, 1687 & 1689). Vol. 1 includes the Bobbio Missal under the title *Liber Sacramentorum Ecclesiae gallicanae.*
Tomasi, Cardinal J.M.,[107] *Codices Sacramentorum nongentis annis vetustiores* (Rome: Bernabò, 1680), containing Old Gelasian Sacramentary (MS Vat. lat. Reg. 316),[108]

Missale Gothicum (MS Vat. lat. Reg. 317),[109] *Missale Francorum* (MS Vat. lat. Reg. 257),[110] and *Missale Gallicanum Vetus* (MS Palat. lat. 493),[111] all four *editiones principes*.

The sacraments during the Enlightenment (1700–99)

Neunheuser, *Storia della Liturgia attraverso le epoche culturali*, pp. 147–51 "L'Illuminismo del secolo XVIII."

Bolton, A., *Church Reform in 18th Century Italy: The Synod of Pistoia 1786* (The Hague: Martinus Nijhof, 1969).

Gerhards, A., "Von der Synode in Pistoia (1786) zum Zweiten vatikanischen Konzil. Zur Morphologie der Liturgiereform in 20. Jahrhundert," *Liturgisches Jahrbuch* 36 (1985), pp. 28–45.

Paoletti, A., "Storia del sinodo diocesano di Pistoia," in C. Lamioni (ed.) *Il Sinodo di Pistoia del 1986*, (Rome: Herder, 1991), pp. 529–33.

Pecklers, K., "The Jansenist Critique and the Liturgical Reforms of the Seventeenth and Eighteenth Centuries," *Ecclesia Orans* 20 (2003), pp. 325–38.

Schotte, H., "Zur Geschichte des Emser Kongresses," *Historisches Jahrbuch der Görres-Gesellschaft* 35 (1914), pp. 86–109, 319–48, 781–820.

Liturgical sources

Johnson, C. & A. Ward (eds) *Missale parisiense anno 1738 publici iuris factum*, BELS 97 (1993).

Missale Romanum [promulgated by Urban VIII] (Antwerp: Plantin & Moreti, 1634).

Pontificale Romanum Benedicto PP. XIV p.m. iussu editum et auctum (Rome: Generosi Salomoni, 1752).

Rituale Romanum Pauli PP. V p. m. iussu editum (Rome: Generosi Salomoni, 1752).

Sodi & Triacca, *Pontificale Romanum: editio princeps 1596.*

Liturgical esources recovered

Le Brun, P., *Explication littérale, historique et dogmatique des prières et des ceremonies de la messe*, 4 vols (Paris: Delaulne, 1716–26).

Martène, E., *De antiquis Ecclesiae ritibus libri tres* (Rouen: Behourt, 1700–2).

Missale Parisense (Paris, Mabre-Cramoisy, 1685), then 1705, 1738 and 1776. The 1738 edition was probably of most importance because it was widely accepted throughout France.[112]

Muratori, L.A. (ed.),[113] *Liturgia romana vetus*, 2 vols (Venice: Pasquali, 1748), containing the Leonine (Verona), Gelasian and Gregorian Sacramentaries, *Missale Gothicum*, *Missale Francorum*, two other Gallican missals and *Ordines* I and II.

The sacraments during the romantic Restoration (1800–1909)

Neunheuser, *Storia della Liturgia attraverso le epoche culturali*, pp. 153–56 "La Restaurazione nel secolo XIX."

Liturgical sources

Missale Romanum [promulgated by Benedict XIV] (Rome: Collini, 1752).

Pontificale Romanum Benedicto PP. XIV p.m. iussu editum et auctum, 1st edn (Rome: Typis Generosi Salomoni, 1752).

Pontificale Romanum Benedicto Clementis VIII ac Urbani VIII jussu editum, postremo a SS. Domini nostro Benedicto XIV. Recognitum et castigatum (Venice: Balleoni, 1823) reprinting of 1752 edition.

Pontificale romanum summorum pontificum iussu editum a Benedicto XIV et Leone XIII p. m. Recognitum et castigatum (Regensburg: Pustet, 1888).

Rituale Romanum Pauli PP. V p. m. iussu editum, 1752.

Rituale romanum Pauli V. pontificis maximi jussu editum et a Benedicto XIV auctum et castigatum, cui ad usum missionariorum apostolicorum nova nunc primum accedit benedictionum et instructionum appendix (Rome: Typis s. Congregationis de propaganda fide, Roma 1864).

Liturgical resources recovered

Bryennios, Philotheos (ed.), *The Didache: Teaching of the Twelve Apostles* (New York: Scribner, 1884).

Duchesne, *Étude sur le Liber pontificalis.*

—— *Le Liber pontificalis: texte, introduction et commentaire.*

Feltoe, C.L. (ed.), *Sacramentarium Leonianum* (Cambridge: Cambridge University Press, 1896).

Hauler, E. (ed.), *Didascaliae apostolorum fragmenta Veronensia latina* (Leipzig: Tebner, 1900), pp. 101–21.

Warner, G.F. (ed.), *The Stowe Missal (MS. D.II.3 in the Library of the Royal Irish Academy, Dublin),* HBS 31–2 (1906, 1915), vol. 1 facsimile, vol. 2 text.

The sacraments during the liturgical movement (1909–59)

Neunheuser, *Storia della Liturgia attraverso le epoche culturali,* pp. 157–65 "Il movimento liturgico classico."

—— "Gli inizi del movimento liturgico," "Il movimento liturgico tra affermazioni e contrasti," *Anàmnesis* 1 (1979), pp. 20–9.

—— "L'avvio dell'ultima riforma liturgica," *Anàmnesis* 2 (1978), pp. 246–9.

Bugnini, A., *The Reform of the Liturgy: 1948–1975* (Collegeville: Liturgical Press, 1990), pp. 5–10.

Chupungco, A.J., *Cultural Adaptation of the Liturgy* (New York/Ramsey: Paulist Press, 1982), pp. 3–41 "A History of Liturgical Adaptation," esp. pp. 37–8.

Maas-Ewerd, Th., "Papst Pius XII. und die Reform der Liturgie im 20. Jahrhundert," in *Liturgiewissenschaftliche Quellen und Forschungen* 88 (Münster: Aschendorff, 2002), pp. 606–28.

Ponsard, B., "Réforme et liturgie sous Pie X (1903–14)," in *LQF* 88/2 Aschendorff, Münster, 2002, pp. 592–605.

Liturgical sources

Sodi & Triacca, *Missale Romanum: editio princeps 1570.*

Pontificale romanum summorum pontificum iussu editum a Benedicto XIV et Leone XIII p. m. Recognitum et castigatum (Regensburg: Pustet, 1888).

Pontificale Romanum, editio typica emendata, 2 vols (Vatican City: Typis Polyglottis Vaticanis, 1961); also M. Sodi & A. Toniolo (eds) MLP 3 (2008).

Rituale Romanum Pauli PP. V p. m. iussu editum (Regensburg: Pustet, 1913).

Rituale Romanum Pauli PP. V p. m. iussu editum aliorumque pontificum cura recognitum atque ad normam Codicis Iuris Canonici accomodatum (Rome: Typis Polyglottis Vaticanis, 1925).

Rituale Romanum Pauli PP. V p. m. iussu editum aliorumque pontificum cura recognitum atque ad normam Codicis Iuris Canonici accomodatum, ss.mi D.N. Pii pp. XII auctoritate ordinatum et auctum (Vatican City: Typis Polyglottis Vaticanis, 1952); also MLP 2 (2008).

Liturgical resources recovered

Andrieu, M. (ed.), *Les Ordines Romani du haut moyen âge,* Études et documents 34, 23 (Louvain: Spicilegium Sacrum Lovaniense, 1959, 1948).

Bannister, H.M. (ed.), *Missale Gothicum: A Gallican Sacramentary,* HBS 52, 54 (1917, 1919).

B. Capelle, "L'œuvre liturgique de S. Gélase," *Journal of Theological Studies* 2 (1951), pp. 139–43.

A. Chavasse, *Le Sacramentaire Gélasien* (Paris, Tournai, New York & Rome: Desclée, 1957).

Lowe, E.A. (ed.), *The Bobbio Missal, A Gallican Mass-Book,* HBS 53, 58–9, (1917, 1920, 1924).

The sacraments and the Second Vatican Council (1960–2009)

Neunheuser, *Storia della Liturgia attraverso le epoche culturali,* pp. 167–76 "Il Concilio Vaticano II e il rinnovamento della liturgia dopo il Concilio."

Liturgical sources

Missale Romanum, editiones varia (1970–)

Pontificale Romanum: De Ordinatione diaconi, presbyteri et episcopi, editio typica (Vatican City: Typis Polyglottis Vaticanis, 1968).

Pontificale Romanum: De Ordinatione episcopi, presbyterorum et diaconorum, editio typica altera (Vatican City: Typis Polyglottis Vaticanis, 1990).

Pontificale Romanum Ordo Confirmationis, editio typica (Vatican City: Typis Polyglottis Vaticanis, 1971).

Rituale Romanum ex decreto Sacrosancti Oecumenici Concilii Vaticani II instauratum auctoritate Pauli PP. VI promulgatum: Ordo Baptismi parvulorum, editio typica (Vatican City: Typis Polyglottis Vaticanis, 1969), editio typica altera (Vatican City: Typis Polyglottis Vaticanis, 1973).

Rituale Romanum: Ordo Celebrandi Matrimonium, editio typica (Vatican City: Typis Polyglottis Vaticanis, 1972), editio typica altera (Vatican City: Typis Polyglottis Vaticanis, 1991).

Rituale Romanum: Ordo Initiationis Christianae Adultorum (Vatican City: Typis Polyglottis Vaticanis, 1972), [reimpressio emendata 1974].

Rituale Romanum: Ordo Paenitentiae, editio typica (Vatican City: Typis Polyglottis Vaticanis, 1974).

Rituale Romanum: Ordo Unctionis infirmorum eorumque pastoralis curae, editio typica, (Vatican City: Typis Polyglottis Vaticanis, 1972), [reimpressio 1974].

Chapter 10

THE DIVINE OFFICE IN HISTORY

†Lázló Dobszay

The Divine Office (*Officium divinum*) is, besides the Eucharist (the Holy Mass), the other principal element of the Christian liturgy. Its essence is the common—and in principle the sung—prayer of the psalter along with some complementary elements (see below), distributed on the days of the year and different times or hours ("horae") of the day.

The origins of singing the Office (first–fourth centuries)

The Office is of the same age as Christian piety, since the communities of faithful prayed "psalms, hymns and spiritual songs" (Col. 3:16; Eph. 5:19) regularly and in common as early as the time of the Apostles. In accord with the practice of antiquity this was done always in common chant (at least recitation or cantillation). The order of the Office as a whole has been, however, developed during a longer time, by the confluence of several motives.

The material of the Office

The psalter is the common prayer book of the Old and New Testament. The psalter of the Office is completed by further chants (canticles) which are similar in their constitution and content to the psalms and are selected from both testaments of Sacred Scripture. The psalms were performed in different ways, and the result was the emergence of other kinds of genres (antiphons, responsories, etc. (see below)). The most appropriate context for *reading* Sacred Scripture was given—within the night worship (Vigils/Matins). In addition to the Bible, other poetic texts were given a place—perhaps similar to those mentioned as "spiritual chants" by Apostle Paul. As prose compositions they were similar to the psalms, and their number greatly increased during the centuries, mainly in the Eastern churches. The Latin Church—because of theological considerations—resisted their entry into the Office, except—not without reluctance—the *Te Deum*, attributed to St Ambrose. Some short verses (versicles) were included as introductions and transitions, performed in most cases in dialogical form. From antiquity, the solemn celebration of the Office included ritual *actions*, such as the use of incense, processions, rituals involving light and gestures of the body. Based on the practice of the Church of Apostles, these elements developed up to the fourth century into the organism of the Divine Office.

The hours

The arrangement of the hours cannot be traced back to one individual ecclesiastical decision. The individual components grew from different roots independently from each other. The most important of all was the prayer at dawn and at sunset, which was solemn and common worship in most religions, including the Jewish liturgy. These are not only the ritual sanctification of the beginning and end of working days, but also a mystical-liturgical celebration of the start and end of the day of the cosmos.

The Christians followed suit in their turn—remembering Christ's doctrine and the monition of St Paul (below). The celebration of the nightly watch for dawn, the origins of which might be of private nature that was not fixed, but which soon became common worship following a more or less fixed order, particularly on the eve of Sundays and feasts, moreover on the death of martyrs and other members of the community. The spiritual writers insisted from early times that the faithful should interrupt their work several times during the day and lift up their mind to the Lord. These short prayers were linked to the hours distinguished in civil life, too, and noteworthy also because of their links with sacred events: *hora tertia* (9 a.m.) the advent of the Holy Spirit; *hora sexta* (noon) the crucifixion; *hora nona* (3 p.m.) the death of the Lord. The needs of Christian communities living in common added two hours for sanctifying the beginning and close of daily activity. Fixing hours for prayer was justified by St Paul's monition "pray without ceasing" (1 Thess. 5:17), regarding praying at the set times every day as ceaseless prayer.

Two fields of development

Throughout Christianity the common celebration of praying psalms in the daily celebration of morning and evening prayer and of the occasional observance of the night watch came to be part of the observance of the faithful, clergy (bishops, priests, and deacons), and the men and women consecrated to God in the monastic life. Prayer at the other hours was practised less by individuals. The material of the universally observed hours was taken from a few mostly unchanging psalms, sung in responsorial or antiphonal performance, with the addition of priestly blessings and deprecations, and in some cases also of readings. These celebrations with the participation of a great number of lay people were accompanied with spectacular rites. The scholarly literature calls this form the "cathedral" (where "cathedral" would include what we call parishes today).

The communities of hermits and monks which spread widely during the third and fourth centuries observed the monition to "pray without ceasing" more severely. The psalmody penetrated their daily life perfectly, not only in times reserved for prayer but also during their manual work. Except for the morning and evening prayer one cannot speak of an Office in the strict sense of the word, rather of the practice of continually reciting the psalter, either in common or in alternation with a cantor.

While the cathedral Office for laity and the secular clergy comprised short and selected psalmody following a fixed liturgical order, the monastics' Office was more akin to commonly performed private prayer which included the whole psalter. The difference between the two systems could be seen until the twentieth century reforms to the Office: some parts include fixed, almost unchanged, selected psalms, while other parts comprise the recitation of the full psalter, in order, distributed over days (*psalmodia currens*). In the Ambrosian Office, the two systems are separated so deeply that the selected psalms are prayed again when the *psalmodia currens* arrives at them.

The formation of the set order of Office

Out of these elements a unified system developed, probably in the third–fourth century, with an arrangement for the full day. A synthesis between the "cathedral" and "monastic" Office was facilitated when "urban monasticism" (communities of monks living in or near the secular churches) came into existence.

In the strict sense of the word, one may speak of the "Office" if: the hours of different origin are united into a fixed system; the hours are celebrated every day; and the psalms are arranged in an order extended to all hours. The hours in the set Office are: *Vigils* (the nightly watch, "night praise," later called "matins"); *Lauds* (dawn prayer, earlier also called "morning praise"); *the Little Hours* ("minor hours"), namely *Prime* at the start of daily work, *Terce* at 9 a.m., *Sext* at noon and *None* at 3 p.m.; *Vespers* (evening prayer); and *Compline* at the start of night.

The number of hours is grounded in the tradition articulated in psalm 118: "Seven times a day I praise thee" (v. 164) and "at midnight I rise to praise thee" (v. 62).[1] The times should not be taken literally: the history of Office shows examples of linking or anticipating some hours (e.g. Vigils and Lauds were often linked; the Little Hours connected, Vespers anticipated in the afternoon, etc.).

While the main role of monks was to offer prayer throughout the day, in secular churches it was a norm to sing Lauds and Vespers solemnly every day, and Vigils on solemnities. According to the modern saying "chorus facit monachum" (Office in common makes the monk), the monk is a monk by means of his participation in the common singing of the Office. The difference between secular and monastic celebrations of the Office remained in the Eastern Church practically up to our days; in the West, praying all the hours became the obligation of the priests also, coinciding with the gradual recess of the Office from the liturgical life of parish churches. As a result all the hours developed enormously during the Middle Ages, producing a rich repertory of antiphons, responsories etc., covering the whole liturgical year.

The distribution of the psalter

Though the distribution of psalms was different according to geographical areas and ecclesiastical jurisdictions, several components of individual hours were widely accepted, in some cases throughout the whole of Eastern and Western Christianity (e.g. psalms 50, 148–150 in Lauds, 118 in the Little Hours). In Christian Antiquity, the structure of individual hours (the number and selection of psalms) could differ amongst dioceses and monasteries. In general, however, one may say that the psalms of the Little Hours, and in great part of Lauds, were stable each day, while the *psalmodia currens* (continuous psalmody) survived in Vespers and Vigils.

Chanting of the Office

The Office was celebrated everywhere in chant, either in simple or richer modulations. Whilst there are no musical documents from the first Christian centuries one can reconstruct the main types of musical genres.

In a great part of the Office, the different kinds of recitation were dominant. In the earliest period, when the text was not still memorized, the psalm might be performed in simple recitation. The use of refrains can be documented from the third century onward. The psalmist went through the psalm, and the community joined in from time to time with a refrain. It was a simple recitation similar to what was called from the sixth century at latest the "responsorium breve" (short responsory). The responsorial psalmody disappeared later and had only two remnants: the Invitatory before Vigils (psalm 94 recited throughout by the cantors, with the refrain by the community) and the short responsory, limited later to one verse and the refrain. In the fifth century at the latest, the responsorial psalmody became merely an *addition* instead of being a given form of regular psalmody.

There is another form of responsory, however, which consists of two verses which are highly melismatic, embellished music (almost a "Konzertstück"—a concert piece—within the Office as it were). It is an open question whether it derives from the responsorial psalmody or whether—which is more probable—it had its separate origin. At any rate, at the beginning of the sixth century it was in use: it followed the readings of Vigils. This *responsorium prolixum* became one of the most beautiful, artistic pieces of the Gregorian repertory.

The style which predominated over the short responsory was the *antiphonal* psalmody. The word "antiphon" had several meanings (singing in parallel octaves, in alternation between men and women, with an added refrain). At any rate, its meaning by the beginning of the sixth century was the same as three centuries later: the psalm is recited alternatively between two half-choirs who came together at the end in a song-like refrain, with text taken from the psalm itself, or from other biblical—or later, a poetical—text. Some scholars suggest that the refrain returned several times during the psalmody.

There are very short and simple antiphons whose music is hardly more than a recitation. Other antiphons consist of three, four or more phrases. It is possible that the two categories are the products of two different ages, or are independent chants ("spiritual songs") inherited from the third or fourth century and integrated into the Office. At any rate, the antiphon of the Roman Office is an organic part of the psalmody itself.

How the early communities could learn so many pieces is an enigma for the musician of our day. No doubt, the number of antiphons and responsories was smaller than in the Middle Ages. Furthermore, the demands on the community were less than that on the solo cantor. Also, improvisation was in everyday use— improvisation means here not a free expression of ideas, but the adaptation of musical models. Today the Eastern Churches, Jewish practice, etc., offer good examples of the discipline of model melodies which regulate the performance but also make it easier.

The versicles which introduce or separate longer parts of the Office are simple recitations with an inflexion at the end (sometimes ornate, with a short melisma). It is intoned by a solo singer and the congregation responds in the same melody. The relatively small number of versicles facilitated their memorization. Some introduce or separate sections of the Office: such are the "Deus in adjutorium" as a start of each day hour, the versicle separating the psalmody and readings in Vigils, or the Hymn and Magnificat at Vespers; others introduce the priest's prayer.

The Hymn is strophic; all verses are sung in the same tune. As to the form, most follow the first hymnographer, St Ambrose (four iambs in each line, four lines in each strophe). Some later pieces adapted the metric pattern of antiquity (sapphic, asclepiadic). The melodies were originally rather simple, but became more and more ornate in the Middle Ages.

The readings of Vigils were recited in special tones with inflexions which corresponded to the grammatical structure of the text. The biblical readings in the day hours (the "capitulum") were not regarded as readings and were recited on a special tone by the celebrant rather than a lector.

Integral and additional parts of the Office

When we study the liturgical books we may be surprised to see that several familiar elements of the hours are absent in the Office for the Sacred Triduum. There is no hymn, no invitatory, no introductory versicle, capitulum or doxology (*Gloria Patri* ...). It is still more astonishing that the monastic Office is not only similar to the secular one, but that its structure was more akin to the secular arrangement rather than with the monastic rite. The symbolic explanation of the omission of these elements was the austerity and sorrow adopted for the days commemorating the Lord's passion and death. But this is surely not the case: neither the doxology nor the capitulum has anything to do with exultation. The real cause might be that these elements are younger than the original Office of the Sacred Triduum and these "innovations" were not adopted for these holy days, not even by the monastics. The hymn is typical: it spread in the sphere of *some* traditions during the fifth or sixth centuries, and still later in Rome herself. The doxology was also an addition at the time when the expression of orthodox doctrine in respect of the Holy Trinity was important.

Therefore, these elements are a second layer in the development of the Office. Since these elements were integral parts of the monastic office of other days but that it does not have them for the Triduum either allows us to suppose that the Office of the Sacred Triduum was already in place at the time of St Benedict, in the sixth century, at the beginning of the monastic Office.

What remains apart from these additions are the psalms (responsorial or antiphonal) and the Vigil readings with their responsories which are integral to the Office. All other elements are additions of the fifth century or possibly earlier.

The emergence of the Roman Office (fifth–eighth centuries)

The development of the Office in the East and West took different paths from the fourth or fifth centuries onward, in spite of some mutual influences. In the East, the Office is enriched with a repertory of poetic works linked to biblical texts. The West, on the other hand, largely retained the biblical texts.

One cannot, however, speak of a homogeneous Latin rite Office. Its development remained multi-centric for many centuries. It is hard to study these developments as they are mostly mentioned in sparse and laconic references and almost nothing concerning their structure, repertory, and texts survives documentarily. Some fragments have been recorded in the Beneventan choirbooks (Southern-Italy). Nothing of the respected Italian sees (Ravenna, Aquileia) remains and hardly anything of the Gallican or Celtic Office chant. The documentation is more abundant from the Iberian peninsula: the Office of Milan survived in the medieval liturgical books due to the pre-eminence of St Ambrose. Of the old Latin rites, the Ambrosian Office came closest to Rome, which added a rich chant repertory, while the arrangement of the Office as a whole was less rational. The structure of some monastic communities' Office survives (Arles: the Rule of Caesarius; Central Italy: the *Regula Magistri*) without, however, comparative material from the subsequent centuries.

With the exception of Milan, the regional rites died out in the period of expansion of the Roman rite (ninth–eleventh century). The universal acceptance of the Roman Office was due to the authority of the Holy See, the influence of the missions which exported liturgical books to the newly Christianized areas, and the centralizing activity of the Carolingians. Its balance of a lucid structure and a pleasant variety also assisted its acceptance.

The two branches of the Roman Office

The surviving liturgical books of the Roman Office from the late ninth century contain the full repertoire in a redaction which makes it possible to reconstruct the arrangement very accurately. These books show clearly that the one and same Roman rite lived in two related forms, one of them being the *cursus saecularis*— how cathedrals, parishes, the secular clergy, and the lay assemblies prayed—and the other the *cursus monasticus*—which was a norm for the communities of Benedictine monks. Their relatedness is striking if they are compared to what we know about other (regional) rites of the Latin Church; that is, a new division originated between the diocesan-parochial and the monastic usage, which cannot be traced back to the first one. There is hardly any difference between them in the structure of the hours; the distribution of the psalms are variations of the same type, the material itself (antiphons, responsories) are a selection from the same sources. The difference was no bigger than that between two dioceses or monasteries. The variations in the assignment of prayers and chants were the consequence of small differences in the structure (see below).

The Rule of St Benedict

Fortunately, the Roman rite is documented in detail about 350 years before the earliest surviving liturgical books. The description of the Office in chapters eight to eighteen of the sixth century Rule of St Benedict was based on the rite of the Roman basilicas and is in harmony with the extant books. The correspondence between the two is noteworthy and manifests the stability of the liturgy over centuries. The Rule is not a liturgical book, and does not contain the liturgical material itself. But it gives evidence as to the structure of the hours, the distribution of psalms, the list of genres, the existence of propers (antiphonary), etc.

The Rule of St Benedict shows that the number and structure of the individual hours had been fixed before the beginning of the sixth century. This remained unchanged during the following centuries. The distribution of the psalms in the hours follows principles identical for the Rule and the later liturgical books. St Benedict distinguishes between the order for weekdays and Sundays, the feasts of the temporal and sanctoral and mentions the proper chants of the individual liturgical days.

The liturgico-musical genres listed by St Benedict and their function in the framework of the Office are the same as the later liturgical books.

The structure of the hours

Hour	*Cursus saecularis* (pre–1911)	*Cursus monasticus*
Vigils: weekdays	Introductory versicles	=
	Invitatory psalm	=
	Hymn only in some churches	Hymn
	One nocturn: 12 psalms with 6 antiphons	1st nocturn: 6 psalms with 3 antiphons
	Versicle	Versicle
	3 readings with 3 long responsories	3 readings with 3 long responsories
		2nd nocturn: 6 psalms with 3 antiphons
		Versicle
		1 short reading with a responsorium breve
	Prayers of conclusion	=
Vigils: Sundays & major feasts	Introductory versicles	=
	Invitatory psalm	=
	Hymn only in some churches	Hymn

(Continued)

Continued

Hour	*Cursus saecularis* (pre–1911)	*Cursus monasticus*
	1st nocturn: 3 psalms with 3 or 1 antiphons	1st nocturn: 6 psalms with 6 antiphons
	Versicle	=
	3 readings with 3 long responsories	4 readings with 4 long responsories
	2nd nocturn as the 1st	2nd nocturn as the 1st
	3rd nocturn as the 1st	3rd nocturn: 3 Old-Testament canticles with 1 antiphon
		Versicle
		4 readings with 4 long responsories
	Te Deum (except Advent and Lent) and prayers of conclusion	Te Deum (every Sunday and feast), Gospel of the day, Hymn "Te decet laus," prayers of conclusion
Lauds	Introductory prayers	=
		Psalm 66
	5 psalms with 5 antiphons	5 psalms with 3–5 antiphons
	Capitulum (biblical)	=
		Responsorium breve
	Hymn	=
	New Testament canticle (Benedictus) with antiphon	=
	Prayer of conclusion	=
Prime	Introductory prayers	=
	Hymn	=
	3 (Sunday – 8) psalms with antiphons	3 psalms with antiphons
	Capitulum	=
	Responsorium breve and versicle	Versicle
	Prayer of conclusion	=
Terce, Sext, None	Introductory prayers	=
	Hymn	=
	3 psalms with antiphons	=
	Capitulum	=
	Responsorium breve and versicle	Versicle
	Prayer of conclusion	=
Vespers	Introductory prayers	=
	5 psalms with 5 antiphons	4 psalms with 4 antiphons
	Capitulum	=
	–	Responsorium breve
	Hymn	=
	Versicle	=
	New Testament canticle (Magnificat) with antiphon	=
	Prayer of conclusion	=
Compline	Introductory prayers	=
	4 psalms (one abbreviated) with 1 antiphon	3 psalms without antiphon
	Hymn, capitulum and versicle	=
	New Testament canticle (Nunc dimittis) with antiphon	
	Prayer of conclusion	=

We should note that the liturgy of Rome was reluctant to integrate a hymn in the Office. Until the end of the Middle Ages there were considerable differences among the local churches concerning the days, hours, a hymn was sung at. Also, from about the year 1000 a *responsorium prolixum* was sung by some local churches · after the *capitulum* of Vespers on great solemnities. About the end of the first millennium, commemorations were added at the end of some hours (firstly at Lauds and Vespers) according to local customs.

There are considerable differences in the length and structure of the individual hours. The longest is Vigils, with abundant psalmody, reading, and long responsories. A longer introductory (and for feasts, also a concluding) section was added. This length emphasized the meditative character of the hour.

Lauds and Vespers have a primarily liturgical character: its medium size, the separation of psalmody and hymnody, the participation of the faithful, rich ceremonial (incense, processions, assistants) all kept alive their origins as the liturgical "hinges" of each day. The correspondence in their structure is conspicuous (five psalms, capitulum, hymn with versicle, New Testament canticle). The Little Hours are short: in their essence they are no more than the recitation of three short psalms—all others elements are additions (as is clear from the Office of Sacred Triduum).

The monastic and secular offices are the same in all essential points. Vigils are somewhat longer for monastics (though abbreviated during summer!) and are distributed in two nocturnes in the weekdays, the second one having only one reading and a *responsorium breve*. The monastic Office does not have the *responsorium breve* in the Little Hours. The symmetry between Lauds and Vespers is limited by the shortening of Vespers (4 instead of 5 psalms). There is no canticle at Compline. A survey of the distribution of the psalms will help us to understand these differences.

The distribution of the psalms

The distribution of the psalms goes back to very old principles such as the distinction between *selected psalmody* and *psalmodia currens*; the harmony between the nature of the individual hours and the assignment of particular psalms to them, and the assignment of some eminent psalm to given hours: psalms 50, 62, 148–150 to Lauds; psalm 140 to Vespers; the praying of psalm 118 in the Little Hours. The distribution of psalms 1–108 to the nocturnal Office and of psalms 109–147 goes back to an early tradition.

The distribution of psalms in the Roman Office:

Hour	*Cursus saecularis* (pre–1911)	*Cursus monasticus*
Vigils: introductory psalm		3
Vigils Sunday	1–20	20–31
Vigils Monday	26–37	32–44
Vigils Tuesday	38–51	45–58
Vigils Wednesday	52–67	59–65, 67–72

(*Continued*)

Continued

Hour	*Cursus saecularis* (pre–1911)	*Cursus monasticus*
Vigils Thursday	69–79	73–84
Vigils Friday	80–96	85–100
Vigils Saturday	97–108	101–08
Lauds: introductory psalm		66
Lauds Sunday	92, 99, 62+66, canticle, 148–50	Throughout the year: 50, 117, 62, canticle
		Easter & Ascensiontide & great feasts: 92, 99, 62, canticle
		All Sundays: 148–50
Lauds Monday	50, 5, 62+66, canticle, 148–50	50, 5, 35, canticle, 148–50
Lauds Tuesday	50, 42, 62+66, canticle, 148–50	50, 42, 56, canticle, 148–50
Lauds Wednesday	50, 64, 62+66, canticle, 148–50	50, 63, 64, canticle, 148–50
Lauds Thursday	50, 89, 62+66, canticule, 148–50	50, 87, 89, canticle, 148–50
Lauds Friday	50, 142, 62+66, canticle, 148–50	50, 75, 91, canticle, 148–50
Lauds Saturday	50, 91, 62+66, canticle, 148–50	50, 91, canticle I and II, 148–50
Prime Sunday	21–25, 117, 118/I–II	118/I–IV
Prime weekdays	53, 118/I–II	1–2, 6-19
Terce Sunday	118/III–V	118/V–VII
Terce Monday	118/III–V	118/XIV-XVI
Sext Sunday	118/VI–VIII	118/VIII-X
Sext Monday	118/VI–VIII	118/XVII-XIX
None Sunday	118/IX–XI	118/XI-XIII
None Monday	118/IX–XI	118/XX-XXII
Terce, Sext, None, weekdays	118/III–XI	119–21, 122–24, 125–27
Vespers Sunday	109–13	109–12
Vespers Monday	114–16, 119–20	113–28
Vespers Tuesday	120–24	129–32
Vespers Wednesday	125–29	134–37
Vespers Thursday	130–32, 134–35	138–140
Vespers Friday	136–40	141–144/I
Vespers Saturday	141, 143–47	144/II–147
Compline	4, 30 (vv. 1–6), 90, 133	4, 90, 133.

Selected psalms are assigned according to their liturgical function while the *psalmodia currens* continues in the biblical order. The *psalmodia currens* runs from 1–108 (*cursus monasticus:* 20–108) in Vigils, and from 109–147 in Vespers. Psalms prayed in other hours (3–5, 21–25, 42, 50, 62, 64, 66, 89, 90, 91, 92, 94, 117, 118, 133, 142) are omitted in the *psalmodia currens*. The (long) Prime of Sunday contained psalms 20–25. This may be the remnants of an older (undocumented) period with 2 × 12 psalms in the nocturnes. For the same reason psalms 1+2+3+6, 7+8+9+10 and 11+12+13+14 are taken as one in Sunday Vigils; so the three psalms of the 1st nocturne in fact contains 3 × 4 psalms. The series of psalms in the Little Hours and Compline corresponds to the obligation to pray briefly throughout the working day and at its end. Their unchanging nature makes it possible to pray them by heart.

The forms of the Office before these developments (protracted Sunday Vigils, the transposition of psalms 21–25 into the Sunday Prime, the difference between *psalmodia currens* and the use of psalm pericopes) are not documented. Since no trace of them can be found in the Rule of St. Benedict, the process probably happened in the fourth or fifth century.

The comparison of the monastic and secular cursus permits some conclusions concerning the question of precedence and some problems of chronology. From the secular side, one can refer to nothing other than late sources, but this fact does not invalidate the argumentation. The two arrangements concur in their main lines. The differences (from at the end of the ninth century) are from some distance negligible. The number and structure of hours of St Benedict's Rule is the same as the secular cursus and allows us to go back centuries in the history. The relatively small differences in their composition and in the distribution of psalms, demonstrate that the *psalmodia currens* of both Vigils and Vespers has been abbreviated. The longer psalms have been divided in two and the number of psalms in Vespers has been reduced from five to four disturbing the symmetry with Lauds.[2]

	Cursus saecularis (pre–1911)	Cursus monasticus
Psalmodia currens Vigils Sunday	1–20	20–31
Psalmodia currens Vigils weekdays	26–38; –52; –67; –79; –96; –108	32–44; –58; –72; –84; –100; –108
3rd psalm of Lauds through the week	62+66	62, 35, 56, 63,[3] 87, *divisio cantici*
Prime Sunday	21–25, 117, 118/I–II	118/I–II
Prime weekdays	118/I–II	1–2, 6–19
Little Hours Sunday	118/III–XI	118/III–XI
Little Hours Monday	118/III–XI	118/III–XI
Little Hours other weekdays	118/III–XI	119–27
Psalmodia currens Vespers	109–16, 119–47 (ex. 133, 142)	109–16, 128–47 (exc. 133, 142)

Some scholars regard the *cursus saecularis* (the "Roman Office") as a product under the influence of the Benedictines. In this view, the relatively late secular choir books reflect the influence of St Benedict's Rule, and cannot say anything as to the early form of Roman Office. Others find in their great similarity evidence of a different history: the Rule is a witness of St Benedict's wish to let the Office be prayed "sicut psallit Ecclesia romana" (Rule, ch. 13), i.e., in conformity with the churches of Rome.

What is the reason for the differences above? The first is a tendency of abbreviating the *psalmodia currens* with a reduction of its psalmody, the division of longer psalms, and making the daily portion somewhat more equal.[4] Also, Vespers became shorter, partly by the divisions, partly by reducing the number of psalms to four (omitting psalms 119–27). Prime lost its stable order of psalms and Lauds received one more psalm which changed according to the weekday. The Little Hours became shorter (the psalm verse of a single hour is approximately two-thirds of the secular Office) and the arrangement simpler by the omission of the *responsorium breve*. Overall the Office became a little shorter, but the number and distribution of stable elements has not changed.

Having no liturgical book of the Roman Office from St Benedict's time, one has to take his arrangement itself into account. That St Benedict adapted an existing Roman office to the daily schedule of monks seems to me more probable than the other way round. Some aspects of the monastic Office are illogical without presuming this. What is the reason to distribute psalm 118 on two days? While psalms 109–47 comprise just what is needed for Vespers (7 × 5 psalms, omitting psalms 117, 118, 133, 142), the monastic Office has a different portion which can be distributed on four days with the transposition of 119–27 to the Little Hours. It is true, the secular Sunday Prime with psalms 21–25 is also awkward, but the problem with Prime is not solved by the Rule. Thus the secular Office might be the parent for the *cursus secularis*. A relatively integral and coherent monastic Office could hardly be produced from the elements of an uneven secular arrangement.

Another argument can be drawn from the responsories to the psalms at Vigils. The style of these responsories is like the *responsoria prolixa*, while their length is similar to the *responsorium breve*. This might be a cycle of early origin sung throughout the ordinary period (like the Ambrosian arrangement), but which survived later in the time after Epiphany and which is mixed with other responsories in some late sources. Their selection and distribution is coordinated with the psalmody of the given day[5]:

Vigils	Cursus saecularis (pre-1911)		Cursus monasticus	
	Daily psalmody	Responsories	Daily psalmody	Responsories
Sunday	1–20	6, 9, 15, 17, 23, 24, 25	20–31	6, 9, 15, 17, 23, 24, 25
Monday	26–38	26, 30, 33	32–44	30, 33, 36
Tuesday	39–52	38, 39, 40	45–58	38, 39, 40
Wednesday	43–67	56, 58	59–72	56, 58, 60
Thursday	68–79	70	73–84	70
Friday	80–95	85, 93	85–100	85, 93
Saturday	97–108	100, 101	101–8	101

As can be seen, the responsories in the monastic Office correspond less well to their daily psalms, than to those of the secular Office. Parenthetically, the list contains psalms 24, 24, 25, i.e. part of Sunday Prime of the secular Office. There can hardly be any other reason for that than parts of the Prime in the monastic Office originated in a period when these psalms were recited in Vigils, i.e. in an unrecorded period of the Roman Office, and survived in their original position. These observations suggest that the secular rite was prior to the monastic one and that it was St Benedict who adapted the Office of the Roman basilicas to the life of his monks.

If this is so the *cursus saecularis* existed (in its basic lines, at least) before the beginning of the 6th century, i.e. before the compilation of the Rule. While in saying "sicut psallit Ecclesia romana," St Benedict is referring specifically to the selection and arrangement of the Old Testament canticles of Lauds, his overall approach is grounded in the Roman tradition. Going further, we may suppose that this tradition, alive in St Benedict's period, was from time immemorial—at least one or two generations. Considering the ecclesiastical history of Rome, the most appropriate period for such an arrangement is probably that of Pope St Damasus I (c. 305; 366–84), who reformed administration, organized the clergy, advanced social care, restored and took particular care of the catacombs, and other aspects of worship.

This analysis reveals traces of a still earlier period. There are also analogies in the Ambrosian rite, which is not dependent on Rome (nor vice-versa), but which may share common roots—such as the genre and function of the Vigils responsories as stock material for ordinary time. Thus we may say that these kinds of structural elements as they appear in the ninth-to-tenth-century sources are survivals of a much earlier period. This, of course, is predicated on having more confidence in the stability of liturgical culture during the period of oral tradition that is sometimes usual.

The development and spread of the Roman Office

As the documents show, after this time the number and composition and the distribution of psalms did not change over the following centuries. It was in the antiphonal and in respect of different additional elements that development occurred.

The antiphonal: antiphons and responsories

The size of the antiphonal was probably very limited in the age of St Benedict. In my calculation approximately 200 antiphons set to 10–15 melodic models (approximately 100 for the ordinary psalter, 40–50 for the temporal feasts, 60–80 for the common of saints and for the Proper of some outstanding saints) and 100–150 responsories (30 for the ordinary psalter, 100 for the common and Proper of saints) might be enough to cover the full year. These pieces might have been, of course, improvised by the cantor, but the stipulation of chapter 14 of the Rule might be regarded as a reference to proper antiphons.[6]

In the following centuries, up to the *translatio imperii* to the Franks, the repertory increased. In the temporal the introduction of the seasons of Advent and Christmas, the fixing of gospel pericopes (which became source of antiphons, e.g. for Lenten weekdays and other major antiphons for the Benedictus and Magnificat), the use of *scriptura occurrens* (the distribution of the Old Testament books during ordinary time), inspired new responsories and a few antiphons: taking the text from the given book might be a creative incentive.

Another impetus for new development was the increasing cult of saints: people wanted to make the common of saints complete and to add proper chant for some individual saints—mainly those venerated in single communities.

The earliest source of the Roman Office (Albi 44, end of the ninth century),[7] contains approximately 1,000 antiphons. The number of antiphons in the old Roman antiphonary is also about 1,000. Though both books originated later than the reception of the Roman rite by the Franks, the archaic feature of Albi 44 and the similar figures in the later old Roman antiphonary make plausible that they essentially reflect the state of the period of "translation" (the second half of the eighth century). The material common to both sources is near to 600. The argumentation has a paradoxical support: the Compiegne antiphonary (of Parisian origin),[8] compiled at the same time as Albi 44, has 1,700 antiphons, which probably include the new Carolingian compositions. Albi 44 has hardly more than half of them; and the reason for the difference should be the "archaism" of Albi and the "progressive" nature of Compiegne. If this is true, the increase of material in the antiphonary would be by about 500 per cent between the sixth and eighth centuries.

Additional elements

The hymns take the same place in the Rule as they do in the monastic sources 400–500 years later, or as in the post-Trent *Breviarium Romanum*. All hours have hymns in all liturgical seasons (except the Sacred Triduum, and in the secular Office, the octave-week of Easter). They are sung in the middle of the hour, before the canticle in Lauds, Vespers and Compline and at the beginning of all other hours. The number of hymns in this rudimentary period was very low: 8–10 for ordinary time and another 10–15 for feasts and the saints' common.

Rome itself rejected the reception of the hymn—as a non-biblical text. As late as the twelfth and thirteenth centuries, no Office hymns were sung in Rome. Many churches in Europe (mainly the conservative German churches) were very selective concerning the hymn: they sang a hymn in some hours and not in others, or sang one on Sundays but not on weekdays (or vice-versa), or on some liturgical days or seasons, but not on others.

At first the hymnal was imported (where it was tolerated at all) from Milan—the home of the genre—and was completed with some Italian products following the Ambrosian repertory. This is the first hymnal. After the spread of the Roman rite in the Trans-Alpine regions, some churches (or rather, monastic communities), added new hymns or substitutions for the old ones. This is the second hymnal, which became popular and influential in the next period, including *Veni Creator, Ave maris stella, Conditor alme siderum, Audi benigne conditor,* hymns for Lauds and Vespers on weekdays. Except for these generally accepted pieces, however, individual churches differed significantly in selecting and distributing hymns.

In the Rule of St Benedict the selection of what is to be read at the Office is decided by the Abbot. In the following centuries the lectionary for the Office crystallized into different systems according to the tradition of the individual churches. The general framework, however, became more stable prior to the eighth century. Sacred Scripture was read in the first nocturne, assigned according to the feast or following a set order of biblical books for ordinary time (Advent: Isaiah; post Epiphany: St Paul's letters; from Septuagesima: the Pentateuch; from Passion Sunday: Jeremiah; Eastertide: Acts of Apostles, Letters of Sts Peter, John and James, Revelation; after Pentecost: The Books of Kings; August: the Wisdom Books; September: Job, Tobias, Judith, Esther; October: Maccabees; November: Ezechiel, Daniel, the lesser Prophets).

This order of biblical books regulated the series of *responsoria prolixa* (or *historiae*) and the Magnificat antiphons of the Sunday first Vespers. The patristic sermons and homilies following the biblical books were first chosen by the leader of the community (St Benedict warns his sons to read only orthodox texts), later by the local or regional traditions. This system was accepted and adapted by the individual churches (dioceses and monasteries) gradually during the sixth to the tenth centuries.

The spread of the Office

The Office described above originated in the urban liturgy of Rome. Other diocesan and monastic centres of the early church had their own customs, though in many respects shared common elements with each other. With the missionary apostolate from the beginning of the seventh century, which carried the faith to the pagan (or half-pagan) nations, the Roman Office (and Mass) books accompanied them and were taught to the singers of England, Ireland, some German churches, and so on. This also influenced the 'old' Christian dioceses in Italy, Southern Gaul, and later (indirectly) Iberia, who gave up their specific rite for the sake of the Roman one. So the Office of urban Rome gradually became the leading, or nearly the only rite, of the Western hemisphere.

After 750 the process sped up. The Carolingian rulers decided for political reasons to adopt the Roman rite and chant. Since their power increased quickly and covered a large area—they directly influenced those parts of the continent which were under their government, and indirectly those outside—this rite became the quasi-official liturgy of the whole of Latin Christianity.

The Office in the early Middle Ages

The period discussed can be counted as approximately two and a half centuries starting with the beginning of the Frankish reception of the *Cantus Romanus* until the close of the missions and relative stabilization of the political and ecclesiastical situation of the continent. As seen above, the Office transmitted to the Franks and other nations is, in essence, the Roman rite as fixed in the seventh century. What did this period add to this legacy?

A system of ecclesiastical structures established by Charlemagne guaranteed the continuity of the liturgico-musical practice of the Office. What later became the network of cathedral and collegiate chapters came into being and the singers, clergy, and scholars gathered in this workshop were obliged to celebrate the liturgical hours daily. They also had to maintain schools where pupils were trained in the sung liturgy and at least the important hours of the Office were prayed with the full participation of pupils. The most eminent chapters (such as Metz) formed not only a liturgical choir but also an assembly of experts who cooperated in developing the repertory and its theoretical articulation.

The theoretical approach—the will to *understand* the intellectual context of phenomena—was an overall trend for the scholars of the Carolingian and post-Carolingian age. They wanted to systematize the musical structure also, and render it accessible by introducing notation. The Office, mainly the antiphons, was of great importance in this theoretical activity. The antiphons were the primary examples of all art in chant: intervals, modes, and melodic turns.

Most likely these workshops were responsible for a decisive change of musical shape of the liturgical chant. Though there is no agreement about the origins of the Gregorian repertory among the scholars of our age, most of them think it was the Carolingian ecclesiastical centers which produced the repertory which was presented as chant by Pope Gregory. The richly ornate form of chant recorded later in a few choir books—called today "Old Roman chant"—might seem too strange and difficult to receive and spread among people of different taste and experience. The clergy of the Carolingian schools simplified it and, without major changes in the form, mode, and melodic outlines, produced a repertory easier to learn. This development touched upon the Office music, which resulted in a universally received set of antiphons and responsories—the seeds of a shared European tradition.

The repertory itself was considerably augmented in these decades. The important but limited temporal and common of the saints grew rapidly during the ninth century: the repertory of the Compiegne antiphonal is about five times bigger than the original of the sixth century might be, and the double amount of either Albi 44 or the old Roman set written down four centuries later. New pieces have been composed for all parts of the antiphonal (the temporal included), after the ninth century. However, this part—as the Mass proper apart from the Alleluia—became regarded as a closed and canonized body, and the increase focused on the Proper of saints. The cult of the saints was ancient, but without (or with a very limited) proper. The new Offices—non-biblical free compositions of clerics of epic or praiseworthy content—were needed for those venerated in a restricted geographical area or simply a local church.

The new Offices occasioned a change of style. While the old Roman repertory retained the old style—clear melodic content of modes, conjunct move of melody, set of standard figures—the new style, influenced also by the theoretical definition of modes, was free in its melodic invention and used larger ambits both within the individual lines and the piece as a whole. At the same time the modal structure was more or less simplified or neglected by them. The modes resting on the same final intermingled, and the principle of *series tonorum* (the subsequent pieces of the cycle of antiphons or responsories written in a numerical sequence of modes) functioned as the means of theoretical organization.

The later Middle Ages

The eleventh century was the period of crystallization. Missionary endeavors meant that almost all people in Europe accepted Christianity together with its forms of worship. The relationship between ecclesiastical centers (cathedrals, chapters, parishes, religious communities) had been settled, their continuous activity and liturgical tradition started and preserved over centuries, the invention of staff notation (by Guido of Arezzo in the eleventh century) assisted in the production of compositions and in keeping them alive and pure. Oral tradition, even if did not disappear, diminished in its importance.

The antiphons and responsories transmitted from Rome to Trans-Alpine regions took their place in the individual traditions according to local decisions. Local personnel added new compositions without imposing any obligation on others to adopt them. In the lists of the twelve most ancient antiphonaries collected by Dom Hesbert,[9] one may find a clearly circumscribed, limited group of pieces more or less on the same position in each church. Another group contains the same pieces but placed in a changed liturgical position. A third group is one of local production often known only in a given church. And so while the Office chant can be called on one hand "universal," on the other hand there are also variants in liturgical, reportorial (and musicological) respects. The Office developed this way became the proper tradition of the local Churches. In other words, the Roman rite acquired the feature of having proper local usages—a feature retained in many places during the whole of the Middle Ages or beyond. In this sense we may speak of the Divine Office of Salisbury, Paris, Mainz, Braga, etc.

Monks followed the tradition of their monastery. Though the principles were determined partly by the Roman urban heritage and partly by St Benedict's Rule, they had and preserved a customary proper to their own community. Occasionally monastic "congregations" were organized, sometimes following the same liturgical customs (primarily in the Office) in spite of the fact that monasteries were often more separate from each other than the parishes of a given diocese.

The new orders founded after 1100 took a different approach which manifested itself first of all in their Office. The "secular" (i.e. non-monastic) orders such as the Norbertines accepted the Office of the church of their origins. Others, such as the Cistercians, defined a proper variant as the common usage and imposed the rite on individual communities by centralized authority.

The Franciscans are a special case. Rome itself followed the old Roman usage up to the twelfth and thirteenth centuries. Subsequently they gave it up (supposedly for musical reasons), and introduced a middle-Italian rite as the proper of Rome, eminently of the Roman curia. The Franciscans, taking over the control of some Roman churches, regarded the rite of the curia as the original Roman liturgy and appropriated it as the rite of their order. This rite of the papal court and of the Franciscan movement spread rapidly through the whole continent and displaced the traditional rite of many dioceses.[10]

Another characteristic change in the Office was the spread of new additions and of its private recitation. The most traditional "addition" is the *preces* selected from psalms, as supplication for the pope, bishop, king, and people at the end of set hours. Another was to add shortened "little offices" (of the Holy Virgin, of the Dead) to the daily Office: this considerably prolonged its length.

Both priests and members of religious orders became burdened with more and more obligations (diplomacy, royal bureaucracy, preaching, missionary work). Therefore, the regular choral singing of the Office was often left to paid cathedral staff (the chapter, chaplains, and schoolboys). While the choral service corresponded with the psalter, antiphonal, and lectionary, the new situation required a new and smaller book containing all the texts—the breviary. Thus "to pray the breviary" became the normal manner of fulfilling the obligation of daily prayer, radically changing the attitude to the Office in subsequent centuries.

The great majority of the proper chants of Mass were the same as received from Rome: they functioned, as it were, as a canonized stock material of the liturgy. Although the ancient set of Office material retained its position, the Office as a whole became the object of a continuous growth. An almost completely new cycle served the cult of saints—the number of days dedicated to saints with a proper or common Office growing up to the end of the Middle Ages.[11]

What was new in these developments was that they were not a collection of single antiphons and responsories, but composed as whole Offices with a logical sequence to the individual pieces. Such a cycle was called "historia." After the turn of the first millennium the strophic or rhymed prose Offices came into fashion. Similarly, its music was conceived as a unit (*series tonorum*). To give a picture of the composition here is the list of antiphons in Matins for St Gregory (all antiphons are 4 × 8 syllables, except the first which has five lines):

Position	Incipit	Content	Mode
1st Noct. Ant. 1	Gregorius ortus Romae	Born in an illustrious family	1
Ant. 2	Lineam sui generis	From his childhood he became worthy of his ancestors	2
Ant. 3	Adhaerebat moralibus	He kept in mind the requirement of an honest life without any break	3
2nd Noct. Ant. 1	Gregorious ut reditur	He was vigilant in his and the Church's life	4
Ant. 2	Studiis liberalibus	He was a diligent student of the liberal arts who became an eminent *praetor* of the City	5
Ant. 3	Hic ab adolescentia	He longed for the fruits of grace from his youth	6
3rd Noct. Ant. 1	Sex struxit in Sicilia	He founded six monasteries in Sicily and one in Rome, where he became a monk	7
Ant. 2	Hiis sane monasteriis	He gave his possessions to the monasteries and to the poor	8
Ant. 3	Qui solebat in sericis	He who wore fine vestments earlier now casts them away, and serves the poor as a poor person.	1

It became customary to insert a long melisma (with repetition of motives) in the repeat (*repetenda*) of the responsories. In some places these melismas were provided with text, each note with a syllable. These tropes (or *verbeta*) were not the only ornamentation of the item, but also gave scope for the creativity of singers to update the inherited material. Such tropes have been very rarely added to antiphons, and either their liturgical position or syllabic shape made way for them in the traditional cycles.

New compositions were also produced in another genre: the hymn, as an independent poem (i.e. often not a part of the *historia*), inspired many ecclesiastical poets. In most cases these items spread only in a limited area or even in one diocese. Some of them are charming poems, often describing the life and miracles of the saint, but only a few had the theological depth of the old hymns.

The age of humanism and the following centuries

The Roman rite did not escape the trends of the late fifteenth to seventeenth centuries. Humanism, early rationalism, the Reformation and the Counter-Reformation, and the inclination to centralism all influenced the liturgy. Their impact manifested itself first of all in the Office, it having a less defined role than the Mass. The reform movements inspired by these intellectual and spiritual changes can be grouped into two seemingly opposite groups: proposers of a radical modernity, and proponents of a return to older, purer traditions.

The first was characterized by a kind of anti-traditionalism. The supporters of modernization wished to introduce a more "logical" system into the Office both in respect of its structure and its material. They wanted to replace the "barbarian" medieval Latin with the more polished Ciceronian style. A new hymnal was published with a papal approbation in 1523, prepared by Bishop Zacharias Ferreri. Ferreri's proposal for the breviary itself aimed at a shorter prayer-book, with removal of every kind of "errors."[12] As the eminent scholar Suitbert Bäumer noted, Popes Leo X, Clement VII, and Paul III were influenced by the pagan-Greek and Roman literature and had no sense of, or taste for, the beauty of the medieval Liturgy.[13]

The most extreme realization of this reform appeared in the breviary by Francis Cardinal Quignonez, a friend of Popes Clement VII and Paul III. Published in 1535, 100 new editions were printed in the following forty years. Its popularity was due to its shortness and simplicity. The chanted parts (antiphons, responsories, versicles and most of the hymns) were omitted. It provided hymns only for the beginning of Vespers and Compline. The text was reduced to biblical passages to be read across the year. The psalms were entirely rearranged: three psalms in each hour; none was repeated; the feasts lost their proper psalms; the structure on Sundays, feasts, and weekdays was similar. As a result, the obligatory portion became nearly the same on every day. The number of readings at Vigils was unchanged (1. Old Testament; 2. New Testament; 3. Life of saints or homily). The legends of saints were reworked or "purified." The whole arrangement reveals that the breviary had been prepared for private prayer. Thus the long process of transition from the choral Office to a private one ended with the triumph of the latter.

Quignonez's breviary was published with papal approbation, but was also harshly received, particularly by John of Arze from Paris. In the end Paul IV abolished it.[14]

Another direction of reform was the desire to restore the old and pure traditions. When printing became possible in the late fifteenth century, most dioceses took care to edit their traditional rites, both the Mass and Office. The impact of humanism (particularly Erasmian philology), prompted new redactions based on the best manuscripts. Bishops or chapters commissioned experts with the aim of presenting a faultless, clear text and structure. These books were destined for use in the whole diocese or ecclesiastical province and often influenced neighboring dioceses. They did not want to produce a new liturgy, but simply present their local tradition in its best form.

Proposals were made in the years between 1520 and 1550 for a "purification" of the Office and the correction of some obvious errors. An outstanding example of these reformed breviaries—"reformed" in a good sense of the word—was that of the Theatine order, who had also the chance of testing it with the permission of the Holy See.[15] Their Office was in some respect a precursor of that of the Council of Trent.

The main concern of the Council of Trent (1545–63) was theological; the content and structure of the liturgy was marginal. The Council laid down some basic principles of liturgical reform and established a commission to implement them with new editions of the breviary and missal.[16] Trent adopted the traditional approach: the new breviary had to be the old one improved. The result, though, was a breviary and the read Office retained its predominance. The "private" (read) Office was to be identical with the common (choral) one.

Trent's commission accomplished its task quickly and the breviary of the Council, the "*Breviarium Pianum*," was published in 1568.[17] The changes to the old Office were not numerous, thus the new edition is truly a development of the old Office—the breviary of the Roman curia without the Frankish (and post-Frankish) accretions (*historiae*, many proper offices, hymns, and tropes). In the structure of hours and distribution of psalms one change was made: Sunday Prime was abbreviated and psalms 21–25 (i.e. the prefix before the proper psalms of the hour—psalm 117 and divisions of psalm 118—were distributed to weekdays (except Saturday)). Otherwise the old Roman structure remained intact. The antiphonal of the medieval Office of the Curia was preserved (except as mentioned above).

The most conspicuous changes are in the lectionary and calendar of saints. The number of saints venerated was reduced, their ranks simplified, and the calendar rearranged accordingly. Instead of having a proper Office, most of the feasts were celebrated with a common Office, or were commemorated. The saints' lives were edited and "legendary" elements removed. Many readings were replaced by better ones. Nevertheless, it is clear that the Office of Trent is nothing other than the ancient traditional Roman Office, revised in some points of secondary importance.

From Trent to Pius X's *Divino afflatu* (1911)

In his Bull "Quod a nobis" promulgating the new breviary, Pius V decreed that the very short breviary composed by Cardinal Quignonez, as well as other unauthorized kinds of breviaries, were abolished, as well as those not used during the previous 200 years. Those which had been in use for 200 years could be changed to the form of the new breviary, provided that the bishop and the chapter were agreed.[18]

In spite of the permission to keep the old local Offices, practically all the dioceses gave them up one after the other, and turned over to the new Roman breviary. This gesture manifested their loyalty to the Holy See, adherence to central papal power (emphasized in the counter-reformation age), and indeed it seemed to be simpler to purchase the newly printed breviary because of the great number of exemplars rather than to print a breviary for their own diocese. By around 1650, the majority of dioceses had been "Romanized". Few persisted in keeping their proper tradition during the following 150 to 200 years.

This concerns, however, only the text of the Office. In spite of some urgent demands, Rome did not regulate the chants of the antiphonal. The coordination of chant and text caused insignificant difficulties. The melodies could survive only if their text was identical with the *Breviarium Pianum*. It was difficult to use their large old chant books and the newly printed breviary simultaneously. When the selection of texts for the Curial–Tridentine Office differed from the local tradition, new melodies were required. In addition, the musical ideals of late humanism were adverse to the Gregorian style. The editors tried to surmount the conflict by transcribing the melodies (shortening their size, transposing melismas, harmonizing musical and textual accents, etc.): in other words, they changed the melody according to the spirit of age. This way, a new branch of Gregorian music emerged, regarded later by the nineteenth- to twentieth-century chant experts as "corrupt." Dozens of Italian and French editions were received and remained—on the level of private compositions—up to the mid-nineteenth century, when the firm Pustet in Regensburg obtained the privilege to publish the "official" Vatican musical editions of Gregorian chant. Since the sung Office was rather rarely celebrated and the private, read Office held dominion over the common, chanted celebration, this concern remains something of mostly academic interest in the history of the Office.

The reformed hymnary

Reforming the hymnary in the spirit of humanism was something frequently demanded for about 100 years. The "barbarian" medieval Latin seemed to be outdated and its language, rhythm, and expression seemed in need of reform. It was held that the language should be made to conform to the Latin of antiquity, the rhythm improved to conform more to the "pure" metric schemes, and that the text be revised according to the contemporary taste for classical and pagan names and terms. The contemporary poets had no sense for the singable quality, simplicity, and noble popularity of the medieval hymns.

After several experiments, Urban VIII commissioned four Jesuits (Matthias Sarbieski, Famianus Straba, Tarquinius Galluzzi, and Hieronymus Petrucci) to prepare a revised hymnary. They identified nearly 1,000 errors in the old hymns and corrected 962. The pope promulgated their work in 1643, although the Benedictines, Dominicans, Premonstratensians, etc. preserved the traditional texts. Critics reacted to this sharply and accused the authors of arbitrariness: "Accessit latinitas et recessit pietas"— Latinity arrived and piety went away, they said.[19]

To illustrate the "revision" I compare one strophe of the *Urbs beata Jerusalem / Caelestis urbs Jerusalem*:

Omnis illa Deo sacra	Alto ex Olympi vertice
et dilecta civitas	Summi Parentis Filius
plena modulis in laude	Ceu monte desectus lapis
et canore jubilo	terras in imas decidens,
Trinum Deum Unicumque	domus supernae et infimae
cum fervore praediat	utrumque junxit angulum.

The Proper of Saints

In the subsequent decades, even centuries, while the possibility of further reform was often discussed, no essential change was made to the Roman breviary. The only field where the proposals were realized was in the cult of saints. The calendar was revised several times: saints were added and abolished, and the ranking of feasts changed considerably. Trent was quite radical in diminishing the categories of veneration. However, it became clear that these categories were not enough to distinguish the importance of saints, doctors, founders of orders, martyrs etc. And so the number of categories grew again between the seventeenth and eighteenth centuries. The four classes of duplex feasts (1st and 2nd, duplex maius, duplex) and the addition of the semiduplex and simplex resulted again in a rich diversity (and even more so in the calendar of some religious orders).

Another area of change was the readings for saints' feasts. The "legendary" elements were eliminated again and again, and the historical authenticity asserted. It is not possible to enumerate all such changes approved by the Holy See here.[20] One may observe, however, that the calendar and lectionary of the late nineteenth century breviary was not identical with that promulgated by Pius V—nor with the 1961 *Breviarium Romanum* either.

French and German reformed breviaries

Pius V, whilst abolishing the breviary of Cardinal Quignonez, gave permission to dioceses to preserve their Office provided that it was either approved or in use for at least 200 years. On the other hand, any diocese might adopt the new *Breviarium Romanum*. Accordingly, some dioceses published their own proper Office whilst most accepted the "Roman" breviary with the addition of the proper saints of their diocese.

Some followed a third way: to keep the proper Office whilst integrating more or less of the breviary of Pius V. These hybrids included the revised sanctorale, homilies, and biographies of saints, while the antiphons, responsories, and hymns remained as they was earlier. The Parisian Office is characteristic of this: several variants were published (1584, 1607, 1643, 1658); they became more and more Roman in nature. This process of "infiltration" of the Roman Office into the proper Office of dioceses was in progress during the seventeenth century. Often not only spiritual and theological but also political affairs influenced when and how individual churches adopted the Roman uses.

The Roman breviary itself also met some minor changes in the seventeenth and eighteenth centuries. The revision of the Vulgate was been carried over into the Office (Clement VIII), the number of saints grew again (Urban VIII), and the selection and texts of readings were modified.

A more radical transformation took place in the late seventeenth century, first of all, in France. Two reasons motivated this change. One of them was the anti-Roman inclination of the French Church. This "gallicanism" strove for a national Church, and favored the omnipotence of the local political and ecclesiastical government.

The other tendency changing the content of the liturgy was Jansenism. Its heterodoxy went together with the rejection of liturgical tradition and attacked liturgical structures and devotional customs, rejecting the *lex credendi* as the deposit of traditional theological treasure. Neo-gallican Jansenism was a step toward Protestantism and atheism. In its last phase the cult of "reason" paved the way for the Enlightenment and revolution.

The first of these French "reformed" breviaries was published in 1678 by Henri de Villars, the Archbishop of Vienne, France. It purged many non-biblical elements from the Office. The subsequent editions of the Paris breviary went further: replacing the responsories with biblical texts and abolishing many hymns. The intention was to present a book of studies edifying in nature, rather than a book of prayer, and the common sung celebration in choir practically disappeared. Finally, the Roman liturgy was fully abrogated in 1791 and all dioceses produced an Office of their own.

In Germany, breviaries in Cologne, Münster, Mainz, etc., were modelled on those of the French dioceses. The breviary of St Maur was profoundly influential: it gave up practically all Roman legacy and collected its material from the Bible, even reconstructing the arrangement of the hours. This breviary found a home in the Benedictine monastery of Pannonhalma in Hungary, which used it up to the Second Vatican Council.

The French and German reformed breviaries followed the main lines of Quignonez; some in fact urged a return to this abolished Office. Both the breviary of Quignonez and the reformed Offices of the seventeenth to eighteenth centuries took the same path as later would the Office of the Second Vatican Council.

The re-introduction of the "Roman" office promulgated following Trent started in the first half of the ninteenth century. In France, it was Abbot Prosper Guérenger who played an outstanding role in the criticism of the gallican breviaries and fought for the restoration of the Roman rite. The gallican-jansensist breviaries and the Offices of the German dioceses were eventually abandoned by the second half of the nineteenth century.

The motu proprio *Divino afflatu* of Pius X (1911) and the psalter of Pius XII

In the hundred years leading up to the twentieth century, the abbreviation of the breviary was repeatedly demanded. In response a new breviary was promulgated by the motu proprio *Divino afflatu* of Pius X dated 1 November 1911.

The argument was that the breviary should better serve priests praying the hours and that it was not suitable for this given the demands of clergy engaged in pastoral activity. *Divino afflatu* observed that many bishops, including at the First Vatican Council, had asked that "the ancient custom of reciting the whole psalter within the week might be restored as far as possible, but in such a way that the burden should not be made heavier for the clergy, whose labours in the vineyard of the sacred ministry are now increased because of the diminution in the number of the labourers."

Formerly the Roman Office was based on two principles. The first was articulated by St Benedict:

> But we strongly recommend, if this arrangement of the psalms be displeasing to anyone, that he arrange them otherwise, as shall seem better to him; provided always that he take care that the psalter with its full hundred and fifty psalms be chanted every week and begun afresh every Sunday at Matins.
>
> For those monks show themselves very slothful in their sacred service, who in the course of the week sing less than the psalter and the customary canticles, whereas we read that our holy fathers strenuously fulfilled in a single day what I pray that we lukewarm monks may perform in a whole week (Rule, ch. 18).

Of course, this concerns, first of all, the monks of St Benedict. As Pius X states: "With good reason was provision made long ago, by decrees of the Roman pontiffs, by canons of the councils, and by monastic laws, that members of both branches of the clergy should chant or recite the entire psalter every week" (*Divino afflatu*).

The second principle was the duality of both *psalmodia currens* and the selection of particular psalms for some hours. This second principle determined the structure of the hours, making distinction between the long Vigils of contemplative character, as well as Vespers, and the Little Hours breaking daily work, often praying the same psalms every day. A third possibility, which could well preserve both principles, i.e. to keep the Roman Office intact but making a distinction between the *vita contemplativa* and *vita activa* did not emerge.

This reform abandoned one the Roman "principles:" they decided to keep the weekly order, but neglected the distinction between the two groups of psalms. Practically that meant that half the Vigils psalms were transposed to the Little Hours, Compline, and Lauds. The consequence was that both the *psalmodia currens* and the standard distribution of psalms disappeared. The structure of some hours changed also: Vigils had nine psalms every day (without making difference between the Sunday and weekday). The portion for each hour and day became nearly the same. At the same time, the breviary became even more a prayer-book for individuals and lost its choral nature. Seventy years later (before the Second Vatican Council) there were already three generations of priests who had grown up without any experience of the harmony of the *psalmodia currens* and the traditional distribution of psalms.

No change was made in the antiphonal, except for the psalter, which needed new chants because of the rearrangement of psalms. The antiphons and responsories of the temporal and sanctoral remained intact. Some of the religious orders (Dominicans, Premonstratensians, etc.) adopted the new Roman psalter; the monastic Office retained the traditional arrangement. The new breviary reduced the number of venerated saints in order to keep the Sunday and weekday Offices free for the temporal.[21]

The psalter of Pius XII

In 1945, Pius XII approved a new version of the psalter: a Latin translation of the Jerusalem Bible which was itself based on the "Masoreta" text supposed to be the original Hebrew Bible. In addition to striving for "authenticity," in many instances merely stylistical arguments—similar to those of the seventeenth-century reform of the hymns—motivated the reworded composition. The new psalter, which was gradually published in breviaries—though the old "vulgate" psalter continued to be published also—detached the clergy and the faithful from the traditional text of the Office which was integral to the chant, theology, and spirituality. In short, it was a significant departure from received tradition.[22]

A comparison of the old and new texts of psalm 66 will demonstrate the difference:

Deus misereatur nostri et benedicat nobis, illuminet vultum suum super nos, et misereatur nostri.	Deus misereatur nostri, et benedicat nobis; serenum præbeat nobis vultum suum,
Ut cognoscamus in terra viam tuam, in omnibus Gentibus salutare tuum.	Ut cognoscant in terra viam eius, in omnibus gentibus salutem eius.
Confiteanur tibi populi, Deus, confiteantur tibi populi omnes.	Celebrent te populi, Deus, celebrent te populi omnes.
Laetentur et exsultent gentes, quoniam judicas populos aequitate, et gentes in terra dirigis.	Lætentur et exsultent nationes, quod regis populos cum æquitáte, et nationes in terra gubernas.
Confiteanur tibi populi, Deus, confiteantur tibi populi omnes:	Celebrent te populi, Deus, celebrent te populi omnes.
terra dedit fructum suum.	Terra dedit fructum suum:
Benedicat nos Deus, noster,	benedixit nobis Deus, Deus noster.
Benedicat nos Deus,	Benedícat nobis Deus,
et metuant eum omnes fines terrae.	et tímeant eum omnes fines terræ!

The Second Vatican Council's constitution *Sacrosanctum Concilium*

Many regard this document as a turning point—positive or negative—in the history of liturgy. Scholars today rightly distinguish between the document approved by Council Fathers and the products of the commission entrusted with its implementation.

Sacrosanctum Concilium's principles are both theological and practical, namely: the liturgy is primarily an *opus divinum, Christ's work*. He offers Himself to the Father and presents to him our prayers and sacrifice united with his. It is not about individuals or groups who produce sacred actions or celebrate their own community identity. Liturgy is the *source and summit* of the Church's activity. It is not a means to achieve didactic or organizational aims. These activities prepare the faithful for celebration or are fruits of it. Ultimately, the liturgy is eschatological: heavenly realities are made present and bring about our union with God which is fulfilled in the eternal kingdom.

Both the clergy and the lay communities should regularly celebrate the Office in its public and choral form. The Office should regain its common character instead of being merely the private prayer of the priest. It should be built in to the formation of future priests and it should again become an organic part of parishes and religious or lay communities.

The liturgy demands the *participation* of the faithful. The religious life transcends the merely social and is defined by its spiritual goal.

This participation *has two aspects*: one, and most important is the intimate spiritual activity in the liturgy, the other has an external quality (words, singing, gestures). Participation does not mean all doing everything: everybody must carry out that, but no more than that, which is his proper liturgical role.

For that all must have a basic and authentic *liturgical formation*: for acquiring both theological and "practical" familiarity with the liturgy. Priests, assistants, singers, laity should be introduced in this according to their specific ministries.

The individual Hours should be celebrated *quantum possible* at their proper time each day.

None of these principles are novelties for the Church. The Council did not correct a neglected, distorted, or erroneous teaching of the past. What it desired was to emphasize their meaning and importance of the Divine Office in the life of the clergy and in the spiritual life of lay communities.

Chapter four of *Sacrosanctum Concilium* provided for some structural changes in the Office. These should be read in conjunction with the above principles. Prime is abolished. Of the day hours (Terce, Sext, None), it is enough to pray one, omitting the other two. (Though this is a new provision in respect of the genuine rhythm of prayer, it touches upon the obligation (discipline) and not the structure of hours.) Matins (Vigils) would be rearranged so that it could be prayed at any time of the day, regardless of the sequence of other hours. The length of psalmody at Matins would be diminished and the readings prolonged. The Office should be better adapted to the demands of those active in apostolic ministry.

The *psalmody* would be revised so that the full psalter would be prayed not during one week but over a longer period. The text of the psalter itself would be revised, rejecting the psalter of Pius XII in favor of the "Neo-Vulgata" instead of the traditional vulgate translation. The Council did not make any provision in respect of the *Antiphonale*.

In the "additional" components, the hymnal is to be revised to replace the seventeenth century ones when it seems useful. The Lectionary agrees with the long sequence of corrections made periodically from the seventeenth century onward: a rich choice from the Bible is required as is a better selection from the Patristic sermons, as well as historically more precise legends of the saints.

Overall, the traditional theological considerations are in great part confirmed; a few somewhat equivocal hints can be discerned concerning the changes of material and demands repeated in the recent decades have been implemented. The proposals for change have no doctrinal implication and are thus freely debatable. The Council's Constitution itself is therefore not radically new in respect of the Office (except perhaps in its abolition of Prime), at least not in the light of the 1911 reform.

However, the *Consilium* set up for the implementation of the Constitution produced a brand-new breviary. Let us consider some of the more important features in this radical innovation.[23]

In respect of the structure of the Office, Prime is abolished. Instead of following the Constitution's disciplinary regulation that two of the other Little Hours can be omitted (n. 89 e), a new "hora media" or Middle Hour with its own psalms has been composed, resulting in the disappearance of the Little Hours: an attack against the *nature* of Little Hours as a whole. The diminution of psalmody at Matins did not accompany an augmentation of the readings; there are fewer, and so Matins lost its meditative character. The function of the Invitatory—which was misunderstood— is practically transposed to Lauds. All hours have been equalized with a number of three psalms (with the exception of Compline). A new genus has been introduced in Lauds and Vespers: the bidding prayers—their freely-worded texts became the gateway for radically new theology, taking the place of the commemorations (made by selected psalm verses from the Middle Ages and the penitential period of recent centuries). The historical function of the hymn has been reinterpreted (transferred onto the beginning of each hour), and thus this genre lost its role in the dramatic and individual structure of the individual hours.

The Constitution spoke only of "some longer period" for praying the *Psalter* (n. 91). The new arrangement fixed this is four weeks both for those who live the *vita comtemplativa* or the *vita activa*. As a result both elements of the Roman Office—*psalmodia currens* and psalms selected for use in particular hours—disappeared. All hours, Sundays, weekdays, and feasts have three psalms (or psalm divisions). The ancient structure which connected some psalms to given hours has been abandoned. Though the Council did not speak of such a possibility, special psalms have been linked to the "hora media." While traditionally Lauds and Vespers had Old Testament canticles before the *Capitulum*, the new breviary included a New Testament canticle for Vespers.

The influence of the new distribution of psalms on the *Antiphonale* was, although indirect, devastating. The new distribution changed the basic set of antiphons. But beyond this, much of it was been replaced or omitted (of the thirty-five Christmas antiphons, fourteen remained). The responsories were changed more radically. A principle was established which required a connection between the content of reading and the responsory. Since few responsories corresponded to this, dozens of new texts were created. It is significant that during the decades since the promulgation of the new Liturgy of the Hours, no complete choral *Antiphonale* has been published,[24] rendering the breviary a private prayer book, a collections of texts rather than "libretto" of psalms to chant, with antiphons and responsories. In spite of the Council, the private Office is more predominant than before.

The changes in the "additional" elements are also numerous. The lectionary had variants in the Middle Ages, certainly, but these are negligible if compared with the totally new lectionary. The Constitution countenanced a revision of the *Hymnal*, but surely in the expectation of the restoration of the authentic texts. In fact, the number of hymns has multiplied; parts of the old treasury have been reintroduced, but some texts have been re-written (in the light of new theological spiritual trends), and the chair of the relevant subcommission expanded the collection up with his own poems.[25]

If one considers the post-conciliar Liturgy of the Hours from the Constitution's requirement of organic development in continuity (cf. n. 23), one may say that this breviary is a radically new product which makes use of a few components of the Roman heritage. One could ask whether an organic development of the Roman heritage in the light of the conditions of our day would be possible. While I think it would, the *Consilium* was clearly not interested in exploring this. Rather, it seems that they took as models the breviary of Quignonez, the revolutionary decisions of the experiments of the seventeenth and eighteenth centuries (such as those of the synod of Pistoia),[26] and the neo-gallican liturgies which provoked Guéranger's criticism.

One may say, then, that the history of the Roman Office ended with the publication of the *Liturgia Horarum* in 1971. It belongs to future generations to re-examine this history and its implications for the liturgical tradition and life of the Western Church.

Notes

1 The Vulgate numeration of the psalms is used throughout this chapter.

2 Other differences of less importance: in Sunday Vigils (*cursus monasticus*) there are three Old-Testament canticles instead of psalms; the number of readings in the *cursus monasticus* is four instead of three; Vigils on weekdays has been interrupted with readings after six psalms; the number of readings here is different for the summer and the winter half-year, the short responsory (a small section is probably a remnant of an earlier full responsorial psalms) is adopted in Laudes and Vespers instead of the little hours of the *cursus saecularis*.

3 Psalm 63 comes second and 64, which is common with the *cursus saecularis*, is third.

4 For example, the *cursus saecularis* of Saturday Vigils includes twelve psalms just as in other days, in spite of some very long psalms belonging to this day.

5 The table gives the typical order based on most sources.

6 "On the feasts of saints and on all festivals let the Office be performed as we have prescribed for Sundays, except that the psalms, the antiphons and the lessons belonging to that particular day are to be said."

7 See: John A. Emerson, Lila Collamore (ed.), *Albi, Bibliothèque Municipale Rochegude, Manuscript 44: A Complete Ninth-Century Gradual and Antiphoner from Southern France* (Ottawa: The Institute of Mediaeval Music, 2002); Marie-Noël Colette, "Le Graduel-Antiphonaire, Albi, Bibliothèque Municipale, 44: une notation protoaquitaine rythmique," in László Dobszay (ed.), *International Musicological Society Study Group Cantus Planus: Papers Read at the 6th Meeting in Eger, Hungary, 1993*, (Budapest: Hungarian Academy of Sciences, Institute for Musicology, 1995), pp. 117–39.

8 Paris, Bibliothèque Nationale, lat. 17436. See: R. Jacobsson, "The Antiphoner of Compiègne" in M. Fassler & R.A. Baltzer (eds), *The Divine Office in the Latin Middle Ages: Methodology and Source Studies, Regional Developments, Hagiography* (Oxford: Oxford University Press, 2000), pp. 147–79.

9 René-Jean Hesbert, *Corpus Antiphonalium Officii*, 6 vols (Rome: Herder, 1963–79).

10 See: S.J.P. Van Dijk & J.H. Walker, *The Origins of the Modern Roman Liturgy: The Liturgy of the Papal Court and the Franciscan Order in the Thirteenth Century* (London & Westminster, MD: Darton, Longman & Todd, 1960).

11 For example *Ordinarium Agriense* for July had eleven proper Offices and fourteen more days with a full common Office. Only a few of the new Offices won acceptance by churches in a wider region and almost none of them obtained a nature of universality. Sometimes a given church left a free choice to pray the proper Office or the common. See: L. Dobszay (ed.) *Liber Ordinarius Agriensis 1509* (Budapest: Magyar Tudományos Akadémia, Zenetudományi Intézet, 2000), n. 539.

12 See: P. Battifol, *History of the Roman Breviary*, 3rd edn (London, New York, Bombay & Calcutta: Longmans, Green & Co., 1912), pp. 178–81.

13 S. Bäumer, *Histoire du Bréviaire*, vol. I (Paris: Letouzey et Ané, 1905), p. 117–18.

14 See: Battifol, *History of the Roman Breviary*, p. 191; A. Reid, *The Organic Development of the Liturgy*, 2nd edn (San Francisco: Ignatius Press, 2005), pp. 34–8.

15 See: Battifol, ibid., pp. 191–4.
16 See Chapter 6 "The Roman Missal of the Council of Trent."
17 M. Sodi, & A.M. Triacca (eds), *Breviarium Romanum: Editio Princeps 1568,* MLCT 3 (1999).
18 See: ibid., p. 3.
19 See: Bäumer, *Histoire du Bréviaire,* vol. I pp. 290–4.
20 See further the works of Battifol and Bäumer given in the bibliography.
21 See: L. Dobszay, *The Bugnini-Liturgy and the Reform of the Reform* (Front Royal, VA: Church Music Association of America, 2003) pp. 56–8; Reid, *The Organic Development of the Liturgy*, pp. 74–8.
22 See: ibid., pp. 131–3.
23 See: Dobszay, *The Bugnini-Liturgy and the Reform of the Reform.* pp. 57–68; L. Dobszay, *The Restoration and Organic Development of the Roman Rite* (London & New York: T&T Clark, 2010), pp. 99–124; A. Bugnini, *The Reform of the Liturgy 1948–1975* (Collegeville: Liturgical Press, 1990), chapter 31 "Composition of the Liturgy of the Hours"; S. Campbell, *From Breviary to Liturgy of the Hours: The Structural Reform of the Roman Office 1964–1971* (Collegeville: Liturgical Press, 1995).
24 Only in 2009 did the Abbey of Solesmes begin the publication of the *Antiphonale Romanum* with volume II, *Ad Vesperas in Dominicis et Festis.* A Latin-French edition of the Liturgy of the Hours (except for the Office of Readings) with Gregorian chant notation has been published by the Communauté Saint-Martin: *Heures Grégoriennes*, 3 vols, 2nd edn (Flavigny: Traditions Monastiques, 2012).
25 Anselmo Lentini OSB; see: Bugnini, *The Reform of the Liturgy 1948–1975,* pp. 547–51.
26 See: Reid, *The Organic Development of the Liturgy*, pp. 51–5.

Bibliography

Battifol, P., *History of the Roman Breviary*, 3rd edn (London, New York, Bombay & Calcutta: Longmans, Green & Co., 1912).
Baudot, J., *The Roman Breviary: Its Sources and History* (London: Catholic Truth Society, 1910).
Bäumer, S., *Histoire du Bréviaire*, 2 vols (Paris: Letouzey et Ané, 1905).
Billet, Jesse D., *The Divine Office in Anglo-Saxon England: 597–c.1000* (Henry Bradshaw Society Subsidia, 2014).
Bugnini, A., *The Reform of the Liturgy 1948–1975* (Collegeville: Liturgical Press, 1990).
Burton, E. & E. Myers, *The New Psalter and its Use* (London, New York, Bombay & Calcutta: Longmans, Green & Co., 1912).
Cabrol, F., *La Réforme du bréviare et du calendrier* (Paris: Bloud, 1912).
Campbell, S., *From Breviary to Liturgy of the Hours: The Structural Reform of the Roman Office 1964–1971* (Collegeville: Liturgical Press, 1995).
Dobszay, L., "Reading an Office book," M.E. Fassler & R.A. Baltzer (eds), *The Divine Office in the Latin Middle Ages* (Oxford: Oxford University Press, 2000), pp. 48–73.
—— *The Bugnini-Liturgy and the Reform of the Reform* (Front Royal, VA: Church Music Association of America, 2003).
—— *The Restoration and Organic Development of the Roman Rite* (London & New York: T&T Clark, 2010).

Fassler, M. & R.A. Baltzer (eds), *The Divine Office in the Latin Middle Ages: Methodology and Source Studies, Regional Developments, Hagiography* (Oxford: Oxford University Press, 2000).

Fillion, L.C., *The New Psalter of the Roman Breviary*, 3rd edn (London & St. Louis: Herder, 1923).

Hesbert, R.-J., *Corpus Antiphonalium Officii*, 6 vols (Rome: Herder, 1963–79).

Quigley, E.J., *The Divine Office: A Study of the Roman Breviary* (Dublin: M.H. Gill & Son, 1920).

Roguet, A.-M., *The Liturgy of the Hours: The General Instruction on the Liturgy of the Hours with a Commentary* (Collegeville: Liturgical Press, 1971).

Salmon, P., *The Breviary Through the Centuries* (Collegeville: Liturgical Press, 1962).

Taft, R., *The Liturgy of the Hours in East and West: The Origins of the Divine Office and its Meaning for Today*, 2nd edn (Collegeville: Liturgical Press, 1993).

Trilhe, R., *La Constitution "Divino Afflatu" et les nouvelles rubriques du Bréviaire romain* (Paris & Tournai: Casterman, 1912).

Chapter 11

GREGORIAN CHANT

Susan Treacy

Introduction

Gregorian chant, defined by Pope St Pius X as "the chant proper to the Roman Church,"[1] has held this name since the eighth century. Strictly speaking, though, Gregorian chant is one of several dialects of liturgical chant in the Western Church.[2] These monophonic melodies, traditionally sung unaccompanied, are known more generally as plainchant or plainsong. Current essays on Gregorian chant usually reflect two different approaches to the topic—Gregorian chant as an object of musicological research, with acknowledgement of its practical use, or Gregorian chant as the music integral to the Roman rite, restored and enriched through musicological research. This brief survey of a vast field will take the latter approach.

Modern liturgical books containing Gregorian chant can be reduced to two, yet history presents a greater variety. The book that holds the Proper chants for Mass is the gradual (*graduale*), which often includes the Ordinary chants in a separate *kyriale* section. The chant book for the Divine Office is known variously as the antiphoner, antiphonary, or antiphonal (*antiphonale*). Analogous to these two books are the missal (*missale*)—which has the texts of the Mass—and the breviary (*breviarium*)—which contains the texts for the Divine Office. The missal and the breviary generally do not contain musical notation, but there are 'notated' editions. Prior to 1200, however, there were separate books for the chants, prayers, and Scripture readings at Mass. The medieval gradual (also sometimes called the antiphoner) contained the chants, the sacramentary the prayers of the celebrant, and the lectionary of the Scripture lessons. There was even a *cantatorium*; the late seventh or early eighth-century *Ordo romanus I* mentions it as the cantor's book containing the gradual, alleluia and tract. Since the Second Vatican Council, the practice of using the gradual, the sacramentary, and the lectionary has been revived. The Divine Office, too, could be celebrated using several books—most commonly psalter and hymnal.

Types of Gregorian chant

Gregorian chant can be classified in various ways: by text, melody, form, modality, manner of performance, and liturgical function. Most of the Mass propers have biblical texts, and of those, selections from the psalter predominate. Most chants with non-biblical texts are Ordinary chants, hymns, and numerous psalm antiphons of the Divine Office, processional antiphons, sequences, litanies, among others.

The melodic style of a chant is defined by its text setting, i.e., the level of ornateness with which the melody clothes the liturgical text. The text setting of every chant is predominantly, but not exclusively, syllabic, neumatic, or melismatic. Syllabic chant is the simplest style, with one note per one syllable of text, and is used for priest-faithful dialogues, prayers, readings, Office psalm antiphons and hymns, the Credo, and some settings of the Gloria. Chants with several notes per syllable—from two to about nine—are said to be neumatic or semi-ornate; thus the style is more flowing and perhaps more contemplative. Neumatic chants include some of the Ordinary chants and some Proper chants (introit, communion). Chants with many notes per syllable (occasionally even fifty or more) are called melismatic, and their style is even more flowing and contemplative. Melismatic chants include the great responsories of the Office and the gradual, alleluia, and tract of the Mass. The amount of elaboration is dependent upon each text and its liturgical function.

A chant can also be categorized by its form, that is, by the way its melody is constructed. Three main categories of chants are those that consist of simple recitation formulae, those that are strophic or contain an element of repetition, and those that are generally referred to as "free."

The simplest chants are the tones for prayers, readings, dialogues, and prefaces. These syllabic recitation formulae are barely more than elevated speech. They feature a single reciting tone articulated by brief melodic formulae at grammatical punctuation points: musical cadences representing comma, colon, and full-stop (period). The collect, epistle, and gospel of the Mass each have distinctive cadences that embellish the reciting tone. The priest-faithful dialogues, especially the preface dialogue, depart from the reciting tone more frequently and are more like true melodies.

More elaborate than these simple liturgical recitatives are the tones used for psalms, canticles, introit verses, and communion verses. These are also chanted mainly on one note—a reciting tone—but this is articulated in order to delineate the two-part structure (hemistichs) of psalm verses. Thus, brief melodic cadence formulae—intonation, mediation, and termination—are sung at the beginning, middle, and end of a psalm verse. Verses with an extra section may be punctuated by a flex—a temporary drop in pitch. There are also degrees of ornateness among tones, with Office psalms being chanted to a simple psalm tone, introit and communion tones having more ornate tones, while canticles such as the Magnificat can have slightly more elaborate tones.

The hymn and the sequence are syllabic chants that exhibit a strophic or repetitive form. Typically, the Office hymn is strophic, with several four-line strophes of metrical poetry, each chanted to the same melody. The sequence, on the other hand, often has a repetitive form with paired melodic phrases, although each couplet may differ in length.

Among the "free" chants, the Gregorian melodies vary considerably, as each genre of chant has its own form, which is dictated by its syntax and liturgical function. Melodic cadences usually articulate the syntax.

Gregorian chants are musically distinguishable from one another through their use of a system of eight modes. A mode can be defined as a melodic type or pattern but also as a melodic scale. In seeking to organize and classify hundreds of liturgical chants, medieval theorists noticed that most chants had a final note (*finalis*) of D, E, F, or G. They also noticed that each melody inhabited a tonal area (melodic range, *ambitus*) either above the *finalis* or around it. Thus there are four pairs of modes that are either authentic (odd-numbered modes)—where the *finalis* is at the bottom of the range—or plagal (even-numbered modes)—where the *finalis* is four notes above the lowest note of the range. An example would be mode 1 (authentic), in which the modal scale ranges from the *finalis* D, to D an octave above and mode 2 (plagal), which ranges from A to A, with D positioned four notes up from A.

Often chants of a particular genre share common melodic phrases, especially in relation to their modal content, and because of centonization. This is a method of composition that involves patching together into a new chant, common melodic phrases that many chants share. For example, *Viderunt omnes* (Christmas Day) and *Timebunt gentes* (3rd Sunday after Epiphany) are just two of the many graduals (almost half) in mode 5 that feature similar turns of phrase.

Traditionally, there are three ways of performing Gregorian chant—antiphonal, responsorial, and direct. Antiphonal chants, sung in alternation (*alternatim*) by two groups, consist of psalms and antiphons of the Office, as well as introits and communions of the Mass.[3] Responsorial chants feature alternation between solo and group singing. Responsorial chants of the Office include the brief and great responsories, while for the Mass the following are all considered to be responsorial— gradual, alleluia, and offertory. Direct chants are those sung throughout by the whole choir, or by a soloist or celebrant, they include, among others, collects, prefaces, and the *Pater noster*.[4]

The Proper chants, with their varying texts appropriate to the liturgical occasion, are the cream of the Gregorian repertoire. These chants, traditionally for the *schola*, run the gamut from neumatic style to virtuosic, melismatic pieces best sung by soloists.

The introit originally accompanied the procession of the ministers to the sanctuary, but as processions became shorter it was eventually chanted as the celebrant mounted the steps to the altar. The use of the term antiphon implies that it framed a psalm, but introits in the most ancient books of liturgical texts (late eighth and ninth centuries) often contain just one verse and a doxology. Apparently, the original method of chanting enough verses to accommodate the length of the procession had been discontinued relatively early.[5] The form of the introit features an antiphon in neumatic style, followed by a verse and the lesser doxology (*Gloria Patri*) set to a more ornate version of a psalm tone; traditionally the antiphon is repeated. The neumatic introit antiphon is more ornate than a simple Office psalm antiphon, thus testifying to the Mass's liturgical pride of place. The stylistic contrast between the neumatic antiphon and its verse and doxology make the introit's form easy to discern, and contribute to the sometimes striking, almost fanfare-like quality of this proclamation of the day's liturgical mystery.

The chants between the readings do not accompany a liturgical action; they are more reflective and contemplative, and thus are very melismatic in style. There is also more flexibility in the use of these chants—gradual, tract, and alleluia— according to the liturgical season. The gradual, following the epistle, is a responsorial chant with a choral respond followed by a solo verse. An older tradition has a repetition of the respond, but this practice died out after the Middle Ages. Some scholars believe the gradual is an elaboration of an originally much simpler responsorial psalm in which a cantor sang the verses, to which the faithful responded with a simple melody, though this hypothesis is disputed.[6] The alleluia, chanted between the gradual and the gospel, is likewise highly melismatic. Its structure consists of the alleluia, a type of choral respond, followed by a solo verse proper to the day, and then the repetition of the alleluia. The word "alleluia" is derived from the Hebrew *hallelujah*, and typically the syllable -ia is set to a melisma. Scholars refer to this melisma as the *jubilus*, and the words at the end of the verse are often sung to the same melody as the jubilus, though this repetition is a later addition stemming from the post-Carolingian era. Thus the alleluia is the latest Proper chant to have developed its final form. The alleluia was at first chanted only on Easter Sunday, but later extended to all Sunday Masses outside of Lent.[7] During Eastertide the gradual is replaced by an alleluia; thus there are two alleluias, to emphasize the joy of the Resurrection. The sequence, a chant that traditionally follows the alleluia, is a syllabic chant with metrical text. It arose in the ninth century, flourished through the thirteenth century, and survived until the sixteenth century, when thousands of sequences were reduced to four after the Council of Trent. During Lent, the alleluia is replaced by the tract. This melismatic chant is an example of direct psalmody, a psalm that is sung without the interruption of refrains. Only two modes—modes 2 and 8—are used for the tracts. Another use of the tract occurs during the Easter Vigil, in the mode 8 canticles sung after the readings.

Besides the introit, another processional chant is the offertory, which originally accompanied an offertory procession. The earliest chant manuscripts show verses following the offertory antiphon, which would then be repeated—either whole or partially—after the verses. The antiphon itself is usually melismatic, although less so than the gradual and alleluia, but the verses are likewise elaborate and require the expertise of soloists. Over time the offertory procession became shorter, finally dying out during the late Middle Ages.[8] Correspondingly, the offertory verses began to be absent from chant books, starting in the eleventh century.[9]

The third processional chant is the communion antiphon, whose original function was to accompany the procession of the faithful going forward for Holy Communion. There is stylistic variety among the communions, but generally this antiphon is neumatic. Witnesses from the early Church provide evidence of psalm singing during communion. St Cyril of Jerusalem, in his *Mystagogical Catechesis*

(V, 20), exhorts his catechumens: "After these things, listen to the singer (ψαγγοντος), who invites us with a sacred melody to communion in the holy mysteries, and says: 'Taste and see that the Lord is good.'"[10] The use of psalm 33:9 is also mentioned in the *Apostolic Constitutions* (Treatise VIII, 14–17) and by St Jerome (*In Isaiam*, II, V, 20). An eighth-century witness, the *Ordo romanus I*, describes the practice of singing psalm verses in addition to the antiphon:

> As soon as the priest begins to administer the sacrament, the choir should intone the *antiphona ad communionem*. Afterwards the psalm is sung. When the communicants have filed past, the signal is given to the choir to end the chant with the [lesser] doxology and the repetition of the verse [i.e. the antiphon].[11]

During the eleventh and twelfth centuries, the psalm verses *ad repetendum* began to be discontinued, and by the twelfth century the only Communion to retain its verses was *Lux æterna* from the Requiem Mass. In the 1958 Instruction *De musica sacra et liturgia*, the Sacred Congregation of Rites restored the option to sing the verses, following the format described above in *Ordo romanus I*.[12]

The texts of the Ordinary chants remain stable from Mass to Mass. Nineteenth-century chant scholars grouped these chants together into sets numbered I–XVIII in the *Graduale*; a separate section contains a further twenty chants *ad libitum* and six settings of the Credo, but the known number of these chants far exceeds those in the *Graduale Romanum*. For instance, there are more than 200 melodies each for the Kyrie, Sanctus, and Agnus Dei, while medieval codices contain more than fifty melodies for the Gloria. Generally, the chants of the Ordinary are syllabic or neumatic in style and capable of being sung by the congregation, though there are some of later composition that give evidence—through their melismatic style—of having been composed to be sung by the schola.

The Kyrie, originally a litany, is the one Ordinary chant that remains in Greek, and is sung immediately after the introit. Kyries can be found as early as the tenth century in French and German manuscripts. Other parts of Europe are generously represented in manuscripts of the eleventh and twelfth centuries. Many of the most popular Kyrie melodies in modern chant books are from this early period, especially the tenth and eleventh centuries. Most of these Kyries appear with a Latin subtitle, for example Kyrie XI (*Orbis factor*), Kyrie I *ad libitum* (*Clemens Rector*), or Kyrie II (*Fons bonitatis*). These subtitles are a vestige of the phenomenon of added text and/or music that many scholars have traditionally called a trope.[13] Each petition is sung three times, resulting in a nine-fold Kyrie,[14] and the A-B-A form of the text invites musical settings that mirror this symmetrical layout.

The Gloria is a prose hymn, much like the hymns of Eastern liturgies. The *Ordines romani* describe the Gloria in its traditional place in the Mass, after the Kyrie, and there is evidence that before the ninth century the Gloria was sung by both clergy and congregation.[15] Thus scholars believe that the simpler melodies, such as Gloria XV and the so-called 'Ambrosian' Gloria, date from this pre-ninth-century era, and that after this, when the singing of the Gloria was assumed by the *schola*, the newer Gloria melodies were too ornate to be sung by the people. One interesting aspect of the Gloria chants is the way they are constructed of small melodic units or motives that are expanded, contracted, or otherwise subtly altered to accommodate text phrases of different lengths.

Although mandated in 798 by the Council of Aix-la-Chapelle to be sung in the Frankish liturgy,[16] the Credo did not become part of the Roman liturgy until as late as 1014; thus the number of Credo melodies is correspondingly smaller.[17] There are six melodies in the *Graduale Romanum*, reserved in a separate section after the other Ordinary chants. But one could say that there are actually only four melodies, as Credo II and V are simply variants of the original eleventh-century Credo I. Moreover, these six melodies represent only a small selection of extant Credo melodies (especially post-1600).[18] The style of the Credo is usually syllabic and, similar to the Gloria, comprising small motives that can be repeated, expanded, or contracted.

Medieval sources often mention congregational chanting of the Sanctus.[19] The Sanctus is sung between the preface and the canon of the Mass. Some scholars believe that the oldest of the Sanctus melodies is no. XVIII in the *Graduale*; its melody closely follows the contours of the preface melody and because of this it seems to flow naturally from the preface.[20] Starting in the eleventh century, the Sanctus melodies became increasingly more ornate, for example Sanctus II and VII, thus implying that the *schola* had taken over this chant. The text includes a number of repetitions that invite melodic repetitions; thus, very often both acclamations of *Hosanna in excelsis* use the same melody.

The Agnus Dei, another chant—like the Kyrie—with ties to the litany, originally featured many petitions. The *Liber pontificalis* documents the addition of the Agnus Dei to the Roman liturgy by Sergius I (687–701) as a fraction chant sung by clergy, choir, and people.[21] The fraction ceremony became shortened when small morsels of unleavened bread were substituted for loaves of leavened bread that took more time to be broken. Thus the need for multiple petitions in the Agnus decreased and the number eventually became fixed at three. This occurred in the tenth century, and increasingly during this century and the next, the words *dona nobis pacem* were added to the end of the chant. After the eleventh century, newer and more elaborate melodies began to be composed, which would explain the hegemony of the choir during this time. With this chant, too, the text presents a clearly delineated form (AAA'), but composers have responded in multiple ways. Of twenty Agnus Dei melodies in the *Graduale*, nine have an AAA (or AAA') structure and nine follow the form ABA. The two remaining settings are Agnus VII, with the form AAB and Agnus XI, which is ABC.[22]

The Divine Office has more variety than the Mass, and its chants are correspondingly more numerous. Therefore, this chapter can cover only distinctive stylistic aspects of the main Office chants.

The invitatory, *Venite exsultemus Domino*, which begins the Office of Matins, is a setting of psalm 94 that, unlike regular Office psalms, features a rearrangement of the psalm's eleven verses into five longer verses. Thus, each verse has a tripartite division analogous to the doxology of the introit, which has an extra phrase with its own intonation and mediation. The antiphon repeats in full after verses one, three, and five, but after verses two and four, only the second half is repeated. The psalm tones used for the verses are not the standard psalm tones, though they do correspond to the eight modes. Interestingly, there are almost no invitatories in either mode 1 or mode 8.[23]

The chanting of psalms framed by simple, syllabic antiphons forms the core of the Divine Office. Each psalm and its antiphon share the same mode, and the eight psalm tones feature different melodic endings, or cadences, in order to facilitate an efficient transition back to the antiphon. The antiphons furnish Proper texts to the *cursus* of the psalms, which is unchanging.

While the other chants of the Office (and Mass) have prose texts, hymn lyrics are non-biblical, metrical poetry. About two-thirds of the Latin Office hymns are in iambic dimeter, the meter of the four fourth-century hymns attributed by St Augustine to St Ambrose.[24] This alone gave a certain authority to hymns in this meter, which the Rule of St Benedict (c. 530) termed "ambrosiani." Hymns generally have a strophic form, with each stanza being set to the same melody, which is syllabic in style.

Responsorial chants of the Office are the brief responsories (*responsoria brevia*)—chanted after the *capitulum*, or short reading, at Compline and the Little Hours in secular use (also at Lauds and Vespers in monastic use)—and the great responsories (*responsoria prolixa*), sung at Matins after each scripture lesson. The principle behind each genre is the same, i.e., a choral response to solo singing.

The brief responsory features a respond, a verse, and the first part of the lesser doxology. The verse and doxology are chanted by a soloist, while each occurrence of the respond is chanted by the choir, except the first and last time, when the choir sings after the cantorial intonation. Although historically there were many melodies for the brief responsory, in current practice there are just a few simple melodies, three of which are used with various texts.

The great responsories are based on the same principle of respond, verse, and doxology but exhibit more variety of form. Usually the respond melodies are ornate and sometimes feature a long melisma. The verses are sung to an elaborate psalm tone corresponding to the mode of the respond. As with other types of psalm tones, there are eight, each one corresponding to a mode.[25] Because Matins is the longest and most complex of the Offices, the great responsories outnumber all other Office chants. Additionally, the great responsories are chanted at Vespers on solemn feasts, and at processions.[26]

Three of the Offices feature New Testament canticles. At Lauds the *Benedictus Dominus Deus*, the canticle of Zechariah (Lk 1:68–79), is chanted, and its counterpart at Vespers is the *Magnificat*, the canticle of Mary (Lk 1:46–55). Each canticle is chanted to one of eight tones that are somewhat more ornate than an Office psalm tone (almost identical to an introit tone).[27] The *Benedictus* and *Magnificat* are each framed by a proper antiphon in neumatic style. *Nunc dimittis*, the canticle of Simeon (Lk 2:29–32), is chanted at Compline in the secular use. An example of direct psalmody, the *Nunc dimittis*, is chanted to a simple psalm tone and often has no antiphon. One antiphon, *Salva nos*, is typically associated with the *Nunc dimittis*.

The history of Gregorian chant

Reconstructing the history of Gregorian chant is an ongoing task that is made more formidable by the fact that liturgical manuscript sources from the pre-Carolingian era have no musical notation. No evidence exists until the late seventh century of an organized series of Proper chants for the liturgical year. James McKinnon attributes this process to the Roman *schola cantorum*, which he believes to have been formed between 650 and 700 as the only known cantorial body dedicated to chant.[28] McKinnon sees the selection process as continuing on into the early eighth century, especially during the pontificate of Gregory II (715–31). Thus this standardized set of Proper chants initiated in Rome made its way to Gaul when the Carolingians decided to replace their chant with Roman chant. This would explain why the Frankish chant manuscripts—the first to be completely notated—are so uniform overall.

Liturgical traditions in the West were generally not uniform before c. 750, although two pre-Carolingian exceptions are worth mentioning. In the late 600s, Spanish bishops in Toledo mandated uniformity in the celebration of the Old Spanish liturgy throughout the Visigothic Church. Meanwhile, in Anglo-Saxon England the Church moved towards a unified liturgical practice on the Roman model. In 597, Pope St Gregory I (the Great) had sent St Augustine of Canterbury to evangelize England. At first, the Anglo-Saxons seem to have used a variety of rites borrowed from Celtic, Gallican, and Roman practices, but in 747 the Second Council of Cloveso changed this. Cuthbert, Archbishop of Canterbury, enjoined the whole Anglo-Saxon Church to adopt Roman liturgical practices. Along with that came adoption of the Roman chant, which had already happened at the twin monasteries of Wearmouth and Jarrow, as described by St Bede (672/3–735).[29]

The Anglo-Saxon Church held dear its connection with Gregory the Great through St Augustine of Canterbury, and David Hiley has advanced the idea that the legendary association of Gregory with Gregorian chant could have originated in Anglo-Saxon England.[30] Thus Hiley believes that the acknowledged impact of the golden age of English monasticism on Carolingian education and liturgy could also have extended to the perception of Gregory as an authority figure in relation to liturgical chant. This is an attractive idea, although it is at variance with the usual explanation for Gregory's perceived eminence in relation to Gregorian chant, which centers on the unification of the Frankish kingdom.

Like the Anglo-Saxons, the founding generations of the Carolingian dynasty saw a practical reason to impose liturgical uniformity on their realm,[31] and by associating Gregory the Great with the composition and promotion of Gregorian chant, they were assured of gaining the authority needed to get the Roman chant accepted. A uniform liturgy would increase the unity of their kingdom, so they subsumed the various Gallican liturgical usages into the Roman rite.

Learning the texts of the Roman liturgy was no problem for the Franks as manuscripts were plentiful, but learning the Roman chant presented challenges because of the lack of musical notation; the vast repertory of chants was learned by rote and memorized. Indeed, St Isidore of Seville (c. 560–636) attested to the lack of musical notation when he commented that "unless sounds are held in the memory by man they perish, because they cannot be written down."[32] The extent to which this lack affected the transmission of Roman chant to Francia and the subsequent development of Gregorian chant is a question that continues to occupy scholars down to the present day. What is the exact relationship of the Roman chant to the Gallican chant sung in the Frankish kingdom?

Aurelian of Réôme's treatise, *Musica disciplina* (840s), provides the first unmistakable evidence of notation. This and a few other examples of neums, however, do not represent a systematic notation of Frankish liturgical manuscripts until the very late 800s, when the first completely notated missals begin to emerge;[33] fully notated manuscripts for the Divine Office do not exist earlier than the end of the tenth century. This earliest neumatic notation does not represent specific pitches or intervals, but only the shape of the melody. It was assumed that cantors had already memorized a melody; the neums merely reminded them of the melody's general direction. Thus the notated chant manuscript was, in effect, a reference copy rather than a performance copy from which singers read the notation.

Not until the eleventh century are there any Roman notated liturgical manuscripts. The chants in the Frankish and Roman manuscripts share many melodic characteristics, yet there are enough variants that both repertories merit being considered as discrete. The Frankish manuscripts contain the repertory that has come to be called Gregorian, while the Roman repertory is commonly referred to as Old Roman. The relationship between these two repertories and the question of how accurately the Franks learned the Roman chant is one that has stimulated much scholarly discussion in the last sixty years. Helmut Hucke's hypothesis has been generally accepted.[34] Basing his argument on the ninth-century accounts of Notker Balbulus and John the Deacon, Hucke posits that "Gregorian chant resulted from the imperfect transmission of the music sung in Rome to Frankish cantors and the virtual separation of the two repertories from around 800 when Charlemagne decreed that all Frankish cantors were to learn the 'Roman' rite from the *schola cantorum* at Metz."[35] Subsequently, this Gallicanized Roman chant was adopted in Rome itself and became known as Gregorian chant.

Exact pitches began to be notated in practical liturgical manuscripts only in the eleventh century, although such notation had already appeared in late ninth-century theory treatises. Aquitanian liturgical manuscripts of the early eleventh century preserve heighted neums, which indicate relative positions of pitches in *campo aperto* (without a staff). Another type of early notation is an alphabetical system, found in the St Bénigne de Dijon tonary (Montpéllier, Faculté de Médecine, H. 159) and in some Norman and English codices. Also during the eleventh century, Guido of Arezzo devised a musical staff that was more compact and usable than earlier attempts at staff notation. Guido employed a red line to designate F and a yellow line for C, which transformed chant pedagogy. The square notation that appears in modern Gregorian chant books originated in late twelfth-century France and subsequently made its way to Italy.

At about the same time the first chant manuscripts were being notated, a new development—polyphony—that would threaten the primacy of Gregorian chant was beginning. The earliest polyphony was merely an added voice, singing in parallel motion with the chant. Over time, however, the chant often became buried under, or within, several vocal lines. Polyphony caught on so successfully that by the time of the Council of Trent (1545–63) it was common for composers to consider a Gregorian melody as only a potential *cantus firmus* for a polyphonic work.[36]

Following the Council of Trent, Pius IV (1559–65) set up a commission in October 1563 to reform the missal and breviary. The new Roman breviary was promulgated on July 9, 1568, and St Pius V (1566–72) promulgated the new Roman missal in his bull *Quo primum* of July 14, 1570. Seven years later Pope Gregory XIII (1572–85) commissioned Giovanni Pierluigi da Palestrina and Annibale Zoilo to edit the chants for the new breviary and missal. Their work was halted in 1578 and lay fallow for thirty years, during which time Palestrina died (1594).[37] Finally, in 1608 Paul V (1605–21) appointed six editors to work on the new Roman Gradual, and privileged the Roman printer Giovanni Battista Raimondi. He was founder of the Medicean Printing Company, named after its patron, Ferdinando Cardinal de' Medici. Giovanni Guidetti, chaplain to Gregory XIII and a singer in the papal chapel, had already published in 1582 his *Directorium chori*, a handbook for singers; it featured a new kind of proportional notation for chant. Meanwhile, the six editors appointed by Paul V had shrunk to two, Felice Anerio and Francesco Soriano, whose work resulted in the Medicean Gradual (1614–15). Their revisions of the chant reflected the influence of Renaissance humanists in their focus on melodic expression of the words. The texts were "improved" by replacing the "barbarisms" of medieval Latin with elegant Ciceronian Latin. The modal sound was modernized through the regular use of B-flat. Melismas were shortened and placed only on syllables carrying the tonic accent, never on weak syllables. As the reformed *Graduale Romanum*, the Medicean Gradual has received much attention from historians, but there were also other versions of the gradual published at the time by religious orders and various local publishers in, for example, Venice, Antwerp, and Paris.[38]

In late seventeenth- and eighteenth-century France, Gallicanism had its effect on liturgy and liturgical chant through the introduction of what is termed neo-Gallican chant, an even more drastic revision of Gregorian chant. Neo-Gallican chant also included newly-composed pieces, and some hallmarks of its style were the use of instrumental accompaniment, accidentals, and metrical rhythms. This chant was often referred to as 'chant figuré' or 'plain-chant musical'; vocal ornamentation was also a feature. An important theorist and composer of neo-Gallican chant was Guillaume-Gabriel Nivers (1632–1714), and another, Henri Dumont (1610–84), stood the test of time with his *Cinq messes en plain-chant* (Paris, 1669), still used in France during the first half of the twentieth century.

The middle years of the nineteenth century saw the burgeoning of Gregorian chant reform. In France, the triumph of ultramontanism, one of whose adherents was Dom Prosper Guéranger (1805–75), abbot of Solesmes, resulted in a gradual forsaking of Gallicanism—and thus neo-Gallican chant—and a turn towards the Roman rite. This stimulated interest in Gregorian chant, but also disagreement as to what exactly was the true chant. Three positions emerged: those who advocated the use of the seventeenth-century Medicean Gradual, those who favored eleventh- to thirteenth-century manuscripts in staff notation, and those who sought to go back even earlier, to manuscripts with the earliest neumatic notations, despite their near indecipherability. A breakthrough occurred in 1846 when Jean-Louis-Félix Danjou (1812–66) found an eleventh-century manuscript featuring both neumatic and alphabetical notations. This was the tonary of St Bénigne de Dijon (Montpellier, Faculté de Médecine, H. 159), which would enable subsequent transcriptions of these ancient manuscripts.

In other countries, too, Gregorian chant was being revived. In Germany, the Cecilian movement (Cäcilien-Verein), under the guidance of Franz Xaver Witt (1834–88) and Franz Xaver Haberl (1840–1910), looked to the Medicean Gradual as a model. After all, reasoned Haberl, this gradual had been the official one endorsed by Pope Paul V, and none other than Palestrina had been one of the editors, so it must have canonical status. Thus in 1871, the Regensburg publisher Friedrich Pustet published a new Gradual that was a reprint of the Medicean Gradual. This was followed, in 1878, by Pustet's antiphoner, modeled on two other post-Tridentine era publications. Pius IX granted a thirty-year monopoly in August 1871 to Pustet's editions as the official and authentic form of Gregorian chant.

Meanwhile, in France at L'Abbaye Saint-Pierre de Solesmes, refounded in 1833 by Dom Guéranger, a monumental revision of Gregorian chant was about to begin. What distinguishes the work of the Solesmes monks from other reformers was their insistence on consulting the very earliest manuscripts of staffless neums. Research was begun around 1856 by Dom Paul Jausions (1834–70); in 1860 he was joined by Dom Joseph Pothier (1835–1923). Together they worked for twenty years on the project of supplying all the chant books needed for liturgical use at the abbey. They did this through painstaking examination and comparison of all the available manuscripts of chant in neumatic notation. Dom Pothier would become one of the leading forces in Solesmes's mission to restore Gregorian chant. In his first publication, *Les mélodies grégoriennes d'après la tradition* (1880), he presented the guiding principles of his research, an explanation of the neums, and a discussion of his theory of oratorical rhythm in chant. The manuscript sources seemed not to provide much information on the rhythmic interpretation of Gregorian chant, so this left much room for discussion. Pothier's interpretation had as its foundation the idea that chant notation did not indicate exact note values, thus each note was equal in duration. This resulted in a free-flowing and non-metrical rendition, with attention to the tonic accents of the words.

Dom Pothier saw to it that a new Gregorian chant font was designed, based on thirteenth- and fourteenth-century French notation, and this made its debut in his *Liber gradualis* (1883). The publication of the *Liber gradualis* sparked off contention over this seeming new style of chant. Some opponents wanted the chant performed only the way it had been done within their memories, while others supported the post-Tridentine style of chant represented by the Pustet Gradual. This dispute occasioned the beginning, in 1889, of *Paléographie musicale*,[39] a series of publications of chant manuscript sources in photographic facsimile. Dom André Mocquereau (1849–1930) inaugurated this series as a way to defend the researches of his mentor Dom Pothier. Mocquereau reasoned: "If we could manage to prove beyond a doubt that the melodies of the Medicean edition were merely a miserable caricature of the early cantilenas, the battle would be won."[40]

In volume I of *Paléographie musicale* Mocquereau compared the tenth-century gradual *Universi*, as given in Pustet's *Graduale*, with the version in Pothier's *Liber gradualis* and a facsimile of the original manuscript from the monastery of Saint Gall. It was clear that Pothier's edition was an exact transcription from the ancient manuscript, whereas the Pustet version was greatly altered. The Regensburg camp, however, would not accept this. Undeterred, Dom Mocquereau delivered the fatal blow to the Germans in volumes II and III of *Paléographie musicale*. Here he presented one chant, the gradual *Iustus ut palma*, as represented in 219 codices dating from the ninth to the seventeenth centuries. Barring a few minor variants, all agreed with the melody transcribed in Pothier's *Liber gradualis*. Pustet's monoply as publisher of the Vatican chant books expired in 1901 and Pope Leo XIII declined to renew it. Solesmes had prevailed; from now on the restored Gregorian chant, based on the monks' researches, would be privileged by the Church.

On November 22, 1903, a few months after Pius X was elected pope, he issued *Tra le sollecitudini*, a motu proprio in which he proclaimed Gregorian chant "the music proper to the Roman church" and favorably recognized the researches and publications of Solesmes. On January 8, 1904, the Sacred Congregation of Rites published an exhortation that the restored chant be adopted in all churches without delay. During a general congress on the Thirteenth Centenary of the Death of Saint Gregory the Great (April 4–9), the new Vatican edition was officially promulgated. Later that month, on April 25, Pius X issued a second motu proprio, *Col nostro*.[41] This announced that the Holy See would retain publishing rights for the new chant books; that the restored chants should agree with the manuscript sources; that the Solesmes monks were to serve as the redactors; and that Dom Pothier would preside over a ten-member *ad hoc* commission, assisted by ten consultants, to oversee the new editions. The process was difficult on account of disagreement over which manuscripts were to be used for the Vatican editions. One faction rejected the use of any but the most ancient manuscripts; this was the position of Solesmes, represented by Dom Mocquereau, who was a commission member. The other side insisted on including manuscripts of later periods; this was the position of Dom Pothier (now abbot of Saint Wandrille) and Peter Wagner, among others. On June 24, 1905, a papal directive established that the Vatican editions would be based on Pothier's *Liber gradualis* (2nd edition), thus effectively excluding Dom Mocquereau and Solesmes.[42]

During this time another dispute was underway; this one centered on how Gregorian chant should be performed. In general, the manuscript sources give no clear indications of rhythm; however, three of the earliest manuscripts contain a number of signs that are indicators of rhythm, stress, or dynamics.[43] The dispute involved two factions, each disagreeing among themselves. Pothier and Mocquereau represented the "equalist" faction, holding that each note of Gregorian chant was equal in duration; however, the two monks disagreed on one point. Pothier's oratorical interpretation gave primacy to the words, represented by the Latin tonic accent, whereas Mocquereau asserted the primacy of the music in his interpretation of chant rhythm. The "mensuralists" advanced the idea that the notes were not of equal value and had a proportional relationship of 2:1. How this was realized, nonetheless, varied considerably in the theories of these scholars, among whom were Antoine Dechevrens, Eduard Bernoulli, Hugo Riemann, Oskar Fleischer, and Peter Wagner.

Before the momentous publication of the *Graduale* (1908), the Vatican first issued its *Kyriale* (1905); simultaneously, Desclée published a *Kyriale* with Solesmes rhythmic signs. These signs had been developed by Dom Mocquereau as a practical representation of his theory of free rhythm.[44] Mocquereau's approach was a mixture of musicological research, intuition, and practical exigency. His disciple, Dom Joseph Gajard (1885–1972), assiduously promoted the classic Solesmes method, and especially through sound recordings of the monastic choir, made in the 1950s and 1960s. In this way the Solesmes style became known worldwide.

After Gajard's death, a new approach to the rhythm of plainchant emerged at Solesmes. Dom Eugène Cardine (1905–88) coined the term *Sémiologie grégorienne* (Gregorian Semiology) to describe the fruits of his closer reading of the rhythmic signs in the ancient neumatic manuscripts, especially manuscripts of Saint Gall and Laon. Chant books published by Solesmes since 2000 do not contain any rhythmic signs.

The place of Gregorian chant in the Church's liturgical life

Gregorian chant has always held a privileged position within the Church, whether implicitly or explicitly. It cannot be said that its privileging began only with the motu proprio of Pius X. Although the first official Church document on music was not issued until the Bull *Una Res* of Leo IV (847–55), the writings of earlier popes contain liturgical pronouncements, which mention regulation of chant. *Una Res* is of a disciplinary nature; in it Pope Leo castigated an abbot for not using the Roman ecclesiastical chant at his monastic liturgies. Because chant arose as an integral part of the liturgy, it was assumed to be the foundational music of the Church's liturgy, thus there was no need to assert its primacy. One of the concerns of Church councils and synods during the Middle Ages was the safeguarding of the Church's traditional liturgical chant. As mentioned above, the Second Council of Clovesho (747) enjoined the Anglo-Saxon Church to accept Roman liturgical use, including the Roman chant. In 1324–5, John XXII (1316–34), the second Avignon pope, issued a Bull, *Docta sanctorum patrum*, in which he wrote against the elaborate fourteenth-century polyphony that was obscuring the chant, which he assumed to be the fundamental musical patrimony of the Church.[45]

By the time of the Council of Trent and in the ensuing years, Gregorian chant was still the official chant of the Church, so much so that Pius V ordered the chant books to be revised, resulting in the Medicean Gradual of 1614–15. Nevertheless, practically speaking, chant was most often sung at the Divine Office, less often at Mass.

Benedict XIV, in his 1749 encyclical *Annus qui*, wrote of Gregorian chant in connection with the Divine Office, yet he commended monks for their excellent chanting, as opposed to the chanting of secular priests, and he referred to it as "the chant that excites the souls of the faithful to devotion and piety . . . more willingly listened to by devout men and rightly preferred to chant called figurative."[46] In a later document (1753), the Pope referred to the fact that "Gregorian chant is seen to be everywhere accepted, and in addition, is heard devotedly by the Christian faithful."[47]

In the nineteenth century, Pope Pius IX granted his approval to the Cäcilien-Verein, founded in Regensburg in 1868. His 1870 brief, *Multum ad commovendos animos*, supported the Cecilians in their mission to promote Gregorian chant, and the pope mentioned that their first object was that "the Gregorian chant or plain chant be everywhere cultivated."[48] Actions of Leo XIII and Pius X promoting Gregorian chant have been cited above.

Starting with Pius X and *Tra le sollecitudini* (1903), the twentieth century saw more explicit promotion of Gregorian chant than any previous century. Pius XI celebrated the silver jubilee of the *Tra le sollecitudini* with his Apostolic Constitution *Divini cultus sanctitatem* (1928). Pius XII made reference to chant in his 1947 encyclical, *Mediator Dei*, and also wrote an encyclical devoted to sacred music, *Musicae sacrae disciplina* (1955). In 1958, the Instruction *De musica sacra et liturgia* followed, in which the Sacred Congregation of Rites explained how to implement the 1955 encyclical. Gregorian chant was extolled as "the sacred music proper to the Roman church" and "music characteristic of the Roman Church." (nn. 5, 16)

The Second Vatican Council's Constitution on the Sacred Liturgy, *Sacrosanctum Concilium* (1963) and the post-conciliar documents implementing it, reference earlier twentieth-century popes and speak of Gregorian chant in the same glowing way, but also contains loopholes. For instance, chapter VI of the Constitution proclaims that Gregorian chant "should be given pride of place [*principum locum*, the "principal," or "first" place] in liturgical services" (n. 112). However, in the 1967 Instruction *Musicam sacram*, a similar sentence is preceded by the qualifier: "In sung liturgical services celebrated in Latin" (n. 50a). This, of course, limits the privileging of Gregorian chant to Mass celebrated in Latin. *Musicam sacram* evinced the tensions between progressive liturgists and traditional Catholic musicians—they prepared twelve drafts of the document before its release. Documents promoting Gregorian chant were released under Paul VI and by John Paul II; the latter wrote a *Chirograph on Sacred Music* in 2003 to commemorate the centenary of Pius X's *Tra le sollecitudini*.[49]

Conclusion

Benedict XVI made many references to the importance of Gregorian chant in works written before he assumed the Chair of St Peter.[50] However, it is his Apostolic Exhortation *Sacramentum Caritatis* (2007) that most appositely underlines the place of Gregorian chant in the liturgical life of the Western Church today: "while respecting various styles and different and highly praiseworthy traditions, I desire, in accordance with the request advanced by the synod fathers, that Gregorian chant be suitably esteemed and employed as the chant proper to the Roman liturgy."[51]

Notes

1   Pius X, Motu Proprio *Tra le sollecitudini* (On the Restoration of Church Music) 22 November 1903, n. 3; NL, p. 5.
2   Chant dialects (outside of Gregorian) are Old Roman, Ambrosian, Beneventan, Ravenna chant, Aquileia chant, Gallican, Celtic, and Mozarabic (Old Spanish) chant. Of these repertories, only Gregorian, Old Roman, and Ambrosian remain intact. See: K. Levy, J.A. Emerson, J. Bellingham, D. Hiley, & B. Zon, "Plainchant," *The New Grove Dictionary of Music and Musicians,* 2nd edn (Oxford: Oxford University Press, 2001), 19, pp. 825–86 (p. 826).
3   Opinions differ on the classification of some chants; moreover, performance style changed over time in the case of some chants. One example is the introit, which was originally an antiphonal chant, but by the sixth century had taken on responsorial characteristics. Ibid., (p. 836).
4   Ibid.
5   The Instruction of the Sacred Congregation of Rites *De musica sacra et sacra liturgia* (On Sacred Music and Sacred Liturgy) of September 3, 1958 restored the possibility of chanting the introit verses (n. 27a); NL, p. 263.
6   See: P. Jeffery, *Re-envisioning Past Musical Cultures: Ethnomusicology in the Study of Gregorian Chant* (Chicago: University of Chicago Press, 1992), p. 80, also pp. 83–4.
7   See: R.F. Hayburn, *Papal Legislation on Sacred Music 95 A.D. to 1977 A.D.* (Collegeville: Liturgical Press, 1978), pp. 4–5.
8   The Sacred Congregation of Rites permitted the chanting of the Offertory verses in *De musica sacra et sacra liturgia* (n. 27b) NL, pp. 263–4. This Instruction also provides for psalm verses sung, presumably, to psalm tones like those used for the introit. The melismatic verses can be found in: C. Ott, ed., *Offertoriale sive versus offertoriorum cantus gregoriani* (Tournai: Desclée, 1935).
9   See: D. Saulnier, *Gregorian Chant: a Guide to the History and Liturgy* (Brewster: Paraclete Press, 2009), p. 75.
10 J. McKinnon, *Music in Early Christian Literature* (Cambridge: Cambridge University Press, 1987), p. 77.
11 H. Hucke & M. Huglo, "Communion," *The New Grove Dictionary of Music and Musicians* (London: Macmillan, 1980), 4, pp. 591–94 (p. 592).
12 *De musica sacra et sacra liturgia* (n. 27c) NL, p. 262. These verses can be found in: *Versus psalmorum et canticorum ad usum cantorum pro antiphonis ad introitum et ad communionem repetendis iuxta codices antiques* (Tournai: Desclée, 1961).

13 R.L. Crocker in "Kyrie eleison," *The New Grove Dictionary of Music and Musicians,*
2nd edn (Oxford: Oxford University Press, 2001) 14, pp. 71–3 (p. 72) and D. Hiley, *Western
Plainchant* (Oxford: Clarendon Press, 1993) p. 152, disagree, basing their opinions on
the research of D.A. Bjork, "The Kyrie trope," *Journal of the American Musicological
Society,* 33 (1980), pp. 1–41. They believe that many Latin-texted Gregorian Kyries, like
Kyrie *fons bonitatis,* in *Cantus selecti ex libris Vaticanis et Solesmensibus excerpti*
(Solesmes: Abbaye Saint-Pierre, 1949), p. 81*, are *prosulae,* chants which have Latin
words added to an already-existing melody. These words transform a melismatic Kyrie
into one that is syllabic.

14 After the Second Vatican Council Kyries with much melodic repetition were truncated
so as to become six-fold, e.g., Kyrie XI.

15 J. Jungmann, *The Mass of the Roman Rite: Its Origins and Development* (New York:
Benziger Brothers, 1950), 1, pp. 357–8.

16 See: R.L. Crocker & D. Hiley, "Credo," *The New Grove Dictionary of Music and
Musicians,* 2nd edn (Oxford: Oxford University Press, 2001), 6, pp. 657–9 (p. 658).

17 Hiley, *Western Plainchant,* p. 169.

18 Ibid., p. 171.

19 Jungmann, *The Mass of the Roman Rite,* 2, pp. 129–31.

20 See: Hiley, *Western Plainchant,* pp. 161–2, however, for a discussion of Sanctus
XVIII.

21 Jungmann, *The Mass of the Roman Rite,* 2, pp. 335–6.

22 Saulnier, *Gregorian Chant,* p. 103. For a further refinement of this, see: W. Apel,
Gregorian Chant (Bloomington: Indiana University Press, 1958), p. 418.

23 To see the Invitatory psalm set to each of the tones (plus some variants) consult: *Liber
hymnarius cum invitatoriis & aliquibus responsoriis* (Solesmes: Abbaye Saint-Pierre de
Solesmes, 1983), pp. 133–73.

24 *Æterne rerum Conditor, Deus Creator omnium, Iam surgit hora tertia, Veni Redemptor
gentium.*

25 For a table of all eight responsorial tones, see: T. Bailey, "Psalm, §II, 11: Responsories of
Mass and Office," *The New Grove Dictionary of Music and Musicians,* 2nd edn (Oxford:
Oxford University Press, 2001), 20, pp. 459–61 (p. 461).

26 See: *Antiphonale monasticum pro diurnis horis juxta vota RR. DD. Abbatum
Congregationum Confoederatarum Ordinis Sancti Benedicti a Solesmensibus Monachis
Restitutum* (Paris: Desclée, 1934), pp. 1183–204, and *Processionale monasticum ad
usum Congregationis Gallicae Ordinis Sancti Benedicti* (Solesmes: E Typographeo
Sancti Petri, 1893).

27 For a comparative table see: Bailey "Psalm, §II, 11: Responsories of Mass and Office,"
pp. 455–7.

28 See: J. McKinnon, *The Advent Project: The Later-Seventh-Century Creation of the
Roman Mass Proper* (Berkeley: University of California Press, 2000).

29 L. Sherley-Price, trans., *Bede: A History of the English Church and People,* revised edn
(Baltimore: Penguin, 1965), p. 231.

30 Hiley, *Western Plainchant,* pp. 506–7.

31 Pepin the Short (751–68), Charlemagne (768–814), Louis the Pious (814–40).

32 Isidore of Seville, *Etymologiarum sive originium libri xv,* quoted in: P. Weiss & R.
Taruskin, *Music in the Western World: A History in Documents,* 2nd edn (Belmont, CA:
Schirmer Cengage Learning, 2008), p. 34.

33 For ninth-century examples of neums see: D. Hiley & J. Szendrei, "Notation, §III, 1:
Plainchant: Origins and earliest examples," *The New Grove Dictionary of Music and*

Musicians, 2nd edn (Oxford: Oxford University Press, 2001), 18, pp. 84–119 (p. 89), table 4.
34 H. Hucke, "Die Einführung des Gregorianischen Gesangs im Frankenreich," *Römische Quartalschrift* 49 (1954), pp. 172–85.
35 Levy et al., "Plainchant," p. 830.
36 See: Hayburn, *Papal Legislation on Sacred Music,* p. 36.
37 For the more complex and dramatic story of this first phase of the Medicean Gradual see: ibid., pp. 36–57.
38 See: Levy et al., "Plainchant", p. 851.
39 A. Mocquereau, ed., *Paléographie musicale: fac-similés photoypiques des principaux manuscrits de chant grégorien, ambrosien, mozarabique, gallican* (Solesmes: Imprimerie Saint-Pierre, 1889–92).
40 P. Combe, *The Restoration of Gregorian Chant: Solesmes and the Vatican Edition* (Washington: Catholic University of America Press, 2003), p. 105.
41 See: Hayburn, *Papal Legislation on Sacred Music,* pp. 256–7.
42 See: ibid., pp. 264–5.
43 St Gallen (Stiftsbibliothek, Mss. 359, 339), Einsiedeln (Benediktinerkloster, Musikbibliothek, Ms. 121), and Laon (Bibliothèque municipale, Ms. 239).
44 Later published in A. Mocquereau, *Le nombre musical grégorien: A Study of Gregorian Musical Rhythm,* vol 1, parts 1–2 (Tournai: Desclée, 1932).
45 E. Richter & E. Friedberg, *Corpus Iuris Canonici* (Leipzig: Tauchnitz, 1881), 2, pp. 1255–7, ET: Hayburn, *Papal Legislation on Sacred Music,* pp. 20–1.
46 Quoted in Hayburn, ibid., p. 95. "Figurative" chant is polyphony.
47 Ibid., p. 109.
48 Ibid., p. 128.
49 Sacred Congregation of Divine Worship, Letter *Voluntati obsequens* (Letter to the Bishops on the Minimum Repertoire of Plain Chant), April 14, 1974; John Paul II, *Chirograph of the Supreme Pontiff John Paul II for the Centenary of the Motu Proprio Tra le Sollecitudini on Sacred Music,* 22 November 2003.
50 See: JRCW 11, part D.
51 Benedict XVI, Apostolic Exhortation *Sacramentum Caritatis,* February 22, 2007, n. 42.

Bibliography

Documents of the Holy See

Benedict XVI, Apostolic Exhortation *Sacramentum Caritatis,* February 22, 2007.
John Paul II, *Chirograph of the Supreme Pontiff John Paul II for the Centenary of the Motu Proprio Tra le sollecitudini on Sacred Music,* November 22, 2003.
Pius X, Motu Proprio *Tra le sollecitudini* (On the Restoration of Church Music), November 22, 1903.
Pius XI, Apostolic Constitution *Divini cultus sanctitatem* (On Divine Worship), December 20, 1928.
Pius XII, Encyclical Letter *Musicae sacrae disciplina* (On Sacred Music), December 25, 1955.
Sacred Congregation of Rites, Instruction *De musica sacra et sacra liturgia* (On Sacred Music and Sacred Liturgy), September 3, 1958.
Sacred Congregation of Divine Worship, Letter *Voluntati obsequens* (Letter to the Bishops on the Minimum Repertoire of Plain Chant), April 14, 1974.

Sacred Congregation of Rites, Instruction *Musicam sacram* (On Music in the Liturgy), March 5, 1967.

Published chant books

Antiphonale monasticum pro diurnis horis juxta vota RR. DD. Abbatum Congregationum Confoederatarum Ordinis Sancti Benedicti a Solesmensibus Monachis Restitutum (Paris: Desclée, 1934).
Cantus selecti ex libris Vaticanis et Solesmensibus excerpti (Solesmes: Abbaye Saint-Pierre, 1949).
Graduale de tempore et de sanctis iuxta ritum sacrosanctae Romanae Ecclesiae cum cantu Pauli V. iusso reformato . . . cum privilegio (Regensburg: Pustet, 1871).
Liber hymnarius cum invitatoriis & aliquibus responsoriis (Solesmes: Abbaye Saint-Pierre de Solesmes, 1983).
Pothier, J., *Liber gradualis* (Tournai: Desclée, 1883).
Ott, C. (ed.), *Offertoriale sive versus offertoriorum cantus gregoriani* (Tournai: Desclée, 1935).
Processionale monasticum ad usum Congregationis Gallicae Ordinis Sancti Benedicti (Solesmes: E Typographeo Sancti Petri, 1893).
Versus psalmorum et canticorum ad usum cantorum pro antiphonis ad introitum et ad communionem repetendis iuxta codices antiques (Tournai: Desclée, 1961).

Other studies

Apel, W., *Gregorian Chant* (Bloomington: Indiana University Press, 1958).
Bailey, T., "Psalm, §II, 11: Responsories of Mass and Office," *The New Grove Dictionary of Music and Musicians,* 2nd edn (Oxford: Oxford University Press, 2001), 20, p. 461.
Bjork, D.A., "The Kyrie trope," *Journal of the American Musicological Society,* 33 (1980), pp. 1–41.
Cardine, E., *Gregorian Semiology* (Solesmes: Abbaye Saint-Pierre de Solesmes, 1982).
Combe, P., *The Restoration of Gregorian Chant: Solesmes and the Vatican Edition* (Washington: Catholic University of America Press, 2003).
Crocker. R.L., "Kyrie eleison," *The New Grove Dictionary of Music and Musicians,* 2nd edn (Oxford: Oxford University Press, 2001), 14, pp. 71–3.
—— and Hiley, D., "Credo," *The New Grove Dictionary of Music and Musicians,* 2nd edn (Oxford: Oxford University Press, 2001), 6, pp. 657–9.
Hayburn, R.F., *Papal Legislation on Sacred Music 95 A.D. to 1977 A.D.* (Collegeville: Liturgical Press, 1978).
Hiley, D., *Western Plainchant* (Oxford: Clarendon Press, 1993).
—— *Gregorian Chant* (Cambridge: Cambridge University Press, 2009).
—— and Szendrei, J., "Notation, §III, 1: Plainchant: Origins and earliest examples," *The New Grove Dictionary of Music and Musicians,* 2nd edn (Oxford: Oxford University Press, 2001), 18, pp. 84–119.
Hucke, H., "Die Einführung des Gregorianischen Gesangs im Frankenreich," *Römische Quartalschrift* 49 (1954), pp. 172–85.
—— and Huglo, M., "Communion," *The New Grove Dictionary of Music and Musicians* (London: Macmillan, 1980), 4, pp. 591–4.
Jeffery, P., *Re-envisioning Past Musical Cultures: Ethnomusicology in the Study of Gregorian Chant* (Chicago: University of Chicago Press, 1992).

Jungmann, J., *The Mass of the Roman Rite: Its Origins and Development*, 2 vols (New York: Benziger Brothers, 1950).

Levy, K., Emerson, J.A., Bellingham, J., Hiley, D., and Zon, B., "Plainchant," *The New Grove Dictionary of Music and Musicians,* 2nd edn (Oxford: Oxford University Press, 2001), 19, pp. 825–86.

McKinnon, J., *The Advent Project: The Later-Seventh-Century Creation of the Roman Mass Proper* (Berkeley: University of California Press, 2000).

—— "Gregorian chant," *The New Grove Dictionary of Music and Musicians,* 2nd edn (Oxford: Oxford University Press, 2001), 10, pp. 373–4.

—— *Music in Early Christian Literature* (Cambridge: Cambridge University Press, 1987).

Mocquereau, A., *Le nombre musical grégorien: A Study of Gregorian Musical Rhythm*, vol 1, parts 1–2 (Tournai: Desclée, 1932).

—— ed., *Paléographie musicale: facsimilés photoypiques des principaux manuscrits de chant grégorien, ambrosien, mozarabique, gallican* (Solesmes: Imprimerie Saint-Pierre, 1889–92).

Pothier, J., *Les mélodies grégoriennes d'après la tradition* (Tournai: Desclée,1880).

Richter, E., and Friedberg, E., *Corpus Iuris Canonici* (Leipzig: Tauchnitz, 1881), 2, pp. 1255–7.

Saulnier, D., *Gregorian Chant: a Guide to the History and Liturgy* (Brewster: Paraclete Press, 2009).

Part III

THE LITURGY OF THE SECOND VATICAN COUNCIL

Chapter 12

THE VISION OF THE CONSTITUTION ON
THE LITURGY

†Anscar J. Chupungco OSB

The aims of the Second Vatican Council

1. The general aims of the Council

> This Sacred Council has several aims in view: it desires to impart an ever increasing vigor to the Christian life of the faithful; to adapt more suitably to the needs of our own times those institutions that are subject to change; to foster whatever can promote union among all who believe in Christ; to strengthen whatever can help to call the whole of humanity into the household of the Church. The Council therefore sees particularly cogent reasons for undertaking the reform and promotion of the liturgy. (*Sacrosanctum Concilium*, 1)

The Latin text is a single sentence the gist of which is: since the Council desires to renew the life and institutions of the Church, foster ecumenical understanding, and strengthen the Church's mission in the world, it is impelled to undertake also the reform and promotion of the liturgy. The Council considers the reform of the liturgy as a necessary step toward the achievement of its other aims. The text echoes the famous saying of Dom Lambert Beauduin that ignorance of the liturgy is the root of religious ignorance. The succeeding article (n. 2) expands this: "For the liturgy, 'making the work of our redemption a present actuality,' most of all in the divine sacrifice of the Eucharist, is the outstanding means whereby the faithful may express in their lives and manifest to others the mystery of Christ and the real nature of the true Church." Article 10 concludes with the lapidary statement that the liturgy is the *culmen et fons* (summit and source) of all the activities of the Church. It will be recalled that Pope Pius X named the liturgy in his 1903 motu proprio *Tra le sollecitudini* as "the Church's most important and indispensable source."

The Constitution enumerates five conciliar aims. They represent the responses of the episcopate and the faculties of theology and canon law to the Vatican's inquiry regarding possible topics for the ecumenical council that Pope John XXIII had announced on January 25, 1959.[1] The number of times the liturgy was brought up was overwhelming: there were 1,855 proposals dealing with it—a significant 20 per cent of the total number of scattered responses.[2]

The general tenor of the responses is pastoral, which is decidedly nuanced by the Pope's catchword *aggiornamento,* or renewal of the Catholic Church. The first two and the fifth of the aims concern directly the life and institutions of the Church. Several conciliar documents address them, such as *Sacrosanctum Concilium* (on the liturgy), *Lumen Gentium* (on the Church), *Dei Verbum* (on Sacred Scripture), *Christus Dominus* (on bishops), *Optatam Totius* (on priests), *Apostolicam Actuositatem* (on the laity), and *Perfectae Caritatis* (on religious life). The third aim relates to ecumenism, while the fourth bears on the place and role of the Church in the modern world.[3] The conciliar documents that address these are *Unitatis redintegratio* and *Gaudium et Spes* respectively.

The pertinent conciliar documents define and articulate the five aims set forth by Vatican II. The aims have become the vision, and the vision a programme to guide and direct the life and activities of the Church after the Council. The recovery of the primacy of God's Word, the reform of worn-out ecclesiastical institutions, ecumenical dialogue, and the active role of the laity, are blessings that the Church has received through the Council. But as we shall have the occasion to discuss, no conciliar vision or its implementation has been the subject of such close scrutiny and heated debate even after almost half a century as the liturgy.

2. *The shaping of the Constitution on the Liturgy*

When the schema on the liturgy was presented to the Council, it was ripe for discussion. It did not appear out of the blue. It was heralded and prepared by two liturgical movements. The first began in the nineteenth century when, after the French Revolution, Prosper Guéranger restored the Benedictine Abbey of Solesmes. The liturgical celebrations in his monastic community effectively revived interest in the liturgy. The second liturgical movement had its beginning in 1909 at a workers' congress in Malines in Belgium where Lambert Beauduin, a monk of Mont-César, expounded his belief about the transforming power of the liturgy.[4] In the face of the upsurge of religious indifference and the threats of emerging political and economic systems in Europe, Beauduin proposed the full and active participation of the faithful in the liturgy as effective response to the perils that beset the Church in the modern world.

These two movements had different orientations, although both were rooted in the same solid grounds of liturgical science, supported especially by the monumental publications of Fernand Cabrol and Henri Leclercq, monks of Farnborough, England. But Guéranger, who strongly opposed the revival of the Gallican liturgies in France, upheld absolute fidelity to the Roman rite as necessary expression of catholicity. Beauduin and his followers, on the other hand, envisioned a type of Roman liturgy that would encourage active participation. To this end it was felt that the rites had to be simplified so that they could be easily understood.

Edmond Bishop's article "The Genius of the Roman Rite" was influential.[5] It describes the classical form of the liturgy that had existed in Rome before the German popes (Clement II, Damasus II, Leo IX, Victor II, and Stephen IX) introduced the hybrid Roman-Germanic rites in the tenth century. The Roman liturgy was originally marked by sobriety, simplicity, and practical sense. These were the classical qualities that could render the liturgy accessible to the greater number of the faithful. The twentieth-century liturgical movement thus earned the title "classical".[6]

Both movements converged in the drafting of *Sacrosanctum Concilium*. This document should not thus be regarded either as an overall refutation of the preceding 400 years or as unreserved adoption of the agenda of the twentieth-century liturgical movement.[7] It represents the convergence of two liturgical movements that characterized the liturgical life of the Church in that period.

In 1947, Pope Pius XII published *Mediator Dei*, an historic encyclical dealing exclusively with the liturgy. It cautioned against the liturgical abuses that were being committed by over-zealous proponents of change. However, it officially recognized the liturgical movement and inaugurated a series of liturgical changes. For example, in that year Belgium received permission for the celebration of evening Mass on Sundays and holydays; in 1949, the translation of the *Missale Romanum* (excepting the Roman canon) into the Mandarin language was approved; and in 1955, the rites for Holy Week were reformed.[8] At the conclusion of the international liturgical congress held at Assisi in 1956, the 1,400 participants travelled to Rome to listen to the address of Pope Pius XII. In his address the Pope affirmed that the liturgical movement was "a sign of the providential dispositions of God for the present time, of the movement of the Holy Spirit in the Church, to draw men more closely to the mysteries of the faith and the riches of grace which flow from the active participation of the faithful in the liturgical life."[9]

At the time the Constitution on the Liturgy was being shaped, many of the ideals of the classical liturgical movement were already a partial reality in several parts of the world. However, there were reservations and even forces of resistance. Liturgically, the Church was in a period of transition from the Tridentine and scholastic frame of mind to a new pastoral sense grafted on scholarly research on the history and theology of the liturgy. The drafters of the Constitution on the Liturgy obviously did not undermine the teachings of the Council of Trent, but the new developments in the Church had to be addressed with a new methodology.

The list of the members and consultors involved in the drafting of the Constitution explains why the general orientation and provisions of the *schema* closely resembled the direction of the fifty-year old liturgical movement. After Pope John XXIII had announced the Second Vatican Council, a preparatory commission on the liturgy was established on June 6, 1960 with Cardinal Gaetano Cicognani as president (succeeded by Cardinal Arcadio Larraona in 1962), and Annibale Bugnini as secretary. The members were Karel Calewaert, Bernard Capelle, Enrico Cattaneo, Romano Guardini, Josef Jungmann, Joseph Malula, Johannes Quasten, Mario Righetti, and Aimon-Marie Roguet. Among the consultors are the names of Bernard Botte, Antoine Chavasse, Godfrey Diekmann, Balthasar Fischer, Pierre-Marie Gy, Anton Hänggi, Johannes Hoffinger, Pierre Jounel, Theodor Klauser, Boniface Luykx, Frederick McManus, Aimé-Georges Martimort, Herman Schmidt, Cipriano Vagaggini, and Johannes Wagner.[10] A good number of them were pastors and scholars who supported and promoted the classical liturgical movement.

Throughout the Constitution there is interplay between *traditio* and *progressio*. Article 23 is significant: "That sound tradition may be retained and yet the way remain open to legitimate progress, a careful investigation is always to be made into each part of the liturgy to be revised." The investigation should be theological, historical, and pastoral, and at the same time attentive to existing liturgical laws and the experience derived from recent liturgical reform and indults conceded to various places. In several of its provisions, the Constitution may be regarded as a transition document, a work of healthy compromise or *via media* between the past and the present and between the traditional and progressive elements of the liturgy. The phrase "sound tradition and legitimate progress" aptly describes this conciliar document.

The following are some examples of the application of *via media*. The first concerns the liturgical language. *Sacrosanctum Concilium* 36 states: "Particular law remaining in force, the use of the Latin language is to be preserved in the Latin rites." Yet because of the advantage the vernacular language offers to the people, bishops' conferences are "empowered to decide whether and to what extent the vernacular is to be used." The second example relates to the question of receiving the chalice. Article 55 states: "The dogmatic principles laid down by the Council of Trent remain intact. In instances to be specified by the Apostolic See, however, communion under both kinds may be granted both to clerics and religious and to the laity at the discretion of the bishops." The third example is about liturgical music. According to article 116, "The Church acknowledges Gregorian chant as distinctive of the Roman liturgy; therefore, other things being equal, it should be given pride of place in liturgical services."[11]

The schema prepared by the preparatory commission included areas that needed particular attention especially in regard to the revision of texts and rites. These are the mystery of the sacred liturgy and its relation to the life of the Church, the Mass, concelebration, Divine Office, sacraments and sacramentals, liturgical calendar, use of vernacular language, liturgical formation, participation of the faithful in the liturgy, adaptation to the culture and traditions of peoples, liturgical vestments, sacred music, and sacred art. The schema addressed the whole range of the Church's liturgical life. With few changes this schema was presented to the Council Fathers as the draft for the Constitution on the Liturgy.

Thereafter, the conciliar commission on liturgy was formed, with Cardinal Arcadio Larraona as president and Ferdinando Antonelli as secretary. The task of the commission was to edit the draft of the Constitution on the basis of the amendments (*emendationes*) and changes (*modi*) proposed by the Conciliar Fathers. The conciliar discussions, which lasted from October 22 to November 13, 1962, took fifteen general congregations or about fifty hours of deliberation on 328 oral interventions and 297 written proposals.[12] The lively debate on the schema, especially on the issue of Latin and the vernacular languages, revealed an awakened interest of the Church leaders in the needed reform of the official worship. The majority of the Fathers favoured the proposals because they were pastorally responsive. However, members of the Roman curia and some diocesan bishops expressed serious concern because the schema seemed to empower the conferences of bishops at the expense of the juridical prerogatives of the Holy See. On November 14, 1962 a vote was taken. The result was overwhelming: of the 2,215 Fathers 2,162 voted in favour.[13]

Pope John XXIII died on June 3, 1963. He was succeeded by Pope Paul VI, who presented the liturgy schema to the council on November 22 supposedly for final vote. 2,158 out of 2,178 Council Fathers approved the schema. It is astonishing that the Pope, for some reason, decided to submit it once again for the vote of the Council before he promulgated it on December 4, 1963. Four opposed the Constitution on the Liturgy, while 2,147 voted in its favour.

Numbers speak. At the Second Vatican Council the worldwide episcopate made the historic decision of owning the course of liturgical reform that was heralded in the preceding century and pastorally realigned by the classical liturgical movement. The Constitution on the Liturgy became the *magna carta* of the Church's life of worship and remains such until another ecumenical council shall decide otherwise. People can argue about the merits and demerits of its implementation, but adherence to it is a firm sign of loyalty to the Church that spoke through the council.

At the conclusion of the second period of the council Pope Paul VI said:

> The difficult, complex debates have had rich results. They have brought one topic to a conclusion, the sacred liturgy. Treated before all others, in a sense it has priority over all others for its intrinsic dignity and importance to the life of the Church ... The liturgy is the first gift we must make to the Christian people united to us by faith and the fervour of their prayers. It is also the primary invitation to the human race, so that all may lift their now mute voices in blessed and genuine prayer ...[14]

The Pope named three of the general aims of the Council, namely Church renewal, ecumenical understanding, and the Church's mission in the world. The liturgy is Vatican II's instrument to achieve them.

The Constitution on the Liturgy: vision and revision

1. The Vision of *Sacrosanctum Concilium*: active participation

The promoters of the classical liturgical movement envisioned a renewed liturgical life marked by full, active participation of the faithful. To achieve this, it was deemed necessary to revise the post-Tridentine liturgical books in order to align them with the requirements of active participation. Revision had to stand on the solid grounds of liturgical principles.

Active participation is the bedrock of the Constitution on the Sacred Liturgy. Without it the Constitution falls apart. It is also the spirit that permeates the entire project of liturgical reform. Article 14 is purposeful: "In the reform and promotion of the liturgy, full and active participation by all the people is the aim to be considered before all else. For it is the primary and indispensable source from which the faithful are to derive the true Christian spirit." The Latin text is worded in the strongest possible terms: *in instauranda et fovenda sacra Liturgia, [actuosa participatio] summopere est attendenda*. Further, article 79 affirms that intelligent, active, and easy participation by the faithful is the "primary criterion" to be observed when revising the rites of sacramentals.

The liturgy is the fountainhead of genuine Christian life. In the thinking of *Sacrosanctum Concilium*, the most effective way for the faithful to avail themselves of the spiritual benefits of the liturgy is through full and active participation. We note the determination and precision in the words used by article 14: reform and promotion; full and active participation; all the peoples; aim before all else; primary and indispensable source; true Christian spirit. The nature of the liturgy demands (*postulatur*) active participation, which is the right (*ius*) and duty (*officium*) of the Christian people by virtue of their baptism.[15]

To ensure the promotion of active participation, article 21 directs that "both texts and rites should be so drawn up that they express more clearly the holy things they signify and that the Christian people, as far as possible, are able to understand them with ease and take part in the rites fully, actively, and as befits a community." Clarity of the liturgical rites and texts, understanding with ease on the part of the assembly, and full and active participation should be the hallmark of the reform of liturgical books. The Constitution does not spare words—the Latin text is sometimes more strongly worded than the English translation—to put across the importance of active participation.

The breadth of reform extends beyond congregational acclamations, songs, and gestures. As article 29 wants us to understand, active participation includes the ministerial functions exercised by servers, readers, commentators, and members of the choir. They exercise "a genuine liturgical function," which they should discharge "with the sincere devotion and decorum demanded by so exalted a ministry and rightly expected of them by God's people." The faithful exercise their baptismal right and duty not only by being actively involved as members of the assembly but also by ministering to its needs in the measure permitted by the hierarchical nature of the liturgy.[16]

Full, intelligent, and active participation is the template for Vatican II's liturgical reform. To advance it, the Council Fathers approved the use of the vernacular, the revision of the existing rites, the creation of new rites if opportune, greater involvement of the laity in liturgical ministries, and the adaptation of the liturgy to the culture and traditions of peoples.

Certain styles of active participation have at times given such prominence to external action that silence and contemplative prayer are neglected.[17] It is timely to remember what article 30 says on this matter: "To promote active participation, the people should be encouraged to take part by means of acclamations, response, psalmody, antiphons, and songs, as well as by actions, gestures, and bearing." Active participation consists principally of such external activities. The Latin substantive *actuositas*, adjective *actuosus*, and adverb *actuose* refer primarily to external action done with energy, though of course they do not exclude inner disposition. Thus, what is intended by the Decree on the Apostolate of Lay People (*Apostolicam actuositatem*) is not principally a contemplative participation in the mission of the Church but external apostolate.

However, the succeeding sentence of article 30, which is sometimes carelessly passed over, is of utmost importance to the definition of active participation: "And at the proper times all should observe a reverent silence."[18] The Latin text is worded in such a manner as to make it clear that silence is a ritual action like the rest. Silence in the liturgy is not a pause from activities; it is a rite in itself, a rite that is meant to deepen the awareness of the presence of the divine mystery. In this sense the appointed time for silence imparts spiritual meaning to active participation.

Some people have commented that Vatican II's active participation does not foster prayerful and contemplative celebration. They claim that while the Tridentine liturgy encourages contemplation, the Vatican II liturgy, with its manifold acclamations and responses, does not leave enough room for contemplation. The critique can probably be traced to the mistaken conception that action and contemplation are mutually exclusive. Right at the beginning of the Constitution such anxious concern is allayed: "It is of the essence of the Church to be both human and divine, visible yet endowed with invisible resources, eager to act yet intent on contemplation, present in this world yet not at home in it" (n. 2). We are made to understand that in the liturgy "the human is directed and subordinated to the divine, the invisible likewise to the invisible, action to contemplation." The contrasting binomials are consistent with the time-honoured description of the Church: it is human yet divine, visible yet invisible, eager to act yet intent on contemplation. What is significant in all this is the unqualified subordination of action to contemplation. Active participation should lead the worshipers to the contemplation of the sacred realities they celebrate.

2. The premises of revision

Sacrosanctum Concilium 21 is loud and clear: "In order that the Christian people may more surely derive an abundance of graces from the liturgy, the Church desires to undertake with great care a general reform (*generalem instaurationem*) of the liturgy itself." The reform was not going to be piecemeal. Its scope was going to be general, covering the whole span of the Roman rite. Vatican II's "hermeneutic of continuity" had to be understood, as far as the external shape of the liturgy was concerned, not with the post-Tridentine liturgy but with the classical form.

The premise on which the conciliar reform stands is likewise loud and clear in article 21: "For the liturgy is made up of immutable elements, divinely instituted, and of elements subject to change. These not only may but ought to be changed with the passage of time if they have suffered from the intrusion of anything out of harmony with the inner nature of the liturgy or have become pointless". Actually, the Latin text speaks of "an immutable part" and "parts subject to change." The history of the liturgy records how the different doctrinal and cultural epochs of the Church had their respective impact on the way the liturgy was understood and celebrated. The unchanging Christian mystery was expressed and re-expressed in different rites that in more ways than one shifted the emphasis or accent from one aspect of the same doctrine to another. Understandably, as the culture of peoples evolved, those liturgical practices that were originally bound to a particular era could indeed become pointless in another.[19]

The type of active participation contemplated by the Constitution required effectively a revision of the existing liturgical books. *Sacrosanctum Concilium* itself lays down the general norm for introducing changes in the liturgy in article 23: "That sound tradition may be retained and yet the way remain open to legitimate progress, a careful investigation is always to be made into each part of the liturgy to be revised. This investigation should be theological, historical, and pastoral." In a word, revision should be premised on theology, history, and pastoral concerns.

Chapter One of the Constitution expounds the premises under separate headings:

1. nature of the liturgy and its importance in the life of the Church;
2. promotion of liturgical instruction and active participation;
3. general norms for liturgical reform;
4. norms drawn from the hierarchic and communal nature of the liturgy;
5. norms based on the teaching and pastoral character of the liturgy;
6. norms for adapting the liturgy to people's culture and traditions;
7. promotion of liturgical life in dioceses and parishes; and
8. promotion of pastoral liturgical action.[20]

The theological and pastoral premises that directly concern the Eucharist, sacraments, sacramentals, divine office, liturgical year, music, and arts and furnishings serve as introductory articles to each of them.

The theological premises named in Chapter One are worthy of attention: they explain the nature of the liturgy and formulate a theological definition of it. Article 7 is particularly rich in doctrine. The first paragraph affirms the presence of Christ in the Church, especially in liturgical celebrations. Christ is present in the Eucharist, in baptism, in the proclaimed word of God, and in the assembly of worshipers. The second paragraph moves on to say that in the liturgy "Christ always truly associates the Church with himself." The third concludes with these lapidary words: "Rightly, then, the liturgy is considered (*habetur*) as an exercise of the priestly office of Jesus Christ." The last paragraph is equally memorable: because every liturgical celebration is an action of Christ the Priest and the Church his Body, "it is a sacred action surpassing all other actions" of the Church.[21] This is echoed in article 10 by the famous phrase *culmen et fons*: "The liturgy is the summit toward which the activity of the Church is directed; at the same time it is the fount from which all the Church's power flows."

The above theological premise is reminiscent of Pope Pius XII's *Mediator Dei* (n. 25). It defines the liturgy as "the public worship, which our Redeemer as head of the Church renders to the Father, as well as the worship which the community of the faithful renders to its Founder, and through him to the heavenly Father. In short, it is the worship rendered by the Mystical Body of Christ in the entirety of its head and members."

Since *Sacrosanctum Concilium* has embraced the early, classical form of the Roman rite as the model for the reform of the ritual shape (plan of the celebration, texts, symbols, and gestures) of the liturgy, it directs in article 21 that "in this reform both texts and rites should be so drawn up that they express more clearly the holy things they signify and that the Christian people, as far as possible, are able to understand them with ease and to take part in the rites fully, actively, and as befits a community." In the thinking of the framers of the Constitution, clarity and intelligibility are the premises of active participation. This is further developed in article 34, which details the qualities of the classical Roman rite: "The rites should be marked by a noble simplicity; they should be short, clear, and unencumbered by useless repetitions; they should be within the people's power of comprehension and as a rule not require much explanation." Noble simplicity, sobriety (*sobrietas romana*), clarity, brevity, and practical sense: these are the qualities that the Constitution wanted to restore to the Roman liturgy in order to foster active and intelligent participation.

Thus, on the level of ritual criteria, the reform desired by Vatican II was premised on the classical properties of the Roman liturgy, which the Franco-Germanic Churches justifiably modified after the eighth century to suit their cultural temperament. They enriched and gave color to the ritual shape of the austere Roman liturgy, but in the process its simplicity, sobriety, and practical sense had to give way to repetitions, allegorical interpretation of rites, and the mystery-laden symbols that were typical of the northern people at that time.[22]

3. Areas for revision

Which are the areas that needed revision in the light of active participation? The answer is the whole range of the Roman liturgy and those areas that relate to it, such as formation of the clergy, adaptation, and popular piety. What are the Constitution's specific provisions on how the revision of the liturgical books is to be carried out?

Earlier we noted that in a number of instances, like the question of language, *Sacrosanctum Concilium* applied the principle of compromise with existing liturgical rites or *via media*. There are, however, some instances where it calls for a thorough, almost radical, revision of the post-Tridentine books. It is not a question of doctrinal alteration but a pastoral solution to the pastoral problem of active participation. In a word, what the Constitution wants to achieve is a liturgy that will "express more clearly the holy things they signify and that the Christian people, as far as possible, are able to understand them with ease and to take part in the rites fully, actively, and as befits a community." It is useful information that the plan or structure of liturgical rites is preserved by and large and that the liturgical formularies, especially those in the Roman missal, are almost always kept intact.

The chief example of the conciliar revision concerns the Order of Mass. Article 50 directs that "the Order of Mass is to be revised in a way that will bring out more clearly (*clarius pateant*) the intrinsic nature and purpose of its several parts, as also the connection between them, and will more readily achieve (*facilior reddatur*) the devout, active participation of the faithful." The type of revision envisaged here is not a cosmetic and superficial one. For article 50, revision means that "the rites are to be simplified, due care being taken to preserve their substance; elements that, with the passage of time, came to be duplicated or were added with but little advantage are now to be discarded (*omittantur*); other elements that have suffered injury through accident of history (*temporum iniuria*) are now, as may seem useful or necessary, to be restored to the vigour they had in the tradition of the Fathers (*ad pristinam sanctorum Patrum normam*)."[23] This provision implies a revision that involves notable changes.[24] In fact, the product, which is the post-conciliar Missal of Paul VI, differs considerably from its predecessor in pastoral orientation, ritual elements, and a number of texts.

The following historical note sheds light on the deeper motive of article 50. After his accession to the papal throne in 1072, one of Gregory VII's immediate priorities besides the eradication of investiture and simony was the reform of the Roman clergy. For this he adopted the strategy of imposing on the clergy a quasi-monastic discipline and of strengthening their ministry of worship. A Roman by origin, he felt that the Germanic liturgy that his German predecessors introduced in Rome was not helpful. He therefore set forth to re-establish the traditional liturgical usages of the Roman Church before the Germans took over its government. He advocated the restoration of the Roman *regula sanctorum patrum*, the *ordo romanus*, and the *mos antiquus*, which he claimed to have examined.[25] Pope Gregory's reform took definitive shape in the twelfth-century revision of the Romano-Germanic Pontifical using the method of elimination in accord with the *romana sobrietas*. Things outside the scope of a pontifical, like didactic elements, or that were contrary to Roman sensitivity, like the Masses for energumens and the blessing of instruments of ordeal, were eliminated. The simplified product is known as the Roman pontifical of the twelfth century.[26] *Sacrosanctum Concilum*'s directive to revise the post-Tridentine books re-echoes the eleventh-century Gregorian reform, albeit for a different motive.

The revision of post-Tridentine books was mandated for the sacraments as well. The Latin subjunctive *recognoscatur/recognoscantur* is used throughout in a normative, mandatory sense: "The rites for the baptism of adults are to be revised" (n. 66). Likewise, "the rite for the baptism of children is to be revised" (n. 67). "The rite of confirmation is also to be revised" (n. 71). "The rite and formularies for the sacrament of penance are to be revised" (n. 72). "The prayers that belong to the rite of anointing are to be revised" (n. 75). "Both the ceremonies and texts for the ordination rites are to be revised" (n. 76). And "the marriage rite now found in the Roman ritual is to be revised" (n. 77). Article 62 offers the reason for revision: "With the passage of time certain features have crept into the rites of the sacraments and sacramentals that have made their nature and purpose less clear to the people of today; hence some changes have become necessary as adaptations to the needs of our own times." In most cases, the ritual revision desired would mean, in practice, a departure from the post-Tridentine rites. The theory of the hermeneutic of continuity with the ritual tradition handed by the post-Tridentine liturgy is not sanctioned by the explicit intention of *Sacrosanctum Concilium* to produce new liturgical books that do not trace direct ancestry to their immediate predecessors.

The brevity of some of the conciliar directives often requires a kind of investigation through exegesis and hermeneutics whereby we are able to read the mind of the lawgiver. An example is the one short sentence that article 72 devotes to the sacrament of penance: "The rites and formularies for the sacrament of penance are to be revised so that they more clearly express both the nature and effect of the sacrament." What is meant by nature and effect of the sacrament? Actually, the Conciliar Commission had a ready explanation of these words. The "nature" of the sacrament refers in this particular instance to its social and ecclesial character, which should mark the celebration of penance. On the other hand, "effect" means reconciliation, which is to be ritually expressed by the restored laying on of hands on the penitent.[27]

The revision of the Divine Office or Liturgy of the Hours affirms the reform initiated by Pope John XXIII. The 1960 Code of Rubrics sought to correct the practice of reciting the hours outside their appointed time contrary to the rule of *veritas horarum*. The Code laid down the norm that the canonical hours are to be recited "at a time nearest to the true time for each canonical hour" (no. 142). *Sacrosanctum Concilium* article 88 repeats the norm: "Because the purpose of the office is to sanctify the day, the traditional sequence of the hours is to be restored so that once again they may, as far as possible, be genuinely related to the hours of the day when they are prayed."[28]

According to *Sacrosanctum Concilium* 107, "The liturgical year is to be revised that the traditional customs and usages of the sacred seasons are preserved or restored to suit the conditions of modern times." Furthermore, Sunday is to hold primacy in such a way that other feasts, unless they be truly of greatest importance, shall not have precedence over Sunday; the annual festival of Easter (the Easter Triduum) is to be celebrated in a most solemn way; and the minds of the faithful must be directed primarily toward those feasts of the Lord on which the mysteries of salvation are celebrated in the course of the year.[29]

Another significant feature of the Constitution is the value it gives to Sacred Scripture. This is to be expected, considering the revival of interest in the Bible at the time of the liturgical movement. *Sacrosanctum Concilium* devotes several articles to the use of Sacred Scripture in the liturgy. According to article 24, "Sacred Scripture is of the greatest importance in the celebration of the liturgy. For it is from Scripture that the readings are given and explained in the homily and the psalms are sung; the prayers, collects, and liturgical songs are scriptural in their inspiration, it is from the Scriptures that actions and signs derive their meaning." Article 35 encourages more biblical readings in the liturgy. They should be more varied and apposite. It recommends bible services in places where no priest is available. Article 51 desires that in the eucharistic celebration "the treasures of the Bible are to be opened up more lavishly, so that a richer share in God's word may be provided for the faithful." Thus "a more representative portion of holy Scripture" should be read in the course of a prescribed number of years. Finally, in order that the Liturgy of the Hours will be a source of devotion and nourishment, article 90 urges the study and deeper understanding of the Bible, especially the psalms.[30]

The Constitution affirms the relationship between faith, which comes through hearing the Word of God, and the sacraments and other liturgical services (cf. article 9). The binomial "word and sacrament" is a fundamental principle in the renewal of the Church's worship. The Word of God prepares and leads to the sacraments, just as faith is required by the sacraments and is nourished by them. Post-conciliar reform would see to it that every liturgical celebration includes the proclamation of God's written Word. No other reading, however noble and venerable, may replace the Word of God in the liturgy. The underpinning theological reason for this is that Christ "is present in his word, since it is he himself who speaks when the holy Scriptures are read in the Church" (n. 7; cf. 33).

Several other provisions emanate from the principle of active participation. They are best understood in the context of active participation. The entire second section of Chapter One deals with ways and means for promoting it. Indispensable is the liturgical formation of the clergy and seminarians. Article 16 rules that "the study of liturgy is to be ranked among the compulsory and major courses in seminaries and religious houses of studies; in theological faculties it is to rank among the principal courses." A sign of effective formation is that "life in seminaries and houses of religious is thoroughly permeated by the spirit of liturgy" (n. 17). Unless the clergy imbibe the genuine spirit of liturgical renewal envisioned by Vatican II, every attempt to promote active participation would be futile (n 14).

The liturgically-formed clergy is expected to engage in the liturgical instruction or catechesis of the faithful. Article 19 considers it "one of the chief duties of pastors as faithful stewards of the mysteries of God." No resources should be spared. When opportune, modern media of communications like radio and television may be used to impart liturgical instruction (n. 20).

The Constitution regards the use of the vernacular as a valuable instrument of active participation. When the Council approved the use of the vernacular in the Roman liturgy, the understanding was that the Latin liturgical books would have to be translated into the local languages. This underpinned article 36 whose formulation drew a good deal of debate in the council hall.[31] The final text is a classic example of the *via media* which reaffirmed, on the one hand, that "the use of the Latin language is to be preserved in the Latin rite," although the use of the vernacular may be extended, and empowered, on the other, the conferences of bishops "to decide and to what extent the vernacular may be used."

While attachment to the Latin liturgy on the part of some Fathers was strongly felt during the council discussion, the implications of a translated liturgy were not lost to others. Directives were needed to safeguard the liturgy's doctrinal purity as well as the intended message of the Latin text. Thus a petition was submitted to the Conciliar Commission to add a clause requiring that "translations from the Latin text into the mother tongue intended for use in the liturgy must be approved by the competent, territorial authority." The reason for the petition was "to avoid dangerous freedom and variety of translations which can threaten the true meaning and beauty of the texts."[32]

Thus, the Constitution regards the use of the vernacular in the liturgy as essential in order to realize its fundamental vision of active participation. This fact should guide the work of translating liturgical texts into the vernacular. Those who specialize in the science of linguistics tell us that not every type of translation effectively transmits the message of the original Latin text. Vernacular texts that do not foster active participation are of little use for the renewed liturgy.

Another means to foster active participation, especially but not exclusively in the missions, is inculturation. *Sacrosanctum Concilium* uses the word "adaptation," but several of its provisions should be read in the context of what is called "inculturation." This word entered into the active vocabulary of the Church only in the 1970s. The Constitution envisages two types of adaptation: those that fall "within the limits set by the *editio typica* of the liturgical books" (n. 39), and those that are "even more radical" (n. 40), because they admit "elements from the traditions and culture of individual peoples."

A brief description of the articles is useful. Article 37 advocates the principle of liturgical pluralism among local churches within the bounds of the substantial unity of the Roman rite. This includes respect for the culture and traditions of local communities and the integration of suitable cultural elements found among them, provided they are not indissolubly bound up with superstition and error.

Articles 38–9 deal with legitimate variations within the body of the Roman rite. It means that the changes introduced by the Conferences of Bishops for their churches fall within the provisions of the *editio typica* published by the Holy See. It does not mean that changes not foreseen by the *editio typica* but approved by the Holy See are not legitimate variations. Article 38 cautions that "the substantial unity of the Roman rite" should be preserved in the process.

Article 40 is about "radical" adaptations of the Roman rite to the culture and traditions of local Churches. It means that the changes have not been envisaged by the *editio typica*. The Conferences of Bishops are given the task to "carefully and prudently weigh" what elements from the people's culture might suitably be introduced into the Roman rite. "Radical" adaptation is initiated by the Conferences of Bishops who submit the project to the Holy See. A period of experimentation follows. Finally the Holy See grants approval and the approved changes are inserted in the particular ritual of the region.

Ultimately, the purpose of *Sacrosanctum Concilium* for permitting adaptation is active and intelligent participation, because the structure, language, rites, and symbols of the liturgical rites evoke the people's authentic cultural values, patterns, and institutions.[33] Local Churches should be able to own and claim the liturgy as their own. The intended recovery of the early, classical form of the Roman rite provides the local Churches with a liturgical model, an *editio typica*, marked by the simplicity of the classical era. It thereby invites them to adapt the revised rites in the same way that the Franco-Germanic Churches had done to the classical Roman liturgy when it migrated to their territory in the eighth century. Thus, the Constitution's point of reference for inculturation is the *editio typica* of the revised liturgical books.

A refreshing feature of the Constitution is the "empowerment" of local bishops and the Conferences of Bishops in liturgical matters directly touching the local Churches. This is what article 22 says: "In virtue of power conceded by law, the regulation of the liturgy (*rei liturgicae moderatio*) within certain defined limits belongs (*pertinet*) also to various kinds of competent territorial bodies of bishops lawfully established." The "empowerment" applies to several areas such as the use of the vernacular, adaptation to local culture, concelebration, and the preparation of particular rituals. *Sacrosanctum Concilium* thus modifies the absolute principle of centralized authority in liturgical matters. This form of moderate decentralization finds a theological basis in article 41 which affirms that "the bishop is to be looked on as the high priest of his flock, the faithful's life in Christ in some way deriving from and depending on him."

Another distinguishing feature of the Constitution is its balanced approach to liturgical laws and rubrics and its strong emphasis on the theology and spirituality of the liturgy. Article 11 reminds pastors that "when the liturgy is celebrated something more is required than the mere observance of the laws governing valid and lawful celebration." The authentic spirit of the liturgy is nourished by the doctrine that the liturgy "is considered as an exercise of the priestly office of Jesus Christ," to which he associated the Church. Christ who is present in all liturgical celebrations (n. 7) can be personally encountered by the faithful when they take part in them actively and devoutly as befits the community of worship. Indeed, "the liturgy is the summit toward which the activity of the Church is directed; at the same time it is the fount from which all the Church's power flows" (n. 10).

Notes

1   The tabulated results of the survey are published in 16 volumes entitled *Acta et documenta Concilio oecumenico Vaticano II apparando. Series praeparatoria* (Vatican City: Typis Polyglottis Vaticanis, 1960–1).

2   See E. Cattaneo, *Il culto cristiano in occidente* (BELS, 1992), p. 521.

3   Ecumenism received special attention during the papacy of John XXIII, a friend of Dom Lambert Beauduin who zealously promoted ecumenical understanding through the liturgy.

4   See: Cattaneo: *Il culto cristiano in occidente*, pp. 492–4,

5   E. Bishop, "The Genius of the Roman Rite", *Liturgica Historica: Papers of the Liturgy and Religious Life of the Western Church* (Oxford: Clarendon Press, 1918), pp. 1-19. See also: B. Neunheuser, "Roman Genius Revisited", M. Francis & K. Pecklers (eds), *Liturgy for*

the New Millennium (Collegeville: Liturgical Press, 2000), pp. 35–48; K. Pecklers: *The Genius of the Roman Rite* (Collegeville: Liturgical Press, 2010).

6 Anthony Cekada writes: "In the early twentieth century, however, the [liturgical] movement took a wrong turn"; *Work of Human Hands: A Theological Critique of the Mass of Paul VI* (Ohio: Philothea Press, 2010), p. 15. My opinion is that it was not a "wrong" turn, but a different turn that addressed pastorally the socio-cultural and religious changes that were affecting the Church at the beginning of the twentieth century.

7 H. Schmidt (ed.), *La costituzione sulla sacra liturgia: testo, genesi, commento, documentazione* (Rome: Herder, 1966); V. Noè: "Storia della Costituzione liturgica. Punti di riferimento," Congregazione per il Culto Divino (ed.), *Costituzione liturgica 'Sacrosanctum Concilium': Studi* (BELS, 1986), pp. 9–24; S. Maggiani: "La riforma liturgica: Dalla Sacrosanctum Concilium alla 'IV Istruzione La Liturgia romana e l'inculturazione,'" G. Angelini, C. Ghidelli, et al., *A trent'anni dal Concilio* (Rome: Studium, 1995), pp. 39–83.

8 For these and other transitional concessions see: K. Pecklers: "History of the Roman Liturgy from the Sixteenth until the Twentieth Centuries," A. Chupungco (ed.), *Handbook for Liturgical Studies*, vol. I (Collegeville: Liturgical Press, 1997), pp. 153–77 (pp. 174–5).

9 NL, p. 234.

10 C. Braga, "La Sacrosanctum Concilium nei lavori della Commissione preparatoria," Congregazione per il Culto Divino, *Costituzione liturgica 'Sacrosanctum Concilium'*, pp. 25–68. For the list of persons involved in the preparatory and conciliar commissions and in the *Consilium*, see the appendices of: A. Bugnini, *The Reform of the Liturgy 1948-1975* (Collegeville: Liturgical Press, 1990); Italian original: *La riforma liturgica 1948-1975* (BELS, 1983).

11 Other examples of *via media* can be seen in the modifications introduced by the conciliar commission into the text of the Constitution: the insertion of phrases like *pro opportunitate* and *ex more*, the elimination of radical-sounding words like *funditus* and *ex integro*, and the softening of some words like *admittatur* by *admitti liceat*; see: *Schema Constitutionis de Sacra Liturgia, Emendationes a Patribus conciliaribus postulatae, Emendationes* VII (Vatican City: Typis Polyglottis Vaticanis, 1963), pp. 9–10.

12 The record of the amendments and changes is published under the title *Schema Constitutionis de Sacra Liturgia: Emendationes a Patribus conciliaribus postulatae & Modi a Patribus conciliaribus propositi* (Vatican City: Typis Polyglottis Vaticanis, 1963); see P. Marini, "Le premesse della grande riforma liturgica," Congregatio per il Culto Divino, *Costituzione liturgica 'Sacrosanctum Concilium,'* pp. 69–101.

13 P. Marini, *A Challenging Reform: Realizing the Vision of the Liturgical Renewal* (Collegeville: Liturgical Press, 2010), pp. xix–xxi. See also the detailed treatment by Cattaneo, *Il culto cristiano in occidente*, pp. 529–34.

14 Paul VI, "Address to the Fathers", 4 December 1963, DOL, pp. 27–28.

15 For a fuller discussion on participation see: A. Kai-Yung Chan, "Participation in the Liturgy", A. Chupungco (ed.), *Handbook for Liturgical Studies*, vol. II (Collegeville: Liturgical Press, 1998), pp.145–59.

16 T. Krosnicki, "Liturgical Ministrie," ibid., pp. 161–71.

17 A. Reid, "Sacrosanctum Concilium and the Organic Development of the Liturgy," U.M. Lang (ed.), *The Genius of the Roman Rite* (Chicago: Hillenbrand, 2010), pp. 198–215 (p. 200): "Of course we know that, in English, the word 'active' poorly translates the meaning of the Latin *actuosa*, which speaks primarily of that internal and

contemplative participation of mind and heart in the liturgical rites rather than an activist concern for everyone to be doing externally observable things as frequently as possible."

18 M. Downey, "The Liturgical Role of Silence," P. Fink (ed.), *The New Dictionary of Sacramental Worship* (Collegeville: Liturgical Press, 1990), pp. 1189–90; I. Dougherty, "Silence in the Liturgy," *Worship* 69 (1995), pp. 142–54.

19 The classic works touching on the influence of different cultural traditions on Christian worship are: Cattaneo, *Il culto cristiano in occidente*; G. Dix, *The Shape of the Liturgy* (London: A&C Black, 1986); L. Duchesne, *Les origines du culte chrétien: Etude sur la liturgie latine avant Charlemagne,* 5th edn (Paris: Boccard, 1925); J. Harper, *The Forms and Orders of Western Liturgy from the Tenth to the Eighteenth Century* (Oxford: Clarendon Press, 1991); J. Jungmann, *The Early Liturgy to the Time of Gregory the Great* (London: Darton, Longman & Todd, 1980); T. Klauser, *A Short History of the Western Liturgy* (Oxford: Oxford University Press, Oxford University Press); M. Metzger, *History of the Liturgy: The Major Stages* (Collegeville: Liturgical Press, 1997); B. Neunheuser, *Storia della liturgia attraverso le epoche culturali* (BELS, 1999); C. Vogel, *Medieval Liturgy: An Introduction to the Sources* (Washington, DC: Pastoral Press, 1986); and G. Willis, *A History of Early Roman Liturgy: To the Death of Pope Gregory the Great* (HBS, 1994).

20 In his posthumous *The Reform of the Liturgy*, pp. 39–48, A. Bugnini lists the fundamental principles of the liturgical reform under two headings: guiding principles and operational principles. Among them he mentions *culmen et fons*, active participation, communal celebration, substantial unity of the Roman rite, and inculturation. He considers inculturation as the third phase of liturgical reform coming after the translation and revision of the liturgical rites.

21 See: A. Chupungco, *What, Then, is Liturgy? Musings and Memoir* (Collegeville: Liturgical Press, 2010), pp. 130–8.

22 Klauser devotes a great part of his work *A Short History of the Western Liturgy* to the influence of the Franco-Germanic Churches on the classical liturgy that they had imported from Rome. A useful reference book for this period is Vogel's *Medieval Liturgy: An Introduction to the Sources.*

23 According to the preparatory commission, "Nonnulla tamen [Ordinis Missae] passim recognoscenda et aliquatenus emendanda videntur, ope studiorum quae, nostra aetate, peracta sunt sive circa originem sive circa evolutionem singulorum rituum Missae", *Schema Constitutionis de Sacra Liturgia: Emendationes a Patribus conciliaribus postulatae,* VI, p. 32.

24 For background reading see: A. Nocent, *La célébration eucharistique avant et après Pie V* (Paris: Beauchesne, 1977); R. Cabié, "The Medieval Origins of the 1570 Order of Mass", A.G. Martimort (ed.), *The Church at Prayer: Introduction to the Liturgy – Vol. II: The Eucharist* (Collegeville: Liturgical Press, 1986), pp. 149–71.

25 *Regula Canonica,* in G. Morin (ed.), *Etudes textes, découvertes: Contributions à la littérature et à l'histoire des douze premiers siècles – Anecdota Maredsolana,* vol. 2, series 1 (Paris: Picard, 1913), pp. 459–60. Pope Pius V invoked the *pristina sanctorum Patrum norma* for the Tridentine Missal of 1570; so did Pope Paul VI for the Missal of 1970.

26 See: M. Andrieu (ed.), *Le pontifical romain du XIIe siècle,* ST 86 (1938); Vogel, *Medieval Liturgy,* pp. 230–9

27 See: A. Chupungco, *Liturgies of the Future* (New York: Paulist Press, 1989), pp. 113–15.

28 A.G. Martimort, "The Liturgy of the Hours," A.G. Martimort (ed.), *The Church at Prayer,* vol. IV (Collegeville: Liturgical Press, 1986), pp. 153–275; V. Raffa: "L'Ufficio

divino: la Veritas Horarum," Congregazione per il Culto Divino, *Costituzione liturgica 'Sacrosanctum Concilium' Studi*, pp. 415–40; A. Chupungco, "The Conciliar Debate on the *Veritas Horarum*," *Ecclesia Orans* 8 (1991), pp. 219–29.

29 For background reading see: A. Adam, *The Liturgical Year* (New York: Pueblo, 1981); M. Augé, "The Liturgical Year in the Roman Rite," A. Chupungco (ed.), *Handbook for Liturgical Studies* vol. V (Collegeville: Liturgical Press, 2000), pp. 177–210.

30 T. Federici, "Parola di Dio e Sacrosanctum Concilium," Congregazione per il Culto Divino, *Costituzione liturgica 'Sacrosanctum Concilium' Studi*, pp. 269–305.

31 J. Lamberts, "Vatican II et la liturgie en langue vernaculaire," *Questions liturgiques* 66 (1985), pp. 125–54; A. Chupungco, "The Translation, Adaptation and Creation of Liturgical Texts," *Notitiae* 208 (1983), pp. 694–700.

32 *Schema Constitutionis de Sacra Liturgia*, Emendationes IV, p. 15.

33 See: A. Chupungco, *Cultural Adaptation of the Liturgy* (New York: Paulist Press, 1982); *Liturgies of the Future; Liturgical Inculturation: Sacramentals, Religiosity, Catechesis* (Collegeville: Liturgical Press, 1992); "Liturgy and Inculturation," *Handbook for Liturgical Studies* II, pp. 337–75; "Inculturation," P. Bradshaw (ed.), *The New Westminster Dictionary of Liturgy & Worship* (Westminster: John Knox Press, 2002), pp. 244–51.

Bibliography

Bishop, E., "The Genius of the Roman Rite," *Liturgica Historica: Papers of the Liturgy and Religious Life of the Western Church* (Oxford: Clarendon Press, 1918), pp. 1–19.

Bugnini, A., *The Reform of the Liturgy 1948–1975* (Collegeville: Liturgical Press, 1990); Italian original: *La riforma liturgica 1948–1975* (BELS, 1983).

Braga, C., "La Sacrosanctum Concilium nei lavori della Commissione preparatoria", Congregazione per il Culto Divino (ed.), *Costituzione liturgica 'Sacrosanctum Concilium': Studi* (BELS, 1986), pp. 25–68.

Cabié, R., "The Medieval Origins of the 1570 Order of Mass," A.G. Martimort (ed.), *The Church at Prayer: Introduction to the Liturgy - Vol.* II: *The Eucharist* (Collegeville: Liturgical Press, 1986), pp. 149–71.

Cattaneo, E., *Il culto cristiano in occidente* (BELS, 1992).

Marini, P., *A Challenging Reform: Realizing the Vision of the Liturgical Renewal* (Collegeville: Liturgical Press, 2010).

Neunheuser, B., "Roman Genius Revisited," M. Francis & K. Pecklers (eds), *Liturgy for the New Millennium* (Collegeville: Liturgical Press, 2000), pp. 35–48.

Nocent, A., *La célébration eucharistique avant et après Pie V* (Paris: Beauchesne, 1977)

Pecklers, K., *The Genius of the Roman Rite* (Collegeville: Liturgical Press, 2010).

Reid, A., "Sacrosanctum Concilium and the Organic Development of the Liturgy," U.M. Lang (ed.), *The Genius of the Roman Rite* (Chicago: Hillenbrand, 2010), pp. 198–215.

Chapter 13

THE IMPLEMENTATION OF
SACROSANCTUM CONCILIUM

†Anscar J. Chupungco OSB

Introduction

At the outset it is useful to note that the postconciliar reform of the liturgy is the result of the work done after Vatican II to implement the provisions of the Constitution on the Sacred Liturgy, *Sacrosanctum Concilium*. The expression, "reform of the reform," that is in vogue in some Church quarters today is not directed to the conciliar document but to the manner in which it was implemented. People may debate about the expediency of the latter, but it is not in their domain to reform the Constitution.

The burning issue is whether the implementation matches the conciliar agenda of liturgical reform. Does the liturgy of Vatican II represent *Sacrosanctum Concilium*, or has it gone way beyond its provisions? People may challenge the way active participation is articulated in the postconciliar liturgical books, but it is not in their authority to dispute article 14: "In the reform and promotion of the liturgy, this full and active participation by all the people is the aim to be considered before all else." There can be differences in interpreting concretely the meaning of "full and active," but there can be no legitimate reason to cross them out from the Constitution.

The story behind its implementation

The intricate and at times tangled history of *Sacrosanctum Concilium*'s implementation is written authoritatively and in great detail by three of its witnesses: Annibale Bugnini,[1] Enrico Cattaneo,[2] and Piero Marini.[3] Any serious study or critique of the postconciliar reform should be rooted in a personal appreciation of the expertise and zeal that accompanied the delicate and demanding task of realizing the Constitution's vision. The books of the three authors offer an absorbing insight on how the agencies of the Holy See handled the challenge of postconciliar reform. It is not necessary nor is it possible to even summarize here the different stages of implementation. The process took several years of undaunted struggle on the part of implementers who worked in an atmosphere of tension brought about by opposition to liturgical changes on a large scale. Students of liturgy are advised to read the aforementioned titles carefully.

1. Pope Paul VI

The successful implementation of *Sacrosanctum Concilium* hinged on several persons and factors. Foremost was Pope Paul VI, who can rightly be named the architect of the postconciliar liturgical reform. He was assisted in the onerous task by two competent persons: Giacomo Cardinal Lercaro, Archbishop of Bologna and a world-renowned liturgist, and Fr. Annibale Bugnini who had been secretary of the Preparatory Commission on Liturgy. As early as 1963, while the Council was still in session, the Pope wanted to issue a motu proprio that would be a kind of provisional application of some of the Constitution's provisions that could be given to the Council Fathers before they left Rome.[4] There was a sense of urgency in the plan of the Pope to start the work of implementation even before the conclusion of the Council. This manifests the importance he gave to the liturgical reform of Vatican II.

Paul VI followed hands-on the progress of liturgical implementation. He made personal interventions to preserve some ancient practices that were rich in symbolism but of little practical consequence. A classic example is his decision to retain the washing of hands during Mass. But the challenge that he faced was to balance the requirements of Vatican II's liturgical reform with the centuries-old prerogatives of the Congregation of Rites. The years immediately following the Council were a time of uneasy, agonizing transition. He was zealously promoting the changes spelled out by *Sacrosanctum Concilium*, but he had to contend with the bureaucracy of the Roman curia and the conservatism in some Church sectors.[5] He reached an inspired solution: he established the implementing commission, called the *Consilium ad exsequendam Constitutionem de sacra Liturgia*, at first under the shadows of the Congregation of Rites and later as an independent body. In the end, he suppressed it to give way to the new Congregation for Divine Worship. By that time a good number of items in the agenda of liturgical reform were already in place. Although some writers judge his seeming indecisions to be "limitations of his pontificate," they can be regarded not as signs of weakness but as acts of prudence and wise judgment.

2. The Consilium

There is no need to repeat here the story of the *Consilium*, which Bugnini, Cattaneo, and Marini narrate. One salient feature of the story was the prolonged conflict between the *Consilium* and the Congregation of Rites. The *Consilium* walked on uneven ground as long as it was a section dependent on the Congregation. The other, and this is absolutely amazing, was the ability of the *Consilium* to launch the reform amidst opposition. Assured of the support of a great number of conferences of bishops, Paul VI, Cardinal Lercaro, Bugnini, and the members of the *Consilium* remained undaunted and pushed through with the implementation. Frequent consultations across the globe with the bishops, who were in reality the primary stakeholders of the reform, gave universal character to the work of the *Consilium* and rooted the reform in local Churches.

Foremost among the tasks assigned to the *Consilium* is "to apply, according to the letter and the spirit of the Council, the Constitution it approved, by responding to the proposals of the conferences of bishops and to questions that arise involving the correct application of the Constitution." This is the content of a letter of the Vatican Secretariat of State to Cardinal Lercaro on February 29, 1964.[6] The *Consilium* fulfilled this task by issuing various norms on the implementation of *Sacrosanctum Concilium*, inclusive of the correction of abuses and the revision of the current liturgical books. It was a period in the modern history of the Catholic Church when the Holy See was in constant consultation with the conferences of bishops across the globe listening to their desiderata concerning the reform of the liturgy.

Implementation is basically a work of interpretation. Interpretation requires exegetical and hermeneutic knowledge of the intention behind the vision. In the case of *Sacrosanctum Concilium*, its provisions for reform had to be carefully studied and interpreted. It is heartening to know that several *periti* of the Conciliar Commission on the Liturgy that drafted the Constitution were later appointed as consultors of the *Consilium*. Many others who were appointed were liturgists known for their support of and dedication to the conciliar reform.[7]

Prominent names in the world of liturgy that were in both the Conciliar Commission and the *Consilium* are: Annibale Bugnini, Ansgar Dirks, Josef Andreas Jungmann, Aimé-Georges Martimort, Frederick McManus, Johannes Overath, Mario Righetti, Pierre Salmon, Cipriano Vagaggini, and Johannes Wagner. Other eminent liturgists and ecclesiastical experts in the *Consilium* were, to mention a few: Henry Ashworth, Theodor Bogler, Pietro Borella, Bernard Botte, Louis Bouyer, Placide Bruylants, Ignazio Calabuig, Eugène Cardine, Enrico Cattaneo, Irénée Dalmais, Balthasar Fischer, Joseph Gélineau SJ, Pierre-Marie Gy, Anton Hänggi, Johannes Hoffinger, Bruno Kleinheyer, Emmanuel Lanne, Boniface Luykx, Juan Matéos, Christine Mohrmann, Burkhard Neunheuser, Adrien Nocent, Josef Pascher, Michele Pellegrino, Jordi Pinell, Johannes Quasten, Aimon-Marie Roguet, Herman Schmidt, Theodor Schnitzler, Xavier Seumois, Damien Sicard, François Vandenbroucke, Pelagio Visentin, Cyrille Vogel, and Johannes Wagner.[8]

The names of the above-mentioned liturgists are a guarantee that the implementation of the Constitution was carried out in accord with the conciliar vision of an earlier, more classical form of liturgy that would promote active participation. The group consisted of pastors and scholars who were advocates of the classical liturgical movement. Many of them played active roles during the Council. They knew what they were doing. Obviously they did not agree on every detail; they debated, and they consulted other pastors and experts around the world, leaving the final decision to Paul VI. In the end, the overall vision of the Council prevailed. Instructions on proper implementation were regularly issued and gradually the liturgical books were revised and disseminated among the conferences of bishops.

Nothing is perfect, but what the *Consilium* produced was an authoritative interpretation of the provisions of *Sacrosanctum Concilium*. It is quite meaningless to claim that the members and consultors of the *Consilium* misinterpreted the mind of the Constitution, or worse, that they misread the provisions. Most of them were personally involved in the unfolding of the conciliar document: they knew both the letter and the spirit of *Sacrosanctum Concilium*. Personal preferences on how the reform should have progressed are not a legitimate ground for casting misgivings about the validity of the *Consilium*'s interpretation of the Constitution and the authenticity of the postconciliar reform.

Worldwide reception

What would be a reasonable gauge for the usefulness of the work of the *Consilium*? The answer that is likewise reasonable is its reception by the local Churches. We are dealing with a reception that is worldwide, at least among developing nations and continents. In a quarter of a century, the postconciliar reform had taken root in Asia, Africa, Latin America, and Oceania.[9] The reception in these places may not match the experiences of other local Churches, especially those that possess a long and sustained tradition, but it stands as a convincing proof that a liturgical reform such as that of Vatican II had been much awaited and desired in those parts of the world. The papers read at the "Convegno delle Commissioni Nazionali di Liturgia" organized by the Congregation for Divine Worship and held in the Vatican in October 1984 are convincing testimonies of the success of the *Consilium*'s work of implementation.[10]

It is therefore a myopic appraisal of the postconciliar reform to view it largely from the spectrum of some traditional Churches. It is desirable that the critics of the liturgical reform of Vatican II take time and effort to experience the global Church, especially outside the northern hemisphere, and realize thereby that the Church is indeed Catholic and embraces a variety of approved forms for celebrating the liturgy. Culture has something to say about differences in liturgical rites. In Asia alone, the style of celebrating the liturgy varies according to the religious culture of the people. Catholic faithful in India and Thailand are comfortable with a contemplative environment for public worship, while the islanders of the Philippines value festive or jovial songs, gestures, and symbols.

When we evaluate the merit of the postconciliar implementation of *Sacrosanctum Concilium*, our chief criterion is not primarily whether or not the reformed liturgy is in continuity with medieval tradition represented by the post-Tridentine rites. The issue about rupture of liturgical tradition is a polemic question that overlooks the history of liturgical tradition, which has undergone adjustments in its textual and ritual expressions in the course of time in order to respond to new Church situations. Surely the essential elements of the sacraments have been preserved faithfully in the process of change, but a comparative study of the rites of the sacraments discloses some strong dissimilarity in their format, formularies, and rubrics. The baptismal rite in the fifth century appears externally different from the medieval and the Vatican II rites, but the essence of the sacrament has not changed.

At the end of the day, the true issue is whether the postconciliar reform has promoted the Church's "earnest desire" that the faithful worldwide are led to "full, conscious, and active participation in liturgical celebrations" (*Sacrosanctum Concilium*, 14) and as a community of worshipers are enabled to encounter Christ and his Church through the liturgical *ritus et preces* of Vatican II. It is a type of elitism to claim that the post-Tridentine liturgy is still the only effective or valid means for all the faithful in the world to enter into the mystery of Christ.

Leave the liturgy of Vatican II alone!

On July 7, 2007, Pope Benedict XVI published the Apostolic Letter *Summorum Pontificum* allowing a wider use of the Tridentine missal. It will be recalled that through *Quattuor abhinc annos* in 1984 and his Apostolic Letter *Ecclesia Dei* in 1988 Pope John Paul II permitted a limited use of the Tridentine missal. Pope Benedict XVI also granted to priests the permission to use the Tridentine rituals of baptism, marriage, penance, anointing of the sick, and funerals. Bishops may use the Tridentine ritual of confirmation. Clerics in major orders may use the Roman Breviary of 1961 (Lauds, Prime, Terce, Sext, None, Vespers, Compline, and Matins). The sacrament of holy orders and the Easter Triduum are glossed over.

Benedict XVI's intention in allowing a wider use of the preconciliar liturgy was to seek "interior reconciliation in the heart of the Church," that is with those who still hold on to the Missal of Pius V. According to *Summorum Pontificum*, the 1970 Missal of Paul VI, revised by authority of Vatican II, remains in force as the *forma ordinaria* of the Mass in the Catholic Church. On the other hand, the missal of Pius V, published in 1962 by Pope John XXIII, is the *forma extraordinaria*. To be in full communion with the Church, priests who opt to celebrate according to the 1962 missal cannot, as a matter of principle, exclude the 1970 missal.

To avoid misunderstanding, Benedict XVI explains that the two forms do not result in two Roman rites. Rather they are twofold form and use of one and the same rite. In fact, they can mutually enrich each other: new saints and some prefaces can be inserted in the 1962 missal, while more attention should be given to the rubrical directives of the 1970 missal.

Benedict XVI makes a timely reminder to observe with greater attention the rubrical directives of the 1970 missal. The *editio typica* of this missal should be kept unless the conferences of bishops with the approval of Rome have inserted rubrical changes. But at all times silence, noble simplicity, and prayerfulness while engaged in active participation should be the hallmark of every Eucharist. These are celebrative elements that ought to be recovered where they have been neglected. Indeed the missal of Paul VI offers opportunities for interior participation and spiritual enrichment.

Benedict XVI acknowledges that the use of the 1962 missal "presupposes a certain degree of liturgical formation and some knowledge of the Latin language" on the part of the community. Since neither of these, especially Latin, is often the case, he admits that the missal of Paul VI will certainly remain the ordinary form of eucharistic celebration in the Roman Church.

Now that the post-Tridentine liturgy has been officially declared as "extraordinary form" of Catholic worship, the two forms should remain distinct from each other. A combination of elements derived from either form will result in a hybrid liturgy that will certainly cause confusion among the faithful. The two forms are intended to coexist, giving to each of the faithful the right to choose which liturgical form suits best their religious needs. For this reason, Benedict XVI wisely and prudently allowed the bishop of the diocese to establish a personal parish where the Tridentine rituals may be used, or he may appoint a chaplain for such group of faithful. Thus there is no reason to "reform the reformed liturgy of Vatican II" using the criteria of post-Tridentine liturgy. To do so is to manifest disrespect for the 1970 missal and the worldwide Catholics who claim it as their own. In a word, we should leave the reformed liturgy alone and insist rather on how to foster greater interiority in its celebration.

Some norms of implementation

In the early years of the *Consilium*, several important documents were issued in order to launch the reform properly. Among these the following are worthy of mention: the First Instruction *Inter Oecumenici* in 1964 for the orderly carrying out of the provisions of *Sacrosanctum Concilium*; the Letter *Le renouveau liturgique* in 1965 on furthering the liturgical reform; the Second Instruction *Tres abhinc annos* in 1967; the Letter *Dans sa récente allocution* of 1967 on several issues regarding the reform; the Rescript in 1969 for India on adaptations of the Mass to the Indian culture; and the Instruction *Comme le prévoit* in 1969 on the translation of liturgical texts. In 1970, the Congregation for Divine Worship published the Third Instruction *Liturgicae instaurationes* to curb on abuses.

Many of the early documents, especially the first two Instructions, dealt with concrete changes in the liturgy in order to advance the reform envisaged by the Constitution. Some, especially the Third Instruction, reacted to abuses committed by individuals. It was unfortunate that the reform was incorrectly interpreted by some "euphoric" sectors, some of which engaged in irresponsible experimentations, such as the creation of personal eucharistic prayers and the reduction of the sacred rites to some type of social gathering. Some of the more important documents on the reform of the liturgy after the approval of *Sacrosanctum Concilium* are discussed below.[11]

1. The motu proprio *Sacram Liturgiam*

The motu proprio *Sacram Liturgiam* was published on January 29, 1964.[12] This initial document contained nothing earth-shaking in terms of radical changes in the liturgy, but it laid the solid foundation for the future reform. It rated the liturgical formation of the clergy as key to the success of the liturgical reform. *Sacrosanctum Concilium* articles 15–17, which makes the study of liturgy compulsory in seminaries and requires trained liturgy professors who were to teach it under theological, historical, ascetical, and pastoral aspects, was to be implemented starting the following academic year. In keeping with articles 45–6, every diocese is to have a liturgy commission working under the direction of the bishop. Other provisions concern the homily, the celebration of confirmation and marriage during Mass, and the recitation of the Divine Office. The motu proprio concludes with a decree that "for the present" article 22, 2 of the Constitution, which entrusts the regulation of the liturgy within specific limits to competent territorial assemblies of bishops, is to be understood on a national level.

But what ignited controversy was *Sacram Liturgiam* n. 9, regarding translations. Although the draft versions were silent about the requirement to submit translations for Rome's approval, the published version in the *Osservatore Romano* (January 29, 1964) carried it. Several conferences of bishops expressed disappointment, deeming it a curtailment of the authority of bishops' conferences to approve translations without further recourse to the Holy See. The conciliar text in question is *Sacrosanctum Concilium* article 36, 4: "Translations from the Latin text into the mother tongue intended for use in the liturgy must be approved (*approbari debet*) by the competent, territorial ecclesiastical authority." The preceding paragraph (36, 3), empowers the conferences of bishops to decide (*statuere*) whether and to what extent the vernacular is to be used in their respective territories. It adds however that their enactments "are to be approved (*probatis*), that is, confirmed (*seu confirmatis*) by the Holy See." This is a condition that is not repeated in paragraph 4, which is about the translations themselves.[13]

Subsequently the debate arose whether or not the translations made by the conferences of bishops still needed the Holy See's approval. A practical reason for the omission of the phrase *probatis seu confirmatis* is the obvious incapability of the Holy See to check the accuracy of translations in possibly hundreds of vernacular languages throughout the world. Such predicament could not have escaped the mind of the Council Fathers. Once the Holy See empowers the conferences of bishops to make liturgical translations, it can only trust the latter's orthodoxy as teachers of the faith.

To put an end to the embarrassing controversy, Annibale Bugnini was asked by the Secretariat of State to formulate an acceptable compromise that could be inserted into the motu proprio before its official publication in the *Acta Apostolicae Sedis*.[14] What Bugnini actually did was to apply the directive of the Constitution, article 36, 3. Thus the definitive, official text of *Sacram Liturgiam* 9 reads: the vernacular translations approved by national conferences of bishops "require due approval, that is confirmation, of the Holy See. This is the course to be taken whenever any Latin liturgical text is translated into the vernacular." We have here a *via media* compromise that tried to satisfy two contrasting positions. The Congregation of Rites wanted to preserve its centuries-old right to approve all liturgical changes, while several conferences of bishops clamored for the application of *Sacrosanctum Concilium* article 36, which empowered them to translate liturgical texts without further approval from Rome. The compromise seemed to have satisfied both sides, but it left in its wake a crucial issue: is Bugnini's intervention an authentic interpretation of article 36, 4?

2. The Instruction *Inter oecumenici*

The Instruction, which took six months of hard work by the *Consilium*, began to be implemented on March 7, 1965. Bugnini writes:

> March 7 thus became a historical date and a milestone in the history of liturgical reform. It was the first tangible fruit of a Council that was still in full swing and the beginning of a process in which the liturgy was brought closer to the assemblies taking part in it and, at the same time, acquired a new look after centuries of inviolable uniformity.[15]

Marini writes:

> The instruction *Inter oecumenici* marked the victory of the more open view of the implementation of the Vatican II liturgy advocated by the *Consilium*, in which the bishops' conferences would be associated with the responsibility of the Holy See. It also marked the end of the Tridentine mentality, which had considered the liturgy as an unchangeable reality reserved solely to the Congregation for Rites.[16]

What was the aim of the Instruction? It explains:

> Necessary before all else is the shared conviction that the Constitution on the Liturgy has as its objective not simply to change liturgical forms and texts but rather to bring to life the kind of formation of the faithful and ministry of pastors that will have their summit and source in the liturgy (see *Sacrosanctum Concilium*, 10). That is the purpose of the changes made up to now and of those yet to come (n. 5).[17]

The liturgy is the *culmen et fons* of the Church's spiritual life and apostolic works. To achieve this with greater effect it had become necessary to make the liturgy more accessible to the faithful. Changes had to be made not for the sake of change but for superior pastoral and spiritual motives.

The Instruction prudently cautions that in order that the faithful will more readily embrace the new liturgy, the implementation should "proceed step by step in stages" and should be explained by pastors through catechesis (n. 4).

The Instruction has five chapters: General Norms, Mystery of the Eucharist, The Other Sacraments and the Sacramentals, Divine Office, and Designing Churches and Altars to Facilitate Active Participation of the Faithful. Except for the liturgical year and sacred music, which the Instruction treats only in passing, the document represents the chapters of *Sacrosanctum Concilium*.

The chapter on general norms lays down the basic premises and requirements for the proper carrying out of the reform everywhere (cf. n. 2). The Instruction devotes several numbers to the liturgical formation of the clergy and the faithful: "Professors appointed to teach liturgy shall be trained as soon as possible, in keeping with the norms of the Constitution art. 15" (11b). Thus the liturgical formation of future pastors should be solidly grounded on the theology, history, and pastoral aspects of divine worship as enjoined by the Constitution. The chief aim of the conciliar liturgical reform, namely the full, conscious, and active participation of the faithful, should be the guiding principle of liturgical study and pastoral liturgy.

Since the Instruction was intended to launch the liturgical reform, its norms on the Mass, sacraments, the Divine Office, and liturgical furnishings were of transitional nature. Nonetheless, it set forth changes many of which would be picked up by the respective *editio typica* of liturgical books. In the case of the Order of Mass, for example, several provisions were incorporated in the 1970 typical edition such as the omission of Psalm 42 at the foot of the altar and the suppression of the last gospel and the Leonine prayers (n. 48). The Instruction also specifies in which parts of the Mass the vernacular may be used (n. 57). Chapter three, which deals with the sacraments, carries important norms such as the laying on of hands by all the bishops present at the consecration of a bishop and the celebration of marriage within Mass (nn. 69–70). The title of chapter five reflects the chief agenda of the conciliar reform: "Designing Churches and Altars to Facilitate Active Participation of the Faithful." Article 90 reads: "In building new churches or restoring and adapting old ones every care is to be taken that they are suited to celebrating liturgical services authentically and that they ensure active participation by the faithful." Perhaps to foster active participation article 92 recommends that "the main altar should preferably be freestanding, to permit walking around it and celebration facing the people."

3. The Instruction *Eucharisticum mysterium*

This momentous Instruction was published by the Sacred Congregation of Rites on May 25, 1967. The key collaborators of Cardinal Lercaro and Bugnini for the draft were Vagaggini (secretary for the group), Martimort, and Wagner.[18] The hand of liturgical theologian Vagaggini is evident especially in the doctrinal sections of the Instruction. The Instruction can rightly be considered a masterpiece of eucharistic theology and a rich source of catechesis.

"The purpose intended for these norms is both to provide the broad principles for catechesis of the faithful about the eucharistic mystery and to make more understandable the signs through which the Eucharist is celebrated as the memorial of the Lord and worshiped in the Church as a lasting sacrament" (no. 4). It is worthy of note that during the early stages of the reform catechesis held a prominent place in the scheme of successful implementation of *Sacrosanctum Concilium*.

The Introduction names "the most noteworthy doctrinal themes" that should be a basic content of catechesis. It presents a balanced approach to the definition of Mass as the sacrifice that perpetuates the sacrifice of the cross, the memorial of Christ's death and resurrection, and the sacred banquet through communion of his Body and Blood (n. 3). Part I offers other doctrinal themes for catechesis, such as the Eucharist in the life of the local Church, the unity of Christians, different modes of Christ's presence, the connection between Word and Eucharist, universal and ministerial priesthoods, and active participation. In Part III, a recommendation is made regarding an issue that continues to be a subject of debate: "It is recommended that as far as possible the tabernacle be placed in a chapel set apart from the main body of the church, especially in churches where there frequently are marriages and funerals and in places that, because of their artistic or historical treasures, are visited by many people" (n. 53).

4. The Instruction Comme le prévoit on liturgical translations

In 1969, the Concilium published the Instruction *Comme le prévoit* on the translation of liturgical texts. The Instruction, which guided the difficult and delicate work of translation into modern languages for thirty-two years, stands on solid scientific grounds. According to the Instruction, the purpose of liturgical translation is to "faithfully communicate to a given people, and in their own language, that which the Church by means of this given text originally intended to communicate to another people in another time" (n. 6). What does the Instruction mean by faithful translation? "A faithful translation cannot be judged on the basis of individual words: the total context of this specific act of communication must be kept in mind, as well as the literary form proper to the respective language." The context includes the message itself, the audience for which the text is intended, and the manner of expression. The method of translation generally, not absolutely and in every circumstance, favored by the Instruction is called "dynamic equivalence," which is recommended by experts of cultural anthropology and linguistic sciences.[19]

Thus *Comme le prévoit* does not judge "formal correspondence" an adequate method of translation because it does not take into account the culture represented by both the source and the receptor languages. It merely renders the original text word by word or phrase by phrase, often unmindful of the cultural underpinnings in them.[20]

Translators are to work on existing liturgical texts that originate in different epochs of Church history and were authored by various people for the use of a given assembly in a given occasion. *Comme le prévoit* exhorts that "to discover the true meaning of a text, the translator must follow the scientific methods of textual study as used by experts" (n. 8). Liturgical hermeneutics is now regarded as a foundational component of the study of liturgy. It consists, among other things, of philological analysis of the text, textual identification (authorship, theological and cultural ambient, literary qualities), and establishment of the redaction sources of the text and its ritual context. It is understood that translators read Latin. A translation from a translated text is anomalous. The importance of Latin was vindicated by Paul VI who himself "had taken every step to have all the modern languages introduced into the liturgy." He affirmed that "without the knowledge of Latin something is altogether missing from a higher, fully rounded education—and in particular with regard to theology and liturgy."[21]

Comme le prévoit tells us that "a liturgical text is a linguistic fact designed for celebration" (n. 27). Liturgical texts are a medium of the relationship between God and the assembly in the here-and-now of a local Church. It is essential that the message be contextualized, made alive and relevant to the particular ecclesial situation. After all, the liturgy is not merely a remembrance of what God has done in ages past. It is also the celebration of what God does for the people gathered here and now. As the Instruction points out:

> The prayer of the Church is always the prayer of some actual community, assembled here and now. It is not sufficient that a formula handed down from some other time or region be translated verbatim, even if accurately, for liturgical use. The formula translated must become the genuine prayer of the congregation and in it each of its members should be able to find and express himself or herself (n. 20).

Hence "in the case of liturgical communication, it is necessary to take into account not only the message to be conveyed, but also the speaker, the audience, and the style" (n. 7).

To achieve this, Paul VI reminded translators that the vernacular texts should be "within the grasp of all, even children and the uneducated," though "set apart from the everyday speech of the street and the marketplace." The translated text must recreate the original message, though without departing from it, so that the assembly is able to perceive the vernacular text as if it had been thought out and written for them. Implied is the avoidance, where liturgically possible, of archaic and antiquated speech, words, and phrases that give the impression of transporting the assembly to some remote past. Without this method of translation advocated by *Comme le prévoit*, translated texts, especially from the earlier strata of the corpus of liturgical texts, will hardly speak in context to the assembly and enjoy ownership by the local Church.

5. The Instruction *Varietates legitimae* on inculturation

The Instruction *Varietates legitimae,* or "The Roman Liturgy and Inculturation," was issued by the Congregation for Divine Worship on January 25, 1994. Its chief purpose is to set down the general norms regarding the application of *Sacrosanctum Concilium* articles 37–40 on inculturation.

A significant achievement of the Instruction is the shift of focus from "adaptation" to "inculturation." As a preliminary observation the Instruction explains that the change of vocabulary is understandable, even in the liturgy: the word "adaptation" could lead one to think of modifications of a somewhat transitory and external nature (n. 4). On several occasions Pope John Paul II used the word "inculturation" to express "the incarnation of the Gospel in autonomous cultures and at the same time the introduction of these cultures into the life of the Church." Echoing the Synod of 1985, he defines inculturation as the "intimate transformation of the authentic cultural values by their integration into Christianity and the implantation of Christianity into different human cultures."[22]

The Instruction covers four areas: first, the historical process; second, the theological requirements emerging from the nature of the liturgy; third, some principles and practical norms; and fourth, the areas open to inculturation.

The lengthy historical section sets the tone of the Instruction. The Instruction recalls the Church's efforts from the time of the Apostles down to the last ecumenical council to "create and develop the forms of Christian celebration according to local conditions." During all this time, however, the Church has always been attentive to its Jewish roots and to the need to critique contemporary culture (nn. 15, 17 & 19). Respect for our Jewish heritage and the obligation to critique certain cultural practices of our own time are two fundamental principles of inculturation. Thus we are not to dismiss from our liturgy such elements as the Scripture, baptismal water, eucharistic bread and wine, oil for the sick, and hand-laying. Nor should we presume that sin and error have not infected our culture. The following quotation from the Instruction expresses an accurate historical perception: "During the course of the centuries, the Roman rite has known how to integrate texts, chants, gestures and rites from various sources and to adapt itself in local cultures in mission territories, even if at certain periods a desire for liturgical uniformity obscured this fact" (n. 17). History sets before local Churches models and ideals to be imitated as well as mistakes to be avoided.

The Instruction notes that the degree and depth of liturgical inculturation depend upon the situation of local Churches (n. 29). The situation of Churches in those countries that were evangelized centuries ago and where faith has left its mark on culture (Churches in traditionally Christian countries) is obviously different from the situation of young Churches in mission lands.

It is useful to note that the Instruction distinguishes two types of inculturation. The first type corresponds to the specifications of the official liturgical books, while the second goes beyond what is specified in these books.[23] The Instruction foresees that for Churches with traditional background "the possibilities of adaptation envisaged in the liturgical books should, on the whole, be considered sufficient" (n. 7). Nonetheless, the Instruction does not deny them the possibility of a more radical type of inculturation, provided their respective conferences of bishops try first the adaptations offered by the liturgical books (n. 63).

The Instruction dutifully cautions that not everything cultural may automatically be integrated into the liturgy and that "fidelity to traditional usages must be accompanied by purification and, if necessary, a break with the past" (n. 48). This is a principle of inculturation which recurs time and again in the Instruction.

The substantial unity of the Roman rite about which *Sacrosanctum Concilium* article 38 speaks has been an object of debate among some liturgists. What does the phrase mean? The Instruction resolves the debate by affirming that "this unity is currently expressed in the typical editions of liturgical books, published by authority of the Supreme Pontiff, and in the liturgical books approved by the episcopal conferences for their areas and confirmed by the Apostolic See" (n. 36). Inculturation works within the framework of approved liturgical books. Because of this, it preserves the substantial unity of the Roman rite. Inculturation is, strictly speaking, not the creation of new families of rites, but the dynamic translation of the Roman liturgy into local languages, symbols, and ritual actions. John Paul II reminded the plenary assembly of the Congregation for Divine Worship on January 26, 1991 that inculturation does not mean "the creation of alterative rites," but the incorporation of suitable cultural elements into the Roman liturgy.

6. The Instruction *Liturgiam authenticam* on liturgical translation

The fifth Instruction *Liturgiam authenticam* was published by the Congregation for Divine Worship and the Discipline of the Sacraments on March 28, 2001. The Instruction sets forth the principle that "the translation of the liturgical texts of the Roman liturgy is not so much a work of creative innovation as it is of rendering the original texts faithfully and accurately into the vernacular language" (n. 20). Although the Instruction consents to the re-arrangement of words and the style of translation for the sake of rhythm, it firmly states that "the original text, insofar as possible, must be translated integrally and in the most exact manner, without omissions or additions in terms of their content, and without paraphrases or glosses. Any adaptation to the characteristics or the nature of various vernacular languages is to be sober and discreet." In a word, what the Instruction wants is formal correspondence. Preference for this method is the reason why it prohibits translations from other translations: "new translations must be made directly from the original texts, namely the Latin, as regards the texts of ecclesiastical composition" (n. 24). How realistic is this norm?

The Instruction suggests the retention of "a certain manner of speech which has come to be considered somewhat obsolete in daily usage" (n. 27). This suggestion is, however, prefaced by a caution to avoid "excessively unusual or awkward" expressions that hinder comprehension. Furthermore, translation "should be free of an overly servile adherence to prevailing modes of expression." On the other hand, words or expressions, "which differ somewhat from usual and everyday speech," are memorable and capable of expressing heavenly realities. Why permit the use of the unusual or awkward and somewhat obsolete words? The answer is pragmatic: to "free the liturgy from the necessity of frequent revisions when modes of expression may have passed out of popular usage."

Liturgiam authenticam replaced *Comme le prévoit*. Formal correspondence replaced dynamic equivalence. Whether or not the assembly will understand more fully the message of the liturgical texts and derive spiritual benefit from them is a question that only time can answer.

7. The Instruction *Redemptionis sacramentum*

On March 25, 2004, the Congregation for Divine Worship and the Discipline of the Sacraments issued a new instruction on the eucharist entitled *Redemptionis sacramentum*. The Instruction is virtually a roll-call of Eucharistic dos and don'ts and the naming of delicts and abuses. It is a response to John Paul II's encyclical letter *Ecclesia de Eucharistia* (April 17, 2003) in which he called upon the Congregation to prepare an instruction that would include "prescriptions of a juridical nature," explaining the "deeper meaning of liturgical norms" in the light of liturgical abuses that violate those norms. The encyclical letter reminds the Church that the mystery of the Eucharist "is too great for anyone to permit oneself to treat it according to his or her own whim."

The Instruction names two chief causes of abuse in the liturgy, especially the Eucharist. The first is "a false sense of liberty;" the second is ignorance of the nature and norms of the liturgy. The shift of focus of Vatican II from rubricism to intelligent and active participation unfortunately sent the wrong signal to the enthusiastic upholders of liberty that the Holy See had adopted an open sky policy or something like the sky is the limit. There are people who have taken absolute ownership of the liturgy. The other cause of abuse is ignorance of the nature and norms of the liturgy. Liturgy is taught more than ever before in seminaries and religious houses. Liturgy seminars and conferences are held with regularity and frequency. Yet the list of delicts and abuses indicate a deficient liturgical formation.

Some abuses are really quite serious, like the use of unauthorized eucharistic prayers, distribution of its parts among deacons and laypersons, the joining of the Mass with a meal, and the use of unapproved creedal formulas and non-biblical readings in place of Sacred Scripture. However, a good number of the so-called abuses are no more than minor rubrical offences or liturgical variations, some of which are approved local practices like wearing a stole over a white chasuble-alb cassock instead of a stole over an alb. Some deviations may not really be abuses but lack of propriety and decorum as in the case of improper vestments or the use of unsuitable plastic vessels that lack style and dignity.

What are the remedies put forward by the Instruction? The Instruction admits that the best remedy for liturgical abuses is biblical and liturgical formation of both pastors and faithful, "so that the Church's faith and discipline concerning the liturgy may be accurately presented and understood." But "where abuses persist," there are corresponding sanctions in accordance with canon law. For example, delicts pertaining to sacrileges are reserved to the Congregation for the Doctrine of Faith. The diocesan bishop, who is responsible for addressing abuses in his diocese, may impose canonical sanctions. In the case of more serious abuses he may refer the matter to the Congregation for Divine Worship and the Discipline of the Sacraments.

The Instruction concludes with a note that the issue of abuse in the celebration of the Eucharist is the concern of all. Hence, abuses should be reported to the diocesan bishop, who in turn may refer the serious deviations to the Holy See. The Instruction is a timely measure to curb abuses in the liturgy, but it should not be taken as a signal to return to rubricism that undermines the theological, spiritual, and pastoral nature of liturgical worship.

The revision of liturgical books

The task given to the *Consilium*, and later to the Congregation for Divine Worship, was to revise the existing liturgical books according to the directives of the Council. The work of revision was not piecemeal but total, covering the whole range of liturgy. From 1968–92, twenty-eight liturgical books have been revised. Foremost among them are the Rite of Ordination of 1968 (with a second edition in 1989), the Rite of Marriage of 1969 (with a second edition in 1990), the Roman missal of 1970 (with a second edition in 1975 and a third in 2002), the Lectionary of 1970 (with a second edition in 1981), the Rite of Infant Baptism of 1970, the four volumes of the Liturgy of the Hours of 1971, the Rite of Confirmation of 1971, the Rite of Christian Initiation for Adults of 1972, the Rite of Anointing of the Sick and Pastoral Care of 1972, the Rite of Penance of 1973, and the Book of Blessings of 1984.[24] In less than thirty years the Latin Church was able to take possession of the reformed liturgy desired by the Council.

An examination of these books reveals the *Consilium*'s and the Congregation's concern to preserve liturgical tradition, while adapting them to the pastoral needs of local Churches. In their introduction, a section deals with the possible adaptations of the book to local traditions. The Word of God is given great prominence. Active participation is carefully spelled out and so are the different forms of ministry involved in the celebration.

Under the leadership of Pope Paul VI, the work of reform included not only revision but also introduction or reintroduction of certain liturgical elements and practices that were judged beneficial. In 1968, the *Consilium* issued the Decree *Prece eucharistica*, promulgating three new eucharistic prayers, followed in 1974 by the Congregation's Decree *Postquam de precibus* on the Eucharistic Prayers for Masses with Children and for Masses of Reconciliation.

Changes were made in the rites of the sacraments as well. In 1968, Pope Paul VI approved in his Apostolic Constitution *Pontificalis Romani recognitio* the substitution of the Veronese formula for the ordination of bishops with a revised formula from the third-century *Apostolic Tradition*. In 1971, he promulgated the new formula for confirmation in his Apostolic Constitution *Divinae consortium naturae*. In 1972, by his motu proprio *Ministeria quaedam* he reformed the "minor orders" reducing them to two (lector and acolyte) which were henceforth called "ministries" to distinguish them from the clerical orders. In 1972, the Pastoral Norms *Sacramentum Paenitentiae* on general absolution was released by the Congregation for the Doctrine of Faith. In 1972, Pope Paul VI published the

Apostolic Constitution *Sacram Unctionem infirmorum*, approving the new formula for anointing, allowing the use of another kind of oil besides olive oil, provided that it is derived from plants, and reintroducing the practice which existed until the thirteenth century to repeat anointing during the same illness if the person's condition worsens.

Conclusion

Thus the work of postconciliar reform not only revised the existing rites, but supplemented and filled in the lacunae of the conciliar liturgical reform. There were instances of reform not mentioned in *Sacrosanctum Concilium*, like the new eucharistic prayers and the repetition of anointing. It can be argued that the reform went beyond the letter of the Constitution, but certainly not its spirit and fundamental intention to make Christian worship a veritable means of enriching the spiritual life of the faithful. If not for this courageous act of the Holy See after the Council, the Church today would have been sadly deprived of a richer liturgical life and of a concrete response to real pastoral needs experienced by local Churches throughout the world. That the official Church went beyond the letter of *Sacrosanctum Concilium*, though within its spirit and the parameters of liturgical tradition, is a sure sign of a trustworthy stewardship that knows not only how to preserve but also how to develop what has been entrusted to it by the Council.

Notes

1 *The Reform of the Liturgy 1948-1975* (Collegeville: Liturgical Press, 1990).
2 *Il culto cristiano in occidente: Note storiche* (BELS, 1992), pp. 539–91.
3 *A Challenging Reform: Realizing the Vision of the Liturgical Renewal 1963–1975* (Collegeville: Liturgical Press, 2007).
4 Bugnini, *The Reform of the Liturgy*, pp. 54–9; Marini records the existence of an initial draft *Primitiae* that did not prosper. His treatment of the story behind the *motu proprio* is detailed and extensive; *A Challenging Reform*, pp. 17–39.
5 See: E. Cattaneo, *Il culto cristiano in occidente,* pp. 538–58.
6 See: DOL p. 214.
7 See list of *periti* of the Conciliar Commission and the consultors of the *Consilium* in Bugnini, *The Reform of the Liturgy*, pp. 940–52.
8 This author had the unique privilege to have had some of them as mentors in the Pontifical Liturgical Institute in Rome and as colleague-consultors in the Congregation for Divine Worship.
9 In the span of thirty years this author had a first-hand experience of vibrant liturgical celebrations according to Vatican II's reform in dioceses, parishes, and religious communities in several countries of Asia, Africa, Latin America, and Oceania.
10 Congregation for Divine Worship, *Atti del Convegno dei presidenti e segretari delle Commissioni nazionali di Liturgia* (Padua: Edizione Messaggero, 1986).
11 The complete list of official documents and acts of the different agencies of the Holy See dealing with liturgical reform from 1963 to 1979 is in DOL, Appendix, pp. 1405–23.

12 ET: ibid., pp. 84–7.

13 It is noteworthy that the Constitution uses different verbs: *approbare* for the conferences of bishops and *probare* for the Holy See. To ascertain that the two do not mean the same thing, the Latin explains *probatis* with the phrase *seu confirmatis*. The Holy See does not approve again what the conferences of bishops have already approved; rather it confirms it, that is, endows it with juridical force by acknowledging its legality.

14 For a detailed report on the controversy see: Marini, *A Challenging Reform*, pp. 19–29.

15 Bugnini, *The Reform of the Liturgy*, p. 100. Marini records the history of the uphill struggle of the *Consilium* to draft the Instruction; see: ibid., pp. 67–79.

16 Ibid, p. 78.

17 DOL, p. 89.

18 Marini, *A Challenging Reform*, p. 8. These three consultors would later be the nucleus and key figures of the *Consilium* when it was separated from the Sacred Congregation for Rites.

19 See: C. Kraft, *Christianity in Culture. A Study in Dynamic Biblical Theologizing in Cross-cultural Perspective* (New York: Orbis Books, 1994), p. 265; see especially chapters 13–15, pp. 261–312.

20 Although "formal correspondence" aims to be faithful to the original text, its fidelity centers almost exclusively on the surface level of the source language and on the literal transference into the receptor language. Sometimes formal correspondence tries to recast the system of the receptor language forcing it to conform to the source language. This often does untold violence to the receptor language.

21 Address to Latinists, *Notitiae* 4 (1968), pp. 144–5; DOL, p. 282.

22 Encyclical Letter *Slavorum Apostoli*, June 2, 1985, n. 21; Discourse to the Plenary Assembly of the Pontifical Council for Culture, January 17, 1987, n. 5; Encyclical Letter *Redemptoris Missio*, December 7, 1990, n. 52.

23 See A. Chupungco: *Cultural Adaptation of the Liturgy* (New York, 1982); "The Magna Charta of Liturgical Adaptation," *Notitiae* 139 (1978), pp. 75–89: "Adaptation of the Liturgy to the Culture and Traditions of Peoples," *Notitiae* 220 (1984), pp. 821–6.

24 See the partial list of the *editio typica* of revised liturgical books in Cattaneo, *Il culto cristiano in occidente,* pp. 592–3.

Bibliography

Baldovin, J., *Reforming the Liturgy: A Response to Critics* (Collegeville: Liturgical Press, 2008).

Bugnini, A., *The Reform of the Liturgy 1948–1975* (Collegeville: Liturgical Press, 1990).

Cattaneo, E., *Il culto cristiano in occidente* (BELS, 1992).

Chupungco, A., "Adaptation of the Liturgy to the Culture and Traditions of Peoples," *Notitiae* 220 (1984), pp. 821–6.

—— *Cultural Adaptation of the Liturgy* (New York: Paulist Press, 1982).

—— "The Magna Carta of Liturgical Adaptation," *Notitiae* 139 (1978), pp. 75–89.

Congregation for Divine Worship, *Atti del Convegno dei presidenti e segretari delle Commissioni nazionali di Liturgia* (Padua: Edizione Messaggero, 1986).

Kraft, C., *Christianity in Culture: A Study in Dynamic Biblical Theologizing in Cross-cultural Perspective* (New York: Orbis Books, 1994).

Marini, P., *A Challenging Reform: Realizing the Vision of the Liturgical Renewal* (Collegeville: Liturgical Press, 2010).

Chapter 14

AFTER *SACROSANCTUM CONCILIUM*— CONTINUITY OR RUPTURE?

Alcuin Reid

The question

The title of the April 1969 Apostolic Constitution of Blessed Paul VI (1897; 1963–78) *Missale Romanum* which prefaces editions of the Roman missal published since 1970 to this day, and which authoritatively establishes the revised rites and texts of the Mass, states that it is "Revised by Decree of the Second Vatican Ecumenical Council." The other liturgical books carry similar and due approbation and repeat the same assertion.

There is no question that the Second Vatican Council called for a general liturgical reform, as its Constitution on the Sacred Liturgy, *Sacrosanctum Concilium,* promulgated by Paul VI on December 4, 1963 makes clear. And it is by no means extraordinary that a commission was established to carry out this work: this was foreseen at the Council and had been the *modus operandi* for the implementation of the liturgical reforms following the Council of Trent.

Yet the work of the commission established by Paul VI in 1964 to implement the reform, the *Consilium ad Exsequendam Constitutionem de Sacra Liturgia,* attracted severe criticism. The Italian writer Tito Casini (1897–1987) even gained a preface from the renowned Latinist, Antonio Cardinal Bacci (1885–1971), for his popular and controversial 1967 work *La tunica stracciata,* a work intended as a public rebuke of the *Consilium's* President, Giacomo Cardinal Lercaro (1891–1976).[1] However, it was the promulgation of the new *Ordo Missæ* in April 1969 (the complete *Missale Romanum* was not published until 1970, though the revised *Calendarium Romanum* and *Ordo Lectionum Missæ* had been published in March and May 1969 respectively), and the approach of the first Sunday of Advent 1969—the date it was to come into force—that provoked the greatest controversy.

This took the form of what has become known as "The Ottaviani Intervention"— a critical study of the new *Ordo Missæ* prepared by a group of Roman theologians in June 1969. It was prematurely published in the Italian press on September 14 and only put into the hands of Paul VI with a covering letter signed by Alfredo Cardinal Ottaviani (1890–1979), former prefect of the Holy Office, and by Bacci, on September 29.[2] Endorsing this study, the cardinals submitted that "the *Novus Ordo Missæ* ... represents, both as a whole and in its details, a striking departure from the Catholic theology of the Mass as it was formulated in Session 22 of the Council of Trent," and that "the pastoral reasons put forth to justify such a grave break ... do not seem to us sufficient."[3]

The cardinals were both Fathers of the Council. Ottaviani had voted for and duly signed *Sacrosanctum Concilium* in 1963.[4] Bacci was on record defending the Constitution against an "application of this Constitution in practice which certain frenzied and fanatical innovators have been seeking at all costs to impose."[5] That they chose to support this impugnation of the core product of that reform, the *Ordo Missæ,* is evidence that a grave question existed in their minds and in those of others as to whether that which the *Consilium* had prepared and Paul VI had promulgated was in fact that which the Council had mandated, or whether it was the result of other, divergent influences.

Controversy about the reform was by no means limited to this incident, and the liturgical changes were a catalyst in the widespread unrest and turmoil experienced by Catholics in the years following the Council.[6] The new liturgy was also abused, sometimes as a platform upon which to give vent to differing ideological positions.[7] The wide range of popular literature and media debate generated at the time deserves further analysis.[8]

In 1971 an English layman wrote of the new rite of Mass:

> To some its plainness, freedom from traditional ceremonies, imagery and mystery and its popular and social character will undoubtedly appeal; and there will be a slowly growing number of priests who know no other Mass. But something intangible and precious will have been lost to the Christian world; and we know of very many priests who are acutely distressed at the destructive character of many of the changes, and who are convinced that the full and intelligent participation of the faithful and the other advantages of the new order could be attained without the impious jettisoning of ... valued and significant acts and words. It is not unreasonable to hope that they may be restored. It is not a good thing for the Church to take the heart out of her most devoted priests.[9]

This assessment, calm and measured for its time and by no means opposed to *Sacrosanctum Concilium,* wondered whether another, less "destructive" path, might not have been possible for the liturgical reform.

The question at the heart of the controversy, then, which became increasingly explicit, is whether the reforms promulgated were in accordance with what was mandated by the Council, or whether Paul VI had promulgated something beyond and different from which the Council had authorized.

The continuing importance of the question

This question did not disappear. In the following years and decades the older liturgical rites were clung to by individuals and groups who rejected the reformed rites. It is important to note that these people did not necessarily reject the Council's liturgical Constitution. Archbishop Marcel Lefebvre (1905–91), who founded the Priestly Society of Saint Pius X in 1970, is perhaps the most prominent example.[10]

In his 1989 tribute to the German liturgist Klaus Gamber (1919–89), the then Prefect of the Congregation of the Doctrine of the Faith, Joseph Cardinal Ratzinger (1927–; Pope Benedict XVI 2005–13), himself an enthusiast for the liturgical reform as a Council *peritus*, gave voice to the concern that persisted in the minds of many:

> After the Council . . . in the place of the liturgy as the fruit of organic development came fabricated liturgy. We abandoned the organic, living process of growth and development over centuries, and replaced it—as in a manufacturing process— with a fabrication, a banal on-the-spot product.[11]

Ratzinger's assertion thus refined the question somewhat into a discussion of whether the liturgical reform was a legitimate, organic development of liturgical tradition (as desired by the Council), or an unprecedented radical innovation (contrary to the Council's wishes).

This question assumes that the Fathers of the Second Vatican Council, in approving the Constitution on the Sacred Liturgy, were intending a moderate pastoral reform rather than a substantial, radical innovation. It can be asserted that a study of the nuanced language of the Constitution and the many clarifications given during its debate at the Council supports this assumption,[12] even though it is true that many of the specific provisions of *Sacrosanctum Concilium* are phrased in somewhat pliable language.

As Pope Benedict XVI, Ratzinger gave the discussion of the correct implementation of the Second Vatican Council—by no means only its liturgical reform—a new vocabulary in his December 22, 2005 Address to the Roman curia, where he contrasted "a hermeneutic of discontinuity and rupture" with "the 'hermeneutic of reform,' of renewal in the continuity of the one subject-Church which the Lord has given to us." In short, "Continuity or rupture?"— where "continuity" does not exclude development or *proportionate* change or innovation, whilst consciously remaining connected with the riches handed on in living tradition, and where "rupture" sees no difficulty in dismissing that which has been handed down and developed through the ages and starting afresh in the light of perceived contemporary needs without regard for what has gone before.

In the light of the controversy occasioned by the liturgical books promulgated by Paul VI and the questions about them which have persisted in the decades since, it is therefore impossible to read "Revised by Decree of the Second Vatican Ecumenical Council" and accept these words at face value. The question of the accordance of these rites with that mandated by the Second Vatican Council, and of their continuity with or rupture from the liturgical tradition it sought to develop, stands.

The question, then, is whether the official liturgical reform—as found in the Latin "typical editions" promulgated by Paul VI (as distinct from the often faulty vernacular translations of them)—is a reform in continuity with liturgical tradition, or a rupture?

Upon this much rests. If the Council's intentions were distorted or ignored in whole or part, or interpreted according to particular ideologies, etc., one may legitimately critique the products of the liturgical reform without calling into question the Second Vatican Council. On that basis one may also consider the merits of, or even insist upon, a "reform of the liturgical reform." Such a critique may also inform considerations for future liturgical development. So too, it may necessitate a reassessment of the treatment that critics of the liturgical reforms received in the charged years following their promulgation.

Those for whom the question has no importance

It should be noted that some scholars and other writers have no qualms in asserting that what followed the Council was a desirable "radical reform of the liturgy" which represents a "radical shift in Catholic theology and piety."[13] One liturgist has asserted:

> The real radicalism of the 1960s was represented by the revolutionary reforms of Vatican II. Breaking with a tradition that stretched back almost 1300 years, *Sacrosanctum Concilium* proposed to substitute popular, pastoral liturgy for papal liturgy; a rite celebrated by redeemed "amateurs" (the pilgrim people of God) for a rite dominated by pushy specialists and experts.[14]

For this school of thought, "with regard to the Church's worship there is no going back,"[15] and any accommodation of those who have questioned the reforms following the Second Vatican Council—liturgical and otherwise—should, according to one popularist, "be a cause of great alarm to those of us who still believe that something monumental happened at Vatican II, that there were developments, reforms and—yes—points of rupture with the past (despite [Benedict XVI's] unconvincing arguments to the contrary)."[16]

These scholars and commentators reject the necessity for ritual and theological continuity in reform. They do not accept that authentic liturgical development in the Western rite is organic,[17] and that this principle is one which ecclesiastical authority must itself respect *a priori*.[18] They frequently deprecate liturgical developments beyond a given point (c. sixth century) and regard such as illegitimate corruptions of supposedly "pure" liturgical forms which they seek to reinstate— though only after careful editorial redaction.[19] They also maintain that substantial discontinuity is a feature of liturgical history.[20]

Whilst they answer the question "Continuity or rupture?" clearly, as above, they regard the answer as having no importance. Rather, not being concerned with the "technical details" of reform, they thereby at least implicitly devalue the content of the principles and norms laid down in the Constitution on the Sacred Liturgy. This they interpret as but one component of the "event" Vatican II, where "something happened," asking "how much of *Sacrosanctum Concilium* is present in Vatican II, and how much of Vatican II is present in the first constitution, *Sacrosanctum Concilium.*"[21] Therefore, that which the Council set down in the Constitution must be read in the light of other aspects of this "event," even if such a reading goes beyond or even contravenes *Sacrosanctum Concilium*—the specifics of which are thus left behind.

The historical impossibility of this hermeneutic for studying the liturgical reform—the Fathers of the Council, the *Consilium* and Paul VI neither asked this question nor operated from its assumptions, or from the agenda articulated *a posteriori* by this school of thought—renders it untenable. Those engaged in the reform were engaged in implementing the Constitution, and began doing so immediately (as the Constitution instructed), without waiting for any such "event" to take its final form.

Yet this view enjoys popularity amongst Italian and Anglophone liturgists and theologians and more, possibly because it underpins the "leave the door open" school of liturgical reform—a stance of some who worked on the reform, certainly,[22] but an attitude that cannot be imputed to the Council as a whole or to *Sacrosanctum Concilium* in particular.

In spite of the positions of these scholars, the question of continuity or rupture in the liturgical reform stands. It is the Conciliar Constitution itself, not some virtual "event" that has been turned into a super-dogma, which must be the basis of research. What is necessary is a methodology that respects the realities involved.

Beginning with the Constitution itself

A sound assessment of the liturgical reform promulgated by Paul VI must therefore be based on the Constitution on the Sacred Liturgy. It is its text and principles read integrally which enjoy the authority of a Constitution of an Ecumenical Council of the Church, not the initiatives—private or official—which others may have subsequently initiated. Understanding its text correctly is crucial. An uncritical reading of isolated articles or statements of the Constitution is as dangerous as taking the same approach to verses of Sacred Scripture.

The Constitution opens with four introductory articles which explain the pastoral and theological motivation for the liturgical reform (articles 1–2), and noting the relation of the Constitution to the liturgical life of Catholics not of the Roman rite, and expressing respect for the same (articles 3–4).[23]

Articles 5–13 present the theological rationale that underpins the pastoral and practical principles that follow. In this rich theological *exposé* we find the theology of the Paschal Mystery articulated in article 5, the differing manners in which Christ is present in the Sacred Liturgy in article 7, and the statement that the Sacred Liturgy is the "*culmen et fons*" ("source and summit") of the life of the

Church in article 10. Article 11 provides the reminder that for the liturgy to bear its fruit the faithful must be connected to it by participating in the liturgical action and underlines that facilitating such participation is a duty of all pastors. Articles 12–13 assert the ongoing importance and value of private and devotional prayer subject to the primacy of the Sacred Liturgy.

Articles 14–20 then lay down two fundamental principles; the first is *"participatio actuosa."* The Council says: "In the restoration and promotion of the Sacred Liturgy the full and active participation by all the people is the aim to be considered before all else, for it is the primary and indispensible source from which the faithful are to derive the true Christian spirit." Its resonance with the fundamental principle of Pius X's 1903 motu proprio *Tra le sollecitudini* is clear.

This provides both the clear pastoral rationale (the "why") and the desired outcome (the ultimate end or "what") of the liturgical reform mandated by the Council, namely facilitating "liturgical piety"—that Christ's faithful would ordinarily find the necessary nourishment for Christian life through conscious connection with and contemplation of the faith of the Church as it is celebrated in the liturgical rites and prayers throughout the annual round of seasons and feasts of the liturgical year, taking due priority over the practice of an unrelated, however worthy, devotional exercise.

Article 14 envisages that this reform requires an *a priori* improvement of the liturgical education and formation of the clergy and the laity, stating:

> It would be futile to entertain any hopes of realizing [*participatio actuosa*] unless the pastors themselves, in the first place, become thoroughly imbued with the spirit and power of the Liturgy, and undertake to give instruction about it. A prime need, therefore, is that attention be directed, first of all, to the liturgical instruction of the clergy.

This is the Constitution's second fundamental principle—the *a priori* necessity of liturgical formation. It is the primary means (the "how") of bringing about the desired outcome of the reform.

These calls for actual participation and for widespread liturgical formation are the first practical policies adopted by the Council Fathers for the liturgical reform and, I submit, we read the rest of *Sacrosanctum Concilium* correctly only if we give *participatio actuosa* and liturgical formation the fundamental primacy that is theirs in the Constitution itself. Thus formation in "the spirit and power of the Liturgy" (as this phrase was understood by the Council Fathers *in aula* in 1962), is essential for the realization of the liturgical renewal of the Church, for achieving *participatio actuosa,* so desired by the Council.

These two principles are inseparable as article 14 itself emphasizes and as the subsidiary articles 15–20 underline. Divorcing them, or allowing one to predominate to the detriment of the other, could not be without severe consequences. Ritual reform not underpinned by the requisite formation might well be said to be at risk of being built on sand (cf. Mtt. 7:26–27), just as an activist interpretation of *participatio actuosa* would risk adopting the error of Martha to the exclusion of the indispensable contemplative role of her sister Mary (cf. Lk. 10:38–42).[24] The interdependence of these principles provides one foundation for a critical appraisal of the implementation of the reform.

Further principles are articulated in the remainder of the first chapter of the Constitution (articles 21–46). Without doubt articles 21–25 are essential for a correct understanding of the reform envisaged by Council. They assert the desire of the Church to undertake a "general restoration" ("*generalem instaurationem*") of the liturgy and that the development of the liturgical rites is legitimate and sometimes necessary (21); clarify the authority competent for aspects of the reform (22); assert the need to retain sound tradition whilst being open to legitimate progress where the good of the Church genuinely and certainly requires it (23); insist that Sacred Scripture is of the greatest importance and that it is essential to promote warm and living love for Scripture (24); and stress that the work is to be begun as soon as possible with the help of experts and the worldwide consultation of bishops (25).

Each of articles 21–4 requires close study and exegesis.[25] They set down principles in respect of the secondary means of the liturgical reform—secondary in that their efficacy will depend on the achievement of the primary means, liturgical formation. They must be read entire, together, and in context. In isolation or in part they can too easily be taken from as justification for positions utterly foreign to the Constitution read integrally.

This is perhaps nowhere more the case than with article 21. Its distinction between divinely instituted elements of the liturgy and "elements subject to change" can seem to render by far the greater part of the liturgical rites—which have developed in the Church's tradition and are not directly of divine origin—"merely" ecclesiastical and seemingly changeable or disposable at will. Such a reading fails to take account of the *liturgical* and *sacramental* role of elements not of divine origin in the developed, multivalent complex that is Catholic liturgy, and takes no account of the stipulations of article 23 in respect of ritual development or those regarding due authority in respect of the liturgy asserted in article 22.[26]

The following principles build on these: articles 26–32 specify implications of the hierarchic and communal nature of the liturgy; articles 33–6 draw out applications from the pastoral and didactic nature of the liturgy; articles 37–40 outline the steps to be followed in liturgical inculturation; articles 41–2 call for specific means of renewal in dioceses and parishes; and articles 43–6 require the establishment of diocesan and supra-diocesan bodies to promote pastoral-liturgical action.

In reading these principles (articles 26–46) we must be careful to note that they are subsidiary to articles 21–5 which in turn find their rationale in articles 14–20. Here, too, there is a danger of taking principles out of context and elevating them into quasi-dogmas. In this respect, the over-enthusiastic 1965 assertion of J.D. Crichton (1907–2001), erroneously attributed to Dom Cipriano Vagaggini (1909–99), that article 34's call for noble simplicity "is the principle of principles of liturgical reform," is illustrative. Whatever its import, article 34 is not "the principle of principles"—*participatio actuosa* and liturgical formation are, as Vaggagini in fact asserts.[27] Noble simplicity is consequent to and dependent upon these, and reforms adopted in the light of this subsidiary principle may be assessed in their light.[28]

Chapters II–VII of the Constitution lay down specific norms for the reform of particular rites and areas of the Sacred Liturgy based on the principles outlined in chapter I. That the specific measures laid down in these chapters are subsidiary to the principles of the first chapter must not be forgotten. The Council's policies laid down in each area require careful consideration in the light of their dependence on the principles of chapter I and of the hierarchy therein.[29]

The redaction of the text of the Constitution

Sacrosanctum Concilium was the product of drafting, discussion, debate, and further redaction from the first draft of the Preparatory Liturgical Commission in August 1961 to the text promulgated by Paul VI in 1963. A study of the development of the text as a whole and of its articles individually reveals the intentions of the drafters and of the revisions made to the draft, of those proposing amendments at the Council, and in the end of the Council itself. The principal redactions are:

1. Pontificia Commissio de sacra Liturgia praeparatoria Concilii Vaticano II, *Constitutio de Sacra Liturgia fovenda atque instaurandus*, 10 August 1961
2. Pontificia Commissio de sacra Liturgia praeparatoria Concilii Vaticano II, *Emendatio capitis I Constitutio de Sacra Liturgia*, 11–13 October 1961
3. Pontificia Commissio de sacra Liturgia praeparatoria Concilii Vaticano II, *Constitutio de Sacra Liturgia* Schema transmissum Sodalibus Commissionis die 15 Novembris 1961
4. Pontificia Commissio de sacra Liturgia praeparatoria Concilii Vaticano II, *Documenta Sessionis Plenariae mensis ianuarii 1962*
5. Pontificia Commissio de sacra Liturgia praeparatoria Concilii Vaticano II, *Constituto de Sacra Liturgia*, Textus approbatus in Sessione plenaria diebus 11–13 ianuarii 1962.
6. *Schema Constitutionis De Sacra Liturgia*, 23 July 1962 & 22 October 1962
7. *Schema Constitutionis De Sacra Liturgia textus emendatus*, 3 October 1963
8. *Constitutio De Sacra Liturgia*, 4 December 1963

The first four texts are published in Angelo Lameri's comprehensive edition, *La « Pontificia Commisio de sacra liturgia praeparatoria Concilii Vaticani II » Documenti, Testi, Verbali*.[30] Francisco Gil Hellín (1940–) provides the final four texts in parallel columns in his *Concilii Vaticani II Synopsis: Constitutio de Sacra Liturgia Sacrosanctum Concilium*. This volume also provides the *Declarationes*, or explanations of the articles, prepared by the Preparatory Commission and explaining their intended application, which were missing from the (same) text (n. 6) that was sent to the Council Fathers and presented *in aula* at the Council's fourth General Congregation on October 22, 1962. The *Declarationes* were only made available to the Fathers the following month. Gil Hellín also provides the texts of aural and written interventions by the Council Fathers—though not all— cross referencing them to the pertinent articles, rendering his work a valuable tool for study of the Constitution.

Whilst this synopsis is indeed helpful, the *Acta Synodalia Sacrosancti Concilii Oecumenici Vaticani II* are also a necessary reference. Students will need access to the four 'parts' of volume I (the first session), and the six 'parts' of volume II (the second session), which publish the chronological acts of the daily congregations as well as texts of emendations to the schema, etc. The *Acta et Documenta Concilio Oecumenico Vaticano II Apparando* publish texts from the preparatory commissions and the acts of the Central Preparatory Commission. The responses received in the worldwide consultation of the episcopate and others prior to the Council and the revision of the *schema* of the Constitution by the Central Commission are of particular interest.

The study of the debate and redaction of the text at the Council itself is crucial, for whatever the intentions of those who prepared the *schema*—and their work is certainly of interest—it is the Pope and the Council who gave the text its ultimate meaning and authority. That is to say, regardless of what experts may have hoped that the Council would approve, or may even have read it as approving, then or afterwards, an accurate reading of the Constitution is one that is in accord with the Council Fathers' intentions expressed *in aula* and the consequent explanations and redactions of the Conciliar Liturgical Commission which were again considered by the Fathers before the text was finally approved and promulgated.

The Council's consideration of what became article 50 of the Constitution (originally n. 37)—on the revision of the rite of Mass—is illustrative.

As part of chapter II, article 50 was discussed beginning in the ninth general congregation on October 29, 1962. Some Fathers saw it as a licence for revolution and protested strongly. Whilst the opening intervention of Francis Cardinal Spellman (1889-1967), and that of Ottaviani on the following day are noteworthy for their critical content, those of Frederico Melendro SJ (1889-1978) and George Dwyer (1908-87) on October 30, as well as that of Alberto De Voto (1918-84) on the 31st, called for clarification. Later the same morning Léon-Arthur Elchinger (1908-98) intervened:

> I propose that the entire text of this article be conserved but that it may be clarified by the publication of the complete *declaratio* prepared by the preparatory commission under this article. So to "calm the spirits" of those that fear a complete revolution of the Order of Mass and the death of the Roman rite, this *declaratio* does not propose for us a revolution but only an evolution—a pastoral evolution—something sound and prudent.[31]

In the next session (November 5) Bishop Henri Jenny (1904-82), intervened. A member of the liturgical preparatory and conciliar commissions, he set forth the content of the *declaratio* on the reform of the Order of Mass. Before outlining the specific reforms, the assurance was given that: "Hodiernus Ordo Missæ, qui decursu saeculorum succrevit, certe retinendus est." ("The current *Ordo Missæ*, which has grown up in the course of the centuries, certainly is to be retained.")[32] The resonance of article 23's principle—that sound tradition is to be retained whilst the way is to be open for legitimate progress—is clear in both Jenny's and Elchinger's interventions.

When the text of chapter II, as revised in the light of the Fathers' interventions, was presented during the Council's second session in October 1963, a printed copy of this *declaratio* was given to each of the Fathers, again including the assurance "Hodiernus Ordo Missæ, qui decursu saeculorum succrevit retinendus est."[33] Also, the text of article 50 had a second sentence summarizing the *declaratio* added, which included the statement that the "rites are now to be restored to the vigour which they had in the days of the Holy Fathers."

If we ask what the Fathers understood and intended by this article in approving chapter II of the Constitution, this history must be borne in mind. Whilst the addition of the reference to "the vigour" had "in the days of the Holy Fathers" may have subtly opened a door through which much later passed,[34] *from the Conciliar debate and redaction of this article itself*, it is difficult to assert that the Fathers of the Council intended anything beyond a moderate reform of the rite of the Mass as specified in the *declaratione* they were given before voting—along the lines of what appeared in the *Ordo Missæ* jointly promulgated by the Sacred Congregation for Rites and the *Consilium* on January 27, 1965 prefaced by a decree mandating that it be adopted in new editions of the missal.[35] The sources make clear, though, that the *Consilium* charged with implementing the Constitution, at least, regarded this as a merely provisional step.[36]

The correct interpretation of this article alone requires much further study,[37] and the material available from the work of the Council is vast as Roberto de Mattei rightly observes in his "Bibliographical Note."[38] Whilst other material must be considered, if we are faithfully to assess what *the Council's* intentions were, we must first make a thorough examination of the material generated by the Council itself, placing ourselves in the shoes of the Fathers *in aula*.

The meaning of the Constitution

Sacrosanctum Concilium captured the popular attention of the Church and the media, with the result that there is an abundance of contemporary articles and other publications on the "changes" to the liturgy. Whilst all these have value, some are indispensible in reading the Constitution accurately.

A number of commentaries were published by key personnel. Amongst them, that edited by Bugnini and Carlo Braga CM, *The Commentary and the Instruction on the Sacred Liturgy*, stands out for assembling a large number of such experts. The commentary "Constitution on the Sacred Liturgy" by the renowned Joseph A. Jungmann SJ (1889–1975) is an essential reference. The two volumes of *The Liturgy of Vatican II*, edited by William Baraúna OFM, bring together the reading of other experts on various aspects of the reform, and should be consulted. Whilst each of these was translated into English, one important commentary that unfortunately was not is that of Herman Schmidt SJ, *La Consititution de la Sainte Liturgie*.

Commentaries appeared rapidly in all languages and whilst some may not have achieved the international standing of those above, they demonstrate the contemporary understanding of the Constitution. In English, that of Frederick R. McManus (1923–2005) appeared in *Worship* from May 1964 and was revised and reprinted for his book *Sacramental Liturgy*. England's J.B. O'Connell (1888–1977) published *Active Sharing in Public Worship*, which, whilst not extensive, retains its value. Austin Flannery OP edited *Vatican II: The Liturgy Constitution*. Shorter articles abound in liturgical and other contemporary journals.

When consulting commentaries it is useful to make the distinction between the information about and explanation of the Constitution that they provide and any interpretations that belong solely to the authors themselves. Whilst contemporary commentaries tend to the former, and their concord is often striking, in seeking the meaning of the Constitution it is useful to read commentaries with an historically critical eye.

The implementation of the Constitution

Here we must distinguish between *Sacrosanctum Concilium* as promulgated by Paul VI on December 4, 1963 and the uses to which its provisions were put afterwards. Two examples from the pen of Annibale Bugnini CM (1912–82), underline the reality of this distinction.

The first is the provision in article 36 § 2 to "extend" the use of the vernacular in the liturgy. As elsewhere, the provisions of article 36 are somewhat elastic, but its four paragraphs read integrally clearly envisage an extension of the vernacular to parts of the rite which retains Latin as the overall norm. This is what the Council Fathers approved and Paul VI promulgated. And yet an almost universal vernacularization of the liturgy quickly ensued, facilitated if not promoted by key personnel associated with the *Consilium*, the Secretary of which (Bugnini) writes:

> It cannot be denied that the principle, approved by the Council, of using the vernaculars was given a broad interpretation. But this interpretation did not spring from a desire to take risks or from an itch for novelty; it was adopted after deliberation, with the approval of competent authority, and in line with the spirit of the conciliar decrees.[39]

Bugnini's explanation raises other factors: the influence of "deliberation," the employment and exercise of competent authority, and the appeal to a "spirit" of the conciliar decrees. These are significant and each must be studied. Here it suffices to note that there is clear evidence of the difference between the provisions of *Sacrosanctum Concilium* and the reality of its implementation.

The second example is stark. Whereas a hallmark of the Roman rite for over a thousand years was its single "eucharistic prayer," the "Roman canon"—a text which developed from the patristic period onward—the 1970 Missal of Paul VI contains four eucharistic prayers (first promulgated in May 1968), and others were approved subsequently. Yet there is no authorization for this significant if not substantial innovation in the Constitution, the second chapter of which lays down what is to happen in the reform of the rite of Mass. Nor was it specified in the clarifying *declaratione* or in any other explanation given to the Fathers after they expressed anxiety about drastic changes to the *Ordo Missæ*.

The chapter in which Bugnini relates the history of this reform opens with a sentence which illustrates something of the dynamic operative within the *Consilium*: "Once euchological pluralism and rubrical flexibility had been rediscovered after centuries of fixism, it was unthinkable that a monolithic approach to the eucharistic prayer should long endure."[40] As Bugnini's account substantiates, scholars may evaluate this innovation without in any way calling into question the liturgical reform mandated by the Council.[41]

In studying the Constitution's implementation, Bugnini's mammoth work *The Reform of the Liturgy: 1948–1975*, stands as a lasting gift to history. It recounts in detail the work of the *Consilium* from its establishment in 1964 to 1969, and of the work for liturgical reform of the Congregation of Divine Worship, of which Bugnini was Secretary from 1969–75. The lists of the members and consulters of the official bodies established to work on liturgical reform from 1948 onward provided in an appendix are a particularly useful tool which can alert researchers to possible archival and published sources.

It stands as the primary reference, save two caveats. Firstly, the English edition reproduces some inaccuracies present in the first Italian edition. These were corrected by A.G. Martimort (1911–2000) for the second Italian edition, which must be checked to verify any matters of importance. The second is that Bugnini wrote this book after his dismissal in 1975 as an *apologia pro* the liturgical reform. It was published in 1983, a year after his death. It is therefore not a detached historical memoir, and must be read in this light.

A less dispassionate account still is found in Piero Marini's *A Challenging Reform: Realizing the Vision of the Liturgical Renewal*. Marini was a young collaborator at the *Consilium* from 1965 and makes available some useful material—particularly in respect of the *Consilium's* assertion of and ensuing battle for its independence from the Sacred Congregation for Rites (which it won). At times, however, his work betrays the desire to perpetuate a partisan vision of liturgical reform.

Nicola Giampietro's *The Development of Liturgical Reform* chronicles the involvement of Ferdinando Antonelli OFM (1896–1993; created cardinal 1973). Antonelli, who had been involved in the official work of reform for as long as Bugnini, was appointed Secretary to the Conciliar Liturgical Commission in 1962—and not Bugnini, who may reasonably have expected the appointment. He was thus involved in the minutiae of the redaction of the Constitution at the Council itself, giving the archival material studied here importance. As Antonelli was not a 'trusted member' of the *Consilium*'s inner circle, and as he himself did not compile this study, it is both important and more dispassionate. Another significant and "alternative'" perspective is provided by the *Mémoires* of Louis Bouyer.

The published documents of the Holy See, including those of the *Consilium*, provide a framework for study, and the three abovementioned works serve to give them context. Reference to the original language texts provides an important corrective to some faulty translations and interpretations based on them.

The *Consilium* published its own journal *Notitiae* from 1965 which is a basic point of reference. Articles appeared in *Notitiae*—as well as other liturgical journals—explaining aspects of the reform, often written by the relators or other members of the working groups responsible for their preparation. Later still *Notitiae* and other journals such as *Ephemerides Liturgicae* and *La Maison-Dieu* published valuable articles about aspects of the reform.[42]

The largely unpublished working documents of the *Consilium* are an important resource. In the first place there are the various *schemata*—the drafts—prepared by its working groups for consideration by the members of the *Consilium*. These demonstrate different influences and sometimes a less than smooth development in the reform. Those concerning the reform of the order of Mass are published.[43] *Notitiae* published a 320-page elenchus of the *schemata* in 1982 (pp. 453–772) which is both illustrative and an important reference for archival research.

Other unpublished documents shed light on the process and issues arising during the reform. For example, following the *debacle* resulting from the presentation of the "Missa normativa" at the October 1967 Synod of Bishops,[44] at the ninth plenary session of the *Consilium* the following month, a letter from the Secretariat of State (November 24, 1967) was distributed conveying Paul VI's injunction not to indulge personal desires but to proceed "wisely and prudently" keeping the good of the People of God before their eyes.[45] Clearly Paul VI judged that this admonition was warranted.

The *Consilium* secretariat kept its collaborators informed by means of *Res Secretariae*. Some, such as that of December 6, 1967 (n. 33), in which Bugnini informs *periti* that he had been summoned by Paul VI who was "preoccupied" that the new rite of Mass should not be impoverished, that the *Confiteor* and (some) prayers at the Offertory be retained, that medieval formulae not be despised, etc.,[46] relate significant events in the course of the reform and demonstrate the positions of different interested parties. That of October 9, 1968 (n. 34), which documents the disagreement between the *Consilium* and Paul VI and the latter's wish to retain the sign of the cross at the beginning of Mass, not to omit the *Kyrie* when the *Gloria* is sung, to insert the words "quem/quod tibi offerimus" into the proposed new formulae for the offertory and to retain the *Orate fratres*, makes another significant contribution to the history of the reform.

Such material critically augments published accounts of the reform. Other contemporary sources—diaries and letters of Council Fathers, *Consilium* members, and *periti*, etc.—are similarly valuable. Diocesan and other archives surely contain much unexplored material of this type.

A posteriori recollections abound and have a value, albeit one which must be read in the light of the sources and of issues which have arisen in the time elapsed since the events recalled.[47] Other studies, such as those published in the "Bologna-school's" *History of Vatican II,*[48] must be critiqued similarly, taking into account any prevailing ecclesiological/political ideology. The Italian account of Enrico Cattaneo (1912–86), a consulter to the *Consilium,* is a useful reference.[49] *The Reform of the Roman Rite: Its Problems and Background,* by Klaus Gamber (1919–89), is an important critical study.

One exemplary study of an aspect of the reform is that of Professor Lauren Pristas, *The Collects of the Roman Missals: A Comparative Study of the Sundays in Proper Seasons before and after the Second Vatican Council.*[50] Her painstaking work, involving careful linguistic and historical analysis, demonstrates a clear grasp of the intent of the Constitution, of the influence of the *Consilium,* and of the intentional theological difference if not divergence in the Latin texts of the collects of the reformed missal. Her work provides one part of the answer to the question, "Continuity or rupture?"

Pristas' study also demonstrates the imposition of contemporary theological ideas on the liturgical reform which have tenuous links at best with the theology of the Constitution itself (articles 5–13). The years between 1963 and 1970 were ones of acute theological turbulence. This historical reality, combined with the ongoing fluid interpretation of the "event" or "spirit" of Vatican II, as well as a desire to be "open to the world" and a self-conscious "ecumenical sensitivity," are also factors that must be studied in assessing the products of the liturgical reform. In this task, journals and other popular literature can be particularly helpful in identifying the influences and, as ever, archival research can shed light on its exact impact on the liturgical reform.

Conclusion

It is the purpose of this chapter to underline the importance of the question of "Continuity or Rupture?" in the liturgical reform and to propose a methodology for its study. A scholarly response must be one based on the sources themselves and that makes the necessary distinctions. The liturgical reform must be assessed by the criteria laid down by the Council itself in its Constitution on the Sacred Liturgy, not by any eisogesis of it.

Such a response must also be one that not only considers the different ritual elements of the reform, but which also takes into account realities which are integral to it. Certainly, the theological content of the reformed rites ranks highly in this task, but factors including liturgical art, music, architecture, etc., are realities which also bespeak reform in continuity, or rupture, and are important elements for study.

Additionally, one may apply this question to the psychological and cultural impact of the reform: the experience of the reform in the local Churches is an important reality. Whilst this consideration moves beyond the scope of assessing the reform as promulgated, it opens up significant areas for further research.

The vision of Council Fathers such as Bishop Elchinger, who believed that the liturgical reform would involve an "evolution" that would be "sound and prudent," not "a complete revolution of the Order of Mass" or "the death of the Roman rite," differs sharply from the view of the prominent French liturgist Joseph Gelineau SJ (1920–2008), speaking but seven years after the appearance of the Missal of Paul VI: "In fact it is a different liturgy of the Mass. We must say it plainly: the Roman rite as we knew it exists no longer. It is [destroyed (détruit)]. Some walls of the structure have fallen, others have been altered; we can look at it as a ruin or the partial foundation of a new building."[51]

If Gelineau is right, there is *prima facie* evidence of rupture. The exact ritual, theological and cultural extent of this difference, and its causes, demand much patient scholarship—scholarship which will serve the coming generations in assessing not just recent liturgical history, but also appropriate paths for the Roman rite in the future.

Notes

1　Tito Casini, *The Torn Tunic: Letter of a Catholic on the Liturgical Reform* (Rome: Fidelity Books, 1967). See also: Annibale Bugnini CM, *The Reform of the Liturgy 1948–1970* (Collegeville: Liturgical Press, 1990), chapter 20 "Opposition."

2　It is said that many other cardinals and bishops had agreed to sign the presentation of the study, but withdrew when this became public; cf. Anthony Cekada, ed., *The Ottaviani Intervention: Short Critical Study of the New Order of Mass* (Rockford: TAN Books and Publishers, 1992), pp. 3–4.

3　Ibid., pp. 27–8.

4　*Acta Synodalia Sacrosancti Concilii Oecumenici Vaticani II: vol II pars IV* (Vatican City: Typis Polyglottis Vaticanis, 1973) p. 441. The signature of Cardinal Bacci is not recorded.

5　Foreword, Casini, *The Torn Tunic*, p. iii.

6　See: Alcuin Reid, *A Bitter Trial: Evelyn Waugh and John Carmel Cardinal Heenan on the Liturgical Changes*, 3rd edn (San Francisco: Ignatius Press, 2011). Of particular note is the 1971 petition to Paul VI by distinguished scholars, writers, artists and historians reproduced in an appendix, pp. 120–3.

7　Cf. Bugnini, *The Reform of the Liturgy*, pp. 257–9.

8　Michael Davies' *Pope Paul's New Mass* (Dickinson, Texas: Angelus Press, 1980) chronicles many contemporary reports and opinions. One of the most interesting publications of the period is: Roger P. Kuhn, *The Mass Reformed: A New Draft Liturgy of the Mass with Commentary* (Notre Dame: Catholic Action Office, 1965).

9　John Eppstein, *Has the Catholic Church Gone Mad?* (London: Catholic Book Club, 1973), p. 74. In spite of the title the author's consideration of the liturgical reform is measured.

10　Lefebvre's remarks from 1965 demonstrated that he was not opposed to liturgical reform: see Alcuin Reid, "Active Participation and Pastoral Adaptation" in: *Liturgy, Participation and Sacred Music* (Rochester: CIEL UK, 2006), pp. 35–50.

11　"Was nach dem Konzil weithin geschehen ist, bedeutet etwas ganz anderes: An die Stelle der gewordenen Liturgie hat man die gemachte Liturgie gesetzt. Man ist aus dem lebendigen Prozess des Wachsens und Werdens heraus umgestiegen in das Machen. Man wollte nicht mehr das organische Werden und Reifen des durch die Jahrhunderte hin Lebendigen fortführen, sondern setzte an dessen Stelle—nach dem Muster technischer Produktion—das Machen, das platte Produkt des Augenblicks;" in: Wilhelm Nyssen. ed., *Simandron. Der Wachklopfer. Gedenkschrift für Klaus Gamber (1919-1989)* (Köln: Luthe Verlag, 1989), pp. 14-15. The English text given here was published on the cover of: Klaus Gamber, *The Reform of the Roman Rite: Its Problems and Background* (San Juan Capistrano & Harrison NY: Una Voce Press & Foundation for Catholic Reform, 1993). A later translation is given in JRCW 11, pp. 537-8.

12 For the development of the text, the interventions of the Council Fathers and the clarificatory *Declarationes* provided by the Conciliar Liturgical Commission, see: Francisco Gil Hellín, *Concilii Vaticani II Synopsis: Constitutio de Sacra Liturgia Sacrosanctum Concilium* (Vatican City: Libreria Editrice Vaticana, 2003).

13 John F. Baldovin SJ, *Reforming the Liturgy: A Response to the Critics* (Collegeville: Liturgical Press, 2008), pp. 102, 139. For further examples of the assertion of discontinuity see also pp. 43, 59, 100, 103, 116, 130, 137.

14 Nathan D. Mitchell, "Back to the Future?" *Worship* 73 (1999), pp. 60-9 (p. 68).

15 Baldovin, *Reforming the Liturgy*, p. 157.

16 Robert Mickens, "Mickens on SSPX" posted on the blog *In All Things* of the journal *America*, January 30, 2009.

17 Alcuin Reid, *The Organic Development of the Liturgy: The Principles of Liturgical Reform and Their Relation to the Twentieth Century Liturgical Movement Prior to the Second Vatican Council*, 2nd edn (San Francisco: Ignatius Press, 2005). A consideration of scholarly responses to this work will appear in *Continuity or Rupture: A Study of the Liturgical Reform of the Second Vatican Council* (forthcoming).

18 The unpublished doctoral thesis of Ole Martin Stamnestro, "The liturgical reforms of the Second Vatican Council considered in the light of the preceding liturgical movement" (University of Oxford, 2008), seeks to assert the priority of ecclesiastical authority over the principle of organic development. This contrasts with the stance of the *Catechism of the Catholic Church*, § 1125: "Even the supreme authority in the Church may not change the Liturgy arbitrarily, but only in the obedience of faith and with religious respect for the mystery of the Liturgy," and with that of Joseph Cardinal Ratzinger: "The pope's authority is bound to the Tradition of faith, and that also applies to the Liturgy. It is not 'manufactured' by the authorities. Even the pope can only be a humble servant of its lawful development and abiding integrity and identity . . .," *The Spirit of the Liturgy*, Ignatius Press, 2000, p. 166; JRCW 11, p. 103. The same principle was asserted in respect of all acts of ecclesiastical authority in the homily of Benedict XVI in the Lateran Basilica on the occasion of his taking possession of the chair of the Bishop of Rome on May 7, 2005: "The Pope is not an absolute monarch whose thoughts and desires are law. On the contrary: the Pope's ministry is a guarantee of obedience to Christ and to his Word. He must not proclaim his own ideas, but rather constantly bind himself and the Church to obedience to God's Word, in the face of every attempt to adapt it or water it down, and every form of opportunism." The legitimate, organic development of the Sacred Liturgy, as a constituent element of Tradition, is not subject to ecclesiastical authority; authority is at its service, which service includes ensuring that development is organic.

19 As a comparison of texts of "Eucharistic Prayer II" and the so-called "Anaphora of Hippolytus" demonstrates.

20 Cf. John F. Baldovin SJ, "*Sacrosanctum Concilium* and the Reform of the Liturgy: Forty-Five Years Later," *Studia Liturgia* 39 (2009), pp. 145–57 (p. 146). The scholarship upon which Baldovin relies in fact demonstrates the organic development of the Roman rite in history and does not support his assertion that "serious and radical reform of the liturgy in the Western Church did not begin in the 1960s and 1970s" (p. 145).

21 Massimo Faggioli, *True Reform: Liturgy and Ecclesiology in Sacrosanctum Concilium*, (Collegeville: Liturgical Press, 2012), p. 3.

22 See: ibid., p. 4.

23 To interpret the words of article 4 "the sacred Council declares that holy Mother Church holds all lawfully acknowledged rites to be of equal right and dignity; that she wishes to preserve them in the future and foster them in every way," as an assertion that the Council envisaged a new rite but nonetheless wished to preserve or "protect" the *Missale Romanum* 1962 is historically inaccurate. The text refers primarily to the Eastern rites and the non-Roman Latin rites (of the primatial sees or religious orders).

24 See: Joseph Cardinal Ratzinger, Homily: "Mary and Martha," Alcuin Reid (ed.), *Looking Again at the Question of the Liturgy* (Farnborough: St Michael's Abbey Press, 2003), pp. 13–15.

25 On article 23 see: Alcuin Reid, "*Sacrosanctum Concilium* and the Organic Development of the Liturgy," Uwe Michael Lang (ed.), *The Genius of the Roman Rite: Historical, Theological, and Pastoral Perspectives on Catholic Liturgy* (Chicago: Hillenbrand Books, 2010), pp. 198–215.

26 As Dom Beauduin asserted: "The whole priestly influence is exercised on the members of the Church only by means of sensible, authentic forms, which are its vehicle. Formulas, readings, chants, rites, material elements, in short, all the externals of the Liturgy, are indispensable for sharing in the thoughts, the teachings, the acts of adoration, the sentiments, the graces which Christ and His visible priesthood destine for us. Hence, to minimize this visible contact under the pretext that the soul can then better achieve something interior, or that invisible communion suffices, is at the same time to diminish the priestly influence of the hierarchy and consequently the action of Christ in our souls;" Lambert Beauduin OSB, *Liturgy: The Life of the Church* 3rd edn (Farnborough: St Michael's Abbey Press, 2002), p. 17.

27 J.D. Crichton, *The Church's Worship* (London: Geoffrey Chapman, 1965), p. 90. In fact, Vagaggini is asserting that the principle of ritual perspicacity is at the service of actual participation, which latter is the "principio dei principi di ogni riforma liturgica;" cf. "I principia generali della riforma liturgica approvati dal Concilio," *L'Osservatore Romano*, December 8, 1963, p. 3.

28 See: Alcuin Reid, "Noble simplicity revisited," D. Vincent Twomey SVD & Janet E. Rutherford (eds), *Benedict XVI and Beauty in Sacred Art and Architecture* (Dublin & New York: Four Courts & Scepter, 2011), pp. 94–111.

29 I have attempted to do this in respect of chapter VI (on Sacred Music) in: Alcuin Reid, "*Ut mens nostra concordet voci nostrae*: Sacred Music and Actual Participation in the Liturgy," Janet E. Rutherford (ed.), *Benedict XVI and Beauty in Sacred Music* (Dublin & New York: Four Courts & Scepter, 2012), pp. 93–126. Some notes in this publication are not correctly reproduced. A complete version appears in *Sacred Music* 139 (2012), pp. 8–33.

30 Angelo Lameri, ed., *La « Pontificia Commisio de sacra liturgia praeparatoria Concilii Vaticani II » Documenti, Testi, Verbali* (BELS, 2013). See also: Carlo Braga CM, "La *Sacrosanctum Concilium* nei lavori della Commissione Preparatoria," *Notitiæ* 20 (1984), pp. 87–134.

31 "Propono ut textus huis numeri omnino servetur sed ut clarificetur publicatione integrae declarationis a commissione praeparatoria sub isto numero elaboratae. Ita mente reficerentur qui timent universam Ordinis Missæ revolutionem et mortem ritus romani. Haec declaratio etenim nobis proponit non revolutionem sed tantum evolutionem—evolutionem pastoralem—et quidam sanam et prudentem." *Acta Synodalia Sacrosancti Concilii Oecumenici Vaticani II*, vol. I part II, (Vatican City: Typis Polyglottis Vaticanis, 1970) p. 80.

32 Ibid., p. 121.

33 *Acta Synodalia Sacrosancti Concilii Oecumenici Vaticani II*, vol. II part II (Vatican City: Typis Polyglottis Vaticanis, 1972), p. 289.

34 See: Joseph A. Jungmann SJ, "Constitution on the Sacred Liturgy" Herbert Vorgrimler (ed.), *Commentary on the Documents of Vatican II*, vol. I (London & New York: Burns & Oates & Herder & Herder, 1967), pp. 1–87 (pp. 36–7).

35 *Ordo Missæ: Ritus Servandus in Celebratione Missæ et De Defectibus in Celebratione Missæ Occurrentibus*, Editio Typica (Vatican City: Typis Polyglottis Vaticanis, 1965). Whilst this *Ordo Missæ* is decared an "editio typica," it is to be noted that no such edition of a "1965 Missal" exists. The closest typical editions are 1962 and 1970. The various and varying missals published from 1965 are the result of editorial choices made locally. Professor Hans-Jürgen Feulner of the University of Vienna has promoted research into the various missals published in the wake of the 1965 *Ordo Missæ*.

36 See: Marizio Barba, *La riforma conciliare dell' "Ordo Missæ,"* 2nd edn (BELS, 2008), pp. 157–65. The difference between the 1965 *Ordo Missæ* and those of the working drafts ("schemata") of the *Consilium* preceding or succeeding it (n. 44, October 22, 1964; n. 106, September 19, 1965; Barba, pp.365–9, 375–87), is striking.

37 See: Alcuin Reid, "*Sacrosanctum Concilium* and the Reform of the *Ordo Missæ,"* Antiphon, 10 (2006), pp. 277–95.

38 See: Roberto de Mattei, *The Second Vatican Council: An Unwritten Story* (Fitzwilliam NH: Loreto Publications, 2012), pp. xxi–xxiv.

39 Bugnini, *The Reform of the Liturgy*, p. 110.

40 Ibid., p. 448.

41 See also: Cipriano Vagaggini, *The Canon of the Mass and Liturgical Reform* (London: Geoffrey Chapman, 1967).

42 See: Congregatio de Cultu Divino et Disciplina Sacramentorum, *Notitiae: Indices 1965–2004*, (Vatican City: Libreria Editrice Vaticana, 2007).

43 See: Barba, *La riforma conciliare dell' "Ordo Missæ,"* Appendix I.

44 This has been studied in a 2012 doctoral dissertation. See the published extract: Christiaan W. Kappes, *The 'Missa Normative' of 1967: Its History and Principles as Applied to the Liturgy of the Mass*, Excerptum (Pontificum Athaneum S. Anselmi de Urbe, Pontificum Institutum Liturgicum: Rome, 2012).

45 "Sanctitas Sua putat Sibi opus non esse in mentem revocare gravitatem muneris vobis demandati, cum Ipsi probe comperta sit officii conscientia, qua in exemplum praestatis. Hoc tantummodo vos commonere disiderat, nempe in vos omnium sacrorum Pastorum et christifidelem oculos converses esse, qui quidem postulant ut labores vestri non properanter, sed sapienter ac prudenter procedant, et vos ne privatis inclinationibus, etsi consideratione dignis, in modos expendendis indulgeatis, sed prae oculis semper habeatis necessitates Populi Dei, quales suffragia Synodi patefecerunt."

46 "In reformationem Missæ bene attendendum est ne ritus depauperetur, sive quoad formulas, sive quoad gestus. Quaedam formulae in se expressivae, ut. ex.gr. quaedam formulae ad Offertorium, vel Confiteor, sunt retinendae. Formulae non sunt reciendae

ex eo quod non sunt antiquissimae: omni aetate Ecclesia de thesauro suo profert et servat in Missa pretiosas margaritas: hac ratione et novae formulae, si quae dignae sint, admittuntur. Attamen formulae aliorum saeculorum, ex.gr. mediae aetatis, ne despiciantur. Super hos conceptus ter rediit sermo Sumi Pontificis quasi cum quadam praeoccupatione."

47 See: Alcuin Reid, "The Fathers of Vatican II and the Revised Mass: Results of a Survey," *Antiphon* 10 (2006), pp. 170–90.

48 See: Guiseppe Alberigo & Joseph A. Komonchak, eds, *History of Vatican II*, 5 vols (Maryknoll & Leuven: Orbis & Peeters, 1995–2006). The differing views in Agostino Marchetto, *The Second Vatican Council: A Counterpoint for the History of the Council* (Scranton: University of Scranton Press, 2010) and De Mattei, *The Second Vatican Council: An Unwritten Story*, should be considered.

49 Enrico Cattaneo, *Il culto cristiano in occidente: Note storiche* (BELS, 2003), pp. 518–94.

50 Lauren Pristas, *The Collects of the Roman Missals: A Comparative Study of the Sundays in Proper Seasons before and after the Second Vatican Council* (London: T&T Clark, 2013).

51 Joseph Gelineau SJ, *The Liturgy Today and Tomorrow* (London, New York & Toronto: Darton, Longman & Todd, Paulist Press & Ramsey, 1978) p. 11. Translation corrected to accord with the orginal: *Demain La Liturgie* (Paris: Cerf, 1977) p. 10.

Select bibliography

Documents of the Holy See

Acta Synodalia Sacrosancti Concilii Oecumenici Vaticani II, vols I & II (Vatican City: Typis Polyglottis Vaticanis, 1970–73).

Gil Hellín, Francisco, *Concilii Vaticani II Synopsis: Constitutio de Sacra Liturgia Sacrosanctum Concilium* (Vatican City: Liberia Editrice Vaticana, 2003).

ICEL, *Documents on the Liturgy: 1963-1979* (DOL)

Kaczynski, Reiner, *Enchiridion Documentorum Instaurationis Liturgicae,* vol. I 1963–73 (Rome: Centro Liturgico Vincenziano, 1990).

Seasoltz, Kevin, OSB, *The New Liturgy: A Documentation 1903-1965* (NL)

Other sources

Baraúna, William, OFM (ed.), *The Liturgy of Vatican II,* 2 vols (Chicago: Franciscan Herald Press, 1966).

Botte, Bernard, OSB, *From Silence to Participation: An Insider's View of Liturgical Renewal* (Washington DC: Pastoral Press, 1988).

Bouyer, Louis, *Mémoires* (Paris: Cerf, 2014).

—— ET: *The Memoirs of Louis Bouyer* (Kettering, OH: Angelico Press, 2015).

Bugnini, Annibale, CM, *The Reform of the Liturgy 1948-1975* (Collegeville: Liturgical Press, 1990).

—— *La riforma liturgica 1948-1975,* 2nd edn (BELS, 1997).

—— & Braga, Carlo, CM, *The Commentary and the Instruction on the Sacred Liturgy* (New York: Benzinger, 1965).

Flannery, Austin, OP, *Vatican II: The Liturgy Constitution* (Dublin: Scepter, 1964).

Gamber, Klaus, *The Reform of the Roman Rite: Its Problems and Background* (San Juan Capistrano CA & Harrison NY: Una Voce Press & Foundation for Catholic Reform, 1993; Fort Collins: Roman Catholic Books, 2006).

Giampietro, Nicola, *The Development of the Liturgical Reform: As Seen by Cardinal Ferdinando Antonelli from 1948–1970* (Fort Collins: Roman Catholic Books, 2009).

Jungmann, Joseph A., SJ, "Constitution on the Sacred Liturgy," Vorgrimler, Herbert (ed.), *Commentary on the Documents of Vatican II*, vol. I (London & New York: Burns & Oates, Herder & Herder, 1967), pp. 1–87.

Lameri, Angelo (ed.), *La « Pontificia Commisio de sacra liturgia praeparatoria Concilii Vaticani II » Documenti, Testi, Verbali* (BELS, 2013).

Marini, Piero, *A Challenging Reform: Realizing the Vision of the Liturgical Renewal* (Collegeville: Liturgical Press, 2007).

McManus, Frederick R., *Sacramental Liturgy* (New York: Herder & Herder, 1967).

O'Connell, J.B., *Active Sharing in Public Worship* (London: Burns & Oates, 1964).

Schmidt, Herman, SJ, *La Consitituion de la Sainte Liturgie* (Brussels: Éditions Lumen Vitae, 1966).

Wagner, Johannes, *Mein Weg zur Liturgierform 1936–1986* (Freiburg, Basel & Wien: Herder, 1993).

Chapter 15

A REFORM OF THE REFORM?

Thomas Kocik

Introduction

It is not easy to define what the phrase "reform of the reform" designates other than in very general terms. For present purposes we shall think of it as a movement in Latin-rite Catholicism dating to the mid-1990s and consisting of loosely affiliated organizations and individuals united around the goal of redirecting the reform of Roman rite liturgy originating from the Second Vatican Council. The advocates of a "reform of the reform" generally regard the Council's Constitution on the Sacred Liturgy, *Sacrosanctum Concilium* of 1963, as having been justifiable and pastorally well oriented—the culmination of the sound ideals of the preconciliar liturgical movement. At the same time, they maintain that the official liturgical reform that followed Vatican II involved changes that were unwarranted by the Council and that, in many instances, break with liturgical and theological tradition.

For this reason, they believe it is necessary to reshape Catholic liturgical practice according to the original intentions of the Council Fathers and in the light of postconciliar experience. The "reform of the reform" can thus be understood, and possibly justified, as a response to the call of Joseph Cardinal Ratzinger, the future Pope Benedict XVI, for "a new Liturgical Movement, which will call to life the real heritage of the Second Vatican Council."[1]

This chapter presents an anatomy of the "reform of the reform" movement: its origins and representative figures, its possible methodologies and the specific proposals advanced in its interests (if not explicitly in its name), and its place among other strategies for further development of the Roman rite. Criticisms leveled at the movement will also be addressed, before concluding with a consideration of the movement's practical feasibility.

I. A prehistory of the movement

To understand the impetus for a "reform of the reform" it is useful to begin by recalling in broad strokes what the Second Vatican Council mandated with regard to liturgical renewal and the changes that occurred in response to that mandate. With the approval of *Sacrosanctum Concilium* on November 22, 1963 and its subsequent promulgation on December 4 of the same year, an ecumenical council had endorsed the most important fruits of the liturgical movement's research and made them the common aims of the Church. A glance at this document reveals its principal concern for the inner spirit or essence of the liturgy from which the outer forms grow.

Echoing Pius XII's encyclical *Mediator Dei* (November 20, 1947), the Constitution describes the liturgy as "an exercise of the priestly office of Jesus Christ" involving the whole Mystical Body of Christ, both the Head and its members (n. 7).[2] As such, "the liturgy is the summit toward which the activity of the Church is directed; it is also the fount from which all her power flows" (n. 10). Continuing on the path opened up by St Pius X in his motu proprio on sacred music, *Tra le sollecitudini* (November 22, 1903), it points to the "full and active participation by all the people" as "the aim to be considered before all else" (n. 14). In liturgical celebrations, the lay faithful are not merely spectators watching or an audience listening. All the faithful, clergy and laity alike, have in virtue of baptism their proper liturgical roles to carry out (n. 28).

The Council Fathers cautioned that the renewal of the liturgy needed to be done in organic continuity with the past (n. 23) and must preserve the "substantial unity" of the Roman rite (n. 38). The "substance" or "substantial unity" denotes what remains the same even in the course of modification, so that an identity of the rite across time can be affirmed and perceived. To understand this principle of development, a comparison can be made with the human body, which changes considerably in appearance and in what it can physically manage as it ages; whatever these changes, the person remains the same.

If the Church's "liturgy is made up of unchangeable elements divinely instituted" there are also "elements subject to change" (n. 21). These latter elements "not only may be changed but ought to be changed with the passage of time, if they have suffered from the intrusion of anything out of harmony with the inner nature of the liturgy or have become less suitable." Moreover, "In this restoration both texts and rites should be drawn up so as to express more clearly the holy things which they signify," and the Christian faithful, "as far as is possible, should be able to understand them with ease and take part in them fully, actively, and as a community" (n. 21). Hence, "The rites should be distinguished by a noble simplicity": brief, clear, without "useless repetitions" and not normally requiring much explanation (n. 34).

Article 50 applies these principles to the very jewel in the crown on the Church's liturgy: "The rite of the Mass is to be revised in such a way that the intrinsic nature and purpose of its several parts, as well as the connection between them, may be more clearly manifested, and that devout and active participation by the faithful may be more easily achieved." How this was to be done is subsequently spelled out: "For this purpose the rites are to be simplified, due care being taken to preserve their substance. Parts which with the passage of time came to be duplicated, or were added with little advantage, are to be omitted. Other parts which suffered loss through accidents of history are to be restored to the vigor they had in the days of the holy Fathers, as may seem useful or necessary" (n. 50).

A greater portion of Scripture was to be read, "so that a richer fare may be provided for the faithful at the table of God's word" (n. 51). The homily was not to be omitted on days of precept without a serious reason (n. 52). General intercessions or "bidding prayers" were to be offered especially on days of precept (n. 53). A suitable place was to be allotted to the vernacular, provided that the faithful may still be able "to say or to sing together in Latin those parts of the Ordinary of the Mass which pertain to them" (n 54). It was recommended that Communion be administered using hosts consecrated at the same Mass, and that on special occasions the faithful receive Communion under both species (n. 55). Pastors were to instruct the faithful to take part in the entire Mass, both the liturgy of the Word and the eucharistic liturgy proper (n. 56). Permission was extended to priests to concelebrate Mass on specific occasions (n. 57); a rite of concelebration was to be drawn up and inserted into the Roman missal and Roman pontifical (n. 58).

In 1964, Pope Paul VI established the *Consilium ad Exsequendam Constitutionem de Sacra Liturgia* ("the *Consilium*"), the committee tasked with implementing the reform called for by the Constitution. Here we pass from principles authenticated by the Council to prudential application of those principles by an international body of bishops and experts. From the beginning, battles ensued over how much change was too much and, perhaps equally important, who got to decide. Early on, Paul VI backed a broadly progressive vision in terms of both content (for example, supporting a move into the vernacular languages more sweeping than the Council envisioned) and process (letting episcopal conferences rather than Rome call many of the plays).[3]

The Council made possible some immediate changes to the missal of St Pius V in its most recent edition, the one approved by St John XXIII in 1962.[4] On September 26, 1964, the Sacred Congregation of Rites and the *Consilium* issued *Inter œcumenici*, the first instruction on the implementation of the Constitution. The instruction permits some use of the vernacular and the celebration of Mass "facing the people." In the light of this document, a revised Order of Mass was promulgated in early 1965, taking effect before the close of the Council. Among the many changes found in the 1965 *Ordo Missæ*, the prayers at the foot of the altar are truncated, several signs of the cross and the so-called last Gospel are omitted, in public Masses the celebrant may go to the *sedilia* after first kissing the altar and the celebrant does not read privately the texts of chants if they are sung or read by another. More radical simplification came in the wake of the second instruction, *Tres abhinc annos* (May 4, 1967): there are even fewer signs of the cross and kisses of the altar, the whole canon may be prayed aloud, the "private" Communion of the priest before the people is abolished and the maniple need not be worn. In May 1968 three newly composed eucharistic prayers were authorized as alternatives to the 1,500-year-old Roman canon.

On April 3, 1969, Paul VI promulgated a new *Ordo Missæ*, which took effect the First Sunday of Advent of that year, although the Roman missal incorporating this new *Ordo* was not published until March 26, 1970. Until now the structure of the

Roman Mass remained virtually indistinguishable from that of the four previous centuries. By contrast, the missal of Paul VI breaks with the pattern of precise rubrics in favor of variations and options. Moreover, it significantly adds to and subtracts from the traditional Order of Mass. The prayers accompanying the offering of the bread and wine are altogether different, and the "prayer over the offerings" (formerly the "secret") is prayed aloud. In the institution narrative, the clause "quod pro vobis tradetur" has been added after the consecration of the bread; after the consecration of the wine, "Haec quotiescumque faceritis, in mei memoriam facietis" is replaced by "HOC FACITE IN MEAM COMMEMORATIONEM" (in capitals), no longer preceded but followed by the "Mysterium fidei," which cues the people's memorial acclamation. The 1970 missal contains the new eucharistic prayers authorized in 1968.[5] Gone are what remained of the prayers at the foot of the altar, the *Aufer a nobis* (as the priest ascends to the altar), the *Oramus te, Domine* (as the priest kisses the altar for the first time), the prayers for the blessing of incense and the censing of the gifts and altar, and the *Placeat tibi* (before the final blessing).

More significant both quantitatively and qualitatively are the changes in the *Proprium Missæ*: quantitatively, in that only 17 percent of the orations (collects, secrets, and postcommunions) in the 1962 missal were brought over intact into the missal of 1970, although the latter provides many more prefaces, especially for feast-days, liturgical seasons, and special occasions;[6] qualitatively, in that the *Consilium* reformers systematically expunged or edited prayers deemed too negative or jarring to perceived modern sensibilities.[7]

The number of biblical readings was expanded such that every Mass now has three obligatory readings, the first of which is usually taken from the Old Testament. In addition, the 1969 Order of Readings for Mass presents a three-year cycle of Sunday readings. Its abandoning of the very ancient annual Roman cycle of Sunday epistles and gospels has been criticized for obliterating the immemorial connection between Sundays and their pericopes.[8]

The Roman calendar, which already had undergone revision in phases between 1955 and 1960, was drastically reorganized in 1969. The *Consilium* removed many of the features of the traditional Proper of Seasons (gone are the ember days, Epiphanytide, Septuagesima, Passiontide, and the octave of Pentecost). A number of saints' days were removed and shifted (sometimes by only one day) for reasons worthy in themselves (e.g. to give priority to the ferial days of Advent and Lent), but, as some critics claim, at the cost of weakening the link between faith and culture.[9] As regards the Church's official daily prayer, it has been argued that the Roman Office, already lethally wounded in the reform of St Pius X, was effectively killed with the abandonment of its three essential components—the structure of the hours, the distribution of the psalms, and the stock material of the antiphonary; thus its successor, the Liturgy of the Hours of 1971, represents something altogether different.[10]

We should also note the many changes not proceeding directly from the decisions of the Council. In churches the world over, portable altars were positioned in front of existing altars to allow for Mass "facing the people" (*Inter œcumenici* permits but does not prescribe this), and altar rails were removed (often at considerable expense) as greater numbers of people stood to receive Communion. By 1970, the liturgy in most parishes was wholly in the vernacular, despite the Constitution's prescription that "the use of the Latin language, with due respect to particular law, is to be preserved in the Latin rites" (n. 36 §1; cf. n. 54, quoted above). Paul VI's motu proprio *Ministeria quædam* (August 15, 1972) suppressed the ancient order of subdeacon and the other minor orders (in the Latin Church only) and opened their appertaining liturgical roles to laymen. By the late 1970s, the hitherto long-defunct option of receiving Communion in the hand was tolerated by indult in many countries. Subsequent concessions by the Holy See permit the presence of cremated remains at funeral Masses (1997 in the USA) and female altar servers (1994).[11]

It is understandable that the liturgical reform could be perceived (to the satisfaction of some and the disquiet of others) as a revolution rather than a renovation. The Council Fathers could not have anticipated that in the space of a few years the backbone of the existing Roman rite would be broken, nor could they have anticipated the departures from longstanding disciplines that successive permissions would involve.

How did this state of affairs come about? Much of the liturgy reform was carried out in the decade following Vatican II, a time of great cultural upheaval in the West. Where the liberationist ideologies of the 1960s and the dynamics of secularization took hold, the liturgy was emptied of a sense of mystery, destabilized by arbitrary distortions and gimmickry, or made a platform for radical feminism (North America, chiefly) and "liberation theology" (Latin America). The complete vernacularization of worship and the "turning around" of altars encouraged priests to adopt a conversational tone for the sake of "engaging" the assembly, with the effect that too often the sacred proceedings appeared to be primarily a didactic affair with little direct address to God.

II. The movement crystallizes

It is difficult to date the genesis of the "reform of the reform" as a distinct category of ongoing liturgical renewal. A key to its approach, however, can be found as early as 1985. While St John Paul II (1978–2005) strove to reinvigorate the Church doctrinally and morally, address aberrant practices in the celebration of the Eucharist, and pastorally accommodate those Catholics who preferred the older Latin forms of worship,[12] Cardinal Ratzinger, who in 1981 was appointed Prefect of the Congregation for the Doctrine of the Faith, worked in a complementary manner to open up a renewed and frank discussion about the liturgy. Since his time as a professor of theology, Ratzinger had lamented the banality that impoverished liturgical practice in many places. In a book-length interview with the cardinal, the Italian journalist Vittorio Messori notes that it is in the liturgy sphere where Ratzinger finds "one of the clearest examples of the contrast between what the authentic text of Vatican II says and the way in which it has been understood and applied."[13] Soon after, Ratzinger began to speak of the need for a new phase of the liturgical movement, a "reform of the reform." Such candor from one so highly placed naturally encouraged, and perhaps inspired, efforts to publicize the problems with the liturgical reform and to find avenues for an eventual solution.

In 1995, two independent organizations were established in the United States on principles that reflect the tension between the positive gains of the reform and its troublesome aspects. The Adoremus Society for the Renewal of the Sacred Liturgy, cofounded by Joseph Fessio SJ (Ratzinger's former student and the founder of Ignatius Press), aims to restore "the beauty, the holiness, and the power of the Church's rich liturgical tradition while remaining faithful to an organic, living process of renewal."[14] The society publishes a monthly newsletter, the *Adoremus Bulletin*. Monsignor M. Francis Mannion, then rector of the Cathedral of the Madeleine in Salt Lake City, Utah, founded the Society for Catholic Liturgy, a multidisciplinary association of Catholic pastors, scholars, architects, and musicians "committed to promoting scholarly study and practical renewal of the Church's liturgy." Its peer-reviewed journal, *Antiphon*, is published three times per year.[15]

If one event could signify the birth of the "reform of the reform" movement, it would be the conference held in June 1996 at Westminster College, Oxford, under the theme, "Beyond the prosaic: human culture and divine liturgy."[16] Its participants, constituted as the "Liturgy Forum" of the Centre for Faith and Culture, agreed upon a declaration that succinctly set forth the case for a revived liturgical movement. Briefly put, the Oxford Declaration on Liturgy speaks positively of the liturgical movement that culminated with the Constitution on the Sacred Liturgy, and recognizes as its good fruits "the introduction of the vernacular, the opening up of the treasure of the Sacred Scriptures, increased participation in the liturgy, and the enrichment of the process of Christian initiation."[17] At the same time, it denounces the thwarting of the Council's intentions by "powerful contrary forces, which could be described as bureaucratic, philistine, and secularist" (n. 1). A considerably impoverished liturgy stands in need of enrichment and resacralization (n. 3). This new phase of reform should emphasize the liturgy's eschatological quality, looking at the Eastern Christian liturgies for important perspectives. The declaration concludes with an appeal for a greater liturgical pluralism as well as a period of critical reflection grounded in "a thorough understanding of the organic nature of the liturgical traditions of the Church" (n. 6).

In the Jubilee Year 2000, Ignatius Press published an English translation of Ratzinger's masterwork, *The Spirit of the Liturgy*, in which Ratzinger (now famously) calls for "a 'liturgical movement,' a movement toward the liturgy and toward the right way of celebrating the liturgy, inwardly and outwardly."[18] At the French abbey of Fontgombault in July 2001, the cardinal presided over a conference that sought to lay the groundwork for a revived liturgical movement.[19] The symposium did not formulate short-term policies or juridical measures; rather, a vigorous discussion took place with a view toward a lasting and organic solution to the liturgical crisis.

III. Reforming the reform: premise, proponents, and proposals

The Rupture Premise

The "reform of the reform" takes its name probably, and its primary inspiration certainly, from Monsignor Klaus Gamber, co-founder and director of the liturgical institute at Regensburg.[20] A specialist in the ancient Roman liturgy and the Eastern Rites, Gamber used the phrase "reform of the reform" in a publication that appeared shortly before his death in 1989. Thereafter Cardinal Ratzinger repeated the phrase a number of times in lectures and interviews.[21]

All of Gamber's important contributions to liturgical scholarship remain in German except for a collection of essays published in 1993 under the title *The Reform of the Roman Liturgy: Its Problems and Background* and another collection originally published in 1972.[22] The 1993 book received great notoriety, in part because of the laudatory introduction by Ratzinger that appears in the 1992 French edition. The testimonial printed at the beginning of the English edition quotes Ratzinger's acclamation of Gamber as "the one scholar who, among the army of pseudo-liturgists, truly represents the thinking at the center of the Church."[23]

Gamber believed that the Mass needed reform because it had "become ossified into a form of rubricism,"[24] but that the conciliar reform was carried out too hastily and radically. His fundamental thesis is that the missal of Paul VI presents a new, totally different, rite rather than a renewal of the historic Roman rite as slowly developed over the course of many centuries. For Gamber, the *Ordo Missæ* of 1965 adequately expresses the organic reform envisaged by the Council. Significantly, Father (later Archbishop) Annibale Bugnini CM, secretary of the *Consilium* from 1964 to 1969, dismisses the 1965 *Ordo* as insufficient because its alterations were merely "peripheral," insisting that "a radical restoration" was necessary in order "to take an ancient building in hand and make it functional and habitable."[25]

Although Ratzinger has never criticized the missal of Paul VI *per se*, he did express misgivings about the way in which it was prepared and imposed, bluntly declaring: "We abandoned the organic, living process of growth and development over centuries, and replaced it—as in a manufacturing process—with a fabrication, a banal on-the-spot product."[26]

The contrast between "organic" development and "revolution" is also at the heart of Alcuin Reid's *The Organic Development of the Liturgy*, the second edition of which carries a preface by Cardinal Ratzinger. This is a much fuller consideration of the development of the Roman rite than Gamber's essays, and has a detailed discussion of the gradual changes that were made from the beginnings of the liturgical movement up to the eve of Vatican II.[27] For Reid, the principle of organic development is "the one fundamental principle of liturgical reform in which all Catholic liturgical reform finds its legitimacy."[28] He acknowledges that "organic development" is a metaphor, but points out that it is the metaphor employed by the Council in speaking of liturgical reform.

Gamber's "rupture premise" (to give it a name) is widely accepted by the critics of the reform. This is why the American liturgist John Baldovin SJ is correct in observing that the notion of a rupture in liturgical continuity is "a kind of prolegomenon to many of the criticisms brought against the reform."[29] As we shall see in Section IV below, the question of organic continuity is complex and requires important distinctions.

Who's who in the "reform of the reform"

Authors have attempted to characterize the "reform of the reform" by distinguishing groups with an individual profile.[30] The first of these typologies was presented in 1996 by Mgr Mannion at the aforementioned Oxford conference. It distinguishes five separate, albeit overlapping, "agendas for liturgical reform" operative in Anglophone Catholicism at that time:

1. advancing official reform;
2. restoring the preconciliar;
3. reforming the reform;
4. inculturating the reform;
5. recatholicizing the reform.

The category most relevant to this chapter is, of course, the third, but before we examine it let us briefly take note of the others. We may pass over the second agenda because its designation is self-explanatory.

What Mannion styles "advancing official reform" is the program for liturgical renewal set forth in Vatican II's Constitution on the Sacred Liturgy and institutionalized in the postconciliar *Consilium*, in the Congregation for Divine Worship (into which the *Consilium* was subsumed in 1969), and in the various initiatives undertaken by that and other Roman dicasteries and by the Pope himself. "The inspiration and ideal of the official agenda," says Mannion, "was the early Roman liturgy, the general features of which it sought to uncover and reappropriate in a methodologically scientific and historically critical manner."[31]

The agenda to inculturate the reform has its roots in the official reform, but seeks "a new phase of creativity ... by which the officially revised liturgical rites will be adapted to the various cultures of the world, including those of the modern West."[32] It claims theoretical legitimacy by reference to articles 37–40 of *Sacrosanctum Concilium*, which concern the adaptation of the Roman liturgical books to new and diverse cultural circumstances.[33] In academic circles especially, this agenda has been influenced by liberation and feminist theologies.

Mannion's preferred agenda, "recatholicizing the reform," seeks to recreate "the ethos that has traditionally imbued Catholic liturgy at its best—an ethos of beauty, majesty, spiritual profundity and solemnity." It does not seek to rewrite the liturgical books, but rather to "recover the sacred and the numinous in liturgical expression which will act as a corrective to the sterility and rationalism of much modern liturgical experience."[34]

We come now to the category of "reforming the reform." After discussing Gamber's foundational work, Mannion describes the central program espoused in this agenda as "a revisitation of the 1962 missal (and its 1965 and 1967 revisions) and a revision of the order of Mass in a less severe direction than actually occurred, in light of what proponents perceive to be the true intentions of the preconciliar liturgical movement and of the Second Vatican Counci."[35]

The noted proponents of a "reform of the reform" are a varied company of clergy and laity representing different academic disciplines. Mannion names Joseph Fessio, the Adoremus Society in general, and Aidan Nichols as representatives of the movement. A more recent typology adds to this group Joseph Ratzinger/ Benedict XVI, Klaus Gamber, László Dobszay, James Hitchcock (historian, St Louis University),[36] Kieran Flanagan (sociologist, University of Bristol),[37] and the present author.[38] Also meriting inclusion are the Italian priests Claudio Crescimanno and Nicola Bux, and the Sri Lankan cardinal Albert Malcolm Ranjith. While secretary of the Congregation for Divine Worship and the Discipline of the Sacraments, Archbishop Ranjith contributed forewords to two books of relevance to the "reform of the reform:" one by Monsignor Nicola Giampietro, an official of the same Vatican congregation, and the other by the abovementioned Claudio Crescimanno. In the former, he declares: "We need to identify and correct the erroneous orientations and decisions made, appreciate the liturgical tradition of the past courageously, and ensure that the Church is made to rediscover the true roots of its spiritual wealth and grandeur even if that means reforming the reform itself . . ."[39]

Methodology and proposals

Among those who advocate some kind of "reform of the reform" there are differences of opinion about where to begin and how to proceed. Some authors construe the project as a moderate revision of the preconciliar Roman liturgy in accordance with the directives of *Sacrosanctum Concilium* (Nichols, Harrison, Parsons).[40] Others see it as a realignment of the rite of Paul VI so that it more closely resembles the traditional rite (Ratzinger,[41] Elliott,[42] Barthe,[43] Fessio,[44] Dobszay[45]). Depending on one's perspective, the preconciliar Roman rite would serve either as a point of departure or as a point of orientation, since that is the rite which the Council sought to renew.

The first detailed scheme for a "reform of the reform" type of Mass was published serially in *Adoremus Bulletin,* which from November 1995 to January 1996 featured a tripartite essay by the Australian priest Brian W. Harrison OS. Using *Sacrosanctum Concilium* as a benchmark, Harrison considers how its relevant paragraphs might have been more faithfully applied to the 1962 missal. The Constitution's prescriptions for simplification, the elimination of certain repetitions, and a clear distinction to be made between the principal parts of the Mass: these he considers met by having the priest at the sedilia until the Liturgy of the Eucharist, eliminating the double *Confiteor,* shortening the *Lavabo* prayer, and dropping the Last Gospel as well as some of the signs of the cross. The result is something like the 1965 *Ordo Missæ,* but with a triennial cycle of Sunday readings (consisting of the epistle, responsorial psalm, and Gospel), an offertory procession, and exclusive use of the Roman canon in Latin.

In *Looking at the Liturgy*, the English Dominican theologian Aidan Nichols encourages "the prayerful, dignified, correct, and, where appropriate, solemn celebration" of the Mass of Paul VI, with parts of the Ordinary in Latin and the celebrant and people facing the same direction for the eucharistic prayer. "But none of this," he asserts, "will restore an adequate continuity with the textuality of the Roman rite in its earlier incarnation or with its ritual integrity as a unity of word and action." He therefore recommends that the traditional rite be reinstated as normative for the Church, but with the best aspects of the reform incorporated: a fuller cycle of readings, the new prefaces, and, where opportune, concelebration and Communion under both species.[46]

Nichols supports Harrison's scheme in the main, but would preserve those repetitive and seemingly excessive features of the rite that contribute to what the Anglican scholar Catherine Pickstock calls the "stammering" quality of the medieval liturgy.[47] He thus argues for the retention of the double *Confiteor* ("a beautiful expression of the sacramental fraternity of lay and ordained") and the Last Gospel ("a coda that sums up the meaning of the whole eucharistic action that has preceded it").[48] The other point on which Nichols is more "conservative" than Harrison concerns the lectionary. While he favors some augmentation of Scripture readings, he opposes a triennial (or even biennial) cycle of readings, for "Such cycles have as their inevitable result ... the obscuring of the properly integrated character of a liturgical day."[49]

The proposals suggested by Harrison and Nichols, along with other possible outlines for a re-reformed liturgy, were published in 2003 as appendices in the present author's book, *The Reform of the Reform? A Liturgical Debate: Reform or Return*. This volume presents an imaginary debate between a "reformer" (of the reform) and a "traditionalist" who argues for a wholesale return to the old Roman rite.

In the same year, a collection of essays was published by László Dobszay († 2011) under the title, *The Bugnini-Liturgy and the "Reform of the Reform."* Dobszay, a Hungarian musicologist and expert on medieval plainsong, elaborates a "reform of the reform" encompassing not only the Ordinary and Propers of the Mass but also the lectionary, the Roman calendar, the Divine Office, and the rites of Holy Week. With regard to the Mass, he proposes no essential change in the structure, texts, and ceremony as given in the old missal: the penitential act takes place before the introit; the traditional series of orations is augmented (not supplanted) by texts taken from the ancient sacramentaries for use *ad libitum* on weekdays; the prayer *super oblata* is prayed aloud, as are the doxology at the end of the canon and the embolism of the Lord's Prayer; the 1962 repertory of prefaces is moderately expanded; the Roman canon regains its privileged position, possibly by means of a rubric requiring its use on Sundays and feast-days, etc.

Outside the English-language field, Claudio Crescimanno has published his own vision of the Vatican II Mass in *La riforma della riforma liturgica* (2009). Like the other proposals we have noted, this one envisages Mass as it was celebrated in the immediate wake of the Council. The rite would be mostly in Latin, with the old offertory prayers restored and the Roman canon as the sole eucharistic prayer (spoken *sotto voce* and in Latin), but with vernacular readings taken from an enhanced lectionary. The general intercessions would follow a set form, and the priest would face towards the "liturgical" (if not geographical) east of the apse when addressing God.

IV. Criticisms directed at the movement

We turn now to criticisms brought against the "reform of the reform." Much of the criticism seems to be based on the assumption that the products of the liturgical reform constitute the renewal of the Roman rite as mandated by Vatican II and adopted (and adapted) by the national bishops' conferences. From this standpoint, any critical scrutiny of the reformed rites is denounced as a devaluation, if not an outright rejection, of the Council itself. The "reform of the reform" is thus identified with Tridentine restorationism or something close to it.[50]

Rita Ferrone contests Mannion's casting of the "reformers of the reform" as moderates. She points to Gamber's opinion that the "active participation" of the faithful intended by the Council could have been achieved without making major changes to the traditional rite, and from this concludes: "The only way that such an evaluation might appear justifiable is if the sedevacantists and Lefèbvrites loom very large on one's mental horizon."[51]

The conciliar historian Massimo Faggioli seeks to develop a critical understanding of the "reform of the reform" by making connections to the theological priorities of Vatican II. Without bothering to describe the "reform of the reform" on its own terms (i.e., on the basis of the views commonly held by its representatives), Faggioli portrays the movement as waffling "between nostalgia for the pre-Vatican II era and the undeniable contribution of *Sacrosanctum Concilium*."[52] When he uses the term "new liturgical movement" he modifies it with the damning epithet "anti-Vatican II."[53]

It is sometimes asserted that the liturgical reform has been the object of criticism stemming from a poor understanding of tradition. The "reform of the reform," its detractors say, is based on "a 'restorationist-revisionistic' reinterpretation" of reform,[54] or on an "a-historic vision" emblematic of postmodernity's "flee from history,"[55] or on an erroneous identification of revealed doctrine with particular (specifically, late-medieval) theories of eucharistic sacrifice and priesthood.[56]

From the perspective of comparative liturgy, Nathan Mitchell dismisses the notion of the "substantial unity of the Roman rite" (*Sacrosanctum Concilium*, 38) as a "myth" arising:

> From an uncritical assumption that the Roman liturgy has had, from time immemorial, an unbroken history of invariable rites and rubrics, texts and gestures, that everyone recognizes as *Roman* in origin, content and structure. But even the slightest acquaintance with Western liturgical history would expose this myth as little more than wishful thinking or euphoric recall. In one sense, there *is* no "Roman rite" and never has been.[57]

Now, one could contrast the ignorance of liturgy to which Mitchell ascribes the "myth" of substantial unity with László Dobszay's historically informed (and finely nuanced) definition of the "traditional Roman liturgy" as:

> The liturgical practice of Rome continuously living and organically developing from the 4th century at the latest (if its basic features are meant) and fixed in the 8th–9th centuries; which preserved its identity during diffusion both geographical (in cathedrals) and institutional (in orders), as also amid the local and temporal variations regulated by the liturgical hierarchy. Or more briefly put: the Roman rite is that which emerges in the uniformity of the organic temporal and coherent spatial variety of its daughter-liturgies.[58]

To be fair, Mitchell's qualifying phrase, "in one sense," acquits him of having set up a straw man. One *can* speak of a "Roman rite" (or, for that matter, a "Byzantine rite"), so long as one understands liturgical forms as they develop in their particular historical contexts while keeping in mind that the various rites occasionally influence one another.

Many of the prayers of the Paul VI missal were taken, either in whole or in some parts recycled, from early Roman sources which were not available when St Pius V, at the behest of the Council of Trent, codified the Roman curial rite as the basis for the Roman missal of 1570. It is possible, therefore, to defend the 1970 missal as a recapturing of older elements and thus "more traditional" than the "Tridentine" missals of 1570–1962. Even Gamber, as critical of the reform as he was, did not believe that the restoration of earlier liturgical forms necessarily constitutes a change in the rite.[59] But it must also be noted that the *Consilium* used those older texts, as well as many prayers it constructed *ex novo*, more often to replace the existing euchological material than to augment it.[60] In so doing, did the reformers violate the stipulation that "any new forms adopted should in some way grow organically from forms already existing" (*Sacrosanctum Concilium*, 23)?

The question can be debated interminably because no precise set of criteria exists for determining which texts and ceremonies must be retained in any given reform if substantial continuity is to be preserved. "Organic development" is a metaphor and, like all metaphors, is capable of various applications. Rita Ferrone, for instance, raises the possibility of an "organic connection" between ancient precedents and new forms on the basis of "an inner logic that inspired both practices" rather than on uninterrupted historical continuance.[61] By way of illustration, she relates the *Pascha annotinum*—the early Christian practice of commemorating the anniversary of baptism on or near the octave day of Easter by saying the Creed—to the renewal of baptismal promises practiced in the Easter Vigil as it was restored by Pius XII in 1951. She faults Alcuin Reid for not taking account of the *Pascha annotinum* in his study *The Organic Development of the Liturgy*, implying that had he done so he would not have deemed the public renewal of baptismal vows "totally novel."[62] On the other hand, the qualifier "from forms already existing"—that is, existing not simply as codified in ancient liturgical books but in extant liturgical practice—would seem to rule out Ferrone's elastic view of organic development.

V. Changed circumstances and future prospects

The liturgical landscape has changed markedly since the 1996 Oxford conference, largely because of two developments that took place in the latter half of St John Paul II's pontificate. First, the bishops who were appointed and the priests who were ordained in that period were on the whole more theologically and socially conservative than the previous generation, a reversal of the classic pattern.[63] If one is conservative in theological outlook, one will likely be less susceptible to interpretations of Vatican II that favor liturgical deformations.

Secondly, in the 1990s the Holy See began to exercise more direct control over liturgical reform.[64] *Varietates legitimæ*, the fourth instruction for applying *Sacrosanctum Concilium* (January 25, 1994), on liturgical inculturation, states that the aim of inculturation is not the creation of new families of rites, but rather the adaptation of the Roman rite to different cultures while maintaining its "substantial unity;" moreover, the Congregation for Divine Worship is to oversee proposals for inculturation. The concern with the Roman rite to the exclusion of any newer rite is reiterated in the fifth instruction, *Liturgiam authenticam* (March 28, 2001). This document affirms that the Roman rite itself is a precious example and instrument of liturgical adaptation to various cultures. It further requires that newly composed vernacular texts contain nothing inconsistent with the meaning, structure, or theological content of the texts found in the Latin typical editions of the liturgical books.[65] The revised English translation of the Roman missal approved by the Holy See in 2010 is an early fruit of *Liturgiam authenticam*.

With the election of Cardinal Ratzinger as Pope Benedict XVI in April 2005, conditions for a "reform of the reform" seemed more favorable than ever.[66] Unity in *cultus*, or continuity of liturgical forms over time, is a common thread running through his writings and statements on the liturgy over the years. Thus it was an evolutionary sensibility in renewal that motivated him, as the Pope, to state in his post-synodal apostolic exhortation *Sacramentum Caritatis* (February 22, 2007) that "the changes which the Council called for need to be understood within the overall unity of the historical development of the rite itself, without the introduction of artificial discontinuities" (art. 3).

That same sensibility motivated Benedict XVI to issue the motu proprio *Summorum Pontificum* (July 7, 2007), which removed restrictions on the celebration of the older Roman liturgy. In the "Letter" accompanying *Summorum Pontificum*, the Pope writes:

> In the history of the liturgy there is growth and progress, but no rupture. What was holy for earlier generations remains holy and great for us; it cannot all of a sudden be entirely forbidden or even harmful. It behooves us all to preserve the

riches that have grown up in the faith and prayer of the Church, and to give them their proper place.

Here we have an important application of the "hermeneutics of continuity" in interpreting Vatican II—the Pope acting on the principle he affirmed in his address to the Roman curia on December 22, 2005.[67]

"This motu proprio," observes French bishop Dominique Rey, "is part of a long-evident desire by Joseph Ratzinger to promote the organic development of the teaching and the liturgy of the Church." As such, it "is to be seen against the horizon of the plan for a *reform of the reform*." Rey describes the "reform of the reform" as a twofold process involving "the rediscovery of *the spirit of the liturgy*" and "the progressive resacralization of worship."[68] If, however, we keep with the Mannion typology, this description seems better suited to the "recatholicization" program than to the "reform of the reform." In any event (and without wanting to put too fine a point on nomenclature), it seems obvious that the first step in any structural "reform of the reform" would have to concern the *spirit* in which the modern rites are celebrated.

In *Sacramentum Caritatis*, Benedict XVI urges bishops and priests to attend to "the *ars celebrandi*, the art of proper celebration" of the liturgy as the "primary way to foster the participation of the People of God in the sacred rite" (art. 38). In this context he speaks about the role of silence in fostering *actuosa participatio* (which is primarily, but not solely, interior), the preeminence of liturgical song (especially Gregorian chant), and the role of sacred art and architecture in connecting beauty and the liturgy. Papal liturgies during Benedict's pontificate exemplified "recatholicization" ideals, demonstrating to the world the highest standard of decorum, God-centeredness, and visible continuity with the older form of the Roman liturgy.[69]

It is to be observed, however, that Benedict as pope did not take up the question of "reforming the reform," if by that term is meant the correction of the "fabricated" modern rites. Nor has his successor, Pope Francis (2013–), whose pastoral priorities do not appear to involve the pursuit of further liturgical restoration along lines followed by Benedict XVI.[70] In terms of practical execution, then, the "reform of the reform" remains a task for the future, a phase of the new liturgical movement subsequent to "recatholicization" and formation in the spirit of the liturgy. This follows from what Benedict said as cardinal: any new reform "ought in the first place to be above all an educative process."[71] Without a proper understanding of the "why" of liturgical change, another season of liturgical turmoil would be inevitable.

In the meantime, the wide availability (since 2007) of the centuries-old Roman rite affords Catholics of a certain age unprecedented exposure to their liturgical heritage. Rather than simply reading about or hearing about the transformation of Roman Catholic worship that occurred after Vatican II, they can now experience firsthand what was lost and what was gained in the liturgy reform. Pope Benedict, in his letter accompanying *Summorum Pontificum*, expressed hope that the older, "extraordinary" form of the liturgy and the postconciliar, "ordinary" form would prove mutually enriching, adding by way of illustration that "new Saints and some of the new prefaces can and should be inserted in the old missal."[72] In terms of existing legislation, *Summorum Pontificum* permits vernacular readings in the 1962 low Mass, although one may question whether this constitutes a true enrichment or simply a welcome option.

Of greatest import to the present study is whether, at some point in the future, the two forms of liturgy can converge, such that we may have the ancient Roman rite as inherited by Vatican II (and by Trent four centuries earlier) and amended as prescribed by the Constitution on the Sacred Liturgy. As Joseph Ratzinger, Benedict had raised the possibility of a new edition of the Roman missal, which would "make it quite clear that the so-called missal of Paul VI is nothing other than a renewed form of the same missal to which Pius X, Urban VIII, Pius V and their predecessors have contributed, right from the Church's earliest history."[73] But is this possible, given that the reform was so radical a deconstruction and reconstruction of the Roman heritage? To stay with that privileged metaphor: if the process of organic development was in fact interrupted, can it really be restarted from within the framework of the reformed liturgy? That is the question dividing the "reform of the reform" theorists between those who believe the basis for a new liturgical movement should be the older form of the Roman rite and those who believe it should be the reformed liturgy.

Conclusion

The "reform of the reform" movement is a big umbrella, with plenty of room under it for discussion and honest disagreement about the means, as well as the precise contours of the solution. Whatever modifications in either form of the Roman rite such a project might involve, whatever reform of either missal in either direction, it is important to proceed with caution, lest past mistakes be repeated, and to adhere carefully to the "law of organic growth within the universality of the common tradition."[74] Otherwise there is no reason to expect that any sort of "reform of the reform" could foster a renewal of the Church's liturgical life that would be more consonant with what the vast majority of the Vatican II Fathers had thought themselves to be approving and with the pastoral needs of the present.

Notes

1   J. Ratzinger, *Milestones: Memoirs 1927–1977* (San Francisco: Ignatius Press, 1998), p. 149.
2   All citations of *Sacrosanctum Concilium* are drawn from: A. Flannery (ed.), *Vatican Council II: The Conciliar and Post Conciliar Documents*, revised edn (Northport, NY: Costello Publishing, 1988).
3   For historically valuable accounts of the *Consilium's* operations see: A. Bugnini, *The Reform of the Liturgy 1948–1975* (Collegeville: Liturgical Press, 1990); M. Barba, *La*

riforma conciliare dell' « *Ordo Missæ* » (BELS: 2002) (on the Order of Mass, specifically); N. Giampietro, *The Development of the Liturgical Reform: As Seen by Cardinal Ferdinando Antonelli from 1948 to 1970* (Fort Collins, CO: Roman Catholic Books, 2009).

4 For a fuller treatment of the 1965 and 1967 reforms of the Mass see: A. Reid, "*Sacrosanctum Concilium* and the Reform of the *Ordo Missae*," *Antiphon* 10 (2006), pp. 286–91.

5 The second *editio typica* of the missal of Paul VI, published in 1975, features additional new eucharistic prayers: two "for Reconciliation" and three "for Masses with Children." The third typical edition of 2002 contains still more eucharistic prayers "for Various Occasions."

6 The number of prefaces has greatly varied over the centuries. On Sundays the preface of the Most Holy Trinity, in use since the thirteenth century (but not prescribed until 1759), has been replaced by new prefaces highlighting the Paschal Mystery.

7 See: A. Cekada, *The Problems with the Prayers of the Modern Mass* (Rockford: TAN Books, 1991); L. Pristas, *The Collects of the Roman Missals: A Comparative Study of the Sundays in Proper Seasons before and after the Second Vatican Council* (London & New York: Bloomsbury, 2013).

8 See: K. Gamber, *The Reform of the Roman Liturgy: Its Problems and Background* (San Juan Capistrano, CA & Harrison, NY: Una Voce Press & Foundation for Catholic Reform, 1993), pp. 63–75.

9 See: M. Drew, "The spirit or the letter? Vatican II and liturgical reform," S. Caldecott (ed.), *Beyond the Prosaic* (Edinburgh: T&T Clark, 1998), pp. 49–67; P. Stravinskas, "Epilogue," T. Kocik, *The Reform of the Reform?* (San Francisco: Ignatius Press, 2003), pp. 105–12.

10 See: L. Dobszay, *The Bugnini-Liturgy and the 'Reform of the Reform'* (Front Royal, VA: Catholic Church Music Associates, 2003); *The Restoration and Organic Development of the Roman Rite* (London & New York: T&T Clark/Continuum, 2010).

11 The allowances for the reception of Holy Communion in the hand and the use of female altar servers resulted from papal concessions to the liturgical "progressives" (often working in seminaries or on the liturgical commissions of the episcopal conferences) who actively undermined the official restriction or prohibition of those practices. These concessions betrayed those priests who, whatever their personal preferences, had obeyed liturgical norms even in the face of scorn from their peers.

12 See: Congregation for Divine Worship, Letter *Quattuor abhinc annos*, October 3, 1984; John Paul II, Apostolic Letter "motu proprio data," *Ecclesia Dei adflicta*, July 2, 1988.

13 J. Ratzinger with V. Messori, *The Ratzinger Report: An Exclusive Interview on the State of the Church* (San Francisco: Ignatius Press, 1985) p. 122.

14 For the Adoremus Society mission statement, see: http://www.adoremus.org/faq.htm

15 For the Society for Catholic Liturgy mission statement, see: http://www.liturgysociety. org. In early 2000, Francis Cardinal George OMI, Archbishop of Chicago, appointed Mannion as head of a new liturgical institute located at the archdiocesan seminary in Mundelein, Illinois.

16 The proceedings are published as: S. Caldecott (ed.), *Beyond the Prosaic: Renewing the Liturgical Movement* (Edinburgh: T&T Clark, 1998).

17 Ibid., pp. 163–5.

18 J. Ratzinger, *The Spirit of the Liturgy* (San Francisco: Ignatius Press, 2000), pp. 8–9; JRCW 11, p. 4.

19 The proceedings are published as: A. Reid (ed), *Looking Again at the Question of the Liturgy with Cardinal Ratzinger: Proceedings of the July 2001 Fontgombault Liturgical Conference* (Farnborough: St Michael's Abbey Press, 2003).

20 On the liturgical legacy of Gamber and his influence on Ratzinger see: M. Hauke, "Klaus Gamber: father of the 'new liturgical movement'," N.J. Roy & J.E. Rutherford (eds), *Benedict XVI and the Sacred Liturgy* (Dublin: Four Courts Press, 2010), pp. 24–69.

21 See the bibliography in: P. Post, "Dealing with the past in the Roman Catholic liturgical 'Reform of the Reform movement'," *Questions liturgiques* 87 (2006), pp. 264–79 (p. 268 n. 11). On the same page Post incorrectly has Gamber extolling Ratzinger's scholarship, not vice versa.

22 K. Gamber, *The Modern Rite: Collected Essays on the Reform of the Liturgy* (Farnborough: St Michael's Abbey Press, 2002).

23 Gamber, *The Reform of the Roman Liturgy*, p. xiii.

24 Ibid., p. 3.

25 Bugnini, *The Reform of the Liturgy*, p. 115.

26 This text appears on the back cover of Gamber, *The Reform of the Roman Liturgy*, translating that published in K. Gamber, *La Réforme Liturgique en Question* (Le Barroux: Éditions Sainte-Madeleine, 1992), p. 8 (JRCW 11, pp. 537–8). See also: Ratzinger & Messori, *The Ratzinger Report*, p. 121; Ratzinger, *Milestones*, p. 148; *The Spirit of the Liturgy*, p. 82 (JRCW 11 p. 50); and his July 1988 address to the bishops of Chile and Colombia in: C. Barthe, *Beyond Vatican II: The Church at a New Crossroads* (Fort Collins, CO: Roman Catholic Books, 2004), pp. 141–8.

27 A subsequent volume by Reid will address the liturgical changes made during and after the Council.

28 A. Reid, *The Organic Development of the Liturgy: The Principles of Liturgical Reform and their Relation to the Twentieth Century Liturgical Movement Prior to the Second Vatican Council*, 2nd edn (San Francisco: Ignatius Press, 2005), p. 307.

29 J. Baldovin, *Reforming the Liturgy: A Response to the Critics* (Collegeville: Liturgical Press, 2008), p. 52.

30 See: M. Mannion, "The catholicity of the liturgy: shaping a new agenda," S. Caldecott (ed.), *Beyond the Prosaic* (Edinburgh: T&T Clark, 1998), pp. 11–48; R. Weakland, "The liturgy as battlefield: What do 'restorationists' want?" *Commonweal*, 11 January 2002, pp. 10–15; Baldovin, *Reforming the Liturgy*.

31 Mannion, ibid., p. 14.

32 Ibid., p. 21.

33 The separation of the "official reform" and "inculturation" agendas in Mannion's schema has been criticized as supporting "a tendency to regard articles 37–40 of the constitution as a kind of Trojan horse;" R. Ferrone, *Liturgy: Sacrosanctum Concilium* (New York/Mahwah, NJ: Paulist Press, 2007) p. 82.

34 Mannion, "The catholicity of the liturgy: shaping a new agenda," pp. 27–8.

35 Ibid., pp. 18–19.

36 Hitchcock's analysis of the liturgical reform following Vatican II, *The Recovery of the Sacred*, was first published in 1974, towards the end of the first stage of official implementation, a period accompanied by much unauthorized experimentation and undisciplined enthusiasm for change. When the second edition was published more than twenty years later, the reform had become more stabilized, but Hitchcock's original analysis was still largely pertinent; e.g., "Although both the revived Tridentine Mass and solemn celebrations of the *Novus Ordo* are deeply moving to many people,

suburban American culture has had its effect, so that for perhaps a majority the regimen of guitar songs, casual styles of celebration, and churches almost as bare as meeting halls are considered signs of progress;" J. Hitchcock, *The Recovery of the Sacred: Reforming the Reformed Liturgy* (San Francisco: Ignatius Press, 1995), p. 10.

37 Flanagan's central argument is that liberal theologians in the pursuit of relevance adopted a pastoral-liturgical strategy of modernization that was sociologically misconceived. Modernity was seen as a solution to problems in the liturgy rather than a symptom of them, when in fact "Modernity embodies a particular plight, a blindness that disables appreciation of liturgical transactions;" K. Flanagan, *Sociology and Liturgy: Re-presentations of the Holy* (London & New York: The Macmillan Press & St Martin's Press, 1991), p. 286.

38 See: Baldovin, *Reforming the Liturgy*.

39 N. Giampietro, *The Development of the Liturgical Reform: As Seen by Cardinal Ferdinando Antonelli from 1948 to 1970* (Fort Collins, CO: Roman Catholic Books, 2009), p. xiv.

40 See: B. Harrison, "The postconciliar Eucharistic liturgy: planning a 'reform of the reform'," Kocik, *The Reform of the Reform?* pp. 170–93; A. Nichols, *Looking at the Liturgy: A Critical View of Its Contemporary Form* (San Francisco: Ignatius Press, 1996) and "Salutary dissatisfaction: an English view of 'reforming the reform'," Kocik, *The Reform of the Reform?* pp. 195–210; J. Parsons, "A Reform of the Reform?" Kocik, *The Reform of the Reform?* pp. 211–56.

41 "It is clear that the proposal of a 'reform of the reform' refers to the missal of 1970 and not to that of 1962, even if the ultimate aim of this reform would be a liturgical reconciliation;" quoted in *The Latin Mass*, Spring 1997, p. 8. Also: "the 'reform of the reform' refers of course to the reformed missal, not to the missal in previous use;" Reid, *Looking Again at the Question of the Liturgy with Cardinal Ratzinger*, p. 150; JRCW 11, p. 564.

42 See: P. Elliott, "A question of ceremonial," Kocik, *The Reform of the Reform?* pp. 257–73.

43 Barthe, *Beyond Vatican II*, p 107.

44 http://www.newliturgicalmovement.org/2008/03/fr-joseph-fessio-speaks-to-nlm-about.html

45 In *The Bugnini-Liturgy and the 'Reform of the Reform,'* Dobszay understands the "reform of the reform" as applying to the postconciliar liturgy (pp. 10, 178), but in his subsequent *The Restoration and Organic Development of the Roman Rite* he rejects as "unworkable" the task of revising the contents of the reformed liturgy so as to reconcile the older and newer rites (p. 66).

46 See: Nichols, *Looking at the Liturgy*, pp. 118, 119 & 120–1; "Salutary dissatisfaction: an English view of 'reforming the reform'," p. 203.

47 Nichols, *Looking at the Liturgy*, pp. 84–6.

48 Nichols, "Salutary dissatisfaction: an English view of 'reforming the reform'," pp. 206–7.

49 Ibid., p. 207.

50 E.g.: K.W. Irwin, *What We Have Done, What We Have Failed to Do: Assessing the Liturgical Reforms of Vatican II* (New York & Mahwah, NJ: Paulist Press, 2013), p. 125: "With this phrase ['the reform of the reform'], nothing less than confidence in the liturgical reform of Vatican II is at stake . . ." See also: Weakland, "The liturgy as battlefield: What do 'restorationists' want?" *Commonweal*, 11 January 2002, pp. 10–15.

51 Ferrone, *Liturgy: Sacrosanctum Concilium*, p. 84

52 M. Faggioli, *True Reform: Liturgy and Ecclesiology in 'Sacrosanctum Concilium'* (Collegeville: Liturgical Press, 2012) p. 10.

53 Ibid., p. 16 et al. Against Faggioli's assertion that the "anti-Vatican II" new liturgical movement rejects the theological *ressourcement* that precipitated and in large part inspired the Second Vatican Council, see: T. Kocik, "The 'Reform of the Reform' in broad context: re-engaging the living tradition," *Antiphon* 12 (2008), pp. 26–44.

54 M. Johnson, "The 'real' and multiple 'presences' of Christ in contemporary Lutheran liturgical and sacramental practice," T. Fitzgerald & D. Lysik (eds), *The Many Presences of Christ* (Chicago: Liturgy Training Publications, 1999), pp. 105–20 (p. 118).

55 Post, "Dealing with the past in the Roman Catholic liturgical 'Reform of the Reform movement'," p. 278.

56 J. Baldovin, "Idols and icons: reflections on the current state of liturgical reform," *Worship* 84 (2010) pp. 386–402 (pp. 392–7).

57 Cited in: Baldovin, *Reforming the Liturgy,* p. 57.

58 Dobszay, *The Bugnini-Liturgy and the "Reform of the Reform,"* p. 151.

59 See: Gamber, *Reform of the Roman Liturgy,* p. 31.

60 See: Pristas, *The Collects of the Roman Missals.* Referring to the ancient Roman sacramentaries (named after the popes with whom it is believed they were connected), Nicola Bux asks: '[I]f it is true that the ancient Gelasian and Leonine patrimony was introduced into the missal of Paul VI, why must the Gregorian patrimony in the Tridentine missal be abandoned?' *Benedict XVI's Reform: The Liturgy between Innovation and Tradition* (San Francisco: Ignatius Press, 2012), p. 106.

61 See: Ferrone, *Liturgy: Sacrosanctum Concilium,* pp. 41–2.

62 Ibid., p. 114 n. 22.

63 See: D. Hoge, *Future of Catholic Leadership: Responses to the Priest Shortage* (Kansas City, MO: Sheed & Ward, 1987) and *The First Five Years of the Priesthood: A Study of Newly Ordained Catholic Priests* (Collegeville: Liturgical Press, 2002); S. Siptroth, "The correlation between political and ecclesial ideologies of Catholic priests: a research note," *Sociology of Religion* 66 (2005), pp. 419–29.

64 It bears noting the work of Jorge Arturo Medina Cardinal Estévez, who served as Pro-Prefect of the Congregation for Divine Worship from 1996 to 1998 and Prefect of the same Roman dicastery from 1998 to 2002. See: N. Roy, "The contribution of Jorge Arturo Medina Estévez," *Antiphon* 10 (2006), pp. 2–11; N. Roy & J.E. Rutherford (eds), *Benedict XVI and the Sacred Liturgy: Proceedings of the First Fota International Liturgy Conference* (Dublin: Four Courts Press, 2010).

65 The Instruction was met with anxiety and hostility by 'progressives' who saw it as an arbitrary exercise of Roman authority to the detriment of inculturation, episcopal collegiality, and biblical scholarship. For a sampling of reactions in early press releases (mostly negative), see: http://www.adoremus.org/1601responses.html

66 See: Bux, *Benedict XVI's Reform,* chapter VII.

67 AAS, 98 (2006), pp. 44–5.

68 M. Aillet, *The Old Mass and the New: Explaining the Motu Proprio Summorum Pontificum of Pope Benedict XVI* (San Francisco: Ignatius Press, 2010), pp. 9–10.

69 See: D. Bonagura, "The future of the Roman Rite: reading Benedict in the light of Ratzinger," *Antiphon* 13 (2009), pp. 228–46; A. Reid, "The Liturgical Reform of Benedict XVI," N. Roy & J. Rutherford (eds), *Benedict XVI and the Sacred Liturgy* (Dublin: Four Courts Press, 2010), pp. 156–80.

70 See: A. Reid, "The New Liturgical Movement after the Pontificate of Benedict XVI," *Sacred Music* 141 (2014), pp. 10–26.

71 J. Ratzinger with P. Seewald, *God and the World: Believing and Living in Our Time. A Conversation with Peter Seewald* (San Francisco: Ignatius Press, 2002), p. 416.

72 About what else "mutual enrichment" might mean in practice, see: T. Finigan, "'Mutual enrichment' in theory and practice," *Usus Antiquior* 2 (2011), pp. 61–8.
73 J. Ratzinger, *The Feast of Faith: Approaches to a Theology of the Liturgy* (San Francisco: Ignatius Press, 1986), p. 87; JRCW 11, p. 525. This position is clearly inconsistent with Ratzinger's earlier remarks about "fabricated liturgy;" see: T. Kocik, "A juggler on a tightrope: Benedict XVI and the 'Tridentine' question," *Saint Austin Review* 7 (2007), pp. 4–7 (pp. 4–5); & "The 'Reform of the Reform' in broad context: re-engaging the living tradition," pp. 29–31. The third typical edition of the postconciliar missal was promulgated by John Paul II in 2000, published in 2002, and emended in 2008. It restores some of the Mass formularies found in the 1962 missal but does not, as some had hoped, reinstate any of the rubrics and practices eliminated after 1963.
74 Ratzinger, *The Feast of Faith*, p. 66.

Bibliography

Aillet, M., *The Old Mass and the New: Explaining the Motu Proprio Summorum Pontificum of Pope Benedict XVI* (San Francisco: Ignatius Press, 2010).
Baldovin, J.F., *Reforming the Liturgy: A Response to the Critics* (Collegeville: Liturgical Press, 2008). This book surveys the "critics" of the reform under the heads of the philosophical, the historical, the theological, and the sociological/anthropological.
Baldovin, J.F., "Idols and icons: reflections on the current state of liturgical reform," *Worship* 84 (2010), pp. 386–402.
Barba, M., *La riforma conciliare dell' « Ordo Missæ »* (BELS: 2002).
Barthe, C., *Beyond Vatican II: The Church at a New Crossroads* (Fort Collins, CO: Roman Catholic Books, 2004).
Bonagura, D.G., "The future of the Roman Rite: reading Benedict in the light of Ratzinger," *Antiphon* 13 (2009), pp. 228–46.
Bugnini, A., *The Reform of the Liturgy 1948–1975* (Collegeville: Liturgical Press, 1990).
Bux, N., *Benedict XVI's Reform: The Liturgy between Innovation and Tradition* (San Francisco: Ignatius Press, 2012).
Caldecott, S. (ed.), *Beyond the Prosaic: Renewing the Liturgical Movement* (Edinburgh: T&T Clark, 1998).
Cekada, A., *The Problems with the Prayers of the Modern Mass* (Rockford: TAN Books, 1991).
Crescimanno, C., *La riforma della riforma liturgica: ipotesi per un 'nuovo' rito della messa sulle tracce del pensiero di Joseph Ratzinger* (Verona: Fede e Cultura, 2009).
Dobszay, L., *The Bugnini-Liturgy and the 'Reform of the Reform'* (Front Royal, VA: Catholic Church Music Associates, 2003).
—— *The Restoration and Organic Development of the Roman Rite* (London & New York: T&T Clark/Continuum, 2010).
Drew, M., "The spirit or the letter? Vatican II and liturgical reform," S. Caldecott (ed.) *Beyond the Prosaic* (Edinburgh: T&T Clark, 1998), pp. 49–67.
Elliott, P., "A question of ceremonial," T. Kocik, *The Reform of the Reform?* (San Francisco: Ignatius Press, 2003), pp. 257–73.
Faggioli, M., *True Reform: Liturgy and Ecclesiology in 'Sacrosanctum Concilium'* (Collegeville: Liturgical Press, 2012).
Ferrone, R., *Liturgy: Sacrosanctum Concilium* (New York/Mahwah, NJ: Paulist Press, 2007).
Finigan, T., " 'Mutual enrichment' in theory and practice," *Usus Antiquior* 2 (2011), pp. 61–8.

Flanagan, K., *Sociology and Liturgy: Re-presentations of the Holy* (London & New York: The Macmillan Press & St Martin's Press, 1991).

Flannery, A. (ed.), *Vatican Council II: The Conciliar and Post Conciliar Documents*, revised edn (Northport, NY: Costello Publishing, 1988).

Gamber, K., *Die Reform der römischen Liturgie: Vorgeschichte und Problematik* (Regensburg: Pustet, 1979).

—— *Fragen in der Zeit. Kirche und Liturgie nach dem Vatikanum II* (Regensburg: Pustet, 1989).

—— *La Réforme Liturgique en Question* (Le Barroux: Éditions Sainte-Madeleine, 1992). Extracts appear on the back cover of the 1993 English edition.

—— *The Modern Rite: Collected Essays on the Reform of the Liturgy* (Farnborough: St Michael's Abbey Press, 2002).

—— *The Reform of the Roman Liturgy: Its Problems and Background* (San Juan Capistrano, CA & Harrison, NY: Una Voce Press & Foundation for Catholic Reform, 1993). This edition consists of two previously published books, *Die Reform der römischen Liturgie* (1979) and *Zum Herrn hin!* (1987). In combining these books there is some duplication of material, which makes for a certain amount of repetition especially regarding the topic of celebrating the Eucharist *ad orientem*. Extracts of the 1992 French edition are printed on the back cover.

Giampietro, N., *The Development of the Liturgical Reform: As Seen by Cardinal Ferdinando Antonelli from 1948 to 1970* (Fort Collins, CO: Roman Catholic Books, 2009).

Harrison, B.W., "The postconciliar Eucharistic liturgy: planning a 'reform of the reform'," T. Kocik *The Reform of the Reform?* (San Francisco: Ignatius Press, 2003), pp. 170–93.

Hauke, M., "Klaus Gamber: father of the 'new liturgical movement'," N. J. Roy & J.E. Rutherford (eds), *Benedict XVI and the Sacred Liturgy* (Dublin: Four Courts Press, 2010), pp. 24–69.

Hitchcock, H.H., "A new era of liturgical renewal: foundations and future," *Antiphon* 10 (2006), pp. 12–31.

Hitchcock, J., *The Recovery of the Sacred: Reforming the Reformed Liturgy* (San Francisco: Ignatius Press, 1995).

Hoge, D.R., *Future of Catholic Leadership: Responses to the Priest Shortage* (Kansas City, MO: Sheed & Ward, 1987).

—— *The First Five Years of the Priesthood: A Study of Newly Ordained Catholic Priests* (Collegeville, Liturgical Press, 2002).

Irwin, K.W., *What We Have Done, What We Have Failed to Do: Assessing the Liturgical Reforms of Vatican II* (New York & Mahwah, NJ: Paulist Press, 2013).

Johnson, M.E., "The 'real' and multiple 'presences' of Christ in contemporary Lutheran liturgical and sacramental practice," T. Fitzgerald & D. Lysik (eds), *The Many Presences of Christ* (Chicago: Liturgy Training Publications, 1999), pp. 105–20.

Johnston, W. H., *Care for the Church and Its Liturgy: A Study of "Summorum Pontificism" and the Extraordinary Form of the Roman Rite* (Collegeville, MN: Liturgical Press, 2013).

Kocik, T.M., *The Reform of the Reform?* (San Francisco: Ignatius Press, 2003).

—— "A juggler on a tightrope: Benedict XVI and the 'Tridentine' question," *Saint Austin Review* 7 (2007), pp. 4–7.

—— "The 'Reform of the Reform' in broad context: re-engaging the living tradition," *Antiphon* 12 (2008), pp. 26–44.

Mannion, M.F., "The catholicity of the liturgy: shaping a new agenda," S. Caldecott (ed.), *Beyond the Prosaic* (Edinburgh: T&T Clark, 1998), pp. 11–48; reprinted in idem,

Masterworks of God: Essays in Liturgical Theory and Practice (Chicago/Mundelein, IL: Hillenbrand Books, 2004), pp. 202–35.

Nichols, A., *Looking at the Liturgy: A Critical View of Its Contemporary Form* (San Francisco: Ignatius Press, 1996).

—— "Salutary dissatisfaction: an English view of 'reforming the reform,'" T. Kocik, *The Reform of the Reform?* (San Francisco: Ignatius Press, 2003), pp. 195–210.

Parsons, J.P., "A Reform of the Reform?" T. Kocik, *The Reform of the Reform?* (San Francisco: Ignatius Press, 2003), pp. 211–56.

Post, P., "Dealing with the past in the Roman Catholic liturgical 'Reform of the Reform movement,'" *Questiones liturgiques* 87 (2006), pp. 264–79.

Pristas, L., *The Collects of the Roman Missals: A Comparative Study of the Sundays in Proper Seasons before and after the Second Vatican Council* (London & New York: Bloomsbury, 2013).

Ratzinger, J., with V. Messori, *The Ratzinger Report: An Exclusive Interview on the State of the Church* (San Francisco: Ignatius Press, 1985).

—— *The Feast of Faith: Approaches to a Theology of the Liturgy* (San Francisco: Ignatius Press, 1986).

—— *Milestones: Memoirs 1927–1977* (San Francisco: Ignatius Press, 1998).

—— *The Spirit of the Liturgy* (San Francisco: Ignatius Press, 2000).

—— with P. Seewald, *God and the World: Believing and Living in Our Time. A Conversation with Peter Seewald* (San Francisco: Ignatius Press, 2002).

Reid, A. (ed.), *Looking Again at the Question of the Liturgy with Cardinal Ratzinger: Proceedings of the July 2001 Fontgombault Liturgical Conference* (Farnborough: St Michael's Abbey Press, 2003).

—— *The Organic Development of the Liturgy: The Principles of Liturgical Reform and their Relation to the Twentieth Century Liturgical Movement Prior to the Second Vatican Council*, 2nd edn (San Francisco: Ignatius Press, 2005), with a foreword by Joseph Cardinal Ratzinger (JRCW 11, pp. 589–94).

—— "Do we need a new liturgical movement?" *Liturgy, Participation and Sacred Music: The Proceedings of the Ninth International Colloquium of Historical, Canonical and Theological Studies on the Roman Catholic Liturgy* (London: CIEL UK, 2006), pp. 239–54. This is the text of an address given on May 15, 2004 at the annual CIEL UK conference.

—— "*Sacrosanctum Concilium* and the Reform of the *Ordo Missae*," *Antiphon* 10 (2006), pp. 277–95.

—— "The liturgical reform of Pope Benedict XVI," N.J. Roy & J.E. Rutherford (eds), *Benedict XVI and the Sacred Liturgy* (Dublin: Four Courts Press, 2010), pp. 156–80.

—— "The New Liturgical Movement after the Pontificate of Benedict XVI," *Sacred Music* 141 (2014), pp. 10–26. This is the text of an address presented to the Church Music Association of America on October 15, 2013.

Roy, N.J., "The contribution of Jorge Arturo Medina Estévez," *Antiphon* 10 (2006), pp. 2–11.

—— & J.E. Rutherford (eds.), *Benedict XVI and the Sacred Liturgy: Proceedings of the First Fota International Liturgy Conference* (Dublin: Four Courts Press, 2010).

Siptroth, S.M., "The correlation between political and ecclesial ideologies of Catholic priests: a research note" *Sociology of Religion* 66 (2005), pp. 419–29.

Stravinskas, P., "Epilogue," T. Kocik, *The Reform of the Reform?* (San Francisco: Ignatius Press, 2003), pp. 105–12.

Weakland, R., "The liturgy as battlefield: What do 'restorationists' want?" *Commonweal*, January 11, 2002, pp. 10–15.

Part IV

THEMES IN CONTEMPORARY LITURGICAL STUDIES

Chapter 16

PASTORAL LITURGY REVISITED

Alcuin Reid

Introduction

Courses and publications promoting "pastoral liturgy" are well known in Catholic dioceses and liturgical institutes. At their best, they take as their starting point the assertion of the Liturgical Constitution of the Second Vatican Council that "the liturgy is the summit toward which the activity of the Church is directed; at the same time it is the font from which all her power flows" (n. 10), and carefully expound the interdependence between authentic liturgical celebration and the pastoral life and ministry of the Church.

At their worst, proponents of "pastoral liturgy" are heirs to those "fervid and courageous initiatives [which] became widespread [and] which proved to be a great attractive force on the new generations" following the promulgation of the Constitution on the Sacred Liturgy in 1963.[1] Such initiatives historically included the "marijuana Mass, Mass with crackers and whisky used as the elements for consecration, 'teen-age' Masses with Coca Cola and hot dog buns," etc.[2] Whilst these have been recognized since as the grave abuses they in fact were, involving "a certain one-sidedness, especially in musical forms, verbal inflation, isolation from a true path of faith of the Christian community, new formalisms, etc," the "purportedly positive aspects" of this liturgical devolution—"communitarian preparation, dynamic and festive style, atmosphere of brotherhood and communion, life-liturgy relation, strong influence on young people and adults, etc."—are proposed still.[3]

The numerous "pastoral" suggestions of the widely published and translated liturgist, Anselm Grün OSB, in *The Seven Sacraments* are but one example. In the rite of baptism, "to help meditate on the mystery of the baptismal water, a source-of-life or circle dance round the font is a possibility ... to indicate our desire that this life-giving water should flow in us too,"[4] he proposes. At Mass:

> The congregation, especially in a small group, can shape the greeting and penitential rite in a particular way. They might open the service with a meditation dance and announce special intentions for the celebration. Instead of the formal confession they can mention their own problems or dangers for their

environment, or represent them in dramatic form ... at Pentecost one group mimed a pool which they could enter, and showed what could be left there, and what could be washed away.[5]

In this approach the liturgical rites as officially promulgated are viewed as a resource to be adapted according to the judgment of those planning the liturgical celebration. It is perceived local or "pastoral" needs and circumstances that drive such adaptations. This results in liturgical celebrations that are self-consciously "pastoral"—that reflect the identity and concerns of the gathered community as discerned by liturgy planners, and it is these which give rise to the liturgical style and sometimes even the content of the rites themselves. This is perhaps the most widely understood meaning of "pastoral liturgy" in theory and in practice.

Yet there is no justification for this in the liturgical reform called for by the Second Vatican Council. Neither *Sacrosanctum Concilium* nor the decades of official documentation that followed support this stance. In the light of this dichotomy, and because the liturgy is truly the *culmen et fons* (the source and summit) of the life and mission of the Church, there is grave need urgently to revisit precisely what is meant by "pastoral liturgy."

The pastoral nature of Catholic liturgy

The adjective "pastoral" when prefixed to the noun "liturgy" creates an entity which is difficult to define theologically, philosophically, or even liturgically. To speak of the pastoral importance and nature of the Sacred Liturgy—as the Liturgical Constitution does often—is comprehensible and its study is straightforward. *Sacrosanctum Concilium* also speaks of "pastoral-liturgical action." But what precisely is "pastoral liturgy"?

The theological content of "pastoral" is rooted in Psalm 23 with its image of the Lord leading his people, like sheep, to "green pastures" (v. 2). We should note that the indication that this new pasture is to be "forever" (v. 6), gives an explicitly eschatological content to this reality. This image is developed further in Christ's description of himself as "the Good Shepherd" in the tenth chapter of St John's Gospel, again with an unquestionably eschatological end in view; the Good Shepherd gives "eternal life" (v. 28) to his sheep.

In theological discourse then, we may say that to qualify a noun with "pastoral" is to assert that the area under examination is to be considered in light of the Church's duty of shepherding all of God's people towards heaven. Given this, one might be forgiven for objecting that "pastoral" when predicated to "liturgy" is somewhat tautological, for surely the liturgy cannot be other than pastoral in this ultimate sense? As a liturgist once asked, "Can someone please explain to me precisely what liturgy is *not* pastoral?"

Catholic liturgy is the public and official worship of Almighty God by His Church in which we encounter Christ's saving action today, ecclesially and sacramentally. All manner of created goods—ministers, material things, sounds, ritual actions, etc—serve to facilitate that salvific encounter and in so doing they themselves serve as privileged sacramentals. This encounter, in which Christ's action has absolute priority, gives the Church her identity.

Consequent to this encounter, the Church is able to articulate something of its content and meaning. Following the ancient maxim *lex orandi, lex credendi* – "the law of prayer is the law of faith: the Church believes as she prays,"—Catholic liturgy is *theologia prima*, and is nothing less than a constitutive element of living Tradition.[6]

The liturgy is intrinsically latreutic. Its primary purpose is to render to Almighty mGod mthe worship that is His due. But this is not a burdensome obedience, for it is in the act of observing this fundamental duty of giving thanks and praise to the Creator for the work of the Redeemer that through the power of the Sanctifier mankind receives the gift of God's life and love, His grace. This consequence—the sanctification of mankind—is the secondary purpose of the liturgy.

Catholic liturgy is, then, of its very nature "pastoral," though we must note that this is not its only, nor indeed its primary, purpose: to invert the purposes of the liturgy is to subvert its nature. Nevertheless, it is in and through liturgical worship that we are initiated into eternal life, are strengthened and daily nourished for life and mission amidst the challenges this world presents to the life of Christ established in us at baptism, are healed from the wounds these conflicts occasion, and are given the consolation of a foretaste of this life's fulfilment, into which the liturgy finally accompanies us. Almighty God remains utterly free to act as He wills, but ordinarily He acts ecclesially and sacramentally—in His Church and through sacramental signs in the Church's liturgy.

The liturgy is something received, something given to us by the Church in her living Tradition. Its forms develop as those of a living organism,[7] and may even be adapted to local cultures according to authoritative principles and norms. But the liturgy is not a subjective or fluid collection of customs, words and rites that have little or no importance other than in the context of the particular group of Christians who assemble for worship. It is not something *to which* a particular gathered assembly gives meaning, nor is it primarily the forum for them to express aspects of their Christian identity, life or mission. Such an approach to worship finds its origin in the intentionally distinct stance of the Protestant Reformation which rejected Catholic liturgy, radically subjectivizing worship and dismissing its developed and multivalent sacramental signs and symbols. The great pastoral reformer of the Counter-Reformation, St Charles Borromeo (1538–84), himself expended much energy on ensuring correct liturgical observance.[8] It must be noted, also, that the Eastern Churches remain firmly rooted in the ancient tradition of liturgical worship and that many Anglicans have found the need to recover the tradition of liturgical worship from the nineteenth-century Oxford Movement onward.

Thus the forms of Catholic liturgy enjoy a theological and ecclesiological—indeed a ritual—objectivity which challenges much of what appears under the banner of "pastoral liturgy." We are simply not free to decide at a local level that this or that element of the liturgical rites can be changed, omitted or substituted, or that other rites may be introduced, unless the liturgical books and norms themselves give us the possibility of so doing,[9] just as we are not free to choose to omit particular articles of the creeds or to compose new ones.

The emergence of "pastoral" liturgy

As has been asserted elsewhere, the *raison d'être* of the twentieth-century liturgical movement was to assert the pastoral efficacy of the liturgy and to facilitate peoples' connection with the action of Christ in the Sacred Liturgy optimally celebrated.[10] The "participation" promoted was participation in the action of Christ in the liturgy, which could not but bear fruit. Put simply, the liturgical movement sought to awaken the Church—clergy, religious, and laity—to the pastoral nourishment to be found in the riches of liturgical Tradition, which had to a greater or lesser extent been ignored for too long.

The practices of the pioneers of this movement, which has roots in the previous centuries,[11] are illustrative and remain instructive. In 1907, the English polyglot Adrian Fortescue (1874–1923) accepted the mission of founding a new parish in Letchworth, Hertfordshire. Whilst he had never aspired to parish ministry, Fortescue "had that originality among few others to be able to realise in his priestly, artistic and intellectual life his ideal for the beauty of Christian worship in all its fullness, and to make the liturgy a living reality."[12] This entailed extensive formation of his people in the Sacred Liturgy. Notable here is *Latin Hymns*, a book he published containing translations of the hymns of Vespers used in his parish each Sunday evening, with translations almost entirely prepared himself. He prefaced it:

> There is not, and there is never likely to be, any religious poetry in the world worthy to be compared with the hymns of the Latin office ... our old Latin hymns are immeasurably more beautiful than any others ever composed ... from every point of view, we ... cannot do better than sing to God as our fathers sang to Him during all the long Ages behind us. Nor shall we find a better expression of Catholic piety than these words, hallowed by centuries of Catholic use, fragrant with the memory of the saints who wrote them in that golden age when practically all Christendom was Catholic.

"If people do not understand what is sung, all this is lost,"[13] he maintained.

The ongoing formation and training of an organist and choir whose repertoire in chant and polyphony would have been considered admirable for a parish many times the size, the building and equipping of a small church as beautifully as means made possible, "long valuable hours ... spent in doing little trifling things in church and sacristy,"[14] etc., were integral to this priest's responsibilities as a pastor. "All this trouble," one of his parishioners remarked after his early death, "Dr Fortescue took for a mere handful of ordinary people."[15]

Other "ordinary people" and parishes were the beneficiaries of similar initiatives. One only needs to consult the papers of the August 1924 Liturgical Congress at Malines—the first such congress held in Belgium after the First World War—to appreciate the extent of these. Their conviction that promotion of participation in the worthy celebration of solemn Mass every Sunday stood at the centre of the renewal of the liturgy and indeed of the life of the parish is notable. So, too, is their emphasis on liturgical formation at every level.[16] The Benedictine Archbishop of Milan from 1929–54, Blessed Alfredo Ildelfonso Schuster (1880–1954), stands out as one who formed his great diocese in the pastoral nature and importance of the liturgy (in his case the Ambrosian rite) fully celebrated, through his personal example and constant teaching from the very first moments of his reign.[17]

These endeavours were grounded in the pastoral imperative of all having a vital connection with the Church's liturgy, and of the necessity that liturgical life of the parishes be as rich as possible: a clear and calm ideal. Yet the twentieth century was not calm—its world was marked by war and unimaginable atrocities, revolution, and the triumph of political ideologies; it experienced rapid technological advances and the increasing ease of travel and communication. These and other factors created "modern man"—an increasingly self-conscious sociological entity whose environment and lifestyle was markedly different to that of the pre-industrialized post-reformation world, and even further from the medieval synthesis of life, faith, and worship that, perhaps, lingered in the fabric of the Church's liturgy with which the liturgical movement sought to connect him.[18]

Is it possible for this entity, "modern man," to connect fruitfully with liturgical tradition? The question is important—indeed crucial—in understanding the emergence of "pastoral liturgy."

The 1932 liturgical week in Namur considered practical questions related to the liturgy and Christian life. The Curé of Notre-Dame d'Espérance in Paris, a parish he described as entirely set in an "evil location" ("totus locus positus est in maligno"), asked whether the liturgy was adapted to the needs of the people. His question arose not out of the assumption that ritual reform was necessary to facilitate fruitful connection between the people and Christ's saving action in the liturgy, but from the conviction that the manner, indeed the quality, of the celebration of the liturgy needed to be adapted to meet the needs of his urban population in the modern world. This pastoral adaptation, he maintained from experience, ought to be threefold: beautiful liturgical celebrations, beautiful singing at Mass and at Vespers, and a beautiful church, or at least one made as beautiful as possible in accordance with the feasts and seasons. All of these, he insists, the people love and want.[19] The other speakers operated from the same assumption: that liturgy's true pastoral effect is achieved when its various rites and seasonal observances are integral to parish life and are celebrated as fully as possible, and when thorough liturgical catechesis and formation at all levels grounds participation in them.

This was the fundamental vision of the liturgical movement which increasingly employed the word "pastoral" in its endeavours,[20] and which included the foundation of a *Centre Pastorale Liturgique* in France in 1943.[21] Yet as early as the

1930s, "modernity" questioned the possibility of achieving this vision. One writer observed:

> The liturgy is found to be no longer a part of the life of the people. In its place have arisen those expressions of devotion which are to the liturgy what every modern corruption is to the reality for which it is substituted. There is need for reform—but at which end shall the reformers start? . . . You may cut down [the peoples'] 'devotions' and drive them to Vespers in the evening, but their attendance, as a general rule, at these services is unnatural and incompatible with the principles upon which their daily life is built. It is these which must first be changed.[22]

This writer rightly identifies the need for reform in the light of the impact of modernity. More importantly, he identifies the fundamental need of formation in the Sacred Liturgy as the pre-condition for fruitful participation in it. In other words, in response to the increasingly urgent question—Should the Church adapt her liturgy so that it speaks to the man of "today," or should the Church seek to educate people in the culture and ways of the Sacred Liturgy so that they might come to it and partake of its riches?—he advocates no short-cut. Rather, he identifies the need to reform and rebuild daily life and culture based on Christian and liturgical principles rather than hastily to reform the liturgy to accommodate the exigencies of modern man.

The pastoral efficacy of the liturgy is not in doubt here, and indeed there is a sagacity in recognizing that the long, hard work of formation of people in the ways of the Sacred Liturgy is the *sine qua non* of achieving its the pastoral fruitfulness—one that is firmly rooted in liturgical tradition and which will nourish *even* modern Christians in their rapidly changing world. This is not to say that the question of liturgical reform itself is excluded *a priori*. The Sacred Liturgy develops organically and is not a rigid monolith tumbling down through the centuries untouched or untouchable. Nor, however, is the Catholic liturgy the subjective response to the perceived needs of each passing age. As a constituent element of Tradition, the Sacred Liturgy enjoys an objectivity, theologically and ritually, which renders it *persuadable* by new circumstances and needs, but not *subject* to them.[23]

The necessity of a sound theological grounding for pastoral liturgical efforts was underlined in the preface to the edition of *La Maison-Dieu* marking the death of the liturgical theologian Dom Odo Casel (1886–1948). Its editors noted their conscious efforts "to give the French liturgical movement a parish base," whilst emphasizing that the theological work of Casel and other monks "have given us light and grace which is particular to them, and without which our liturgical effort would have quickly lost its freshness and as its specific density, to be lowered to the level of very ordinary pastoral action indeed, of a 'movement' in the most pejorative sense of the term, which is that of an agitation."[24]

In the middle of the twentieth century, the objectivity of liturgical tradition and the necessity for liturgical formation were understood, as is evidenced in the 1947 encyclical letter *Mediator Dei* of Pius XII (1876; 1939–58). At the same time Pius XII established a commission to prepare a general reform of the liturgy.[25] Whilst it worked in secret, the emerging products of this commission, beginning with the 1951 reform of the Paschal Vigil, gave considerable momentum to questions of ritual reform—questions which were taken up and discussed throughout the 1950s at international conferences and liturgical weeks.

This momentum and its fruits are studied elsewhere.[26] Some reforms, such as the restoration of the authentic times of the celebration of the ceremonies of the Paschal Triduum—celebrating the Paschal Vigil during the night on Saturday rather than early on Saturday morning, etc.—may be said to be pastoral in the sense of facilitating greater participation in the ceremonies themselves. The rites regained some liturgical integrity thereby—the rites and prayers of the Mass of the Lord's Supper, of the Good Friday liturgy and of the Vigil belong in the evening, afternoon and night respectively. Enhancing liturgical authenticity thus could not but be of pastoral benefit.

Some reforms, however, betrayed a certain liturgical antiquarianism, fuelled by decades of liturgical research. Others, perhaps influenced by the momentum of reform, may be described as innovation out of what may be called a pastoral expediency—a desire to introduce new practices so as quickly to facilitate liturgical participation. A "pastoral" desire for cutting down and simplifying the rites was also to be found.

So, too, the question of the use of vernacular languages in the liturgy continued to be argued. Countries of continental Europe had increasingly used the vernacular for rites other than the Mass. During the 1950s, this practice increased, impacting even upon the somewhat more rigid Anglophone countries.

In 1955, Dom Oswald Sumner (†1964) argued powerfully that the exclusion of the vernacular meant that "the food that could be taken from the Mass into daily life is absent save, in part, for those who have had the courage to struggle with the columns of a missal. The hearing of the Word of God would have a different effect."[27] Clifford Howell SJ (1902–81) made a stronger claim, that "for more than ten centuries the celebration of Mass has ... failed to effect the distribution of the 'Bread of God's Word' to the people at large," and expressed the hope of the future introduction "into public Masses of a sufficient use of the vernacular."[28] Their hopes were partially realized in the Sacred Congregation of Rites' 3 September 1958 Instruction on Sacred Music and the Liturgy, *De musica sacra*, which stated that it was "desirable" for a lector to read the Epistle and Gospel in the vernacular at Low Mass on Sundays and Feasts (n. 14 c).

Whilst uncritical personal preferences are sometimes expressed in respect of the reforms enacted in the decade from 1951 onward, and valid critiques of the various aspects of them are certainly possible, there is no doubt that the overriding motivation for their promulgation was to facilitate peoples' more fruitful participation in the Church's liturgical rites. As Joseph A. Jungmann SJ (1889–1975), *the* liturgical historian of the era, asserted at the First International Congress of Pastoral Liturgy held in Assisi in 1956: "the living liturgy, actively participated in, was itself for centuries the most important form of pastoral care."[29] The publication of popular works such as *Liturgy in the Parish* and *Teaching Liturgy in Schools*,[30] demonstrates the progress this conviction was making. Yet reform of the liturgical rites themselves was increasingly seen as a means once again to render the liturgy "living" and thereby pastorally effective. Some scholars—pre-eminently Jungmann—also argued concomitantly for reform to correct what they regarded as the medieval "corruption" of the liturgy.[31]

The crucial question here—and later—is one of proportionality: was objective liturgical Tradition "persuaded" of the value of these reforms, as it were, or was the liturgy subjected to the growing pastoral and scholarly enthusiasms of liturgists as the momentum for ritual reform increased? The risks were real: liturgical reform could outrun the liturgical formation it necessarily presupposed; the theological and ritual riches of the liturgy as developed in tradition could be unduly devalued or even jettisoned; the pastoral benefits desired might not be achieved. There has not been sufficient research to answer this question in respect of the decade leading up to 1962, but it is clear that the desire that the liturgy be more pastorally efficacious and the desire to enact reform in order to achieve that end increase during this time.[32]

In calling the Second Vatican Council in 1959 St John XXIII (1881; 1958–63) had primarily pastoral ends in view. He emphasized the pastoral importance of the Sacred Liturgy often, as the journal *Worship* underlined in 1963 by collecting relevant extracts from his discourses. One example:

> How we would like to see priests and the faithful always be careful about preparing for this divine action and carrying it out perfectly! An altar with nothing missing, where everything is just as it should be; servers who are well-trained, devout and attentive; a few words from the priest that are short but to the point, well-adapted to the audience, listened to with the attention and respect that the Word of God deserves; active participation, through dialogue and chant, yet with that discretion which leaves room for personal, silent prayer; finally and above all, holy Communion, as frequently as possible, to make participation in the sacrifice really complete.[33]

John XXIII inherited the commission established by Pius XII and its decade of work provided a natural basis for the liturgical preparatory commission for the Council. Their work from 1960–62 was certainly intended to prepare a general reform of the liturgy of the Roman rite to facilitate participation so as to render the liturgy more pastorally efficacious. The work of this commission also invites further research.[34]

The consideration of the Sacred Liturgy at the Council itself is discussed in another chapter.[35] Its resultant Constitution on the Sacred Liturgy, *Sacrosanctum Concilium* (4 December 1964), is clearly a mandate for moderate ritual reform with the aim of imparting "an ever increasing vigour to the Christian life of the faithful" (n. 1). It is clear that "the liturgy is the summit towards which the activity of the Church is directed" and "at the same time it is the fount from which all her power flows" (n. 10).

Article 14 articulates the fundamental principles of the reform desired by the Council:

> Mother Church earnestly desires that all the faithful should be led to that fully conscious, and active participation in liturgical celebrations which is demanded by the very nature of the liturgy. Such participation by the Christian people as "a chosen race, a royal priesthood, a holy nation, a redeemed people" (1 Pet. 2:9; cf. 2:4–5), is their right and duty by reason of their baptism.
>
> In the restoration and promotion of the Sacred Liturgy, this full and active participation [*participatio actuosa*] by all the people is the aim to be considered before all else; for it is the primary and indispensable source from which the faithful are to derive the true Christian spirit; and therefore pastors of souls must zealously strive to achieve it, by means of the necessary instruction, in all their pastoral work.
>
> Yet it would be futile to entertain any hopes of realizing this unless the pastors themselves, in the first place, become thoroughly imbued with the spirit and power of the liturgy, and undertake to give instruction about it. A prime need, therefore, is that attention be directed, first of all, to the liturgical instruction of the clergy ...

These principles—of the pastoral need for true or actual participation in the liturgy,[36] and of the necessary precondition for achieving this, namely widespread liturgical formation—reiterate with the highest authority the sound principles that motivated the liturgical movement of previous decades. Indeed, the Council directly draws upon the 1903 motu proprio of St Pius X (1835; 1903–14) *Tra le sollecitudini.*

It is important to underline the interdependence of these principles. This is perhaps best done by reiterating the Council's own words: "it would be futile to entertain any hopes of realizing this [*participatio actuosa*] unless the pastors themselves, in the first place, become thoroughly imbued with the spirit and power of the liturgy, and undertake to give instruction about it."[37] The Council foresaw that there were indeed no short-cuts to the widespread realization of the pastoral efficacy of the Sacred Liturgy.

In seeking to realize this pastoral goal *Sacrosanctum Concilium* mandated "the reform and promotion of the liturgy" (n. 1). Its desire "that the sacrifice of the Mass, even in the ritual forms of its celebration, may become pastorally efficacious to the fullest degree" (n. 49) is illustrative. Whilst a study of the implementation of the Council's mandate lies elsewhere, there is no doubt that, in the words of the Council *peritus* Pierre-Marie Gy OP (1922–2004), at a press conference given in Rome in November 1962 during the first session of the Council and published by *L'Osservatore Romano*, "at the centre of everything ... there is a simple idea, namely: the liturgy is pastoral, and if it is not pastoral it does not attain its end."[38] Whilst noting Gy's strong emphasis on the *secondary* end of the Sacred Liturgy here— which almost obscures its primary latreutic end—it is to an examination of what "pastoral liturgy" came to mean following the 1963 promulgation of *Sacrosanctum Concilium* that we must now turn.

Pastoral liturgy after *Sacrosanctum Concilium*

Father Gy continued his press conference by asking: "What is the meaning of the term 'pastoral liturgy'?" His answer is illustrative:

> In the first place, that the faithful who assist at the liturgy must understand it, must participate consciously and actively in a living assembly. In the second place, that pastors are responsible for such an active understanding and participation, that the active participation of the faithful in the liturgy is a very important part of their responsibility as pastors.[39]

His answer resonates with the substance of what would be promulgated as article 14 of *Sacrosanctum Concilium* (above).

Gy also correctly observed that a "pastoral objection" to the "great changes in the liturgy envisaged by the Council" could be made: "in general the faithful do not like their piety to be disturbed, and a pastor always prefers patient instruction to sudden change." He continues:

> This is true, no doubt, but we must take into account here the purpose and the grace proper to an ecumenical council ... The grace of a council is not only to make the different parts of the Church intensely aware of each other, but also to see beyond the present day into the future ...
>
> In all the parishes of the Church the people of the baptised and their pastors are invited to go beyond the pastoral needs of the local community in order that the Church with all its members may become capable in a great renewal to respond to the men of tomorrow, and to offer to them also the environment for that prayer in spirit and in truth of which our Lord Jesus Christ speaks in the Gospel.[40]

Gy foresaw that "none or very few" of the Council's liturgical reforms "will be susceptible of immediate application," envisaging that the new liturgical books "could still take several years." "While we wait," he advised, "we shall have to practice patience and strive to inculcate in the faithful a true liturgical spirit so that later on the application of the new norms will be understood, accepted and lived."[41]

Again, the *a priori* need for liturgical formation resonates, and rightly. However Gy's view, which anticipates "great" and "sudden" changes which necessarily disturb piety in order to establish a liturgy that is pastoral in the view of future generations, is one that finds no basis in *Sacrosanctum Concilium*. This clear step beyond the Council, which speaks more moderately of the need "to adapt more suitably to the needs of our own times" (*Sacrosanctum Concilium*, n. 1), is not beyond the vision of this *peritus*—who would play an important role in the Constitution's implementation.[42]

There is a critical dichotomy here between the position of the Council—which is consonant with the initiatives of the decades preceding it—and talk of a "necessary" disturbance by great and sudden changes so as to make of the liturgy something pastoral for future generations. This raises the question of the fidelity of the implementation of the Constitution to the Council itself. In respect of pastoral liturgy, we must ask whether the Council's nuanced vision was achieved, or simply left behind?

The Council speaks of the "promotion of pastoral-liturgical action" through the establishment of liturgical commissions at a national and diocesan level which will foster "the promotion and restoration of the liturgy" (*Sacrosanctum Concilium*, nn. 43–6). These provisions, read in the light of article 14, surely give such commissions the duty of facilitating liturgical formation so as to enable true participation in the liturgical rites—rites moderately reformed in accordance with the other provisions of the Constitution. Whilst the Constitution contains clear "Norms for adapting the Liturgy to the culture and traditions of peoples" (nn. 37–40),[43] it does not give a licence for adaptation of the liturgy at a local level according to perceived pastoral needs. Indeed, it states exactly the opposite (n. 22 § 3).

It is true that the *Consilium* charged with the implementation of *Sacramentum Concilium* 'amplified' its provisions. Annibale Bugnini CM (1912–82) would state clearly: "It cannot be denied that the principle, approved by the Council, of using the vernaculars was given a broad interpretation."[44] On this question it can be argued that whilst the liturgical use of the vernacular can serve participation and its pastoral end, the wholesale vernacularization of the liturgy substantially changes the nature of the rite.[45] Whilst Bugnini states that this change was "in line with the *spirit* of the Conciliar decrees" and relies on "the approval of competent authority," the departure in this and in other areas from the reform authorized by the Council itself is clear.[46]

This "competently approved" largesse in respect of the provisions of *Sacrosanctum Concilium,* which was principally the result of the desires and even the enthusiasms of the liturgists working on the reform itself, coincided with widespread unofficial adaptation of the liturgy according to the supposedly pastoral judgment of individual celebrants and communities. Some such were cited in the Introduction to this chapter. Bugnini himself laments "the free composition of texts, including the eucharistic prayer; the substitution of secular readings for biblical ones; celebrations outside sacred places (homes, meeting rooms, refectories); use of ordinary bread; rejection of the vestments; use of noisy music unsuited to a sacred action; dialogue homilies that at times became discussions rather than a listening to the Word of God; ritual eccentricities."[47] Such practices spread rapidly and, again in Bugnini's words, "did harm to the faithful and to the reform generally."[48] Nor were they by any means a mere temporary phenomenon. At a local level liturgical practice moved very far from the nuanced provisions of *Sacrosanctum Concilium* in a very short time indeed whereby "pastoral liturgy" came to mean improvisation and a "creativity" which went well beyond the rites as given—an approach which, unfortunately, is not yet extinct.[49]

Such liturgical dissolution obscures the nature of the Sacred Liturgy as the public worship *of the Church*—and not merely of the local assembly—as developed and handed on in the Church's Tradition, and renders participation in the liturgy facile. In part, this phenomenon can be traced to an ecclesiological shift following the Council's description the Church as "the new people of God" (*Lumen Gentium*, 9). According to one *peritus*, "the emphasis with which the idea of the people of God was seized on during the Council meant that the emotion surrounding this discovery far exceeded what the biblical foundations could bear." One implication of this is that: "'People' appears as a concept to be dealt with in sociological and political terms: if the Church can be defined by the concept 'people,' then its nature and its legal structure are best determined on the basis of sociological points of view. In this way the 'people of God' becomes the vehicle of an anti-hierarchical and anti-sacral idea of the Church, indeed a revolutionary category suitable for dreaming up a new Church."[50]

In 1965 the *Consilium* consulter Johannes Wagner (1908–99) prefaced an edition of *Concilium* dedicated to the liturgy by observing that:

> In the course of its history [the liturgical movement] has . . . become much more aware of its true nature, and the word "pastoral" is no longer adequate to designate this nature. One could . . . give a deeper meaning to "pastoral" . . . and describe it as pastoral care through liturgy, or pastoral care starting at the altar, but all this is hardly satisfactory . . . something has come to the fore which goes beyond pastoral activity and is the very basis of pastoral work.
>
> Today we see the foundation of all pastoral work in a new and growing self-awareness of the Church . . . The people of God become aware of themselves in public worship. In this public worship they become visibly manifest as a whole and in the various parts . . . In the celebration of the liturgy the Church becomes an "event", as Rahner said . . .
>
> Basically, therefore, the liturgical movement which brought about a new awareness of all this, is nothing but a part, a specific expression and an important interpretation of a much wider process which has been developing in the Church for a long time already, and through which the image of the Church comes to be seen again in a new light, and is realised in an even deeper way.[51]

Wagner captures the "spirit" of the time which was indeed that of a "new Church" with a "new" theology of worship. The Spanish *peritus* and advisor to the liturgical *Consilium*, Casiano Floristán (1926–2006), developed this new theology in an article "The Assembly and Its Pastoral Implications" published in 1966. Drawing on sociological and psychological considerations Floristán raises eight questions pertinent to the liturgical "assembly:"

1. Does each member of the assembly feel he *belongs*?
2. How *active is the participation* of each member of the assembly?
3. How *hierarchical* should the structure of each Christian assembly be?
4. How *universal* or *catholic* is the assembly in its composition?
5. Does the assembly perform a *pastoral* service, initiating and strengthening the faith of its members?
6. How *suitable* is the *place* of worship?
7. What are the *relations* between the *assembly* and the *broader human community*?

8. What is the relationship between the *parochial* assembly and the *diocesan* assembly?[52]

Some of Floristán's questions, and aspects of his reflections upon them, are sound. Other aspects, however, provide fuel for a radical subjectivization of the liturgy whereby the assembly itself, a somewhat "hyper-conscious" gathering of the people of God, and perhaps not God Himself, becomes the focus of worship. Once liturgy has gone down this path it soon arrives at the need constantly to appease human sensibilities anew (i.e. to entertain): "The ever-threatening temptation to mechanical repetition must be avoided," Floristán warns. "This requires that at each epoch of time the celebration must be sufficiently 'new' for everyone to take part full of expectation."[53]

As a result of this prevailing theological wind, "pastoral liturgy," whether Wagner, Floristán, and their colleagues intended it or not, rapidly came to mean liturgy that was devolved, deregulated, and denuded of its ritual heritage and theological objectivity. "Liturgy" as "the expression in worship of the Church as God's people" as *Concilium* defined it in 1972,[54] resulting in widespread liturgical "rationalistic relativism, confusing claptrap and pastoral infantilism."[55]

That this was not the intention of the Council is clear from a study of its Constitution on the Sacred Liturgy. However this liturgical de-formation spread widely.[56] In the face of this ecclesiastical authority attempted to reassert liturgical discipline and the true nature of the reform,[57] efforts which, if not completely, have nonetheless laid the foundations for a renewal of authentic liturgical theology and praxis—indeed of authentically pastoral liturgy.

Liturgy that is truly pastoral

Liturgy that is authentically pastoral is liturgy that is authentic to its nature as liturgy: liturgy which is truly that of the Church—that which we receive in her living tradition—and which is celebrated as the Church intends it to be celebrated, namely primarily as an act of the worship of Almighty God that is His due.

This principle excludes the subjective concept that "the liturgy *itself* must be pastoral and must be able to adapt to the needs of the people" and that "differentiated forms of eucharistic celebration" should be "introduced within the bounds of the same locality,"[58] with a "ritual practice" that is "existentially effective and culturally meaningful."[59] It challenges the post-conciliar assumption that young people and adults fail to connect with the liturgy because of supposed "widespread expectations ... regarding adaptation, participation and communion," and that "greater creativity ... greater interpretive freedom ... new symbols ... a festive atmosphere ... celebrations that engender courageous choices ... [and] small groups capable of significant relationships" are the hallmarks of truly pastoral liturgy.[60]

Nor does it accept that the Sacred Liturgy has a primarily catechetical or pedagogical function—an error that the *Directory for Masses with Children* issued by the Congregation for Divine Worship on 1 November 1973 and the three eucharistic prayers for children it occasioned the following year promoted—if not intentionally, at least in its widespread application. Decades later the Directory's hope that its measures would form children for liturgical participation in the future (nn. 8–15), so enthusiastically seized on by "pastoral" liturgists,[61] seem not to have been fulfilled. Children thus formed do not seem to be any different to their contemporaries in their liturgical (non) practice. A comprehensive study of this question would be revealing.[62]

No, the Sacred Liturgy is an act of worship and a privileged *locus theologiae*, not a catechetical tool or a panacea for initiatives or enthusiasms of the gathered community. If the liturgy becomes primarily an instrument for catechesis it is easily subjected to and reshaped in accordance with any programme or ideology. When the legitimate distinction between *interior* worship of the heart and mind and the *external* forms of the liturgy is used as a basis for subjective alteration of the latter to serve transient ends, that which the liturgical rites and prayers make present—the action of Christ in His Church—itself becomes secondary. What is left is the action of man with his own limited vision and preoccupations. The danger then is that it is simply the community and its desires (howsoever worthy), and not Almighty God, that such liturgical celebrations worship.

This is not Catholic liturgy, nor is it authentic pastoral action. Truly pastoral liturgy is not "liturgy-lite," nor is it "liturgy *à-la-carte*." The liturgy it is fundamentally latreutic—it is by its very nature cultic. It is worship: the Church's worship of Almighty God. And when its nature as ecclesial worship is respected, its pastoral efficacy is optimal: "A true and fruitful celebration of the liturgy at once demands and secures a truly Christian life."[63] As one liturgist wrote as early as 1969: "Since 'liturgy' means worship itself, the addition of the word 'pastoral' is superfluous: there is no such thing as a 'pastoral Mass' or a 'pastoral baptism' alongside of the celebration of Mass or baptism."[64]

We have noted that the Second Vatican Council's Constitution on the Sacred Liturgy promoted "pastoral-liturgical action" rather than "pastoral liturgy" (nn. 43–6).[65] In 1965, a study of pastoral liturgical action was published by Aimon-Marie Roguet OP (1906–91), one of the founders of France's *Centre de pastorale liturgique* in 1943 and its co-director until 1964, as well as a member of the liturgical Preparatory Commission and a consulter of the post-conciliar *Consilium*. It appeared as a chapter in the widely published work of Aimé-Georges Martimort (1911–2000), *L'Église en prière*,[66] and in English translation in 1968 in *The Church at Prayer – Introduction to the Liturgy*. Although this article was omitted from subsequent editions of Martimort's book, its value as an articulation of the Constitution's understanding of the pastoral effects of the Sacred Liturgy remains.

Roguet defines pastoral-liturgical action as: "the part of this art [of pastoral ministry] which consists in helping the faithful to participate actively and consciously in the liturgical celebration, the primary and indispensable source from which the faithful are to derive the true Christian spirit."[67] It is not primarily missionary in that "it has for its object the celebration of the mysteries by and for the faithful" and "does not as such envisage non-believers."[68] Such activity is educative and essentially formative, seeking to lead people "progressively to a profounder penetration of the most authentic Christian mystery."[69] Pastoral liturgical action:

> Is not directed to apparent success, nor to adapting itself only to the immediate needs of the Christian people, especially to a segment of this people geographically and socially confined. It ought to bring the faithful into the worship of the Church and teach them to respect and love everything which constitutes her patrimony of thought and prayer. It does not aim so much at forming small, sincere and coherent communities as to incorporate them in the community of all countries and times, the Church. Thus, it has to be founded on a vast and precise knowledge of liturgical tradition, without which it risks being reduced to a short-sighted pragmatism, extemporaneous rites and anarchical experiments.[70]

Once again we find that the key to unlocking the pastoral efficacy of the Sacred Liturgy is the patient work of liturgical formation. This is of the essence of pastoral-liturgical activity. It is the necessary precondition for a participation in liturgical celebrations that are pastorally efficacious. Indeed, as early as 26 September 1964 the Instruction of the Sacred Congregation of Rites, *Inter Oecumenici*, would clarify that the intention of the Constitution on the Sacred Liturgy is "not simply to change liturgical forms and texts but rather to bring to life the kind of formation of the faithful and ministry of pastors that will have their summit and source in the liturgy (see n. 10). That is the purpose of the changes made up to now and of those yet to come" (n. 5).

The Constitution certainly envisaged ritual reforms to facilitate such pastorally efficacious participation, in particular the increased (but not exclusive) use of the vernacular. However, as we have seen, their efficacy is predicated by the Council itself on thorough liturgical formation (see *Sacrosanctum Concilium*, 14, cited above).

Roguet considers various requirements for the celebration of the liturgy and even regards the turning of the altar towards the people as desirable; something not asked for by the Council and, in the opinion of this author, unnecessary if not misleading in respect of efficacious participation in the liturgy. In this, and in his enthusiasm for the "commentator" in the liturgy, his application of these principles reflects some of the enthusiasms of the period.[71] Yet his principles retain their value:

> The first concern of [pastoral-liturgical] action should be to promote a celebration which is exact, worthy, beautiful and true. Liturgy is a sacred action. Pastoral action consists in introducing the people into this action, in making the signs meaningful to them with a view to participation. For this reason it is necessary that this action be authentic, the signs be recognisable and participation possible.[72]

And Roguet is clear that "a beautiful liturgical celebration should be the point of departure for a deeper and purer personal religion and for a more charitable and more radiant communal life."[73] The pastoral importance of beauty should be underlined here. As Hans Anscar Reinhold (1897–1968) wrote in 1958: "Voluntary poverty certainly helps the spreading of the Gospel, but liturgical destitution and parsimony are hardly the things the poor demand of Christ's Church."[74]

There is a clear resonance between Roguet's principles, which arise from those of the Council itself, and the 22 February 2007 Apostolic Exhortation of Benedict XVI (1927–; 2005–13), *Sacramentum Caritatis*. With a freshness that leaves aside the 'pastoral' liturgical dross of previous decades, Benedict XVI teaches:

> Like the rest of Christian Revelation, the liturgy is inherently linked to beauty: it is *veritatis splendor.* The liturgy is a radiant expression of the paschal mystery, in which Christ draws us to himself and calls us to communion. As St Bonaventure would say, in Jesus we contemplate beauty and splendour at their source. This is no mere aestheticism, but the concrete way in which the truth of God's love in Christ encounters us, attracts us and delights us, enabling us to emerge from ourselves and drawing us towards our true vocation, which is love (n. 35).

Benedict XVI then moves to the practical application of this theological reality:

> The primary way to foster the participation of the People of God in the sacred rite is the proper celebration of the rite itself. The *ars celebrandi* is the best way to ensure their *actuosa participatio.* The *ars celebrandi* is the fruit of faithful adherence to the liturgical norms in all their richness; indeed, for two thousand years this way of celebrating has sustained the faith life of all believers, called to take part in the celebration as the People of God, a royal priesthood, a holy nation (see *1 Pet* 2:4–5, 9) (n. 38).

We have here two fundamental principles of liturgy that is truly pastoral. Indeed, Part II of *Sacramentum Caritatis* is nothing less than a directory of pastoral liturgy drawn up in the light of decades of varying post-conciliar liturgical experience. Its specific provisions pertain to the modern rites, certainly, but its principles are also applicable to the *usus antiquior*—the older form of the Roman rite—the pastoral efficacy of which is an increasingly evident fact in the life of the Church of the twenty-first century and which dispels many myths about the absolute necessity of particular ritual reforms.[75] So too the liturgical theology taught in Part I of the exhortation, and the pastoral implications of liturgical participation drawn out in Part III, place the question of authentic liturgical celebration in its rightful ecclesial and missionary context. Indeed, the whole of *Sacramentum Caritatis* is a fundamental resource for a renewed and integrated understanding of the theological, pastoral and missionary aspects of the Sacred Liturgy which will serve the Church of the twenty-first century, and beyond, very well indeed.

In striving towards an authentic renewal of the Sacred Liturgy, a renewal that bears true pastoral fruit, the words of the "father" of the new liturgical movement serve as a reliable guide:

If the liturgy appears first of all as the workshop for our activity, then what is essential is being forgotten: God. For the liturgy is not about us, but about God. Forgetting about God is the most imminent danger of our age. As against this, the liturgy should be setting up a sign of God's presence. Yet what happens if the habit of forgetting about God makes itself at home in the liturgy itself and if in the liturgy we are thinking only of ourselves? In any and every liturgical reform, and every liturgical celebration, the primacy of God should be kept in view first and foremost.[76]

Conclusion

In January 1969, Father Annibale Bugnini rather ambitiously claimed that as a result of the reforms enacted, "millions and hundreds of millions of the faithful . . . have at last achieved worship in spirit and truth" and "can at last pray to God in their own languages and not in meaningless sounds."[77] His later memoirs were somewhat more measured, speaking of the "long and difficult" road of liturgical reform, expressing the hope that "at the end the Church will have a renewed liturgy that will give God's people once again a sense of the sacred mystery and help them to enter into it."[78]

The 1983 reflections of the President of the North American Academy of Liturgy, Mark Searle (1941–92), are perhaps more realistic:

Looking back over our accomplishments, we liturgists can rightly claim to have achieved a success beyond the wildest dreams of the early pioneers of the liturgical movement, especially at the structural level. Where the effects of such structural reform are concerned, however, the verdict is not quite so unanimous. It must be admitted that the liturgical pioneers who pressed for change had no special competence to foresee what the results of those changes would be. Whereas they were equipped with profound knowledge of the liturgical tradition and a deep insight into the centrality of the liturgy in the life of the church, theologically understood, the conviction that the reforms would generate renewal was based on little more than a hunch, validated by the enthusiasm of some monastic communities and of lay and clerical followers who, in the words of Miss Jean Brodie, "like that kind of thing." In short, historical awareness and theological depth were enough to persuade church authorities to reform the liturgy, but they were insufficient to ensure any controlled connection between the reform of the liturgical books and the renewal of Christian life.[79]

Indeed, the previous year Searle had soberly observed that:

It was never in anyone's dreams that . . . many of the most devout and active faithful would look for sustenance in their religious lives to sources outside the Church, finding themselves alienated from the liturgy they once loved. Such, however, is often the case. Many whose vocation is to prayer either suffer parish liturgy or avoid it . . . We are in danger of being left with those of the faithful who have neither the sense of conviction nor clarity of vision to go anywhere else.[80]

"This has to change,"[81] Searle concluded. He was, and is, correct: the pastoral renewal expected to follow from the ritual reforms enacted after the Second Vatican Council has not occurred. Indeed, the effect of predicating "pastoral" to "liturgy" in the decades following the Council obscured the true nature of the Sacred Liturgy and led to liturgical practices foreign to it and to the principles espoused by the Council. This reality has not facilitated the widespread renewal of Christian life, which is why this reality most certainly needs urgently to be revisited.

Every pastoral activity of the Church finds in the Sacred Liturgy the source of all its endeavours. So too, all pastoral activity finds in the liturgy its end: the praise and adoration of God the Father, through His Son Jesus Christ in the power of the Holy Spirit in the ecclesial assembly, His Church (see: *Sacrosanctum Concilium*, n. 10). It is in this sense that the Sacred Liturgy is truly pastoral. It is the foretaste of the eschatological pasture to which the Good Shepherd guides His sheep—a foretaste which is both a motivation and a consolation, and a missionary and evangelical imperative, by means of which we already rejoice in "green pastures", "beside still waters," our cups overflowing.

But we can only realize this end if we ensure that liturgical celebrations are grounded in a profound respect for the nature of liturgy itself. The folly of recent decades should be enough to warn us away from paths that are a dead-end. The vision and practice of the pioneers of the liturgical movement can still provide encouragement and inspiration. And the principles of *Sacrosanctum Concilium* read with the wisdom of *Sacramentum Caritatis* can chart our route. Then, working from the conviction that "the true celebration of the Sacred Liturgy is the centre of any renewal of the Church whatever,"[82] we may approach the pastoral goal St John XXIII espoused for the renewal of the Sacred Liturgy: "to enable the Christian life of the faithful to grow more and more every day."[83]

Notes

1   Domenico Sartore CSJ, "Pastoral Liturgy," Anscar J. Chupungco OSB (ed.), *Handbook for Liturgical Studies*, vol. II (Collegeville: Liturgical Press, 1998), pp. 65–95 (p. 82).
2   Andrew Greely, "Religious Symbolism, Liturgy and Community," Herman Schmidt SJ (ed.), *Liturgy in Transition* (New York: Herder, 1971), pp. 59–69 (p. 66).
3   Sartore, "Pastoral Liturgy," p. 82
4   Anselm Grün OSB, *The Seven Sacraments* (Mumbai: St Paul's, 2007), p. 70. An earlier edition with different pagination is published by Continuum, New York & London, 2003.
5   Ibid., p. 30.
6   *Catechism of the Catholic Church*, n. 1124.
7   See: Alcuin Reid, *The Organic Development of the Liturgy: The Principles of Liturgical Reform and Their Relation to the Twentieth Century Liturgical Movement Prior to the Second Vatican Council*, 2nd edn (San Francisco: Ignatius Press, 2005).

8 "That such a cardinal, such a Saint, thought the vast labour expanded on the reformation of ceremonial of his province worthwhile is, for us, a much needed lesson in value judgement;" M.A. Chapman, "The Liturgical Directions of Saint Charles Borromeo: Terminal Essay," *Liturgical Arts* 7 (1939), pp. 10–13 (p. 13). Other essays in this series may be found in *Liturgical Arts* 3 (1934), pp. 142–8; 4 (1935), pp. 109–18; 5 (1936), pp. 60–3, pp. 105–9; 6 (1938), pp. 91–4

9 See: *Sacrosanctum Concilium*, n. 22.

10 See: Chapter 8 "The Twentieth Century Liturgical Movement."

11 See: R.W. Franklin, "Guéranger and Pastoral Liturgy: A Nineteenth Century Context," *Worship* 50 (1976), pp. 146–62. The account of the liturgical formation and practice of the parish of Mesnil-St-Loup on pages 160–2 is illustrative.

12 Henri Leclerq, cited in: Reid, *The Organic Development of the Liturgy*, p. 89.

13 Ibid, p. v.

14 John G. Vance & J.W. Fortescue, *Adrian Fortescue: A Memoir* (London: Burns, Oates & Washbourne, 1924), p. 29.

15 Edith Cowell, "Adrian Fortescue," *Blackfriars* IV (1923), pp. 1029–34 (p. 1032). See also: Aidan Nichols OP, *The Latin Clerk: The Life, Work and Travels of Adrian Fortescue* (Cambridge: Lutterworth Press, 2011), chapter 8 "The Practice of the Liturgy."

16 See: *Cours et Conferences des Semaines Liturgiques*, Tome III (Louvain: Abbaye du Mont-César, 1925).

17 See: Alfredo Idelfonso Schuster, Inos Biffi (ed.), *La Sacra Liturgia "Il cuore della Chiesa orante,"* (Piemme: Casale Monferrato, 1996), which provides extracts from many of Schuster's writings as well as an overview essay by the editor (the latter unfortunately seeks to identify Schuster with the reforms implemented over a decade after his death).

18 For an account of the pastoral nature of medieval liturgy see: Virginia Reinburg, "Liturgy and the Laity in Late Medieval and Reformation France," *The Sixteenth Century Journal* 23 (1992), pp. 526–47.

19 F.J. Godet, "La Liturgie: est-elle adaptée aux besoins du people?" *Prière Liturgique & Vie Chrétienne: Questions Actuelles – Cours et Conferences des Semaines Liturgiques*, Tome X (Louvain & Gembloux: Abbaye du Mont-César & Duclot, 1932), pp. 151–67.

20 For the emergence of the term "pastoral" see: Heinrich Rennings, "What is the Liturgy supposed to do?" *Concilium* 2 (February 1969), pp. 60–8 (pp. 62–3).

21 See: Pie Duployé OP, *Les Origines du Centre de Pastorale Liturgique 1943–1949* (Mulhouse: Salvator, 1968).

22 From a letter published in no. 3 of an English journal *Order* (c. 1930), quoted in: Donald Attwater, "Two Years Later—and a Query," in: *Orate Fratres* 4 (1929/30), pp. 151–5 (p. 152). Attwater does not cite the author's name.

23 See: *Catechism of the Catholic Church*, n. 1124.

24 "Nous avons assez travaillé, depuis les origines du C.P.L., à donner au mouvement liturgique français une base paroissiale pour pouvoir aujourd'hui, au début de ce cahier consacré à un grand moine, déclarer que nos amis bénédictins nous ont communiqué une lumière et une grâce qui n'appartiennent qu'à eux, et sans lesquelles notre effort liturgique aurait vite perdu sa fraîcheur et comme sa densité spécifique pour être ravalé au niveau d'une très quelconque pastorale, d'un « mouvement » au sens le plus péjoratif du terme, qui évoque celui d'une agitation;" "Sommaire," *La Maison-Dieu* 14 (1948), pp. 3–4 (p. 4). See also: A. Nichols OP, "Odo Casel Revisited," *Antiphon* 3 (1998), pp. 12–20; P. Duployé & A.M. Roguet OP (eds), *Études de pastorale liturgique: Vanves 26–28 Janvier 1944*, 'Lex Orandi' 1 (Cerf, Paris, 1944), especially the insightful

contribution of Louis Bouyer, "Après les journées de Vanves: Quelques mises au point sur le sens et le rôle de la Liturgie," pp. 379–89.

25 See: Reid, *The Organic Development of the Liturgy*, pp. 150 ff.

26 See: ibid., chapter 3.

27 Oswald Sumner, "The Conversion of England," Charles R.A. Cunliffe (ed.), *English in the Liturgy: A Symposium* (London: Burns & Oates, 1955), pp. 134–50 (p. 142).

28 Clifford Howell SJ, "The Liturgical Approach", ibid., pp. 50–91 (pp. 90, 91).

29 J.A. Jungmann SJ, "The Pastoral Idea in the History of the Liturgy," *The Assisi Papers: Proceedings of the First International Congress of Pastoral Liturgy* (Collegeville: Liturgical Press, 1957), pp. 18–31 (p. 29). See also: J.A. Jungmann SJ, *Pastoral Liturgy* (London: Challoner Publications, 1962).

30 W. Rafferty, *Liturgy in the Parish* (London: Challoner Publications, 1958); E. Athill, *Teaching Liturgy in Schools* (London: Challoner Publications, 1958).

31 See: Reid *The Organic Development of the Liturgy*, pp. 164 ff.

32 One of the most radical proposals of this period was published by H.A. Reinhold, *Bringing the Mass to the People* (London: Burns & Oates, 1960). It argues that significant ritual reform is required to adapt the Mass to the needs of modern man.

33 "Pope John on Pastoral Liturgy" in: *Worship*, vol. 37 (1962/3), (pp. 464–97), p. 481.

34 See: chapter 14. Also: Angelo Lameri, ed., *La « Pontificia Commisio de sacra liturgia praeparatoria Concilii Vaticani II » Documenti, Testi, Verbali* (BELS: 2013). A study of their work will form one chapter of Alcuin Reid, *Continuity or Rupture: A Study of the Liturgical Reform of the Second Vatican Council* (forthcoming).

35 See: chapter 14.

36 Whilst "participatio actuosa" is translated as "*active* participation," in the context of the liturgical movement and the intention of the Council Fathers, this activity is primarily a connection with the action of Christ in the Sacred Liturgy, being actively engaged with it, which connection the Council certainly believed would be enhanced by external activity such as singing and responding, but which does not exclude participation without external activity, such as attentively following the rites, prayers, chant, etc.

37 See: Alcuin Reid " 'Thoroughly imbued with the spirit and power of the Liturgy'— *Sacrosanctum Concilium* and Liturgical Formation," A. Reid (ed.), *Sacred Liturgy: The Source and Summit of the Life and Mission of the Church* (San Francisco: Ignatius Press, 2014), pp. 213–36.

38 P.M. Gy OP, "Pastoral Liturgy," *Worship* 37 (1962/3), pp. 559–63 (p. 559). The press conference was given on 14 November 1962 and published as: "La conferenza stampa di Padre Pietro Maria Gy. La liturgia è pastorale. I fedeli devono essere 'spettatori muti,' " *L'Osservatore Romano*, n. 263, 16 novembre 1962, p. 2.

39 Ibid.

40 Ibid., p. 562.

41 Ibid., p. 562–3.

42 For Gy's involvement see the Appendix "Members and Consultors of the Organisations for Liturgical Reform" to: Annibale Bugnini CM, *The Reform of the Liturgy 1948–1975* (Collegeville: Liturgical Press, 1990), pp. 937–55, and the index entries on pp. 970–1.

43 A correct interpretation of these articles must respect the antecedent principles outlined in the Constitution. See also: Benedict XVI, Apostolic Exhortation, *Sacramentum Caritatis*, 22 February 2007, n. 54.

44 Bugnini, *The Reform of the Liturgy*, p. 110.

45 See further: Uwe Michael Lang, *The Voice of the Church at Prayer: Reflections on Liturgy and Language* (San Francisco: Ignatius Press, 2012), pp. 179–80.

46 Bugnini, *The Reform of the Liturgy,* p. 110. Emphasis added. Some of the more prominent 'pastoral' changes that were introduced—the celebration of Mass facing the people, the reception of Holy Communion on the hand, the practical exclusion of Latin by the vernacular, the introduction of new eucharistic prayers, the relegation of Gregorian chant and sacred polyphony, etc—have no basis in the Constitution on the Sacred Liturgy. See also chapter 14.

47 Ibid., p. 258.

48 Ibid., p. 259.

49 The present author personally experienced almost all of the abuses of which Bugnini complained in seminaries in Australia between 1982–89. Whilst such abuses seem now to occur less often, some still surface. See for example the utterly inappropriate performance of the "Sister Act" ensemble at the noon Mass in St Stephen's Cathedral, Vienna, on Tuesday, 18 September 2012, featured on YouTube at: www.youtube.com/watch?v=Ki-HuVqWFeU. The blog *Rorate Coeli* continues to report on similar abuses.

50 Joseph Cardinal Ratzinger, *Church, Ecumenism and Politics* (Slough: St Paul Publications, 1988), p. 21.

51 Johannes Wagner, "Preface," *Concilium* 2 (February 1965), pp. 3–4.

52 Casiano Floristán, "The Assembly and Its Pastoral Implications," *Concilium* 12 (1966), pp. 33–44 (pp. 40–43).

53 Ibid., p. 43.

54 David Power, Herman Schmidt SJ & Helmut Hucke, "Editorial," Herman Schmidt SJ (ed.), *Liturgy: Self Expression in the Church—Concilium: Religion in the Seventies* (New York: Herder & Herder, 1972), pp. 7–8 (p. 7).

55 Joseph Cardinal Ratzinger with Vittorio Messori, *The Ratzinger Report: An Exclusive Interview on the State of the Church* (San Francisco: Ignatius Press, 1985) p. 121. For an analysis see: Joseph Cardinal Ratzinger, *A New Song for the Lord: Faith in Christ and Liturgy Today* (New York: Crossroad, 1997), pp. 32, 112–15. JRCW 11 (pp. 443–47) contains pp. 112–15 of *A New Song for the Lord.*

56 The literature generated in this period is illustrative. See: Robert W. Hovda & Gabe Huck, *There's No Place Like People—Liturgical Celebrations in Home and Small-Group Situations* (Washington DC: The Liturgical Conference, 1969); John P. Mossi SJ (ed.), *Modern Liturgy Handbook* (New York: Paulist Press, 1976); Robert W Hovda, *Strong, Loving and Wise: Presiding in Liturgy* (Washington DC: The Liturgical Conference, 1976) [later: Collegeville: Liturgical Press]. A more nuanced publication is: Harold Winstone (ed.), *Pastoral Liturgy: A Symposium* (London: Collins, 1975).

57 See: Alcuin Reid, "From rubrics to *ars celebrandi*—Liturgical Law in the 21st Century," *Antiphon* 17 (2013), pp. 139–67 (pp. 157–63).

58 Sartore, "Pastoral Liturgy," p. 66. Emphasis added.

59 Ibid., p. 69.

60 See: ibid. p. 83.

61 See: ibid. pp. 81–2.

62 Chapter III of Athill's, *Teaching Liturgy in Schools* discusses "Children and the Mass." See also: Alain de Sauvebouef, *Our Children and the Mass: How to Make it Live for Them* (London: Challoner Publications, 1958). Peter Kwasniewski argues: "The ultimate 'children's Mass'—and I mean for everyone, from the wee lad to the ancient, who seeks to live out the vocation of *spiritual* childhood, not for those who remain (or who would have others remain) locked at a childish stage of human development—is a Tridentine Mass with all the stops pulled, thundering orthodoxy and whispering mystery to all present. If you want a church full of Catholics who know their faith, love their faith and

practice their faith, give them a liturgy that is demanding, profound, and rigorous. They will rise to the challenge," *Resurgent in the Midst of Crisis: Sacred Liturgy, the Traditional Latin Mass, and Renewal in the Church* (Kettering, OH: Angelico Press, 2014), p. 27.

63 William J. O'Shea SS, *The Worship of the Church* (London: Darton, Longman & Todd, 1960, p. 30.

64 Rennings, "What is the Liturgy supposed to do?" p. 62.

65 The only occurrence of the term "pastoral liturgy" in *Sacrosanctum Concilium* is in article 44: "It is desirable that the competent territorial ecclesiastical authority mentioned in Art. 22, 2, set up a liturgical commission, to be assisted by experts in liturgical science, sacred music, art and pastoral practice. So far as possible the commission should be aided by some kind of Institute for Pastoral Liturgy [Institutum Liturgiae Pastoralis], consisting of persons who are eminent in these matters, and including laymen as circumstances suggest. Under the direction of the above-mentioned territorial ecclesiastical authority the commission is to regulate pastoral-liturgical action throughout the territory, and to promote studies and necessary experiments whenever there is question of adaptations to be proposed to the Apostolic See."

66 A.-G. Martimort, *L'Église en prière – introduction à la liturgie* (Tournai, Rome & New York: Desclée, 1965).

67 Aimon-Marie Roguet OP, "Pastoral-Liturgical Action," A.-G. Martimort (ed.) *The Church at Prayer—Introduction to the Liturgy* (Shannon: Irish University Press, 1968), pp. 220–34 (p. 223).

68 Ibid. Keith Pecklers SJ perpetuates the subjective view: "Unlike its Tridentine form, Vatican II worship was to reach out widely to embrace all of God's world. Liturgy, then, was necessarily concerned about life outside of the sanctuary walls: human liberation, justice and mercy for the poor and oppressed, dialogue with other Christians and with non-Christian believers;" "*Ressourcement* and the Renewal of Catholic Liturgy, On Celebrating the New Rite," Gabriel Flynn & Paul D. Murray (eds), *Ressourcement: A Movement for Renewal in Twentieth Century Catholic Theology* (Oxford: Oxford University Press, 2012), pp. 318–32 (p. 331).

69 Ibid., p. 225.

70 Ibid., pp. 225–26. Roguet footnotes *Sacrosanctum Concilium* 23.

71 See: ibid., pp. 226–27.

72 Ibid., p. 226.

73 Ibid., p. 232–33.

74 H.A. Reinhold, *The American Parish and the Roman Liturgy* (New York: Macmillan, 1958), p. 90.

75 See chapter 21. For a powerful argument asserting the pastoral value of the *usus antiquior* see Kwasniewski's *Resurgent in the Midst of Crisis: Sacred Liturgy, the Traditional Latin Mass, and Renewal in the Church.*

76 Joseph Cardinal Ratzinger, "Preface" to Reid, *The Organic Development of the Liturgy,* p. 13; JRCW 11, pp. 593–94.

77 Bugnini, *The Reform of the Liturgy,* p. 283, n. 16.

78 Ibid., p. 48.

79 M. Searle, "New Tasks, New Methods: The Emergence of Pastoral Liturgical Studies" *Worship* 57 (1983), pp. 291–308 (pp. 292–93).

80 M. Searle, "Reflections on Liturgical Reform," *Worship* 56 (1982), pp. 411–30 (p. 427).

81 Ibid.

82 Joseph Cardinal Razinger, cited in: Roberto de Mattei, "Reflections on the Liturgical Reform," Alcuin Reid (ed.), *Looking Again at the Question of the Liturgy with Cardinal Ratzinger* (Farnborough: St Michael's Abbey Press, 2003), pp. 130–44 (p. 141).
83 Cited in: Sartore, "Pastoral Liturgy," p. 65. See also: Dante Balboni, "La liturgia pastorale nel pensiero di Papa Giovanni XXIII," *Ephemerides Liturgicae* 72 (1958), pp. 384–87.

Select bibliography

ICEL, *Documents on the Liturgy: 1963–1979* [DOL].
Athill, Emmanuel, *Teaching Liturgy in Schools* (London: Challoner Publications, 1958).
Beauduin, Lambert, OSB, *Liturgy: The Life of the Church*, 1st & 2nd edns (Collegeville: Liturgical Press, 1926 & 1929); 3rd edn (Farnborough: St Michael's Abbey Press, 2002).
Benedict XVI, Apostolic Exhortation *Sacramentum Caritatis*, February 22, 2007.
Bugnini, Annibale, CM, *The Reform of the Liturgy 1948–1975* (Collegeville: Liturgical Press, 1990).
O'Shea, William J., SS, *The Worship of the Church* (London: Darton, Longman & Todd, 1960), chapter 3 "The Purpose of the Liturgy," pp. 26–46.
Rafferty, William, *Liturgy in the Parish* (London: Challoner Publications, 1958).
Reid, Alcuin, "Active Participation and Pastoral Adaptation," *Liturgy, Participation and Sacred Music: Proceedings of the Ninth International Colloquium of Historical, Canonical and Theological Studies on the Roman Catholic Liturgy* (Rochester: CIEL UK, 2006), pp. 35–50.
—— "Noble Simplicity Revisited," D.V. Twomey SVD & Janet E. Rutherford (eds), *Benedict XVI and Beauty in Sacred Art and Architecture* (Dublin & New York: Four Courts & Scepter, 2011), pp. 94–111.
—— "'Thoroughly imbued with the spirit and power of the Liturgy'—*Sacrosanctum Concilium* and Liturgical Formation," A. Reid (ed.), *Sacred Liturgy: The Source and Summit of the Life and Mission of the Church* (San Francisco: Ignatius Press, 2014), pp. 213–36.
—— "*Ut mens nostra concordet voci nostrae*: Sacred Music and Actual Participation in the Liturgy," Janet E. Rutherford (ed.), *Benedict XVI and Beauty in Sacred Music* (Dublin & New York: Four Courts & Scepter, 2012), pp. 93–126.
Rodheudt, Guido, "Pastoral Liturgy and the Church's Mission in Parishes—The Dangerous Hermeneutic of a Concept," A. Reid (ed.), *Sacred Liturgy: The Source and Summit of the Life and Mission of the Church* (San Francisco: Ignatius Press, 2014), pp. 273–89.
Roguet, Aimon-Marie, OP, "Pastoral-Liturgical Action," A.-G. Martimort (ed.), *The Church at Prayer—Introduction to the Liturgy* (Shannon: Irish University Press, 1968), pp. 220–34.
Sartore, Domenico, CSJ, "Pastoral Liturgy," Anscar J. Chupungco OSB (ed.), *Handbook for Liturgical Studies*, vol. II (Collegeville: Liturgical Press, 1998), pp. 65–95.

Chapter 17

THE LITURGY AND SACRED LANGUAGE

Uwe Michael Lang

Introduction

Languages exist in the context of a structured system that is determined by a variety of factors (social, cultural, psychological, and so on). The languages used in Christian worship have developed under certain conditions and circumstances that need to be considered to understand their characteristics. For this purpose, the work of Christine Mohrmann and the Nijmegen School on Latin in the liturgy is still essential, despite the valid criticism of the idea of Christian Latin as a "special language" that would be marked by particularities in morphology, lexis, and syntax.[1] Mohrmann's approach to liturgical language is based on Ferdinand de Saussure and other representatives of the Geneva school of linguistics, who propose to see language not only as a means of social communication in ordinary life, but also as a medium of expression of persons in a comprehensive sense. Human speech is not just a utilitarian instrument that serves to communicate facts, and should do so in the most simple and efficient manner; it also provides the forms of expressing and interpreting the rich and subtle workings of the human mind, including the arts, philosophy, and religion.[2]

Language is also the medium in which religious thoughts and experiences are expressed. It reaches its limits in two extreme forms of expression: "speaking in tongues" and "mystical silence." Speaking in tongues, or *glossolalia*, a phenomenon familiar to us from St Paul's First Letter to the Corinthians and has had an astonishing revival for the last hundred years or so in the charismatic movements; it also known also in other religion traditions, for example, the Oracle of Delphi. *Glossolalia* makes human communication impossible; the person who speaks "in tongues" can only be understood with the help of an interpreter. Paul clearly has reservations about *glossolalia* and prefers "prophecy," because this is in the service of charity and builds up the church (1 Cor. 14). In "mystical silence," human communication is excluded as well, as in the experience Augustine and his mother Monica shared at Ostia, described in book nine of the *Confessions*.[3]

"Sacred language" does not go as far as *glossolalia* and mystical silence in excluding human communication completely, or at least attempting to do so.

However, it reduces the element of comprehensibility in favor of other elements, notably that of expression. Mohrmann proposes to see in sacred language, and in particular in its vocabulary, a specific way of organizing religious experience. She also argues that every form of belief in the supernatural, in the existence of a transcendent being, leads necessarily to adopting a form of sacred language in worship—just as a consistent secularism leads to rejecting any form of it.

Sacred language is the medium of expression not just of individuals, but of a community living according to certain traditions. Its linguistic forms are handed down from generation to generation; they are often deliberately "stylized" and removed from contemporary language. There exists a similar phenomenon in the field of literature, the stylized language of the Homeric epos with its consciously archaic and colorful word forms. The language of the *Iliad* and the *Odyssey*, which is also found in Hesiod and in later poetic inscriptions, was never a spoken language used in everyday life.[4]

With Mohrmann, we can name three characteristics of sacred or, as she also says, "hieratic" language. First, sacred language is conservative; it shows tenacity in holding on to archaic linguistic forms. In the pagan Roman tradition, this characteristic was so pronounced that that for centuries prayers were used, while their meaning was not even understood by the priests who recited them. In the early Middle Ages, command of Latin was sometimes so poor that even basic mistakes were made in the most crucial sacramental formulas.[5] Secondly, foreign elements are introduced in order to associate with ancient religious tradition; a case in point is the Hebrew Biblical vocabulary in the Latin use of Christians. Augustine makes pertinent observations on this in his *De doctrina christiana*: "In some cases, although they could be translated, the original form is preserved for the sake of its solemn authority," such as "*amen*" and "*alleluia.*" Other words "are said to be incapable of being translated into another language . . . This is especially true of interjections, which signify emotion, rather than an element of clearly conceived meaning;" as an example, he cites "*osanna.*"[6] Thirdly, sacred language uses rhetorical figures that are typical of oral style, such as parallelism and antithesis, rhythmic clausulae, rhyme, and alliteration.[7]

From a theological perspective, the use of sacred language in the liturgy belongs to the "solemnity" that is observed in the celebration of the sacraments, especially of the Eucharist.[8] The idea of *solemnitas* is central to St Thomas Aquinas' understanding of the liturgy.[9] The German philosopher Josef Pieper proposed a broad definition of "sacred language," which includes gestures and signs as well as the words used in public worship; this would more or less cover the same ground as Aquinas' idea of *solemnitas*.[10] However, here, I follow the more restricted sense of the "sacred language," that is, the linguistic forms and expressions used in the Church's public worship.

It should be noted that by "sacred language" I do not mean to refer here to the Patristic tradition of the *tres linguae sacrae* of Christianity, Hebrew, Greek, and Latin, which were used on the title of the Cross according to John 19:20. Hilary of Poitiers refers to these three languages as "sacred," because in those languages "is preached above all the mystery of the will of God and the expectation of the coming Kingdom of God."[11] For Latin Church Fathers, such as Hilary and Augustine, and the Medieval tradition, these three languages are "sacred" not because of some outstanding inherent quality, but because they played a crucial role in the economy of salvation and in the preaching of the Gospel. Augustine comments on the title of Christ's Cross in John 19:20: "These three languages were prominent there before all others: Hebrew on behalf of the Jews who boasted in the law of God; Greek on behalf of the wise men among the pagans; Latin on behalf of the Romans who at that time were dominating many and almost all peoples."[12] However, this idea is quite different from the principle of "trilinguism," according to which the liturgy could only be celebrated in Hebrew, Greek, and Latin. In fact, recent scholarship has shown that "trilinguism," a charge that was brought up in the polemics surrounding the missionary work of St Cyril and St Methodius, was never held by Western theologians. Their reflections on the *tres linguae sacrae* rather referred to their use within the Latin rites.[13]

Early Eucharistic prayers

The aforementioned characteristics of sacred language emerge clearly from the early history of eucharistic prayers. It is generally agreed that these were relatively fluid in the first three centuries. Their exact wording was not yet fixed, and the celebrant had some room to improvise. However, as Allan Bouley notes, "Conventions governing the structure and content of improvised anaphoras are ascertainable in the second century and indicate that extempore prayer was not left merely to the whim of the minister. In the third century, and possibly even before, some anaphoral texts already existed in writing." Bouley speaks of an "atmosphere of controlled freedom,"[14] because concerns for orthodoxy limited the celebrant's liberty to vary the texts of the prayer. This need became particularly pressing during the doctrinal struggles of the fourth century; hence this era saw the emergence of fixed eucharistic prayers, such as the Roman canon, the Anaphora of St John Chrysostom, and others.

There is another important aspect of this development: the freedom to improvise existed only in a framework of fixed elements of content and style, which was, above all, biblically inspired. In a recent study on improvisation in liturgical prayer, Achim Budde analyses three oriental anaphoras used over a considerable geographical area, the Egyptian version of the Anaphora of St Basil, the West Syrian Anaphora of St James, and the East Syrian Anaphora of Nestorius. With his comparative method, the German liturgist identifies common features of structure, style, and rhetoric. Budde argues that these patterns and stable elements go back to the pre-literary history of these eucharistic prayers and that they was studied and even memorized by priests in the early Church.[15] As noted by the Norwegian exegete Sigmund Mowinckel, known especially for his work on the psalms, rapid development of fixed forms of prayer corresponds to an essential religious need and constitutes a fundamental law of religion.[16] Budde's methodological approach is an important supplement and corrective to that of

Bouley and other liturgical scholars, who would appear to underestimate the significance of repetition and memorization in an oral culture.[17] The formation of stable liturgical texts can thus be ascertained from early on as a strong force in the process of handing on the Christian faith.

In the Western tradition, the freedom to improvise remained for a longer time than in the East, especially in certain liturgical prayers, such as the introductory part of the eucharistic prayer we now call "preface."[18] This is the reason why there is such a great variety of prefaces in the early Roman sacramentaries. Mohrmann concludes that it is "this system which leads to a marked traditional prayer style."[19] A similar phenomenon can be observed in the earliest Greek epos: the freedom of individual singers to improvise on the given material led to a stylized language. In the liturgy, the early tradition of oral improvisation in prayer helped to create a sacred style.

Mohrmann introduces a useful distinction between sacred languages of a "primary" and a "secondary" kind. "Primary" sacred languages were formed as such from the beginning, for example, the language of the Greek oracles that was close to the *Kunstsprache* of the Homeric epos. "Secondary" sacred languages have come to be experienced as such only in the course of time. The languages used in Christian worship would seem to fall under this category: Greek in the Byzantine tradition; Syriac in the Patriarchate of Antioch and the "Nestorian" Church of the East with its missions reaching to India and China; Old Armenian; Old Georgian; Coptic; Old Ethiopian (*Geʿez*); Church Slavonic; not to forget the Elizabethan English of the *Book of Common Prayer* and the German used in the Lutheran books of worship (from the *Brandenburgisch-Nürnbergische Kirchenordnung* of 1533 to the *Lutherische Agende I* of 1955); and, of course, the Latin of the Roman Rite and other Western liturgical traditions.

There are stylistic features in all these liturgical languages that separate them from the ordinary languages of the people. This distance was often the result of linguistic developments in the common language that were not adopted in the liturgical language because of its conservative nature. However, in the case of Latin as the language of the Roman liturgy, a certain distance existed right from the beginning: the Romans did not speak in the style of the canon or of the collects of the Mass. As soon as Greek, originally the prevalent language of Christian communities in Rome, was replaced by Latin in the liturgy, a highly stylized medium of worship was created.[20]

This contribution focuses on the Latin tradition, and in particular on the Roman liturgy which became dominant in the Christian West. The field of research is of course much wider and it would be desirable to study the sacred languages of the Eastern Christian liturgies.[21]

The language of the Roman liturgy

The most important early source for the Roman eucharistic prayer is St Ambrose of Milan, who in his *De sacramentis*, a series of catecheses for the newly baptized that was held around 390, quotes extensively from the eucharistic prayer employed at that time in his city.[22] The passages quoted are earlier forms of the prayers *Quam oblationem, Qui pridie, Unde et memores, Supra quae,* and *Supplices te rogamus.* Elsewhere in *De sacramentis,* the Bishop of Milan emphasizes that he desires to follow the use of the Roman Church in everything; for this reason, we can safely assume that the same eucharistic prayer he quotes was also used in Rome.[23]

The wording of the prayers cited by Ambrose is different from the canon that was settled by Pope Gregory the Great in the late sixth century and has come down to us, with only a few minor changes, in the oldest extant liturgical books, especially the Old Gelasian Sacramentary, dating from the middle of the eighth century, but believed to reflect the liturgical use of the middle of the seventh century. The differences between Ambrose's eucharistic prayer and the Gregorian canon are far less remarkable than their similarities, given that the almost 300 years lying between the two texts were a period of intense liturgical development.[24] It is therefore a most remarkable fact that a mature version of the Roman canon emerges without any antecedents in the late fourth century.[25]

The available evidence strongly suggests that the transition from Greek to Latin in the Roman liturgy happened slowly and gradually.[26] Parts of the liturgy were already in Latin before the second half of the fourth century, notably the readings from Holy Scripture. By the late fourth century, the ancient version of the psalms used in the liturgy had acquired such a sacrosanct status that St Jerome only revised it with caution. Later he translated the psalter from the Hebrew, as he said, not for liturgical purposes, but to provide a text for scholarship and controversy.[27] It is also likely that the baptismal liturgy was celebrated in Latin at an early stage.

This development took more than 100 years and that it was completed in the pontificate of Damasus, who died in 384; from then on, the liturgy in Rome was mostly celebrated in Latin. In later periods, Greek elements were introduced into the Roman liturgy, most notably the invocation *Kyrie eleison,* adopted from stational processions. In the seventh century, there was a strong influx of Eastern Christians in Rome, which is reflected in the inclusion of the *Trisagion* in the *Improperia* of the Good Friday liturgy and the use of bilingual readings on several solemn celebrations in the liturgical year, such as Christmas and Easter (Sunday and Monday), the Vigils of Easter and Pentecost, the four Ember Saturdays, and the Mass for the ordination of a pope.[28] An interesting case is the so-called "*Missa graeca,*" which is attested in several manuscripts from the Carolingian age. Texts of the Roman Ordinary of the Mass are written in Greek, but in Latin letters and they are sometimes provided with neumes, indicating that they would have been sung. This phenomenon spread throughout Europe even to places where Greek culture was quite remote and illustrates the prestige of Greek as a liturgical language in Western Christendom.[29]

Peter Burke, a major contributor to the relatively new academic discipline of "sociolinguistics" or the "social history of language," has alerted us to the fact that "the choice of one language over another is never a neutral or transparent one."[30] As for the question why the move towards a Latin liturgy in Rome occurred rather late, various answers have been given, and there is something to be said for all of them. The German liturgist Theodor Klauser attributed this to the general conservatism of Romans and their tenacity in keeping religious traditions. This is certainly true for the Roman Church as well. According to Allan Bouley, the need for a carefully formulated orthodox language, especially during the Arian crisis of the fourth century, provided the leaven for creating an official Latin form of the prayers of the Mass. Bouley's thesis that it was the need for orthodox prayers that advanced the creation of Latin rites is certainly borne out by the efforts of St Ambrose to formulate the orthodox faith in liturgical hymns and prayers against the current Arianism of the barbarian tribes. Christine Mohrmann argues that the formation of liturgical Latin became possible only after the Peace of the Church, established by the Emperor Constantine. There was no longer such a strong need for Christian communities to define themselves in opposition to the surrounding pagan culture. Their new secure status gave the local churches in the West greater freedom to draw, at least for purposes of style, not for contents, on the religious heritage of Rome for the development of their liturgies.

Moreover, the formation of a Latin liturgical language should be seen as part of a wide-ranging effort to Christianize Roman culture. The popes of the late fourth and the fifth century, beginning with Damasus, made a conscious and comprehensive attempt to appropriate the symbols of Roman culture for the Christian faith. Parts of this attempt were the appropriation of public space through extensive building projects and the appropriation of public time with a cycle of Christian feasts throughout the year replacing pagan celebrations, as with the Philocalian calendar of the year 354. The formation of liturgical Latin was part of this effort to evangelize Roman culture and attract the influential elites of the Empire to the Christian faith. It would not be accurate to describe this process as an adoption of the "vernacular" language in the liturgy. The Latin of the Roman canon, of the collects and prefaces of the Mass was removed from idiom of the ordinary people. It was a highly stylized language that required some effort fully to understand and appreciate by the average Roman Christian of the fifth century or later, given especially that the rate of literacy was very low compared to our times.[31]

These prayers of the ancient sacramentaries were formed according to technical rules of composition.[32] Liturgical prayer is a form of public speech, and hence it is not surprising that in Christian antiquity, the threefold *officia* of classical rhetoric were applied to it as well. The reasons for this are presented succinctly by Mary Gonzaga Haessly in work on *Rhetoric in the Sunday Collects of the Roman Missal*:

> All these devices of the art of language are necessary for us, for they enable us:
> (1) to grasp clearly the lessons embodied in the Prayers (*docere*); (2) to make these lessons more acceptable to us through the charm of diction and structure, in a word, through their appeal to our aesthetic sense (*delectare*); (3) to persuade us (*movere*) to mold our conduct in accordance with the principles of faith set forth in the prayers. This explains why rhetoric is, and must be, found in the liturgy: it is to dispose us to pray "ut oportet," as we ought to pray.[33]

It was by no means a foregone conclusion that the Western Church would generally adopt Latin as its liturgical language. There were native languages in the Western Empire, such as Gothic, Celtic, Iberic, or Punic. It is possible to imagine a Western Church with local languages in its liturgy, as in the East, where, in addition to Greek, Syriac, Coptic, Armenian, Georgian, and Ethiopic was used. However, the situation in the West was fundamentally different; the centralizing force of the Roman Church was such that Latin became the only liturgical language. This was an important factor in furthering ecclesiastical, cultural and political unity. *Latinitas* became one of the defining characteristics of Western Europe.

From late antiquity to the Middle Ages: decay and renewal

Studies of liturgical Latin, such as those of Christine Mohrmann, used to concentrate on what may be called the "classical" period of formation of the Roman rite from the fourth to the sixth century. Recently, more attention has been devoted to liturgical texts from a later period and originating not from Rome, but from Gaul, Spain, and other parts of the Latin Church.[34] Els Rose has published a substantial study of liturgical Latin in the *Missale Gothicum*, along with her critical edition of this late seventh-century witness to the Gallican tradition.[35] Whilst the merits of this research in the wider field of liturgical Latin are beyond doubt, Rose uses the opportunity for some harsh criticism of Mohrmann's approach. She charges Mohrmann with promoting a "one-sided view of liturgical Latin [i.e. a hieratic, highly stylized language with hardly any popular features]," because she confined her interpretation "to the liturgical texts of the *Patres* and the liturgy of the church of Rome, choosing her examples from these undoubtedly rich but restricted treasuries," passing over other traditions, such as the Gallican or Visigothic ones. Thus Mohrmann is said to present "an opinion on liturgical Latin based on a select corpus of sources but presented as a general view on the subject."[36] As mentioned above, scholars have presented important correctives to Mohrmann's methodology, but this does not mean that it needs to be discarded entirely. There can be no doubt that she was aware of non-Roman Latin liturgical sources,[37] but she chose as the scope of her studies an in-depth analysis of the characteristically *Roman* prayer style, which liturgical scholars before her, such as Edmund Bishop,[38] had identified. This approach can and should be enlarged, and Rose's research, leaving aside unnecessary polemics, serves this purpose.

In her study of the *Bobbio Missal*, another manuscript from the Gallican tradition dating from the turn of the eighth century, Rose takes issue with Robert Coleman, because he considers non-Roman liturgical sources of the seventh and eighth centuries as evidence of extensive vulgarization. As an example, Coleman observes that the Roman canon appears in the *Bobbio Missal* in a truncated form that obscures its meaning. He rightly speaks of a "garbled form" and concludes that "in a religion where departures from the prescribed form of words could raise doubts about the validity of the rites enacted by them, the motivation to restore was strong."[39] I cannot see how one could reasonably question this conclusion. In fact, Rose herself provides several examples of how the _Bobbio Missal_ radically shortens prayers of the _Missale Gothicum_ to the point that their grammar becomes confused and their contents can be understood only with difficulties.[40] This is not just a question of orthographic peculiarities that would be typical of a period of transition from Latin to the Romance vernaculars. In fact, Rose herself concedes that in some cases "the scissor and paste work of the compiler of the _Bobbio Missal_ has led to grammatically incorrect and incomprehensible texts."[41] This is just one aspect of the decay of Latin literary culture in the Merovingian period, which prompted the efforts of churchmen and scholars under Charlemagne to purify and standardize liturgical books. The Carolingian Renaissance restored the classical form of liturgical Latin; however, by doing so, at the same time it created a greater distance between the language of the liturgy and the developing vernacular of the people.[42]

Speech and silence

Liturgical prayer is a form of public speech and it is to be expected that it would be said or sung by the officiating clergy in an audible voice, as would seem to have been the universal rule for Christian worship in the first centuries. In the case of the Eucharist, the celebrant bishop or priest recites prayers in the name and on behalf of the whole assembly, and the people usually respond with "Amen," as elicited by the concluding formula of the prayers themselves.

However, from the early Middle Ages certain parts of the Roman rite of Mass were recited by the celebrant in a low voice, most notably the centre of the eucharistic liturgy, the canon. Its silent recitation became the norm until the liturgical reforms following the Second Vatican Council and continues to this day in what Pope Benedict XVI has established as the "extraordinary form," or _usus antiquior_, of the Roman rite.[43] This practice is by no means limited to the Western tradition; on the contrary, Eastern liturgies, such as the Byzantine Anaphora of St John Chrysostom, also contain prayers that are to be said _submissa voce_ by the celebrant bishop or priest.[44]

The earliest clear evidence for a partial recitation of the eucharistic prayer in silence is from the East Syrian tradition and is found in the _Homily on the Mysteries_ attributed to Narsai, the head of the theological schools of Edessa and of Nisibis (d. 502).[45] The liturgical practice emerging from Narsai's homily is confirmed by subsequent witnesses to the East Syrian tradition that are only a little later than Narsai: a short description of the liturgy by Catholicos Iso'yahb I (518–95/6),[46] which is included in the _Synodicon Orientale_, and the more detailed liturgical commentary of Gabriel of Qatar (written between 615 and 625).[47]

The custom of reciting large parts of the anaphora in silence also spread to Greek-speaking churches by the middle of the sixth century, as we can infer from the Emperor Justinian's legislation against it in his _Novella_ of March 26, 565.[48] By the year 565, the practice of reciting the canon silently had not yet made its way to Rome.[49]

Between the latter part of the sixth century and the second half of the eighth century, liturgical practice in Rome developed in such a way that by the year 800, the canon of the Mass was recited by the celebrant in a low voice. The *Ordines Romani* of the eighth century present the canon of the Mass, now understood to begin with *Te igitur*, as a "holy of holies," into which only the Pontiff could enter.[50] This idea would eventually lead to an entirely silent recitation of the canon.[51] It is conceivable that this practice was introduced in Rome by the popes of Greek and Syrian origin that were elected to the See of Peter in the second half of the seventh century and the first half of the eighth century.

The development towards a recitation of liturgical prayers *submissa voce* is usually attributed to the increasing sense of reverence and awe towards the mysteries celebrated in the liturgy, which is tangible especially in the Eastern Christian traditions from the fourth century onwards. Two decisive factors are identified: the emphasis on the divinity of Christ in opposition to Arianism and the concern to protect the sacred from the uncatechized masses that were flocking into the church after the Constantinian settlement.[52]

In the case of the Roman liturgy, there might be another consideration that should not be neglected: the architectural setting of the solemn celebrations of the Roman Pontiff. When the pope celebrated Mass in one of the large Roman basilicas, such as the Lateran, St Peter's in the Vatican, or St Paul's Outside the Walls, before the existence of electrical amplification, it would be impossible in most parts of the church to follow the prayers he recited or chanted at the altar. Even in a smaller church like St Sabina, the audibility of the liturgical prayers would be much limited. Just as there were visible barriers, such as the relatively high *cancelli* separating the various precincts of the church's interior, a ciborium over the main altar, sometimes decorated with curtains, so the physical dimensions of the church interior created an audible barrier between the pope and his assistants at the altar and the faithful in the naves.[53]

The *Ordines Romani*, describing liturgical practice in the city of Rome, would not need to specify this, but when they were adapted to Frankish conditions, and thus to churches of medium or small size, it was actually written down that the canon was to be recited in a low voice. This interpretation would in my view give justice to the development observed from *Ordo Romanus* I to *Ordo Romanus* V. Thus the emergence of the silent canon in the Western tradition should also be seen in the context of the liturgy's architectural setting that had a decisive impact on the relation between speech and silence.

Latin and the vernacular in the Modern Age

In the course of the Middle Ages, the formation of national languages and cultures in Europe meant the language of the liturgy became more and more removed from the language of the people. However, it would be an exaggeration to conclude that the use of Latin as a sacred language was a barrier to understanding of and participation in the Mass. In the first place, as the (Lutheran) liturgical scholar

Frank Senn argues, such a conclusion rests on a narrow understanding of participation that "sees liturgy only as text and limits participation to speaking roles." Senn continues:

> The laity have always found ways to participate in the liturgy, whether it was in their language or not, and they have always derived meaning from the liturgy, whether it was the intended meaning or not. Furthermore, the laity in worship were surrounded by other 'vernaculars' than language, not least of which were the church buildings themselves and the liturgical art that decorated them.[54]

Senn also notes in passing that the common accusations against Latin in the liturgy have been greatly overstated. This would certainly hold in countries where the vernacular developed from Latin. Augustine Thompson shows in his study of ordinary religious practice in Italian cities in the high Middle Ages that, contrary to the claim made by heretical groups, such as the Waldensians, there was a basic understanding at least of the meaning conveyed in Latin liturgical texts, and that this was so even among the lesser educated, at least if they chose to follow attentively.[55] Historical sources provide interesting examples: in 1296, a synod in Grado decreed that deacons were not to use melismatic tones in their chanting of the Gospel "these impeded the understanding of the hearers and so the devotion in the minds of the faithful is reduced." The elaborate tones were permitted only for the proclamation of the genealogies of Christ on Christmas and Epiphany and for "the first Gospel chanted by a newly ordained deacon."[56] In Italy, the spoken language of the people was still close enough to the Latin that comprehension of liturgical texts was by no means restricted to the educated clergy. Writing about early modern Europe, Peter Burke records that an increasing part of the laity was studying Latin, including the small but growing group of learned women.[57] The cultural impact of the sacred language in everyday speech is also evident from the resonances of liturgical Latin in the vernacular languages of the Romance countries, some of which go back to the early modern period.[58]

The use of Latin in this period still provided an example of "diglossia," which means that "it was considered appropriate to use that language in some situations and domains."[59] It was the language of the cultural elites and served to bind together international communities of ideas, above all the Church and the Republic of Letters. None the less, the objections to the use of Latin not only in the liturgy, but in public life at large and in other aspects of the Church's life, became more widely spread in the Renaissance and Reformation periods. The humanists' movement for a return to the purity of Ciceronian Latin aggravated this situation, because it meant that Latin as a "living second language" was discarded in favour of reviving a language that had been truly "dead."[60]

The problem became acute in the sixteenth century, when the Protestant Reformers, in continuity with dissident movements of the later Middle Ages, attacked the use of Latin in the liturgy. There was also a theological rationale at the root of this critique: the Protestants' idea of divine worship being essentially a proclamation of the Word of God made them conclude that using a language that was not intelligible to the assembly was contrary to the Gospel. Martin Luther was happy to allow for some Latin, as far as it was understood by the people, and this custom was followed for some time in Lutheran communities. John Calvin, on the other hand, categorically rejected the use of Latin in worship.[61]

At the Council of Trent, the question of liturgical language was much debated, and the arguments produced by the Protestant Reformers were considered very seriously. The *Decree on the Sacrifice of the Mass* of the Council's 22nd Session in 1562 contains a carefully-worded doctrinal exposition on the subject, stating that it did not seem *expedient* to the Fathers that the Holy Mass should be celebrated in the vernacular, although they recognize the value of the texts of the Mass for the instruction of the faithful. However, pastors should preach frequently about what is read at Mass, especially on Sundays and feast days.[62] Moreover, canon nine of the same *Decree on the Sacrifice of the Mass* declares anathema anyone who says that the vernacular language *must* be used in the celebration of Mass; again, the subtle wording of this conciliar text is to be noted.

The question of Latin and the vernacular in the Church's liturgy continued to be discussed in the centuries after Trent, especially in the Catholic Enlightenment of the eighteenth century, and came to the fore especially in the twentieth century,[63] but this will be the topic of the next chapter.

Notes

1   R. Coleman, "Vulgar Latin and the Diversity of Christian Latin," J. Herman (ed.), *Actes du 1er Colloque international sur le latin vulgaire et tardif (Pécs, 2–5 septembre 1985)* (Tübingen: Niemeyer, 1987), pp. 37–52 (p. 58), rightly insists that any attempt to distinguish characteristics of "Christian Latin" needs to differentiate between the various registers of discourse that existed from early on: "the vulgarized Latin of Bible and Psalter, the plain but unvulgarized style of ecclesiastical administration, the more sophisticated idiom of expository and hortatory literature and finally the products of high literary culture—the hymns and collects of the Liturgy and Offices." Thus "Christian Latin is no illusion," as put by D. Sheerin, "Christian and Biblical Latin," F.A.C. Mantello & A.G. Rigg (eds), *Medieval Latin: An Introduction and Bibliographical Guide*, (Washington, D.C: Catholic University of America Press, 1996), pp. 137–56 (p. 150). J.J. O'Donnell, *Augustine, Confessions. Introduction, Text, and Commentary*, 3 vols, (Oxford: Clarendon Press, 1992), vol. I, lxiii, writes: "the question of 'Christian Latin' as *Sondersprache* is ripe for fresh and venturesome treatment."

2   Thus C. Mohrmann, *Liturgical Latin: Its Origins and Character. Three Lectures* (London: Burns & Oates, 1959), pp. 1–26; see also the author's collected studies: *Études sur le latin des chrétiens*, 4 vols, Storia e letteratura 65, 87, 103, 143 (Roma: Edizioni di Storia e Letteratura, 1961–77).

3   O'Donnell (ed.), Augustine, *Confessions*, IX,10,25.

4   See: Mohrmann, *Liturgical Latin*, pp. 10–11. See the seminal work by K. Meister, *Die Homerische Kunstsprache* (Leipzig: Jablonowski, 1921).

5   See the correspondence between Pope Zacharias and Boniface, *Ep. 68*: Monumenta Germania Historica, Epistulae Selectae I, 141 (dated July 1, 746).

6 R.P.H. Green (ed. & trans.), Augustine, *De doctrina Christiana* II, xi, 16, Oxford Early
   Christian Texts (Oxford: Clarendon Press, 1995), p. 73. On the meaning of "*os(i)anna*"
   there is an interesting exchange of letters between Pope Damasus and Jerome: *Ep. XIX
   et XX*: CSEL 54, pp. 103–110.

7 See: C. Mohrmann, "The Ever-Recurring Problem of Language in the Church," in
   Études sur le latin des chrétiens, vol. IV, pp. 143–59 (pp. 151-2).

8 Thomas Aquinas, *Summa Theologiae* IIIa q. 64 a. 2 ad 1, IIIa, q. 83, a. 4, and IIIa, q. 66,
   a 10, resp.

9 See: T.A. Becker, "The Role of *Solemnitas* in the Liturgy According to Saint Thomas
   Aquinas," M. Levering & M. Dauphinas (eds.), *Rediscovering Aquinas and the
   Sacraments: Studies in Sacramental Theology* (Chicago: Hillenbrand, 2009),
   pp. 114–35.

10 J. Pieper, *In Search of the Sacred* (San Francisco: Ignatius Press, 1991), p. 41.

11 Hilary of Poitiers, *Tractatus super psalmos, prol.* 15: CSEL 22, p. 13.

12 Augustine of Hippo, *In Joan. Ev. tract.* 117, 4: CCL 36 p. 653.

13 See, for instance, how Thomas Aquinas takes up and develops Augustine's exegesis in
   his commentary on John: *Super Io.*, cap. 19 l.4. See: F.J. Thompson, "SS. Cyril and
   Methodius and a Mythical Western Heresy: Trilinguism. A Contribution to the Study
   of Patristic and Mediaeval Theories of Sacred Languages," *Analecta Bollandiana* 110
   (1992), pp. 67–122; T. M. Kolbaba, *The Byzantine Lists: Errors of the Latins*, Illinois
   Medieval Studies (Chicago: University of Illinois Press, 2000), pp. 66-7. Thus
   K. Pecklers, *Dynamic Equivalence: The Living Language of Christian Worship*
   (Collegeville: Liturgical Press, 2003), pp. 4–7, needs to be taken with caution.

14 A. Bouley, *From Freedom to Formula: The Evolution of the Eucharistic Prayer from Oral
   Improvisation to Written Texts*, Studies in Christian Antiquity 21 (Washington: Catholic
   University of America Press, 1981), p. xv; on the emergence of fixed forms in
   eucharistic prayers, see also A. Gelston, *The Eucharistic Prayer of Addai and Mari*
   (Oxford: Clarendon Press, 1992), pp. 11–21.

15 A. Budde, "Improvisation im Eucharistiegebet. Zur Technik freien Betens in der Alten
   Kirche," *Jahrbuch für Antike und Christentum* 44 (2001), pp.127–44, esp. p. 138. See
   also: J. Hammerstaedt & P. Terbuyken, "Improvisation," *Das Reallexikon für Antike und
   Christentum* 17 (1996), pp. 1212–84.

16 See: S. Mowinckel, *Religion und Kultus*, trans. A. Schauer (Göttingen: Vandenhoeck &
   Ruprecht, 1953), pp. 8, 14, 53.

17 See: Budde, *Improvisation im Eucharistiegebet*, p. 137.

18 See: B. Botte & C. Mohrmann, *L'ordinaire de la messe: Texte critique, traduction et
   etudes*, Études liturgique 2 (Paris & Louvain: Cerf & Abbaye du Mont César, 1953),
   pp. 39–40; C. Mohrmann, "Sur l'histoire de Praefari-Praefatio," *Études sur le latin des
   chrétiens*, vol. III, pp. 291–305 (originally published in *Vigilae Christiane* 7 [1953],
   1–15).

19 Mohrmann, *Liturgical Latin*, p. 24.

20 See: U.M. Lang, "Rhetoric of Salvation: The Origins of Latin as the Language of the
   Roman Liturgy," U.M. Lang (ed.), *The Genius of the Roman Rite: Historical, Theological
   and Pastoral Perspectives on Catholic Liturgy. Proceedings of the 2006 Oxford CIEL
   Colloquium* (Chicago: Hillenbrand Books, 2010), pp. 22–44.

21 For a brief discussion of rhetorical elements in Greek anaphoras, see H. Engberding,
   "Die Kunstprosa des eucharistischen Hochgebetes der griechischen Gregoriusliturgie,"
   Alfred Stuiber & Alfred Hermann (eds), *Mullus: Festschrift Theodor Klauser* (Münster:
   Aschendorff, 1964), pp. 100–10.

22 Ambrose, *De sacramentis* IV, 5, 21–2; 6, 26–7: CSEL 73, pp. 55, 57. Note that the so-called *Traditio Apostolica*, attributed to Hippolytus of Rome, cannot be used as a source for early Roman liturgical practice, because of uncertainties about its date, origin and authorship. See: B. Steimer, *Vertex traditionis: Die Gattung der altchristlichen Kirchenordnungen* (Berlin & New York: de Gruyter, 1992), M. Metzger, "À propos des règlements ecclésiastiques et de la prétendue *Tradition apostolique,*" *Revue des sciences religieuses* 66 (1992), pp. 249–61, and P.F. Bradshaw, M.E. Johnson & L.E. Philips, *The Apostolic Tradition: A Commentary*, Hermeneia (Minneapolis: Fortress Press, 2002). This most recent research confirms the insights of L. Bouyer, *Eucharist: Theology and Spirituality of the Eucharistic Prayer* (Notre Dame & London: University of Notre Dame Press, 1968), pp. 188–91.

23 Ambrose, *De sacramentis* III, 1,5: CSEL 73, p. 40.

24 See: J. Beumer, "Die ältesten Zeugnisse für die römische Eucharistiefeier bei Ambrosius von Mailand" *Zeitschrift für katholische Theologie* 95 (1973), pp. 311–24; Bouley, *From Freedom to Formula*, pp. 200–15; G. Jeanes, "Early Latin Parallels to the Roman Canon? Possible References to a Eucharistic Prayer in Zeno of Verona," *Journal of Theological Studies* 37 (1986), pp. 427–31; M.J. Moreton, "Rethinking the Origin of the Roman Canon," *Studia Patristica* 26 (1993), pp. 63–6.

25 See: Botte & Mohrmann, *L'ordinaire de la messe*, p. 17.

26 Mohrmann, *Liturgical Latin*, pp. 50–3; J. A. Jungmann, *The Mass of the Roman Rite: Its Origins and Development (Missarum Sollemnia)*, (New York: Benziger, 1951 & 1955), vol. I, pp. 50–1; Bouley, *From Freedom to Formula*, pp. 203–7; *pace* T. Klauser, "Der Übergang der römischen Kirche von der griechischen zur lateinischen Liturgiesprache," *Miscellanea Giovanni Mercati: 1. Bibbia, letteratura cristiana antica*, ST 121 (1946); see now also: M.K. Lafferty, "Translating Faith from Greek to Latin: Romanitas and Christianitas in Late Fourth-Century Rome and Milan," *Journal of Early Christian Studies* 11 (2003), pp. 21–62.

27 See Jerome's two prefaces to the Psalter in *Biblia sacra iuxta Vulgatam versionem*, R. Weber and R. Gryson (eds) (Stuttgart: Deutsche Bibelgesellschaft, 4th edn, 1994), pp. 767–9; See: C. Mohrmann, "The New Latin Psalter: Its Diction and Style," *Etudes sur le latin des chrétiens*, vol. II, pp. 109–31 (pp. 110–11).

28 See: C. Vogel, *Medieval Liturgy: An Introduction to the Sources* (Washington, DC: The Pastoral Press, 1986), pp. 296–7.

29 See C.M. Atkinson, "Missa graeca," L. Lütteken (ed.), *Messe und Motette* (Bärenreiter & Metzler: Kassel & Stuttgart, 2002), pp. 18–19; W. Berschin, *Griechisch-lateinisches Mittelalter. Von Hieronymus zu Nikolaus von Kues* (Bern & München: Francke, 1980), pp. 31–8.

30 In the words of Lafferty, *Translating Faith from Greek to Latin*, p. 24, referring to P. Burke, *The Art of Conversation* (Ithaca: Cornell University Press, 1993).

31 Mohrmann, *Liturgical Latin*, pp. 53–4; see also M. Klöckener, "Zeitgemäßes Beten. Meßorationen als Zeugnisse einer sich wandelnden Kultur und Spiritualität," R. Meßner, E. Nagel & R. Pacik (eds.), *Bewahren und Erneuern. Studien zur Meßliturgie. Festschrift für Hans Bernhard Meyer SJ zum 70. Geburtstag*, Innsbrucker theologische Studien 42 (Innsbruck & Wien: Tyrolia, 1995), pp. 114–42 (pp. 126–7).

32 See: E. Norden, *Die antike Kunstprosa vom VI. Jahrhundert v. Chr. bis in die Zeit der Renaissance*, 2nd edn, 2 vols (Leipzig: Teubner, 1909), vol. II, p. 457; C. Mohrmann, "Problèmes stylistiques dans la littérature latine chrétienne," *Études sur le latin des chrétiens*, vol. I, pp. 147–70 (pp. 147–8).

33 M.G. Haessly, *Rhetoric in the Sunday Collects of the Roman Missal: with Introduction, Text, Commentary and Translation* (Cleveland: Ursuline College for Women, 1938), p. 5. See also the various contributions in: J.G. Leachman & D.P. McCarthy (eds), *Appreciating the Collect: An Irenic Methodology* (Farnborough: St Michael's Abbey Press), 2008.

34 For the Visigothic tradition, see, for instance: R. Wright, *Late Latin and Early Romance in Spain and Carolingian France* (Liverpool: Cairns, 1982), pp. 73–8; M.C. Díaz y Díaz, "El latín de la liturgia hispánica," J.F. Rivera Recio & L. Brou (eds), *Estudios sobre la liturgia mozárabe*, (Toledo: Diputación Provincial, 1965), pp. 55–87.

35 H.G.E. Rose (ed.), *Missale gothicum e codice Vaticano Reginensi latino 317 editum*, CCL 159D (2005); see also: "Liturgical Latin in the Missale Gothicum (Vat. Reg. Lat. 317). A reconsideration of Christine Mohrmann's approach," *Sacris Erudiri* 42 (2003), pp. 97–121.

36 E. Rose, "Liturgical Latin in the Bobbio Missal," Y. Hen & R. Meens (eds), *The Bobbio Missal: Liturgy and Religious Culture in Merovingian Gaul* (Cambridge: University Press, 2004), pp. 67–78 (p. 70).

37 See: Mohrmann, *Quelques observations sur l'évolution stylistique*, p. 235, n. 21.

38 E. Bishop, "The Genius of the Roman Rite," *Liturgica Historica* (Oxford: Clarendon Press, 1918), pp. 1–19. Bishop's assessment of the distinctive Roman and Gallican features is generally correct, even if one need not follow his value judgment that is implied in his comparison; see: P. Bradshaw, "The Genius of the Roman Rite Revisited," U.M. Lang (ed.), *Ever Directed Towards the Lord: The Love of God in the Liturgy Past, Present, and Hoped For* (London: T&T Clark, 2007), pp. 49–61.

39 Coleman, *Vulgar Latin and the Diversity of Christian Latin*, p. 47.

40 See: Rose, *Liturgical Latin in the Bobbio Missal*, pp. 71–6.

41 Ibid., p. 72.

42 See: E. Auerbach, *Literatursprache und Publikum in der lateinischen Spätantike und im Mittelalter* (Bern: Francke, 1958), pp. 88, 197.

43 Benedict XVI, *Apostolic Letter Motu Proprio data "Summorum Pontificum"* (July 7, 2007).

44 See: A. Hänggi & I. Pahl, *Prex eucharistica. Volumen I: Textus e variis liturgiis antiquioribus selecti*, 3rd edn, Spicilegium Friburgense 12 (Freiburg/Schweiz: Universitätsverlag, 1998), pp. 223–9.

45 See A. Gelston, "The Meaning of šl' in Theodore of Mopsuestia's Sixteenth Catechetical Lecture and the Silent Recitation of the Eucharistic Prayer," *Journal of Theological Studies* 60 (2009), pp. 191–2; likewise G.G. Willis, *Further Essays in Early Roman Liturgy* (London: SPCK, 1968), p. 126. There is an English translation of the Syriac original by R.H. Connolly, *The Liturgical Homilies of Narsai* (Cambridge: University Press, 1909), pp. 1–32.

46 See his *Letter to James, Bishop of Darai*, J.B. Chabot (ed.), *Synodicon Orientale ou Recueil de synodes nestoriens*, (Paris: Imprimerie Nationale, 1902), pp. 168–9 (Syriac text) and p. 428 (French translation); See: S.Y.H. Jammo, *La structure de la messe chaldéenne du début jusqu'à l'anaphore*, Orientalia Christiana Analecta 207 (Rome: Pontificium Institutum Orientalium Studiorum, 1979), p. 21.

47 Gabriel of Qatar, *Memra V*, 2, 66–7 (British Library, Or. 3336, fol. 201v–202r), published in the Syriac original and in an English translation by S.P. Brock, "Gabriel of Qatar's Commentary on the Liturgy," *Hugoye: Journal of Syriac Studies* 6 (2003), pp. 197–248 (pp. 235–6 [Syriac text]; p. 215 ET). See also: S.Y.H. Jammo, "Gabriel Qatraya et son

commentaire sur la liturgie chaldéenne," *Orientalia Christiana Periodica* 32 (1966), pp. 39–52.

48 Justinian, *Nouellae*, CXXXVII, vi, R. Schoell (ed.), *Corpus Iuris Civilis*, vol. 3, 6th edn (Berlin: Weidmann, 1954), p. 699. See also the slightly later anecdote from John Moschus, *Pratum spirituale*, 196: PG 87, 3080-4.

49 See: G.G. Willis, *A History of Early Roman Liturgy to the Death of Pope Gregory the Great*, Henry Bradshaw Society (1994), pp. 36–8.

50 *Ordo Romanus* I, 88: M. Andrieu, *Les Ordines Romani du haut moyen âge*, Spicilegium Sacrum Lovaniense (Louvain: Peeters, 1931–61), vol. II, pp. 95–6.

51 *Ordo Romanus* XV, 37–43: Andrieu, vol. III, pp. 103–4; *Ordo Romanus* V, p. 58: Andrieu vol. II, p. 221.

52 See, for instance, E. Bishop, "Observations on the Liturgy of Narsai," Connolly, *The Liturgical Homilies of Narsai*, pp. 85–163 (pp. 92–7); G. Kretschmar, "Die frühe Geschichte der Jerusalemer Liturgie," *Jahrbuch für Liturgik und Hymnologie* 2 (1956-7), pp. 22–46 (pp. 30–3).

53 See: Willis, *Further Essays in Early Roman Liturgy*, pp. 128–9.

54 F.C. Senn, *The People's Work: A Social History of the Liturgy* (Minneapolis: Fortress Press, 2006), p. 145.

55 A. Thompson, *Cities of God: The Religion of the Italian Communes 1125–1325* (University Park, PA: The Pennsylvania State University Press, 2005), pp. 239–41.

56 Quoted after Thompson, *Cities of God*, p. 240.

57 See: P. Burke, *Languages and Communities in Early Modern Europe: The 2002 Wiles Lectures given at Queen's University, Belfast* (Cambridge: University Press, 2004), p. 49.

58 Ibid., pp, 50-1, provides a few delightful examples; see also R. Bracchi, "Il latino liturgico sulla bocca del popolo," E. dal Covolo & M. Sodi (eds), *Il latino e i cristian: Un bilancio all'inizio del terzo millennio*, MSIL 17 (2002), pp. 489–507.

59 Burke, *Languages and Communities*, p. 43.

60 See C. Mohrmann, "The Ever-Recurring Problem of Language in the Church," *Études sur le latin des chrétiens*, vol. IV, pp. 143–59 (p. 152); Burke, *Languages and Communities*, pp. 144–5.

61 H.A.P. Schmidt, *Liturgie et langue vulgaire. Le problème de la langue liturgique chez les premiers Réformateurs et au Concile de Trente*, Analecta Gregoriana 53 (Romae: Apud Aedes Unversitatis Gregorianae, 1950).

62 Council of Trent, 22nd Session (September 17, 1562), *Decree on the Sacrifice of the Mass*, ch. 8; DZ 1749.

63 A lot of useful material is assembled in Pecklers, *Dynamic Equivalence*.

Bibliography (excluding primary sources)

Atkinson, C.M., "Missa graeca," L. Lütteken (ed.), *Messe und Motette*, MGG prisma (Bärenreiter & Metzler: Kassel & Stuttgart, 2002), pp. 18–19.

Auerbach, E., *Literatursprache und Publikum in der lateinischen Spätantike und im Mittelalter* (Bern: Francke, 1958).

Bardy, G., *La question des langues dans l'Église ancienne*, Études de Théologie Historique (Paris: Beauchesne, 1948).

Becker, T. A., "The Role of *Solemnitas* in the Liturgy According to Saint Thomas Aquinas," M. Levering & M. Dauphinas (eds), *Rediscovering Aquinas and the Sacraments: Studies in Sacramental Theology* (Chicago: Hillenbrand, 2009), pp. 114–35.

Berschin, W., *Griechisch-lateinisches Mittelalter. Von Hieronymus zu Nikolaus von Kues* (Bern & München: Francke, 1980).

Beumer, J., "Die ältesten Zeugnisse für die römische Eucharistiefeier bei Ambrosius von Mailand" *Zeitschriftfür katholische Theologie* 95 (1973), pp. 311–24.

Bishop, E., "Observations on the Liturgy of Narsai," R.H. Connolly, *The Liturgical Homilies of Narsai*, Texts and Studies 8,1 (Cambridge: University Press, 1909), pp. 85–163.

—— "The Genius of the Roman Rite," *Liturgica Historica* (Oxford: Clarendon Press, 1918), pp. 1–19.

Botte B. & Mohrmann, C., *L'ordinaire de la messe: Texte critique, traduction et etudes*, Études liturgique 2 (Paris & Louvain: Cerf & Abbaye du Mont César, 1953).

Bouley, A., *From Freedom to Formula: The Evolution of the Eucharistic Prayer from Oral Improvisation to Written Texts*, Studies in Christian Antiquity 21 (Washington: Catholic University of America Press, 1981).

Bouyer, L., *Eucharist: Theology and Spirituality of the Eucharistic Prayer*, C.U. Quinn (trans.), (Notre Dame & London: University of Notre Dame Press, 1968).

Bracchi, R., "Il latino liturgico sulla bocca del popolo," E. dal Covolo & M. Sodi (eds), *Il latino e i cristian: Un bilancio all'inizio del terzo millennio*, MSIL 17 (2002), pp. 489–507.

Bradshaw, P., "The Genius of the Roman Rite Revisited," U.M. Lang (ed.), *Ever Directed Towards the Lord: The Love of God in the Liturgy Past, Present, and Hoped For* (London: T&T Clark, 2007), pp. 49–61.

—— Johnson, M.E. & L.E. Philips, *The Apostolic Tradition: A Commentary*, Hermeneia (Minneapolis, MN: Fortress Press, 2002).

Budde, A., "Improvisation im Eucharistiegebet. Zur Technik freien Betens in der Alten Kirche" *Jahrbuch für Antike und Christentum* 44 (2001), pp. 127–44.

Burke, P., *The Art of Conversation* (Ithaca: Cornell University Press, 1993).

—— *Languages and Communities in Early Modern Europe: The 2002 Wiles Lectures given at Queen's University, Belfast* (Cambridge: University Press, 2004).

Coleman, R., "Vulgar Latin and the Diversity of Christian Latin," J. Herman (ed.), *Actes du 1er Colloque international sur le latin vulgaire et tardif (Pécs, 2–5 septembre 1985)* (Tübingen: Niemeyer, 1987), pp. 37–52.

Díaz y Díaz, M.C., "El latín de la liturgia hispánica," J.F. Rivera Recio & L. Brou (eds), *Estudios sobre la liturgia mozárabe*, (Toledo: Diputación Provincial, 1965), pp. 55–87.

Engberding, H, "Die Kunstprosa des eucharistischen Hochgebetes der griechischen Gregoriusliturgie," in *Mullus: Festschrift Theodor Klauser*, JAC. Ergänzungsband 1 (Münster: Aschendorff, 1964), pp. 100–10.

Gelston, A., *The Eucharistic Prayer of Addai and Mari* (Oxford: Clarendon Press, 1992).

—— "The Meaning of *šl* in Theodore of Mopsuestia's Sixteenth Catechetical Lecture and the Silent Recitation of the Eucharistic Prayer," *Journal of Theological Studies* NS 60 (2009), pp. 191–2.

Haessly, M. G., *Rhetoric in the Sunday Collects of the Roman Missal: with Introduction, Text, Commentary and Translation* (Cleveland: Ursuline College for Women, 1938).

Hänggi, A. & I. Pahl, , (3rd edn), Spicilegium Friburgense 12 (Freiburg/Schweiz: Universitätsverlag, 1998).

Hammerstaedt J. & P. Terbuyken, "Improvisation" *Das Reallexikon für Antike und Christentum* 17 (1996), pp. 1212–84.

Jammo, S.Y.H., "Gabriel Qatraya et son commentaire sur la liturgie chaldéenne," *Orientalia Christiana Periodica* 32 (1966), pp. 39–52.

—— *La structure de la messe chaldéenne du début jusqu'à l'anaphore*, Orientalia Christiana Analecta 207 (Rome: Pontificium Institutum Orientalium Studiorum, 1979).

Jeanes, G., "Early Latin Parallels to the Roman canon? Possible References to a Eucharistic Prayer in Zeno of Verona," *Journal of Theological Studies* 37 (1986), pp. 427–31.

Jungmann, J.A., F.A. Brunner (trans.), *The Mass of the Roman Rite: Its Origins and Development (Missarum Sollemnia)*, 2 vols (New York: Benziger, 1951, 1955).

Klauser, T., "Der Übergang der römischen Kirche von der griechischen zur lateinischen Liturgiesprache," *Miscellanea Giovanni Mercati: 1. Bibbia, letteratura cristiana antica*, ST 121 (1946).

Klöckener, M., "Zeitgemäßes Beten. Meßorationen als Zeugnisse einer sich wandelnden Kultur und Spiritualität," R. Meßner, E. Nagel & R. Pacik (eds), *Bewahren und Erneuern. Studien zur Meßliturgie. Festschrift für Hans Bernhard Meyer SJ zum 70. Geburtstag*, Innsbrucker theologische Studien 42 (Innsbruck & Wien: Tyrolia, 1995), pp. 114–42.

Kolbaba, T.M., *The Byzantine Lists: Errors of the Latins*, Illinois Medieval Studies (Chicago: University of Illinois Press, 2000).

Kretschmar, G., "Die frühe Geschichte der Jerusalemer Liturgie," *Jahrbuch für Liturgik und Hymnologie* 2 (1956–7), pp. 22–46.

Lafferty, M.K., "Translating Faith from Greek to Latin: Romanitas and Christianitas in Late Fourth-Century Rome and Milan," *Journal of Early Christian Studies* 11 (2003), pp. 21–62.

Lang, U.M., "Rhetoric of Salvation: The Origins of Latin as the Language of the Roman Liturgy," U.M. Lang (ed.), *The Genius of the Roman Rite: Historical, Theological and Pastoral Perspectives on Catholic Liturgy. Proceedings of the 2006 Oxford CIEL Colloquium* (Chicago: Hillenbrand Books, 2010), pp. 22–44.

—— *The Voice of the Church at Prayer: Reflections on Liturgy and Language* (San Francisco: Ignatius Press, 2012).

Leachman, J.G. & D.P. McCarthy, (eds), *Appreciating the Collect: An Irenic Methodology*, Liturgiam Aestimare: Appreciating the Liturgy, 1 (Farnborough: St Michael's Abbey Press, 2008).

Meister, K., *Die Homerische Kunstsprache* (Leipzig: Jablonowski, 1921).

Metzger, M., "À propos des règlements ecclésiastiques et de la prétendue *Tradition apostolique*" *Revue des sciences religieuses* 66 (1992), pp. 249–61.

Mohrmann, C., *Liturgical Latin: Its Origins and Character. Three Lectures* (London: Burns & Oates, 1959).

—— *Études sur le latin des chrétiens*, 4 vols, Storia e letteratura 65, 87, 103, 143 (Roma: Edizioni di Storia e Letteratura, 1961–77).

Moreton, M.J., "Rethinking the Origin of the Roman Canon," *Studia Patristica* 26 (1993), pp. 63–6.

Mowinckel, S., A. Schauer (trans.), *Religion und Kultus* (Göttingen: Vandenhoeck & Ruprecht, 1953).

Norden, E., *Die antike Kunstprosa vom VI. Jahrhundert v. Chr. bis in die Zeit der Renaissance*, 2nd edn, 2 vols (Leipzig: Teubner, 1909).

O'Donnell, J.J., *Augustine, Confessions. Introduction, Text, and Commentary*, 3 vols (Oxford: Clarendon Press, 1992).

Pecklers, K., *Dynamic Equivalence: The Living Language of Christian Worship* (Collegeville: Liturgical Press, 2003).

Pieper, J., L. Krauth (trans.), *In Search of the Sacred* (San Francisco: Ignatius Press, 1991).

Rose, E., "Liturgical Latin in the Missale Gothicum (Vat. Reg. Lat. 317). A reconsideration of Christine Mohrmann's approach," *Sacris Erudiri* 42 (2003), pp. 97–121.

—— "Liturgical Latin in the Bobbio Missal," Y. Hen & R. Meens (eds), *The Bobbio Missal: Liturgy and Religious Culture in Merovingian Gaul*, Cambridge Studies in Palaeography and Codicology (Cambridge: University Press, 2004), pp. 67–78.

Rose, H.G.E. (ed.), *Missale gothicum e codice Vaticano Reginensi latino 317 editum*, CCL 159D (2005).

Schmidt, H.A.P., *Liturgie et langue vulgaire. Le problème de la langue liturgique chez les premiers Réformateurs et au Concile de Trente*, Analecta Gregoriana 53 (Romae: Apud Aedes Unversitatis Gregorianae, 1950).

Senn, F.C., *The People's Work: A Social History of the Liturgy* (Minneapolis: Fortress Press, 2006).

Sheerin, D., "Christian and Biblical Latin," F.A.C. Mantello & A.G. Rigg (eds), *Medieval Latin: An Introduction and Bibliographical Guide*, (Washington, DC: Catholic University of America Press, 1996), pp. 137–56.

Steimer, B., *Vertex traditionis: Die Gattung der altchristlichen Kirchenordnungen*, BZNW 63 (Berlin & New York: de Gruyter, 1992).

Thompson, A., *Cities of God: The Religion of the Italian Communes 1125–1325* (University Park, PA: The Pennsylvania State University Press, 2005).

Thompson, F.J., "SS. Cyril and Methodius and a Mythical Western Heresy: Trilinguism. A Contribution to the Study of Patristic and Mediaeval Theories of Sacred Languages," *Analecta Bollandiana* 110 (1992), pp. 67–122.

Vogel, C., W.G. Storey, N.K. Rasmussen (rev. & trans.), *Medieval Liturgy: An Introduction to the Sources* (Washington, DC: The Pastoral Press, 1986).

Willis, G.G., *Further Essays in Early Roman Liturgy*, Alcuin Club Collection 50 (London: SPCK, 1968).

—— *A History of Early Roman Liturgy to the Death of Pope Gregory the Great*, Henry Bradshaw Society, Subsidia 1 (1994).

Wright, R., *Late Latin and Early Romance in Spain and Carolingian France* (Liverpool: Cairns, 1982).

Chapter 18

ENGLISHING THE MASS

Bruce E. Harbert

Vernacular translation following the Second Vatican Council

Sacrosanctum Concilium article 36 contains the following:

> § 1. Particular law remaining in force, the use of the Latin language is to be preserved in the Latin rites. § 2. But since the use of the mother tongue ... frequently may be of great advantage to the people, the limits of its employment may be extended. This will apply in the first place to the readings and directives, and to some of the prayers and chants.

The four categories enumerated in the last sentence, though somewhat vaguely defined, do not embrace the whole body of liturgical texts. There is no mandate here for a total transformation of the language of the liturgy. Moreover, the official English translation (quoted here) is somewhat misleading, in that "in the first place" seems to imply that a future process of gradual vernacularization is envisaged, but that is not what the Latin *imprimis* means. A more accurate rendering would be: "This will apply *principally* to the readings and directives, and to some of the prayers and chants ..."

Few people imagined in the early 1960s that the entire Catholic liturgy would be celebrated in the vernacular, and those who did could find no support for their view in the documents of the Council.

One man who did foresee what was to come, and the challenges it would bring, was Dom Placide Bruylants, a monk of the Abbey of Mont-César in Louvain, Belgium. He was already well known for his comprehensive study of the text and history of the orations in the preconciliar missal and his Concordance to the Veronese Sacramentary. His translation of the missal into Flemish is still an invaluable guide for translation of Roman orations. Because of his unrivalled knowledge, he seemed the obvious choice when picked after the Council to head the study group for the revision of orations and prefaces in the missal. Unfortunately, his health was poor, and he died in October 1966. Had he lived longer, we should doubtless have had a post-conciliar *Missale Romanum* of higher quality.

In 1964 he published a brief article in which he summarized the character of the prayers of the Roman Rite:

> How should we approach these texts, which could be called the classics of Christian prayer? Do they deserve this title in the sense in which Cicero is called the classic of Latin eloquence? Or are they classics in the manner of a Corneille or a Racine, for the depth with which they have succeeded in depicting the constants of the human soul and heart?
>
> We would be tempted to say that they have both of these characteristics, though in different ways.[1]

Firstly, he argued, the oldest texts can be called classic because of their style, which set a standard for later compositions: "Without doubt, the orations that we call 'ancient'... exhibit a literary perfection that has hardly been successfully imitated later, or outside the purely Roman tradition. In this sense, one could speak of a classic period, stretching roughly from Leo I (440–61) to Gregory I (590–604)."[2] Secondly, they are a classic expression of the depths of the Christian heart:

> They express in a classic manner what is most fundamental in our attitude towards God. They teach us how to enter by prayer into the mystery of God, and more especially into the mystery of God's redemptive love.
>
> Beyond their literary form, which reflects the Christian culture and civilisation of a quite specific period, they express the permanent religious reality of the Christian mystery, which transcends the contingencies of time and space.[3]

In Bruylants' view, it was this latter characteristic that had to be transmitted to future generations, but its vehicle had to be a different style of liturgical prayer suitable to modern culture. He foresaw the difficulties that awaited translators of the missal: "If we are to transmit into the texts that we shall be praying tomorrow in our own language all the religious density of their Latin originals, our language, like theirs, will need to have a clearly sacred character, which translators will probably take a long time to discover."[4]

By distinguishing style from substance in this way, Bruylants identified an issue that was to be central in liturgical history for the next half-century, and is still unresolved: is it possible to change the language of liturgical texts while retaining their substance?

The first ICEL translation

On January 31, 1967, the last bastion of Latin fell, as Pope Paul VI gave permission for the use of the vernacular for the whole of the canon and for the sacramental forms of ordination. The English-speaking world was ready, since as early as 1963 a group of English-speaking bishops attending the Council had established the

International Commission on English in the Liturgy (ICEL). In those early years it remained relatively inactive, awaiting the publication of the new missal. But on March 13, 1967 the Director of ICEL, Fr Frederick McManus, wrote to Mgr Wagner of the Trier Liturgical Institute to tell him that an English version of the Roman canon was being prepared in the ICEL office, though not by the Bishops of the Commission, or indeed in response to their wishes:

> We have reached the stage of first revision, but have said nothing to the bishops of the ten countries involved ... We have rigorously eliminated from the text any traces of the Latin rhetorical flourishes, excessive use of adjectives, etc. which might in any way detract from the nature of our own language and the contemporary tone we wish to give to the translation.[5]

It is already well documented that, with regard to the Latin form of the liturgy, the specialists entrusted with the remodeling of the rites took matters into their own hands and introduced changes that went far beyond what the Council had envisaged. This letter of McManus shows the same process in an Anglophone context. The "we" who have decided the style of the canon are not the bishops of ICEL, but the author and his colleagues.

The Roman canon is the most elaborately composed of all the Roman liturgical texts. It is full of the rhetorical flourishes that McManus deplored, such as *hostiam puram, hostiam sanctam, hostiam immaculatam*, which became simply "this holy and living sacrifice," and the five-fold use of adjectives in *benedictam, adscriptam, ratam, rationabilem acceptabilemque*, which became "Bless and approve our offering, make it acceptable to you, an offering in spirit and in truth." Honorific terms were suppressed, so that the Blessed Virgin was no longer "glorious" and St Joseph and the Apostles no longer "blessed." McManus had succeeded in his aim of uprooting a text formed in the court-milieu of late Antiquity and transplanting it into the democratic world of the late twentieth century West.

ICEL's early methods received semi-official support in 1969 with the publication by the *Consilium* for executing the Constitution on the Sacred Liturgy of *Comme le prévoit*,[6] a document offering guidance on liturgical translation. It was much influenced by the writings of Eugene Nida of the American Bible Society. He developed a theory of translation designed to make the Bible accessible to new readers in a wide variety of languages. Central to his recommendations was a contrast between "formal equivalence," where the translator renders the original word for word, and "dynamic equivalence," which allows a freer approach, seeking to reproduce the effect, rather than the structure, of the original. Nida saw these two approaches as complementary, both to be used as appropriate in the same text, whereas the *Consilium*'s document recommended dynamic above formal equivalence.

Nida was a fine scholar, with a broad and up-to-date knowledge of linguistic theory. Perhaps the best-known fruit of his work is the *Good News Bible*, also known as *Today's English Version*. It was designed to be approachable, so as to introduce the Scriptures to new readers, and was undoubtedly successful in achieving that aim. It was aimed principally at the lone reader, and has never been considered suitable for Catholic worship, which requires a more formal style suited to public proclamation. Although he was the leading translation theorist of his day, his methods were ill suited to the needs of the liturgy.

Towards the end of his long life, Nida expressed regret that his ideas had been misunderstood and misused. In particular, he criticized the widespread view that dynamic equivalence was good and formal equivalence bad. Though he named no names, one can hardly doubt that Catholic liturgical translators were among those he had in mind.

Comme le prévoit also addressed a matter that Nida had not had to consider: the fact that liturgical prayer is public utterance. Translators were encouraged to consider the aural and oral aspect of their texts in order to ensure euphony and intelligibility.

These writings articulated the principles that guided ICEL in producing its first translation of the Roman missal, which showed the same characteristics as the 1967 version of the canon, with a simple syntax and vocabulary. ICEL's translation of the missal was completed in 1973, and soon came into use throughout the English-speaking world, replacing earlier versions.

A striking feature of this translation is that *Dominus* was frequently translated as "Father" rather than "Lord," which is its more exact translation. There are two possible reasons for this. In the liturgy, all three Persons of the Holy Trinity are referred to and addressed as "Lord," an important way of affirming that all three are God, since "Lord" is a divine title. But translators may have felt that this can lead to confusion, especially when "Lord" is used for two different persons in close proximity, as in the anamnesis of the Roman canon, where ICEL translated *Domine* as "Father," and at the end of the same prayer, where it was left untranslated. The second possible reason is that "Lord" may have been felt to belong to an outmoded social structure. This illustrates how, despite Bruylants, style and substance cannot easily be separated. Linguistic choices are often made for non-linguistic reasons.

Revising the 1973 translation

From the beginning, ICEL's bishops realized that their first translation of the missal would need to be revised. In 1982, they instituted a consultation on the 1973 texts to discover what people found good or bad about them. The results of this consultation suggested principles for the revision, which began in 1984. A Progress Report on the project published in 1988 listed some of these principles:

> ...Careful attention to a substantive fidelity to the Latin originals; a fuller vocabulary with a greater use of adjectives and strong verbs; greater attention to speech stresses or the rhythm and cadence of the prayers; use of connectives that results in somewhat longer sentences but conveys the subordination of ideas in the text.[7]

As the work went on, sections of it were circulated to ICEL's member Bishops' Conferences and gradually voted on and approved, until the work was completed in 1998, and it seemed that the new translation would be in use by the new millennium. But opposition was also growing among bishops, particularly in the USA, who found the new texts too imprecise theologically and too contrived in their language, especially in their avoidance of masculine terms, such as "man," when both genders were being referred to. For instance, it was proposed to include in the Nicene Creed:

For us and for our salvation
he came down from heaven.

The objection to this is that it fails to translate *homines*. "Human beings," which is an accurate translation of this Latin word, was presumably thought stylistically inappropriate, and the translators did not want to use "men" for fear of excluding women. There is an important dogmatic point here, since the Fathers of Nicaea could simply have said "for us," but they inserted "human beings" to indicate that Christ died for the whole of the human race, not for a part of it, or for any other beings, such as angels. Here is a case of stylistic considerations being allowed to outweigh the substance of the text.

These reservations were shared in Rome, with the result that in 2002 the Prefect of the Congregation for Divine Worship and the Discipline of the Sacraments wrote to Presidents of English-speaking Bishops' Conferences to say that the Congregation would not be able to grant the *recognitio* to the 1998 text. Here is a sample of the Congregation's *Observations:*

> The Structure of the collects: Relative clauses often disappear in the proposed text (especially the initial *Deus, qui* ..., so important in the Latin collects), so that a single oration is divided into two or more sentences. This loss is detrimental not only to the unity of the structure, but to the manner of conveying the proper sense of the posture before God of the Christian people, or of the individual Christian. The relative clause *acknowledges* God's greatness, while the independent clause strongly conveys the impression that one is *explaining* something about God to God. Yet it is precisely the *acknowledgement* of the *mirabilia Dei* that lies at the heart of all Judaeo-Christian euchology. The quality of supplication is also adversely affected so that many of the texts now appear to say to God rather abruptly: "You did a; now do b." The manner in which language expresses relationship to God cannot be regarded merely as a matter of style.[8]

The Congregation had already in the previous year published its Fifth Instruction "for the right implementation of the Constitution on the Sacred Liturgy of the Second Vatican Council," entitled from its first words *Liturgiam authenticam* (March 28, 2001). The title of this document is sometimes misunderstood, when *authenticam* is taken to mean "authentic" in the modern English sense of "real," "true" or "genuine," which is not what *authenticus* means in Latin. Applied to documents, as it most frequently is, it means "in accord with the original." Applied to people, it means "authoritative" or "worthy of belief." For liturgy to be *authenticus*, it must be faithful to the tradition from which it derives.

Nor is the status of the Fifth Instruction always well understood because it is often presented as a replacement for *Comme le prévoit*, substituting an official predilection for dynamic equivalence with one for formal equivalence. In fact, the Fifth Instruction, issued with the full authority of the Congregation and with the approval of the Pope, has a far higher status than one simply published by the *Consilium*. Nevertheless, taken together, the two documents offer parameters within which translators can work: the former warning against undue slavishness and the latter against undue liberty. It is true that in places *Liturgiam Authenticam* contradicts *Comme le prévoit,* but for the most part what needed saying in 1969 still had value in 2001 and remains valuable now. The authors of *Comme le prévoit* knew the texts of the Roman rite well, and identified perceptively many pitfalls that await the incautious translator.

Liturgiam authenticam was animated by a desire to safeguard the Church's doctrine and spiritual traditions by controlling the language of liturgical texts, that is, to protect their substance by prescribing their style, as the preamble indicates:

> The greatest prudence and attention is required in the preparation of liturgical books marked by sound doctrine, which are exact in wording, free from all ideological influence, and otherwise endowed with those qualities by which the sacred mysteries of salvation and the indefectible faith of the Church are efficaciously brought into prayer by means of human language, and worthy worship is offered to God the Most High (n. 3).

But the document repeatedly modifies its prescriptions with phrases like "as far as possible," thus increasing the latitude available to the translator. For example: "The connection between various expressions, manifested by subordinate and relative clauses, the ordering of words, and various forms of parallelism, is to be maintained as completely as possible in a manner appropriate to the vernacular language" (n. 57 a).

ICEL worked for seven years on a new translation, sending sections as usual to Bishops' Conferences for approval. When the work was done, the Conferences submitted their texts, with necessary local adaptations, to the Congregation for *recognitio*. By now, the Congregation had the assistance of the *Vox Clara* Committee, composed of about a dozen bishops drawn from several countries but predominantly from the United States of America, to advise them on English-language liturgical texts. This committee availed itself of the assistance of half a dozen collaborators, a striking contrast to the hundreds who had contributed to the work of ICEL. In 2010, the new translation was promulgated, its final form being the responsibility of the Congregation, and it came into use around the world in the following year.

A critique of aspects of the 2010 translation

Nobody can predict how long it will remain in public use, but a widespread feeling has become evident that, although it went a good way toward satisfying the desire for a more formal style, and transmitted more faithfully the content of the original, there is still ample room for improvement. Consequently, the remainder of this chapter will be concerned with aspects of the text that merit reconsideration.

Some of the remaining issues arise from the nature of the Latin language itself, and its structural differences from English.

Latin has no article, either definite or indefinite, so that a translator often has to choose which one to use, or whether to use an article at all. Omission of the article will give the text a more allusive character, as in the prayer after Communion for Wednesday in the Second Week of Eastertide:

> lead those you have imbued with heavenly mysteries
> to pass from former ways to newness of life.

"Heavenly mysteries" can be taken to mean not only the Eucharist just celebrated, but the Sacraments of Initiation celebrated at the Easter Vigil, and indeed the entire paschal experience. Often, when *sacra* modifies *mysteria* in the Latin the translation uses the definite article to show that the reference is precisely to the Eucharist:

> Abide graciously, O Lord, with your people
> who have touched the sacred mysteries . . .

But sometimes it goes further, using the demonstratives "this" or "these" where the Latin has no equivalent:

> Show unceasing favour, O Lord,
> to those you refresh with this divine mystery . . .

> . . . look upon the hearts dedicated to you
> by means of these sacred mysteries . . .

There is a theological point here as well as a linguistic one. Scholastic theology seeks precise and exhaustive definition whereas the theology of the first Christian millennium is more content with allusion. The classic prayers of the Roman rite come from the latter period, but now they are being translated in a post-scholastic age whose attitudes are exemplified by the use of demonstratives to achieve a more assertive precision than is offered by the originals. The overuse of "this" and "these" in the interest of greater definiteness is a characteristic that has passed over from the former English translation of the Mass to the new one.

This tendency comes to a head in the Roman canon when the celebrant says that we offer to God: "this pure Victim, this holy Victim, this spotless Victim, the holy Bread of eternal life, and the Chalice of everlasting salvation." It would be possible to use the indefinite article: "a pure victim, a holy victim, a spotless victim" without losing the identification of the eucharistic elements with Christ. The definite article could also be used: "the pure victim, the holy victim, the spotless victim," which would emphasize more the uniqueness of what is being offered. The official translation, with its triple use of "this," which seems to point repeatedly and insistently at what lies on the altar, exemplifies the clarity and force of post-Tridentine eucharistic catechesis. A patristic text has been translated with a post-scholastic mentality. A further difficulty arises from the use of "victim," which in English is used only for animates, to translate *hostia*, which can also be used for inanimates, as in the phrase *hostiam laudis* ("the sacrifice of praise") from Ps 115,8, quoted at Heb 13,15. To identify a victim, who must be a person or animal, with "bread" and a "chalice" sounds odd.

Students of Latin learn early on not to translate the ablative absolute construction by following the Latin syntactical pattern too closely, that is, not to write "Gaul having been conquered, Caesar returned home," but to prefer "When Gaul had been conquered, Caesar returned home." Appropriately, then, on Friday in the Fourth Week of Lent we pray:

> Grant, we pray, O Lord,
> that, as we pass from old to new,
> so, with former ways left behind,
> we may be renewed in holiness of mind.
> Through Christ our Lord.

In line 3, "former ways having been left behind" would be a wooden, over literal translation.

An ablative absolute is often used in connection with the intercession of the saints. For instance, the latter part of the collect for St Pius X might be literally translated: "grant us, with him interceding, to participate in your mysteries with lively faith and fruitful charity." The official version is in fact: "grant, through his intercession, that we may participate in your mysteries with lively faith and fruitful charity."

But a problem arises with the use of "through" in such cases. "Through" is the normal English translation for the Latin preposition *per*, which plays an important role in the liturgy. The majority of orations in the missal and elsewhere in the liturgy are addressed to God the Father and end in a formula beginning with *Per*, which we translate "Through our Lord Jesus Christ, your Son …" The eucharistic prayers similarly end with *Per Ipsum*, "Through him." In the Nicene Creed, we say of Christ "through him all things were made." All these formulae indicate that, as St Paul teaches, "there is one mediator between God and men, the man Christ Jesus" (1 Tim. 2:5). Consistently with this doctrine, it is a constant feature of the Roman euchology that God is never asked to grant or do something "through the intercession" (*per intercessionem*) of anybody. In the current Latin missal, there is only one exception, tucked away in the collect of the Common for Several Founders of Churches, a prayer newly composed for the

1970 missal, presumably composed by an author unaware of this convention and its implications.

It is to be regretted, therefore, that the official English version frequently asks God to grant favors "through the intercession" of one or more saints. This will lend support to Protestant critics who claim that Catholics do not take seriously the uniqueness of the mediation of Christ.

Latin, like any other language, changed during the many centuries in which it was in use. An example is the use of the conjunction *cum*, which in classical Latin is temporal (meaning "when") when followed by an indicative verb and causal (meaning "because") when followed by a subjunctive. However, this distinction lapses in later Latin, so that *cum* with an indicative in later texts can properly be translated "since."

The beginning of the paschal prefaces, which is first found in the mid-eighth century Gelasian Sacramentary, is:

> Vere dignum et iustum est, aequum et salutare
> Te quidem, Domine, omni tempore confiteri,
> sed in hoc potissimum gloriosius praedicare
> cum Pascha nostrum immolatus est Christus.

The official version follows the classical rule for the interpretation of *cum*, translating:

> It is truly right and just, our duty and our salvation,
> at all times to acclaim you, O Lord,
> but in this time above all to laud you yet more gloriously,
> when Christ our Passover has been sacrificed.

This is strange, because "when" with a have-tense usually refers to the future, as in "When you have lifted up the Son of Man, then you will know that I am he," whereas here it can only refer to the past, Christ having been sacrificed already. In the background to this text are the words of St Paul: "Christ our Passover has been sacrificed; therefore let us keep the feast."

Paul indicates a causal link between Christ's sacrifice and the Easter festivities, which would surely make better sense in the Paschal prefaces that he has inspired. Remembering the late-Latin use of *cum*, we could translate them thus: "but in this time above all to laud you yet more gloriously, *since* Christ our Passover has been sacrificed."

The use of "when" in the official version, if it makes any sense at all, reduces Easter to an anniversary commemoration, whereas "since" makes of it what St Paul understood it to be, the celebration of an enduring reality that arises from the Paschal Mystery.

It was only in the second Christian millennium that *sacramentum* acquired its now familiar sense, denoting one of the group of seven sacraments defined by the Church. In earlier Christian Latin, it was applied to many sacred objects and events. It is used to refer to the sacred season of Lent in both the collect and the prayer over the offerings for the First Sunday of Lent, both of which are translated accurately in the official English text, which does not use the English word *sacrament*. But a more complex situation arises with the prayer that follows the seventh reading in the Paschal Vigil, which contains the phrase *totius Ecclesiae sacramentum*. This, together with many other texts from the patristic period, may well have been in the mind of the Fathers of Vatican II when they spoke of the Church as a sacrament, without indicating how such nomenclature might be integrated with a scholastic view of sacramentality. Their words led many in subsequent years to explore the theme of the sacramentality of the Church. Their work, however, seems not to have impressed the authors of the official translation, which translates this phrase as "the wondrous mystery of the whole Church." Here is a striking example of the common tendency to translate texts of the patristic period with the mentality of the scholastic era.

To call a person *pius* in classical Latin indicates that that person is faithful to his obligations. Aeneas shows that he is *pius* by rescuing his father from the fire that is destroying the city of Troy. *Pius* could denote fidelity to religious and moral obligations as well as familial ones, and this has given us the modern words "pious" and "piety." It has also given us "pity." Representations of Our Lady holding her dead son show her exercising the familial duty of care for the dead, and also expressing her grief in a way that evokes our compassion. Appropriately, English-speakers often borrow the Italian word *pietà* for such statues, for example the famous one by Michelangelo. Similarly, the motif of "the pelican in her piety," popular in medieval iconography, shows a mother bird taking pity on her young and feeding them with her own blood.

The prayer over the offerings for the seventh Sunday of Eastertide, given for the same Sunday in the 1570 *Missale*, and found already in the Veronese Sacramentary, contains the petition *ut per haec piae devotionis officia / ad caelestem gloriam transeamus*. Frederick Husenbeth (1796–1872), one of the earliest translators of the Mass into English, was content with a translation that is little more than a transliteration: "that, by these offices of pious devotion, we may pass to heavenly glory," and was followed closely by many subsequent translations, both before and after the Second Vatican Council. Adrian Fortescue, detecting an earlier sense of *pius*, wrote "loving devotion." His lead was followed later in the century by Caraman and Walsh with "these acts of filial homage." Other versions offered flabby approximations to the Latin.

Liturgical texts often call God *pius*, but it hardly seems appropriate to call God "pious"—an earlier sense of the word must be involved here. A scholarly translator would perhaps choose "fatherly." The collect for Wednesday of the Fifth Week of Lent asks God to enlighten the hearts of his children and give them *pium auditum*, "a fatherly hearing:" the paternal note is barely missable, granted the earlier reference to childhood. But the official translation is content with "a gracious hearing."

In early Latin, *devotio* denoted a specific act of self-consecration to the gods, often ending in the death of the person performing the act. In the Vulgate of the

Acts of the Apostles, when a group of Jews vow to fast until they have killed Paul, they say *devotione devovimus nos nihil gustaturos* "we have bound ourselves by a vow to taste nothing" (Acts 23:14). In the Christian centuries, *devotio* lost this sense, and came to mean only a habit, and never an act, of devotion. But the prayer after Communion for the Twelfth Week of the Year contains the phrase *devotione frequenti*, which implies that here *devotio* is a single act, repeated at frequent intervals: it might be translated "frequent acts of self-sacrifice." Moreover, in the 1962 *Missale* and its predecessors, *devotione* here was modified by *pia*. It was the 1970 revisers who restored the original reading *frequenti* from the Veronese Sacramentary. Nevertheless, the official version translates the phrase blandly with "constant devotion."

Humanus in classical Latin can mean "human" in the sense of "belonging to the human race" as in Terence's famous dictum *Homo sum; nihil humani alienum a me puto*, "I am a human being; there is nothing human that I imagine to be alien to me." It can also mean "humane," in the sense of "gentle" or "kindly." Cicero in particular developed the notion of *humanitas* as a mark of a civilized person. Much later, in the context of Christological controversy, *humanitas* came to be used to denote human nature in contrast with *divinitas*, particularly in the case of Christ. This development is exemplified especially in the writings of Pope St Leo the Great, who wrote in 449 to the Emperor Theodosius that the martyrs of Rome had no motive for their suffering other than "the confession of true divinity and true humanity in Christ." In English we have two words for these two senses: "humaneness" and "humanity."

Both senses of *humanitas* are found in the Roman missal: the collect for the Night Mass of Christmas, very possibly from the pen of Pope St Leo the Great himself, prays "that we may share in the divinity of Christ, who humbled himself to share in our humanity." By contrast, in a recently composed prayer for refugees and exiles, *humanitas* is appropriately translated "true compassion." But when on the Memorial of the Queenship of the Blessed Virgin Mary we are asked to pray "to be given strength by the humanity of Christ," the translation seems to stray from orthodox belief. It is contrary to Christian faith to imagine the human nature of Christ operating independently from his divinity in giving us strength. A better translation would have us pray: "that the kindness of Christ may come to our aid."

A principal vehicle for conveying deference in liturgical texts is provided by the catenative verbs, so called after the Latin word for "chain," *catena*, because they cannot stand alone, but must link with another verb. A familiar example comes in the words said during the preparation of the gifts about Christ, who "humbled himself to share in our humanity," where "humbled himself" translates *dignatus est*. The word *dignor*, which has given us modern English "deign," occurs well over seventy times in the missal. In not all of these cases is it as well used as in the one just quoted, which probably originates with Pope St Leo the Great. The collect for the Feast of the Holy Family, for instance, which was newly composed for the 1970 missal, begins "O God, who were pleased to give us / the shining example of the Holy Family," where "were pleased" translates *dignatus es*, adding little to the sense.

The use of catenatives increases as the Roman rite develops. There are relatively few in the Veronese Sacramentary, far more in the Gelasian, and a large number in the prayers newly composed for the 1970 missal.

When "deign" was proposed as a translation for *dignor*, widespread outcry ensued. It was pointed out that in modern speech, "deign" is mostly used in negative or interrogative expressions, and then ironically ("Would you deign to come to my party?"; "She didn't deign to visit me in hospital"). Without "deign," translators struggle to find an acceptable translation for *dignor*. "Be pleased to" is used, as is "graciously" but both can often seem like unnecessary padding, and so in the official version, *dignor* has sometimes been left untranslated, despite the requirements of *Liturgiam authenticam*. An example comes in the collect for the Solemnity of the Sacred Heart: "O God, who in the Heart of your Son, wounded by our sins, bestow on us in mercy the boundless treasures of your love," where "deign to bestow on us in mercy" would be a more scrupulous translation of the third line. It is a pity to have lost the note of condescension in the prayer, since awareness of divine condescension is so central to devotion to the Sacred Heart.

The liturgy often uses *dignor* in requests made to God, as in the epiclesis of the third eucharistic prayer: "graciously make holy these gifts." In these cases, there is an accurate translation available, namely "please": "please make holy these gifts," but when this was suggested, it met with a strongly negative response, even from people who had argued for the use of everyday language in the liturgy.

The most problematic of the catenatives is *mereor*. From it is derived modern English "merit," which is used as an equivalent to "deserve" as in "such a crime merits severe punishment" or "that song merits a wider audience." But *mereor*, when used in Christian Latin does not always mean "deserve," for we can deserve nothing of God: when God responds favorably to our good works, he is not paying us a "just wage" for them. As Augustine says, when God crowns our merits, he is crowning his own gifts. For this reason, presumably, the translators have avoided using "deserve" as a translation for *mereor*. But they have made abundant use of "merit," which is understood today as synonymous with "deserve." This will require careful catechesis to explain that in the missal, "merit" does not mean "deserve," lest worshippers think they can score points with God, and Protestants, who have opposed Catholic teaching on merit ever since Martin Luther, say "I told you so." Again, there is an accurate translation of *mereor* available, namely "get to," indicating an unearned favour, as in "I got to have tea with the Queen." But again, this is too colloquial.

Another catenative is *valeo*, meaning "to be able to." This also has often been left untranslated, since it seems to add little to the sense. For instance, in the blessing of palms on Palm Sunday, the Latin prays "that we may be able to reach the heavenly Jerusalem," which has been reduced to "that we may reach the heavenly Jerusalem." There seems to be little loss of sense here: we are hardly like to be able to reach heaven but decide not to reach it. But again, a perfectly natural translation is available for *valeo*, namely "manage." "That we may manage to reach the heavenly Jerusalem" conveys the effort required, as the official translation fails to do. But again, its register is too colloquial to be widely accepted in the liturgy.

The reader may feel that the use of "that we may" in the last paragraph is slightly foreign to modern English, and that it would be more natural to say "so that we can." Another example is in the collect for the twenty-fourth Sunday *per annum*:

Look upon us, O God,
Creator and ruler of all things,
and, that we may feel the working of your mercy,
grant that we may serve you with all our heart.

Here, "so that we can feel the working of your mercy" would probably sound more contemporary to most hearers. In other cases, "will" may seem more appropriate, for example in a text for the blessing of water in the Paschal Vigil: "May he graciously renew us, that we may remain faithful to the Spirit," where "so that we will remain faithful" might be preferred. Sometimes "might" is used, as in a preface for the dead: "he accepted death, so that we might all escape from dying." Here "could" or "would" might seem preferable. However, "that + may / might," rather than "so that + can / will" seems widely acceptable, another example of a non-colloquial usage being accepted into the liturgy.

The distinction between "may" and "might" is in flux in contemporary English. More fastidious readers may be troubled at finding "might" after present tenses and "may" after past tenses, but maintenance of the classic distinction seems to be becoming archaic. A comparison of versions of John 3:16 will illustrate many ways of expressing purpose. To give but two examples, the New American Bible has "For God so loved the world that he gave his only Son, so that everyone who believes in him might not perish but might have eternal life," whereas the Revised Standard Version has "For God so loved the world that he gave his only Son, so that everyone who believes in him may not perish but may have eternal life."

Uncertainty in the use of these words has produced a problem in the language of the missal. As we have seen, they are associated with ability, which seems inappropriate in God's case. We surely should not pray, on Tuesday of the Fifth Week of Lent: "We offer you, O Lord, the sacrifice of conciliation, that . . . you may . . . pardon our offences," since this gives the impression that our sacrifice enables God to pardon us, that is, that we can increase God's ability—"will" would be better than "may" here.

Purpose-clauses are an area where the arrival of God into human language raises unique issues. We act with a purpose that may or may not be fulfilled, whereas God's purpose is always fulfilled. Nor does God need to do one thing in order to be able to do another. In fact, it would seem prudent to avoid altogether the use of "may" and "might" in dependent clauses with God as subject. Another way of expressing purpose that can be useful in such cases is "so as to." Thus, in the preface to the fourth eucharistic prayer, "yet you . . . have made all that is, so that you might fill your creatures with blessings," would become "yet you . . . have made all that is, so as to fill your creatures with blessings."

Though such considerations will be dismissed by some as unduly minute, one contributor to formal style is a greater regularity of syntax than is common in ordinary speech. The King James version of the Bible is a well-known example of this, and it may be regretted that in some ways the missal falls unnecessarily short of the standards of the KJV. There is a constant temptation in the liturgical field of human action to be content with the second-best on the grounds that "it will do," but the truth is that nothing is too good for the Sacred Liturgy.

Liturgical change invariably encounters strong resistance. Hence, *Liturgiam authenticam* number 64 says: "Without real necessity, successive revisions of translations should not notably change the previously approved vernacular texts of the eucharistic prayers which the faithful will have committed gradually to memory."

However, a special challenge was posed by several texts in the Order of Mass which had been translated, not by ICEL but by ICET, the International Consultation on English Texts, an interdenominational body whose proposals ICEL had accepted. This body was influenced by Thomas Cranmer's translations in the Anglican Book of Common Prayer and its progeny, with the result that several of its proposals were in fact drawn from that book. Many of these were changed, but some were not, among them the translation of *Sursum corda* as "Lift up your hearts." Study of the Latin and underlying Greek originals suggested that these words should not be translated as a command from the celebrant but rather as an invitation, more appropriately for the Roman rite, in which commands are usually given by the deacon. Scholarship also strongly suggested that what the people are invited to do at that point in the Mass is not to raise their hearts, but to hold them on high. The Italian translation *In alto i nostri cuori* ("Let our hearts be on high") seemed to provide a suitable model. The people's response, far from expressing an obedient compliance with a command from the celebrant, as Cranmer's version suggests ("We lift them up unto the Lord") indicates that they are already doing what he has invited them to do: "We hold them before the Lord." The sixteenth-century Book of Common Prayer translation was born of a clerical age, whereas the preface dialogue itself dates from at least as early as the third century, and reflects the more collegial, participatory ecclesiology of those days, which Vatican II was concerned to reinstate. But Cranmer won the day with "Lift up your hearts; We lift them up to the Lord."

He also influenced the conclusion to the collects, which he had translated: ". . . through Jesus Christ our Lord, who with thee and the Holy Ghost liveth and reigneth, ever one God, world without end." The 1973 translation had adopted Cranmer's phrase "one God" in its own version of the Conclusion: ". . . through our Lord Jesus Christ, your Son, who lives and reigns with you and the Holy Spirit, one God for ever and ever."

This failed to translate *in unitate Spiritus Sancti* ("in the unity of the Holy Spirit"), a formula unique to the Western liturgies, which expresses the distinctively Western theology of the Spirit as the bond of unity between Father and Son. The 2010 version translates this faithfully, but without removing Cranmer's "one God," so that *unitate* is translated twice and the syntax seems to indicate that Christ is "one God," implying that there are others. The Italians use a more accurate version, which would translate into English thus: "Through our Lord Jesus Christ, your Son, who is God, living and reigning with you in the unity of the Holy Spirit for ever and ever." But this is markedly different from what people have become accustomed to, and would for that reason meet resistance.

Conclusion

A translator who approaches the *Missale Romanum* is faced with a collection of texts from a wide range of sources. Their dates extend from Old Testament times to the present century. Mostly composed in Europe or the Holy Land, they exhibit a variety of regional styles. The provenance of the *Missale* is far wider than that of the Bible. A scholarly translator will aim to reflect the nuances that distinguish these texts. The author of a devotional translation, by contrast, will highlight elements helpful to the contemporary worshipper. The liturgical translator is under greater pressure, because he is producing a text for public use. His work will pass through several revisions, over which he has no control. Eventually, it will come before a committee composed largely if not entirely of bishops, whose minds will be, not only on the text before them, but on its likely reception by their colleagues. Eventually, all the bishops of the language-group will be invited to judge the text. They will be asking, not only if the proposed version is faithful to its original, but also whether it will be acceptable to their clergy and laity, and the latter consideration will often carry more weight with them than the former. Moreover, not all of them will be experienced Latinists, and those who are may only have read a narrow range of writings, in canon law, for example, or scholastic theology, which will have limited their awareness of the range of meaning a Latin word can have acquired over more than two millennia.

A single striking example of the effect that such pressures can have is to be found in the second eucharistic prayer, where *astare coram te*, which unambiguously means "to stand in your presence" has been translated as "to be in your presence" because of the custom in many parts of the world of kneeling rather than standing during the eucharistic prayer.

No translation is perfect, but the experience of the last half-century has shown that many influences militate against the production of a faithful translation of the *Missale Romanum* for liturgical use that will be universally well received. What we have is a translation of texts from the first Christian millennium produced under the influence of scholasticism, of popular piety, of ecclesiastical politics, and of many other pressures. How long it will last, one cannot say but, since these pressures will remain, it seems unlikely that any future liturgical translation could succeed in being more faithful.

The question arises, whether large international committees are best suited to the translation of liturgical texts. That is not, after all, how they were first produced. Although scholars gave early sacramentaries titles that associated them with popes—Leonine, Gelasian, and Gregorian—the origin of their individual items remains for the most part uncertain. The idea that there should be a single missal promulgated for use throughout the world dates from, and was only feasible in, the age of printing. In the manuscript age, there was inevitably more variation from place to place.

The Fathers of Vatican II were not envisaging vernacular liturgy. They said: "Therefore no other person, even if he be a priest, may add, remove, or change anything in the liturgy on his own authority" (*Sacrosanctum Concilium*, 22 § 3). But once celebrants began to use their own language, they began to improvise, changing the printed text according to their views. This almost universal practice should not be attributed solely to disobedience or ill-will. When reading aloud a text written in an idiom close to their own, most people will unconsciously make changes to what is printed. The introduction of options into the rite, sometimes arising from dissent among those responsible for its production, has increased the unpredictability of what will happen at a celebration, and consequently the celebrant's sense of freedom.

The age of print is now giving way to the age of electronic communication. This was apparent in 2010, as the new translation was promulgated. A missal was presented to the Pope, but was found to contain a text so chaotically inaccurate that it never came into use. A stream of corrections emanated from the Congregation, so that several versions were in circulation at once. Thus the Church entered the era of Wikiliturgy.

Electronic communication can serve the liturgy by facilitating the exchange among celebrants of modifications to the printed text, leading to a sifting process that sorts the good from the bad and recommends the former. Recourse to the Latin text will always be necessary, to avoid the vernacular straying too far from the tradition. This means that not only the official book must be studied, but the manuscripts on which it is based, which can reveal defects in the official text, as this article has sought to demonstrate. And those who love the ancient, classic texts of the Roman rite will still need to read and pray them in Latin, as the Fathers of the Second Vatican Council envisaged.

Notes

1 Bruylants, Placide, "En quête d'un nouveau style de prière," *Questions Liturgiques* 45 (1964), pp. 150–4 (p. 151).
2 Ibid.
3 Ibid., pp. 153–4.
4 Ibid., p. 154.
5 Archive of the International Commission on English in the Liturgy, Washington, DC.
6 DOL n. 123.
7 International Commission on English in the Liturgy, *Progress Report on the Revision of the Roman Missal* (ICEL: Washington, DC, 1988), p. 10.
8 Jorge A. Cardinal Medina Estevez, Letter, March 16, 2002, Prot. n. 429/02/L.

Bibliography

Baker, Mona, *Routledge Encyclopedia of Translation Studies* (London: Routledge, 1998).
Beall, Stephen M., "Verbal Iconicity: A Problem in Liturgical Translation," *Downside Review* 117 (1999), pp. 133–44.

Bruylants, Placide, *Concordance verbale du Sacramentaire Léonien* (Louvain: Éditions de l'Abbaye du Mont César, 1945).

—"En quête d'un nouveau style de prière," *Questions Liturgiques* 45 (1964), pp. 150–54.

— *Les oraisons du Missel Romain: texte et histoire*, Études Liturgiques, 1 (Louvain: Centre de Documentation et d'Information Liturgiques—Abbaye du Mont César, 1952).

Congregation for Divine Worship and Discipline of the Sacraments, "Fifth Instruction 'For the right implementation of the Constitution on the Sacred Liturgy of the Second Vatican Council' *Liturgiam authenticam*," March 28, 2001.

Consilium ad exsequendam Constitutionem de Sacra Liturgia, Instruction: "*Comme le prevoit*, on the translation of liturgical texts for celebrations with a congregation," January 25, 1969; DOL n. 123.

Day, Juliette J., *Reading the Liturgy: An Exploration of Texts in Christian Worship* (London: Bloomsbury/T&T Clark, 2014).

Dumas, Antoine, "Pour mieux comprendre les textes liturgiques du missel romain," *Notitiae* 6 (1970), pp. 194–213.

Gallagher, Daniel B., "What Has Language to Do with Beauty? The Philosophical Foundations of Liturgical Translations," Janet E. Rutherford & James O'Brien (eds), *Benedict XVI and the Roman Missal* (Dublin: Four Courts Press, 2011), pp. 226–44.

Harbert, Bruce E., "Ancient Rhetoric and Modern Prayer: The Case of the Roman Canon," *Antiphon* 5 (2000), pp. 30–6.

—"Implementing *Liturgiam Authenticam*: A Case Study," *Antiphon* 6 (2001), pp. 20–26.

International Commission on English in the Liturgy, *Progress Report on the Revision of the Roman Missal* (ICEL: Washington, DC, 1988).

— *Second Progress Report on the Revision of the Roman Missal* (ICEL: Washington, DC, 1990).

— *Third Progress Report on the Revision of the Roman Missal* (ICEL: Washington, DC, 1992).

Jeffery, Peter, "A Chant Historian Reads 'Liturgiam Authenticam' 3: Languages and Cultures," *Worship* 78 (2004), pp. 236–65.

Lang, Uwe Michael, "Translating the *Missale Romanum*: Towards a Sacral Vernacular," Janet E. Rutherford & James O'Brien (eds), *Benedict XVI and the Roman Missal* (Dublin: Four Courts Press, 2011), pp. 245–59.

—*The Voice of the Church at Prayer: Reflections on Liturgy and Language* (San Francisco: Ignatius, 2012).

Magee, Michael K., "The Liturgical Translation of the Response 'Et Cum Spiritu Tuo'," *Communio* (2002), pp. 152–71.

Munday, Jeremy, *Introducing Translation Studies: Theories and Applications* (London: Routledge, 2001).

Nida, Eugene A. & Charles R. Taber, *The Theory and Practice of Translation* (Leiden: E.J. Brill, 1969,1982).

Ostdiek, Gilbert, Jeremy Driscoll & Dennis D. McManus, *The Voice of the Church: A Forum on Liturgical Translation* (Washington DC: United States Conference of Catholic Bishops, 2001).

Pecklers, Keith F., *Dynamic Equivalence: The Living Language of Christian Worship* (Collegeville: Liturgical Press, 2003).

Serratelli, Arthur, "The New Roman Missal; a Moment in the Church's Liturgical Renewal," Janet E. Rutherford & James O'Brien (eds), *Benedict XVI and the Roman Missal* (Dublin: Four Courts Press, 2011), pp. 275–91.

Silva-Tarouca, C. (ed.), *Sancti Leonis Magni Epistulae Contra Eutychis Haeresim*, vol. 1. Textus et Documenta 15 (Romae: Apud aedes Pontificiae Universitatis Gregorianae, 1934).

Walsh, Christopher, "Minding Our Language: Issues of Liturgical Language Arising in Revision," *Worship* 74 (2000), pp. 482–503.

Chapter 19

LITURGICAL MUSIC

Timothy McDonnell

Introduction

The contemporary practice of liturgical music in the Roman Catholic Church is a subject viewed from starkly divergent perspectives. The documents of the Church, their official and unofficial interpretations, the views of practitioners as well as academics all vie for dominance in the arena of liturgical music praxis. The explanation for this condition is likely the process of continual reform in which the liturgy has labored for the last century—a reform that escalated in the period following the Second Vatican Council (1962–65).

The total measure of contemporary musical practice in the Catholic liturgy is so extensive as to preclude a comprehensive treatment here. Additionally, some of the musical fashions in common use exceed the traditional categories of the Catholic liturgical music, and would require extensive commentary to parse out fully.[1] This survey will avoid an indiscriminate catalog of musical items and their uses as well as a perfunctory recitation of liturgical regulations regarding music. Rather, it will focus on the practice of liturgical music in view of the principles established by the Church since the Second Vatican Council to ensure the Catholic character and identity of the liturgy.

The chapter will also address to some extent the tension that exists between the received musical forms and the provisions of the reformed Mass liturgy mandated by the Council. An examination of these provisions and how they impact the practice of music in the ritual life of the Church forms the heart of this study. Finally, we will examine the challenges, choices, and adaptive initiatives that the revised liturgy occasions, and the philosophical questions attached to those conditions. The scope of this project, then, is to present the *status quaestionis,* and is intended to be suitably broad to furnish an informed beginning to the study of liturgical music and its current practice in the Church.

Music in the liturgy after the conciliar reforms

The pattern of liturgical reform in the period between the reign of Pius X and the commencement of the Second Vatican Council was one of incremental and contiguous adjustment, such that the inherited musical forms and elements were continually useful and useable throughout the process. The reform of Holy Week in the decade or so preceding the Council, however, intimated a new approach toward reform that resulted in the obsolescence of some musical elements.[2] Because liturgical music is always tied to a ritual, the fate of the former is intrinsically wed to that of the latter. The period following the Council saw the advent of a new paradigm that would abandon the pattern of reform by gradual degrees. It also was less concerned about the historical continuity of the rites, often appealing to periods of liturgical history that predate many of the ritual and textual elements around which the pre-Conciliar Mass was structured.

The reformers' approach required a kind of historical leap to what the scholarship of the time considered a more pristine proto-liturgy of Roman origin (see *Sacrosanctum Concilium,* 50). The consolidation of the Roman rite historically hinges on the period between the papacy of Gregory I (†604 AD) and the subsequent formation of the Holy Roman Empire under Charlemagne (†814). Alongside the refinements of ritual and text, the creation of the chant repertory attached to those elements was a major undertaking of that era. Consequently, the modern search for and appropriation of liturgical forms and concepts anterior to the formational age of the classical Roman rite presented substantial challenges for the repertory of music which came into existence during the period of coalescence in the Gregorian-Carolingian era.[3] The struggle to maintain the ritual identity to which these older musical forms were attached in the face of a clear demand on the part of the renovated rites for new ones frames the cultural crisis in liturgical music during the latter twentieth century.

The documents of the first phase of reform (1962–69) are ambiguous on the point of preserving the received musical patrimony. The *Constitution on the Sacred Liturgy* supported the continued use of Latin and gave a position of privilege to Gregorian chant (n. 116). At the same time, it strongly encouraged the active participation of the faithful (n. 14). It is important to note that when Pius X first coined this expression in his 1903 motu proprio, the supposition was that the faithful would assume their roles in the singing of the liturgical chants that belonged to them—in Latin.[4] Even as late as the Constitution, this ideal was preserved, and the Council seemed optimistic in this document that the project of educating the faithful in the use of Latin chant was achievable (*Sacrosanctum Concilium,* 54).

There were, however, concessions within the Constitution that gave rise to the most significant development in the common experience of the Church's life: the vernacular liturgy. The Constitution was adamant that the Latin tongue would remain the norm for the Roman Church, but the vernacular was to be admitted (always with the approval of the national conferences of bishops) wherever its use would seem to be of pastoral advantage (*Sacrosanctum Concilium,* 36 § 2). Although it was never a documented decision on the part of the Church, the idea of educating the hundreds of millions of Roman Catholics in the ancient tongue of their rite appeared to be gradually surrendered in favor of the obvious advantages of the vernacular. The common tongue was introduced at Mass in phases throughout the mid-1960s, and by the time of its promulgation in the fall of 1969, the new Mass, in effect, ushered the arrival of the thoroughly vernacular liturgy.[5]

The conciliar language on the received musical tradition led to contrary perceptions, and proponents of both traditional music and progressive music have found themselves citing the same document against each other since its publication. Despite strong passages favoring the prominence of Gregorian chant, for instance, other expressions introduce the possibility of supplanting the traditional plainsong with other forms for cultural reasons (*Sacrosanctum Concilium*, 119). The effect of these accommodations has had pastoral consequences that include a preponderance of confusion about what is permitted and what is not, but also, and more critically to the continuity of Catholic culture, was an ensuing apathy toward the traditional forms. This neglect for the traditional music was compounded by the practical experience immediately following the reform, which found a popular, mass-produced, and ready-made repertoire too convenient to disdain.

The Pope too, at the time of the promulgation of the new Mass, was ambiguous if not fatalistic on the point of preserving the use of Gregorian chant in the liturgy. In a general audience during the week in which the new Missal came into force, Paul VI reflected on the changes being introduced and their consequences:

> It is here that the greatest novelty will be recognized, the novelty of the language. No longer will Latin, but the common language be the principal language of the Mass. The introduction of the vernacular will surely amount to a great sacrifice for those who know the beauty, the power, and the expressive holiness of Latin ... We will lose a great part of that stupendous and incomparable artistic and spiritual accomplishment, the Gregorian chant. We have reason indeed for regret, almost to lose heart.[6]

In exchange for these losses Paul VI points to easy intelligibility and plainness of speech that trumps the style of the liturgy. Accessibility is clearly made the chief motivation for decisions relative to the liturgy.

The new conditions outlined by Paul VI identified the principal challenge for the old repertoire—the language barrier. As the new liturgy was accepted and the faithful became accustomed to encountering the liturgy through the immediacy of the spoken word rather than the well-thumbed pages of a hand missal, the foundational vision proposed by Pius X at the dawn of the new century, which placed the Latin liturgical chant on the lips of devoted congregations, dissipated.[7] The precipitous pace at which these developments took place (some six years lay between the Constitution on the Sacred Liturgy and the promulgation of the new *Missale Romanum*) resulted in a kind of musical vacuum. The old repertoire had not been integrated into the new ritual format, and a comprehensive program of adaptation of these treasures of the classical liturgy had yet to be undertaken. Nevertheless, their absence was met with two principal substitutes:

hymns, largely drawn from Protestant sources, and songs in folk- and pop-inspired style. A discussion of the approaches to substitutions will be taken up at the end of the chapter.

Principal documents in the reform of the liturgy and its music

The chief document, and cause for the process of reform, was the Constitution on the Sacred Liturgy (known also by its Latin title *Sacrosanctum Concilium*), promulgated on December 4, 1963 by Pope Paul VI. The document treating the Sacred Liturgy was the first item of consideration for the Second Vatican Ecumenical Council, which was celebrated between 1962 and 1965. The Constitution is principally concerned with fostering liturgical piety among the faithful, toward which pastoral end it makes several specific pronouncements. The most notable changes called for in the document include the possibility of using the vernacular extensively in Mass, the reinstitution of the Universal Prayer of the Faithful, an expansion of the biblical readings used at Mass, the reception of Holy Communion under both kinds, and the possibility of concelebration by several priests. The task of implementing the commands of the Council was entrusted by Pope Paul VI to the *Consilium for the Implementation of the Constitution on the Sacred Liturgy.*

Several documents followed the Constitution, but the most important document on music that followed the Council was the 1967 Instruction from the Sacred Congregation of Rites entitled *Musicam sacram*. This document provided a more specific interpretation of the Council's wishes as they applied to liturgical music. The purpose was to give those responsible for the practice of liturgical music a reasonable basis upon which to navigate the many options of the new liturgy. Speaking of principles, *Musicam sacram* was intended to quell voices in the extreme, particularly those on the conservative side of the liturgical reform.[8] Despite its profile as a clarifying text, there are several paragraphs that seem to make some matters cloudier. For instance, the document includes the following conclusion: "No kind of sacred music is prohibited from liturgical actions by the Church as long as it corresponds to the spirit of the liturgical celebration itself and the nature of its individual parts, and does not hinder the active participation of the people."[9]

There are at least two revolutionary ideas in this one excerpt. The first is providing a non-musical measure for the propriety of a given musical selection for the liturgy. Just six decades earlier, Pius X had set Gregorian chant as the exemplar and model for liturgical music.[10] The new Instruction appealed to a vague "spirit of the liturgical celebration." In the sense that music is the most proximate model for other music, this criterion is less clear than the previous paradigm. Further, we see for the first time in this passage a blanket reference to the people's active participation as the standard against which liturgical music would be evaluated in the reformed liturgy. On the surface these principles are not really new, but the fact that they were advanced without due regard for extant models from the tradition presented new challenges for Catholic liturgical music.

Like the Constitution on the Sacred Liturgy, the Instruction *Musicam sacram* emphasizes the objective value of the Latin liturgical tradition and its music. The Council had endorsed the opinion of previous popes in bestowing upon Gregorian chant the principal place among the liturgical repertories of music. The Instruction, however, places a qualification on that privileged position, saying:

In sung liturgical services celebrated in Latin:

(a) Gregorian chant, as proper to the Roman liturgy, should be given pride of place, other things being equal. Its melodies, contained in the "typical" editions, should be used, to the extent that this is possible.

(b) It is also desirable that an edition be prepared containing simpler melodies, for use in smaller churches.

(c) Other musical settings, written for one or more voices, be they taken from the traditional heritage or from new works, should be held in honor, encouraged and used as the occasion demands (n. 50).

While this article makes a clear reference to the principality of Gregorian chant derived from the Constitution on the Sacred Liturgy, and is followed by a paragraph admitting of the use of Latin chants in the vernacular liturgy, it is difficult to see how the opening qualifier—"services celebrated in Latin"—is anything less than a circumscription of the principle found in the Constitution. The Constitution itself makes no such qualification, but the effect of this expression in *Musicam sacram* has been felt in direct proportion to the extreme infrequency of "services celebrated in Latin" in modern Catholic practice.

In an effort to fortify the place of Gregorian chant, Paul VI gave the Church a collection of simpler chants under the title *Jubilate Deo* in 1974 with the intention of establishing a small but solid international repertory of Latin chants for the Catholic world. The motivation here was to preserve Latin singing particularly at international gatherings, such as those associated with the Holy Year. In addition to a simple composite setting of the Mass ordinary, the booklet contains just over a dozen chants to be used ad libitum.

The introduction to the work, entitled "The Bond of Unity," makes clear that this publication is to be viewed as an encouragement for the use of Gregorian chant and Latin. Quoting the Council's Constitution on the Liturgy, it emphasizes: "Steps should be taken so that the faithful may also be able to say or to sing together in Latin those parts of the ordinary of the Mass which pertain to them."[11] By and large, this encouragement held little sway in the period following the initial reforms. The excitement and enticement of new "worship styles" virtually eclipsed the former and venerable repertory of chant and polyphony.

These circumstances were not countered by impressions emanating from the Vatican in subsequent years. A little noticed 1987 document issued by the Congregation for Divine Worship called "Concerts in Churches," made several oblique statements, which while they do not bear directly on the liturgy, do reveal an attitude that seems to skirt the gist of the Constitution. Under the title "The

Importance of Sacred Music," the document draws the following conclusion about the patrimony, which had been developing right up to the eve of liturgical reform:

> Any performance of sacred music which takes place during a celebration, should be fully in harmony with that celebration. This often means that musical compositions which date from a period when the active participation of the faithful was not emphasized as the source of the authentic Christian spirit are no longer to be considered suitable for inclusion within liturgical celebrations.
>
> Analogous changes of perception and awareness have occurred in other areas involving the artistic aspect of divine worship: for example, the sanctuary has been restructured, with the president's chair, the ambo and the altar *versus populum*. Such changes have not been made in a spirit of disregard for the past, but have been deemed necessary in the pursuit of an end of greater importance, namely the active participation of the faithful. The limitation which such changes impose on certain musical works can be overcome by arranging for their performance outside the context of liturgical celebration in a concert of sacred music.[12]

The admissions contained in this excerpt are surprising given the assurances of reverence that the Constitution on the Sacred Liturgy advanced during the Council on behalf of sacred music *in the liturgy*, which it called "a treasure of inestimable value, greater even than that of any other art," and that it should be "preserved and fostered with great care" (nn. 112, 114). The relegation of the liturgical patrimony of music to concerts outside of the liturgy on the basis of its obsolescence is a dramatic departure from the sense of continuity that the Constitution proposed for sacred music. The most startling element is the position that "active participation" might result in the disinheritance of the patrimony of sacred music. Even Gregorian chant, which had been specifically given a place of privilege (n. 116),[13] is mentioned among the musical orphans in the document: "The *Scholae cantorum* have not had frequent occasion to execute their traditional repertory of sacred polyphonic music within the context of a liturgical celebration ... the same has happened with Gregorian chant, which has come to form part of concert programs both inside and outside the church."[14] It is difficult to conclude from this document what the perspective of the Holy See really was during this period. The sense that the exile of the traditional repertory was a cause for regret is not apparent in the tone of the document. Rather, it suggests a concession that churches become concert venues, converting the sacred repertory into museum pieces out of the need for cultural preservation.

The last decade has seen a resurgence of interest and official concern about the state of the liturgy, and in particular its musical tradition. In 2003, marking the one hundreth anniversary of the motu proprio of Pius X on sacred music, Pope John Paul II issued a *chirograph* which summarized the current view of sacred music. Although the document celebrates the principles laid down by Pius X, particularly that music destined for liturgical use should be holy, of good form, and universal, the document stresses the same themes brought out by *Musicam sacram* in 1967.

It even goes so far as to repeat that Gregorian chant should enjoy preferment in the liturgy, but also repeats the qualification "in Masses celebrated in Latin."[15] The document also strongly endorses the formation and activity of the *schola cantorum* (see n. 8). Whereas *Musicam sacram* fell short of providing a sound and solid model for the creation of new liturgical music (other than that it should primarily serve the goal of active participation), John Paul II takes the occasion of this *chirograph* to restore Gregorian chant as the supreme model for liturgical composition (n. 12). Far from dislocating the traditional repertory, the document is a considerably strong witness for the practice of the musical patrimony in the liturgy.

Pope Benedict XVI had vigorously championed the musical tradition of the Church before his election to the papacy, and has taken several specific steps to return it to a place of esteem in the liturgy. His February 22, 2007 Apostolic Exhortation *Sacramentum Caritatis* takes care to address certain aspects of the liturgical celebration that touch on sacred music. For one thing, he offers a vision of "active participation" (nn. 52–63) that comprehends not only physical activity, but also and primarily an inward disposition of willful engagement in the liturgical celebration (see n. 52). This bears directly on sacred music of the past in that much of it does not contemplate the physical participation of the congregation. The document is also noteworthy in that it is the most recent exhortation of the faithful to learn to pray and sing liturgically in the Latin tongue.

Benedict XVI took several occasions to praise the excellent practice of sacred music in allocutions and messages throughout his papacy.[16] No decision has borne a greater impact for sacred music than the rehabilitation of the pre-Conciliar liturgy, the so-called "1962 Missal," with the motu proprio *Summorum Pontificum*, promulgated on July 7, 2007. This bold step reintroduces the liturgical habitat in which the musical tradition of the Catholic liturgy developed and thrived, and presents a context in which to reconsider the role of music in the new Order of Mass.[17]

The books of the reformed liturgy of the Mass[18]

One of the results of the reform of the liturgy is an entirely new set of books for the performance of the Liturgy. The principal collection of books, of course, pertains to the celebration of the rituals themselves. They are initially promulgated according to their "typical editions," which means the original Latin version published by the Holy See. These are then translated into the various languages in cooperation with the regional conferences of bishops and with the approval of the Holy See. The chief book published after the reform for the Mass liturgy is the *Missale Romanum* (the Roman missal). This book, called the Sacramentary in English until recently, contains the prayers that belong to the celebrant at Mass.[19] Additionally, the evangeliary and the lectionary complete the principal books of the Mass. The former contains only the Gospel readings for the Mass, while the latter contains all the readings, as well as the texts of the chants between them.

It should been clearly noted that the striking feature of the new lectionary (and evangeliary) is the introduction of a three-year cycle of readings. The purpose in this initiative was to provide a fuller representation of biblical readings in the Mass, according to the wishes of the Constitution on the Sacred Liturgy (n. 51).

In addition to these ritual books there are several other items that fill out the ceremonies that take place in the sanctuary. The Roman ritual, first published in 1976 and subsequently reissued, is a pair of volumes that includes special prayers associated with blessings and other special rituals. To this we add the *Ceremonial of Bishops*, which gives a detailed description of the liturgy when celebrated by a bishop (published in 1984).

The music books of the liturgy appeared over a long period of time on account of the detailed level of scholarship and musicological work necessary to bring them to completion in light of the reform. The earliest musical publications for the new Mass were the two graduals, the *Graduale Romanum* (1972)[20] and the *Graduale Simplex* (1967).[21]

The *Graduale Romanum* had long been the book containing the proper chants of the Mass (the introit, the gradual or first Alleluia in Eastertide, the tract or the Alleluia before the gospel, the offertory, and the communion) to be performed by the choir, the *schola cantorum*. In the modern versions, the Roman Gradual has been appended with the *Kyriale*, which is the collection of chants for the ordinary of the Mass. In essence, the new *Graduale* includes all the chants necessary for the choir to sing the plainchant of the Mass liturgy. It includes some twenty Gregorian chants that had fallen out of use over the centuries.[22] Further, several chants that had been created for newer feasts were excluded from the collection because of their "neo-Gregorian" origin. This was not uniformly done, and several of these remain for recently created feasts such as the Sacred Heart and Christ the King.[23] The most significant development in the new *Graduale Romanum* was the redistribution of the chants to accommodate the new lectionary. The lectionary, as we have seen, consists of three yearly cycles (A, B, and C). Consequently, the chants of the Mass proper had to be adjusted to match this variability in theme and content in the readings. The result is that the *Graduale Romanum* has frequent cross-referencing throughout its pages, directing the choir to various locations in the book to locate the chant appropriate to the lectionary readings.

In contrast to this fastidious attachment of the proper chants to a three-year cycle, the concept of the *Graduale Simplex* comprises a rotation of seasonal texts that may or may not be relevant to the readings. So, for the Advent Season, there are two sets of propers to be used during the whole season. On any given day in Advent, then, the cantor or *schola cantorum* could chant one of two introits from this collection as opposed to the specific chant appointed for the day by the *Graduale Romanum*. For most of the seasons there are a few sets that can be employed *ad libitum*. For the Sundays of Lent and for several other feasts and solemnities, the collection provides proper sets. In these cases, the *Graduale Simplex* could be said to offer an alternate proper to those found in the *Graduale Romanum*. The *Graduale Simplex*, or Simple Gradual, was compiled in order to respond to the recommendation in Vatican II's Constitution on the Sacred Liturgy that called for the preparation of an edition "containing simpler melodies, for use in small churches" (n. 117). Like the *Graduale Romanum*, this simpler gradual is also appended with a collection of chants called the *Kyriale Simplex*.[24] The melodies in the *Simplex* are indeed much easier than those found in the *Graduale Romanum* and are modeled on the more syllabic chant genres used in singing the Divine Office.

The collection is also notable for its approach to the chants between the readings. Again, there are several options. The responsorial psalm is provided in each of the sets of propers, excluding Eastertide, which has two "alleluiatic" psalms, or a simple antiphonal alleluia with verses. The responsorial psalm is somewhat different in format to those appearing in the lectionary. In the lectionary, a whole line of a psalm is provided as the "respond." In the Simple Gradual, the respond is generally the last few words of a psalm line. This tag is repeated as the respond after each verse. The alleluiatic psalm can be substituted for the simple Alleluia wherever given in the collection. It is similar in form to the responsorial psalm here described. Each verse of a psalm is answered with a very short Alleluia.

Also unique to the Simple Gradual are the options for the chant before the Gospel during Lent. The lectionary provides for an acclamation of praise to Christ, followed by a verse and a repetition of the praise refrain. The *Graduale Romanum* places the ancient tract at this point, which is a rather ornate psalmodic chant of varying lengths. In addition to a very simple psalm-tone tract, the Simple Gradual provides the option of performing an antiphon with at least one verse from the preceding psalm. The acclamation antiphons themselves are pre-existing items borrowed from the *Antiphonale* repertory of the Divine Office.[25]

While these two Graduals approach the issue of the Mass proper with divergent rationales, neither has found widespread use in the Church. The infrequency of the Latin celebration of the liturgy coupled with the perceived impediment of language has rendered these books nearly obsolete. Obviously, these circumstances present special challenges for the idea of the "sung proper" of the Mass, challenges which have met with solutions of various kinds. A discussion of the trends and issues associated with the departure from the prescribed chant-texts follows a survey of the musical appointments for the sung liturgy in the General Instruction of the Roman missal.

The challenge of chant adaptation to the vernacular

The official documents of the Church esteem Gregorian chant as the native music of the Roman liturgy. But with the near universal predominance of vernacular liturgies, the opportunity for its use has virtually disappeared. The circumstances have suggested to many, especially given the singular honor accorded to Gregorian chant by the Council, that a clear need exists for English versions of the chant for use in the vernacular liturgy. The efforts of those who undertook this challenge reflect some of the dilemmas encountered by those members of Protestant sects who undertook the sweeping revision of their liturgical norms in the sixteenth century.

As much now as then, there are two points of resistance in the process of converting the Latin plainsong into functional English plainsong. The epicenter of this conflict is the necessity to prefer one element over the other, either the text or the music. On the one hand, the transcriber could choose to compromise the original melody, placing intelligibility and idiomatic clarity above regard for the native tune. The second approach insists on retaining the melodic content of the tune, adapting the translation to the prosody of the musical line.

Historically, liturgical reform movements have attempted both approaches with varying degrees of success. Luther preferred the text over the music in the examples of liturgical recitative that he proposed for the German Mass, but some of his hymns are notably deferential to their Gregorian melodic origins. In any event, he deprecates harshly the twisting of the German language to conform to Gregorian melodies.[26] Most other sixteenth-century reformers shared Luther's emphasis on text over musical sources, such as the Englishman, John Merbecke. Still, there have been cases of reformers opting to retain the integrity of the original melodies, crafting the translation of the text to a pre-existing melodic form.

This was the case with the nineteenth-century Oxford Movement within the Anglican Church. The critical questions that inspired the Oxford Movement were theological in nature, and the answers they arrived at were all the time more in line with positions held by the Catholic Church. Throughout the ninteenth century this more Catholic disposition within some quarters of Anglicanism led to an increased interest not only in the Catholic theological heritage, but the Catholic liturgy as well. Reflecting the restorationist initiatives in already begun in France, the Anglican Church saw a remarkable catholicization of its rites and ceremonies in many quarters, and music was an important part of this trend. To maintain the English aesthetic, some musicians worked on an Anglicization of the Gregorian repertoire. For instance, Burgess and Palmer transcribed the whole cycle of the Mass proper chants into English, preserving entire the melodies of the Gregorian originals. In this work of transcription, the words are made to fit to the tunes which remain unaltered.

The post-conciliar years have seen similar efforts on the part of Catholic musicians, but with more of an emphasis on simplification of the melodic material. This is done not only in a spirit of accessibility, but also to maintain the prosody of the English translation which is seen to lose its intelligibility in the melismatic passages of the original Gregorian chants. While these adaptations depart more radically from the Gregorian framework of complexity, they do rely more on the skill and "ear" of the adapter for their musical impact. Several composers have undertaken to create a functional set of propers for the English Order of the Mass in recent years, including Fr. Samuel Webber, OSB, Bruce E. Ford (whose work much resembles that of Burgess & Palmer), Fr. Columba Kelly, OSB, Paul Ford (who adapted the *Graduale Simplex* into English), Adam Bartlett (whose effort has been made widely available through a Creative Commons license), and others. Among the earliest attempts is that of the Rev. Paul Arbogast in 1964. This work preserves a chant-like format for the Mass antiphons, but greatly simplifies the forms. In this work, Fr. Arbogast crafts his adaptations according to the principal of *centonization*, basing his adaptation on modally associated melodic patterns. The integrity of the text is paramount for Arbogast who assures his readers in the introduction that:

> The importance of expressing the text, and of making the melodies a vehicle for this expression, cannot be overemphasized. The accents of the text are the soul of the melodies; they should be given careful attention as the culmination points of the dynamic line, even when the accented syllable itself receives but a single note of melody while the following syllable has many more notes.[27]

This consideration of accent, syllabification, and melisma-distribution is of considerable significance in the discussion of chant adaptation to English. It returns us to the same consideration of the principal criteria for adaptation and whether the prosodic features of the words or the integrity of the original melodies should be given preference in the process of transcription.

Criticism has been lodged against both preferences and not without good arguments for either. For those who favor maintaining textual clarity and the inherent verbal accent of the words in the adaptation, the complaint is that when translations are fit to the melodies rather than the contrary, the words are dominated by music that is indifferent to their meaning. This indifference of the tunes toward the text frequently means that long melismatic passages are sung on insignificant words or unaccented syllables. On the other hand, those who defend the integrity of the melodies counter that melodies are as important an artifact of the Christian patrimony as the texts themselves, and that the preserving their identity maintains one mark of universality so ardently praised by the Church (in particular by Pius X).

In assessing these positions, it is important to consider the relationship that exists between the texts and the tunes in the Gregorian originals. The same criticism of indifference of tune to text could be raised against the Latin chants themselves. It is not infrequent that a Gregorian chant will emphasize an unaccented syllable (typically the last, which is rarely accented in Latin) with many notes, or even an insignificant word like "et," particularly in the more elaborate chant genres.[28] Additionally, many Gregorian melodies served as the basis for *contrafactum*. In these cases, the texts were second considerations, being conformed to pre-existing melodies. In effect then, this criticism against tune dominance is applicable to a significant part of the Gregorian repertoire in its native language.

Nevertheless, Bruce E. Ford, who preserves the original tunes diligently, exercises tremendous good sense in his adaptations. While he strictly guards the melodic integrity, his adaptations also demonstrate solicitude for the singer, especially with respect to the choice of vowels for melismas. The much earlier, but similar *Plainchant Gradual* of Burgess and Palmer preserves not only the tunes, but often the same indifference toward the tonic accent of the words that the Gregorian versions do. Frequently we find in the *Plainchant Gradual* that unstressed syllables receive more notes than their accented counterparts. These adaptations reflect the buoyancy found in the authentic Gregorian versions, which also musically accent syllables that the verbal stress pattern does not. Insofar as the Gregorian redistribution of accent frees the words from their earthbound stress-pattern, the *Plainchant Gradual* enjoys an aesthetic advantage over the more recent attempts at Gregorian adaptation into English.

Prescriptions for music in the General Instruction of the Roman Missal

In the four decades since the promulgation of the new missal of Paul VI (1970), the Church has seen seven editions of the document which most proximately governs the celebration of the Mass, the *Institutio Generalis Missalis Romani,* or, the General Instruction of the Roman Missal (called frequently, the GIRM).[29] Over the years, the Instruction's treatment of music had been more or less consistent. There were minor adjustments to phraseology and word choice, and in some cases to ritual prescriptions for music. For instance, between the 2000 edition and that of 2002, the singing of the sequence was moved from after the Alleluia (the second Alleluia in Eastertide) to before it so as to conform to the order presented in the Lectionary of the Mass.[30] Emphases are also shifted throughout the editions. In the most recent edition of 2002, there are clear preferences for sung liturgical elements over recitation. Further, the latest edition also pre-positions singing as the first action in association with certain parts, hence in n. 68, "The Creed is to be sung or said ..." The preference for a thoroughly sung liturgy is apparent throughout the 2002 edition.

The Instruction concerns itself with setting general norms, but also provides detailed directives on the execution of particular musical elements in the Mass liturgy, and general guidance for the sourcing of particular musical material for these parts. The principal areas of interest for musical praxis are the paragraphs that touch on the proper and ordinary chants of the Mass. The proper consists of the same traditional elements as before the Conciliar reform: the introit (called "entrance" in the English translation of the Instruction), the chants between the readings, the gradual and the Alleluia or tract, the offertory, and the communion. There are other proper texts that are chanted, such as the collect, but that is the role of the priest-celebrant rather than the cantor or choir, to whom the execution of the main musical elements is entrusted. The ordinary chants are likewise those that existed before the reform: the Kyrie, the Gloria, the Credo, the Sanctus, and the Agnus Dei.

The provisions for the proper chants present the most complications for musical praxis in the documents. The texts of the proper are usually short verses drawn from the Psalter, many of which date to the first millennium. Traditionally, these were the heart of the Gregorian repertoire. In the Instruction, the mode of execution for the proper chants is clear enough, but the actual music, its form, and even its textual content are a matter given wide latitude and left to the discretion of the local practitioners. In the case of the introit, the Instruction indicates that the song may be sung by a schola, a cantor, the congregation, or an alternation between these, and that the music may be drawn from the Roman Gradual (the

Gregorian original), the Simple Gradual, a song from another approved collection, or another song. The directives are similar for the communion. For the offertory, there are no recommendations for the source of this chant, except that it is always permitted to be sung at Mass (see: nn. 48, 74, 87).

The case of the chants between the readings is even more nuanced. After the first reading, the responsorial psalm is appointed. The Instruction indicates that it should be taken from the lectionary. However, the document approves substitution, in particular the use of the Gregorian proper antiphon found in the Roman Gradual, or a simpler chant drawn from the Simple Gradual, or even an approved metrical setting of the psalm. As in the other cases of the proper, the substitutions tolerate a broad range of musical genres and forms. It is also important to note that the psalm appointed in the Lectionary is often different from that appointed in the *Graduale*.[31] Given the array of options, the Instruction provides the potential for a widely divergent experience of this element of the Mass (n. 61).

The *Alleluia*, which is sung before the Gospel, is more standardized than the psalm. It is to be drawn from either the lectionary or the Gradual (presumably either version). In either case, the form is essentially the same, despite the aesthetic differences among the options. It consists of the antiphon "Alleluia" followed by a verse and a repeat of the antiphon (nn. 62–3).

Unlike most of the proper elements, the ordinary chants are fixed so far as their texts are concerned. The Instruction stipulates performance norms for each of these five elements, the details of which have implications for the use of pre-Conciliar settings of the some of the texts.

The Instruction characterizes the *Kyrie* as penitential, and therefore it should ordinarily be sung by all together, or the people alternating with the choir or cantor. Although a preference is expressed for the six-fold Kyrie, more repetitions are permissible if the musical form calls for it. It is unclear whether the preference for sung participation of the whole assembly in this chant precludes the use of an exclusively choral setting of the text, but many pre-Conciliar settings could survive this adaptation (n. 52).

The *Gloria*, which is reserved to Sundays outside of Advent and Lent and other principal feasts of the year, is characterized as a hymn (which intensifies its identity as uniquely musical) glorifying and entreating "God the Father and the Lamb." Traditionally, the hymn was intoned by the priest-celebrant exclusively, but the modern practice permits a cantor or the whole choir to introduce the piece. It may be sung by all, by the people in alternation with the choir, or by the choir alone. This last option concedes the use of pre-Conciliar settings of the text (n. 53).

Likewise, the Instruction says "sung" before "said" as the principal mode of execution for the Creed. Also like the Gloria, this text is reserved for Holy Days of Obligation, including Sundays and other major feasts. Unlike the Gloria, however, this text is meant for the whole assembly to render, either in complete tandem, or by alternation between the congregation and the choir. This stipulation would exclude the use of most pre-Conciliar settings (n. 68).

The *Sanctus* (which is always joined to the Benedictus in the reformed liturgy) enjoys the briefest treatment out of the members of the ordinary by the Instruction.

Similarly, it is "sung or said," presuming that the first option is prioritized. The requirement that it be sung or recited by all impedes the use of pre-Conciliar settings in the New Order (n. 79b).

Finally, the *Agnus Dei* is described as accompanying the fraction rite before Holy Communion. The Instruction calls for a sung acclamation by the choir or cantor with the people responding. Once again, the structure of pre-Conciliar settings of this text do not overtly contemplate involvement by the congregation (n. 83).

By and large, the ordinary seems to have been reconceived to such an extent as to preclude the use of polyphonic settings in the reformed liturgy, with the exception of the Gloria. The proper, which even before the Council, rarely employed polyphonic settings, retains access to the original Gregorian settings, albeit through a secondary option. Nothing about the provisions for the ordinary would seem to exclude the Gregorian melodies except that the congregation be fluent enough to render their part in alternation with the choir. The alternation schema poses some difficulty in the case of the Gregorian Sanctus, for no other reason than the fact that the plainsong construction of this chant is not conceived along antiphonal lines.

The issue of the use of pre-Conciliar repertory is dwarfed in significance by the latitude prescribed for the proper of the Mass in the General Instruction. In addition to the manifold possibilities presented, there are unclear indications in places. For example, the first option for the introit indicates that the setting could the "antiphon from the Roman missal or the psalm from the Roman Gradual." While the second source is musical, the first, the Roman missal, lacks musical material for this part of the Mass. Insofar as the antiphons in the missal correspond to those in the Gradual, the missal ends with the antiphon, omitting the psalm with which the introit continues in the Gradual. From a musical perspective then, the first source listed in the first option for the introit is a non-starter. The option to employ the *Graduale Simplex* follows the option for the missal or Roman Gradual.

The final options are yet further removed from the idea of a specifically assigned text for the proper. The Instruction makes a provision for *alius cantus*; that is "another chant" may be substituted in the case of the introit, the offertory and the communion. The provision states that the selection should be from an approved source, but in the absence of approved hymnals in many national bishops' conferences (such as in the United States), the criteria remain largely undefined.

Substitution is in fact the most widely used option in the Church today, and the use of a hymn or other song in the vernacular typically takes the place of the proper antiphon assigned by the Gradual. Prior to the Council, the practice of singing vernacular hymns and popular religious songs at low Mass during these moments in the liturgy was condoned. At the sung, or so called, "Solemn" or "High" Mass the singing was to be done in Latin alone by precept.[32] The precedent of choosing hymns and songs for the Mass provided the basis for the most popular treatment of the liturgical propers in the period since the liturgical reform.

Horror Vacui: hymnody, other songs, and choice in the reformed Mass

Although the convenience of their introduction is easily understood, especially in light of the arrival of the vernacular Mass and the options for substitution permitted by the General Instruction, the use of hymns in the liturgy of the Mass has a complicated history. Strictly speaking, the hymn-form is a native and constituent element in the Divine Office.[33] In the classical form of Lauds and Vespers, for example, the hymn occupies a distinguished location between the Old Testament psalmody and the New Testament canticle.[34] Positioned thus, the hymn is reflective in nature and usually provides a theological or spiritual meditation on the subject of the day's liturgy. The great collection of hymns that adorned the Catholic liturgy of the Office provided some basis for the new music that would serve the reformed liturgies during the period of the Protestant Reformation. Numerous hymns from the medieval and Patristic periods were recast in the language of the people by the Protestant reformers, who like the architects of the twentieth-century Catholic revision were motivated to satisfy the needs of a vernacular liturgical format.

Luther's approach to the introduction of hymns into his *German Mass* during the sixteenth century is a useful historical comparison to the paths taken in Catholic liturgical music after the Second Vatican Council.[35] The need to provide for singing in the wake of his separation from the Catholic Church and its ancient Latin liturgy offered challenges similar to those faced during the 1960s by the modern Catholic musicians. Luther recognized that time and the talent pool needed to create a stylistically cogent and balanced liturgical form were not immediately available after his movement gathered its first adherents.[36] Under these circumstances, there were three principal sources for the new singing that Luther would sanction and advance. The first source was the Latin plainsong that would be adapted for vernacular use. Along similar lines, Luther admitted the use of non-liturgical melodies of the late Middle Ages, fitted, of course, with texts reflecting the new theology.[37] The third and, perhaps, most common path was the composition of entirely new texts and new tunes.

In the wake of the reforms of the 1960s, modern Catholic musicians and liturgical experts took recourse to options very similar to those presented to Martin Luther four centuries earlier. There were certain considerations to be weighed, however. Would the sizeable repertory of vernacular Protestant hymns and the theological perspectives they contain be admitted to Catholic worship? Would the new musical sources also include folk music, and introduce to the Catholic liturgy for the first time a repertory that was not art-music? Would secular music coined in the age of "mass media" supply an acceptable stylistic option? In time, the answer to all of these questions has proven to be "yes" in practice if not by precept, each affirmative having its own set of consequences.

The wholesale borrowing of Protestant hymns was perhaps the first widespread step for vernacular music in the reformed liturgy, especially in America. It was, after all, an easily accessed base of material to supply the new liturgy with a reasonable repertory in short order. The appearance of "Praise to the Lord," among other examples, was a commonplace after the introduction of the new Mass.[38] While the introduction of these items has not necessarily brought with it any of the explicitly heretical tenets of the sects of their origins, they do introduce a new set of theological emphases. Simultaneously, these hymns do not possess all of the theological dispositions necessary to support a thoroughly Catholic doctrinal orientation. On the surface, these pieces are benign in their dogmatic content. The formational effects of these new musical elements, however, deserve some deeper reflection, perhaps more on the basis of what they omit rather than what they contain.

Another serious step that was taken after the inauguration of the reformed liturgy was the adaptation of folk songs for liturgical use. This included a wide range of source material, from such regionally divergent examples as the Scottish "O Waly, Waly" and the Appalachian "Shaker Tune," refitted with religious texts. This approach raises some questions about previous standards, particularly those pronounced by the patron of twentieth century liturgical reform, Pope Pius X. Among the conditions Pius X laid down for sacred liturgical music in his famous 1903 motu proprio, one was that all liturgical music must be "true art" (*Tra le sollecitudine*, 2). Pius X used this term to explain his requirement that liturgical music possess "goodness of form," which is to say the qualities of artistic endeavor and craft that distinguishes some music as art music. Already in 1955 in *Musicae sacrae disciplina*, Pius XII admitted the salutatory use of "popular religious hymns," but this is distinct from the sourcing of folk elements that has been seen since the Council (n. 37). Pius XII qualified his approbation of these musical forms by insisting that they be cultivated "carefully" and that "despite the fact that they are short and easy, they should manifest a religious dignity and seriousness" (n. 63). Moreover, Pius XII implemented Pius X's axiom that "the more closely a composition for church approaches in its movement, inspiration, and savor the Gregorian form, the more sacred and liturgical it seems to be" by observing that there are popular religious hymns that "derive their origin from the liturgical chant itself" (n. 62). The only conclusion that can be drawn is that even on the eve of the Council, non-chant musical sources were still expected to be on the level of art-music, not only by virtue of their origin, but also because of their artistic value.

A further distinction needs to be drawn between the new folk-sourced repertory and the sources to which the Protestant reformers turned in the sixteenth century. On the one hand, there were strains of Protestantism, such as that founded by Calvin, that earnestly labored to banish any hint of art from the church services. In fact, the polyphonic arrangements of the Genevan Psalms (first published in 1543) were intended only for home use by the information provided by Calvinist composer Claude Goudimel in his preface of 1565. The aim of Calvinist liturgy was purposely to present music as untutored and literally artless.[39]

The Lutheran approach was quite the opposite. Largely, the array of pre-Reformation sources for the chorales already had artful histories, particularly in the form of the polyphonic *Leisen* refrains and German-language courtly songs. Many of these works also had explicitly religious sources, such as *Gelobet seist du, Jesu Christ, Christ ist erstanden, Nun bitten wir den heiligen Geist,* and *Gott sei gelobet und gebenedeiet*, all of which are derived from liturgical sequences.[40] Luther was an ardent music lover and a composer of no little accomplishment. He was careful to avoid the iconoclastic excesses of other reformers of the period, and was insistent that the music of the church not slouch toward mediocrity, making the point that music was an inborn inclination for most people, but that "what is natural should still be developed into what is artful."[41]

The resort to new musical forms in post-Conciliar liturgical has tended to model the Calvinist approach over the Lutheran, not only in its sourcing, but also in its presentation, which typically maintained an unschooled approach to the musical elements of the music (accompaniment, vocal inflection, etc.). Moreover, the entry of this body of untutored music into the liturgy marked a departure from the pre-Conciliar model, enunciated by Pius X and developed by subsequent popes. In the very least, the category "art" has been expanded, with no sure indication of what the new borders of that region are.

The condition of genre ambiguity that the introduction of folk music sources leads to further questions, in particular the degree to which popular secular forms of music that have commercial origins can be employed in the liturgical action. Very little in the way of official reaction has been forthcoming from the Church on the legitimacy of this expansion of musical sources since the first Rock Masses in the 1960s. The most prominent and credible criticism voiced about the use of pop and rock music in the liturgy comes from Joseph Cardinal Ratzinger. In *A New Song for the Lord*, Ratzinger makes several bold and elucidating arguments that contextualize a problem for the introduction of this genre into liturgical use. Among the approaches that he takes to the subject, the most interesting is the criticism of rock and pop on the basis of its artificiality and its remote connection to human life and its experiences. He draws a distinction here between mass-produced industrialized media which is created in a record label board room and authentic folk music which has its roots in the work, leisure, life, and death of ordinary people.

Mass society is something completely different from that community bound together for life which produced folk music in the old and original sense. The masses as such do not know experiences firsthand; they only know reproduced and standardized experiences. Mass culture is thus geared to quantity, production, and success. It is a culture of the measurable and marketable.[42]

In this sense, Ratzinger challenges whether such material constitutes a culture at all since it is intrinsically divorced from authentically human motivations, other than the accumulation of wealth. Further he writes: "Music of this type must be excluded from the Church, not for aesthetic reasons, not out of reactionary stubbornness, not because of historical rigidity, but because of its very nature."[43]

By establishing a *genesis-test* for contending genres in the field of liturgical music, Ratzinger deftly removes one of the bases on which the cultural battles for the soul of modern liturgical music had been waged. The kernel of his analysis addresses the assertion that the contemporary cultural relevance of a body of music ranks above that body of music's inherent qualities as a criterion for inclusion in liturgical use. The argument goes that the liturgy and its music must be "of its time" and that the use of traditional or even ancient forms is somehow dishonest because "it is not our music." Ratzinger turns this argument on its head by demonstrating that rock and pop genres are really *no one's* music because they are produced by and for commercial interests.[44] There are other popular genres, like jazz, which although they too pose serious problems for liturgical incorporation, still distinguish themselves as authentically folk music because of their historical origins. The influence of jazz, particularly the blues, on rock and pop cannot be minimized, however, the mass means by which rock and pop were communicated to the world are indicative of centrality of commerce to its nature and existence. Whereas jazz and the blues were uniquely recognized as the aggregate expression of real communities and individuals,[45] rock and pop were predominantly disseminated through mass broadcast media, in particular the radio.

Further considerations can be drawn from Ratzinger's premises. The experience of live performed folk music is intrinsically communal, and in the truest sense, populist. In its pure form, which is always tied to a local community, or even an ethnic group, folk music preserves only the thinnest line between the performer and the audience. In fact, it seems that in folk performance contexts, the performer is perceived as "one of the audience." In this way, folk music derives its authenticity from proximity: between the performer and the listener, between the individual and the aggregate, between real people and places.

Against the communitarian experience of folk music we can characterize the experience of rock and pop as totalitarian, in the sense that there is only monologue. This is not only true of the radio experience of rock and pop, which is by the necessity of the technology a one-way form of communication, but also in its instances of live performance, where the volume of the (usually solo) performer is maximized to the extent that its proportion is only relatable to "the masses." The superhuman impression this creates for the performer simultaneously alienates him from the individual audience member (who can only be seen as puny in this context) and mythologizes him to the masses. While this feeds the cult of celebrity, the sense of musical aggregation such as folk or choral music achieves is annihilated.

The distinction between communitarian and totalitarian provenance seems operative in the discussion over the proper sourcing of liturgical forms of music. The liturgy itself has a communitarian dimension, but it does not stop there. Because it has as its object perfection, the communitarian modes of expression must be formally oriented toward perfection, which is to say, they should as Pius X insisted, be "true art." Setting aside momentarily the question of the legitimacy of sourcing secular material, the question of whether particular pieces have their origins in the folk repertoire does not preclude their "sublimation" to the level of art. In spite of his paradigmatic position among Catholic musicians, Palestrina's sources are frequently no nobler than the modest chorales upon which Bach built his titanic oeuvre.[46] That being said, Ratzinger's perspective encourages a discernment of these things according to their natures, an assessment that looks to origins and motivations, as much to aesthetic features.

Conclusion

The region of cultural tension created by the struggle between common practice and a prescribed ideal is precisely where the modern Catholic liturgy finds itself today, not only with respect to its music, but also in the various other enterprises which serve liturgical ends (architecture, language, etc.). Still, a close reading of the Conciliar and post-Conciliar documents gives good reason to believe that the liturgical principles of sacred music have not changed substantially since Vatican II. The possible perception of contradiction in the documents may take time to resolve, but the attitude today seems to be the attitude that has held sway for most of the Church's history: a reasonable variation within the practice of liturgical music should be accommodated without resulting in a crisis of identity. Such a crisis inevitably emerges when norms or principles are neglected or disregarded. A genuine vision of contemporary Catholic liturgical music will necessarily harmonize these enduring principles with modern praxis.[47]

Notes

1 Although the chapter will make reference to the *Extraordinary Form* of the Mass, the ambitus of this paper is not large enough to include a treatment of musical praxis in that format.

2 The Paschal Vigil was the first major object of reform in 1951, followed by the rest of Holy Week in 1955. See: Annibale Bugnini, *The Reform of the Liturgy: 1948-1975* (Collegeville: Liturgical Press, 1990). This is a remarkably frank account of the work of the *Consilium for the Implementation of the Constitution on the Sacred Liturgy* by its secretary. One example of musical obsolescence through the reform was the loss of the hymn *Vexilla regis prodeunt* in the 1955 Holy Week ceremony for Good Friday.

3 For a revelatory treatment of the origins of the Gregorian chants proper to the Mass Liturgy, see: James McKinnon, *The Advent Project* (Berkeley: University of California Press, 2000).

4 Motu proprio on Sacred Music, *Tra le sollecitudini*, November 22, 1903; NL, pp. 3–10. See the introduction.

5 Bugnini, *The Reform of the Liturgy*, pp. 99–113.

6 Paul VI, General Audience, November 26, 1969: "Qui, è chiaro, sarà avvertita la maggiore novità: quella della lingua. Non più il latino sarà il linguaggio principale della Messa, ma la lingua parlata. Per chi sa la bellezza, la potenza, la sacralità espressiva del latino, certamente la sostituzione della lingua volgare è un grande sacrificio ... perderemo grande parte di quello stupendo e incomparabile fatto artistico e spirituale, ch'è il canto gregoriano. Abbiamo, sì, ragione di rammaricarci, e quasi di smarrirci ..."

7 See: *Tra le sollecitudini*, II, 3.

8 Bugnini, pp. 900–901.

9 Sacred Congregation for Rites, Instruction, *Muscam Sacram*, March 5, 1967, n. 9; DOL n. 508. "Nullum genus musicae sacrae Ecclesia ab actionibus liturgicis arcet, dummodo spiritui ipsius actionis liturgicae et naturale singularum eius partium respondeat et debitam actuosam populi participationem non impediat."

10 See: *Tra le sollecitudini*, II, 3.

11 Sacred Congregation for Divine Worship, *Jubilate Deo* (Boston: Daughters of St. Paul, 1974); see: *Sacrosanctum Concilium*, n. 54.

12 *Concerti nelle chiese*, 5 November 1987; n. 6. Official texts in various languages are given in *Notitiae* 24 (1988), pp. 3–39; "Quando l'esecuzione della musica sacra avviene durante una celebrazione, dovrà attenersi al ritmo e alle modalità proprie della stessa. Ciò obbliga, non poche volte, a limitare l'uso di opere create in un tempo in cui la partecipazione attiva dei fedeli non era proposta come fonte per l'autentico spirito cristiano. Codesto cambiamento nell'esecuzione delle opere musicali è analogo a quello attuato per altre creazioni artistiche in campo liturgico, per motivo di celebrazione: per esempio, i presbiteri sono stati ristrutturati con la sede presidenziale, l'ambone, l'altare 'versus populum.' Ciò non ha significato disprezzo per il passato, ma è stato voluto per un fine più importante, come è la partecipazione dell'assemblea. L'eventuale limitazione che può avvenire nell'uso di codeste opere musicali può essere supplita con la presentazione integrale di esse, al di fuori delle celebrazioni, sotto la forma di concerti di musica sacra."

13 "Ecclesia cantum gregorianum agnoscit ut liturgiae romanae proprium: qui ideo in actionibus liturgicis, ceteris paribus, principem locum obtineat"—the famous phrase granting "principal place" to Gregorian chant in the Roman Liturgy.

14 *Concerti nelle chiese,* no. 2. "Le *scholae cantorum* non hanno avuto molte volte l'opportunità di eseguire il loro repertorio abituale di musica sacra polifonica nel contesto della celebrazione liturgica. Lo stesso è capitato con il canto gregoriano, che è entrato a far parte dei programmi di concerti dentro e fuori della chiesa."

15 John Paul II, Chirograph on Sacred Music, 22 November 2003, n. 7.

16 See, for example: "Letter of His Holiness Benedict XVI to the Grand Chancellor of the Pontifical Institute of Sacred Music on the 100th Anniversary of its Foundation," May 13, 2011; "Address of His Holiness Benedict XVI to Participants in the National Congress of *Scholae Cantorum* Organised by the Italian Association of Saint Cecilia," November 10, 2012.

17 For a comprehensive description of music in the Extraordinary Form see: B. Andrew Mills, *Psallite Sapienter* (Richmond: Church Music Association of America, 2008). Compare with R.R. Terry, *Catholic Church Music* (London: Greening & Co. Ltd., 1907).

18 Here we will concern ourselves with the books attached to the Mass liturgy. The Divine Office consists of multiple liturgical hours on any given day. Several books pertain to the celebration of the Office, but because their use is generally the occupation of the clergy, and because the authoritative books for the music of the Office remain as of yet incomplete, we will limit ourselves to a discussion of the Mass.

19 The term "sacramentary" comes from the earliest Mass books which only contained the parts pertinent to the celebrant. Prior to the liturgical reform, all the texts of the Mass, prayers and readings, were contained integrally in the single Roman Missal. The Missal itself coalesced in the Middle Ages from disparate ritual books (also called sacramentaries, epistolaries, and evangelaries) because of the rise of low Masses, wherein the priest celebrant was the only minister of the Mass. As such, because the priest had to perform all the parts himself, an integral Missal containing all the parts (even the choir's antiphons, which were not sung but recited in the Low Mass) was necessary for the solitary priest to complete the rite.

20 First promulgated by the Sacred Congregation for Divine Worship in the decree *Thesaurum cantus gregoriani;* see: DOL n. 534.

21 The first typical edition of the *Graduale Simplex* was promulgated in 1967 by the decree *Sacrosancti Oecumenici*; see DOL n. 532. A second typical edition was produced and promulgated in 1974 by the decree *Cantus faciliores*; see: DOL n. 536.

22 Sacred Congregation for Divine Worship, *Ordo cantus Missae*, Introduction, June 24, 1974; DOL n. 535.

23 See: Peter Jeffrey, "The New Chantbooks from Solesmes," *Notes* 47 (1991), pp. 1039–63. See footnotes 37 & 38.

24 The *Kyriale Simplex* was the first musical publication following the Constitution on the Sacred Liturgy, having been promulgated in 1964 by the decree *Quum Constitutio*; DOL n. 530. It includes five simpler settings of the Mass ordinary. The introduction to this work makes the interesting point that its contents looked to both the Ambrosian and Mozarabic Rites for source material.

25 For the third Sunday in Lent the Simple Gradual appoints the antiphon "Non in solo pane" which had been the antiphon at Sext on the first Sunday in Lent in the pre-Conciliar Office. One difficulty is that the verse is not provided for with the psalm-tone for the antiphon and it is up to the singer to presumably point the psalm verses on the spot. The rubric in the *Graduale Simplex* for these acclamations reads "Canitur deinde unus saltem versiculus e psalmo responsorio praecedenti, qui non est adhibitus;" (At least one verse from the preceding responsorial psalm is sung, which is not appended here.)

26 Ulrich S. Leupold (ed.), *Luther's Works*, vol. 53 "Liturgy and Hymns" (Philadelphia: Fortress Press, 1965), p. 54.

27 Paul Arbogast, *Complete English Propers for the High Mass for All Sundays and Principal Feasts* (Cincinnati: World Library of Sacred Music, Inc., 1964), pp. 8–9.

28 An example of this music-to-text relationship on the word "et" is illustrated by the gradual chant for the third Sunday in Advent, *Qui sedes*: Abbaye Saint-Pierre de Solesmes, *Graduale Romanum* (Tournai: Desclée & Co., 1974), p. 22.

29 The different editions were published in 1969, 1970, 1973, 1975, 1983, 2000, and 2002.

30 Dennis C. Smolarski, SJ, *The General Instruction of the Roman Missal: 1969–2002: A Commentary* (Collegeville: Liturgical Press, 2003) p. 30. The *Graduale Romanum* still places the sequence in its traditional place immediately before the Gospel.

31 For instance, for the thirteenth Sunday in Ordinary Time, the lectionary calls for Psalm 89, while the Roman Gradual appoints two verses from Psalm 33 for the same day.

32 Pius XII, Encyclical Letter, *Musicae sacrae disciplina*, 25 December 1955, n. 47; NL, p. 226.

33 The *sequence* or *prosa* of the Mass (which is only retained for a few liturgical days in the modern era) is a "hymn" in the sense that it is a meditation on the mysteries of the given liturgical celebration. Nevertheless, the form of most sequences employs a variable strophic model, in which the tune changes during the course of the poem (which, nevertheless retains its regular poetic meter throughout). These hymnodic pieces served a similar role in the Mass as the hymn does in the Office, and their use was widespread throughout the Middle Ages.

34 The revised form of the Office places the hymn before the psalmody.

35 Leupold, *Luther's Works*, vol. 53, p. 17. Martin Luther worked vigorously for the establishment of a German Mass. He was, however, unwilling to mandate the abandonment of Latin in the liturgy, leaving the matter in the hands of local authorities with due discretion for local sensibilities. His principal interest in the use of music was the encouragement of conscious participation on the part of the congregants. In a letter to Nicholas Haussman, bishop of Zwickau, Luther offered several concrete

suggestions on a new "order of Mass." He was, however, solicitous that local governors of churches be responsible for the details of the liturgy, saying, "What is left can be decided by actual practice, as long as the Word of God is diligently and faithfully preached in the church."

36 Ibid., p. 54.

37 Ibid., pp. 36–7.

38 Originally "Lobet den Herrn" in the German by Joachim Neander (1680).

39 Richard Taruskin, *The Oxford History of Western Music,* vol. I (Oxford: Oxford University Press, 2005), pp. 754–6.

40 Stainton Taylor, *The Chorale Preludes of J.S. Bach* (London: Oxford University Press, 1942). For a reappraisal of Luther's sources for his new repertory of hymns see: Robin A. Leaver, *Luther's Liturgical Music: Principles and Implications* (Grand Rapids: Wm. B. Eerdmans Publishing, 2007), pp. 12–18. In this passage, Leaver debunks the suggestion that Luther used secular musical sources reset with religious texts for his revised German Mass.

41 Taruskin, *The Oxford History of Western Music,* vol. I, p. 755.

42 See: Joseph Cardinal Ratzinger, *A New Song for the Lord* (New York: The Crossroad Publishing Co., 1997), pp. 107–8; JRCW 11, pp. 507–9.

43 Ibid., p. 124; JRCW 11, p. 456.

44 For a more progressive view, see: Anthony Ruff, OSB, *Sacred Music and Liturgical Reform* (Chicago: Hillenbrand Books, 2007), pp. 462–63.

45 Localization was essential to the nomenclature of jazz sub-genres: New Orleans Dixieland, St Louis Blues, "Hot" Chicago Jazz, etc.

46 For example, the Masses by Palestrina on the tune *L'homme armé.*

47 Pope Benedict XVI makes this assertion: "An authentic renewal of sacred music can only happen in the wake of the great tradition of the past, of Gregorian chant and sacred polyphony." Greeting to the Domenico Bartolucci Foundation, June 24, 2006.

Bibliography

Arbogast, Paul, *Complete English Propers for the High Mass for All Sundays and Principal Feasts,* (Cincinnati: World Library of Sacred Music, Inc., 1964).

Bartlett, Adam, *Simple English Propers for the Ordinary Form of Mass: Sundays and Feasts.* (Richmond: Church Music Association of America, 2011).

Benedict XVI, Apostolic Exhortation, *Sacramentum Caritatis,* February 22, 2007.

Bugnini, Annibale, *The Reform of the Liturgy:1948–1975* (Collegeville: Liturgical Press, 1990).

Burgess, F. & G.H. Palmer, *The Plainchant Gradual, vols I & II* (Wantage: St Mary's, 1946).

Guéranger, Prosper, OSB, *The Liturgical Year: Advent,* (Cincinnati: Benziger Bros, 1910).

Jeffrey, Peter, "The New Chantbooks from Solesmes," *Notes* 47 (1991), pp. 1039–63.

John Paul II, Chirograph on Sacred Music, November 22, 2003.

Leaver, Robin A., *Luther's Liturgical Music: Principles and Implications* (Grand Rapids: Wm. B. Eerdmans Publishing, 2007).

Leupold, Ulrich S., *Luther's Works,* vol. 53 "Liturgy and Hymns" (Philadelphia: Fortress Press, 1965).

McKinnon, James, *The Advent Project* (Berkeley: University of California Press, 2000).

Mills, Andrew B., *Psallite Sapienter* (Richmond: Church Music Association of America, 2008).

Paul VI, General Audience, November 26, 1969.

Pius X, motu proprio *Tra le sollecitudini,* November 22, 1903.

Pius XII, Encyclical Letter, *Musicae Sacrae Disciplina*, December 25, 1955.

Ratzinger, Joseph, *A New Song for the Lord* (New York: The Crossroad Publishing Co., 1997).

Ruff, Anthony, OSB, *Sacred Music and Liturgical Reform* (Chicago: Hillenbrand Books, 2007).

Sacred Congregation for Divine Worship, Decree promulgating the *Graduale Romanum, Thesaurum cantus gregoriani*, June 4, 1972; DOL n. 534.

—— Introduction to the *Graduale Romanum, Ordo cantus Missae*, June 24, 1974; DOL n. 535.

—— Decree promulgating the *Graduale Simplex (Second Typical Edition), Cantus faciliores,* November 22, 1974; DOL 536.

—— *Jubilate Deo* (Boston: Daughters of St Paul, 1974).

—— *General Instruction of the Roman Missal* (2002).

—— *Concerti nelle chiese*, November 5, 1987; official texts in various languages are given in *Notitiae* 24 (1988), pp. 3–39.

Sacred Congregation for Rites, Decree promulgating the *Kyriale Simplex, Quum Constitutio*, December 14, 1964; DOL n. 530.

—— Instruction, *Muscam Sacram,* March 5, 1967.

—— Decree promulgating the *Graduale Simplex, Sacrosancti Oecumenici*, September 3, 1967; DOL n. 532.

Second Vatican Council, Constitution on the Sacred Liturgy, *Sacrosanctum Concilium,* December 4, 1963.

Smolarski, Dennis C., SJ, *The General Instruction of the Roman Missal:1969–2002: A Commentary* (Collegeville: Liturgical Press, 2003).

Taruskin, Richard, *The Oxford History of Western Music*, vol. I (Oxford: Oxford University Press, 2005).

Taylor, Stainton, *The Chorale Preludes of J.S. Bach* (London: Oxford University Press, 1942).

Terry, R.R., *Catholic Church Music* (London: Greening & Co. Ltd., 1907).

Chapter 20

DISCERNMENT, DECORUM, *AUCTORITAS*: KEYS TO REANIMATING CATHOLIC ARCHITECTURE

Thomas Gordon Smith, AIA, FAAR

Introduction

About the time of Christ's birth, a Roman architect named Vitruvius wrote a book presenting Greek ideas about designing towns, buildings, and means of defense. He promoted responsibility in each field, expecting manual skill, intellectual curiosity, respect for past accomplishments, and decorous professional conduct. His book advocated the use of aesthetic standards and architectural problem-solving drawn from Greek *antiqui*. Those ancient architects built Doric and Ionic temples, theaters with effective acoustics, and civic centers that scholars still examine and publish. Architects traditionally studied them as paradigms, or exemplary models, when designing analogous structures. Vitruvius' prescriptions for disciplined and beautiful buildings have been sustained for two millennia; he provides a perennial resource for instruction and hope through traditional standards of wholeness.

> Architects who have sought to be skilled with their hands without formal education have never been able to reach a position of authority in return for their labors; while those who relied only upon reasoning and scholarship were clearly pursuing the shadow, not the substance. But those who have a thorough knowledge of both, like men fully armed, have more quickly attained their goal with authority (Vitruvius, I, I, 2).

During the past century in the secular Western world, ideals such as *balance, beauty,* and *style* have been prohibited by modernists in the spheres of art and architecture. Around 1900, the attack by iconoclastic modernists against the long-lasting Renaissance that began in fifteenth-century Italy was fundamentally persuasive. Although established European and American architects ignored modernist forays and Catholic patrons perpetuated traditional norms, after the Second World War Western institutions, including the Catholic Church, succumbed to an artistic modernism that enforced iconoclastic abstraction as it gained corporate, governmental, and popular approbation.[1]

As Catholics, we learn from childhood to emulate our spiritual predecessors. This practice allows us to more readily resist and contradict the still-dominant prohibition against emulating ancient churches in new buildings. By using architectural forms and traditional plans for churches and auxiliary structures that stem from our repository of Western historical styles, in conjunction with an inventive method which responds to present circumstances, architects and patrons may build churches that dispose the faithful to prayer and contribute to the holistic artistic legacy the Church has established throughout two millennia.

Catholic leaders and architects today should not feel bound to build new churches modeled on by-now old-fashioned secular precedents that are supposedly "of our time." Since 2000, recognition of the need for fundamental change in Catholic architecture and the allied arts has come primarily from individuals in new Catholic orders, stalwart educational institutions, and reformed branches of old orders. They have engaged with classical architects to build durable, practical, and visually evocative churches. The practice of *ora et labora* within many conventual walls today reflects a reestablishment of discipline similar to others that have occurred during the past eighteen centuries. These movements renew concepts of vocation while simultaneously developing architectural parallels of rigor that are ancient, yet refreshingly new.

A growing number of architects and artists have trained themselves to build and create works of art and architecture that emulate ancient and Catholic exemplars. Their sense of vocation as professionals is similar to the impetus we see in new religious orders. Given the example and teaching of Pope Benedict XVI regarding the tangible renewal of the celebration of the liturgy and its physical setting, we face the wonderful possibility that newly-built churches will serve the practice of Catholic faith and reflect the 2,500 year old heritage of Western architectural and artistic expression.

I share my thoughts as a practicing classical architect, not as an architectural historian. Working with clients to help articulate their needs, understand their aspirations, and design new buildings for them is a far different task from that of a historian. But architects study historical precedents and I will discuss several churches in detail in order to describe methods of architectural practice; the decorum of the "language" of classical architecture; and the concept of style.

I. Patronage requires connoisseurship

The priest's role as patron is essential for achieving churches commensurate with liturgical and pastoral vitality. The architect needs to work directly with the priest, or religious superior, as patron. This is difficult in most dioceses, which have become encumbered with the administrative legacy of corporate models of "convenience" and "efficiency." Such bureaucratic structures perpetuate cronyism, siphon-off professional fees, and, most problematically, replace the incisiveness of a patron with the diffuse tendencies of a committee.

To counterbalance these factors, it is essential for dioceses to select young priests with inherent interest in physical things like buildings and train them in the art of patronage. Our societies no longer provide aristocrats like St Charles Borromeo, who came from a noble line of patrons and learned the discerning art of patronage by shadowing Pope Pius IV.[2] We should heartily fulfill the stipulations in the Second Vatican Council's Constitution on the Sacred Liturgy, *Sacrosanctum Concilium,* to institute seminary courses in the history of art and architecture. The Constitution spoke explicitly about the need to prepare clerics to be capable of serving as informed patrons:

> While they are doing their studies in philosophy and theology, clerics should also be trained in the history of [sacred art] and its development, together with the sound principles on which works of art for worship should be based. They will thus appreciate and preserve the hallowed monuments of the church, and be able to give suitable advice to artists and craftspeople as they bring their work into being (n. 129).

In his 2007 Apostolic Exhortation *Sacramentum Caritatis,* Pope Benedict XVI called for a renewal in this effort:

> A solid knowledge of the history of sacred art can be advantageous for those responsible for commissioning artists and architects to create works of art for the liturgy. Consequently it is essential that the education of seminarians and priests include the study of art history, with special reference to sacred buildings and the corresponding liturgical norms (n. 41).

Sacrosanctum Concilium underscores that education in the history of art is an introduction to connoisseurship. Pope Benedict reinforces the importance of this learning for good patronage. These studies are not undertaken simply to gain awareness of Catholic cultural patrimony and preserve artifacts; they help us imbue contemporary buildings and sacred works of art with the values of earlier artistic achievements. David Watkin presents the most reliable account of Catholic building from 300–1900 in *A History of Western Architecture.*

It is likely that a future Charles Borromeo will amplify seminary studies by a natural inclination that perpetuates life-long study. Cardinal Mundelein of Chicago is an excellent model for this effort during the early twentieth century.[3] Young priests, seminarians, and religious may become cultural leaders and patrons for buildings if they can identify and work with faithful, capable architects dedicated to building Catholic structures. Professionals now exist who have integrated traditional methods of solving architectural problems within contemporary practical demands. When the priest is properly prepared for the responsible role of patron, he will be able to positively participate in the creative process with the architect. This will enable the Church to move forward culturally, rather than remain isolated within secular artistic constraints.

The essential relationship is priest and architect, but it will grow to incorporate the efforts of office staff, other clergy, engineers, contractors, artists, and artisans to carry out the work. Just as the architect may not be sophisticated theologically, the priest need not be an architect. Instead, each must develop a reciprocal relationship to become prime collaborators. The architect should comprehend the advantage of achieving *auctoritas*, or capability to solve problems through manual and cerebral methods with confidence. The professional should also take long-term legal responsibility as "Architect of Record" throughout all phases of design and construction. The architect-of-record is a licensed professional who forms a contract to assume legal responsibility for the architectural design services for a project. This includes signing the final drawings to indicate compliance of the construction documents with relevant building and safety codes. If the architect needs help or local representation, it should be auxiliary, or the design intent may not be carried out with architectural integrity in the resulting church. Just as in liturgy, the details of construction design are essential to achieving the whole: good intentions do not produce the desired result without careful, concerted effort.

The goal of achieving strength, function, and beauty—Vitruvius' simultaneous criteria for a good building—provides a format for considering this balance of responsibilities. Strength is primarily the province of the architect and engineering consultants, who must ensure the structural, mechanical, electrical, and life-safety aspects of the design. The delineation of function lies in the patron's responsibility to articulate requirements for the project and the architect's ability to satisfy both practical details and how the church can enable prayer, spiritually and intellectually. The client should, for example, have a clear idea of how the proposed church and auxiliary facilities will be used for various liturgies, sacraments, and parish activities. He must think carefully about the number of parishioners, the acoustical requirements for organ and choir, readings and oration. The patron should also set goals for the orientation of the church on the site, and functional access to the sacristy, rectory, classrooms, and other parish areas. Considerations of style should be discussed from the beginning. "Traditional" is not a style; Gothic, Romanesque, or Classical are broad categories that can be starting points. The terms not only convey spiritual and cultural overtones, but have constructional and aesthetic implications that require as much development as the resolution of functional requirements.

The third criterion, defining "the beauty of Thy house and the place where Thy glory dwelleth," (Ps. 26:8) is the co-equal task of patron and architect. Since the three criteria flow into one solution, however, the relationships are not territorial, but collaborative through successive phases of development.

The initial program, a list of requirements, becomes the tool used to evaluate the schematic design when functional relationships are first delineated in explicit drawings and simple models. Nuanced change and development of the initial scheme is normal through successive phases of design. The ideal relationship to forge throughout design and construction is a bond of trust and candid interaction between patron and architect, and, eventually, contractor.

Avoiding two extremes in expectations

Two common errors in patron-architect relationships discount the value of vital collaboration. One mistake is the elevation of the architect into a genius whose prescription for the design in a hasty sketch-on-a-cocktail-napkin is accepted by the patron as a *fait accompli*. The opposite problem is when a client insists on receiving three diverse design concepts from which to pick a favorite. It is better to begin with serious discussion of the program for the church, ideas of preferred styles that might be developed, and aspirations for the type of church plan and its relationship to auxiliary buildings. Then, a professional interchange begins.

Aim for durability in churches

The horizontal line of an equilateral triangle represents the idea of strength in a building: a durable base to which function and beauty are hinged. Egyptian pyramids embody the idea of stability and longevity, although they do so with an absolute minimum of usable interiors. Ancient Greek temples were built with great precision and durability; some have survived millennia. In many public buildings of the past century, however, architects did not aspire to longevity. Their patrons and architects saved initial expense by using superficial methods of sheathing a building using thin layers of material, whether glass, stone, or metal, conjoined with fragile connections of steel, that are vulnerable to corrosion and failure within decades. Without being oblivious to economic constraints, Catholics, by building solidly-constructed, load-bearing structures should perpetuate the practical and symbolically rich durability of churches.

II. Paradigmatic architectural methods

To describe how an architect works to resolve problems of strength, function, and beauty to design a church, I rely on the treatise by Marcus Vitruvius Pollio (c. 90 BC–c. 20 BC). He wrote *On Architecture* to describe the architect's methods, which require balancing intellectual and manual skills. Four skills are: 1) mastering several types of drawing; 2) understanding the use of proportioning systems; 3) gaining comprehensive knowledge of what materials are appropriate for a particular project and how they are put together; and 4) knowing how to express meaningful ideas through architectural styles, the heritage of their detail, and the integration of figural and decorative arts.

Before discussing these methods, I would like to acknowledge Vitruvius' invaluable gift to Western culture, in concert with the uncountable builders, patrons, and architects who have perpetuated and developed his standards. Likewise, I appreciate the numerous people who successively copied Vitruvian manuscripts over centuries and those who subsequently published and illustrated his ideas after Guttenberg.[4] One propitious sign for integrated classicism is the spontaneous publication of newly-translated and illustrated Vitruvius editions in recent years; several of these are noted in the bibliography. Historically, when Vitruvius is well-tended, holistic architecture follows!

Vitruvius wrote his treatise to set rigorous standards for young architects serving Caesar Augustus in post-civil war Rome. Vitruvius synthesized his directives from twenty-five now-lost Greek architectural accounts. His education presumably instilled several-hundred-year-old formal and professional norms devised by these *antiqui* who built superb temples to Apollo, Artemis, and Athena in Miletus, Ephesus, and Priene.[5] His professional practice was focused on military architectural work in support of Augustus' war efforts, but Vitruvius' encyclopedic work continues to provide a widespread and long-lasting influence on builders of varied temperaments.

Vitruvius' presentation of a rectangular coordinate system of Ionic plans, for example, spiced with admonitions to utilize subtle optical refinements to impart elegant vitality, provided enough information for the sixteenth-century Catholic architect, Andrea Palladio, to graphically interpret Vitruvius' Ionic details and building configurations in illustrations for Daniele Barbaro's 1556 edition of Vitruvius.[6] Palladio also utilized these Ionic systems in new churches two hundred years before Westerners could actually visit the Ionian temples Vitruvius described.

Balancing intellectual and manual skills

Although architects are visual thinkers, Vitruvius admonishes them to enlist the brain with "careful, serious thought and watchful attention" to be "directed to the agreeable outcome of one's project."[7] To this prudent sense of evaluation, he adds the need for the occasional stroke of genius, that is—invention—spurred by the "lively mental energy" of a versatile mind. The ability to invent is what differentiates paradigmatic architecture from merely copying existing structures; it allows one to develop an idiom at once recognizable and new. A patron and architect should not hesitate to emulate paradigms. A successful new design, infused with ingenuity, will inevitably be "of our time," a cliché that forms the most-feared hurdle to contemporary work in any traditional style.

Learning to draw

Catholic patrons who want to build churches with wholeness need to work with an architect who can both delineate compelling proposals and resolve design conflicts through drawing. Architects collaborate in offices or studios to accomplish work that requires a number of individuals who possess particular talents to solve, develop, and build. In searching for an architect, the patron should look for principals and key staff members able to draw by hand, as well as use computers. This species is scarce in the profession. Computers are excellent for the minute modular precision of bricks and mortar, employing such detail to make construction documents of great precision. Although architects do not carry out construction, their drawings must convey realistic tectonic concepts to the builders.

Computer technology, useful as it may be for a synthesis of components of a design, tends to discourage manual drawing. The type of architect Catholic patrons should seek will prize manual ability that goes from eye to brain to hand, as well as digital technology, because drawings are the most tangible artifacts architects can make. Drawing is a manual activity that depends on natural gifts of visualization enhanced by training. The professional produces both subjective drawings that give impressions of the building, and rational drawings that are used to discuss details with the patron. Eventually these convey exact requirements to the builder. Vitruvius uses the Greek word *diathesis,* or "opening up the problem," to describe the simultaneously inspirational and auto-critical process of drawing. The successive results are prime media for architect and patron to critique in an interactive process that gets closer and closer to resolving refinements of the design.

Vitruvius' Greek architectural heroes developed communication techniques in three types of drawings with extraordinary finesse: the plan, the elevation, and the section. The plan shows wall layouts of the building depicted from above. It is useful in understanding functional relationships, circulation, and locations of

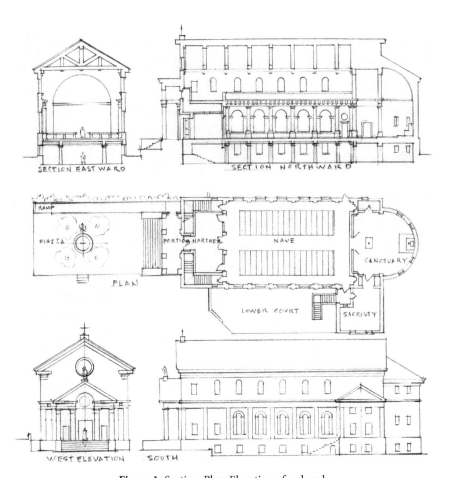

Figure 1 Section, Plan, Elevation of a church

openings. Elevations are perpendicular drawings of façades that indicate heights, details, and materials of exterior elements. The section is conceptually a visual "slice" through a building to show spatial and structural relationships that may not be visible after construction.

Recently discovered full-size plans, elevations, and sections incised into the marble courtyard walls of the Temple of Apollo at Didyma, near Miletus, are working drawings that served successive builders from 300 BC–300 AD, when construction of the temple ceased.[8] These documents were preserved from obliteration because the stone walls never received a final polish. The drawings display the precision and ingenuity of Paeonius the Milesian and Daphnis the Ephesian, architects whom Vitruvius describes as having the "highest renown."[9] The drawings at Didyma also demonstrate the long-term credibility and respect that a set of working drawings done with *auctoritas* may receive.

Scaenographia, or perspective drawing, is a fourth graphic way that the architect stimulates and tests the imagination and communicates ideas to the patron. The Greek word *scaenographia* suggests origins for this type of drawing in one-point perspective architectural backdrops for theatrical scenery. I emphasize Vitruvius' recommendation of perspectives because architects should constantly visualize spatial and constructional concepts in drawings from all angles. Perspectives may reveal three-dimensional problems that could occur in construction, if not anticipated, and corrected, in the design phases.

More artistic perspectives provide comprehensible images of what the architect is proposing as the design develops. The patron is better able to critique when he understands the design through perspectives and can contribute ideas for refinement.

Figure 2 Perspective of a church

Canons: the diverse proportional systems

Building new churches involves winnowing styles and plan-forms from the broad spectrum of Catholic architectural heritage. The elements of classical systems are clearly defined by rational ways of learning how formal elements are inter-related structurally, proportionally, and in poetic, or meaningful, terms. Such evaluation, from multiple points of view, teaches the architect to discern good, better, or best.[10] Because individual taste is shaped by personality and context, evaluations of what is "best" vary. Nevertheless, various "bests" are held up as canons of proportions to be imitated. When the word "canon" is used in relation to a type of architecture, it refers to established standards. Although these are useful guides, they are not universal. Some architects employ one or more established canons for their work; others develop their own ideals.

An architect might draw two parallel versions of Doric columns with the beams they support, following the canons of two Italian Renaissance architects. Andrea Palladio (1508–80) published *I Quattro Libri dell'Architettura* in 1570 and Giacomo Barozzi da Vignola (1507–73) published *Regola delli cinque ordini d'architettura* in 1562. Historically, their canonical proportions and details have exerted the greatest influence on Catholic churches. Initially, the two versions look similar, but their differences can be clarified by comparing *symmetria,* or proportional relationships. Proportion is gauged by establishing a module. The height of the column to a module is the most basic of these ratios. For Doric, the module is one-half the diameter of the bottom of the column shaft. In Vitruvius' Doric, the total height of the column is the multiple of the module × 14, whereas Palladio suggests the module × 15, and Vignola recommends 16.

Figure 3 Comparison of Doric Symmetria from Vitruvius, Palladio, and Vignola

Divisions and multiples of the module are tabulated to establish ratios to define a particular set, or canon, of proportional relationships. The primary beam, or architrave, is substantial while the Doric guttae toward the top are minute. The technique is used, for example, to execute a design for the portico of a church. The results can be presented to the patron for evaluation. Fifteen hundred years after Vitruvius' effort, his treatise became a model for Palladio and Vignola, allowing a fortuitous re-animation of Doric architecture! We can also benefit today.

These three canons for Doric ratios have been the most influential. Each reflects a Hellenistic preference for svelte, or attenuated, proportions. Their symmetria are not the only formulae, however, for determining Doric proportions. Early Doric temples in Athens and Corinth display completely different proportional ratios; the Parthenon is bold and heavy by comparison to Vitruvius, Palladio, or Vignola. In the mid-eighteenth century, Stuart and Revett promoted the Doric symmetria of the Parthenon.[11] Their engravings provoked outrage from the English arbiter of architectural taste, Sir William Chambers: "it may appear extraordinary, that a

Figure 4 Comparison of Parthenon and Hellenistic Doric

people ... so celebrated for poetry, rhetoric, and every sort of polite learning ... should be so deficient in architecture."[12]

Such comments reflect varied opinions of taste. In artistic matters, tolerance ebbs and flows. Despite Chambers' complaint, during the first four decades of nineteenth-century building in Britain and the United States, Classical Greek proportions virtually superseded Hellenistic/Renaissance canonical standards. A later reaction returned to Renaissance proportions. There are possibly ten to one more Doric buildings related to Vitruvius' symmetria than ones following the Parthenon's canon. While consensus may exert dominance, different canons serve valuable expressive purposes.

Using symmetria to define a proportional aesthetic for Doric is a system that can be applied to analyse other types of classical architecture. In addition, late nineteenth/early twentieth century architects and scholars applied the technique to Gothic churches by selecting particular historical examples as models to formulate the standard ratios. Various types of Romanesque churches, Cistercian, for example, can be analysed by the same methods and applied to designs for new churches.

Ratios of symmetria, although fundamental, should not become obsessive. Using one or another should not be touted as a magic key to guarantee a "perfect" column and beam, or the proportion of the arch of another style, or a golden section system for the church as a whole. The aspiration to revive the quality and character of Catholic architecture cannot be solved by formulae. We must learn

Figure 5 Comparison of Senanque and Annunciation Abbey at Clear Creek

how to balance venerable analytical tools with intuitive creative processes through the confidence of *auctoritas*: judging by eye as well as by canon. After all, Vitruvius suggests that the architect exerts invention within a proscribed system. Patron and architect will build beautiful churches when they can make the myriad decisions required through considered balance of manual skills and intellectual analysis.

Oeconomia: comprehensive knowledge of materials and building techniques

Oeconomia is a concept that involves realistic strategies to build the type of church the patron and architect envision. Early consideration of economy poses the question of how to build in a particular place and time. The Greek idea of *oeconomia* is about money, but it also evaluates the long-term durability of construction materials and methods. Patron and architect must prudently evaluate whether building materials are available in the region and if contractors and workers are capable of skillful fabrication to ingeniously resolve the constraints of actual conditions.

In the British Isles, the United States, and most parts of the world today, we build in the inherently superficial building economy of curtain-walls of glass and thin stone panels, hung from a steel or concrete armature. Since World War II, this construction technology has perpetuated the modernist aesthetic and has become the dominant system for institutional buildings. Given the opportunity to build a new church, however, many patrons would prefer to base stylistic aspirations on thick-walled, masonry paradigms. This hope is challenged by an economic culture of material and fabrication geared to the curtain wall. Extreme durability is difficult to achieve in the current economy of building, but it is a worthy goal!

Since 1980, a small percentage of architects have worked against the surface-oriented aesthetic to promote the cultural and physical durability of classical design. In this counter-cultural effort, some architects focused on an apologetic of load-bearing masonry construction versus steel and glass, while others revived the aesthetic concepts of symmetria and decorum. The movement has gained breadth and maturity in recent years, with practitioners merging substantial construction methods and refined expression of architectural form. One practical argument is that a durable building is economical in the long-term. A second is that patrons find it easier to raise construction funds for expressive and beautiful buildings.

Regarding the material and craft of masonry, sustainable construction in brick and stone is more valued in Britain than the United States. The Eastern and Midwestern parts of the United States still have skilled masons and good supplies of brick, but craftsmen and the material have essentially evaporated in California. Even sophisticated engineers in that state react against the idea of brick, although current seismic codes are uniformly enforced throughout the country. Culturally, masonry no longer plays a role in Californian buildings and has become unfamiliar to architects, contractors, and manufacturers.

I am most involved with building economy in the Midwestern United States. In addition to excellent quality brick, we are fortunate to have quarrying and cutting of Indiana limestone and Minnesota granite. Throughout the country, however, many quarries have ceased production. Unfortunately, some have been converted to cold storage depots, or only slightly better, subjected to crushing stone for road-work. Instead, we have tended to import Caen limestone from France and marble from China, Spain, and Brazil.

Despite the "global economy," importing stone from abroad is enormously expensive. Architects should encourage small, sometimes obscure, regional quarries by specifying their products to increase durable and sustainable building practice, but the problem is not new. It demonstrates an aspect of *oeconomia* that Vitruvius recognized: "Economy denotes the proper management of materials and of site, as well as a thrifty balancing of cost and common sense in the construction of works. The architect should not demand things which cannot be found or made ready without great expense. For example, not all places have an abundant supply . . . of marble."[13] He follows with an injunction to locate nearby substitutes.

Andrea Palladio provides an inspiring example of how *oeconomia* requires adaptability and careful, hierarchical evaluation. Between 1540 and 1580, he built civic buildings, palaces, and villas throughout the Veneto integrating regional vernacular building techniques with sophisticated architectural forms imitating ancient and modern Roman buildings. He executed the structures in brick, mortar, and stucco, instead of stone. During the last decade of his life, he erected magnificent churches in Venice and their façades were executed in stone. The august permanence of imported material signifies the spiritual and civic importance of San Giorgio Maggiore and the Redentore. Meanwhile, the less visible parts were built in brick and stucco.

Reality of budgets

Patrons need to exercise prudence when considering architects to design a church, being wary of sumptuous schemes that may be alluring, but impossible to achieve within a realistic budget. The patron needs to learn about the track record of potential architects during the selection process through conversations with previous clients. A close examination of recently-constructed buildings and discussion with the architect about the priorities of budget on previous work should be candid.

When reviewing brochures, one should determine when the projects were constructed. Just as some liturgical arts studios promote magnificently-painted stained-glass windows made in 1925, as though they have such artistic capability now, some architectural successor firms show historical work. The current generation must demonstrate capability.

The patron and architect will expend great time and effort to build within a reasonable financial economy. No matter how generous the patronage, every project has a budget and a program: creating a design that meets functional and financial needs requires setting priorities and accepting limitations. The patron may hope for a more elaborate design than what is feasible and in good faith, the architect might comply. Both must beware of dreams that are completely outside the scope of the budget. While fantasy may be appealing, it is a kind of "eye candy" that ultimately leads to delay and the frustration of back-tracking. Working together with a sense of trust, the patron and architect can achieve a reasonable balance.

Once the architect has been selected, the patron and architect should develop a timeline for completing the steps of design, coordination with the specialist consultants, phases of construction, and fundraising. This will allow information from both sides to be exchanged so schedules can be more realistic than wishful. The duration required to design a beautiful, functional church that will help strengthen the Catholic cultural environment can be great, including the time to forge a working relationship between key participants. Using unusual, durable methods of construction also requires time and effort.

Phases of construction

> According to the grace of God given to me, like a skilled master builder I laid a foundation, and someone else is building upon it. Each builder must choose with care how to build on it. For no one can lay any foundation other than the one that has been laid; that foundation is Jesus Christ.
>
> (St Paul, I Corinthians 3:10–11)

Sometimes construction must be completed in phases, despite the hopes of patron and architect. While inconvenience for the patron is evident, from the architect's point of view, drawn-out construction phases are inefficient. Previously accomplished decisions carried out in working drawings are often re-thought when long intervals occur and construction drawings must be re-done. These problems are overcome with patience and prudence, however, recognizing that the extraordinary challenges and privileges of building for the Church require more effort and skill than typically expended on secular projects.

III. Return to decorum

Architectural decorum tends toward the cerebral faculty more than the manual aspects of *oeconomia*. In both cases, it is usually good to follow rules knowingly and respectfully to gain productive understanding. Decorum is analogous both to the etiquette of social deportment and to self-expression. Architectural decorum stems from knowing correct behavior well enough to devise inventive ways to convey standard and extraordinary meanings through architectural forms. The object of decorum in architecture, despite the relatively mute nature of building-forms, is to express character that people can perceive and discuss.

In everyday behavior, our actions reveal both social conformity and individual personality. Similarly, through fluency with the accrued languages of formal architectural elements, such as Doric, Ionic, and Corinthian types of architecture, architects convey ideas, sometimes called the grammar of architecture. Architects use this grammar to communicate ideas about the dedication of a church, for example, by selecting appropriate columns, beams, and decoration that have traditional meanings. More explicit iconography can be expressed through statuary and paintings. Apt quotations from scripture or the saint's vita can be inscribed within panels or upon entablatures to initiate the process of "reading" church façades and interiors. Classical architectural languages are the most codified and emulated, but other styles, such as various modes of Romanesque and Gothic churches, carry historical and cultural associations the architect and patron can develop.

For over two millennia, architects have periodically revitalized architecture through concepts that stem from decorum. Vitruvius wrote *On Architecture* in the chaotic aftermath of decades of warfare that impeded education for architect and patron alike. He restored Greek analogies between architectural forms and something like narrative communication. He also knew that conceptual associations only make sense if the formal language is used correctly with an understanding that the archaic origins of different types of columns developed within different Greek cultures. As we might do today, Vitruvius complained that buildings of his time betrayed ignorance of conventions, resulting in a conglomeration of forms, and thus lacked decorum. For example, one must not place a Doric entablature over Corinthian columns! Sophisticated rhetoric, or architectural poetry, can thrive with intentional contradiction, but indiscriminate intermingling is foolish.

Centuries after his death, Vitruvius' treatise may have played some part for builders constructing Romanesque churches. Renaissance scholars rediscovered Vitruvius' manuscripts and architects emulated his Greek and Roman forms with fervor and increasing erudition. With time, generations also assimilated his injunctions for professional and artistic integrity.

Beginning a century ago, however, it became prohibited to convey architectural meaning through methods of decorum. Modernist architects set out to invalidate ancient traditions of associating utilitarian and decorative parts of buildings, such as columns, capitals, and metopes, with anthropomorphic and historically-accrued meaning. It is not surprising, then, that few patrons know about Vitruvius' holistic methods and most architects dismiss their relevance. Vitruvius' edicts about the necessity of decorum can help renew this heritage to counter the fiercely-proclaimed strictures of the last century and remedy widespread cultural ignorance.

Catholic patrons should seek architects who have trained themselves to understand the value and methods of decorum. Architects will then be able to bring visual nuance to buildings and astutely convey meaning as part of function and beauty. *The Catechism of the Catholic Church* reminds us, "The whole Church is apostolic, in that she remains, through the successors of St Peter and the other apostles, in communion of faith and life with her origin: and in that she is 'sent out' into the whole world. All members of the Church share in this mission, though in various ways" (nn. 863–5). Churches always have a missionary potential; even during a brief visit attending a wedding ceremony, a non-Catholic may be struck by liturgical and architectural beauty that leads to conversion.

Just as in social interchange, when we recognize and employ the standards of architectural decorum, architects, patrons, and the faithful may think more deeply about their faith. Expressive architectural treatments may catch the eye, lead to recognition, and promote contemplation. Study of the grammar of architectural elements and their associations stimulates comprehension, as literacy allows the pleasure of reading.

Two churches in Rome, dedicated to St Peter and St Susanna, illustrate the rewards of comprehending architectural expression. Each successfully demonstrates the use of appropriate architectural language that "portrays" the saint of dedication.

These churches are also "paradigms," a concept that comes from an ancient building practice of having the master stone-mason carve a capital, or other architectural element, according to the exact specifications of the designer. This piece showed other workers the precise qualities to be copied. Since then, the concept has been enlarged to describe whole buildings that are exemplars of a type; in this usage, paradigms are chosen from among many possible examples because their qualities are worthy of emulation.

San Pietro in Montorio

In 1502 Donato Bramante (1444–1514), signaled the Renaissance in Rome by erecting a cylindrical chapel dedicated to St Peter on the Janiculum Hill, held at that time to be the location of his martyrdom. Bramante employed two ancient concepts of decorum to convey St Peter's character. First, he used sturdy and tectonic Doric architecture to represent Peter; Doric was designated in antiquity for strategic or martial gods of war in pagan temples. Second, Bramante changed the sculptural symbolism in the Doric metopes to essentially baptize their message, substituting Christian images for pagan precedent.

Bramante used architectural elements salvaged from an ancient building to construct the circular portico of San Pietro in Montorio. This *spolia* consists of sixteen granite column shafts quarried in Egypt and imported for use in an unknown Roman structure. Bramante's re-use may have been primarily dictated by economy, but perhaps the transfer from a pagan to a Christian structure was also meaningful. Granite columns inherently represent physical and temporal durability; their Egyptian provenance could even have been associated with God's providential help to Moses, a man comparable to Peter in character and leadership.

Bramante was a classicist working within a conceptually Gothic architectural milieu. He found direction through two Vitruvian methods: associations of decorum and proportional ratios of symmetria. In discussing decorum, Vitruvius advises, "the temples of Minerva, Mars, and Hercules will be Doric, since it is appropriate for temples of these gods to be built without dainty decoration on account of their virile strength."[14] Regarding proportional relationships, he notes that "if anyone wishes to take the trouble to deal with these methods, he can find an explanation of the proportions … to construct perfect and flawless temples in the Doric manner."[15]

Figure 6 Perspective of San Pietro in Montorio

The granite colonnade of San Pietro in Montorio surrounds a cylindrical chapel capped by a dome. I will focus on the exterior columns and beams, called trabeation, because Bramante made changes to ancient decorum that re-vitalized Doric architectural form for Christian use. The proportional ratios of the granite shafts were, of course, pre-determined but Bramante used their diameter to calculate the newly fabricated parts, such as the new capitals that bear the horizontal stone beams, called architraves. The architraves support a horizontal frieze, the intermediate zone that may be decorated for narrative communication. The frieze is capped by a cornice, the overhanging element that sheds water away from the building.

These bands considered together are called the "entablature." The Doric frieze is articulated with alternating vertical triglyphs, elements that, according to an origin myth, represent the ends of wooden cross-beams. Metopes are square, sculpted panels between the triglyphs. On Greek Doric metopes, sculptors depicted events from mythical narratives that could be read sequentially from one metope to another, somewhat like a comic strip. Romans tended to display mementos of sacrifice on metopes, like *bucrania*, or skulls of cattle; often alternated with *paterae*, or bowls used to pour oil upon the altar fire. Bramante transformed antique burnt offerings to bloodless Christian sacrifice in San Pietro's Doric frieze. Instead of a *patera*, he had a chalice and paten carved on one metope.

Not all ancient architectural ideas proved useful in the transition to Christian usage. Vitruvius cites the occasional Greek substitution of female or male statuary, in place of columns, as an example of the kind of historical knowledge that should be familiar; he says architects must be able to explain why maidens support the porch roof at the Erechtheum on the Acropolis, by telling a story of subjugation. Although St John the Baptist and St Peter were imprisoned, their trials of ignominy led to martyrdom and exaltation. Therefore, it would break Christian rules of decorum to depict them as permanently subjected statuary supporting a portico. Instead, it is appropriate to paint or sculpt their humiliation in narrative sequences that celebrate their eventual triumph. In addition, Doric columns sustaining a hefty beam, cross-breams, and a solid roof could be a decorous way to convey the

Figure 7 Parts of the Entablature

fortitude of such saints. Doric columns are abstractly anthropomorphic due to their powerful proportions and narrative associations. More literally, the roof-load is channeled through beams to columns with head-like capitals, finally through a foot-like base to the foundation. These anthropomorphic abstractions lead to an appreciation of different "characters" of column typologies.

Santa Susanna in Rome

We witness a meaningful application of Doric architecture at San Pietro in Montorio, but the brusque Doric would be indecorous for a church dedicated to Saint Susanna. Instead, Corinthian columns and capitals would convey her feminine virginity and piety. A century after Bramante built San Pietro in Montorio, the Catholic Reformation architect Carlo Maderno (1556–1629) designed the façade of Santa Susanna to dignify a boxy, early Christian church dedicated to the virgin martyr. Because Susanna died in defiance of Roman authority, Maderno conveyed her integrity through the delicacy of Corinthian columns and her spiritual triumph through the Composite pilasters above. The Corinthian register can be said to represent the young woman's earthly trials, while the Composite conveys her sainthood.

The Corinthian-type capitals that Maderno designed for the church of *Santa Susanna*, on the Quirinale Hill in Rome, derive from Greek antiquity. Two tiers of delicate acanthus leaves and profuse tendrils mask the bell-shaped structure of the capital. The form was invented about 430 BC by the bronze-sculptor, Kallimachos. According to Vitruvius, his inspiration came from observing a tile-covered basket filled with cherished items, set upon the grave of a young girl near Corinth. Approaching the city gates the spring after her death, Kallimachos' imagination was struck by an accident of nature: he noticed that a perennial acanthus plant, with sprouting leaves and stalks, had grown up around the woven-reed container.

Unlike previous generations of Greeks who worked around Athens and Corinth to develop Doric architecture, and a somewhat similar trial-and-error process to perfect Ionic structures among Ionians near Ephesus, Vitruvius reports that the invention of Corinthian capitals was a stroke of genius. The perennial reanimation of the tenacious, but delicate-looking, plant came to symbolize hope. Vitruvius reserved Corinthian for "delicate divinities, so its slender outlines, its flowers, leaves, and ornamental volutes, will lend decorum where it is due."[16]

Maderno's choice of Corinthian is readily comprehensible. The svelte column shafts are cushioned from the foundation by elegantly profiled bases. For the capital, the basket-like bell is enmeshed by articulate leaves, tendrils, and flowers. Rather than the simple Doric architrave, the Corinthian epistylium, or beam-above-the-columns, is profiled with three horizontal facets so we perceive a refined, not severe, strength.

At Santa Susanna the columns are connected to the walls, closely bundled at the main portal and spaced farther apart in lateral stages. They become pilasters, or flattened versions of the column shaft and capital, at the outside corners and are further reduced to brick piers on the lateral wings. These diverse types of Corinthian carry the same beams, brackets, and cornice.

Figure 8 Façade of Santa Susanna

Maderno employed Composite pilasters upon the upper zone of Santa Susanna's façade. The Composite type, developed by Imperial Roman architects as a fusion of Corinthian and Ionic motifs, was used on triumphal arches to commemorate military victories. Maderno probably designated Composite to express St Susanna's triumph through steadfast faith.

Maderno contributed to a century of intensive Italian development of classical form and meaning in additional ways at Santa Susanna. A platter, bearing her severed head, is sculpted above the portal and graphically displays the end of earthly fidelity. The relic rests in an arrowhead-shaped temple pediment that mediates a transition between Corinthian and Composite. The pediment points up toward a sculpted laurel crown within a triumphal arch in the Composite register.

I hope these details from San Pietro in Montorio and Santa Susanna help explain the concept of decorum. Most of us are already familiar with aspects of

Figure 9 Head of Santa Susanna

meaning in classical buildings because they are a foundational part of Western heritage. Denis McNamara emphasizes this point:

> If an architect could invent a way of designing buildings that has greater subtlety, articulateness, specificity, historical association, and conventional clarity than a living, inherited Classical tradition, then by all means, it should be done! If it expresses the Catholic faith's embrace and fulfillment of history better than has been done before, its Truth will be radiant, its completeness will be obvious, and its clarity will ring true ... But because legibility depends upon conventions of the inherited tradition, replacing Classical architecture proves exceedingly difficult.[17]

IV. The basilican plan

Historically, the basilica, or "royal place" in Greek, is the most common form of Christian church. I will discuss the time-honored basilican-type church, characterized by an axial focus from entry to sanctuary. Interest in reviving the basilica is an antidote to recent asymmetrically-planned churches of irregularly-shaped volume. The floor may also slope, auditorium-style, toward to the altar. Dioceses have built many variations on 1950s expressionistic churches, but they do not serve liturgical functions well.

In November 2000, the United States Conference of Catholic Bishops ratified the first official document about American church architecture published after Vatican II. The publication states that a bishop has discretion to "decide that the tabernacle be placed in the sanctuary apart from the altar of celebration or in a separate chapel suitable for adoration and for the private prayer of the faithful."[18] I recall hearing a radio broadcast of the bishops' discussion about the document. While they did not delve into architectural subtleties, as I recall the coverage, the bishops focused on one point: the reserved Holy Eucharist should be the visual focal point in a Catholic church. The best way Catholics can achieve this objective is to predicate newly built churches, small or large, on the basilican model used in the earliest churches built in Rome under Constantine's sponsorship, and in many locations throughout the empire, including Bethlehem.[19]

The most basic basilican structure has a longitudinally-oriented rectangular nave with a flat ceiling. Ideally, the orientation is eastward. One enters from a western vestibule looking toward a well-defined sanctuary, raised several steps. The sanctuary may be a concave apse with the altar and separated tabernacle on axis.

Flanking side aisles can increase the width of the rectilinear volume. The arches or columns that separate nave and aisles sustain the higher central volume, illuminated by north and south clerestory windows. At the northeast and southeast corners of the nave, outward doors would insure fire code exits for parishioners and supplement emergency passage through the vestibule. An organ and choir loft placed above the vestibule is the ideal location for acoustical effectiveness and

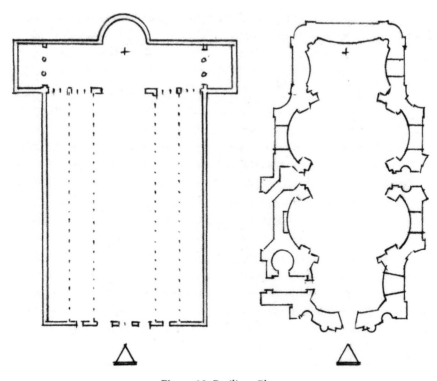

Figure 10 Basilican Plan

liturgical decorum. The overall shape also facilitates acoustics for the readings and preaching.

A modest basilican configuration can be greatly expanded into a massive church or cathedral. One can enlarge the basic components, increase the height of the nave, and add new volumes. A square crossing toward the sanctuary can be extended by north and south transepts to form a cruciform plan.

The patron and architect can determine the exact configuration in response to budget and functional requirements. On any scale, however, the apse shelters the Real Presence and enables the congregation to focus on the eucharistic action of the Mass.

No matter how simple or elaborate the plan, and how modest or lofty its verticality, the basilican-typology does not predict a particular architectural style: the format has served early Christian, Romanesque, Gothic, Renaissance, and Baroque churches and periodic revivals of each style. Although the form originated in ancient Greek civic structures, it was adopted by the Romans, and converted under Constantine to Christian use. Unlike worship in pagan temple complexes, where sacrificial offerings took place outdoors so the altar was placed in front of the stairs and portico of the building, the Christian community worshipped indoors, to focus on the altar and the ambo.[20]

While Byzantine churches eventually developed in a centralized, rather than a basilican manner, Watkin explains the practical and symbolic reasons the Roman church adopted the linear type:

> The new public image of Constantinian Christianity ... sought inspiration not in Roman temple architecture with its obvious pagan associations, but in the aisled basilica which was the most prominent form of public building in Rome and in countless Romanized cities. From the early fourth century the Christian assembly halls consisted of various combinations of the following basilical features: the rectangular plan, the timber roof with trusses either exposed or concealed by a flat ceiling, the side aisles, sometimes colonnaded, the high clerestory, and always the tribunal, often apsed, at the far end, formerly containing the magistrate's seat and now the bishop's seat with the altar in front of him. A splendid early example was ... the Lateran Basilica of San Giovanni in Laterano, which Constantine began in c. 313.[21]

The basilican form spread and developed with the expansion of the faith throughout the Mediterranean and into Northern Europe. Centralized martyria, cylindrical churches, and octagonal baptisteries were exceptions to this dominant form. Central-plan types command a large share in histories of early Christian, Romanesque, and Renaissance accomplishments because they are fascinating. Architects were, and are, attracted to the spatial complexity, grandeur, and mesmerizing concentric symmetry a central plan creates. A center focus is appropriate for special functions, such as the exquisite reliquary chapel Guarino Guarini (1624–84) designed for the Holy Shroud in Torino. Most frequently, however, the seemingly constricted, but remarkably adaptable format of the basilica provides an armature for diverse architectural styles, functional nuances, and methods of construction to flourish.

After 1500 brilliantly persuasive artist/architects like Leonardo da Vinci and Michelangelo proposed monumental centrally-planned churches. Michelangelo's ideas were carried out within three apses defined by gigantic pilasters built to encircle the tomb of St Peter at the Vatican. Although Michelangelo hoped the dome he planned for the Vatican would crown a centralized structure, in the early seventeenth century a Catholic Reformation desire to emulate early Christian basilicas and emphasize the Roman origins of Christianity in Western Europe, resulted in extending a capacious nave toward the Tiber.

The stone-mason turned architect, Francesco Borromini (1599-1667), designed a magnificent elevation for the back wall of Carlo Maderno's extended nave at St Peter's. After beginning independent practice, Borromini designed the tiny San Carlo alle Quattro Fontane in Rome, almost wholly surmounted by a longitudinal oval dome. His design mediated between a centralized and longitudinal arrangement.

Saint John Lateran Basilica, Rome

> What was going on here when these walls were rising, is going on here and now
> when believers in Christ are being gathered together. It's by believing, you see,
> that beams and stones, as it were, are being hewn out of the forests and the
> mountains; but when they are catechized, baptized, formed, it's as though they
> are being chipped and chiseled, straightened out, planed by the hands of
> carpenters and masons. However, they don't make a house for the Lord unless
> and until they are mortised and cemented together by charity. (St Augustine,
> Sermon 336)[22]

For the Jubilee of 1650, Francesco Borromini was entrusted to extensively shore-
up and reconfigure the nave of Rome's cathedral and arch-basilica, San Giovanni
in Laterano, a building so important to the church that its dedication is celebrated
as a feast each November and its full name includes the words "Mother and Head
of all the Churches of the *Urbe* and *Orbe*." Borromini solidified the weakened
structure that had been repeatedly damaged by fire, earthquake, and neglect. In
doing so, he imparted Roman classicism to the grand nave and the unusual pairs
of side aisles parallel to it. After consolidating the armature of what remained of
Constantine's gift to monumental Christian architecture, Borromini created a
unified interior appearance, at once old and new. He merged the Hadrianic
elegance of the Pantheon with the processional monumentality of the new San
Pietro Vaticano. To enhance the progression, Borromini's sculptors reinforced the
history of the apostles through statuary and iconographic panels in relief. A fully-
intact St Bartholomew, for example, lunges outward from an aedicula displaying
his flayed skin over one forearm, while also grasping the knife of his martyrdom.
The fourth-century structural armature of San Giovanni in Laterano persists
beneath the architectural skin. Borromini's consolidation of strength and beauty
remains a testament to Catholic Reformation fervor.

V. Style

We have seen how Vitruvius conveyed Greek distinctions of Doric, Ionic, and
Corinthian proportion, detail and narrative meaning through symmetria and
decorum. Specifics can change in response to a broad question: in what style shall
we build? We can perceive the "beauty of Thy House" within churches that look
different from one another. People who appreciate or detest one stylistic expression
of form and decoration make subjective judgments based on aesthetic norms,
whether cultural, generational, or nationalistic. Diverse styles are not intrinsically
ugly or beautiful; no matter how relativistic this sounds, they are simply different.
How well a style is expressed in a particular building constitutes its beauty,
calculated by connoisseurship.

For over seventeen hundred years, Catholic patrons, architects, and builders
developed many visual modes to convey the spiritual beauty of a church. The job
of architectural historians like David Watkin or John Morley,[23] a historian of

Western furniture, is to explain and illustrate the tangible styles people have developed and subsequent ways others have revived them. Their books are largely illustrated by Catholic buildings and furnishings because the Church was the prime patron and the best preserver between the emperors Constantine and Napoleon.

Morley observes that architects and artists first develop means of expression that distinguish their cultures. These are the primary artifacts by which we perceive cultural change. With time, artisans follow suit. Cabinetmakers, for example, respond to architectural impetus with commensurate furniture to form cohesive environments. We can discuss early Christian, Romanesque, Gothic, or Baroque as meaningful concepts by observing how they are distinct while detecting subtle similarities. The more deeply we understand various styles, the more readily we perceive their diffusion and, in many cases, their incorporation of indigenous traditions.

In this context we may recall the declaration of the Second Vatican Council that the "church has not regarded any style of art as its own: rather, it has taken in what has been current in every age, in the light of the temperaments of peoples, their circumstances, and the needs of the various rites" (*Sacrosanctum Concilium*, 123). This is important to remember in light of the various prejudices as to a particular style, such as Gothic, being the only "true" Catholic architecture.[24] Periodically, patrons and architects redefine aesthetic standards of perfection through both profound study and inchoate influence. They investigate paradigms to emulate and accommodate them to regional and pragmatic factors. This synthetic process reanimates old—even ancient—styles for modern expression. Such emulation is appropriate not only in church structures, but in new liturgical furnishings, implements, and vestments.

I want to define and defend the term *style* as describing distinctly different, yet often recognizable and repeatable visual and intellectual patterns characterized by tenacious longevity. Too often, style is confused with fashion. The style section of a Sunday newspaper is a medium of fashion trends, tracking mercurial shifts for people to change their look or transform the living room. Even the monikers change rapidly. Some years ago the weekend edition of the *Wall Street Journal* replaced the standard above "style, fashion . . . gear, gadgets" to "Off Duty."

I will use an example of furniture to discuss style, instead of the less tangible medium of architecture. Style, for John Morley, "describes the dominant visual culture . . . that dictated the general appearance of furniture" and further, "furniture is judged to be of a particular period or country by its style . . . if the form of a chair were constant and unchanging, it would become superfluous to speak of its 'style.'"[25]

Klismos and Throne

Two examples of Greek chairs tell stylistic stories: the domestic *klismos* and the regal throne. *Klismoi* are depicted on Greek vases more frequently than the rarified seat of power. The curvaceous *klismos* marked distinction, not only in antiquity, but in a late eighteen-century European revival. Architects re-introduced the idea of *klismos*-type chairs while assimilating the Grecian architectural style from publications of archaeological expeditions. Throughout the nineteenth century, European and American designers and chair-makers suitably adapted the elegant *klismos* for Grecian drawing rooms. The style was revived periodically during the twentieth.

The Greek throne, with straight turned legs, arm rests, and a high back, imitated a Persian prototype. The Romans, and then Byzantine Christians, perpetuated the throne-style chair. We also recognize it in manuscript depictions of royal Carolingians and eleventh-century ivory carvings of Christ in benediction. The style of an ancient Persian and Greek throne continues to signify the authority of a bishop.

In 1845, the Italian architect Palagio Palagi (1775–1860) redesigned the interiors of the Royal Palace in Torino. In one corner of the King's Audience Hall he located a chapel recess. A pair of doors could close off view of the altar during secular visitations, but when open for Mass communicants might notice an unusual scene on the front altar panel. A relief carving depicts Christ seated at the center of a wide table in the act of breaking bread. We might think of the Last Supper, but this subject shows the Inn at Emmaus, not the Upper Room. Two disciples on either end are startled once they recognize Our Lord. One disciple is half-standing, braced with hands grasping the table edge, caught in a movement which pushes a *klismos* backward. The other clutches the table-end and seems transfixed upon his throne-like chair. Palagi designed many elaborate *klismos* chairs throughout the palace as well as a regal throne. It is most unlikely that the roadside inn at Emmaus contained chairs of such distinction, but Palagi reflected the dignity of the Gospel account with stylistic furniture that courtiers would recognize as both ancient and current. By depicting them on the altar, Palagi may also have intended a visual metaphor of the Resurrection: Jesus is for East and West, for king and slave, for rich and poor.

We should remember that Catholics have sought classical wholeness and references to antiquity in churches throughout many periods and in diverse places. We should have confidence to open this opportunity again. Early Christian,

Figure 11 Throne and *Klismos* at Emmaus

Romanesque, and Catholic Reformation churches display the classical principles of clarity, balance, and meaningful expressions through columns, round arches, and other elements of architectural vocabulary. The early Christian adaptation of the secular Roman basilica created the linear vestibule-to nave-to sanctuary plan that has served function well through many stylistic changes, including the Gothic. The builders of Romanesque churches in Southern France incorporated ancient spoils of column shafts and capitals into façades with apparent delight. They also carved new imitations to fill-in gaps to literally continue classical tradition. The long Italian Renaissance provides the most thorough synthesis of classical theory, changing some concepts and deepening others. Renaissance architects provided not only opulent structures, but excellent models for *oeconomia*. Palladio called Vitruvius his "master and guide."[26]

Conclusion

I have approached the topic of architecture in the service of the Catholic Church as a broad effort to encourage radically different ways to design and build "of our time." I have spent my career advocating the reintegration of classical planning, *symmetria*, and iconic meanings learned from traditional resources. The ancient and extended Renaissance periods of classical reanimation predominate as personal points of reference. I hope the reader will interpret these venerable techniques in light of other worthy paradigms.

The keen desire of young Catholics to integrate liturgical and theological traditions in vital contemporary practice is parallel, and similarly motivated, for some young architects, painters, makers of statuary, and artisans. I hope this essay helps potential patrons to build churches with light for iconic arts and acoustics for richly developed music. I encourage patrons to integrate the varied skills and responsibilities balanced by their predecessors, who expected great architects to integrate history and archeology for expressive use of renewed architectural languages. Contemporary patrons and architects should work to create churches that express the strength, function, and beauty of our faith.

Notes

1   See for example: Aidan Nichols, *Redeeming Beauty: Soundings in Aesthetics* (Aldershot: Ashgate Publishing, 2007), chapter 6 "The French Dominicans and the Journal *L'Art sacré*."

2   Carlo Borromeo, *Instructiones Fabricae et Supellectilis Ecclesiasticae* (Città del Vaticano: Libreria Editrice Vaticana, 2000). John Alexander's *From the Renaissance to the Counter-Reformation: The Architectural Patronage of Carlo Borromeo during the Reign of Pius IV* is an excellent resource on Borromeo in English (Rome: Bulzoni, 2007).

3   Denis McNamara, *Heavenly City: The Architectural Tradition of Catholic Chicago* (Chicago: Liturgy Training Publications, 2005).

4   Robert Tavernor gives an excellent account of Vitruvius in the introduction to Richard Schofield's translation, *On Architecture* (London: Penguin Books, 2009).

5 J.J. Coulton, *Ancient Greek Architects at Work: Problems of Structure and Design* (Ithaca: Cornell University Press, 1977).

6 Daniele Barbaro: *I Dieci Libri dell'Architecttura di M. Vitruvio, Tradotti & Commentati da Mons. Daniel Barbaro: in piùcommoda forma ridotti* (Venice: Francesco de'Franceschi, 1567; Reprint, Milan: Edizioni II Polifilo, 1987 & Rome: Bardi Editore, 1993).

7 Vitruvius: I, II, 2, Thomas Gordon Smith, *Vitruvius on Architecture* (New York: Monacelli, 2003) p. 67.

8 Lothar Haselberger, "The Construction Plans for the Temple of Apollo at Didyma," *Scientific American* 253 (1985), pp. 126–32.

9 Vitruvius: VII, Introduction, 16; Vitruvius, Morris Hicky Morgan (trans.), *The Ten Books on Architecture* (Cambridge: Harvard University Press, 1914) p. 200.

10 I take this terminology of discernment from Albert Sack's *Fine Points of Early American Furniture* (Atglen PA: Schiffer Publishing; 1950; new edition, 2007).

11 James Stuart and Nicholas Revett, *The Antiquities of Athens, Volume the Second* (London: John Nichols, 1787), pp. 1–12.

12 William Chambers, *A Treatise on the Decorative Part of Civil Architecture*, 3rd edn (London: Smeeton, 1791; reprinted by Benjamin Blom, 1968) p. 19.

13 Vitruvius: I, II, 8, Morgan, *The Ten Books on Architecture*, p. 16.

14 Vitruvius: I, II, 5; Smith, *Vitruvius on Architecture*, p. 68.

15 Vitruvius: IV, III, 3; ibid., p. 123.

16 Vitruvius: I, II, 5; ibid., p. 69.

17 Denis McNamara, *Catholic Church Architect and the Spirit of the Liturgy* (Hillenbrand Books, Chicago, 2009), p. 105.

18 National Conference of Catholic Bishops, *Built of Living Stones: Art Architecture, and Worship* (Washington DC: United States Catholic Conference, 2000), § 74.

19 Richard Krautheimer, *Rome: Profile of a City, 312–1308* (New Jersey: Princeton University Press, 1980).

20 Sabine G. MacCormack, *Art and Ceremony in Late Antiquity* (Berkeley: University of California Press, 1990).

21 David Watkin, *A History of Western Architecture* (New York: Watson-Guptill Publications, 2000), pp. 89–90.

22 St Augustine, Sermon 336, "At the dedication of a Church," *Sermons on the Saints, 306–340A*, Edmund Hill (trans.), *Works of St Augustine* III/9 (Hyde Park, NY: New City Press, 1994), p. 267.

23 John Morley, *The History of Furniture: Twenty-Five Centuries of Style and Design in the Western Tradition* (New York: Little Brown & Co. 1999).

24 Cf. David Watkin, *Morality and Architecture* (Chicago: University of Chicago Press, 1977), who traces the connection between the claim by Pugin in the nineteenth century that Gothic was the only morally acceptable form of architecture to similar claims put forward in favor of Modernism in the twentieth.

25 Morley, *The History of Furniture*, pp. 7, 12.

26 A. Andrea Palladio, *I Quattro Libri* (1570), R. Tavernor & R. Schofield (trans.), *Four Books on Architecture* (Cambridge: MIT Press, 2002), p. 5.

Bibliography

Alexander, J., *From the Renaissance to the Counter-Reformation: The Architectural Patronage of Carlo Borromeo during the Reign of Pius IV* (Rome: Bulzoni, 2007).

Barbaro, D., *I Dieci Libri dell'Architecttura di M. Vitruvio, Tradotti & Commentati da Mons. Daniel Barbaro: in piùcommoda forma ridotti* (Venice: Francesco de'Franceschi, 1567); Reprints: Milan: Edizioni II Polifilo (1987); Rome: Bardi Editore (1993).
Benedict XVI, Apostolic Exhortation *Sacramentum Caritatis*, February 22, 2007.
Borromeo, C., *Instructiones Fabricae et Supellectilis Ecclesiasticae* (1577), (Città del Vaticano: Libreria Editrice Vaticana, 2000).
Boucher, B., *Andrea Palladio: The Architect in his Time* (2nd edn) (New York: Abbeville Press, 2007).
Chambers, W., *A Treatise on the Decorative Part of Civil Architecture,* (3rd edn, 1791); Reprint: (London: Benjamin Blom, 1968).
Connors, J., *Borromini and the Roman Oratory: Style and Society,* (Cambridge: MIT Press, 1980).
Coulton, J.J., *Ancient Greek Architects at Work: Problems of Structure and Design* (Ithaca: Cornell University Press, 1977).
Haselberger, L., "The Construction Plans for the Temple of Apollo at Didyma," *Scientific American* 253 (1985), pp. 126–32.
Krautheimer, R., *Rome: Profile of a City, 312–1308* (New Jersey: Princeton University Press, 1980).
MacCormack, S.G., *Art and Ceremony in Late Antiquity* (Berkeley: University of California Press, 1990).
McNamara, D.R., *Heavenly City: The Architectural Tradition of Catholic Chicago* (Chicago: Liturgy Training Publications, 2005).
—— *Catholic Church Architecture and the Spirit of the Liturgy* (Chicago: Hillenbrand Books, 2009).
Morley, J., *The History of Furniture: Twenty-Five Centuries of Style and Design in the Western Tradition* (New York: Little Brown & Co., 1999).
National Conference of Catholic Bishops, *Built of Living Stones: Art, Architecture, and Worship* (Washington DC: United States Catholic Conference, 2000).
Nichols, A., *Redeeming Beauty: Soundings in Sacred Aesthetics* (Farnham: Ashgate Publishing, 2007).
Palladio, A., *I Quattro Libri* (1570); R. Tavernor & R. Schofield (trans.) *Four Books on Architecture*, 2nd edn (Cambridge: MIT Press, 2002).
Portoghesi, P., *Francesco Borromini,* 2nd edn (Milan: Electa Editrice, 1984).
Rowland, I.D. & T.N. Howe, *Vitruvius: Ten Books on Architecture* (Cambridge: Cambridge University Press, 1999).
Sack, A., *Fine Points of Furniture: Early American* (Atglen, PA: Schiffer Publishing, 1950; revised 2007).
Second Vatican Council, Constitution on the Sacred Liturgy *Sacrosanctum Concilium*, December 4, 1963.
Scott, J.B., *Architecture for the Shroud: Relic and Ritual in Turin* (Chicago: University of Chicago Press, 2003).
Schofield, R. (trans.) & R. Tavernor, *On Architecture* (London: Penguin Books, 2009).
—— (translators), *The Four Books on Architecture,* 2nd edn (Cambridge: MIT Press, 2002).
Smith, T.G., *Classical Architecture: Rule and Invention* (Layton, UT: Gibbs M. Smith, Inc., 1988).
—— *Vitruvius on Architecture* (New York: Monacelli Press, 2003).
Stuart, J. & Revett, N., (1787), *The Antiquities of Athens, Volume the Third* (London: John Nichols, 1787; reprint: New York: Princeton Architectural Press, 2008).

Vignola, B., *Regola delli cinque ordini d'architectettura* (1562); ET: Metrovic, B., *Canon of the Five Orders of Architecture* (New York: Acanthus Press, 1999).

Vitruvius, P., M.H. Morgan (trans.), *The Ten Books on Architecture* (Boston: Harvard University Press, 1914; reprinted: New York: Dover, 1960). See also the translation by R. Schofield (London: Penguin, 2009).

Watkin, D., *Morality in Architecture* (Chicago: University of Chicago Press, 1977).

—— *A History of Western Architecture,* 4th edn (London: Calmann & King, 2005).

Chapter 21

THE *USUS ANTIQUIOR*—ITS HISTORY AND IMPORTANCE IN THE CHURCH AFTER THE SECOND VATICAN COUNCIL

Alcuin Reid

Introduction

On July 7, 2007, the day of the publication of Pope Benedict XVI's (1927–; 2005–13) motu proprio *Summorum Pontificum,* the Italian Bishop Luca Brandolini (1933–), of Sora-Aquino-Pontecorvo, spoke to *La Repubblica*:

> This day is for me a day of grief. I have a lump in my throat and I do not manage to hold back my tears . . . I cannot hide my sadness for the putting aside of one of the most important reforms of the Second Vatican Council . . . I am living the saddest day of my life as a priest, as a bishop, and as a man . . .
>
> It is a day of grief, not only for me, but for many who lived and worked in the Second Vatican Council. Today, a reform for which so many laboured, at the cost of great sacrifices, animated solely by the wish to renew the Church, has been cancelled . . . today an important reform of the Council was undermined . . .
>
> The episcopal ring which I carry on my finger belonged to Archbishop Annibale Bugnini, the father of the Conciliar liturgical reform. I was, at the time of the Council, a disciple of his and a close co-worker. I was close to him when he worked in that reform and I always recall with how much passion he worked for liturgical renewal. Now, his work has been cancelled.
>
> I will obey, because I care for the Holy Father. I have for him the same sentiment that a son has for his father. And then, as a bishop, I am bound to obedience. Yet, in my heart, I suffer deeply. I feel as if wounded in my heart, and I cannot help saying it.[1]

Bishop Brandolini's reaction to the freeing of the *usus antiquior*—the older form of the Roman rite (which is known by different names)[2]—from the strictures that had impeded its celebration since the liturgical rites produced following the Second Vatican Council were promulgated by Blessed Paul VI (1897; 1963–78), is an eloquent testimony to the significance of this act in liturgical history.[3] Whilst his language is emotive, it accurately reflects the passion of many in respect of both the authoritative imposition of the newer liturgical rites and the proscription of the older ones from the 1970s onward.

Those decades are now happily consigned to history, yet a study of them is illustrative both in terms of the liturgical issues of that period, and in respect of the importance of the *usus antiquior* in the Church of the twenty-first century. Although there are some for whom *Summorum Pontificum* will never be seen as anything other than a "step backward,"[4] in the ongoing history of the Roman rite it is a most significant step forward indeed.

The History of the *usus antiquior* following the Council

It is clear that there was no smooth transition from the pre-conciliar to the post-conciliar rites. When demonstrated at the 1967 Synod of Bishops, the rite of Mass proposed by the *Consilium* producing the new rites was not at all well received. Following the promulgation of the new *Ordo Missae* in 1969 and the *Instructio Generalis* that prefaced it, a public controversy ensued as a result of the protest against it endorsed by Alfredo Cardinal Ottaviani (1890–1979) and Antonio Cardinal Bacci (1885–1971).[5] Clergy, bishops and laity saw the "new Mass" as something quite distinct from the "old Mass," regardless of their preferences or assessment. Indeed, at his General Audience days before the introduction of "the liturgical innovation of the new rite of the Mass" Paul VI, whilst judging the change apposite, recognized that its introduction would be a "many-sided inconvenience," and cause "the kind of upset caused by every novelty that breaks in on our habits." He was clear that "this novelty is no small thing."[6]

The older *Ordo Missae,* as modified in 1965 and 1967, was to be permitted in Latin until no later than November 28, 1971, after which only the new rite would be permitted, save for elderly or sick priests celebrating with permission and without others present.[7] In practice almost all public celebrations of the Mass used the new rite in the vernacular as soon as this was possible, although the new *Missale Romanum* did not appear until 1970 and it took some time for vernacular versions of the liturgical texts to be finalized.

Prompt and unquestioning obedience to papal authority was a virtue prized by loyal Catholics of all ranks at that time. As John Cardinal Heenan (1905–75), a Council Father and Archbishop of Westminster (who had criticized the direction of the reform at the 1967 Synod of Bishops), wrote in 1969 to a correspondent upset by the prospect of the liturgical changes: "If the Holy Father has decided to reform the liturgy, we must accept it."[8]

As the end of the *vacatio legis* in respect of the adoption of the new *Ordo Missae* approached in November 1971, an historical initiative was coordinated by the London-based Austrian poet and novelist Alfred Marnau (1918–99). Marnau brought together fifty-seven "distinguished writers, scholars, artists and historians" who signed an "ecumenical and non-political" petition to Paul VI which called "to the attention of the Holy See the appalling responsibility it would incur in the history of the human spirit were it to refuse to allow the Traditional Mass to survive, even though this survival took place with other liturgical forms."[9] It was sent to Rome; its text and signatories were made public in *The Times* on July 6, 1971.[10]

Cardinal Heenan, who had continually manifested sympathy towards those upset with the liturgical changes, agreed to help. Paul VI received Heenan on October 29, 1971. After the audience Heenan wrote to ask permission for the occasional celebration of the "so-called Tridentine Mass" in the future, submitting that whilst "most Catholics are quite happy with the new rite … some of the older people (like some of the older priests) would be grateful" if such a permission was granted.[11] The following day Paul VI instructed Father Bugnini (1912–82), Secretary of the Sacred Congregation of Divine Worship, to prepare "a favourable answer."[12]

What came to be known as "the Heenan Indult" was signed on November 5, 1971. It stated that:

> It is permitted to the local Ordinaries of England and Wales to grant that certain groups of the faithful may on special occasions be allowed to participate in the Mass celebrated according to the rites and texts of the former Roman missal. The edition … to be used on these occasions should be that published again by the decree of the Sacred Congregation of Rites (27 January 1965), and with the modifications indicated in the *Instructio altera* (4 May 1967).
>
> This faculty may be granted provided that groups make the request for reasons of genuine devotion, and provided that the permission does not disturb or damage the general communion of the faithful. For this reason the permission is limited to certain groups on special occasions; at all regular and other parish community Masses, the Order of Mass given in the new Roman missal should be used. Since the Eucharist is the sacrament of unity, it is necessary that the use of the Order of Mass given in the former missal should not become a sign or a cause of disunity … For this reason agreement among the bishops of the Episcopal Conference as to how this faculty is to be exercised will be a further guarantee of unity of praxis in this area.[13]

Bugnini wrote to Heenan in an accompanying letter: "His Holiness knows well that Your Eminence will ensure that this permission is granted with that prudence and reserve that this matter requires. It is also very desirable that the permission be given without too much publicity."[14]

But publicity there was. According to *The Tablet* this led "not only to controversy but to confusion."[15] In response to the blithe statement on the front page of the English Catholic paper *The Universe* on November 26, 1971 that: "As from this Sunday … it is forbidden to offer Mass in the Tridentine rite anywhere in the world," *The Times* of December 2, 1971 ran an article, "Pope sanctions traditional Latin Mass in Britain," reporting on the granting of the indult.[16] Bugnini observes that the indult "caused difficulties: for the Holy See and the bishops of other

countries, who were urged to obtain the same faculty; for the Congregation ...
which the most intransigent rebuked for the grant; for its Secretary [Bugnini],
since the Pope had decided to turn to him rather than to the Prefect."[17]

The indult's application varied according to the will of the diocesan bishop—
some refused all requests. Heenan allowed a monthly Mass in the crypt of
Westminster Cathedral and two Masses a year at the high altar—a permission
maintained by his successor from 1975, George Basil Hume OSB (1923–99). It is
to be noted that whilst the permission was not for the pre-conciliar *Ordo Missae*,
but for that as amended by the Holy See in 1965 and 1967,[18] in practice the
stipulation that the amended rite be used was ignored. In 1974, Marnau, by then
Chairman of the Latin Mass Society, gained a further concession when, at his
request and with the advocacy of Cardinal Heenan, the Low Week meeting of the
English and Welsh hierarchy recogniszed the right of Catholics to leave instructions
regarding the rite to be used for their requiem Mass.

The same bishops revisited the question of the rite of the Mass at their 1975
Low Week meeting, issuing a decree insisting that "the unity of the Church is
endangered if the rules laid down by the Holy See for the celebration of Mass are
not observed." The decree strongly criticized "priests who virtually make up their
own Mass" and those "at the other extreme ... who reject all the liturgical reforms,"
noting that "in both cases it is a question of loyalty and obedience to the Holy See."
It recalled that the Heenan indult was given "on the strict condition that all danger
of division would be avoided."[19]

In May 1977 the Prefect of the Congregation for Divine Worship, following a
meeting of dicastery heads and others held in reaction to the occupation of the
church of St Nicholas du Cardonnet in Paris that February (which resulted in the
Archbishop of Paris offering the use of another church for the celebration of
the *usus antiquior*—a measure that had previously been adopted in the French
city of Saint-Etienne),[20] recommended that it was necessary to curb the Heenan
Indult. The Holy See does not seem to have acted on this recommendation, though
by 1980 only six English bishops were making use of it.[21]

The Heenan indult forms but a small part of this history, but its significance lies
in Paul VI's grant of a concession which Bugnini states had already been proposed
to the members and consulters of the Congregation for Divine Worship in April
1971, of whom all save two rejected the proposal as potentially "harmful to the
liturgical reform and the pastoral efforts of bishops to apply it,"[22] and in the fact
that after granting the indult to Heenan, Paul VI was personally "adamant" not to
grant this indult "to anyone else."[23] Yet in 1972 the Congregation did respond that
a diocesan bishop could grant an occasional permission in restricted cases where
there was no question of dissension or of any disturbance of the faithful.[24]

A large role in the history of the continued celebration of "old" Mass in the years
following the introduction of the "new" was, however, played somewhat
unintentionally by Archbishop Marcel Lefebvre CSSp (1905–91). It needs to be
noted as a matter of historical record that Lefebvre was not opposed to liturgical
reform. He was a member of the Central Preparatory Commission for the Council
and as such was very well acquainted with the schema on the Sacred Liturgy which

that Commission examined in March 1962. As a Father of the Second Vatican Council he voted for the Constitution on the Sacred Liturgy in 1963 and signed it.[25] In 1965 he maintained that "some reform and renewal was needed," explaining:

> The first part of the Mass, intended for the instruction of the Faithful and as a means of expressing their faith, clearly stood in need of a means of achieving these ends more plainly, and in some way, more intelligibly. In my humble opinion, two of the reforms proposed for this purpose appeared useful: first the rites of this first part and some vernacular translations.
>
> Let the priest draw near the faithful, communicate with them, pray and sing with them, stand at the lectern to give the readings from the Epistle and Gospel in their tongue, sing the Kyrie, the Gloria and the Credo with the faithful in the traditional divine melodies. All of these are happy reforms restoring to this part of the Mass its true purpose. The arrangement of this teaching part of the rite should set, in the sung Masses of Sunday, the pattern to which other Masses should conform. These aspects of renewal seem excellent.[26]

As Superior General of the Congregation of the Holy Spirit (1962–8), Lefebvre was no *avant-garde* liturgical reformer: he sought to implement *Sacrosanctum Concilium* faithfully and himself concelebrated Mass *versus populum* at least once.[27] The formation of seminarians that he accepted in 1969 at the insistence of others, after his retirement as Superior General and with the necessary canonical permissions, did not involve a fundamental rejection of liturgical reform or of the new *Ordo Missae*.[28] Whilst Lefebvre's attitude to the new liturgy hardened gradually,[29] reflecting the fact that in this period the acceptance or rejection of the "new" Mass became a touchstone of obedience to ecclesiastical authority and of acceptance of the prevailing (and often questionable) interpretations of the Second Vatican Council—an obedience and acceptance demanded as uncritically as any required "pre-Vatican II" —it is simply untrue to assert that "almost immediately after the Council, an organised opposition [to the liturgical reform was] led by ... Lefebvre."[30]

Nevertheless, in the 1970s the question of the acceptance of the post-conciliar liturgical reform became politicized.[31] This puts the English bishops' 1975 monition that the Heenan indult continue "on the strict condition that all danger of division would be avoided" (above) into context. It was in 1975 that the authorization for Lefebvre's growing seminary was withdrawn at the instigation of the Holy See. In the light of Lefebvre's refusal to close it, by May 1976 Paul VI judged it necessary to speak of Lefebvre's retention of the *usus antiquior* in a Consistorial address:

> We must attach to this refusal to respect the liturgical norms laid down a special grievousness in that it introduces division where Christ's love has gathered us together in unity ... For our part, in the name of tradition, we beseech all our children ... to celebrate the rites of the restored liturgy with dignity and fervent devotion. Use of the new *Ordo Missae* is in no way left up to the choice of priests or people.[32]

In June 1976, Lefebvre proceeded with ordinations against the explicit command of Paul VI and was consequently suspended *a divinis*.[33] After granting Lefebvre's request to be received the following September 11, Paul VI wrote at length explaining his stance. In respect of the liturgical reform and the retention of the *usus antiquior* by Lefebvre he insisted:

> The reason we have made the judgement, as a matter of general principle, to brook no delays in this regard or to allow no exceptions is the spiritual growth and unity of the whole ecclesial community; for Catholics the *Ordo Missae* of the Roman rite is a singular sign of their unity. As for you, the former rite of Mass is a sign of your false ecclesiology and a matter on which to assail the Council and its work of reform ...
>
> In the Church there is room for what is called pluralism, but only in things lawful and only within the limits of obedience. They have no understanding of this who flatly reject the reform of the liturgy ...
>
> We thus cannot bow to your demands, because they involve activities that are the consequences of your rebellion against the one, true Church. You can be sure that this inflexibility does not stem from a refusal to allow concession on points of liturgy or discipline, but from the fact that the import and gravity of your activities are such that to accede would mean our opening the way to an utterly false conception of the Church and tradition.[34]

Paul VI had indeed made a concession in liturgical discipline for Heenan. But the motivation for his refusal to do so for Lefebvre is clear. So too is his constant demand for unquestioning and immediate obedience and trust—something both strikingly ultramontane and, arguably, undermined by Paul VI's *volte face* toward the Primate of Hungary, József Cardinal Mindszenty (1892–1975) in December 1973, whom he stripped of his title and office in spite of earlier assurances to the contrary.[35]

Thus, in the midst of the widespread post-conciliar theological and pastoral turmoil, including liturgical disobedience if not anarchy in some places,[36] the celebration of the *usus antiquior* was excluded *a priori* as a matter of obedience and of loyalty to the Pope and to the Council. Supporters were labelled with the pejorative term *intégristes*, and held *a priori* to be people tied to the past with closed minds who rejected the modern world, for whom the Mass of Paul VI was the last straw, a point of rupture with which there could be no compromise. The old Mass was regarded as the banner under which such ecclesiastical reactionaries—thought also to be linked to political *integrisme*—marched.[37]

This highly charged atmosphere suffocated any consideration of the possible pastoral value of allowing the older rites to continue requiring submission to the "package" that was "the Council" was placed before pastoral concerns. In such an environment, any assertion of a distinction between the mandate of the Council's Constitution on the Sacred Liturgy and the liturgical reforms implemented in its name—by Paul VI—was widely regarded as treasonable.

The ironic reality was that in this period clergy could adapt, change or even mutilate the liturgy of the missal of Paul VI without much fear of sanction, but those who used the older rites could expect prompt proscription by authority. As the Bishop of Metz, France, explained in 1979 (an article republished by the Holy See): "some make the old missal the symbol of their opposition to the Council, the symbol of their opposition to the application [of it] made by the Pope and the bishops of the entire world."[38]

In respect of Lefebvre, an *impasse* was reached to which the personalities of both Lefebvre and Paul VI, and of those who advised them,[39] certainly contributed. Paul VI's remarks in a 1977 interview with Jean Guitton are illustrative: "I would be ready to authorise the Mass of Pius V; I have celebrated it all my life. But this rite has become a symbol ... the symbol of an opposition to the Council. My duty as pope is to apply the Council."[40]

Whilst an evaluation of these factors is beyond our scope here, it is historically important to note that Lefebvre's tenacity was a significant factor in the continuance of the Western Church's older rites following the Second Vatican Council, though individual priests, one other bishop—Antônio de Castro Mayer (1904–91), Bishop of Campos, Brazil—and some religious communities did all they could, in spite of significant pressure, to retain the ancient liturgical rites. Bugnini notes that the French abbey of Fontgombault was "conspicuous" in its wish to do this by arguing that the older rites were more suited to contemplative monks. However in the end its abbot, Dom Jean Roy (1921–77), capitulated and adopted the new liturgical books.[41] Lay organizations, most prominently the *Foederatio Internationalis Una Voce* (founded in 1964), also contributed to the promotion of the ancient rites at different levels.

Another issue in the final years of the pontificate of Paul VI was the question of the canonical status of the older rites. The 1976 study of a Professor of Canon Law at the University of Florence, Count Neri Capponi (1925–), "Alcune considerazioni giuridiche in materia di riforma liturgica," published in English in 1979 as *Some Juridical Considerations on the Reform of the Liturgy*,[42] was not the first of its kind,[43] but was perhaps the most widely circulated. It asserted that the legislative acts promulgating the "new" Mass, and the subsequent statements of the Holy See asserting its exclusivity, did not validly canonically *abrogate* the continued use of the "old" Mass.[44] Furthermore, it held that "at least by virtue of established custom, all celebrants should be free to use [the ancient Roman rite] and all the faithful to take part in it."[45] These arguments gained considerable following and gave a sound canonical foundation to individuals and groups continuing to use the older rites in the pontificate of Paul VI and beyond his death on August 6, 1978.

But thirty-three days after his election, on November 18, 1978, St John Paul II (1920; 1978–2005) received Archbishop Lefebvre in audience. The new pontiff had a different outlook, as Lefebvre's account of the audience relates. In respect of the continued use of the older rites, Lefebvre quotes John Paul II as observing: "these liturgical questions: they are disciplinary questions, disciplinary: perhaps we had better look into the question."[46]

And that the Holy See did.[47] It is clear that by 1980, as the Prefect of the Congregation for the Doctrine of the Faith, Franjo Cardinal Šeper (1905–81), wrote to Lefebvre, "the Holy Father could envisage authorising the celebration of Holy Mass according to the rites of the Roman Missal before the reform of 1969."[48]

Indeed, in June 1980 John Paul II authorized James Cardinal Knox (1914–83), Prefect of the Congregation for Sacraments and Divine Worship, to survey local Ordinaries in respect of the use of Latin in the liturgy and of the presence in their territories of individuals or groups wishing the so-called "Tridentine" Mass. From the results of this enquiry, published in December 1981, the Congregation concluded that the vast majority of the episcopate believed that there was little if any issue to be dealt with and that a concession for the continued use of the older rites was not opportune—in fact that it could bring about "an attitude of contempt in respect of what was established by the Second Vatican Council and by the Holy Father, which would be a grave wound against the communion and unity of the Church."[49]

Lefebvre commented on this survey in a letter to Cardinal Šeper's successor, Joseph Cardinal Ratzinger, in January 1982, asserting that it "served to veil the Pope's eyes to the actual situation." "The bishops themselves are very often unaware of how extensive these groups are, for they are not in touch with them," he claimed.[50] Examination of the published data suggests that he had a point.[51]

As Prefect of the Congregation for the Doctrine of the Faith, Ratzinger held meetings with relevant curial cardinals and officials in November 1982 and April 1983 to consider *both* the question of Lefebvre's regularization and liturgical questions in general. It was in this dual context that the question of a limited extension of permission to celebrate the old Mass was considered anew.[52]

These meetings bore fruit following the April 1984 appointment of Paul Augustin Mayer OSB (1911–2010) as Prefect of the Congregation for Divine Worship when, on October 3, 1984 by means of the circular letter *Quattuor Abhinc Annos* (and not decree)[53] the Congregation granted an indult by means of which diocesan bishops were granted the faculty to permit the celebration of Mass according to the 1962 *Missale Romanum*, in Latin and without any admixture of the new and old rites, by groups who do not "call into question the legitimacy and doctrinal exactitude" of the 1970 missal. These celebrations were permitted in churches or oratories indicated by the bishop, and not normally parish churches "on the days and under the conditions fixed by the bishop." After one year, bishops were required to inform the Congregation of any concessions granted. The indult, "indicative of the common Father's solicitude for all his children," was not to be used in a way to "prejudice the faithful observance of the liturgical reform in the life of the respective ecclesial communities."[54]

Later the same month, a meeting of the Presidents and Secretaries of National Liturgical Commissions convened by the Congregation for Divine Worship took place in Rome. Under the presidency of ICEL Chairman Archbishop Denis Hurley OMI (1915–2004) and with ICEL's Executive Secretary, John R. Page, as secretary, the English language group meeting—the largest, comprising representatives of thirty-two episcopal conferences, including twenty-seven bishops—approved a report containing resolutions. The second resolution expressed "grave concern, regret and dismay" in the light of *Quattuor Abhinc Annos*, and stated that it:

Appears to be a movement away from the ecclesiology of the Second Vatican Council with its insistence on the active involvement of the whole people of God (according to the different functions and ministries) in the eucharistic celebration ...

Seems to give support to those who have resisted the liturgical renewal and seems to demonstrate a lack of consideration for all those who, at great personal cost and with great difficulty, did in fact accept the liturgical reform and who in time wholeheartedly embraced the desires of the Council ...

Seems to violate the collegial sense of the worldwide episcopate, 98 percent of whom ... responded that this was not a problem in the Church but rather ... the concern of a tiny minority who have contrived to create the impression that it is a much greater issue than it is ...

Appears to be a subversion ... in that the responsibility of both the Apostolic See and an Episcopal Conference is removed and the authority over so important a question is left to the local bishop.[55]

Worship adds that these resolutions voiced "concerns expressed in other group meetings or in the reports of the conferences."[56]

These concerns speak for themselves and of their times. The concern that an individual diocesan bishop was competent to grant permission for the use of the 1962 missal is particularly noteworthy for its implicit fear that some bishops might in fact grant such permission in spite of the preferences of their episcopal neighbors, or of what the episcopal conference might approve were the decision to be left to it. So too, the identification of external liturgical participation and the Council's ecclesiology, is of significance.

In 1986, in response to a survey of the indult's application in thirty American dioceses, the editor of *Worship*, Aelred Tegels OSB (1922–2003), concluded that "there is no general demand for a return to the Tridentine Mass." He continued:

There have been relatively few requests, indeed none in many dioceses. Attendance at scheduled celebrations is, on the whole, quite small ... and it does not seem to be increasing. The level of participation is generally minimal and, with very few exceptions there is little or no attempt to distinguish ministerial roles ... It seems that the people who regularly attend these celebrations are simply not receptive to the program of liturgical renewal mandated by Vatican II. If this were not so, why would they not be content with the celebration, in Latin, of the ... Missal of Paul VI? ... there is disturbing evidence that in some places at least, where regular Sunday celebrations are allowed, and particularly where the diocesan chancery does not exercise sufficient control by designating the place of celebration and the presider, the people who attend these celebrations conceive of themselves as forming a quasi-parish and withdraw in effect from the worship and life of the local church.

Tegels concluded that if this situation "throughout this country and throughout the world" was found to be similar, "we should hope for the revocation of what many regarded from the very beginning as an unwarranted and very unwise concession."[57]

No summary of the reports sent by the world's bishops to the Holy See has been published. However, in light of them and of at least one other, submitted by the *Foederatio Internationalis Una Voce*, Cardinal Mayer asked John Paul II to form a commission of cardinals to consider new or amended legislation in the light of experience following *Quattuor Abhinc Annos*. The Pope chose Cardinals Mayer, Ratzinger, Agostino Casaroli (1914–98), Silvio Oddi (1910–2001), Alfons Maria Stickler SDB (1910–2007), Bernard Gantin (1922–2008), Antonio Innocenti (1915–2008), Pietro Palazzini (1912–2000), and Jozef Tomko (1924–).[58]

They met on December 12, 1986. The Cardinals were asked to consider whether Paul VI authorized the bishops to forbid the celebration of the traditional Mass and whether a priest had the right to celebrate the traditional Mass in public and in private without restriction, even against the wishes of the local bishop. They were also asked to advise the Pope as to how the older Mass could be better integrated into ecclesial life—if they judged it to be apposite.

Cardinal Mayer was received by John Paul II on February 7, 1987 and presented the Commission's affirmative response to both questions (to the first, 8 to1, the second, unanimous)[59]—responses consonant with the canonical arguments of Count Capponi and which reflected the jurisprudence of the Holy See, which, on appeal, upheld the right of priests to celebrate the *usus antiquior*.[60] Mayer presented the Commission's recommendations for promoting more Latin in the liturgy and for allowing wider use of the 1962 missal:

1. In the liturgy of the Roman rite, due respect shall be accorded to the Latin language. Bishops shall see to it that in all major locations in their dioceses at least one Mass in Latin is celebrated on Sundays and Holydays. At these Masses the readings may also be recited in the vernacular.
2. In their "private" Masses priests may always use the Latin language.
3. For Masses celebrated in Latin—whether with or without a congregation— the celebrant may choose freely between the Roman missal of Paul VI (1970) and that of John XXIII (1962).
4. If the celebrant chooses the Missal of Paul VI, he must follow the rubrics thereof.
5. If the celebrant chooses the Missal of John XXIII, he must follow its rubrics, but may:
   - use either Latin or the vernacular for the readings
   - have recourse to the additional Prefaces and Prayers of the Proper contained in the Missal of Paul VI and add Intercessions ("preces universales").
6. The liturgical calendar to be used is that applying to the missal which the celebrant has chosen to follow.[61]

These recommendations may be said to be the fruit of more mature consideration made possible by the openness of John Paul II to the "disciplinary" nature of the question of the liturgy, as the review of them given by Darío Cardinal Castrillón Hoyos (1929–) in 2008 indicates.[62] The desire to regularise Lefebvre's growing Society of Saint Pius X was an important factor, certainly, but the Cardinals *also* recognized the wider right of clergy and laity to the older liturgy if they wished.

From July 1987 the Holy See, in particular Cardinal Ratzinger, worked assiduously to achieve the regularization of the Society of St Pius X, in the end without success. In spite of everything that was offered, including an episcopal successor, Lefebvre consecrated four priests to the episcopate without papal mandate on June 30, 1988.[63] The resultant Motu Proprio *Ecclesia Dei Adflicta* of July 2, 1988 stated that:

> It is necessary that all the Pastors and the other faithful have a new awareness, not only of the lawfulness but also of the richness for the Church of a diversity of charisms, traditions of spirituality and apostolate, which also constitutes the beauty of unity in variety: of that blended "harmony" which the earthly Church raises up to Heaven under the impulse of the Holy Spirit (5a).

In it John Paul II decreed that:

> A *Commission* [be] instituted whose task it will be to collaborate with the bishops, with the Departments of the Roman curia and with the circles concerned, for the purpose of facilitating full ecclesial communion of priests, seminarians, religious communities or individuals until now linked in various ways to the Fraternity founded by Mons. Lefebvre, who may wish to remain united to the Successor of Peter in the Catholic Church, while preserving their spiritual and liturgical traditions, in the light of the Protocol signed on 5 May last by Cardinal Ratzinger and Mons. Lefebvre (6 a).

And, most significantly, the Pope decreed that "respect must *everywhere* be shown for the feelings of all those who are attached to the Latin liturgical tradition, by a wide and generous application of the directives already issued..." (6 c, emphasis added).

Whilst decreeing that generosity was necessary, *Ecclesia Dei adflicta* did not expand the provisions of *Quattuor Abhinc Annos*. The *Ecclesia Dei* Commission established in its wake soon found that it had to deal with significant numbers of individuals and groups formerly associated with Archbishop Lefebvre who did not wish to be associated with his schismatic acts. The provisions of *Quattuor Abhinc Annos* were inadequate to deal with people who had retained—and in some cases, who had known nothing other than—a full liturgical and sacramental life according to the *usus antiquior.*

On October 18, 1988 John Paul II granted Cardinal Mayer particular faculties to facilitate the working of the Commission. These included the erection of the Fraternity of St Peter for priests and seminarians formerly of the Society of St Pius X and the faculty of "granting *to all who ask for it* the use of the Roman missal according to the 1962 *editio typica* and according to the norms proposed in

December 1986 by the Commission of Cardinals constituted for that purpose, the diocesan bishop having been advised."[64] To this end the *Ecclesia Dei* Commission regularized many and endorsed their celebration of the sacraments and sacramentals using the liturgical books in use in 1962. It also granted indults for the celebration of Mass to individual priests, secular and religious, without prior consultation with their Ordinaries and regardless of any existing association with the older rites, to the alarm of many bishops and religious superiors—a faculty which younger priests hurried to obtain.

Following *Ecclesia Dei Adflicta*, the journal *Worship* observed that "the extent to which the Holy See may wish to compromise the liturgical principles of Vatican II to win back Lefebvre's followers is an important issue," and expressed the hope that the Commission would not have much impact, that "the voice of authentic tradition with which will not be uprooted"—with which the author identifies the liturgy promulgated by Paul VI—and that "new life will not be stunted by obeisance before the cultural, social and theological shibboleths of the European past."[65] The journal *Concilium* published a "special column" which expressed confusion at "the importance attached to a handful of integralists who seem to be living in the wrong century and who refuse to recognize the living Tradition of the Church on the pretext of remaining faithful to their own cherished traditions," as well as amazement at the patience and indulgence shown them. The author worried that "a number of intransigent Catholics" were seeking "with fervent zeal to make *Traditionalism without Lefebvre* one of the legitimate components of post-conciliar Catholicism," and noted that "on the pretext of giving satisfaction to the eternal pre-conciliar nostalgia seekers, we risk discouraging a multitude ... who continue to experience the Second Vatican Council as an event of grace for the Church and the world."[66]

For commentators such as these, the concessions made are seen as unfair to people who had gritted their teeth, as it were, and accepted the "many-sided inconvenience" of which Paul VI spoke in November 1969. Beyond this however, these commentators betray a concept of Tradition which is utterly positivistic. The new liturgical rites, promulgated by authority, are deemed exclusively normative and their uncritical acceptance is held—almost as a dogma of the Faith—to be an essential component of the living Tradition of the Church regardless of any question of authority itself having to respect Tradition or indeed of the requirement that authority be faithful to what an Ecumenical Council lays down in respect of the legitimate development of the Sacred Liturgy. From this perspective there can certainly be no going back on the liturgical reform of Paul VI; neither can there be any thought of moving forward including the older rites, for their availability is perceived as an ongoing rebuke to the reform imposed by Paul VI, to those who accepted it and to what it represented, including a particular interpretation of the Council itself. Ironically, those who espouse this positivistic concept of Tradition often fail to accord the same authority the right to re-include the *usus antiquior* in the Tradition—or to re-assert its rightful place in it—by another positive act.

But John Paul II and the Commission of Cardinals which had recommended the provision of an indult wider than that of 1984 could see that the Tradition of the Church was able to encompass both. Accordingly Cardinal Mayer worked on the text of a *Notificatio* which would give legal force to the Cardinals' recommendations. Yet this project "became known" by bishops around the world, who lobbied against any extension of permission and the granting of indults. Concern was such that thirty-three USA archbishops met with John Paul II in Rome in March 1989 to make their views known. Nevertheless, the *Notificatio* was submitted to the Pope on May 5. This prompted the Presidents of the episcopal conferences of England and Wales, France, Germany, and Switzerland to fly to Rome to oppose the measures. The three-hour meeting which involved senior curial officials, including the Secretary of State and Cardinal Ratzinger, saw the Pope, "his pen hovering over the paper, [decide] at the last moment not to sign," and accede to the demand that priests' requests for indults would, in the first place, be forwarded to their Ordinary.[67]

Effectively, this ended the possibility of any more permissive legislation in the pontificate of John Paul II, the "wide and generous" application of *Quattuor Abhinc Annos* being left to the discretion of diocesan bishops, the opposition of some of whom was emboldened by the Pope's capitulation in the face of episcopal pressure.[68] Nevertheless, before retiring as President of the *Ecclesia Dei* Commission in July 1991, Cardinal Mayer wrote to bishops to encourage them to "to facilitate the proper and reverent celebration of the liturgical rites according to the Roman missal of 1962 wherever there is a genuine desire for this on the part of priests and faithful." His letter offers "guidelines and suggestions" including the clarification that there is "no reason" why such celebrations could not take place in parish churches, and the suggestion that "a weekly Sunday and holy day Mass be scheduled in a central location and at a convenient time on a trial basis" where people had requested it. It informed the bishops that the Commission would "much prefer" that they themselves grant indults to priests wishing to celebrate the older rites, and raised the possibility of the new lectionary being used in them—noting that this should not be imposed if congregations did not wish it.[69] This letter is certainly indicative of the mind of the Holy See, but its generous tone lacked legal force.

Although the *Ecclesia Dei* Commission continued to regularise individuals and groups—most prominently the Brazilian Society of St Jean-Marie Vianney in 2002—after May 1989 it lost something of its effectiveness.[70] There was little that clergy or laity or indeed the Commission itself could do if the diocesan bishop was opposed, as many were. Liturgists widely regarded the *usus antiquior* as an unfortunate but insignificant survival which fostered a lack of unity. In 1992 Aimé-Georges Martimort (1911–2000) would even ask whether the continuing use of the older rites could have "a spiritual value, strictly speaking?"[71] In the last year of John Paul II's life one liturgist went so far as to propose that the previous permissions should be annulled and that "there should also be a period of compulsory transition implemented for all priests ordained after 1970, with perhaps five years for them to prepare for the celebration of the Novus Ordo exclusively."[72]

In 2000 Cardinal Ratzinger gave a book-length interview in which he said:

> For fostering a true consciousness in liturgical matters, it is . . . important that the proscriptions against the form of liturgy in valid use up to 1970 should be lifted.

Anyone who nowadays advocates the continuing existence of this liturgy or takes part in it is treated like a leper; all tolerance ends here. There has never been anything like this in history; in doing this we are despising and proscribing the Church's whole past. How can one trust her present if things are that way? I must say, quite openly, that I don't understand why so many of my episcopal brethren have to a great extent submitted to this rule of intolerance, which for no apparent reason is opposed to making the necessary inner reconciliations within the Church.[73]

Ratzinger's surprise election to the papacy in April 2005 gave the question of the *usus antiquior* new life. Indeed, in his 2000 interview we find the ground plan for the motu proprio *Summorum Pontificum* he promulgated as Pope Benedict XVI on July 7, 2007: acceptance of the ongoing value of the *usus antiquior* for those who wish it *and* as a means of fostering "a true consciousness in liturgical matters;" reconciliation within the Church (his profound wish to achieve the reconciliation of the Society of St Pius X was demonstrated in his reception of its Superior General, Bishop Bernard Fellay, in private audience on August 29, 2005); reconciliation of the Church with her own history; and overcoming episcopal obstruction.[74]

The promulgation of *Summorum Pontificum* generated more heat than light in some circles, particularly regarding its nonchalant decree that the *usus antiquior* was "never abrogated"—an understandable assertion, surely, for one closely involved in the study of the question on behalf of the Holy See for more than twenty years. Amongst the reactions that of Mark Francis CSV, a professor of Liturgy at San Anselmo in Rome and Santa Clara University, USA, in *The Tablet* stands to the fore: "Until now, the Pope, who is not a trained liturgist, has shown interest and sensitivity in liturgical matters," he concedes. But with *Summorum Pontificum* Pope Benedict demonstrated "a real misunderstanding of the liturgy's role in the life of the Church," and adopted a liturgical "relativism," ignoring "the hallowed patristic axiom *lex orandi, lex credendi*," Francis argued.[75]

Such reactions speak more about the preconceptions of their authors than they do about the motu proprio. *Summorum Pontificum* must be studied carefully, as the act of ecclesiastical law that it is, together with Benedict XVI's letter to the bishops of the same date—which makes manifest the *mens legislatoris*—and in the light of the authoritative clarifications made by the Instruction *Universae Ecclesiae* of April 30, 2011. Some such studies have been published and can be helpful.[76]

Summorum Pontificum's establishment of the rights of laity, religious and clergy to the celebration of Mass, the Divine Office and the sacraments according to the *usus antiquior*, the duty of care for this right that it lays down for pastors and rectors of churches and chapels, and its removal from the bishop the power to forbid the *usus antiquior* in his diocese,[77] giving him, rather, the duty to provide the Mass and sacraments according to the older use for those who request them when priests in his diocese are themselves unable to do so, constitutes a singular act of the exercise of the papal primacy in the face of decades of episcopal obstruction—a most significant event in modern liturgical history.

The importance of the Usus Antiquior

In the decades following the imposition of the Missal of Paul VI the numbers attending or wishing to attend celebrations according to the older rites were proportionately small. Whilst these increased as a result of the 1984 indult and again following this indult's encouragement by John Paul II in 1988, the increase was not momentous, although the post-1988 erection of seminaries, religious communities and chapels in which the *usus antiquior* was fundamental significantly amplified its availability and impact in the wider Church. Certainly *Summorum Pontificum* expanded its possible use and impact further, though even Benedict XVI would observe in his accompanying letter that its impact was unlikely to be wide. What, then, is the importance of a relatively small proportion of the Church retaining the unreformed liturgical rites? Was it, and is it, "much ado about nothing"?

The almost unanimous response to the last question is an emphatic: "No!" However, this apparent unanimity emerges from two distinct perspectives.

The first perspective is that epitomised by the 2003 remark of the *Worship* columnist Nathan Mitchell, that "the combined effect of *Quattuor Abhinc Annos* and *Ecclesia Dei* has had a chilling effect on Roman Catholic liturgical renewal."[78] In the wake of *Summorum Pontificum*, Mitchell proposed three "clarifications" and identified five "issues" that illustrate this stance. He seeks to clarify that the liturgical reform following the Council was not "merely superficial and cosmetic (hence optional, negligible)" but was "substantive" and "theological;" that "what seems historically discontinuous and unprecedented is not the post-conciliar reform's creation *of a new missal that includes and supersedes its predecessors*, but *Summorum Pontificum*'s provisions;" and that there were also plenty of "deformations of the liturgy which were hard to bear"—(he is referring to Benedict XVI's reference to post-conciliar abuses in his letter to the bishops)—in the four hundred years between 1570 and 1970.[79]

Mitchell's "issues" commence with the assertion that the provision of "two liturgical options" may well intensify and not relax the liturgical and therefore the ecclesiological "rift that separates us from one another within the communion of the Church." His second issue is that *Summorum Pontificum* appears to condone "active lobbying and even recruitment" to the *usus antiquior*, "a practice surely not envisaged by either the bishops at Vatican II or by Paul VI's constitution, *Missale Romanum*." This, Mitchell believes, may impede the motu proprio's desire for "reconciliation at the heart of the Church." He believes that the concern for "sacrality" is an issue; that the "neotraditionalist retrieval of the recent past" is an affirmation of consumerist culture and values; and that some liturgical texts of the *usus antiquior* may seem out of sync with "Vatican II's *lex docendi*" in respect of the Jewish people.[80]

This stance is summarized by John Baldovin SJ's 2008 claim that "many people have not accepted the Second Vatican Council and the renewal and reform of the Church that have sprung from it" and that *Summorum Pontificum* "will only give them hope that the last forty years can be reversed."[81] Or, as he wrote in 2010: "we stand at a crossroads with regard to the reception of the liturgical reform and indeed of Vatican II itself."[82]

Proponents of this view argue that historically, discontinuity and rupture are part and parcel of Western liturgical history, that "the attitude that inspired *Summorum Pontificum*, namely that the post-Vatican II reform ... lacked organic continuity with its past, is historically shallow,"[83] and that Paul VI most certainly abrogated the previous edition of the *Missale Romanum*.[84] Theologically, principally ecclesiologically, they argue that the Second Vatican Council was an epochal event and that the liturgical reforms that ensued are an essential part of its whole, and are indeed theologically normative. Permissions to celebrate " 'the old liturgy' ... could not but weaken the theological impact of *Sacrosanctum Concilium* on the living ecclesiology of Catholicism," they argue. Therefore:

> The liturgy of Vatican II is not only the first and foremost medium of Vatican II but also an integral part of the theological message of Vatican II. Its core content is essential for the core content of Vatican II. *The liturgy of Vatican II is constitutionally necessary for the theological survival of Vatican II.* Undoing the reform of Vatican II leads to the dismantling of the Church of Vatican II. This is why it is necessary to understand the deep connections between the liturgical reform and theology of Vatican II in its entirety.[85]

From this demarcation of "the Church of Vatican II" and the elevation of its policies and orientations practically to the level of dogma, flows the view that to celebrate anything other than the rites that go by its name is intrinsically an act of disunity with that same "Church of Vatican II." As one writer put it, "the unreformed liturgy of 1962 is incapable of bringing into being the ecclesial community that *Lumen Gentium* ... describes ... [it] is a liturgy incapable of birthing the Church of empowered laity sought by the bishops of the Second Vatican Council."[86]

Some of those who hold this stance do recognize that pastorally there is "some desire for this rite," but, as Baldovin presumes to assert: "it is the duty of the diocesan bishop not to encourage the pre-conciliar liturgy." Its promotion, he asserts, is "a futile attempt to recreate the past."[87] The "treasures of inestimable value" that are the Missal of Paul VI and its lectionary,[88] they argue, are where our attention and energy should be focussed, and they are ungenerous if not disingenuous in their interpretation of Benedict XVI's legislation.[89]

Others insist that *Summorum Pontificum* introduces a liturgical "virtual reality," as opposed to "real reality," which "raises the risk of radically relativizing the meaning and significance of the [liturgical] reform," for the sake of "tiny minorities that ... make nostalgia their identity and presumption their only hope."[90] And some note that it may even be seen as a "victory by the Church's conservative wing and a positive step in correcting or even negating the Council's liturgical agenda" or that it "actually offers a step forward for the Church—part of what is called a 'new liturgical movement.' "[91]

The second—and clearly distinct—perspective takes as its starting point the reality articulated by Benedict XVI in his 2007 letter to the bishops presenting *Summorum Pontificum*:

In the history of the liturgy there is growth and progress, but no rupture. What earlier generations held as sacred, remains sacred and great for us too, and it cannot be all of a sudden entirely forbidden or even considered harmful. It behoves all of us to preserve the riches which have developed in the Church's faith and prayer, and to give them their proper place.

Its proponents would certainly see the *usus antiquior* as an antidote to the poor and abusive celebration of the rites promulgated by Paul VI, to their defective vernacular translation and questionable adaptation. Some would welcome the freedom established for the older rites by Benedict XVI as a clearly pastoral measure, allowing diversity in what John Paul II described in his 1978 meeting with Archbishop Lefebvre as a "disciplinary matter," so as to further the unity of the Church.

Theologically, following the maxim *lex orandi, lex credendi*, they would note that the Sacred Liturgy "is a constitutive element of the holy and living Tradition" (*Catechism of the Catholic Church* n. 1124; see: *Dei Verbum* n. 8), and assert that continuity with objective liturgical tradition (in its rites and prayers and even in its disposition and attitudes—all of which comprise an organic whole) as it is received in tradition, is fundamental to the doctrinal orthodoxy and sound pastoral practice of the Church. This objectivity, they would argue, in no way excludes proportionate development of the Sacred Liturgy as has happened throughout history and as was called for by the Second Vatican Council.

Nor would they reject the connection between genuine ecclesiological and liturgical renewal—a reality espoused by the pre-conciliar liturgical movement in the light of the 1943 encyclical letter *Mystici Corporis* of Pius XII—or deny that this necessitates a greater attention to the baptismal dignity of all of Christ's Faithful in the liturgical assembly and respect for the corporate nature worship and its differing liturgical roles. But they would not agree that such theological and liturgical renewal necessitates the particular ritual reforms promulgated by Paul VI or substantial rupture with received liturgical Tradition.

Indeed, historically they would question whether what in fact the Council called for was in fact what was implemented, noting especially the stipulation of article 23 of *Sacrosanctum Concilium*: "There must be no innovations unless the good of the Church genuinely and certainly requires them; and care must be taken that any new forms adopted should in some way grow organically from forms already existing," and the teaching of the *Catechism*: "Even the supreme authority in the Church may not change the liturgy arbitrarily, but only in the obedience of faith and with religious respect for the mystery of the liturgy" (n. 1125).

This perspective would hold that the liturgical rites produced by the post-conciliar *Consilium* cannot be described as proportionate, organic developments of the received liturgical tradition, noting research which evidences varying political influences and ideologies operative in the reform.[92] They would agree with Cardinal Ratzinger's observation that: "After the Council . . . in the place of the liturgy as the fruit of organic development came fabricated liturgy. We abandoned the organic, living process of growth and development over centuries, and replaced it—as in a manufacturing process—with a fabrication, a banal on-the-spot product."[93]

Its followers would also draw attention to the ongoing existence of communities who regard their liturgical celebrations as the expression of their own identity, and fashion the liturgy accordingly, and thereby living from a defective ecclesiology in which the local community is not effectively open to substantial unity with the local, let alone the universal, Church, or her millennial liturgical Tradition. They would draw attention to certain predominating ritual dispositions that have theological, pastoral and psychological importance, such as the orientation of the altar, the manner of receiving Holy Communion and the de-sacralization of liturgical art, architecture, and music,[94] which introduce elements of rupture into the celebration of the liturgy *as it is experienced by the vast majority of the faithful* in ways that find no justification in the Council's Constitution on the Sacred Liturgy.

Those who welcome *Summorum Pontificum* thus would agree with Cardinal Ratzinger's rejection of "the suggestion by some Catholic liturgists that we should finally adapt the liturgical reform to the 'anthropological turn' of modern times and construct it in an anthropocentric style." They would hold with him that:

> If the Liturgy appears first of all as the workshop for our activity, then what is essential is being forgotten: God. For the Liturgy is not about us, but about God. Forgetting about God is the most imminent danger of our age. As against this, the Liturgy should be setting up a sign of God's presence. Yet what happens if the habit of forgetting about God makes itself at home in the Liturgy itself and if in the Liturgy we are thinking only of ourselves? In any and every liturgical reform, and every liturgical celebration, the primacy of God should be kept in view first and foremost.[95]

They would assert that, whilst capable of development, the liturgical rites in use in 1962 nevertheless possess an integrity in respect of the Church's liturgical tradition and afford us valuable and substantially unedited access to this tradition.[96] Their use, they hold, safeguards against the liturgical and theological subjectivity and ideologies to which the new rites have too often fallen prey. They are essentially God-centred and intrinsically latreutic, which is essential to Catholic worship.

They would reject charges of nostalgia and point out that the *usus antiquior* nourishes Catholics today, noting with Benedict XVI its real pastoral value: "It has clearly been demonstrated that young persons too have discovered this liturgical form, felt its attraction and found in it a form of encounter with the Mystery of the Most Holy Eucharist, particularly suited to them" (Letter presenting *Summorum Pontificum*). They would hold this up in recognition of the truth that "what earlier generations held as sacred, remains sacred and great for us too," and assert that these rites do have their "proper place" in the liturgical and pastoral life and renewal of the Church at the beginning of the twenty-first century,[97] as the many, and predominantly young and vital communities, personal parishes, seminaries, and religious houses—in communion with the local bishop—for whom worship according to the *usus antiquior* is the *culmen et fons,* the source and summit of their Christian lives (*Sacrosanctum Concilium,* n. 10), bear ongoing testimony. They would note the value to the wider Church of that "mutual enrichment" between the older rites and the new of which Benedict XVI spoke in presenting *Summorum Pontificum.*[98]

They would also point out that the overwhelming majority of contemporary celebrations of the *usus antiquior* evince a level of formation and true liturgical participation that is in perfect harmony with *Sacrosanctum Concilium* article 14. They may even see this as a providential fruit of the post-conciliar proscription of these rites, given that people frequenting them have had to invest and sacrifice substantially to have access to them, and have thereby had a concentrated and at times a costly liturgical formation. In this light they may assert that the ongoing celebration of the older rites is not opposed to the two fundamental principles of the Second Vatican Council's Constitution on the Liturgy: to achieve widespread *participatio actuosa,* and to achieve this by ensuring that the clergy are "thoroughly imbued by the spirit and power of the liturgy" and that they in turn form others in this spirit (n. 14).

Its supporters would point to the value of the ritual demands that the *usus antiquior* places on the worshipper—the demand to find ways of connecting with these rites, or indeed of allowing them to connect with us, because of their ritual complexity: "If you want a church full of Catholics who know their faith, love their faith, and practice their faith, given them a liturgy that is demanding, profound, and rigorous. They will rise to the challenge," Peter Kwasniewski argues.[99] Supporters of this view would emphasize the human and psychological value of the multivalent nature and riches of the *usus antiquior,* which provides more varying means of connection with Christ acting in the liturgy, which can more easily touch different temperaments and psyches.[100]

Some who hold this perspective may well regard the timely and epochal "event" of *Summorum Pontificum* as a victory—of liturgical tradition over substantial innovation posited in its place following Vatican II—and indeed believe it to be a valuable step in correcting the erroneous agendas of some of those responsible for implementing the Second Vatican Council's Constitution on the Sacred Liturgy. Some may see it as a re-connection with received liturgical tradition which may inform liturgical reform in the future—perhaps as the ground for a "reform of the reform." Thus many may well see that *Summorum Pontificum* was in fact a timely step forward for the Church as part of what is called the "new liturgical movement."

Conclusion

In the history of the reform following the Second Vatican Council the proscription of the former liturgical rites from 1971 to 2007, and its attendant political skirmishes, make less edifying reading the more perspective the passing years bring. So too, some of the reactions to and arguments against their newfound freedom appear increasingly partisan—almost an idolization of the liturgical books of Paul VI and of a particular manner of interpreting the Council favored by certain schools of thought.

It must be said clearly that despite the concerns of Bishop Brandolini and others, Vatican II's liturgical reform was not "cancelled" or "undermined" on July 7, 2007. However, it was definitively set in a new context.

The interpretation of *Sacrosanctum Concilium* that predominated throughout the decades following the Council was protected by a closely guarded wall behind which the older rites were kept hidden and forbidden. Demolishing that wall has allowed the unedited liturgical tradition in which the Council Fathers were themselves formed, and from which they spoke of liturgical reform, freely to be experienced and has permitted its riches to speak openly once again. The right to these riches established by Benedict XVI, and the interaction he envisaged that their availability would bring about through "mutual enrichment," has established a new dynamic in the liturgical life of the Western Church at the beginning of the twenty-first century. The rites promulgated by Paul VI are no longer protected by sanctions. These rites, and the prevailing applications of them, can no longer pretend to be the apotheosis of liturgical history that their creators believed. The products of the post-concilar reform, and their proponents, must now dialogue with received liturgical tradition, and do so based on their merits.

What the outcome of this dialogue will be is for future historians to recount. But the more the *usus antiquior* is experienced and celebrated, and its value cherished, the more impetus there will be to look again at the questionable reform that followed the promulgation of *Sacrosanctum Concilium* in December 1963. For through *Summorum Pontificum*, the Church has refused to forget or to hide the riches of her liturgical tradition any longer—riches which increasingly nourish and sustain the Christian faith and life of twenty-first century people, for whom their proscription the attendant disputes are—happily—history.

For these generations the *usus antiquior* is not a rejection of the real Second Vatican Council,[101] or of its true ecclesiology. They are not *intégristes*, but people who have tasted something "sacred and great" and know its value as the source of Christian life and mission in the modern world. For them: "The *usus antiquior* is something much more valuable than a bone to be thrown to disgruntled Catholics as a pacifier. It has a part to play in the work of the new evangelisation since it so effectively resists secularism and satisfies the post-modern hunger for coherent order, beauty and an experience of self-transcendence."[102]

Indeed, it becomes increasingly clear that today and into the future the *usus antiquior* can serve:

"To impart an ever increasing vigour to the Christian life of the faithful . . . to foster . . . union among all who believe in Christ . . . [and] to call the whole of mankind into the household of the Church" (*Sacrosanctum Concilium*, 1).

Notes

1   Orazio La Rocca, Intervisto "Obbedirò al Pontefice ma è un giorno di lutto Si cancella la riforma," *La Repubblica*, July 8, 2007, p. 10. For Brandolini on the relationship between *Mediator Dei* and *Sacrosanctum Concilium*, see: Alcuin Reid, *The Organic Development of the Liturgy,* 2nd edn (San Francisco: Ignatius Press, 2005), p. 139 n. 295.

2   Including "The Old Rite," "The *Vetus Ordo,*" "The Latin Mass," "The Traditional Rite/ Mass," "The Traditional Latin Mass" ["TLM"], "The Tridentine Mass," "The Gregorian Rite," and "The Extraordinary Form." The neutral and descriptive term "the *usus antiquior,*" taken from the "Letter of His Holiness Benedict XVI to the Bishops on the Occasion of the Publication of the Apostolic Letter 'Motu Proprio Data' Summorum Pontificum on the use of the Roman Liturgy Prior to the Reform of 1970," July 7, 2007, is used here so as to avoid other terms which, at least in English, have been used to make comparative and qualitative judgments about the older and newer forms of the Roman rite.

3   J.A. Komonchak of the Catholic University of America and English-language editor of a five-volume *History of Vatican II*, pronounced that *Summorum Pontificum* "was not an event of historic significance,"—an ironic comment given that his is one of no fewer than four commentaries on precisely this "insignificant" event in the edition of *Commonweal* immediately following its publication; Joseph A. Komonchak, "One Cheer," *Commonweal* 134 (2007), pp. 15–16 (p. 15). Indeed, one only need study the two hundred pages of the entire issue of *Rivista Liturgica* (n. 1, January–February 2008) "responding" to *Summorum Pontificum* to see that liturgists understood it to be a most significant moment in liturgical history.

4   See: Rita Ferrone, "A Step Backward," *Commonweal* 134 (2007), pp. 13–15. Ferrone regards *Summorum Pontificum* as: "another step toward a goal that the vast majority of Catholics would not countenance if it were openly acknowledged—namely, the gradual dismantling of the liturgical reform in its entirety;" p. 15.

5   See: chapter 14, "After *Sacrosanctum Concilium*—Continuity or Rupture?"

6   Paul VI, General Audience November 26, 1969; *L'Osservatore Romano*, "Weekly Edition in English," December 4, 1969, pp. 1, 12.

7   See: Sacra Congregatio Pro Cultu Divino, *Instructio De Constitutione Apostolica « Missale Romanum » Graditim Ad Effectum Deducenda*, October 20, 1969, *Notitiae* 6 (1969), pp. 418–23. ET: DOL, n. 209, pp. 534–8. Aimé Georges Martimort mentions a permission granted to Abbé Raymond Dulac on October 12, 1970 by Benno Cardinal Gut, Prefect of the Congregation of Divine Worship, which interpreted this clause widely, but gives no reference or text; see: "La réforme liturgique incomprise: l'*Ordo Missae* face au controverses et aux dissidences," *La Maison-Dieu*, n. 192 (1992), pp. 79–119 (p. 95).

8   Cited in: Alcuin Reid (ed.), *A Bitter Trial: Evelyn Waugh and John Carmel Cardinal Heenan on the Liturgical Changes*, 3rd edn (San Francisco: Ignatius Press, 2011), p. 23. For Heenan's intervention at the 1967 Synod see: pp. 102–14.

9   See: ibid., pp. 120–3.

10 "Appeal to preserve Mass sent to Vatican," in: *The Times*, July 6, 1971, p. 12. Also published in *The Tablet*, July 17, 1971, p. 707.

11 Letter, October 29, 1971, cited in: Reid, *A Bitter Trial*, p. 112.

12 Annibale Bugnini, *The Reform of the Liturgy: 1948–1975*, (Collegeville: Liturgical Press, 1990) p. 298. A reproduction of Paul VI's October 30, 1971 manuscript letter is

published in the "documentazione fotografica" section at the end of Annibale Bugnini, *Liturgie cultor et amator: servì la chiesa* (Rome: Edizione Liturgiche, 2012).

13 Sacra Congregatio Pro Cultu Divino, Letter, November 5, 1971, Prot. N. 1897/71. The author is indebted to Mr Leo Darroch for making available material on the Heenan Indult from his personal archives.

14 Annibale Bugnini, Letter, November 5, 1971, Prot. N. 1891/71.

15 "The Latin Mass Again", *The Tablet,* December 11, 1971, p. 1192. See also the Letters to the Editor, December 18, 1971, p. 1223.

16 "Pope sanctions traditional Latin Mass in Britain", *The Times,* December 2, 1971, p. 2.

17 Bugnini, *The Reform of the Liturgy,* p. 298, n. 42.

18 See: *Ordo Missæ: Ritus Servandus in Celebratione Missæ et De Defectibus in Celebratione Missæ Occurrentibus,* Editio Typica (Vatican City: Typis Polyglottis Vaticanis, 1965); *Variationes in Ordinem Missæ Inducendæ Ad Normam Instructionis S.R.C. Diei 4 Maii 1967* (Vatican City: Typis Polyglottis Vaticanis, 1967).

19 Decree, "The New Roman Missal," *Notitiae,* 11 (1975), pp. 143–4.

20 See: Marcello Olivi, "L'integralismo francese e la riforma liturigca del Concilio Vaticano II," *Ephemerides Liturgicae* 106 (1992), pp. 38–67, 117–52 (pp. 132–5).

21 See: Martimort, "La réforme liturgique incomprise," p. 98.

22 Bugnini, *The Reform of the Liturgy,* pp. 296–7 n. 41. See: ibid, p. 95

23 "il papa fu irremovibile, e non volle concedere l'indulto a nessun'altra;" Bugnini, *Liturgie cultor et amator,* p. 86.

24 In response to a request from a priest of the diocese of Le Mans, France, for a Mass at a Gregorian chant school, the Congregation responded: "quaestionem proponendam esse Ordinario Diocesano, qui pro sua prudentia pastorali iudicabit an opportunam sit concedere celebrationem *unius* sanctae Missae iuxta Missale romanum non instauratum, removo quovis periculo dissentionis et turbationis in communitate fidelium;" "Unicuique suum;" *Notitiae* 9 (1972), p. 48. Bugnini notes: "The petitioner took advantage of this reply to spread the word that it was possible to ask the Ordinary for the habitual celebration of the Tridentine Mass. The inference was false and abusive;" *The Reform of the Liturgy,* p. 296.

25 *Acta Synodalia Sacrosancti Conciliii Oecumenici Vaticani II:* vol II pars VI (Vatican City: Typis Polyglottis Vaticanis 1973) p. 443.

26 Marcel Lefebvre, *A Bishop Speaks: Writings and Addresses 1963–1975* (Edinburgh: Scottish Una Voce, 1976), pp. 37–8.

27 See: Bernard Tissier de Mallerais, *Marcel Lefebvre: The Biography* (Kansas: Angelus Press, 2004), p. 346.

28 See: ibid., pp. 415–17.

29 See: ibid., pp. 461–65.

30 Keith Pecklers SJ, *Liturgy: The Illustrated History* (New Jersey: Paulist Press, 2012), p. 236.

31 See: Olivi, "L'integralismo francese e la riforma liturigca del Concilio Vaticano II," pp. 119–32.

32 DOL, n. 59 p. 178. See also: Michael Davies, *Apologia Pro Marcel Lefebvre: Part I 1905–1976* (Kansas: Angelus Press, 1979), pp. 173–91.

33 See: Davies, *Apologia I,* pp. 193–216.

34 DOL, n. 61, p. 186. See also: Davies, ibid., pp. 301–43.

35 See: Olivi, "L'integralismo francese e la riforma liturigca del Concilio Vaticano II," p. 117–19.

36 See: Alcuin Reid, "From Rubrics to *Ars Celebrandi*—Liturgical Law in the 21st Century," *Antiphon* 17 (2013), pp. 139–67 (pp. 148–57); Olivi, ibid., pp. 60–62; chapter 16 "Pastoral Liturgy Revisited."

37 See: József Cardinal Mindszenty, *Memoirs* (New York: Macmillan, 1974), pp. 239, 245–47.

38 "Le drame est que certains font de l'ancien missel le symbole de leur opposition au Concile, le symbole de leur opposition à l'application qu'en font le Pape et les évêques du monde entier." Paul Joseph Schmitt, "A propos du missel de Saint Pie V" *Notitiae* 16 (1980), pp. 110–15 (p. 114). See also: Aimé-Georges Martimort, "But what is the Mass of Pius V?" *L'Osservatore Romano*, Weekly Edition in English, September 16, 1976, pp. 11–12.

39 On June 5, 1977 Paul VI's Master of Pontifical Liturgical Celebrations (proposed by Bugnini to succeed himself in that role in 1970) and Undersecretary of the Congregation for Divine Worship and Discipline of the Sacraments, Msgr Virgilio Noè (1922–2011), wrote to the French liturgist and Consultor of the Congregation, Pierre Jounel (1914–2004): "Quanto alla Messa di S. Pio V, e a una sua eventuale concessione, fortunamente Roma non cede: e suo questo le posso dire che non pocco peso ha avuto anche la nostra Congregazione, per mezzo di un esposto che abbiamo dovuto presentare, con tutta un'argomentazione che penso sia stata di non pocco conto nel prendere questo orientamento di fermezza. Ne sarebbe adatta di mezzo tutta quanta la riforma liturgica." The letter also relates the "sad" reality that Lefebvre was due to give a conference in Rome the following day. Archive of the Centre National de Pastorale Liturgique, Paris, Fonds Jounel, box 1; Congregation letterhead, non-protocolled.

40 "Je serais tout prêt à autoriser la messe de Pie V: je l'ai célébrée toute ma vie. Mais ce rite est devenu un symbole . . . le symbole d'une opposition au Concile. Mon devoir de pape est d'appliquer le Concile;" cited in: Martimort, "La réforme liturgique incomprise," p. 97.

41 See: Bugnini, *The Reform of the Liturgy*, p. 295 n. 38. Bugnini errs in asserting that the abbot never changed his mind.

42 Neri Capponi, "Alcune considerazioni giuridiche in materia di riforma liturgica," *Archivio Giuridico "Filippo Serafini,"* 190 (1976), pp. 147–73. *Some Juridical Considerations on the Reform of the Liturgy* (Edinburgh: Una Voce, 1979). The author is grateful to Mr Alan Henderson for his assistance in locating these texts.

43 Bugnini lists others in: *The Reform of the Liturgy*, p. 292 n. 30.

44 Indeed, it appears that in 1974 the Secretariat of State decided *against* seeking an authoritative clarification on this point; see: Bugnini, ibid, p. 300.

45 Capponi, *Some Juridical Considerations on the Reform of the Liturgy*, p. 25.

46 Michael Davies, *Apologia Pro Marcel Lefebvre: Part II 1977-1979* (Kansas: Angelus Press, 1983), p. 263.

47 In "Return to the Tradition" (*The Tablet*, 25 April 2009, pp. 14–15), p. 14, Robert Mickens erroneously asserts that "the Holy See's first discussions in years with Archbishop Lefebvre" were the result of an instruction of John Paul II to Cardinal Ratzinger in July 1982. In fact they were the result of an instruction to Cardinal Šeper during the audience granted to Lefebvre in November 1978; see: Davies, *Apologia II*, pp. 264–5.

48 See: Michael Davies, *Apologia Pro Marcel Lefebvre: Part III 1979-1982* (Kansas: Angelus Press, 1988), p. 255.

49 "Un atteggiamento di disprezzo a quanto stabilito dal Concilio Vaticano II e dal Santo Padre, il che sarebbe una grava ferita contro la communione e l'unita della Chiesa," in:

"Investigatio de usu linguae latinae in liturgia romana et de Missa quae « Tridentina » appelari solet," *Notitiae* 17 (1981), pp. 589–611 (p. 611).

50 See: Davies, *Apologia III*, p. 354.

51 For example, Lefebvre was in contact with groups in several dioceses in Australia by 1980 and would open his first Australian Priory—in Sydney—the following year. The survey does not and perhaps could not reflect Lefebvre's knowledge of such groups.

52 See: Martimort, "La réforme liturgique incomprise," pp. 105–6.

53 Martimort underlines the fact that this option left bishops with complete liberty; ibid., p. 106.

54 "De indulto Missale Romanum adhibendi iuxta editionem typicam anni 1962," *Notitiae* 21 (1985), pp. 9–10. The indult was signed by the Prefect, Archbishop Paul Augustin Mayer OSB and the Secretary, Archbishop Virgilio Noè. Noè is rumoured to have been required to be ordered to do so; something consistent with his opposition to the concession (see note 39 above) and his later frequent and drastic intervention to prevent priests celebrating the *usus antiquior* in St Peter's Basilica—by personally surveying priests offering Mass and removing the cruets of those using the old rite—during his period as Archpriest (1991–2002).

55 "Tridentine Mass Permission Criticized," *Origins* 14, pp. 334–5. *Worship* published a fuller report of the meeting: Aelred Tegels OSB, "Chronicle: A Minisynod on Liturgical Reform," *Worship* 59 (1985), pp. 72–8.

56 Ibid., p. 76. "Il disorientamento dei partecipanti al Convegno fu considerevole;" Olivi, "L'integralismo francese e la riforma liturigca del Concilio Vaticano II," p. 147. One Irish liturgist is reported to have labelled the indult "the worst betrayal since Judas;" cited in: B.W. Harrison, OS, "The Postconciliar Eucharistic Liturgy: Planning a 'Reform of the Reform," T. Kocik (ed.), *The Reform of the Reform? A Liturgical Debate: Reform or Return* (San Francisco: Ignatius Press, 2003), pp. 151–93 (p. 154).

57 Aelred Tegels OSB, "Chronicle: The Fortunes of the Tridentine Mass," *Worship* 60 (1986), pp. 169–71 (p. 171).

58 N. Bux & S. Vitiello, "Dossier: The Motu Proprio of Benedict XVI *Summorum Pontificum cura,*" Agenzia Fides, Vatican City, August 1, 2007, p. 2. On October 3, 2008 Cardinal Castrillón Hoyos, Prefect of the *Ecclesia Dei* Commission, published "Risposte del Cardinale Presidente della Pontificia Commissione *Ecclesia Dei* a certi quesiti" on the website of the Congregation for Clergy: http://www.clerus.org/clerus/dati/2008-10/24-20/castrillon_rispost.html (accessed March 12, 2014) which lists only eight members: Mayer, Casaroli, Gantin, Ratzinger, William W. Baum (1926–), Edouard Gagnon PSS (1918–2007), Stickler and Innocenti.

59 Alfons Maria Cardinal Stickler, "The Attractiveness of the Tridentine Mass," *The Latin Mass Magazine,* Summer 1995, pp. 11–17 (p. 14). The work of this Commission and the jurisprudence of the Holy See at the time are areas which invite further research.

60 Bux & Vitiello, "Dossier" p. 3.

61 International Federation Una Voce, Bulletin no. 54, Epiphany 1990, FIUV Archives.

62 Castrillón Hoyos, "Risposte del Cardinale Presidente della Pontificia Commissione *Ecclesia Dei* a certi quesiti."

63 See: Tissier de Mallerais, *Marcel Lefebvre,* pp. 547–60; "Lettera di Giovanni Paolo II al Cardinale Joseph Ratzinger," *Notitiae* 24 (1988), pp. 279–80.

64 Emphasis added. "concedendi omnibus id petentibus usum Missalis Romani secundum editionem typicam vim habentem anno 1962, et quidem iuxta normas iam a commissione Cardinalitia « ad hoc ipsum instituta » mense Decembri anno 1986

propositas, praemonito Episcopo dioecesano;" AAS 82 (1990), pp. 533–4. It is
indicative of some attitudes towards the *usus antiquior* in the Roman curia at this
time that these faculties were not published for more than a year and a half after they
were granted.

65 R.W. Franklin, "Chronicle: The Liturgical Schism," *Worship* 62 (1988), pp. 448–51,
(pp. 448, 451).

66 See: Claude Geffré, "Traditionalsim without Lefebvre," *Concilium* 25 (1989),
pp. xi–xvi, n. 2.

67 International Federation Una Voce, Bulletin no. 54. Damian Thompson, "A Near Miss
for the Old Mass," *The Spectator*, 14 July 1989, pp. 16–17.

68 At the June 1989 meeting of the Bishops of the USA, an *ad hoc* committee chaired
by Archbishop John Quinn of San Francisco recommended norms which: limited
the celebration of "Mass in Latin" to only one location in a diocese; mandated
the new lectionary and calendar; forbade weddings and funerals "in Latin" and
ruled that all sacraments other than the Eucharist must be celebrated in English
according to the modern rite in the person's proper parish. Archbishop Strecker of
Kansas City presented these norms to his people. The President of the USA
Bishops' Conference, Archbishop John May, denied to the *Ecclesia Dei* Commission
that any such norms had been approved; see: International Federation Una Voce,
Bulletin no. 54.

69 See: "Guidelines on Tridentine Mass," *Origins* 21 (1991), pp. 144–5.

70 In 1999 not the Commission, but the Congregation for Divine Worship and
Discipline of the Sacraments, issued official responses clarifying that priests of
Institutes erected by the Commission could celebrate and concelebrate the modern
rites, and could not be prevented from so doing by their superiors: *Notitiae* 35 (1999),
pp. 307–9.

71 "Est-ce une valeur spirituelle proprement dire?" Martimort, "La réforme liturgique
incomprise" p. 118.

72 Andrew Cameron-Mowatt SJ, "Polarisation and Liturgy," *Priests and People* 18 (2004),
pp. 374–9 (p. 378). See also his article published just in advance of *Summorum
Pontificum*: "This day forward," *The Tablet*, February 24, 2007, pp. 10–11, and the
response: Alcuin Reid, "Something old, something new," *The Tablet*, March 10, 2007,
pp. 10–11.

73 Joseph Cardinal Ratzinger, *God and the World: A Conversation with Peter Seewald*
(San Francisco: Ignatius Press, 2002), p. 416. Original German edition published in
2000.

74 The Vatican Press Office statement of August 29, 2005 reads: "The Holy Father
Benedict XVI this morning received, in the Apostolic Palace of Castel Gandolfo, the
Superior General of the Saint Pius X Fraternity, Monsignor Bernard Fellay, who had
requested it. The Pope was accompanied by the Most Eminent Cardinal Darío
Castrillón Hoyos, President of the Pontifical Commission *Ecclesia Dei*. The meeting
took place in an atmosphere of love for the Church and of desire to reach perfect
communion. Albeit aware of the difficulties, the wish to proceed by stages and in
reasonable time was shown." *Summorum Pontificum* was most certainly one of the
"stages" envisaged.

75 Mark Francis CSV, "Beyond Language," in: *The Tablet*, July 14, 2007, pp. 6–7. See
also: Andrew Cameron Mowatt, SJ, "*Summorum Pontificum*: A Response," in: *The
Pastoral Review*, November 2007, pp. 4–11; *Commonweal*, vol. 134 n. 14 (17 August
2007).

76 See: William H. Johnston, *Care for the Church and Its Liturgy: A Study of Summorum Pontificum and the Extraordinary Form of the Roman Rite* (Collegeville: Liturgical Press, 2013). Johnson's study is genuinely sympathetic if a little ponderous and at times historically and canonically naïve. The Spanish study of Alberto Soria Jiménez OSB, *Los Principios de interpretación del motu proprio Summorum pontificum* (Madrid: Ediciones Christiandad, 2014) is comprehensive. Norbert Lüdecke, "Canonical Remarks on the Motu Proprio *Summorum Pontificum*," *Antiphon* 13 (2009), pp. 193–227 is valuable but was written before *Universae Ecclesiae*. See also: the works of Gero P. Weishaupt, *Päpstliche Weichenstellungen das Motu Proprio Summorum Pontificium Papst Benedikts XVI. und der Begleitbrief an die Bischöfe; ein kirchenrechtlicher Kommentar und Überlegungen zu einer "Reform der Reform"* (Bonn: Verlag für Kultur und Wiss, 2010); *Die Instruktion "Universae Ecclesiae": ein kirchenrechtlicher Kommentar* (Kreuzlingen: Benedetto-Verlag, 2013). An English edition of Weishaupt's work is due for future publication by Ignatius Press. For a canonical interpretation of *Summorum Pontificum* which fails to respect its integrity (and the stance of which *Universae Ecclesiae* excludes) see: John M. Huels, "Reconciling the Old with the New: Canonical Questions on *Summorum Pontificum*" *The Jurist* 68 (2008), pp. 92–113.

77 This has not always been well understood by bishops, some of whom have sought to use their duty of moderating the liturgy in their diocese (*Sacrosanctum Concilium* 22) as a licence for imposing their personal will. The only power the diocesan bishop has is to ensure that the provisions of *Summorum Pontificum* and *Universae Ecclesiae* are faithfully adhered to and to intervene to correct abuses. See: Alexander K. Sample, "The Bishop: Governor, Promotor and Guardian of the Liturgical Life of the Diocese," A. Reid (ed.), *Sacred Liturgy: The Source and Summit of the Life and Mission of the Church* (San Francisco: Ignatius Press, 2014), pp. 255–71.

78 Nathan D. Mitchell, "Amen Corner: 'Life Begins at Forty'," *Worship* 77 (2003), pp. 56–69 (p. 63).

79 Nathan D. Mitchell, "Amen Corner: *Summorum Pontificum*," *Worship* 81 (2007), pp. 549–65 (pp. 551–9). Italics original.

80 Ibid., pp. 559–65.

81 John Baldovin SJ, *Reforming the Liturgy: A Response to the Critics* (Collegeville: Liturgical Press, 2008), p. 132.

82 John Baldovin SJ, "Idols and Icons: Reflections on the Current State of Liturgical Reform," *Worship* 84 (2010), pp. 386–402 (p. 402).

83 John Baldovin SJ, "Reflections on *Summorum Pontificum*," *Worship* 83 (2009), pp. 98–112 (p. 102). See also: Arnold Angenendt, "Questionable Praise of the Old Liturgy," *Worship* 85 (2011), pp. 194–210.

84 See: Chad J. Glendinning, "Was the 1962 *Missale Romanum* Abrogated? A Canonical Analysis in the Light of *Summorum Pontificum*," *Worship* 85 (2011), pp. 15–37. This article fails to take account of the work of Neri Capponi or of the 1986 Commission of Cardinals.

85 Massimo Faggioli, *True Reform: Liturgy and Ecclesiology in Sacrosanctum Concilium,* (Collegeville: Liturgical Press, 2012), pp. 8, 158. Emphasis added.

86 Georgia Masters Keightley, "*Summorum Pontificum* and the Unmaking of the Lay Church," *Worship* 86 (2012), pp. 290–310 (pp. 291, 292).

87 Baldovin, "Reflections on *Summorum Pontificum*," pp. 109, 112.

88 Patrick Regan, *Advent to Pentecost: Comparing the Seasons in the Ordinary and Extraordinary Forms of the Roman Rite* (Collegeville: Liturgical Press, 2012), p 305.

89 See: Kevin W. Irwin, *What we have done – What we have failed to do: Assessing the Liturgical Reforms of Vatican II* (Paulist Press: New York, Mawah, NJ, 2013), pp. 11–12, 124–6, 250–1 (nn. 25, 27).

90 Andrea Grillo, *Beyond Pius V: Conflicting Interpretations of the Liturgical Reform*, (Collegeville: Liturgical Press, 2013), pp. 95, 109, 120.

91 Pecklers, *Liturgy: The Illustrated History*, p. 239.

92 See for example examinations of the reform the collects, prayers over the gifts and the post-communion prayers of the Missal of Paul VI: Anthony Cekada, *The Problems with the Prayers of the Modern Mass* (Rockford: Tan, 1991); Lauren Pristas, *The Collects of the Roman Missals: A Comparative Study of the Sundays in Proper Seasons before and after the Second Vatican Council* (London: Bloomsbury, 2013); Anthony Cekada, *Work of Human Hands: A Theological Critique of the Mass of Paul VI* (West Chester: Philothea Press, 2010). There remains a wide scope for further research in identifying the motivations and principles operative in the production of the liturgical books promulgated by Paul VI.

93 "Was nach dem Konzil weithin geschehen ist, bedeutet etwas ganz anderes: An die Stelle der gewordenen Liturgie hat man die gemachte Liturgie gesetzt. Man ist aus dem lebendigen Prozess des Wachsens und Werdens heraus umgestiegen in das Machen. Man wollte nicht mehr das organische Werden und Reifen des durch die Jahrhunderte hin Lebendigen fortführen, sondern setzte an dessen Stelle—nach dem Muster technischer Produktion—das Machen, das platte Produkt des Augenblicks;" in: Wilhelm Nyssen. ed., *Simandron. Der Wachklopfer. Gedenkschrift für Klaus Gamber (1919–1989)* (Köln: Luthe Verlag, 1989), pp. 14–15. See also: "Klaus Gamber: L'intrépidité d'un vrai témoin" K. Gamber, *La Réforme Liturgique en Question* (Barroux: Éditions Sainte-Madeleine, 1992), pp. 6–8; RCW 11, pp. 536–8.

94 See: U.M. Lang, *Turning Towards the Lord: Orientation in Liturgical Prayer* (San Francisco: Ignatius Press, 2004) and its preface by Joseph Cardinal Ratzinger (RCW 11, pp. 393–5); Athanasius Schneider, *Dominus Est—It is the Lord* (Pine Beach: Newman House Press, 2008).

95 Joseph Cardinal Ratzinger, Preface to: Reid, *The Organic Development of the Liturgy*, p. 13; RCW 11, pp. 593–4.

96 This is not to deny that some reforms prior to the 1962 Missal, such as the Holy Week rites, may themselves be in need of reconsideration. Much further scholarship is required in this area.

97 See: Peter Kwasniewski, *Resurgent in the Midst of Crisis: Sacred Liturgy, the Traditional Latin Mass, and Renewal in the Church* (Kettering, OH: Angelico Press, 2014).

98 For some considerations see: Johnston, *Care for the Church and Its Liturgy*, chapter 7; Paul A. McGavin, "Brackets and Footnotes: A Way toward Mutual Enrichment," *Antiphon* 14 (2010), pp. 273–84. In noting these studies the author does not imply concurrence with their proposals, which must be studied critically.

99 Kwasniewski, *Resurgent in the Midst of Crisis*, p. 27.

100 See: Christopher M.J. Zielinski OSB Oliv., "Liturgy, Ritual, and Contemporary Man—Anthropological and Psychological Connections," Reid, *Sacred Liturgy*, pp. 237–54.

101 For a consideration of the "true" Council see the Address of Benedict XVI at his meeting with the parish priests and clergy of the Diocese of Rome, February 14, 2013.

102 Tracey Rowland, "The *Usus Antiquior* and the New Evangelisation," Reid, *Sacred Liturgy*, pp. 115–37, (p. 132).

Select Bibliography

Benedict XVI, Apostolic Letter 'Motu Proprio Data' Summorum Pontificum, July 7, 2007.

—— "Letter of His Holiness Benedict XVI to the Bishops on the Occasion of the Publication of the Apostolic Letter 'Motu Proprio Data' Summorum Pontificum on the use of the Roman Liturgy Prior to the Reform of 1970," July 7, 2007.

Fortescue, Adrian; J.B. O'Connell & Alcuin Reid (eds), *The Ceremonies of the Roman Rite Described*, 15th edn (London: Burns & Oates, 2009).

Johnston, William H., *Care for the Church and Its Liturgy: A Study of Summorum Pontificum and the Extraordinary Form of the Roman Rite* (Collegeville: Liturgical Press, 2013).

Kwasniewski, Peter, *Resurgent in the Midst of Crisis: Sacred Liturgy, the Traditional Mass, and Renewal in the Church* (Kettering, OH: Angelico Press, 2014).

McManus, Frederick R., *Pontifical Rite of the Restored Order of Holy Week* (Paterson, NJ: St Anthony Guild Press, 1958).

O'Connell, J.B., *The Celebration of Mass*, 4th edn (Milwaukee: Bruce Publishing Company, 1964); reprinted by Preserving Christian Publications.

Reid, Alcuin, "Something old, Something new," *The Tablet*, 10 March 2007, pp. 10–11.

—— ed., *Looking Again at the Question of the Liturgy with Cardinal Ratzinger: Proceedings of the July 2001 Fontgombault Liturgical Conference* (Farnborough: St Michael's Abbey Press, 2003).

Tracey Rowland, "The *Usus Antiquior* and the New Evangelisation," A. Reid (ed.), *Sacred Liturgy: The Source and Summit of the Life and Mission of the Church* (San Francisco: Ignatius Press, 2014), pp. 115–37.

Soria Jiménez, Alberto, OSB, *Los principios de interpretación del 'motu proprio Summorum Pontificum'* (Madrid: Edicones Cristianidad, 2014).

Stehle, Aurelius, OSB & Emmeran A. Rettger OSB, *Manual of Episcopal Ceremonies*, 2 vols, 5th edn (Latrobe: St Vincent Archabbey, 1961); reprinted by Preserving Christian Publications.

Weishaupt, Gero P., *Päpstliche Weichenstellungen das Motu Proprio Summorum Pontificium Papst Benedikts XVI. und der Begleitbrief an die Bischöfe; ein kirchenrechtlicher Kommentar und Überlegungen zu einer "Reform der Reform"* (Bonn: Verlag für Kultur und Wiss, 2010)

—— *Die Instruktion "Universae Ecclesiae": ein kirchenrechtlicher Kommentar* (Kreuzlingen: Benedetto-Verlag, 2013). An English edition of Weishaupt's work is due for future publication by Ignatius Press.

Chapter 22

AN ANGLICAN PERSPECTIVE

Benjamin Gordon-Taylor

Introduction

It may fairly be claimed that Anglicans have made a very significant contribution to liturgical scholarship, and have done so most particularly in the period from about 1850 to the present. In the context of this book the present chapter, which is as its title suggests only a "perspective," and cannot claim to be comprehensive, in historical terms is concerned chiefly with those who saw the importance of the shared sources of the Western Catholic tradition. Many of these might broadly be identified as "Anglo-Catholics," but this is at the same time to recognize the problems of definition and interpretation that such a term involves, and to acknowledge the ebb and flow of wider ecclesiological debate past and present. Many individuals were also responsible for the founding and flourishing of corporate bodies which have sought to foster and underpin liturgical studies, such as the Henry Bradshaw Society and the Alcuin Club which have made their contribution through publishing in particular.

Conversely, it must be acknowledged that Anglicans and Anglicanism have always owed a great debt to Catholic liturgical scholars and liturgical life, directly and individually, but also in the influence these have had corporately on both scholarship and processes of liturgical revision within the Church of England and other provinces of the Anglican Communion. Indeed, more than ever before there is among liturgical scholars far less consciousness of confessional boundaries than once there would have been, as the very existence and character of such academic, international, and ecumenical bodies as *Societas Liturgica* bear witness. It is now completely unremarkable for a volume of essays on a liturgical topic to include authors from across the ecumenical spectrum of liturgical expression, especially where the topic is of common interest and significance, just as it is quite normal for an Anglican scholar to be published by a Roman Catholic press and vice versa. Liturgists today are for the most part bound by deep ties, instincts, and sympathies which transcend the debate and controversy which may exist in other areas of ecclesial life, although this is not at all to exclude robust discussion or the fruitful pursuit of differing interpretations—indeed these are strengthened by the character and quality of the inter-confessional nature of liturgical studies today.

The revival of liturgical scholarship in the Church of England

It might be assumed that the foundations of modern Anglican liturgical scholarship lie in the Oxford Movement, but the reality is not that straightforward. While the Oxford Movement undoubtedly prompted a revival of Catholic liturgical practice in the Church of England, by no means all Anglican liturgical scholars in the nineteenth century, nor indeed in the twentieth or twenty-first, were its explicit adherents or descendants, although crucially they had a scholarly interest in the wider Catholic liturgical heritage.[1] Part of the reason for this may have been that there continued in the Church of England a debate about the continuing suitability or otherwise of the Book of Common Prayer that had begun much earlier. As liturgists of the present day would undoubtedly claim, proposals for revision must be underpinned by sound scholarship.

One strand of scholarship in respect of the Book of Common Prayer is that of its origins and composition in relation to the sources on which it draws. There had always been a genre of commentary on the nature and text of the Prayer Book. A notable example was Charles Wheatly's *A Rational Illustration of the Book of Common Prayer of the Church of England*, first published in 1710 and still in print in the second half of the nineteenth century, an edition appearing, for example, in Bohn's Standard Library series in 1853, and another published by Cambridge University Press in 1858.[2] This could be described as the typical precursor of the more sophisticated work which began to emerge, since it drew on and presented in synthesis still earlier scholarship of the sixteenth century as well as presenting a contemporary interpretation. In this respect it is worth quoting the full subtitle of Wheatley's volume, which mentions in review some key early figures: *Being the Substance of every Thing Liturgical in Bishop Sparrow, Mr L'Estrange, Dr Comber, Dr Nichols, and all former Ritualists, Commentators, and others, upon the same Subject.* It should be pointed out that "ritualist" here means simply a student of rites, one concerned with the study of liturgy, not the meaning of the term when later applied to Anglican clergy whose liturgical practices in the Catholic direction caused controversy in the later nineteenth century. The description of the sort of study Wheatley was writing as a "rationale" is significant, and provides a critical link with what could be called the first modern scholarly study of the Prayer Book by Francis Procter, whose *History of the Book of Common Prayer with a Rationale of its Offices* appeared in 1855,[3] itself to be rewritten at the very beginning of the new century by Walter Frere, whose resulting *New History of the Book of Common Prayer with a Rationale of its Offices*, the classic "Procter and Frere," was still in print in at least 1961.[4] Of the names in Wheatley's subtitle, that of Hamon L'Estrange is of particular interest for later developments in scholarship, since he is noted for having examined the text of the Book of Common Prayer and its precursors by the method of comparative columns, in a work entitled *Alliance of Divine Offices* of 1690,[5] a method repeated in terms of the sources of the Book of Common Prayer and in much more extensive and accurate fashion by F.E. Brightman in *The English Rite* of 1915,[6] still a definitive work of its kind.

Most scholars of the Book of Common Prayer had in common the explicit or implied motive of assuring the sufficiency and fitness for purpose of the text as it had become fixed in 1662, a concern which in the case of at least Procter, Frere, and Brightman must involve a measure of assumed continuity with the pre-Reformation liturgy in England since the sources are examined so carefully. This assumed ecclesiological as much as liturgical continuity, the view that the Book of Common Prayer was *the* "English Liturgy" in succession to the pre-Reformation rites, and its demonstration, formed a key element in the approach to liturgical scholarship of many of those who could be described as influenced or convinced by the claims of the Oxford Movement, and whose work came to form part of the intellectual underpinning of the progress and evolution of the Movement in its later forms. Also, however, for the later figures mentioned here their work increasingly served to underpin a growing momentum for the revision of the 1662 Book of Common Prayer by a liturgy which took into account the scholarly advances of the nineteenth and early twentieth centuries. These advances would come to suggest for this group of scholars the need for a revision of the text in what might be loosely described as a Catholic direction, most especially in respect of the Eucharist.

The interest in the pre-Reformation sources of the Book of Common Prayer also suggests a wider interest in the liturgical history of the Church in the West and the East before the Reformation. This forms the second major development in liturgical scholarship among Anglicans in the nineteenth century. One aspect of this interest was specifically the Church in medieval England, and again, there was an ecclesiological implication at work, that of a sense of this era as part of the inheritance of the Church of England, but the results of the scholarship had a much wider potential audience.

Here we encounter once again the significance of individuals. Richard Pfaff in his recent and excellent *History of the Liturgy in Medieval England* usefully reviews the developments in the historiography of medieval English liturgy and the particular contribution of Anglicans.[7] Thus he notes William Maskell (c. 1814–90), "one of the first scholars of the nineteenth century to devote himself to serious liturgical study," author of *The Ancient Liturgy of the Church of England* (1844) and *Monumenta Ritualia Ecclesiae Anglicanae* (1846), the titles of both of which carried clear ecclesiological implication, although Maskell was to become a Roman Catholic in 1850.[8] Pfaff describes F.H. Dickinson (1813–90) as "a lay amateur … a country gentleman, co-founder of Wells Theological College [an Anglican seminary], and High Sheriff of Somerset," whose liturgical scholarship produced works of similar ecclesiological assumption: a *List of Printed Service Books according to the Ancient Use of the Church of England*, and importantly what Pfaff regards as "the first modern edition of a medieval English service book," that of the Sarum Missal, produced in stages between 1861 and 1883.[9] Later figures included Henry Austin Wilson (1854–1927), "an Anglican clergyman (and son of a bishop), lifelong Oxford don, and immensely productive editor of important liturgical texts,"[10] among them the *Gelasian Sacramentary*.[11] Another great figure in this flowering of Anglican liturgical scholarship was the layman John Wickham Legg, a surgeon by formal training, of whom more will be said below in connection with the Henry Bradshaw Society.

Into the twentieth century: "English" or "Western" Use?

It has always been the case that within the bounds of broad definition, there have been varying interpretations of what continuity with the Western tradition and its sacramental emphasis meant in liturgical practice. In the first half of the twentieth century, and particularly evidently in the period between the First and Second World Wars, Anglo-Catholics were essentially divided ecclesiologically, and therefore liturgically, into two main groups. Thus the so-called "Anglo-Papalists" favored a liturgy which resembled as closely as possible, in ceremonial and to varying degrees text (including sometimes the use of Latin) that of the Roman Catholic liturgy of the day, called by them the "Western Use," while those who came commonly to be called "Prayer Book Catholics" placed emphasis on the so-called "English Use" as fully and legitimately expressive of the Catholic heritage of the Church of England: in other words, the Book of Common Prayer and, for some of them, its limited supplementing with material in English translation taken from the Sarum rite of the immediate pre-Reformation period. It is worth examining the nature of this distinction, which can be traced largely in the contemporary reports of the Anglo-Catholic Congresses and in the various unofficial but widely used liturgical books produced in support of each approach.

In 1923, Wilfred Knox, the brother of the convert to Roman Catholicism Ronald Knox, claimed that "the course of events has finally decided in favour of those who advocate a very considerable alteration of the external forms of Anglican worship and the introduction of a very wide measure of Roman practice in matters of devotion."[12] However, this assertion was at the very least somewhat premature, in that there was clearly a serious difference of opinion at the liturgical heart of the movement, and the debate continued throughout the inter-war period. At the 1927 Congress, Stephen Gaselee, and Maurice Child attempted to strike a conciliatory note with "a joint publication of two persons who hold different preferences as to the ceremonial of the Eucharist." They sought to reassure the Congress participants: "We have not come here to make a gladiatorial show for your amusement, and we regret uncharitable words that have been used on both sides: the English usager will not call the other party a 'Romanizer', the Westerner will not speak with a sneer of 'British Museum Religion.'"[13] Instead they set out the relative merits of the "Western [i.e. Roman] Use" and the "English Use."[14]

Yet there is little sign that their irenic approach had any real effect. At the same Congress, Kenneth Mackenzie spoke exclusively in support of Roman forms, and stated that "for all practical purposes the Roman rite has not been unworthy to take its place as the premier rite of Christendom."[15] Child himself, who presented the case for the "Western Use," called the Roman rite "convenient and orderly . . .

worked out by experts," an implied indictment of the liturgical skills of the framers, and probably the contemporary revisers, of the Book of Common Prayer. Child maintained that the Roman rite was "safe guide for anything that we can possibly want."[16] This argument in support of the use of Roman forms reflected an ecclesiological as well as a liturgical point of view which was expressed liturgically in the proposition that "ceremony follows Patriarchate:" the Pope was Patriarch of the Western Church, of which the Anglican Communion was a part, and therefore it was "seemly to follow the Bishop of Rome in the ceremonial which he has succeeded in inducing the rest of the West to adopt."[17] This principle had already been discussed at the Anglo-Catholic Priests' Convention in 1921, when R.L. Langford-James had asked a question as to what was "the nature and scope of the authority which is claimed for the Book of Common Prayer as binding on Western Catholics."[18] Apart from this ecclesiological argument, proponents of the Western Use contended that there was also important pastoral and spiritual justification: Wilfred Knox argued that Roman forms were aids to greater devotion, as opposed to what he termed "the more old-fashioned type of Anglican piety."[19] This suggests a wider agenda in the context of the Anglo-Catholic movement as a whole. One effect of the Oxford Movement and its aftermath had been to restore within the Church of England aspects of belief which had fallen out of currency, especially in respect of the Eucharist, and it was possible to argue that the static character of Anglican liturgical provision meant that such aspects could not be taught and expressed without making use of additional material from contemporary Catholic sources. However, this argument had relatively little airing, and the debate tended to be dominated by ecclesiological concerns.

This form of Anglo-Catholic liturgical expression and rationale had most influence in parishes, and many parishes so influenced continue to use the Roman missal as the basis of their liturgical life. This has become an established part of Anglican life, particularly in England, although for some the ecclesiological anomaly remains, blurred to some degree by liturgical revision in the Church of England which has seen a significant degree of textual and visual convergence, although the presence of a range of theological stances has inevitably shaped the outcome of most elements of the revision process.

Supporters of the other main strand of liturgical usage in the Anglo-Catholic movement between the wars, who favored the so-called "English Use," were on the whole more moderate Anglo-Catholics whose ecclesiology gave far less emphasis to the role of the papacy, and far more to the original Tractarian spirit of the continuity of the Church of England with the Western tradition as expressed in England. To some extent, they shared the view of their opponents that the Book of Common Prayer as it stood was no longer fit for purpose, but argued that the solution was not its abandonment but its revision, and did not believe that they were free to depart from the existing liturgy of the Church of England, however deficient in their opinion it may have become. Nevertheless, they believed that the existing eucharistic rite in the Book of Common Prayer could be interpreted in such a way as to allow enrichment of ceremonial in a correspondingly architecturally appropriate and suitably furnished setting. The sources of such an interpretation lay not in contemporary Roman Catholic but in medieval English liturgical usage and an approach to the Book of Common Prayer which emphasized its Catholic continuity rather than its reformed revolution. In respect of the mediaeval sources, the Use of Sarum with its distinctive character was seen as the true Catholic precursor of the English liturgy of the day.

In the Book of Common Prayer, crucial to the argument was the interpretation of the so-called "Ornaments Rubric," which set out what the liturgical space was to look like, and what those who ministered in it were to wear. The nature of the interpretation and its practical consequences is classically set out in *The Parson's Handbook* by Percy Dearmer, Vicar of St Mary's, Primrose Hill, and a leading supporter of the English Use.[20] First published at the end of the nineteenth century, it remained in print in successive and increasingly enlarged and illustrated editions until the 1960s, and contained meticulously detailed information about the setting and celebration of the "English Liturgy".[21] The visual and performative dimension of the English Use was also encouraged by the Alcuin Club, and particularly in *A Manual of Ceremonial* first published in 1921, which as its title suggests gives directions for and illustrates in drawings and photographs the celebration of the Eucharist using the text of the Book of Common Prayer but with ceremonial adapted from mediaeval English forms, including the presence of celebrant, deacon and subdeacon in the traditional vestments and the use of lights and incense.[22]

This strand of Anglo-Catholic liturgical practice was potentially far more acceptable to the ecclesiastical authorities of the Church of England since it claimed not to depart from the authority of the Book of Common Prayer, although in reality to many the two positions were probably indistinguishable in a largely pre-ecumenical and intellectually unsympathetic era of suspicion of anything perceived as "Roman." Ironically, the Western Use took the contemporary Roman rite as its yardstick, while it could have been said that there was nothing very contemporary about the English Use, hence the jibe of its opponents, quoted by Gaselee and Child, that it was "British Museum Religion." Yet it could be claimed that it has been the English Use in varying degrees that can be said to have done most to influence the liturgical practice of many Anglican cathedrals and greater churches: for example, the wearing of traditional vestments of Gothic rather than Latin shape by the ministers, and of plain albs with apparelled amices by servers, both of which were classic indicators of the English Use. Even in the period between the wars the influence was at work where supporters of the style held high office: the English Use was introduced at Truro Cathedral by its leading proponent, the diocesan bishop himself, Walter Frere,[23] and at York Minster by the dean, Eric Milner White.[24]

The two main strands of Anglo-Catholic liturgical practice in this period gave rise to a number of specially produced liturgical books.[25] These were not authorized publications of the Church of England, unlike the Book of Common Prayer, although they were related to it in varying degrees and often included in some way the texts of the Order for Holy Communion. Their production had begun in the nineteenth century, but the third decade of the twentieth century was perhaps their zenith, and the period by which they most clearly reflected the two schools of thought and practice in their content and appearance. For the proponents of the Western Use, most enduringly the *English Missal* was the preferred book, the latter appearing in several increasingly elaborate editions from 1912 up to the final one in 1958,[26] the altar edition of which contained colored plates; there were many successive hand editions for the laity. It contained the text of the Book of Common Prayer order for Holy Communion, but also the Roman canon in Latin and English and the Ordinary of the Mass, the two forms interspersed. In its manner of decoration it mirrored traditional Catholic practice: texts in black, rubrics in red. The equivalent for the English Use was *The English Liturgy*, edited by Walter Frere, Percy Dearmer, and Samuel Mumford Taylor, first produced in 1903 and going through several editions down to 1950.[27] Unlike the *English Missal* it only appeared in an altar edition. It too had texts in black and rubrics in red, but the texts were those of the Book of Common Prayer only, with notation for singing parts of the liturgy, including the epistle and gospel, according to the chant. Other altar books reflecting this strand of Anglo-Catholic worship were in use, some of which included supplementary material from "English" sources, and still more were produced or modified after 1928 in order to make use of the order for the Eucharist (and the eucharistic prayer) in the proposed 1928 Book of Common Prayer.

With the revision of the liturgy of the Roman Catholic Church from the 1950s, and particularly with the introduction of the Missal of Paul VI in 1970, many of those who had used the *English Missal* abandoned it in favor of the new Roman rite in its entirety, or of a version of the new Church of England order for the Eucharist in contemporary language, initially "Series 3," later Rite A in the *Alternative Service Book* of 1980, and most recently Order 1 in the current *Common Worship* family of rites, often with "Catholic" additions. With the introduction of the English translation of the third typical edition of the Roman missal in Catholic parishes in England in 2011, it remains to be seen how extensive a use this comes to have in those Anglican parishes which have hitherto used its predecessor, especially in view of the decision of Rome to depart from those texts of the ordinary of the Mass previously used in common, and given the consequences of this decision, for example in terms of familiarity and musical resources.

Liturgical scholarship: the Henry Bradshaw Society

The Henry Bradshaw Society was established in 1890 in memory of the eponymous former Librarian of Cambridge University, for the production of scholarly editions and facsimiles of liturgical texts from the medieval period.[28] From the beginning, it was a collaborative work of Anglicans and Roman Catholics whose scholarly interests coincided, and thus from the perspective of today must be seen as a remarkable expression of early ecumenism in which a commitment to sound liturgical scholarship on the basis of common sources to some degree transcended the acknowledged divisions and mutual suspicions of the time, a factor that is still present among the liturgical scholars of the present era, for example in the character and membership of the international *Societas Liturgica*. Of members of the early Council and the longer list of supporters, a majority were Anglicans and included the Archbishop of Canterbury among the supporters, but several prominent Roman Catholic figures were also involved, among them the layman Edmund Bishop, author of the classic collection of essays, *Liturgica Historica*.[29] At the first meeting of the Society there was an unfortunate attempt to exclude Roman Catholics from membership, but this failed,[30] and their participation was thenceforward assured. Nevertheless, as Ward and Johnson conclude, the driving force was the Anglican Wickham Legg:

> If any one man ... typified the enterprise that was the Henry Bradshaw Society in the years of its infancy and fast-achieved maturity, that man was John Wickham Legg. A fine figure of an exacting scholar with a warm and unprejudiced heart, Legg was the soul and guiding principle of the best that Henry Bradshaw Society achieved. Around him other figures clustered, some of whom, despite notable contributions, have left little trace in the annals. We might think for example of the Rev. William John Blew, possessor of a remarkable liturgical library, and a Vice-President of the Henry Bradshaw Society at his death. There were those, too, such as Christopher Wordsworth or the young Frere, whose merits were great and who have met with their biographies.[31]

The authors and editors of the main series of published editions were indeed at first mostly Anglicans, and their names reflect the vigorous and serious interest in the pre-Reformation liturgy shown by late nineteenth and early twentieth-century Anglican scholars. Wordsworth, Frere, Warren, Wilson, and Wickham Legg all edited one or more volumes in the first fifteen years of the Society's existence.

The series is still in progress and now numbers some 120 volumes, and the Henry Bradshaw Society series of volumes is today an esteemed and rich resource for the study of the liturgy of the medieval Church, although not every volume in the series is directly liturgical in character. Since 1994 there has also been a series of occasional volumes, the *Subsidia*; these are mainly extended monographs on themes connected with the main interests of the Society.[32]

Liturgical scholarship: the Alcuin Club

The Alcuin Club was founded in 1897 by four Anglican laymen who met and resolved that: "A club to be called the Alcuin Club be and is hereby constituted." As a historian of the club, George Timms, has written: "The Alcuin Club is unique in its existence and in the number and range of its scholarly publications."[33] In 1897, though, the Alcuin Club took its place among a number of Victorian clubs and societies with liturgical and ecclesiastical interests, for example the English Historical Society, the Camden Society, and the Henry Bradshaw Society. In common with the Camden Society, founded in 1839, a guiding principle of the Alcuin Club in its early years was that "it was not possible to understand the nature of the medieval Church without diligent research into service-books, visitation articles, parochial records and the devotional and dogmatic writings of the Middle Ages in England,"[34] and this perspective came to include the study of vestments and other visual ornaments of the Church.

Initially the Alcuin Club was under the direction of the four lay founders: again John Wickham Legg, also the main founder of the Henry Bradshaw Society; H.B. Briggs, a musician known for his expertise in the chant; W.H. St John Hope, and J.T. Micklethwaite, both experts on church furnishings and architecture. However, eleven more persons were invited to the second meeting of the Committee, among then seven clergymen, among whom were some now regarded as luminaries of Anglican liturgical scholarship: F.E. Brightman, author of *The English Rite*; Walter Frere, later superior of the Community of the Resurrection at Mirfield and then Bishop of Truro; H.A. Wilson, editor of *The Gelasian Sacramentary*; and Christopher Wordsworth, also a skilled editor of early texts. These names were also all associated with the Henry Bradshaw Society in its early years. Thus the laymen of the original foundation were soon joined and eventually outnumbered by clergy, but it has always has been the case that the Alcuin Club has had distinguished lay scholars on its Committee and among its members.

The four lay founders determined that "the object of the said Club be to promote the study of the history and use of the Book of Common Prayer." As Timms comments, "The Prayer Book was to be central in all the Club's activities and the 'touch-stone' and guiding principle of all its publications,"[35] at least in the early period. Indeed, though initially membership was for a time open only to Anglicans, one of the extremely fruitful aspects of the Club as it has developed is its ecumenical character, both in terms of members and of authors of its publications. The scope and subjects of the publications has also reflected this, although the Anglican ethos remains.

The founders also resolved that "the work of the Club be the publication of Tracts dealing with the Object of the Club, and such other works as may seem desirable, with reproductions of miniatures from MSS and photographs of Church Furniture, Ornaments and Vestments."[36] One could sum up the original object and work of the Club as the fostering of liturgical study and publication of liturgical works which have some connection with the Book of Common Prayer. Since 1897, however, the range and scope of publications has expanded and diversified, and today they include works of liturgical theology and wider liturgical history more generally. Since the 1920s there has also been an important strand of encouraging and resourcing good liturgical practice.

The Anglican character of the Club is still very much present, but in the late 1980s a partnership was entered into with the Anglican Evangelical Group for the Renewal of Worship, with a view to publishing a series of booklets on liturgical subjects which covered a wider spectrum of the tradition, and was more widely ecumenical in scope. There are now usually two studies published each year. This has proved a convenient format for the study of one specific issue or the production of an edition and/or translation of a liturgical text.

The Secretary of the Alcuin Club wrote in a Club newsletter in 1988: "There is need (we are convinced of this) for a society that is rigorously scholarly yet thoroughly pastoral in its approach, that is open to the new ecumenical atmosphere in which liturgy is done and yet treasures the Anglican and Catholic emphasis that Alcuin has stood for, and which can do some important work in helping the Church to prepare for [future liturgical revision]." This is still true of the Club, whose publications are of value to scholars and practitioners across the ecclesiological spectrum. The list of authors of Alcuin Club publications continue to include many of the most prominent Anglican liturgical scholars of the day, and the continuing series of the Club are a testimony to the ongoing commitment of Anglicans and ecumenical partners to liturgical research and good practice in a shared liturgical tradition.[37] The value of this work to students has most recently borne fruit in the preparation and publication of *The Study of Liturgy and Worship*, a new guide to liturgical studies on a thematic and ecumenical basis, reflecting contemporary practice in the teaching of liturgy.[38]

Anglican liturgical scholarship: two personalities

Much could be written about many Anglican scholars of the liturgy, past and present, who have or have had an instinctive feel for the shared Western tradition, but it seems most useful to draw brief attention to two particularly distinguished exemplars of the two main strands of Anglican liturgical scholarship and practice in the first half of the twentieth century: Walter Frere and Gregory Dix. They are of considerable and lasting significance and reputation, and their contributions to liturgical scholarship lie behind a great deal of more recent work by both Anglican and Roman Catholic writers. Without their work, liturgical scholarship and liturgical revision in the Anglican Communion would have looked very different. An examination of their work by the student will lead to that of their contemporaries.

Walter Howard Frere (1863–1938)

Walter Frere was one of the original members of the Community of the Resurrection (CR), an Anglican Religious Community founded by Charles Gore (later Bishop of Worcester and of Oxford) in 1892, moving via Radley in Oxfordshire to Mirfield in the West Riding of Yorkshire in 1898. Frere was elected Superior of the Community in 1902, and in 1922 was appointed Bishop of Truro, the first monastic in the Church of England to become a bishop, and still one of only a very few Anglican religious to have been a diocesan bishop. In the latter part of the nineteenth century he established himself as a scholar of church history, liturgical texts, and liturgical music; he was a founder member of the Alcuin Club (later for many years its President), and a contributor to the Henry Bradshaw Society series of scholarly editions of texts. His liturgical interests focused on the history and proposed revision of the Book of Common Prayer, Western liturgical sources, and the history of the chant in the liturgy. He typifies the so-called Prayer Book Catholic in his outlook, interests and interpretations, yet he was also profoundly and pioneeringly ecumenical as a participant in the Malines Conversations in the 1920s. He was a prominent figure in the debates on Prayer Book revision, indeed he had been elevated to the episcopate partly to bring liturgical expertise to that body in that context. He is a figure who invites further study.[39]

Gregory Dix (1901–52)

In contrast to Frere, and his junior by three decades, but by no means in uncreative opposition to him—he wrote a considerable appreciation of Frere in the memorial volume edited by C.S. Phillips—Gregory Dix represents the so-called "Western Use" strand of Catholic Anglicanism in the twentieth century, and his liturgical practice, publications, opinions, and interpretations reflect that expression. Dix was a monk of the Anglican Benedictine community at Nashdom Abbey, and a considerable scholar, whose work on the structure of the Eucharist was especially influential within and beyond the Anglican Communion. It found classic expression in his *magnum opus*: *The Shape of the Liturgy* published in 1947, a massive work still in print and hugely influential on generations of students of liturgy, but since subject to considerable scholarly criticism and revisionist comment. Nevertheless, Dix's achievement would not have been what it was without his comprehensive vision of the Western tradition, and in this sense he typifies an important Anglican view of the shared sources of the liturgy. Dix also merits further study.[40]

The later twentieth century and after

The second half of the twentieth century and the beginning of the twenty-first has seen a vibrant continuity in the tradition of Anglican liturgical scholarship which encompasses the whole spectrum of liturgical history, thus continuing a commitment to the study of shared sources as well as uniquely Anglican aspects. There has, for example, arisen a formidable tradition of liturgical scholarship in the Episcopal Church in the United States which has become an essential and influential part of the wider Anglican liturgical scene, and which has made a significant contribution to the liturgical studies of many denominations in North America and beyond; the Episcopal Church has produced a distinguished line of liturgical scholars of international influence.

In Britain, the commitment to liturgical studies of university departments of theology has been far less enthusiastic than that of many in North America, such that many Anglican liturgical scholars in the United Kingdom, including those of the broadly Catholic tradition, are either teachers in Church of England theological colleges (although usually in this way affiliated to a university) or holders of pastoral appointments in parishes and universities. A positive side to this, however, is that the tradition of the Anglican scholar-parson survives in liturgical studies, and not just among those who would describe themselves as "Anglo-Catholic."

Vitally, in the past fifty or so years, the hitherto almost exclusively male and clerical world of Anglican liturgical studies has been enriched by the emergence of female scholars on both sides of the Atlantic, and a welcome resurgence of lay authors. At the same time, it has become increasingly difficult to identify a clear strand of "Anglo-Catholic" liturgical scholarship, partly since traditions within and beyond the Anglican Communion have become used to co-operation and complementarity rather than competition, and because there has been a growing resistance to ecclesiological "labels," often now seen as unhelpful in the context of ecumenical collaboration and a sense of shared endeavor in studying the worship of the past and the present with a view to a common future. Thus it is very important in the Anglican context to recognize the contribution of evangelical Anglicans to liturgical scholarship in the last fifty years as fully complementing that of the Catholic tradition within Anglicanism, and this must be seen as an essential and indispensible aspect of the Anglican influence on the study of the wider shared tradition.

A new era of liturgical revision in the Church of England (and soon more widely in the Anglican Communion) began in 1955 with the formation of the Liturgical Commission, which included representatives of the various theological traditions in the Church of England.[41] It was in many ways a means of moving on from the rejection by Parliament in 1928 of the proposed revision and replacement of the Book of Common Prayer of 1662.[42] The debates leading to the 1928 book were conducted largely along (theological) "party" lines, and so the new approach heralded not the end of vigorous debate on liturgical matters but at least a more constructive means of taking the range of views into account. The key to future progress lay in the decision not to attempt to replace the Book of Common Prayer, but to produce alternatives to it. The first finally authorized result of this process was the *Alternative Service Book* (ASB) of 1980, which had been preceded since 1966 by the experimental liturgies of Series One, Two, and Three. The ASB was itself replaced by a new family of volumes under the banner of *Common Worship: Services and Prayers for the Church of England*, published from 1997. *Common Worship* signalled a new approach to revision in that it abandoned the assumption stemming from the Book of Common Prayer that all necessary liturgical material could be contained in one book, a fact recognized during the currency of the *Alternative Service Book*.[43] Instead emphasis is placed on common liturgical structures, but with a comprehensive library of material from which to select according to the rules to order the service and the notes provided with each liturgy.

At all points in these processes, the influence of Anglican liturgical scholars and practitioners has been present, as have crucial ecumenical perspectives, for example through the work of successive incarnations of the Anglican-Roman Catholic International Commission. Also, meetings of the Liturgical Commission are attended by observers from other churches, including the Roman Catholic, and the liturgical reform that has taken place in the Roman Catholic Church over the past fifty years has been an essential and often significantly influential part of the wider ecumenical context, and continues in the collaborative study of the shared sources of Western Christendom.

Notes

1 A series of short studies of Anglican liturgical scholars of the nineteenth and twentieth centuries, together with select bibliographies for each, is to be found in: C. Irvine (ed.) *They Shaped Our Worship: Essays on Anglican Liturgists*, Alcuin Club Collections 75 (London: SPCK, 1998).

2 C. Wheatley, *A Rational Illustration of the Book of Common Prayer* (London: Bohn, 1853; Cambridge: CUP, 1858).

3 F. Procter, *History of the Book of Common Prayer with a Rationale of its Offices* (London: Macmillan, 1855).

4 F. Procter & W.H. Frere, *New History of the Book of Common Prayer with a Rationale of its Offices*, 1st edn (London: Macmillan, 1901; repr. 3rd corrected impression, London: Macmillan, 1961).

5 H. L'Estrange, *Alliance of Divine Offices* (London: Broom, 1659; several editions, reissued, Oxford: Parker, 1846).

6 F.E. Brightman, *The English Rite, Being a Synopsis of the Sources and Revisions of the Book of Common Prayer*, 2 vols (London: Rivington's, 1915).

7 R.W. Pfaff, *The Liturgy in Medieval England: A History* (Cambridge: CUP, 2009); see especially pp. 9–12. The contribution of Anglican scholars to our knowledge of this subject is evident throughout Pfaff's study.

8 Ibid., p. 9.

9 Ibid., pp. 9–10.

10 Ibid., p. 10.

11 H.A. Wilson (ed.), *The Gelasian Sacramentary* (Oxford: Clarendon Press, 1894).

12 W.L. Knox, *The Catholic Movement in the Church of England* (London: Philip Allan, 1923).

13 M. Child & S. Gaselee, "Eucharistic Ceremonies," *Report of the Anglo-Catholic Congress; Subject: The Holy Eucharist* (London: Society of SS. Peter & Paul, 1927), pp. 195–203.

14 Ibid., pp. 195–6.

15 K.D. Mackenzie, "Eucharistic Rites," *Report of the Anglo-Catholic Congress; Subject: The Holy Eucharist* (London: Society of SS. Peter & Paul 1927), pp. 183–95 (p. 193).

16 Child & Gaselee, "Eucharistic Ceremonies," p. 200.

17 Ibid., p. 200.

18 *Report of the First Anglo-Catholic Priests' Convention: General Subject: Priestly Efficiency* (London: Society of SS. Peter & Paul, 1921), p. 88.

19 Knox, *Catholic Movement*, p. 236.

20 For an excellent biography of Dearmer, see: Donald Gray, *Percy Dearmer: A Parson's Pilgrmage* (Norwich: Canterbury Press, 2000).

21 The full title is instructive: P. Dearmer, *The Parson's Handbook Containing Practical Directions both for Parsons and Others as to the Management of the Parish Church and its Services According to the Anglican Use, as Set Forth in the Book of Common Prayer*, 12th edition (London: Humphrey Milford, 1932). Earlier editions, for instance that of 1899, had contained "An Introductory Essay on Conformity to the Church of England," thus claiming legitimacy for the liturgical approach taken, remarks taken into the introductions of later editions.

22 *A Manual of Ceremonial*, Alcuin Club Tracts xiii (London: Mowbray, 1921; 4th edition including photographs, 1947).

23 The directions are given in a booklet of which the author is not stated but almost certainly written by Frere (although his initials do appear after the Foreword):

Directions for the Celebration of the Holy Communion by the sacred Ministers in accordance with the alternative Order published in 1928 (Truro: Netherton & Worth, 1935). Although it had been rejected by Parliament, Frere nonetheless authorized the 1928 Order for the Eucharist for use in his diocese.

24 At York Minster, a service booklet was introduced which explained the service and provided devotional material for the worshipper. This too has no stated author but its style strongly suggests Milner-White himself: *The Holy Eucharist in York Minster with Instructions and Private Prayers* (York, n.d.). Here the rite is that of 1662.

25 For a detailed and informative study of Anglo-Catholic liturgical books from the nineteenth century onwards, see M. Dalby, *Anglican Missals and their Canons: 1549, Interim Rite and Roman,* Alcuin/GROW Joint Liturgical Studies 41 (Cambridge: Grove Books, 1998).

26 *Missale Anglicanum: The English Missal* (London: W. Knott, 1912), and many editions thereafter, some with varying titles although essentially in the same series of editions: see Dalby, *Anglican Missals*, pp. 19–20.

27 P. Dearmer, W.H. Frere & S.M. Taylor (eds), *The English Liturgy from the Book of Common Prayer with Additional Collects, Epistles and Gospels* (London: Rivingtons, 1903), and subsequent editions.

28 A.Ward & C. Johnson, "The Henry Bradshaw Society: Its Birth and First Decade 1890–1900," *Ephemerides Liturgicae* 104 (1990), pp. 187–200.

29 E. Bishop, *Liturgica Historica: Papers on the Liturgy and Religious Life of the Western Church* (Oxford: Clarendon Press, 1918).

30 Ward & Johnson, "Henry Bradshaw Society," p. 7.

31 Ibid., pp. 14–15.

32 For an excellent guide to the publications of the Society up to 1992, see: A. Ward, *The Publications of the Henry Bradshaw Society: An Annotated Bibliography with Indexes,* BELS 67 (1992); also the website: www.henrybradshawsociety.org with link to the current list of publications since 1890 and the text of the article by Ward and Johnson cited above.

33 For a more detailed history of the Alcuin Club down to its centenary in 1987, and annotated bibliography up to 1996, see: P.J. Jagger, *The Alcuin Club and its Publications 1897–1987* (Norwich: Alcuin Club/Hymns Ancient & Modern, 1996), in which G. Timms, "The History of the Alcuin Club: Some Insights into Liturgical Study, Writing, and Publishing," pp. 3–21, on which this paragraph largely draws.

34 Timms, "Alcuin Club", p. 3.

35 Ibid., p. 7.

36 Ibid.

37 For current publications of the Alcuin Club see: www.alcuinclub.org.uk

38 Juliette Day and Benjamin Gordon-Taylor (eds), *The Study of Liturgy and Worship: An Alcuin Guide* (London: SPCK, 2013; Collegeville: Liturgical Press, 2013).

39 Further reading on Frere and a guide to his work and publications can be found in the following: Benjamin Gordon-Taylor and Nicolas Stebbing CR (eds), *Walter Frere: Scholar, Monk, Bishop* (Norwich: Canterbury Press, 2011), a new assessment of Frere's life and work, in which see especially essays by John Livesley, Philip Corbett, Benjamin Gordon-Taylor, and Peter Allan CR on Frere's liturgical interests, public and educational role in respect of liturgy, and scholarly context; C.S. Phillips (ed.), *Walter Howard Frere* (London: Faber & Faber, 1947), a memorial volume with essays by, among others, the major Anglican liturgical scholars Gregory Dix OSB and Gabriel Hebert SSM, interesting as near-contemporary assessments of his work;

R.C.D. Jasper (ed.), *Walter Howard Frere: His Correspondence on Liturgical Revision and Construction*, Alcuin Club Collections 39 (London: SPCK, 1954). This annotated collection of Frere's correspondence gives a vivid impression of the concerns and profound scholarly approach of one of those Catholic-minded individuals most intimately involved with Prayer Book Revision in the years leading up to 1928.

40 See: Gregory Dix, *The Shape of the Liturgy* (London: Dacre Press, 1947). One of the most influential works of liturgical scholarship of the twentieth century, subject to much revision and critical study which it is essential to read alongside Dix's work, and yet it remains a classic of its kind, not least for the famous passages of "blue prose" which do much to stir the imagination and underline the central importance of the liturgy in Anglican life as it is set in the wider western tradition. Gregory Dix, *The Apostolic Tradition* (London: SPCK, 1937), an edition of a major early text which still takes its place among the many editions and studies of the *Apostolic Tradition*, but which must be read in conjunction with more recent publications and opinions as to authorship and purpose. Gregory Dix, *A Detection of Aumbries* (London: Dacre Press, 1942), a more eccentric example of Dix's enthusiasms: a study of the reservation of the Blessed Sacrament, with a special emphasis on English practice. This relatively short work was challenged after his death by the response of S.J.P. van Dijk & J.H. Walker, *The Myth of the Aumbry* (London: Burns & Oates, 1957). Simon Jones, "Introduction," G. Dix, *The Shape of the Liturgy*, new edn (London: Continuum, 2005), pp. x–xxviii. This is an essential essay on Dix and his subsequent interpreters which contains further bibliography necessary to any serious study and appraisal of Dix's work. Simon Jones (ed.) *The Sacramental Life: Gregory Dix and His Writings*, Canterbury Studies in Spiritual Theology (Norwich: Canterbury Press, 2007), a Dix "reader," ideal as an introduction to his work, with excellent linking commentary. Simon Bailey, *A Tactful God: Gregory Dix, Priest, Monk and Scholar* (Leominster: Gracewing, 1995).

41 R.C.D. Jasper, *The Development of Anglican Liturgy 1662–1980* (London: SPCK, 1989). The definitive overview of liturgical revision by a scholar who was a member of the Liturgical Commission from its inception in 1955 until after the publication of the ASB, and its Chairman from 1964; also G.J. Cuming, *A History of Anglican Liturgy* (London: Macmillan, 1969).

42 On which process and what led to it see: Donald Gray, *The 1927–28 Prayer Book Crisis: Volume 1. Ritual, Royal Commissions, and Reply to the Royal Letters of Business*, Joint Liturgical Studies 60 (Cambridge: Grove Books, 2005); idem, *The 1927–28 Prayer Book Crisis: Volume 2. The cul-de-sac of the 'Deposited Book' . . . until further order be taken*, Joint Liturgical Studies 61 (Cambridge: Grove Books, 2006).

43 For liturgical revision in the Church of England in the period leading up to the introduction of Common Worship, see: David Hebblethwaite, *Liturgical Revision in the Church of England 1984–2004: the working of the Liturgical Commission*, Joint Liturgical Studies 57 (Cambridge: Grove Books, 2004).

Bibliography

Brightman, F.E., *The English Rite, Being a Synopsis of the Sources and Revisions of the Book of Common Prayer*, 2 vols (London: Rivington's, 1915).

Cuming, G.J., *A History of Anglican Liturgy* (London: Macmillan, 1969).

Dalby, M., *Anglican Missals and their Canons: 1549, Interim Rite and Roman* (Cambridge: Grove Books, 1998).

Day, Juliette & Gordon-Taylor, B. (eds), *The Study of Liturgy and Worship: An Alcuin Guide* (London & Collegeville: SPCK & Liturgical Press, 2013).

Dearmer, P., *The Parson's Handbook Containing Practical Directions both for Parsons and Others as to the Management of the Parish Church and its Services According to the Anglican Use, as Set Forth in the Book of Common Prayer*, 12th edn (London: Humphrey Milford, 1932).

Dix, Gregory, *The Shape of the Liturgy* (London: Dacre Press, 1947).

Gordon-Taylor, B. & N. Stebbing (eds), *Walter Frere: Scholar, Monk, Bishop* (Norwich: Canterbury Press, 2011).

Gray, D., *Percy Dearmer: A Parson's Pilgrmage* (Norwich: Canterbury Press, 2000).

—— *The 1927–28 Prayer Book Crisis: Volume 1. Ritual, Royal Commissions, and Reply to the Royal Letters of Business* (Cambridge: Grove Books, 2005)

—— *The 1927–28 Prayer Book Crisis: Volume 2. The cul-de-sac of the 'Deposited Book' . . . until further order be taken* (Cambridge: Grove Books, 2006).

Irvine, C. (ed.), *They Shaped Our Worship: Essays on Anglican Liturgists* (London: SPCK, 1998).

Hebblethwaite, D., *Liturgical Revision in the Church of England 1984–2004: the working of the Liturgical Commission*, Joint Liturgical Studies 57 (Cambridge: Grove Books, 2004).

Jagger, P.J., *The Alcuin Club and its Publications 1897–1987* (Norwich: Alcuin Club/Hymns Ancient & Modern, 1996).

Jasper, R.C.D., *The Development of Anglican Liturgy 1662–1980* (London: SPCK, 1989).

Jones, S. (ed.), "Introduction", G. Dix, *The Shape of the Liturgy*, new edn (London: Continuum, 2005), pp. x–xxviii.

—— *The Sacramental Life: Gregory Dix and His Writings* (Norwich: Canterbury Press, 2007).

Pfaff, R.W. *The Liturgy in Medieval England: A History* (Cambridge: CUP, 2009).

Phillips, C.S. (ed.), *Walter Howard Frere* (London: Faber & Faber, 1947).

Procter, F., & W.H. Frere, *New History of the Book of Common Prayer with a Rationale of its Offices*, 1st edn (London: Macmillan, 1901; repr. 3rd corrected impression, London: Macmillan, 1961).

Ward A. & C. Johnson, "The Henry Bradshaw Society: Its Birth and First Decade 1890–1900," *Ephemerides Liturgicae* 104 (1990), pp. 187–200.

Part V

A–Z OF THE STUDY OF CATHOLIC LITURGY

Absolution In the sacrament of Penance (confession), absolution is the act by which, praying the formula given in the rite, a priest who has the necessary jurisdiction remits a person's sins. "Absolution" is also used for the prayer after the *Confiteor* at Mass asking forgiveness and for the rite at the end of a requiem Mass where the coffin is sprinkled with holy water and incensed with prayers for the forgiveness of the sins of the deceased. "General absolution" refers to the remission of the sins of a group of people by one priest in situations where individual and integral confession is impossible and there is an urgent need for absolution, such as in a situation of emergency or grave danger. General absolution imparted without the necessary conditions is held to be invalid.

Accolade In medieval rites for the conferral of knighthood, the ceremonial striking ("dubbing") of a new knight, delivered either as a light slap to the face or neck or as a tap with a sword.

Active participation Common translation of the Latin *participatio actuosa*. The term first appears in modern times in Pius X's 1903 motu proprio *Tra le sollecitudine* on sacred music as "partecipazione attiva" and is used to describe a deeper involvement of the faithful in the liturgical services. This has been interpreted variously, but includes the vocal participation in prayers and singing, as well as bodily postures, but above all an interior attentiveness and disposition toward the sacred mysteries being celebrated and connection with the action of Christ in the liturgical rites.

Adoremus: Society for the Renewal of the Sacred Liturgy An association of Catholics cofounded in the USA in 1995 by Helen Hull Hitchcock (author, founder of Women for Faith and Family), Fr Jerry Pokorsky (cofounder of CREDO, an association of priests dedicated to faithful liturgical translation) and Fr Joseph Fessio SJ (founding editor of Ignatius Press). Its purpose is "to rediscover and restore the beauty, the holiness, and the power of the Church's rich liturgical tradition while remaining faithful to an organic, living process of renewal." Adoremus undertakes projects and offers materials to promote a faithful application of the liturgical reform mandated by the Second Vatican Council. The association also assists bishops by occasionally providing analysis and critiques of existing and proposed liturgical practices. Its newsletter, *The Adoremus Bulletin*, is published ten times per year. Website: www.adoremus.org

Alleluia A Hebrew word roughly translated as "praise the LORD." "The Alleluia" refers to the chant sung immediately before the Gospel in the Mass, except during Lent. Traditionally the form consists of an "alleluia" respond intoned by the cantor up to the quarter bar and repeated by the choir, followed by a verse, usually from the psalms. After the verse is sung by a cantor the whole alleluia is repeated by the full choir. In the post-Vatican II lectionary the "Alleluia verse" is a sentence sung before and after which "Alleluia" is said or sung one or more times.

Altar The altar is the table-like structure (*mensa*) on which the Eucharistic sacrifice is offered. From the fourth century it has been customarily made of stone and includes a sepulchre in which the relics of a saint (usually a martyr) are enclosed. Altars are consecrated by a liturgical rite. A portable altar is a smaller piece of stone, containing relics, which can be put in place temporarily for the celebration of Mass. The 1960 code of rubrics permitted the use of the Eastern antimensium in place of a portable altar (n. 525). The General Instruction of the Roman Missal promulgated by Paul VI does not require a portable altar for the celebration of Mass away from a consecrated altar. See: Orientation.

Alternatim Musical alternation between two groups—two choirs, choir and organ.

Ambrosian rite The ancient and venerable liturgical rite of the Archdiocese of Milan, Italy, which takes its name from St Ambrose (337–97), bishop of Milan, although the liturgical tradition of Milan predates him. The Ambrosian rite is considered to be as ancient as the Roman rite and enjoys its own particular calendar, ritual and chant which developed from antiquity. The sixteenth century St Charles Borromeo (1538–84) zealously defended the legitimacy and antiquity of the rite following the Council of Trent. In the twentieth century new editions of the missal and other liturgical books prepared under the archbishops of Milan, Blessed Andrea Ferrari (1850–1921) and Blessed Ildefonso Schuster OSB (1880–1954)—both zealous apostles of the Ambrosian liturgy—were published: an *editio typica* of the missal appeared in 1902 and the last *editio post typicam in* 1954. Following the Second Vatican Council liturgical books were prepared which, while setting aside much of the Ambrosian liturgical heritage in favour of modern Roman tendencies, retain some Ambrosian customs. The traditional Ambrosian liturgy is still celebrated and editions of the older liturgical books can be found at: www.signumambrosianum. it. See: Archdale A. King, *Liturgies of the Primatial Sees* (London, New York & Toronto: Longman's, Green & Co., 1957); Cyrille Vogel, *Medieval Liturgy: An Introduction to the Sources* (Washington DC: Pastoral Press, 1986), pp. 282–3; Cesare Alzati, George Guiver (trans.), *Ambrosianum Mysterium: The Church of Milan and its Liturgical Tradition*, 2 vols (Cambridge: Grove Books, 1999–2000).

Anointing of the Sick (extreme unction) Anointing of the Sick is a sacrament bestowed in a liturgical rite which brings about "the uniting of the sick person to the passion of Christ, for his own good and that of the whole Church; the strengthening, peace, and courage to endure in a Christian manner the sufferings of illness or old age; the forgiveness of sins, if the sick person was not able to obtain it through the sacrament of Penance; the restoration of health, if it is conducive to the salvation of his soul; and the preparation for passing over to eternal life" (CCC, 1532).

Antiphon A brief syllabic chant serving as a frame or refrain for a psalm or canticle in the Divine Office or for the entrance ("introit"), offertory, or communion processions at Mass. Some antiphons lost their associated psalm verses over time (such as the Offertory and the Communion), which modern chant scholarship has worked to restore. There are independent antiphons such as the Marian antiphons, invitatory antiphons for the beginning of the night office, and processional antiphons for feasts, e.g., Palm Sunday.

Antiphonale (Antiphonal) Also antiphonary or antiphoner. A liturgical book containing the chants for the Divine Office. One must distinguish that used for the Roman Office (celebrated by the secular clergy) with its *Antiphonale Romanum*, from the monastic office with its *Antiphonale Monasticum*. In the early Middle Ages, the term antiphoner could also be used to mean any book of liturgical chant.

Antonelli, Ferdinando Guiseppe (1896–1993) An Italian Franciscan of the Order of Friars Minor who served in the Vatican's Sacred Congregation of Rites from 1930 and who was a member of the Pontifical Commission for the Reform of the Liturgy established by Pius XII in 1947 from its inception. In October 1962, John XXIII unexpectedly named Antonelli the secretary for the Conciliar Commission for the Sacred Liturgy at the Second Vatican Council instead of Annibale Bugnini CM, who was expected to fill the position. In 1965, Antonelli was named Secretary of the Congregation of Rites and consecrated archbishop. In 1969 he became Secretary of the Congregation for the Causes of the Saints and, following his retirement in 1973, was created cardinal. Nicola Giampietro's work *The Development of the Liturgical Reform: As Seen by Cardinal Ferdinando Antonelli from 1948–1970* (Fort Collins: Roman Catholic Books, 2009) provides important primary source material for the period and counterbalances other accounts, particularly that of Annibale Bugnini.

Aquileia rite An ancient rite of the northern Italian patriarchal see of Aquileia, which by medieval times had become more a local use of the Roman rite. Following the Council of Trent it was largely abandoned in favor of the *Missale Romanum* promulgated by St Pius V. Not enough remains in manuscript sources to allow for more than speculation about the liturgical use and its chant. See: Archdale A. King, *Liturgies of the Past* (London, New York & Toronto: Longman's, Green & Co., 1959); Cyrille Vogel, *Medieval Liturgy: An Introduction to the Sources* (Washington DC: Pastoral Press, 1986), pp. 283–4.

Ara A Latin word meaning "altar," this term was often used in medieval texts to denote a small consecrated stone that both served as a portable altar for celebrating Mass and as a base upon which to set the Blessed Sacrament for reservation rites on Holy Thursday and Good Friday.

Archa A Latin term meaning "ark," commonly used in medieval texts to identify the tabernacle used for the Holy Thursday reposition of the Blessed Sacrament.

Architrave The main horizontal beam of a church building supported by columns.

Ars celebrandi "The art of proper celebration, and the full, active and fruitful participation of all the faithful. The primary way to foster the participation of the People of God in the sacred rite is the proper celebration of the rite itself. The *ars celebrandi* is the best way to ensure their *actuosa participatio*. The *ars* *celebrandi* is the fruit of faithful adherence to the liturgical norms in all their richness; indeed, for two thousand years this way of celebrating has sustained the faith life of all believers, called to take part in the celebration as the People of God, a royal priesthood, a holy nation (cf. 1 Pet. 2:4-5, 9)" Benedict XVI, Apostolic Exhortation *Sacramentum Caritatis*, February 22, 2007, n. 38 (also nn. 39–42); See: Peter Elliott, "*Ars Celebrandi* in the Sacred Liturgy," Alcuin Reid (ed.) *Sacred Liturgy: The Source and Summit of the Life and Mission of the Church* (San Francisco: Ignatius Press, 2014), pp. 69–85; Alcuin Reid, "From Rubrics to *Ars Celebrandi*—Liturgical Law in the 21st Century," *Antiphon* 17 (2013), pp. 139–67.

Auctoritas The capability to solve problems through manual and cerebral methods with confidence.

Baptism Holy Baptism is the basis of the whole Christian life, the gateway to life in the Spirit (*vitae spiritualis ianua;* Council of Florence: DZ 1314) and the door which gives access to the other sacraments. Through baptism we are freed from sin and reborn as sons of God; we become members of Christ, are incorporated into the Church and made sharers in her mission: "Baptism is the sacrament of regeneration through water in the word" (CCC 1213). The ritual consists of a candidate being immersed in water or having water poured over the head in the name of the Triune God. Catholic, Orthodox, Lutheran, and Reformed churches largely agree on the theology and practice of the Christian sacrament of baptism, especially the place of infant baptism. Arguments for infant baptism came from the baptism of entire households in the New Testament (e.g. Acts 16:33) and the example of the early Church. The Catholic Church teaches that original sin is entirely removed in baptism and that concupiscence (the spark of sin remaining in Christians after baptism) was not itself sin, enabling Christians to do good works without sin.

Baumstark, Anton (1872–1948) A German philologist, orientalist, and liturgist specializing in Eastern liturgy, Baumstark developed the "comparative liturgy" method of studying the historical development of the liturgy as an organic whole, which has not been without its influence since. His two principal works have been translated into English: F.L. Cross (ed.), *Comparative Liturgy* (Westminster, MD: Newman Press, 1958); F. West (ed.), *On the Historical Development of the Liturgy* (Collegeville: Liturgical Press, 2011).

Beauduin, Lambert (1873–1960) A Belgian priest of the diocese of Liège who entered Mont César (now Kiesersberg) abbey in Leuven in 1906 and who discovered the central role of the Sacred Liturgy in the spiritual life during his Benedictine novitiate. Beauduin's September 1909 lecture at the Malines Congress is considered by many to be the start of the modern liturgical movement. He began publication of the periodical *Les Questions Liturgiques et Paroissiales* and organized liturgical weeks for diocesan clergy. His 1914 work, *La Piété de l'Église* (ET: *Liturgy the Life of the Church*) retains its value as a seminal text. Beauduin left Mont César in 1925 to be prior of Amay Priory, later Chevetogne Abbey. See: Alcuin Reid, *The Organic Development of the Liturgy*, 2nd edn (San Francisco: Ignatius Press, 2005), pp. 78–85.

Benedict XVI (Joseph Ratzinger 1927–; 2005–13) A German priest and theologian who was appointed archbishop of Munich in 1977, Prefect of the Congregation for the Doctrine of the Faith in 1981 and elected pope on April 19, 2005, from which office he resigned on February 28, 2013. Sometimes called the "Father of the new liturgical movement" because of his call for the same as Joseph Cardinal Ratzinger in *The Spirit of the Liturgy* and for his openness to the question of reforming the liturgical reform implemented following the Second Vatican Council, Benedict XVI's pontificate brought the question of the liturgical practice of the Western Church to the fore and furthered critical study of the same. The Sacred Liturgy features in numerous discourses and acts of governance from his pontificate. Most noteworthy are his 2007 Apostolic Exhortation *Sacramentum Caritatis* and his motu proprio *Summorum Pontificum* of the same year. A volume of his writings on the Sacred Liturgy before his election to the papacy has been published (RCW 11). See also: Alcuin Reid, "The Liturgical Reform of Pope Benedict XVI," N.J. Roy & J.E. Rutherford (eds), *Benedict XVI and the Sacred Liturgy* (Dublin & Portland, OR: Four Courts Press, 2010), pp. 156–80.

Bechoffen, Johann A sixteenth century Augustinian theologian who authored an important commentary on the ceremonies of the Mass, *Quadruplex missalis expositio* (Basel: Furter, 1505), which was reprinted numerous times. In his discussion of the Roman canon he energetically advocates the genuflection of the celebrant to the Eucharist following the consecration.

Benediction A word meaning "blessing" from the Latin words *bene dicere*, to speak well. A blessing is imparted by a bishop, priest, or deacon to people or to objects for a specific purpose or as a means of sanctification according to the given liturgical rite. "Benediction of the Blessed Sacrament" is a rite involving the blessing of people by a bishop, priest or deacon at the end of a period of adoration of the Blessed Sacrament solemnly exposed in a monstrance (requiring full ceremonial vesture, incense, and chant), or simply, without full ceremonial, in a ciborium (the closed vessel containing the Blessed Sacrament), simply placed on the altar.

Benevento rite An ancient rite of the Lombard duchy of Benevento in southern Italy, which was flourishing in the seventh century but had given way to the Roman rite most probably by the tenth. Eleventh and twelfth century manuscript sources give some indication of its chant. See: Archdale A. King, *Liturgies of the Past* (London, New York & Toronto: Longman's, Green & Co., 1959); Cyrille Vogel, *Medieval Liturgy: An Introduction to the Sources* (Washington DC: Pastoral Press, 1986), p. 284.

Bishop, Edmund (1846–1917) An English layman and autodidact with experience of continental European Catholicism, Bishop made a significant contribution to late nineteenth- and early-twentieth-century liturgical scholarship. His principal works are collected and published in *Liturgica Historica* (Oxford: Clarendon Press, 1918). This volume opens with his famous essay "The Genius of the Roman Rite," which has influenced liturgical scholarship up to the present day. See: Abercrombie, Nigel, *The Life and Work of Edmund Bishop* (London: Longmans, 1959).

Borromeo, Charles (1538–84) Called to Rome to serve his uncle, Pope Pius IV (1499; 1559–65), Borromeo was created cardinal in 1560 (age twenty-one) before even receiving the diaconate. He was entrusted with much administration on behalf of the pope including that of the Archdiocese of Milan. He was consecrated bishop in 1563 and appointed archbishop of Milan in 1564. Having assisted in the final sessions of the Council of Trent, St Charles was one of the great reforming bishops of the Counter Reformation, achieving much in his relatively brief ecclesiastical life. The Sacred Liturgy was central to his reforms and he went to great lengths to ensure the correct arrangements of churches for its celebration. So too, worthy liturgical music was important—whilst in Rome Borromeo was instrumental in advancing the career of Giovanni Pierluigi da Palestrina (c. 1525–94). As archbishop, St Charles ensured the survival of the Ambrosian rite following the Council of Trent.

Botte, Bernard (1883–1980) A Belgian monk of Mont César and the first director of the *Institut Supérieur de Liturgie* in Paris (1956–64) and later Abbot of Mont César. Scholars to whose formation he contributed form a major part of his legacy. In the early 1950s he organized summer study sessions for liturgy professors at Mont César and was deeply convinced of the fact, expressed most notably in *Sacrosanctum Concilium*, that efforts of liturgical renewal would be futile without proper liturgical formation of priests. Convinced of the importance of oriental languages for editorial work, he studied Syriac, Coptic, and Ethiopic before editing *La tradition apostolique de Saint Hippolyte* (Paris: Cerf, 1946; Münster Westfalen: Aschendorffsche Verlagsbuchhandlung, 1963; Albert Gerhards (ed.), Münster Westfalen: Aschendorffsche Verlagsbuchhandlung, 1989), which was highly influential in mid-twentieth-century liturgical thought and reform; recent scholarship has, however, demonstrated the assumptions made about the "apostolic tradition" at that time to be flawed. Botte was the Relator of study group 20, the post-conciliar *Consilium* which worked on the reform of the rites of ordination. See his autobiography: *Le mouvement liturgique: Témoignage et souvenirs* (Paris: Desclée, 1973) ET: *From Silence to Participation* (Washington DC: Pastoral Press, 1988).

Bouyer, Louis (1913–2004) Ordained a Lutheran minister in 1936, the Parisian converted to Catholicism in 1939 and was ordained a priest of the French Oratory. Following his conversion, Bouyer became a leading figure in the biblical and liturgical movements, lecturing and publishing widely in French and English. His books *The Paschal Mystery* (Chicago: Regnery, 1950; London: Allen & Unwin, 1951) and *Life and Liturgy* (London: Sheed & Ward, 1956; also published as *Liturgical Piety,* Notre Dame, IN: University of Notre Dame Press, 1955) were particularly influential. Yet he was appointed a Consultor of the post-conciliar *Consilium* only in 1966. Bouyer's *Mémoires* (Paris: Cerf, 2014), ET: *The Memoirs of Louis Bouyer* (Kettering, OH: Angelico Press, 2015) provide critical insights into key personnel of the *Consilium* and some of its internal operations and dealings with Pope Paul VI. Bouyer was severely critical of the way the Second Vatican Council's liturgical reform was implemented in his 1968 *La decomposition du catholicisme* (Paris: Aubier-Montaigne, 1968)

ET: *The Decomposition of Catholicism* (Chicago: Franciscan Herald Press, 1969). At Bouyer's 2004 funeral, Cardinal Jean-Marie Lustiger described him as *"the least conformist of theologians and among the most traditional."* See also: Alcuin Reid, "The Reformed Liturgy: A 'Cadaver Decomposed'?—Louis Bouyer and Liturgical *Ressourcement*," *Antiphon* 16 (2012), pp. 37–51.

Braga rite The ancient liturgical rite of the Archdiocese of Braga, Portugal, including its particular calendar, ritual and chant. The Braga rite enjoyed a resurgence in the first half of the twentieth century. See: Archdale A. King, *Liturgies of the Primatial Sees* (London, New York & Toronto: Longman's, Green & Co., 1957); Cyrille Vogel, *Medieval Liturgy: An Introduction to the Sources* (Washington DC: Pastoral Press, 1986), pp. 288–9; Alcuin Reid, *The Organic Development of the Liturgy* (2nd edn), (San Francisco: Ignatius Press, 2005), pp. 128–30.

Breviarium (Breviary) The book or volumes of books which collect together the antiphons, psalms, hymns, versicles, readings, and other texts arranged for the celebration of the Divine Office or Liturgy of the Hours. As a book the development of the breviary goes hand in hand with the increase of the obligation of clergy to pray the Divine Office privately, instead of communally in choir. Apart from the *Breviarium Romanum* promulgated in 1568 following the Council of Trent, different dioceses and religious orders retained their own proper breviaries (the *Breviarium Monasticum*, the *Breviarium Ambrosianum*, etc.). Following the Second Vatican Council many dioceses and orders adopted the *Liturgia Horarum* promulgated by Paul VI. See: Abbot Cabrol, *The Books of the Latin Liturgy* (London & St Louis, MO: Sands & B. Herder, 1932).

Bucranion A relief carving of a bull's skull derived from the hanging head of a sacrificed animal on an altar or metope.

Bugnini, Annibale (1912–82) Annibale Bugnini was an Italian Vincentian priest who was editor of the journal *Ephemerides Liturgicae* from 1944–63 and taught liturgy at the Pontifical Urban College and at the Pontifical Lateran University up until 1962. Named secretary of the commission for liturgical reform established by Pius XII in 1946, Bugnini was a key figure in the work of liturgical reform until 1975. He became secretary of the liturgical preparatory commission for the Second Vatican Council (1960–2) but was not named the secretary of the corresponding conciliar commission by John XXIII, losing his teaching posts around the same time. Paul VI rehabilitated Bugnini by naming him secretary of the *Consilium ad exsequendam Constitutionem de Sacra Liturgia* in 1964. Bugnini's organizational skills and personal will, as well as his close relationship with Paul VI, impacted significantly on the direction and shape of the post-conciliar reform of the liturgy. In 1969 Bugnini was named secretary of the newly formed Congregation for Divine Worship and consecrated archbishop in 1972. He was removed from this post in 1975 for reasons that are unclear, and refused the nomination as Apostolic Nuncio in Uruguay. In 1976 he accepted a post as Apostolic Pro-Nuncio in Iran, where he served until his death in 1982. His work, *The Reform of the Liturgy 1948–1975* (Collegeville: Liturgical Press, 1990), written in the months following his 1975 removal, is a primary source for study of liturgical reform. See also his autobiography: *Liturgiae cultor et amator: servì la chiesa* (Rome: Edizione Liturgiche, 2012).

Burchard, John (c. 1450–1506) A papal master of ceremonies, Burckard was a co-editor of the first printed edition of the Roman Pontifical, the 1485 *Pontificalis liber*, and the author of a definitive manual of rubrics for the celebration of Mass, the 1498 *Ordo servandus per Sacerdotem in celebratione missae* (*Order to be Observed by a Priest in the Celebration of Mass*). His diary of papal events provides a valuable record of late-medieval liturgical practice at Rome.

Cabrol, Fernand (1855–1937) A monk and eventually prior of the Benedictine Abbey of Saint Pierre de Solesmes, Cabrol had dreamed of a monastic foundation dedicated to liturgical studies, and this was realised at last at St Michael's Abbey, Farnborough, Hampshire, of which he was the founding prior from 1896 and the first abbot from 1903. He authored numerous liturgical works which are published in both French and English, the most renowned being the *Dictionnaire d'Archéologie Chrétienne et de la Liturgie* published in 28 volumes from 1920–53, which he published with Dom Henri Leclercq. The abbey's liturgical scholarship waned after his death, and following the transfer of the monastery from the Solesmes Congregation to the control of English monks in 1947 its library was dispersed.

Cadence A resting place in a musical work, either temporarily at the end of a phrase, or at the very end of the work. In Gregorian chant, a cadence is often a distinctive melodic formula, especially in the psalm tones.

Caeremoniale (Ceremonial) A *Caeremoniale* is a book giving practical directions for the celebration of liturgical rites. Although there are editions for religious orders and dioceses such as the *Caeremoniale Monasticum* and the *Caeremoniale Ambrosianum*, etc., the most common is the *Caeremoniale Episcoporum* which contains the rules for ceremonies celebrated by bishops. The first edition was published in 1600 and was amended up until the *editio tertia post typicam* of 1948. A new *Caeremoniale Episcoporum* was published following the Second Vatican Council in 1984 (*reimpressio emendata* 2008), which appeared in English translation as *The Ceremonial of Bishops* (Collegeville: Liturgical Press, 1989). See: Abbot Cabrol, *The Books of the Latin Liturgy* (London & St Louis, MO: Sands & B. Herder, 1932).

Calendar The calendar is the specific arrangement of the seasons and feasts of the liturgical year. Liturgical calendars are universal (*Calendarium Romanum*) or particular, that is applying to a local diocese, religious order or religious congregation. Local calendars will adapt the universal calendar to the particular feasts observed in a given place or order, and reflect the decisions of legitimate authority in respect of when certain feasts are observed. From antiquity, the Church of Milan has observed its own proper calendar which is markedly different from the Roman one (the absence of Ash Wednesday, several Sundays of Advent, etc.). The calendar has developed throughout history although periodically there has been a need to prune the number of saints mandated for celebration in the universal calendar. The Roman calendar was changed substantially following the Second Vatican Council, losing many of its ancient features (Septuagesima, the Octave of Pentecost, etc.), and moving many feasts to different dates regardless of popular piety associated with them.

Campo aperto Chant manuscripts that date from before the invention of the musical staff. Neums are *in campo aperto*, "in an open field," i.e., written without staff lines and, thus, lacking in precise pitches.

Canon A term used for the central prayer of the rite of Mass ("the canon of the Mass," "the Roman canon"); *see* Eucharistic prayer and Roman canon. In architecture a canon is a set of proportional relationships for different types of columns and beams based on a module.

Cantus firmus A pre-composed melody used by a composer as the foundation of a new polyphonic work. Very often the *cantus firmus* was a piece of Gregorian chant.

Capida A garment in the form of a hood or veil commonly conferred upon neophytes in late medieval baptismal rites symbolizing the white robes given to the newly baptized in earlier times.

Capelle, Bernard (1884–1961) From 1928–52, Capelle was the second abbot of the Benedictine abbey of Mont César (now Keizersberg) established in Leuven, Belgium, by the Abbey of Maredsous in the late nineteenth century. As Dom Lambert Beauduin was a monk of Mont César, the abbey played a large part in promoting the twentieth-century liturgical movement in its initial phase, hosting liturgical meetings and publishing literature of a popular and scholarly nature. Capelle was a liturgical scholar in his own right and was consulted on the projected reform of Holy Week by the commission for liturgical reform established by Pius XII and gave an address at the 1956 Assisi Congress on pastoral liturgy. See: Bernard Capelle, *Travaux Liturgiques*, 3 vols (Louvain: Abbaye du Mont César, 1955, 1962, 1967); Bernard Cappelle, *A New Light on the Mass*, 2nd edn (Dublin & London: Clonmore & Reynolds & Burns & Oates, 1961); Alcuin Reid, *The Organic Development of the Liturgy*, 2nd edn (San Francisco: Ignatius Press, 2005), pp. 344, 362.

Carmelite rite The liturgical use of the friars of the ancient observance of the Carmelite Order (O. Carm.), otherwise known as "the rite of the Holy Sepulchre and Church of Jerusalem," consisting of some ancient uses, medieval usages from France and somewhat influenced by the Dominican rite. Its liturgical books were reformed following the Council of Trent; the newly formed Discalced Carmelites adopted the Roman rite in spite of the preference of St John of the Cross for the Carmelite rite. The seventeenth century saw further editions of the liturgical books in the light of the reforms of Trent. The Carmelite breviary adopted Pius X's arrangement of the psalter in 1933 and a new edition of the missal was published in 1935. The 1972 General Chapter of the Carmelite order decided to abandon the Carmelite rite in favor of the reformed liturgical books promulgated by Paul VI, though under the provisions of the 2007 motu proprio *Summorum Pontificum* and the 2011 Instruction *Universae Ecclesiae* it continues to be celebrated by some Carmelite friars and communities. See:

Archdale A. King, *Liturgies of the Religious Orders* (London, New York & Toronto: Longman's, Green & Co., 1955).

Carthusian rite This rite owes its origins to the twelfth century liturgy in use in Grenoble, France, where the order was founded, and possibly includes influences from the liturgy of Lyon (the metropolitan see) and Cluny. Its liturgical books remained relatively stable with new editions of the missal and breviary appearing following the Council of Trent in the late sixteenth and seventeenth centuries (editions of the missal were published in 1603 and 1679). Following the Second Vatican Council, the Carthusian order was singular in its wish to retain its own rite, publishing revised liturgical books in 1981. See: Archdale A. King, *Liturgies of the Religious Orders* (London, New York & Toronto: Longman's, Green & Co., 1955).

Casel, Odo (1886–1948) A monk of Maria Laach who promulgated the theory that Christian sacraments originated in the mystery religions of the Greek and Roman empires, rather than in Jewish worship. His most famous work was *Das Christliche Kult-Mysterium* (1932), ET: *The Mystery of Christian Worship and Other Writings* (Westminster, MD & London: Newman Press & Darton, Longman & Todd, 1962). He considered that Aquinas held an understanding of the mystery of the presence of the historical sacrifice of the cross objectively realized in a sacramental mode of existence on the altar. His ideas were developed and taught by Abbot Salvatore Marsili OSB (1910–83), the founder of the Pontifical Institute of Liturgy in Rome, amongst others. See: Aidan Nichols OP, "Odo Casel Revisited" *Antiphon* 3 (1998), pp. 12–20.

Castle of Dolors A funerary term of medieval origin denoting an elaborate catafalque of cloth-draped wood usually mounted with or surrounded by numerous torches or candles.

Celtic rite By "Celtic rite" may be understood a varied, ancient, rich number of liturgical traditions of Ireland and Anglo-Saxon England, rooted in Gallican practices, which gradually fell into disuse following the introduction of Roman customs (including the date of Easter) from the seventh century when St Augustine of Canterbury inaugurated the trend towards Roman chant and liturgy. These had been definitively abandoned by the end of the twelfth century. Celtic chant was in use until the early seventh century, but practically none of this chant survives in manuscript sources. Other manuscript sources, including missals, do (*The Bobbio Missal, The Stowe Missal*). Whilst so-called "Celtic" rites have found a diverse popularity in modern times, which has given rise to much literature which must be studied critically, historians have argued against the notion of a "Celtic Church" which itself suggests that the concept of a unified Celtic rite is not tenable. See: Fernand Cabrol OSB, *The Mass of the Western Rites* (London: Sands & Co., 1934); Archdale A. King, *Liturgies of the Past* (London, New York & Toronto; Longman's, Green & Co., 1959); Cyrille Vogel, *Medieval Liturgy: An Introduction to the Sources* (Washington DC: Pastoral Press, 1986), pp. 280–2; T.M. Charles-Edwards, *Early Christian Ireland* (Cambridge University Press: Cambridge, 2007).

Centonization A compositional process whereby musical motives or formulae, sometimes associated with a mode, are strung together to create a more complex melody. This theory is used to explain the melodic patterns that are found in the chant repertory, particularly for certain genres or modes. This process was also used in the composition of liturgical texts (collects, chiefly) by the post-Vatican II *Consilium*.

Christian Latin The idea of Christian Latin as a "special language" that would be marked by particularities in morphology, lexis, and syntax was developed by the Nijmegen School, especially its leading representative, Christine Mohrmann (1903–88). Today, scholars in the field are generally critical of the theoretical approach of this school, while its contributions to the study of Latin in late antiquity are still valued. The most pertinent criticism of Mohrmann and her disciples is their restrictive selection of sources to substantiate their theoretical claims. However, there are uniting features in the great variety of texts that can be subsumed under the heading "Christian Latin," above all their vocabulary, which is largely derived from the Sacred Scriptures and distinguishes them from pagan and secular texts. Any attempt to characterize the use of Latin among Christians in late antiquity will need to differentiate between the various registers of discourse that existed from early on. Of particular note is the language of the liturgy, which includes the "vulgar," that is, non-classical idiom of the Scriptures as well as the prayers and hymns that are shaped by the Bible in form and content, and at the same time are monuments of a high literary culture. See: C. Mohrmann, *Liturgical Latin: Its Origins and Character. Three Lectures* (London: Burns & Oates, 1959); *Études sur le latin des chrétiens*, 4 vols, Storia e letteratura 65, 87, 103, 143 (Roma: Edizioni di Storia e Letteratura, 1961–77); R. Coleman, "Vulgar Latin and the Diversity of Christian Latin," J. Herman (ed.), *Actes du 1er Colloque international sur le latin vulgaire et tardif (Pécs, 2–5 septembre 1985)* (Tübingen: Niemeyer, 1987), pp. 37–52; D. Sheerin, "Christian and Biblical Latin," F.A.C. Mantello & A.G. Rigg (eds), *Medieval Latin: An Introduction and Bibliographical Guide* (Washington, DC: Catholic University of America Press, 1996), pp. 137–56.

Column A vertical support of Greek and Roman systems of trabeation; columns are circular, piers are square.

Concelebration The offering of Mass by more than priest at the same time in the same liturgical rite. It is necessary to distinguish between "ritual concelebration," where priests attend the same celebration, vested as priests, but do not consecrate the bread and wine (they do not offer Mass as priests), and "sacramental concelebration," where priests do consecrate and offer the Mass as priests. Instances of the former are found frequently in Western liturgical history, as well as in the East (which did not know sacramental concelebration until it was imposed by Rome on those Churches in communion in the eighteenth century). Sacramental concelebration in the West was rare. The Second Vatican Council called for sacramental concelebration to be permitted in certain circumstances, but in spite of the Council's intention to allow its moderate use it has become practically the only way most priests participate in the modern rite of Mass when they are not themselves the principal celebrant. See: Alcuin Reid, "Concelebration Today, Yesterday and Tomorrow," Joseph de Sainte-Marie

OCD, *The Holy Eucharist—The World's Salvation* (Leominster: Gracewing, 2015), pp. xvii–xxxix.

Cistercian rite The liturgical use of the Benedictine reform initiated at Cîteaux in 1098, which quickly became the Cistercian order. In the organization of the order in the twelfth century, of which centralization was a feature, it was decided that each house should follow uniform liturgical practices. The ancient Cistercian rite would seem to be indebted to the Roman rite as developed in Carolingian times and to Cluniac monastic customs in which the first members of the order were formed (though shorn of its "excesses"). The Divine Office sought to be faithful to arrangement laid down in the Rule of St Benedict. Cistercian liturgical books were not revised following the Council of Trent, but the beginning of the seventeenth century saw the erosion of the traditional Cistercian liturgy in the face of Romanizing tendencies, resulting a hybrid rite in the 1656 breviary and the 1657 missal which retained elements of the traditional use. The ritual of 1689 served further to protect the order's liturgical heritage. New editions of the Cistercian liturgical books were published up until the Second Vatican Council. Following the Council, the order adopted the missal promulgated by Paul VI, but retained its own arrangement for the Divine Office. The pre-conciliar Cistercian liturgy has been revived by some houses of the order. See: Archdale A. King, *Liturgies of the Religious Orders* (London, New York & Toronto: Longman's, Green & Co., 1955); Cyrille Vogel, *Medieval Liturgy: An Introduction to the Sources* (Washington DC: Pastoral Press, 1986), pp. 287–8.

Common Liturgical texts and chants can be distinguished between those that are "proper" (to a particular season or feast), those that are "ordinary" (that do not change, such as the order of Mass), and those that are "common" (groups of texts shared for particular types of saints, e.g. apostles, martyrs, virgins, etc.).

Communio (Communion) The *communio* is the proper or common Mass antiphon sung during the communion procession. This chant is usually brief, however the 1958 Instruction *De musica sacra et liturgia* restored the practice of singing several verses from the psalm finishing with the *Gloria Patri* with the antiphon used as a refrain when the text of the antiphon is from a psalm. Following the Second Vatican Council the Gradual supplies all the communion antiphons with psalm verses. The Church Music Association of America (www.musicasacra.com) has republished the chant for these verses and has worked to prepare chants for the modern English texts of the *communio*.

Composite A Roman architectural type that fuses Corinthian and Ionic capital elements.

Confirmation Baptism, the Eucharist, and the sacrament of Confirmation together constitute the "sacraments of Christian initiation." Confirmation perfects baptismal grace; it is the sacrament which gives the Holy Spirit in order to root us more deeply in the divine filiation, incorporate us more firmly into Christ, strengthen our bond with the Church, associate us more closely with her mission, and help us bear witness to the Christian faith in words accompanied by deeds. Confirmation, like Baptism, imprints a spiritual mark or indelible character on the Christian's soul; for this reason one can receive this sacrament only once in one's life (CCC 1285, 1316–17).

Congregation for Divine Worship and Discipline of the Sacraments This Vatican dicastery or department, exercising vicarious papal authority, deals with the promotion and regulation of the liturgy and, primarily, of the sacraments. It promotes pastoral liturgical activity in everything related to the preparation and celebration of the Eucharist, the other sacraments and sacramentals, as well as the celebration of Sunday and other feasts of the liturgical year, the liturgy of hours, blessings, and other liturgical rites. It is the successor to the Sacred Congregation of Rites (established in 1588) and the Congregation for the Discipline of the Sacraments (established in 1908). In 1969, Paul VI abolished the Sacred Congregation of Rites and established the Congregation for Divine Worship, incorporating the *Consilium ad exsequendam Constitutionem de Sacra Liturgia* (established in 1964) which was abolished at the same time. In 1975, Paul VI united the Congregation for Divine Worship with the Congregation for the Discipline of the Sacraments. These were separated by John Paul II in 1984, only to be reunited in his curial reform of 1988.

Consilium The *Consilium ad exsequendam Constitutionem de Sacra Liturgia* was established by Paul VI in 1964 to prepare the implementation of the Second Vatican Council's Constitution on the Sacred Liturgy, *Sacrosanctum Concilium*. Its establishment was seen as unusual given the existence of the Sacred Congregation of Rites, and in its early years a power struggle ensued in respect of its competences. In the end its key personnel, including its Secretary, Annibale Bugnini, obtained the support of Paul VI for its work. Its officials, members, consulters and various study groups worked to produce new liturgical rites until its abolition by Paul VI in 1969, when its responsibilities were incorporated into the new Congregation for Divine Worship. See: Annibale Bugnini CM, *The Reform of the Liturgy 1948–1975* (Collegeville: Liturgical Press, 1990); Piero Marini, *A Challenging Reform: Realizing the Vision of the Liturgical Renewal* (Collegeville Liturgical Press: 2007).

Constitution on the Sacred Liturgy (*Sacrosanctum Concilium*) The Constitution on the Sacred Liturgy, often known by its first Latin words, *Sacrosanctum Concilium*, was promulgated by Paul VI on December 4, 1963 at the end of the second session of the Second Vatican Council. It is to be distinguished from the other three constitutions of the Council, two of which are "dogmatic" constitutions whilst the other is a "pastoral" constitution. *Sacrosanctum Concilium* is simply entitled "constitution" and contains the principles and disciplinary decisions of the Council in respect of the liturgical reform it authorized. By means of the Constitution the Pope and the Council sought to undertake "the reform [renewal] and promotion of the liturgy" (*instaurandam atque fovendam liturgiam curare*) to "to impart an ever increasing vigor to the Christian life of the faithful; to adapt more suitably to the needs of our own times those institutions which are subject to change; to foster whatever can promote union among all who believe in Christ; to strengthen whatever can help to call the whole of mankind into the household of the Church" (n. 1). Studies of the genesis of its text, of its redaction at the Council itself and of its implementation by the *Consilium* have led some scholars to maintain that its legitimate principles and aims were set aside in the years following its promulgation, and to argue that a "reform of the reform" is necessary for a faithful implementation of the Council's wishes. Others hold that the Constitution began a process of ongoing liturgical reform that cannot be limited by its provisions. See: chapters 12–15 of Part III above.

Contrafactum (Contrafacta) A compositional practice whereby a text is set to a pre-existing melody. This process was frequently used in the creation of the repertory of Gregorian music in the Middle Ages.

Corinthian A Greek architectural type with a bell-shaped capital decorated with acanthus leaves and tendrils.

Corpus Christi Literally "the Body of Christ." The term "Corpus Domini" (the Body of the Lord) is also sometimes used. The development of eucharistic adoration in the twelfth and thirteenth centuries gave rise to the practice of celebrating a feast of "Corpus Christi" in honour of the Blessed Sacrament on the Thursday following Trinity Sunday involving the solemn celebration of Mass followed by a procession in which the Blessed Eucharist is carried through the streets. Pope Urban IV (c. 1195; 1261–64) extended this practice to the entire Latin rite in 1264. St Thomas Aquinas (1225–74) composed rich and beautiful texts for the Mass and Office of Corpus Christi which are in use to this day.

Crux This Latin term, which can be used in a literal sense to refer simply to a cross without an image of Christ crucified fastened to it, in a liturgical context from the tenth century onward most often denotes a crucifix, i.e., a cross with the *corpus* of Christ.

Custodia A term in Iberian texts commonly used to denote a monstrance, but also denoting a large portable shrine for carrying the Blessed Sacrament in Corpus Christi processions or for solemnly reserving the Eucharist on Holy Thursday.

Customary A liturgical book providing detailed rubrics for the celebration of Mass, the recitation of the Divine Office, the ordering of processions, and the ceremonies for particular feast days for individual dioceses, monasteries or religious orders.

De Grassis, Paride (c. 1470–1528) A papal master of ceremonies and bishop of Pessaro, De Grassis authored a book of rites for cardinals and bishops, *De caeremoniis cardinalium et episcoporum in eorum dioecesibus* (Rome: In aedibvs popvli Romani, 1580).

Decorum A methodical discernment by the architect to select appropriate and expressive architectural elements.

Dekkers, Eligius (1915–98) The fifth abbot of the Benedictine Abbey of Sint-Pietersabdij, Steenbrugge, Flanders, from 1967 until 1981, Dekkers taught patristics, theology and liturgy at the University of Leuven. Although he would become widely known in the academic world for his *Corpus Christianorum*, a series invaluable for contemporary liturgical research, Dekkers never went to university and was largely self-taught. During his novitiate he had studied philosophy and theology, but most of his academic education came through wide reading. He received numerous accolades, including several honorary doctorates. He was a corresponding Fellow of the British Academy and sat on editorial boards of various scholarly publications. Dekkers was a gentle and modest man whose life of quiet scholarship was devoted to the academic project he himself launched.

Denis the Carthusian (1402–71) A Belgian priest of the Carthusian Order, and a man of extraordinary holiness and one of the most prolific Catholic writers ever. In addition to authoring numerous theological and scriptural treatises, Denis also wrote significant works on the liturgy, including the *Expositio missae* and a commentary concerning hymns.

Depositio A term meaning "Deposition," denoting a Good Friday ceremony commemorating the burial of Christ in which a crucifix, an image of the Lord resting in death, or in some cases the Blessed Sacrament, would be carried to a representation of the Savior's tomb and be symbolically "buried" there.

Devotio moderna From the end of the fourteenth century this spiritual movement (the "modern devotion"), arose stressing personal meditation and internal prayer as distinct from external liturgical ritual. The most famous work of this school is *The Imitation of Christ* by St Thomas à Kempis (c. 1380–1471). In the sixteenth century the individualism of the *devotio moderna* came of age in the Spiritual Exercises of St Ignatius of Loyola (1491–1556). Ignatius excluded the choral celebration of the Divine Office for his Jesuit order so that it would not hinder their availability for apostolic works, whilst insisting on the practice of personal meditation. In other sixteenth century orders for whom choir obligation was retained—the Capuchin Franciscans (founded 1528) and the Discalced Carmelites (founded 1593)—the *recto tono* recitation of the Divine Office was the norm. The *liturgical* celebration of the Office became an official duty to be accomplished efficiently so as to leave room for mediation and prayer after the manner of the *devotio moderna*. The cumulative effect of the *devotio moderna* was the relegation of the liturgical celebration of the Sacred Liturgy to the status of one devotion amongst others (at best) or of a legal duty to be accomplished by the clergy (at worst) and the development, with successive generations, of a spiritual life more distant still from the Church's liturgy.

Diathesis The process of drawing to explore design solutions.

Divine Office (Liturgy of the Hours) The Divine Office is, besides the Eucharist, the other principal element of the Christian liturgy. It is the common—and in principle the sung—prayer of the psalter along with some complementary elements distributed on the days of the year and different times or hours ("horae") of the day, which find their origin in the Jewish tradition expressed in psalm 118: "Seven times a day I praise thee" (v. 164) and "at midnight I rise to praise thee" (v. 62). In Christian tradition, this developed into the hours of Matins, Lauds, Prime, Terce, Sext, None, Vespers, and Compline. In time, the texts of the Divine Office were collected into breviaries for the private recitation of the clergy, detracting from its nature as sung communal prayer. The whole psalter was prayed each week and, until its rearrangement by Pius X in 1911, its arrangement contained features dating back to Jewish observances from at least the time of Christ himself. Different dioceses and religious orders had their own versions of the Divine Office or variations of the Roman form. Monastics did not adopt the rearrangement of the psalter imposed by Pius X. Following the Second Vatican Council, substantial changes were made to the Divine Office including the suppression of Prime, the redesigning of Matins as an Office of Readings for any time of the day, the redistribution of the psalter over four weeks, and the suppression of certain psalms or parts of psalms deemed to be unsuitable. The 2007 motu proprio *Summorum Pontificum* authorized the praying of the 1961 *Breviarium Romanum*, and today religious houses celebrating the more ancient forms of the liturgy pray the older form of the Divine Office proper to their order.

Dominican rite The Sacred Liturgy is central to the life of the Dominican order and its proper liturgical uses, uniformly established in the second half of the thirteenth century under Humbert of Romans (c. 1190/1200–77) who was elected master general in 1256, were a cherished feature of the order. Their liturgy is a use of the Roman rite influenced by contemporary local (particularly French) usages and adapted to the life of the order. It was not reformed in the light of the Council of Trent and survived the seventeenth-century desire of Clement VIII (1536; 1592–1605) to suppress it (and possibly also other uses), developing gradually under the influence of successive masters general and general chapters. Pius X's arrangement of the psalter was adopted in 1923. The twentieth century historian of Dominican liturgy, William Bonniwell OP, is severe in his criticism of the novelty of this reform, observing that "on 1 January 1923 . . . the ancient Roman Office, which the Dominican Order had preserved and guarded with fidelity for seven centuries, ceased to exist." He notes, however, that many older friars asked for and received dispensations to retain the former Office; *A History of the Dominican Liturgy* (Joseph F. Wagner: New York, 1944) pp. 351–2. Following the Second Vatican Council a new edition of the *Missale iuxta ritum Ordinis Praedicatorum* was published in 1965, incorporating elements of the reform of the Roman rite then in progress. In 1969, the master general petitioned the Holy See for permission for the order to adopt the Roman rite; the rescript granting this permission also allowed the master general or provincials to permit the use of the old Dominican liturgy. In recent years, many friars have shown an interest in their order's liturgical tradition, and celebrations of the Dominican liturgy have become more frequent. Resources and studies have been published at: http://dominican-liturgy.blogspot.com. See also: William R. Bonniwell OP, *The Dominican Ceremonial for Mass and Benediction* (New York: Comet Press, 1946); Archdale A. King, *Liturgies of the Religious Orders* (London, New York & Toronto: Longman's, Green & Co., 1955); Augustine Thompson OP, "Preconciliar Reforms of the Dominican Rite Liturgy: 1950–1962," *Antiphon* 15 (2011), pp. 185–201 & "Preconciliar Reforms of the Dominican Rite Liturgy: 1962–1969," *Antiphon* 15 (2011), pp. 299–317.

Doric The earliest and simplest Greek architecture, developed in Attica.

Doxology An acclamation of praise to the Blessed Trinity (from the Greek, *doxa*, "praise" or "glory," and *logia*, "saying"). The "greater doxology" is the *Gloria in excelsis Deo* of the Mass, while the "lesser doxology" is the *Gloria Patri*, used, e.g., at the end of psalms and canticles.

Durandus, William (1237–96) After serving in the Roman curia, in his later years Durandus served as bishop of Mende, France. Arguably the most influential liturgist of late-medieval Christendom, he authored the *Rationale divinorum officiorum*, a massive liturgical commentary providing mystical explanations of a wide range of liturgical ceremonies and practices. The pontifical that he compiled (c. 1294) as well as a manual of instructions for the celebration of Mass that he authored (c. 1294) shaped to a considerable extent the subsequent late-medieval development of the liturgy.

Easter Sepulchre A representation of the tomb of Christ used from Good Friday to Easter Sunday to commemorate his burial and resurrection, within which a crucifix, or an image of Christ resting in death, or the Blessed Sacrament would be enshrined after being carried there in the *Depositio* rite.

Elevatio This Latin term is used both in the context of Mass for the raising of the Sacred Host following the consecration and in the context of Holy Week for medieval rites for Easter Sunday of bringing forth a crucifix, an image of Christ or the Eucharist from a representation of the Lord's tomb to commemorate the resurrection.

Entablature A combination of architrave, frieze, and cornice above columns to support roof structure.

Epistolarium (Epistolary) A book for liturgical use containing the lessons to be chanted before the Gospel during Mass usually arranged according to their liturgical sequence. In the *usus antiquior* the Epistle is chanted by the subdeacon from this book. The epistolarium is often incorporated into the same volume as the evangelarium.

Eucharist *see* Mass

Eucharistic prayers The text of the eucharistic prayer was relatively fluid in the first three centuries; its exact wording was not yet fixed, and the celebrating bishop (or priest) had some room to improvise. However, stable rules regarding structure and contents of the prayers, which were, above all, biblically inspired, emerge already in the second century, and the first written texts of anaphoras go back to the third century. Concerns for doctrinal orthodoxy limited the celebrant's liberty to vary the texts of the prayer. This need became particularly pressing during the doctrinal struggles of the fourth century; hence this era saw the emergence of fixed eucharistic prayers, such as the Roman canon, the Anaphora of St John Chrysostom and others. Another important aspect that should not be underestimated is the significance of repetition and memorisation in an oral culture. The formation of stable liturgical texts can thus be ascertained from early on as a strong force in the process of handing on the Christian faith. Moreover, the early practice of improvisation within a stable framework of biblical motives led to a distinctly traditional style of liturgical prayer. See: A.

Bouley, *From Freedom to Formula: The Evolution of the Eucharistic Prayer from Oral Improvisation to Written Texts*, Studies in Christian Antiquity 21 (Washington DC: Catholic University of America Press, 1981); A. Budde, "Improvisation im Eucharistiegebet. Zur Technik freien Betens in der Alten Kirche", *Jahrbuch für Antike und Christentum* 44 (2001), pp. 127–44; G.G. Willis, *A History of Early Roman Liturgy: To the death of Gregory the Great*, HBS, Subsidia I (1994).

Evangeliarium (Evangeliary/Book of Gospels) A book for liturgical use containing the gospels texts usually arranged according to their liturgical sequence from which the deacon sings the gospel at Mass. Because of the liturgical reverence paid to the proclamation of the gospel this book, which is carried in procession, is often ornately decorated with symbols of Christ.

Extreme unction *see* Anointing of the Sick

Façade The principal front of a building.

Flex If there is an extra section in a psalm verse, before the mediant cadence, the recitation tone drops ("flexes") temporarily, then resuming the recitation tone. The flex is actually a type of cadence, and is signified by a dagger (†).

Frieze The intermediate zone of an entablature, above the architrave and below the cornice.

Gabriel Biel (c. 1425–95) A German priest and theologian, Biel authored a valuable commentary on the ceremonies of the Mass, *Sacri canonis missae expositio* (Reutlingen: Johann Otmar, 1488), that includes an exposition on kneeling and other acts of reverence offered to Christ in the Eucharist following the consecration.

Gallican rite This term can denote various liturgical realities: the rites existing in Gaul before the eighth- and ninth-century reforms of Pepin and Charlemagne, the Roman rite as enriched by the Carolingian liturgists in Gaul and Germany, a French use introduced into Apulia and Sicily by the Normans, the Franco-Roman rite which supplanted the Mozarabic rite in Spain at the behest of Gregory VII (c. 1015/28; 1073–85) at the end of the eleventh century, and the liturgical books introduced into many French dioceses in the eighteenth century. The most common use of the term is in respect of the liturgical tradition of early medieval Gaul, as distinct from the Roman and Milanese rites or the Eastern liturgies. Much scholarship has been devoted to these early liturgical forms and various hypotheses exist as to their origin; see: Cyrille Vogel, *Medieval Liturgy: An Introduction to the Sources* (Washington DC: Pastoral Press, 1986) pp. 275–7. Its liturgical chant predates the adoption of Gregorian chant by the Carolingians in the late eighth and ninth centuries. See: chapter 4 above, also: Fernand Cabrol OSB, *The Mass of the Western Rites* (London: Sands & Co., 1934); Archdale A. King, *Liturgies of the Past* (London, New York & Toronto: Longman's, Green & Co., 1959).

Gamber, Klaus (1919–89) Monsignor Gamber was director of the Liturgical Institute founded in 1957 at Regensburg, and published *The Reform of the Roman Liturgy: Its Problems and Background* (Una Voce Press & Foundation for Catholic Reform: San Juan Capistrano & Harrison, NY, 1993) which asserted that the liturgical books promulgated by Pope Paul VI do not represent a properly organic development or reform of the Roman rite, as called for by article 23 of the 1963 Constitution on the Liturgy *Sacrosanctum Concilium*. Joseph Cardinal Ratzinger's praise of Gamber gave his work a prominence that helped further critical assessment of the liturgical reforms following the Second Vatican Council. See: Klaus Gamber, *The Modern Rite: Collected Essays on the Reform of the Liturgy* (Farnborough: St Michael's Abbey Press., 2002); Joseph Cardinal Ratzinger, "In Memory of Klaus Gamber" JRCW 11, pp. 536–8.

General Instruction of the Roman Missal The English version of the *Institutio Generalis Missalis Romani*, the General Instruction of the Roman Missal is the document providing authoritative directives for the celebration of the rite of Mass promulgated since the Second Vatican Council, replacing the former *Rubricae Generales Missalis* and the *Ritus servandus in celebratione Missae* found in earlier editions of the missal. It is printed at the start of editions of the missal, the most recent edition being that contained in the *Missale Romanum* of 2002 (reprinted with amendments in 2008). Episcopal Conferences are able to petition the Holy See for variations in the General Instruction for their territories.

Graduale (Gradual) A liturgical book containing Mass chants, especially the propers, e.g. the *Graduale Romanum*. The term is also used for the highly melismatic proper chant that is sung after the Epistle at Mass which usually consists of two verses of a psalm. The first verse is sung by the full choir after the cantor intones up to the asterisk. The second verse is usually sung by a solo cantor, the choir joining in at the final asterisk. Both verses are sung straight through without any repetitions. Although there may be some relation to the ancient responsorial psalm, documentary evidence suggests that the gradual underwent either a radical metamorphosis since that time, or was reimagined altogether during the Gregorian-Carolingian period.

Gregorian chant One of several repertories of liturgical plainsong used in the Western Church. Its attribution to St Gregory the Great (c. 540; 590–604) is apocryphal, however the era subsequent to his papacy and up to the reign of Charlemagne is considered to be the period of its coalescence. Over the centuries its influence has been extreme, and it has come to be known as the official music of the Roman rite.

Hearse Within the context of the Holy Week liturgy, this term denotes the wooden candle stand used for the ceremonial extinction of lights during the offices of Tenebrae, usually triangular in shape and able to accommodate fifteen candles which are symbolically extinguished successively during the rite.

Guardini, Romano (1885–1968) Ordained a priest in Germany in 1910, Guardini discovered the liturgy at the Benedictine abbey of Beuron whilst a young man and in 1918 wrote the German original of *The Spirit of the Liturgy* (Sheed & Ward: London, 1930), which was widely translated and became a seminal text for the nascent liturgical movement. Guardini wrote extensively and engaged in liturgical practices seen as *avant garde* for his time. Whilst he is often regarded as a theological precursor of the Second Vatican Council, in 1964 he wrote a famous letter on "the liturgical act," critiquing some contemporary strands of thought ("A Letter from Romano Guardini" in: *Herder Correspondence*, Special Issue, 1964, pp. 24-6.) See: Romano Guardini, *Sacred Signs* (Sheed & Ward: London, 1937), *Liturgische Bildung* (Deutsches Quickbornhaus: Burg Rothenfels am Main, 1923); *Formazione liturgica* (Ed. Morcelliana: Brescia, 2008); Alcuin Reid, *The Organic Development of the Liturgy*, 2nd edn (San Francisco: Ignatius Press, 2005), pp. 92-5.

Guéranger, Prosper (1805-75) Guéranger was a diocesan priest and an author of liturgical works who re-founded the Abbey of Solesmes, France, in 1833. In 1837, Solesmes was raised to the rank of abbey by Gregory XVI (1765; 1831-46) with Guéranger its first abbot. His romantic scholarship raised many questions, though his widely translated fifteen-volume *The Liturgical Year* became a classic of liturgical piety. Guéranger's energetic ultramontanism was a significant factor in the eradication of the eighteenth century Gallican liturgies from France. After his death, Solesmes continued to promote liturgical renewal and research, particularly into Gregorian chant. Guéranger's monastic descendants were foundational for the liturgical movement of the twentieth century. See: Alcuin Reid, *The Organic Development of the Liturgy*, 2nd edn (San Francisco: Ignatius Press, 2005), pp. 56-60; 65-6.

Hebdomadarian The priest or deacon in a community of clergy or religious assigned to preside at the Divine Office for the period of a week.

Heenan indult The singular permission given by Paul VI to the Archbishop of Westminster in 1971 for the continued use, under certain conditions, of the rite of Mass before the missal of Paul VI. See: chapter 21 above.

Heighted neums Also known as diastematic neums, these represent definite pitches by their placement at different heights above and below an imaginary line.

Hermeneutic of continuity In an address to the Roman curia on December 22, 2005, Pope Benedict XVI famously described two contrasting ways of interpreting the Second Vatican Council. One is an erroneous "hermeneutic of discontinuity and rupture," which reads Vatican II as a mandate for radical change, even revolution, in virtually every sphere of the Church's life; the other is an authentic "hermeneutic of reform," which is attuned to the Church's tradition of teaching and worship as it has been handed on and its understanding faithfully developed over the centuries. The latter is also referred to sometimes as the "hermeneutic of reform in continuity" and the "hermeneutic of continuity." In making provisions for wider use of the 1962 *Missale Romanum* (the last "typical edition" of the missal prior to Vatican II), Pope Benedict upheld the hermeneutic of continuity with respect to the Church's liturgical tradition.

Holy water Water that is blessed according to a liturgical rite by a priest or deacon and used in the blessing of oneself (customarily when entering a church or chapel), of others and of places or objects with the intent of making them holy and repelling evil. Holy water recalls the cleansing from sin and purification of the sacrament of baptism and is itself a sacramental. The traditional blessing of holy water involves its exorcism and also that of salt, which is then mixed with the water. Other forms of holy water include "Easter water" which is blessed at the Paschal Vigil, and "Gregorian water" which is prepared with the addition of salt, ashes, and wine, and blessed by a bishop for use in the consecration of a church and an altar or the reconciliation of a desecrated church. See: Archdale A. King, *Holy Water: A Short Account of the Use of Water for Ceremonial and Purificatory Purposes in Pagan, Jewish and Christian Times* (London: Burns, Oates & Washbourne, 1926).

Holy Year Instituted in 1300 by Pope Boniface VIII, the Holy Year of Jubilee is a year in which pilgrimages to the tombs of the Apostles in Rome are encouraged with generous indulgences. Originally intended to occur every 100 years, the interval between jubilee years has been decreased, first to fifty years, and currently to every twenty-five years. Occasionally, popes have declared particular years of "extraordinary" jubilee for given reasons.

ICEL The International Commission on English in the Liturgy is a mixed commission of Catholic Bishops' Conferences in countries where English is used in the celebration of the Sacred Liturgy. It was established in 1963 to prepare English translations of each of the Latin liturgical books and liturgical texts in accord with the directives of the Holy See. On September 15, 2003 the Congregation for Divine Worship and the Discipline of the Sacraments established ICEL as a mixed commission in accordance with the Holy See's Instruction *Liturgiam authenticam.*

Incense Following its use in Jewish worship, Christian liturgy has used incense since at least the fourth century. It is a symbol of worship of the divine and of prayer rising to Almighty God ("Let my prayer be counted as incense before thee, and the lifting up of my hands as an evening sacrifice" Ps. 141:2), and is used as a liturgical sign of reverence and honour. It is blessed before use and is therefore a sacramental.

Innocent III (c. 1160; 1198–1216) Prior to his election as Pope Innocent III in 1198, Lothario of Segni composed one of the greatest medieval commentaries on the rites of the Mass, *De sacro altaris mysterio.*

Inter Œcumenici The first "Instruction for the Right Application of the Constitution on the Sacred Liturgy of the Second Vatican Council," *Inter Œcumenici*, was prepared by the *Consilium* and issued by the Sacred Congregation of Rites on September 26, 1964. It defines the role that episcopal conferences and local bishops were to have in regulating the Vatican II liturgical reform, respecting the principles enunciated in *Sacrosanctum Concilium* regarding the Holy See and territorial ecclesiastical authority. More widespread use of the vernacular is permitted throughout liturgical celebrations, notably for certain parts of the Mass. Other changes made in the Mass include the introduction of general intercessions and ritual simplifications (e.g., fewer genuflections and signs of the cross, omission of the "last Gospel," and the priest no longer says prayers silently that are being sung by the choir or said by the people). Celebration "facing the people" is mentioned (for the first time) but not required. Various reforms were indicated for the other sacraments, the Divine Office, and church architecture.

Initio (Intonation) The distinctive melodic group of notes on which the first word or words of a chant are sung by priest or cantor, and which are followed by the whole congregation or the choir. In a psalm tone, the intonation leads to the recitation tone and is usually sung only on the first psalm verse, by the cantor.

Introit The entrance chant of the Mass which is sung as the clergy and assistants approach the altar. It is taken from the proper or the relevant common in the *Graduale*. The 1958 Instruction *De musica sacra et liturgia* restored the practice of singing several verses from the psalm, and finally the *Gloria Patri*, with the antiphon used as a refrain. The Church Music Association of America (www.musicasacra.com) has republished the chant for these verses and has worked to prepare chants for the modern English texts of the introit.

Ionic A type of Greek architecture characterized by scroll-like elements on the capital, developed in Ionia.

Jugalis A multi-colored ribbon (often white and purple) used for the symbolic action of binding or joining together the bride and groom during medieval Spanish marriage ceremonies to symbolize the couple's reception of the nuptial vocation and their marital union.

Jungmann, Joseph A. (1889–1975) An Austrian priest who became a Jesuit after ordination, Jungmann spent most of his life as a professor of catechetics and liturgy at the University of Innsbruck. His 1948 two-volume work *Missarum sollemnia: Eine genetische Erklärung der römischen Messe*, ET: The *Mass of the Roman Rite: Its Origins and Development*, 2 vols (New York: Benziger, 1951), was profoundly influential in shaping historical assumptions underlying liturgical reform in the coming decades: Jungmann was *the* liturgical historian of the era and his opinions were widely sought and respected; he was a part of all official organs for liturgical reform from 1948–69. His presumption of the corruption of the Western liturgy in its development beyond the patristic period underlines much of the reform proposed before and enacted following the Second Vatican Council. See: Alcuin Reid, *The Organic Development of the Liturgy*, 2nd edn (San Francisco: Ignatius Press, 2005), pp. 164–72.

Kavanagh, Aidan (1929–2006) A Benedictine monk of St Meinrad's Archabbey who studied under Balthasar Fischer (1912–2001) in Trier, then founded the doctoral program in liturgy at the University of Notre Dame, before going to teach at Yale for twenty years. He left an impact on three fronts: the use of ritual studies, the rites of initiation, and the definition of liturgical theology. His fictional creation Mrs Murphy personifies a liturgical theologian who may lack the specialized training of second-order theology, but can be called a theologian, nonetheless, for having absorbed the Church's *theologia prima* by living the liturgy.

Keizersberg Abbey (Abbé Mont César) A Benedictine house of studies established in Leuven in 1888 by nine monks from Maredsous Abbey formally established in 1899 as part of the Beuronese Congregation. The abbey is still known for its connection both with Dom Lambert Beauduin and the origins of the twentieth-century liturgical movement. In 1921, the abbey moved from the Beuronese

Congregation to become part of the new Belgian Mission Congregation of Our Lady (*Belgische Congregatie van Onze-Lieve-Vrouw-Boodschap*). In 1929, the abbey began publication of the theological journal "Recherches de Théologie Ancienne et Médiévale." When the French section of the Catholic University of Leuven moved out of Leuven in 1968, the abbey became a Flemish institution and changed its name from *Mont César* to *Keizersberg*. In 1968, the abbey became part of the Subiaco Congregation. The abbey and the theology faculty of KU Leuven jointly sponsor the *Liturgisch Instituut* and the now French-English liturgical periodical, *Questions Liturgiques: Studies in Liturgy*, founded in 1910.

Kyriale A chant book containing the ordinary chants of the Mass from the *Graduale.*

Latin and liturgical participation in the Middle Ages In the course of the Middle Ages, the formation of national languages and cultures in Europe meant the language of the liturgy became more and more removed from the language of the people. It would be an exaggeration, however, to conclude that the use of Latin as a sacred language was an insurmountable barrier to understanding of and participation in the Mass. Such a conclusion would rest on a narrow understanding of participation that "sees liturgy only as text and limits participation to speaking roles" (Frank Senn). The rite itself provided many possibilities for internal and external participation, and sacred art and architecture had a language of their own that could be read like a "vernacular." Moreover, in Romance countries, there was a basic understanding at least of the meaning conveyed in Latin liturgical texts, and that this was so even among the lesser educated, at least if they chose to follow attentively. The cultural impact of the sacred language in everyday speech is also evident from the resonances of liturgical Latin in Romance vernaculars. The use of Latin in this period still provided an example of "diglossia"; it was the language of the cultural elites and served to bind together international communities of ideas, above all the Church and the Republic of Letters. Nonetheless, the objections to the use of Latin not only in the liturgy but in public life at large and in other aspects of the Church's life became more widely spread in the Renaissance and Reformation periods. The humanists' movement for a return to the purity of Ciceronian Latin aggravated this situation, because it meant that Latin as a living second language was effectively discarded. See: F.C. Senn, *The People's Work: A Social History of the Liturgy* (Minneapolis: Fortress Press, 2006); A. Thompson, *Cities of God: The Religion of the Italian Communes 1125–1325* (University Park, PA: The Pennsylvania State University Press, 2005); P. Burke, *Languages and Communities in Early Modern Europe: The 2002 Wiles Lectures given at Queen's University, Belfast* (Cambridge: Cambridge University Press, 2004).

Latin during the Reformation and at the Council of Trent In the sixteenth century, the Protestant Reformers, in continuity with dissident movements of the later Middle Ages, attacked the use of Latin in the liturgy. There was a theological rationale at the root of this critique: the Protestants' idea of divine worship being essentially a proclamation of the Word of God made them conclude that using a language that was not intelligible to the assembly was contrary to the Gospel. Martin Luther was happy to allow for some Latin, as far as it was understood by the people, and this custom was followed for some time in Lutheran communities. John Calvin, on the other hand, categorically rejected the use of Latin in worship. At the Council of Trent, the question of liturgical language was much debated, and the arguments produced by the Protestant Reformers were considered very seriously. The *Decree on the Sacrifice of the Mass* of the Council's 22nd Session in 1562 contains a carefully worded doctrinal exposition on the subject, stating that it did not seem *expedient* to the Fathers that the Holy Mass should be celebrated in the vernacular, although they recognize the value of the texts of the Mass for the instruction of the faithful. However, pastors should preach frequently about what is read at Mass, especially on Sundays and feast days. Moreover, canon nine of the same *Decree on the Sacrifice of the Mass* declares anathema anyone who says that the vernacular language *must* be used in the celebration of Mass; again, the subtle wording of this conciliar text is to be noted. The question of Latin and the vernacular in the Church's liturgy continued to be discussed in the centuries after Trent, especially in the Catholic Enlightenment of the eighteenth century, and came to the fore especially in the twentieth century. See: H.A.P. Schmidt, *Liturgie et langue vulgaire. Le problème de la langue liturgique chez les premiers Réformateurs et au Concile de Trente*, Analecta Gregoriana 53 (Romae: Apud Aedes Unversitatis Gregorianae, 1950).

Laudes Regiae Liturgical acclamations for the king, his family and his entourage, which were sung on special occasions, such as royal welcome rituals (*adventus*), major liturgical feasts, or royal visitations.

Laus Perennis The perpetual chant of Psalms in shifts.

Lectionary This term denotes a book containing the texts of readings for the liturgy, either for Mass or the Divine Office. Mass readings were formerly contained in the missal, however following the Second Vatican Council a lectionary was published containing the new three-year cycle of readings for the Mass, also including the responsorial psalm and the alleluia and its verse.

Lefebvre, Gaspar (1880–1966) A Benedictine monk of the Abbey of St André, Bruges, Lefebvre made a particularly valuable pastoral contribution to the foundational and pioneering work of the liturgical movement by publishing bilingual missals: Latin-English, Latin-French, Latin-Dutch, Latin-Italian. The Latin-English *St Andrew Daily Missal with Vespers for Sundays and Feasts* was published between 1920 and 1959 at St André, now Sint-Andriesabdij, Zevenkerken, and was widely used in the Anglophone world.

Lefebvre, Marcel (1905–91) A French Holy Ghost missionary, Lefebvre served with distinction in Africa and was consecrated bishop in 1947 at the age of forty-one. Having been archbishop of Dakar and Apostolic Delegate to Senegal, Lefebvre returned to France as bishop of Tulle in 1962 only to be elected superior general of his congregation later the same year. He was a member of the Central Preparatory Commission for the Second Vatican Council. As a Father of the Council, he voted for and signed its Constitution on the Sacred

Liturgy. Following the Council he became increasingly concerned about its interpretation and implementation and resigned as superior general in 1968. In 1969, at the urging of some seminarians, he established a seminary for the formation of seminarians in the traditional manner in Fribourg, Switzerland, with the necessary permission of the local bishop. In 1970, his "Society of St Pius X" was established in compliance with ecclesiastical law. The seminary chose to use the preconciliar liturgical rites. Other bishops regarded the seminary with suspicion and in 1975 a new local bishop canonically dissolved the Society. Lefebvre continued his work and period of bitter, open conflict ensued between the Society and the Holy See in which positions became increasingly entrenched. The rejection of the reformed liturgy became a standard behind which more and more people rallied, but the issues were wider than, and perhaps not fundamentally, liturgical. Paul VI suspended Lefebvre *a divinis* in 1976 after his refusal to halt ordinations. In 1988, Lefebvre consecrated four bishops without pontifical mandate, thereby incurring the canonical penalty of *latae sententiae* excommunication. Lefebvre's stance forced the Holy See to reconsider the prohibition of the older liturgy under John Paul II and led directly to the 1984 indult *Quattuor abhinc annos* and its extension in the 1988 motu proprio *Ecclesia Dei adflicta*—measures which Benedict XVI would extend by his 2007 motu proprio *Summorum Pontificum* and his 2009 rescinding of the excommunication of the four bishops consecrated by Lefebvre. See: chapter 21 above; Bernard Tissier de Mallerais, *Marcel Lefebvre: The Biography* (Kansas City: Angelus Press, 2004).

Leisen A medieval repertory of non-liturgical religious songs, typically in German, they date from as early as the ninth century, but are generally of later medieval origin. The term "leisen" is supposedly derived from "eleison" of "Kyrie eleison."

Leitourgia This term was used for a service performed by an individual for the state, frequently without charge, i.e. a public service, from which the word "liturgy" is derived. The term was then applied to the religious cults performed in the Jewish Temple.

Lenten veil This curtain, commonly decorated with Passion imagery or symbols, would be hung in the church sanctuary for the season of Lent, concealing the altar.

Lex Orandi, Lex Credendi "Lex orandi" is literally, "the law of prayer." It is a grammar of life contained in the liturgical activity of the Church that is the foundation for our belief. "Lex credendi" is literally, "the law of belief." It is also the activity of the liturgical Church working out and sustaining the belief that is founded upon her life of prayer. The *Catechism of the Catholic Church* teaches: "The Church's faith precedes the faith of the believer who is invited to adhere to it. When the Church celebrates the sacraments, she confesses the faith received from the apostles—whence the ancient saying: *lex orandi, lex credendi* (or: *legem credendi lex statuat supplicandi*, according to Prosper of Aquitaine [fifth century]). The law of prayer is the law of faith: the Church believes as she prays. Liturgy is a constitutive element of the holy and living Tradition" (1124).

Liber Sacerdotalis A 1523 compilation of Italian liturgical ceremonies, at least some of which are believed to constitute observances in the see of Venice as recorded and compiled by the Dominican Father Alberto Castellani.

Litanies From the Greek "lite" (prayer), litanies are a series of liturgical petitions, often addressed to the saints, to which the people respond to lines sung by the cantor with a short invocation such as "Kyrie eleison" or "Ora pro nobis." Litanies were in use in the East by the fourth century and spread widely throughout East and West.

Liturgiam Authenticam The fifth "Instruction for the Right Application of the Constitution on the Sacred Liturgy of the Second Vatican Council," *Liturgiam Authenticam*, was issued by the Congregation for Divine Worship and the Discipline of the Sacraments on March 28, 2001. It establishes new norms for translating the Latin liturgical texts into vernacular languages, thereby reversing the approach of the 1969 Instruction *Comme le prévoit*, published by the *Consilium*. Whereas the *Consilium* endorsed the principle of "dynamic equivalence," which aims to convey the general meaning of the original text rather than giving a literal translation, *Liturgiam Authenticam* takes quite a different attitude to translation. Adopting the principle of "formal equivalence," it decrees that the original Latin text, insofar as possible, must be translated integrally and accurately, "without omissions or additions in terms of their content, and without paraphrases or glosses," so as to maintain the Roman rite's particular style, structure, and sacral vocabulary. It also calls for the correction of existing vernacular translations in keeping with these norms, and for the establishment of an oversight committee to ensure the fidelity of future translations.

Liturgicæ Instaurationes This third "Instruction for the Right Application of the Constitution on the Sacred Liturgy of the Second Vatican Council," was published on September 5, 1970 by the Sacred Congregation for Divine Worship, a body that succeeded the Sacred Congregation of Rites and the *Consilium*. This Instruction recalls the purposes of the Vatican II liturgical reform and appeals to bishops to exercise their proper role in the regulation of the liturgy within their domains. In addition, it calls for an end to unauthorized liturgical experimentation (e.g., the substitution of non-biblical readings in the Liturgy of the Word, and the recitation of any part of the eucharistic prayer by the assembly), lists liturgical ministries now open to women (reader, usher, musician), and attends to questions about materials used in the liturgy, specifically bread for the Eucharist and worthy communion vessels.

Liturgical abuse Liturgical abuse is a term designating a serious violation of liturgical law. Such abuses were often the result of unauthorized "pastoral" initiatives and so-called "liturgical creativity" following the Second Vatican Council in spite of the duty of the clergy to celebrate the Church's liturgy according to the norms established in the liturgical books. Liturgical abuses often cause scandal, confusing and alienating faithful Catholics.

Liturgical asceticism *Askesis* meant a kind of training or discipline, often undergone by athletes. When this spiritual discipline overcomes the passions it capacitates a person to participate in the liturgy, and conforms the person to the image of the resurrected Christ. See: David W. Fagerburg, *On Liturgical Asceticism* (Washington, DC: Catholic University of America Press, 2013).

Liturgical formation Liturgical formation is primarily a matter of ongoing immersion in the living celebration of the *ecclesia* (the liturgical life of the Church); catechetical instruction, practical training or academic study should serve that end. First and foremost those responsible for liturgical formation must become "thoroughly imbued with the spirit and power of the liturgy", without which, as the Second Vatican Council insisted, efforts at promoting liturgical renewal "would be futile" (*Sacrosanctum Concilium*, 14). See: Alcuin Reid, "Thoroughly imbued with the spirit and power of the Liturgy— *Sacrosanctum Concilium* and Liturgical Formation," Alcuin Reid (ed.), *Sacred Liturgy: The Source and Summit of the Life and Mission of the Church* (San Francisco: Ignatius Press, 2014), pp. 213–36.

Liturgical law Ecclesiastical ordinances pertaining to divine worship to which liturgical ministers—ordained and lay—owe obedience. Following the establishment of the Sacred Congregation of Rites after the Council of Trent the power of regulating the liturgy has been reserved to the Holy See and is exercised today by the Congregation for Divine Worship and Discipline of the Sacraments. Whilst liturgical law is of ecclesiastical origin, its wilful infringement is at least a matter of disobedience. See: Alcuin Reid, "From Rubrics to *Ars Celebrandi*— Liturgical Law in the 21st Century," *Antiphon* 17 (2013), pp. 139–67; Raymond Leo Cardinal Burke, "Liturgical Law in the Mission of the Church," Alcuin Reid (ed.), *Sacred Liturgy: The Source and Summit of the Life and Mission of the Church* (San Francisco: Ignatius Press, 2014), pp. 389–415.

Liturgical movement The twentieth century liturgical movement sought to place the Sacred Liturgy at the center of the life of the Church so that all of the faithful could draw from its spiritual riches through conscious connection with (participation in) the action of Christ in the liturgy. As the movement progressed it increasingly considered whether some reforms to the liturgical rites themselves would facilitate these ends. In the decade or so before the Second Vatican Council, many of its enthusiasts worked towards such reforms (see: chapter 8, above). The "new" liturgical movement arose in response to the call of Joseph Cardinal Ratzinger in his book *The Spirit of the Liturgy* (San Francisco: Ignatius Press, 2000; also JRCW11) for "a movement toward the liturgy and toward the right way of celebrating the liturgy, inwardly and outwardly" (pp. 8–9), and in the light of a perceived rupture in Western liturgical tradition following the Second Vatican Council. It seeks authentic liturgical renewal and embraces the desire for a faithful implementation of the Council's Constitution on the Sacred Liturgy as well as an openness to the riches and value of the *usus antiquior* in the life of the Church (see: chapters 14, 15 & 21, above).

Liturgical piety Sometimes called "liturgical spirituality," liturgical piety is finding the necessary nourishment for Christian life in the active and conscious contemplation of the faith of the Church as it is celebrated in the liturgical rites and prayers throughout the annual round of seasons and feasts of the liturgical year. Liturgical piety is not one form of spirituality amongst others: because it is nothing other than praying the Church's liturgy itself, it enjoys an objectivity and a priority over the practice of unrelated, however worthy, spiritual or devotional exercises.

Liturgical prayer "*submissa voce*" The earliest incontestable evidence for a partial recitation of the eucharistic prayer in silence is from the East Syrian tradition and is found in the *Homily on the Mysteries* attributed to Narsai, the head of the theological schools of Edessa and of Nisibis (d. 502). The custom of reciting large parts of the anaphora in silence also spread to Greek-speaking churches by the middle of the sixth century, as we can infer from the Emperor Justinian's legislation against it in his *Novella* of 26 March 565. Between the latter part of the sixth century and the second half of the eighth century, liturgical practice in Rome developed in such a way that by the year 800, the canon of the Mass was recited by the celebrant in a low voice. This development is usually attributed to the increasing sense of reverence and awe towards the mysteries celebrated in the liturgy, which is tangible especially in the Eastern Christian traditions from the fourth century onwards. Two decisive factors are identified: the emphasis on the divinity of Christ in opposition to Arianism and the concern to protect the sacred from the uncatechized masses that were flocking into the church after the Constantinian settlement. In the case of the Roman liturgy, there might be another consideration that should not be neglected: the architectural setting of the solemn celebrations of the Roman Pontiff. Even in a smaller church, before the existence of electrical amplification, it would be impossible in most parts of the church to follow the prayers he recited or chanted at the altar. Thus the emergence of the silent canon in the Western tradition can also be seen in the context of the liturgy's architectural setting that had a decisive impact on the relation between speech and silence. See: E. Bishop, "Observations on the Liturgy of Narsai," R.H. Connolly, *The Liturgical Homilies of Narsai* (Cambridge: Cambridge University Press, 1909), pp. 85–163 (pp. 92–7); G. Kretschmar, "Die frühe Geschichte der Jerusalemer Liturgie," *Jahrbuch für Liturgik und Hymnologie* 2 (1956–7), pp. 22–46.

Liturgical theology The examination of liturgical phenomena by academic theologians, or the insight that liturgical realities give to theological subjects, or what emerges from the Church's liturgical act.

Liturgiology The name of an academic discipline practised by "liturgiologists" which examines the development of liturgical rites, liturgical books, and liturgical actions. The discipline borrows methods from source analysis and historical and ritual studies.

Liturgy The Trinity's perichoresis kenotically extended to invite our synergistic ascent into deification. Thin definition: the ceremonies and rituals of the Christian Church.

"The Sacred Liturgy is . . . the public worship which our Redeemer as Head of the Church renders to the Father, as well as the worship which the community of the faithful renders to its Founder, and through Him to the heavenly Father. It is, in short, the worship rendered by the Mystical Body of Christ in the entirety of its Head and members" (Pius XII, Encyclical Letter *Mediator Dei,* November 20, 1947).

"The liturgy is considered as an exercise of the priestly office of Jesus Christ. In the liturgy the sanctification of the man is signified by signs perceptible to the senses, and is effected in a way which corresponds with each of these signs; in the liturgy the whole public worship is performed by the Mystical Body of Jesus Christ, that is, by the Head and His members" (Second Vatican Council, Constitution on the Sacred Liturgy *Sacrosanctum Concilium*, December 4, 1963, n. 7).

Liturgy of the Hours *see* Divine Office

Long ceremonial A book of papal liturgical ceremonies dating from shortly before 1342 attributed to John of Sion.

Malabranca Orsini, Latino (†1294) A Dominican friar and later a cardinal and prelate of the Roman curia, Malabranca is credited with authoring an important manual for the celebration of Mass, the *Ceremonial of a Cardinal Bishop* (c. 1280).

Lyons rite The liturgical use of the French see of Lyons given definitive form under the Carolingian appointee Bishop Leidrade (†c. 821). The rite is Roman in origin and in some ways preserved primitive Roman uses where those of Rome itself developed further. In the seventeenth century, the scholarly Giovanni Cardinal Bona (1609–74) would observe of Lyons: "A Church which knows nothing of novelties, clinging tenaciously, in the matter of chant and ceremonies, to ancient tradition" (King, *Liturgies of the Primatial Sees*, p. 19). In spite of this, the late seventeenth and eighteenth centuries saw the adoption of neo-Gallican liturgical books and the elimination of various customs. This provoked a notorious dispute between the cathedral chapter and the innovating Archbishop Antoine de Montazet (1713–88), eventually settled in favour of the archbishop and enforced by the Paris Parliament. In the nineteenth century, various revisions of the liturgical books sought to correct at least some of the reforms introduced by de Montazet. This century also saw much pressure brought to bear in favor of simply adopting the Roman rite, which was imposed in 1864 with the addition of a diocesan proper and ceremonial. A more-traditional edition of the missal was published in 1904. Today Mass is celebrated according to this missal at least weekly in Lyons at the Church of St Georges and by some other priests of the diocese. See: Archdale A. King, *Liturgies of the Primatial Sees* (London, New York & Toronto: Longman's, Green & Co., 1957); Denys Buenner OSB, *L'Ancienne Liturgie Romaine: Le Rite Lyonnais* (Lyon & Paris: Emmanuel Vitte,1934); Cyrille Vogel, *Medieval Liturgy: An Introduction to the Sources* (Washington DC: Pastoral Press, 1986), pp. 288–9.

Marriage The practice of marriage among Christians was widespread from the earliest days of the Church, based upon the teachings of Jesus and St Paul found in the New Testament (see: John 4 and Matthew 19). Marriage was the last of the seven sacraments of the Catholic Church to be widely acknowledged; it was understood explicitly as a sacrament only from the eleventh and twelfth centuries. The *Catechism of the Catholic Church* teaches: "The marriage covenant, by which a man and a woman form with each other an intimate communion of life and love, has been founded and endowed with its own special laws by the Creator. By its very nature it is ordered to the good of the couple, as well as to the generation and education of children. Christ the Lord raised marriage between the baptized to the dignity of a sacrament. The sacrament of Matrimony signifies the union of Christ and the Church. It gives spouses the grace to love each other with the love with which Christ has loved his Church; the grace of the sacrament thus perfects the human love of the spouses, strengthens their indissoluble unity, and sanctifies them on the way to eternal life ... Since marriage establishes the couple in a public state of life in the Church, it is fitting that its celebration be public, in the framework of a liturgical celebration, before the priest (or a witness authorized by the Church), the witnesses, and the assembly of the faithful (1660–1, 1663).

Marsili, Salvatore (1910–85) Abbot of the Benedictine Abbey of Finalpia, Italy, and later one of the founders of the Pontifical Liturgical Institute, Rome, Marsili focused his attention on the theology of the Liturgy and continued in the line of thought propagated by Odo Casel, presenting liturgy as the exploration of God that takes place in public worship. His work has not been translated into English, nor is he well known outside Italy.

Martène, Edmond (1654–1739) A French Benedictine priest of the Congregation of Saint Maur, Martène compiled two encyclopedic collections of largely medieval liturgical texts, the *De antiquis ecclesiae ritibus* and *De antiquis monachorum ritibus*, works that remain unsurpassed for the sheer breadth of primary sources presented.

Martimort, Aimé-Georges (1911–2000) A priest of the diocese of Toulouse in whose faculty of theology he began to teach in 1938. He became a leading liturgist among the French school after the Second World War and became co-director of the *Centre Liturgique Pastorale de Paris* and of the periodical *La Maison-Dieu*. He served as a *peritus* for the Second Vatican Council's liturgical commission and was a consulter for the post-conciliar *Consilium* from its inception. In that capacity Martimort was the relator of the group charged with preparing the reform of the Divine Office. Msgr Martimort edited the influential four-volume *L'Eglise en prière*, which first appeared in French from 1961 (latest edition 1995), which has been widely translated (ET: *The Church at Prayer*, from 1968, latest edition 1986–8).

Martyrologium (Martyrology) A liturgical book containing names and short biographies of martyrs and other saints arranged according to their *dies natalis* (the day of their martyrdom, their birthday into heaven) or according to the day their feast is kept. A martyrology can be particular to a given Church or religious order, or universal. Typical editions of the Roman Martyrology appeared in 1584, 1749, 1913–14 (updated substantially in 1922 and last updated in 1956) and, following the Second Vatican Council, with a radically rearranged sanctoral in 2001 (last updated in 2004). The martyrology for the day was read in collegiate and cathedral churches at the office of Prime, and in monasteries in chapter. Its Christmas proclamation is sometimes sung before pontifical midnight Mass. See: Alexius Hoffmann OSB, *A Benedictine*

Martyrology (Collegeville: St John's Abbey, 1922); Abbot Cabrol, *The Books of the Latin Liturgy* (London & St Louis, MO: Sands & B. Herder, 1932); J.B. O'Connell (ed.) *The Roman Martyrology* (Westminster, MD: Newmann Press, 1962).

Mass "The Mass" is the term in common use in the West for the liturgical rite of the celebration of the sacrament of the Blessed Eucharist. The term originates in the sending forth at the end of the rite: *Ite missa est* ("Go, it is sent"). The Mass can be known by other terms including "the Eucharist" (from the Greek, "thanksgiving") or, often in the East, "the Divine Liturgy" (see: CCC 1328–32). The Mass is celebrated in obedience to Christ's command at the Last Supper, "Do this in remembrance of me" (Lk 22.19). Borrowing from the writing of St Thomas Aquinas, the Second Vatican Council teaches: "At the Last Supper, on the night he was betrayed, our Savior instituted the eucharistic sacrifice of his Body and Blood. This he did in order to perpetuate the sacrifice of the cross throughout the ages until he should come again, and so to entrust to his beloved Spouse, the Church, a memorial of his death and resurrection: a sacrament of love, a sign of unity, a bond of charity, a Paschal banquet 'in which Christ is consumed, the mind is filled with grace, and a pledge of future glory is given to us'" (*Sacrosanctum Concilium*, n. 47). A "private Mass" as distinct from a public one, is one in which a priest celebrates with only one assistant. A "low Mass" (*missa lecta*), which is not sung, is distinguished from a "solemn Mass" (*missa solemnis*) in which the priest is assisted by other sacred ministers (deacon and subdeacon) with full ceremonial and singing. A "sung Mass" (*missa cantata*) is celebrated without deacon and subdeacon. The missal of Paul VI does not retain these distinctions, allowing the assistance of sacred ministers and singing at any form of Mass. A "pontifical" Mass is one celebrated by a bishop or an abbot, using pontifical ceremonial and insignia.

Mediation (Mediant Cadence, Mediatio) A distinctive melodic formula that signals the resting place at the end of the first half of a psalm verse. Each psalm tone has a distinctive mediant cadence. Hebrew psalm verses are usually in two parallel halves.

Mediator Dei The 20 November 1947 encyclical letter of Pius XII on the Sacred Liturgy. Dom Beauduin described it as explaining "the basic prerogatives that entitle the liturgy to a post of the first order in the spiritual life." See: Alcuin Reid, *The Organic Development of the Liturgy,* 2nd edn (San Francisco: Ignatius Press, 2005), pp. 138–41; Aidan Nichols OP, "A Tale of Two Documents," Alcuin Reid (ed.), *A Pope and a Council on the Sacred Liturgy* (Farnborough: St Michael's Abbey Press, 2002), pp. 9–27.

Melisma A musical passage where a cluster of notes (usually more than a few) are sung on a single syllable.

Metope A square panel between triglyphs in a Doric frieze.

Michel, Virgil (1888–1938) An American Benedictine monk of St John's Abbey, Collegeville, Minnesota, who encountered the nascent liturgical movement and Dom Beauduin during his studies in Europe. Returning to the United States Michel founded the liturgical periodical *Oratre Fratres* (now *Worship*) in 1926 and the Liturgical Press to promote the liturgical movement in the English-speaking world and to provide English translations of its seminal works. Michel's *The Liturgy of the Church: According to the Roman Rite* (Macmillan: New York, 1938) is a popular classic with lasting value. See: Alcuin Reid, *The Organic Development of the Liturgy*, 2nd edn (San Francisco: Ignatius Press, 2005), pp. 97–100.

Missale (Missal) The missal is the book containing the rites and texts necessary for the celebration of the Mass. In ancient times, different books served for the particular functions of diverse minsters. In time these texts became collected into sacramentaries and in due course, with the development of the private Mass, books containing all the texts for the priest-celebrant to pray in the absence of other ministers were compiled. It is this compilation which is the missal, or *missale plenum* (the "full" missal), which was common by the thirteenth century. The missal promulgated by Paul VI in 1970 is not a *missale plenum*, omitting the readings from Sacred Scripture which are published separately in a lectionary.

Missale mixtum A title borne by some missals of late medieval Spain, most notably by the printed missal that the Spanish primate Francisco Cardinal Ximenes de Cisneros (†1517) issued combining ancient Mozarabic rite texts with borrowings from the late fifteenth century archdiocesan missal of Toledo, and intended for the revival of the Mozarabic rite.

Mode Music based on the eight medieval melodic patterns or scales known as modes, Church modes, or ecclesiastical modes. Like the major and minor scales, they are also composed of a series of whole steps and half steps, with each mode having a different arrangement of whole and half steps. Mode I (Dorian): the authentic version of the D mode, in which D, the final (*finalis*), is at the bottom of the scale, which extends the full octave above it to D. Mode II (Hypodorian): the lower-range, plagal version of the D mode, in which the *finalis* is still D, but is no longer the bottom note of the modal scale. The range of the mode is from A up to A, with D (the *finalis*) situated in the middle of the scale. Mode III (Phrygian): the authentic version of the E mode, in which E, the *finalis*, is at the bottom of the scale, which extends the full octave above it to E. Mode IV (Hypophrygian): the lower-range, plagal version of the E mode, in which the *finalis* is still E, but is no longer the bottom note of the modal scale. The range of the mode is from B up to B, with E (the *finalis*) situated in the middle of the scale. Mode V (Lydian): the authentic version of the F mode, in which F, the *finalis*, is at the bottom of the scale, which extends the full octave above it to F. Mode V chants often appear with an added flat on B. The B-flat in the mode changes its sound and makes it sound like a major scale. Mode VI (Hypolydian): the lower-range, plagal version of the F mode, in which the *finalis* is still F, but is no longer the bottom note of the modal scale. The range of the mode is from C up to C, with F (the *finalis*) situated in the middle of the scale. Like mode V, mode VI also often appears with an added flat on B. Mode VII (Mixolydian): the authentic version of the G mode, in which G, the *finalis*, is at the bottom of the scale, which extends the full octave above it to G. Mode VIII

(Hypomixolydian): the lower-range, plagal version of the G mode, in which the *finalis* is still G, but is no longer the bottom note of the modal scale. The range of the mode is from D up to D, with G (the *finalis*) situated in the middle of the scale.

Modernism (architectural) A rejection of classical typologies in favor of abstract forms based on technological models.

Module A measure used in part-to-whole ratios in proportional systems; the diameter of the base of a column is a frequently-used module.

Monophonic Music that consists of a single unaccompanied vocal line. Gregorian chant is monophonic.

Monstrance Also known as an "ostensorium," the monstrance is an ornate vessel used to hold the consecrated Host aloft for the purpose of adoration and Benediction of the Blessed Sacrament. Monstrances are to be distinguished from similar vessels used to hold the relics of saints for public veneration, called "reliquaries."

Monumento (Monumentum) In Spain, this term, meaning "tomb," first used in the twelfth century to denote the repository for the Holy Thursday reservation of the Eucharist, became commonplace in Spanish liturgical texts by the sixteenth century as an expression of the pervasive symbolic association of the repository with the sepulchre of Christ.

Motu proprio A written administrative act in ecclesiastical law given, as the term suggests, at the personal initiative of the competent legislator. Most frequently the term is used for a legislative document issued personally by the supreme authority in the Church, the Pope.

Mozarabic rite Also known as the Hispanic, Visigothic, or Toledo rite, this ancient liturgical rite from the Iberian peninsula betrays early Roman origins with Eastern influences in its ritual, calendar, and chant. Sixth- and seventh-century bishops, pre-eminently St Isidore of Seville (c. 560–636), gave the rite its definitive form and it was developed subsequently under episcopal supervision. The bishop of Toledo, St Ildefonsus (c. 607–67), stands to the fore in this respect. Pope Gregory VII (1015/28; 1073–85) suppressed the "superstition of the Toledan error" (King, *Liturgies of the Primatial Sees*, p. 503) in favor of the Roman rite and Cluniac usages, which were adopted by the Spanish kingdoms in prompt succession by the end of the eleventh century. The rite survived in six ancient Toledan parish churches by way of a concession granted after the death of Gregory VII and enjoyed something of a revival under an archbishop of Toledo at the end of the fifteenth century and the beginning of the sixteenth, when a chapel of Toledo cathedral was established and endowed for its celebration. Political factors diminished the celebration of the rite in the nineteenth century and the Spanish Civil War saw the priests of the Mozarabic chapel slaughtered in 1936. After the war it was partially restored, though with limited means. Following the Second Vatican Council, a revised edition of the missal and lectionary appeared between 1988–95. Today this revised rite is celebrated regularly in the Mozarabic chapel of Toledo cathedral and in a handful of other locations. Chant sources remain from the tenth and eleventh centuries. The sixteenth-century chant had a significant admixture of Gregorian chant and it is not the genuine, pre-Reconquista Mozarabic chant. See: Fernand Cabrol OSB, *The Mass of the Western Rites* (London: Sands & Co., 1934); Archdale A. King, *Liturgies of the Primatial Sees* (London, New York & Toronto: Longman's, Green & Co., 1957); Susan Boynton, "Restoration or Invention? Archbishop Cisneros and the Mozarabic Rite in Toledo," *Yale Journal of Music & Religion* 1 (2015), pp. 5–30.

Muratori, Ludivico Antonio (1672–1750) An Italian priest and scholar famed for his discovery of an early catalogue of New Testament books in the Ambrosian library, Muratori promoted liturgical participation in his day. His 1747 work *Della Regolata Devozione dei Cristiani* moves beyond the promotion of participation and recoils from excessive devotionalism and anything in the liturgy that seemed to have a hint of superstition or magic about it, preferring a liturgical and ceremonial simplicity in keeping with some Enlightenment tendencies. The term "noble simplicity" finds something of its origins in his work. See: J.D. Crichton, *Lights in Darkness: Fore-runners of the Liturgical Movement* (Dublin: Columba Press, 1996), pp. 14–24.

Neum In Gregorian chant, a note, or a group of notes, sung to one syllable of text.

Neunheuser, Burkhart (1904–2004) A monk of Maria Laach, Germany, Neunheuser was one of the founders of the Pontifical Liturgical Institute in Rome in 1961 and its second dean. He specialized in the history of the liturgy and his *Storia della Liturgia attraverso le epoche culturali* (BELS, 1999) is a seminal text. Neunheuser agreed with Abbot Vonier's interpretation of Aquinas on the sacrificial nature of the Mass. On the basis of ST 3, q. 79, a.1 and q. 83, a.1, Neunheuser summarizes Aquinas' teaching on the Eucharist as sacrifice in this way: "The Eucharist is image (*imago repraesentativa*) of the passion of Christ, but image full of effective power."

Noble simplicity A term of Enlightenment origin employed by article 34 of the Second Vatican Council's Constitution on the Sacred Liturgy which says: "The rites should be distinguished by a noble simplicity; they should be short, clear, and unencumbered by useless repetitions; they should be within the people's powers of comprehension, and normally should not require much explanation." Following the Council this *subsidiary* principle of the Constitution was elevated by some to be "the principle of principles of liturgical reform" (J.D. Crichton, *The Church's Worship*, London: Geoffrey Chapman, 1965, p. 90), leading to simplicity being ignobly visited upon liturgical rites, music, architecture, vesture, vessels, etc. A correct understanding of this subsidiary principle of the Constitution is essential. See: Alcuin Reid, "Noble Simplicity Revisited," D.V. Twomey SVD & Janet E. Rutherford (eds), *Benedict XVI and Beauty in Sacred Art and Architecture* (Dublin & New York; Four Courts & Scepter, 2011), pp. 94–111.

Norbertine (Premonstratensian) rite Intrinsically liturgical in its conventual life since its foundation in the twelfth century, the Norbertine order established its own uniform uses early in its history. The origins of the rite lie in the Roman rite in use in the Rhineland in the eleventh century and other French, canonical, and monastic influences, particularly Cistercian ones. The growth of the order saw its spread and successive general chapters legislated on liturgical observance. The general chapter of 1605 sought a harmonization of the order's rite with the Roman rite and by the middle of the seventeenth century liturgical books thus revised were in place, to be revised subsequently. Neo-Gallican editions of the Norbertine liturgical books appeared at the end of the eighteenth century, but their use did not survive the French Revolution. New and more-traditional editions were produced in the nineteenth century and in the first half of the twentieth century the order revised the liturgical books once again, restoring more of the old traditions. A new *Rubricae et Calendarium Breviarii et Missalis Iuxta Ritum Ordinis Praemonstratentis* was approved by the Abbot General in May 1964. Following the Second Vatican Council the order adopted the revised Roman rite, though the pre-conciliar rites and chant are retained in some Norbertine communities. See: Archdale A. King, *Liturgies of the Religious Orders* (London, New York & Toronto: Longman's, Green & Co., 1955).

Obsequiale A term commonly used in late medieval Germany and Austria to denote a liturgical book containing rubrics and prayers for the parochial administration of baptism, penance, and the anointing of the sick, as well as the distribution of Holy Communion, Viaticum, and funeral rites, priestly blessings of persons or objects, and ceremonies for particular feasts.

Octave A custom with Old Testament origins by which during the period of seven days following a great feast, making eight days in total, the liturgy continues to celebrate or at least commemorate the feast. The 1955 simplification of the rubrics reduced the number of octaves in the Roman rite to three (those of Christmas, Easter, and Pentecost). The calendar promulgated by Paul VI in 1969 further abolished the octave of Pentecost. The most ancient octaves are those of the feasts of Easter, Pentecost and Epiphany.

Oeconomia The consideration of construction costs, materials, methods, labor, and hierarchy.

Offertorium (Offertory) The chant of the Mass which is sung as the celebrant goes up to the altar to begin the offering of the bread and wine. It is taken from the proper or the relevant common in the *Graduale*. The 1958 Instruction *De musica sacra et liturgia* permitted the singing of the ancient Gregorian melodies of the original Offertory verses which once were sung after the antiphon and, if the verse comes from a psalm, the practice of singing several verses from the psalm, and finally the *Gloria Patri*, with the antiphon used as a refrain. The Church Music Association of America (www.musicasacra.com) has republished the Latin chant for the *offertorium* and has worked to prepare chants for the modern English texts.

Office *see* Divine Office

Office of Shepherd A medieval liturgical rite for Christmas night constituting a dramatization of the visit of the shepherds to the newborn Christ Child in the manger.

Old Roman chant Liturgical chant of Rome, found in Roman manuscripts of the late eleventh to thirteenth centuries.

Ordination (Holy Orders) "Since the beginning, the ordained ministry has been conferred and exercised in three degrees: that of bishops, that of presbyters, and that of deacons. The ministries conferred by ordination are irreplaceable for the organic structure of the Church: without the bishop, presbyters, and deacons, one cannot speak of the Church (cf. St Ignatius of Antioch, Ad Trall. 3,1). The sacrament of Holy Orders is conferred by the laying on of hands followed by a solemn prayer of consecration asking God to grant the ordinand the graces of the Holy Spirit required for his ministry. Ordination imprints an indelible sacramental character" (CCC 1593, 1597).

Ordinary Liturgical texts and chants are distinguished between those that are "ordinary" (that do not change, such as the order of Mass), those that are "proper" (to a particular season or feast), and those that are "common" (groups of texts shared for particular types of saints, etc.). Occasionally, the ordinary will vary according to season, for example, the chant during the sprinkling immediately prior to solemn Mass is *Vidi aquam* during the Easter Season, and outside of Easter the chant is *Asperges me*. The principal musical parts of the ordinary are the Kyrie, Gloria, Credo, Sanctus, Agnus Dei and the dismissal.

Ordines The ceremonial directions and instructions for the performance of the rite, later called rubrics.

Ordo Missae (Order of Mass) The fixed rite of the celebration of Mass as distinct from the liturgical texts proper or common to a particular season or feast. In the Western rites the *Ordo Missae* of some religious orders and patriarchal sees differs from that of the Roman rite, though all contain the Roman canon. The *Ordo Missae* of the Roman rite promulgated following the Second Vatican Council contains numerous options among which the celebrant may choose.

Orientation The ancient Christian practice of turning toward the East (the direction of the rising sun) when praying, reflected since ancient times in the building of churches where the apse is at the eastern end of the building. Where, for some reason, churches were not built thus the practice of turning to the East to pray was nevertheless maintained. The canon of the Mass (or eucharistic prayer) was prayed with priest and congregation facing eastward, although in the twentieth century the practice of celebrating Mass "facing the people" grew up, based largely on faulty archeology. The value of the traditional practice of liturgical orientation in the celebration of the Mass and other rites as promulgated following the Second Vatican Council is increasingly appreciated. See: U.M. Lang, *Orientation in Liturgical Prayer* (San Francisco: Ignatius Press, 2004); Stefan Heid, "The Early Christian Altar—Lessons for Today," Alcuin Reid (ed.), *Sacred Liturgy: The Source and Summit of the Life and Mission of the Church* (San Francisco: Ignatius Press, 2014), pp. 87–114.

Organic development The principle which holds that "in the history of the liturgy there is growth and progress, but no rupture" (Benedict XVI, Letter to the Bishops on the Occasion of the Publication of *Summorum Pontificum*, 7 July 2007), and that for liturgical reforms to be legitimate "any new forms adopted should in some way grow organically from forms already existing" (*Sacrosanctum Concilium*, n. 23). The question of whether the liturgical books promulgated by Paul VI following the Second Vatican Council were organic developments of liturgical tradition, or radical innovations, underlies much discussion of the need for a "reform of the reform" and of various elements of the new liturgical movement. See: Alcuin Reid, *The Organic Development of the Liturgy*, 2nd edn (San Francisco: Ignatius Press, 2005).

Ottaviani intervention A critical study of the *Ordo Missæ* promulgated by Paul VI prepared by a group of Roman theologians in June 1969 signed by Alfredo Cardinal Ottaviani (1890–1979) and Antonio Cardinal Bacci (1885–1971) and submitted to Paul VI casting doubts on the orthodoxy of the rite and on the prudence of its adoption. Article 7 of the General Instruction of the Roman Missal was substantially revised in the light of the controversy aroused by the intervention, though no ritual changes were made in the *Ordo Missae*. See: chapter 14 above.

Oxford Declaration on Liturgy The *Oxford Declaration on Liturgy* is a succinct, six-point summary of the conclusions and proposals of the international liturgical conference held in Oxford in June 1996 under the auspices of the Liturgy Forum organized by the Center for Faith and Culture, at that time a Catholic research centre at Westminster College. It acknowledges the "positive results" of the liturgical reform following Vatican II (e.g., increased participation in the liturgy, the introduction of the vernacular, more extensive use of Scripture), but also highlights areas of grave concern chiefly relative to modern cultural developments (e.g., the loss of the "sense of the sacred" in much contemporary liturgical practice). An important reference point for the reform of the reform and new liturgical movement, the Declaration is offered as an appendix to the conference's published proceedings, S. Caldecott (ed.) *Beyond the Prosaic: Renewing the Liturgical Movement* (Edinburgh: T&T Clark, 1998).

Oxford Movement The nineteenth century Anglican movement centred on several personalities associated with Oxford University. The aim of the movement was the recovery of lost theological and liturgical traditions since the Reformation. The most famous protagonist in this movement was Blessed John Henry Newman (1801–90) who converted to Catholicism in 1845 and was created a cardinal in 1879.

Palmesel An image of Christ riding a donkey used in some places from the tenth century onward to symbolize the Saviour's triumphal entry into Jerusalem in the procession of Palm Sunday.

Paradigm An exemplar of a type, worthy of emulation.

Paschal Liturgically, "pertaining to Easter," such as the Paschal Vigil, the paschal fire, etc.

Pastoral liturgy A term often used to denote liturgical celebrations or styles intentionally adapted to facilitate people's participation. At its best "pastoral liturgy" means the optimal celebration of the liturgical rites in their fullness so as to afford many and varying points of ritual connectivity with the action of Christ taking place in the liturgy. At its worst "pastoral liturgy" denotes a subjective approach to the liturgical rites which are thus modified at will according to a perceived need or a particular situation, or simply to liturgical abuse enacted in the name of "pastoral" creativity. See: chapter 16 above.

Patera A flat, circular dish for votive use; often carved on a frieze in a decorative sequence.

Paul VI (1897; 1963–78) Elected pope after the first session of the Second Vatican Council, Paul VI continued its work and promulgated its Constitution on the Sacred Liturgy on 4 December 1963. He rehabilitated Annibale Bugnini CM and made him responsible for coordinating the liturgical reform called for by the Council. Paul VI personally reviewed every aspect of the new liturgical rites together with Bugnini and approved them *in forma specifica*. There is evidence that Bugnini was somewhat duplicitous in his dealings with the pope at times and that Paul VI suffered doubts about elements of the rites he had approved— although he had no doubts about the authority with which he insisted on their use. In 1975, Paul VI removed Bugnini from any responsibility for the Sacred Liturgy. His pontificate saw much unauthorised liturgical experimentation and abuse, which troubled Paul VI greatly. There was, however, no room for questioning the liturgical reform he promulgated.

Pax-brede (Pax-Board) The *pax-brede* or *instrumentum pacis* is an ornamented tablet of wood, ivory, or metal with a picture of Christ or a saint kissed by the celebrant of Mass and by those to whom it is passed to signify the exchange of the sign of peace. See: J.B. O'Connell, *The Celebration of Mass*, 4th edn (Milwaukee: Bruce Publishing Co., 1964) pp. 430–31.

Penance (Confession/Reconciliation) "The forgiveness of sins committed after Baptism is conferred by a particular sacrament called the sacrament of conversion, confession, penance, or reconciliation. The sacrament of Penance is a whole consisting in three actions of the penitent and the priest's absolution. The penitent's acts are repentance, confession or disclosure of sins to the priest, and the intention to make reparation and do works of reparation" (CCC 1486, 1491). Penance may also refer to the specific acts of reparation proposed by the priest to the penitent.

Piccolomini, Agostino Patrizio (c. 1435–95). A papal master of ceremonies, Piccolomini was a co-editor of the first printed edition of the Roman Pontifical, the 1485 *Pontificalis liber*, and the compiler of the most expansive edition of a book of papal liturgical rites, the *Caeremoniale Romanum* (c. 1488).

Pilaster A square, pier-like representation of a column applied to a wall.

Pius Parsch (1884–1954) A canon regular of the Austrian Abbey of Klosterneuberg, Parsch worked to promote and popularize liturgical piety following in the first half of the twentieth century. His efforts included the celebration of the liturgy in a nearby chapel of St Gertrude in a manner which was considered *avant-garde* for its time, including a wide use of the vernacular, as well as numerous publications which were widely translated. See: Alcuin Reid, *The Organic Development of the Liturgy*, 2nd edn (San Francisco: Ignatius Press, 2005), pp. 110–15.

Pius X (1835; 1903–14) One of the first acts of the pontificate of Pius X was the motu proprio *Tra le sollecitudine* (November 22, 1903) which laid down the fundamental principle of the twentieth-century liturgical movement: that liturgical piety was normative for the Christian life. This proved to be an authoritative foundation on which others would build. Pius X promoted the frequent reception of Holy Communion and lowered the age for its first reception. In 1911, he promulgated a reform of the breviary which is based on questionable principles and is in some ways a forerunner of later twentieth century reforms. See: Alcuin Reid, *The Organic Development of the Liturgy*, 2nd edn (San Francisco: Ignatius Press, 2005), pp. 74–8.

Pius XII (1876; 1939–58) In 1946, Pius XII established a commission for liturgical reform, appointing its first members two years later. From 1948–60 this commission worked gradually toward a general reform of the liturgy. It is not clear how closely Pius XII followed or monitored their work, however he promulgated the experimental reform of the Paschal Vigil (1951) and of the entire Holy Week liturgy (1955) as well as a simplification of rubrics (1955). A consultation on breviary reform was begun in 1957. Pius XII wrote the encyclical letters *Mediator Dei* (1947) and *Musicae Sacrae Disciplina* (1955) and addressed the participants of the first international congress on pastoral liturgy, held in Assisi in 1956, in Rome. See: Alcuin Reid, *The Organic Development of the Liturgy*, 2nd edn (San Francisco: Ignatius Press, 2005).

Plagal Version of a mode which starts four notes below the final (*finalis*) and ends a fifth above it; the even numbered modes (II, IV, VI, VIII).

Plainsong A term used to describe any number of repertories of single-melody liturgical music, as opposed to polyphony. Gregorian chant is one repertory of plainsong.

Planctus A Good Friday chant of medieval origin in the form of a lament representing the grief of one of those who witnessed the death of Christ, or the grief of the congregation. In a Portuguese context, this term refers to a specific chant, *Heu, heu Domine* ("Alas, alas, Lord"), used in late medieval Portuguese *Depositio* rites.

Polyphonic Music written in more than one voice, as opposed to plainsong, which has only a single line of music.

Pontificale (Pontifical) A liturgical book collecting the rites celebrated by a bishop (pontiff). Manuscript pontificals exist from around the end of the ninth century and the *Pontificalis liber*, published in 1485, was the first printed edition of the *Pontificale Romanum*. See: Abbot Cabrol, *The Books of the Latin Liturgy* (London & St Louis, MO: Sands & B. Herder, 1932).

Premonstratensian rite *see* Norbertine rite

Procession of Prophets A medieval rite particularly common in Spain added to the recitation of Matins on Christmas night in which a cleric representing St Augustine would summon the testimony of various prophets and other biblical personages, enacted by other clerics, to testify to the birth of Christ.

Programme A list of requirements for an architecture project.

Proper Liturgical texts and chants are distinguished between those that are "proper" (to a particular season or feast), those that are "ordinary" (that do not change, such as the order of Mass), and those that are "common" (groups of texts shared for particular types of saints, etc.). The principal musical elements of the proper are the Introit, Gradual, Alleluia or Tract, Offertory, and Communion. Some feasts also have a sequence which is proper to the day. Propers are the most ornate and musically-challenging chants in the repertoire and are best sung by accomplished singers.

Prose *see* Sequence

Prosa (Prosula) Words added to an already-existing chant. One example would be text added to a melisma in a great responsory. The melisma was then transformed into a syllabic chant.

Prosody A term used to describe the patterns of emphasis, articulation, and accent in speech and music which pertains to the composer's approach to syllabification when text setting as well as meter in poetry.

Psalm tone A melodic formula used for chanting the psalms. Gregorian chant uses three types of psalm tones; simple, introit, and canticle. Simple psalm tones are the most common.

Psalmodic Of or pertaining to the psalms.

Psalter The book of Psalms. The basis of much liturgical music, the book of Psalms is generously represented throughout the Gregorian chant repertoire, especially among the antiphons of the Mass. Praying the psalter in its integrity formed the basis of the Divine Office in the West up until the breviary promulgated by Paul VI following the Second Vatican Council.

Quignonez, Francis (Quiñonez) (c. 1482–1540) In 1529, the Franciscan Cardinal Quignonez was entrusted with a reform of the breviary by Clement VII (1478; 1523–34). The resultant breviary, published under Paul III (1468; 1534–49) in 1535 and in a new edition in 1536, was not well received for its radical departure from liturgical tradition. The Quignonez breviary was repudiated by Paul IV (1476; 1555–9) in 1558 and proscribed by Pius V (1504; 1566–72) in 1668. This incident in liturgical history carries much significance in the study of the relationship between positive acts of authority in the development of liturgical tradition, particularly acts of papal authority. See: Alcuin Reid, *The Organic Development of the Liturgy*, 2nd edn (San Francisco: Ignatius Press, 2005), pp. 34–9.

Radulph (Ralph) of Rivo (†1403) A Dutch priest, historian and liturgist, Radulph authored several significant liturgical commentaries, including the *Liber de officiis ecclesiae.*

Range The distance between the lowest and highest note of a melody. In Latin: *ambitus.*

Ratzinger, Joseph *see* Benedict XVI

Ravenna chant Liturgical chant used at Ravenna, which was the Roman imperial capital in the fifth century. Almost nothing is known about this chant, especially whether it was independent of Roman chant.

Recitation (Reciting) tone The main tone on which most of a psalm verse or a liturgical recitative is chanted.

Reform of the Reform The assertion that the liturgical reform as enacted following the Second Vatican Council should itself be reformed so as more faithfully to implement the Council's Constitution on the Sacred Liturgy,

Sacrosanctum Concilium. The emergence of proposals for a reform of the reform may be seen as one of the first steps of the new liturgical movement. See: Thomas M. Kocik, *The Reform of the Reform? A Liturgical Debate: Reform or Return* (San Francisco: Ignatius Press, 2003); also chapter 15 above.

Regula missal This early Franciscan liturgical book, compiled around 1230, was modelled upon a lost papal missal from the pontificate of Pope Honorius III (1216–27).

Relics From the Latin term for "remains," relics are parts of the body of a saint or blessed, or items associated with them or with Jesus Christ (his cross, its nails, etc.) to which liturgical veneration may be paid (particularly on the saint's feast, etc.) if the authenticity of the relic has been duly established. The ancient custom of liturgically entombing the relics of martyrs in or under a new altar is observed to this day. Relics are distinguished between first class (parts of the saint's body), second class (items associated with them, such as clothing they wore), or third class (items touched to a first class relic). The sale of relics is strictly forbidden under Church law. Relics are exposed for veneration in reliquaries, a vessel similar to a monstrance, though often smaller.

Requiem From the Latin word meaning "rest" which is the first word of the introit of the funeral Mass, requiem is used to denote rites and chants pertaining to death and burial, hence "requiem Mass."

Respond A chant that is the response of a choir to a solo verse; also the refrain of a responsory, as opposed to its verses.

Ressourcement A broad intellectual and spiritual movement within the European Catholic community (especially in France) which arose in the 1930s in response to the challenge presented by secularized society and which by the eve of the Second Vatican Council had become a well recognized and influential force in Roman Catholic theology. Its participants were not a tightly organized cadre or self-conscious school, but rather a diverse group of thinkers united in the conviction that the key to theology's relevance to the present situation lay in a recovery or repristination of the timeless dimensions of the Christian tradition. This was not to be achieved by means of an anachronistic restoration of outmoded categories and practices, but rather by plumbing the biblical, patristic, and liturgical sources of Christian faith for insights that might prove helpful in addressing the critical questions of the postmodern era and renewing Christian vitality. One of the most prominent *ressourcement* theologians, the French Dominican Yves Congar (1904–95; created Cardinal in 1994), described the Sacred Liturgy as "the privileged *locus* of Tradition, not only from the point of view of conservation and preservation, but also from that of progress and development," *Tradition and Traditions: An Historical and a Theological Essay* (New York: Macmillan, 1967), p. 429—a view consonant with that of Dom Prosper Guéranger (1805–75), for whom the liturgy was "Tradition itself at its highest degree of power and solemnity," *Institutions Liturgiques* (Paris & Le Mans: Débécourt & Fleuriot, 1840) vol. I, p. 3.

Rituale (Ritual) A liturgical book containing the rites celebrated by a priest or deacon other than the Mass, i.e. the other sacraments, funeral rites, blessings, processions, etc. Its origins lie in variously titled books containing some or more of these rites, and the first *Rituale Romanum* was only published in 1614. The Ritual has always been the least uniform of the Roman liturgical books, permitting of much local variation according to custom. In the middle of the twentieth century permissions were given for increasing amounts of the vernacular to be used in various rites contained in the Ritual. See: Abbot Cabrol, *The Books of the Latin Liturgy* (London & St Louis, MO: Sands & B. Herder, 1932).

Roman canon The ancient eucharistic prayer of the Roman rite in sole use from at least the fifth century up until the introduction of alternatives following the Second Vatican Council. The Roman canon was held in such veneration that it was regarded as "a prayer unaltered and unalterable, the acceptance of which is incumbent on all the churches" (Ildefonso Schuster, *The Sacramentary*, vol. 1, London: Burns, Oates & Washbourne, 1924, p. 318). Differing uses of the Roman rite (those of patriarchal sees and religious orders) respected this principle. The most important early source for the Roman canon is St Ambrose of Milan, who in his *De sacramentis*, a series of catecheses for the newly baptized that was held around 390, quotes extensively from the eucharistic prayer employed at that time in his city. The passages quoted are earlier forms of the prayers *Quam oblationem, Qui pridie, Unde et memores, Supra quae,* and *Supplices te rogamus.* Elsewhere in *De sacramentis*, the bishop of Milan emphasises that he desires to follow the use of the Roman Church in everything; for this reason, we can safely assume that the same eucharistic prayer he quotes was also used in Rome. The wording of the prayers cited by Ambrose is different from the canon that was settled by Pope Gregory the Great in the late sixth century and has come down to us, with only a few minor changes, in the oldest extant liturgical books, especially the Old Gelasian Sacramentary, dating from the middle of the eighth century, but believed to reflect the liturgical use of the middle of the seventh century. The differences between Ambrose's eucharistic prayer and the Gregorian canon are far less remarkable than their similarities, given that the almost 300 years lying between the two texts were a period of intense liturgical development. It is therefore a most remarkable fact that a mature version of the Roman canon emerges without any antecedents in the late fourth century. In the missal of Paul VI, the Roman canon is eucharistic prayer I. See: Ambrose of Milan, *De sacramentis* IV, 5,21–2; 6,26–7: CSEL 73,55 and 57; *De sacramentis* III,1,5: CSEL 73,40; *Sacramentarium Gelasianum*, ed. L.C. Mohlberg, *Liber Sacramentorum Romanae Aeclesiae Ordinis Anni Circuli*, Rerum Ecclesiasticarum Documenta. Series maior. Fontes, IV, 3rd edn, (Rome: Herder, 1981); G.G. Willis, *A History of Early Roman Liturgy: To the death of Gregory the Great*, HBS, Subsidia I (1994).

Rosmini, Antonio (1777–1855) An Italian priest and founder of the Rosminian order, Rosmini saw the lack of the laity's comprehension of the Church's liturgy as a "wound" in the Body of Christ, whilst *not* holding that the vernacular was a simple solution to the problem. So too, he regarded the insufficient education of the clergy and their consequent inability to nourish the faithful through the liturgy, particularly in preaching, as a second "wound." His nuanced positions promoted intelligent participation in the liturgy, which was seen by some as controversial at the time.

Rubrics Rubrics are the ceremonial directions in liturgical books printed in red (*ruber, rubris*) to direct the ministers in carrying out the liturgical rites correctly. Rubrics form part of liturgical law and are binding. See: Alcuin Reid, "From Rubrics to *Ars Celebrandi*—Liturgical Law in the 21st Century," *Antiphon* 17 (2013), pp. 139–67.

Sacra Liturgia An association of Catholics working for an authentic interpretation of the Second Vatican Council's mandate for liturgical reform, promoting an assessment of the implementation of *Sacrosanctum Concilium* that is faithful to the Council, an ongoing consideration of the value of a possible reform of the reform as well as the integral celebration of the *usus recentior* with an optimal *ars celebrandi* (cf. *Sacramentum Caritatis,* 38–42), and maintaining an openness to the value and riches of the *usus antiquior* in the Church today. Website: www.sacraliturgia.org. See: Alcuin Reid (ed.), *Sacred Liturgy: The Source and Summit of the Life and Mission of the Church* (San Francisco: Ignatius Press, 2014).

Sacrament Sacraments are external signs of interior grace celebrated in a liturgical rite which effect that which they signify. Hence when a person is washed with water in the rite of baptism, the person is cleansed from original and personal sin, etc. "Christ instituted the sacraments of the new law. There are seven: Baptism, Confirmation (or Chrismation), the Eucharist, Penance, the Anointing of the Sick, Holy Orders and Matrimony" (CCC 1210).

Sacramentals "Sacred signs which bear a resemblance to the sacraments: they signify effects, particularly of a spiritual kind, which are obtained through the Church's intercession. By them men are disposed to receive the chief effect of the sacraments, and various occasions in life are rendered holy" (*Sacrosanctum Concilium,* n. 60). Sacramentals may be distinguished between blessings of objects, places and persons, particular blessings of persons which are constitutive, and exorcisms. See: CCC 1667–73.

Sacramentary The title of the earliest extant Mass books for the Roman rite (e.g. the *Gelasian Sacramentary*). Following the Second Vatican Council this term was employed in some English-speaking countries for the liturgical book containing the parts said or sung by the priest-celebrant, now entitled "the Roman missal".

Sacramentum Caritatis The 22 February 2007 post-synodal Apostolic Exhortation of Benedict XVI consequent to the 2005 Synod of Bishops on "The Eucharist: Source and Summit of the Life and Mission of the Church." Part II, "The Eucharist, A Mystery to be Celebrated" (nn. 34–69) deals explicitly with liturgical questions.

Sacred Congregation of Rites Founded in 1588 by Pope Sixtus V (1521; 1585–90) and entrusted with the governance and regulation of the Sacred Liturgy, the Congregation was merged with the Congregation for Divine Worship by Paul VI in 1969. See: Frederick R. McManus, *The Congregation of Sacred Rites* (Washington DC: Catholic University of America Press, 1954).

Sacred language The linguistic forms and expressions used in public worship constitute a register that is commonly experienced as "sacred language." Christine Mohrmann proposes to see in this phenomenon a specific way of organizing religious experience. Sacred language is the medium of expression not just of individuals, but of a community living according to certain traditions and hence it is handed down from generation to generation. Three major characteristics can be identified: first, sacred language is stable and shows tenacity in holding on to archaic linguistic forms ("Our Father, who art in heaven …"); secondly, foreign elements are introduced in order to associate with ancient religious tradition, for instance, the Hebrew Biblical vocabulary in the Latin use of Christians (*amen, alleluia, …*); thirdly, sacred language uses rhetorical figures that are typical of oral style, such as parallelism and antithesis, rhythmic clausulae, rhyme, and alliteration. There are stylistic features in all major Christian liturgical languages that separate them from the ordinary languages of the people. This distance was often the result of linguistic developments in the common language that were not adopted in the liturgical language because of its conservative nature. However, in the case of Latin as the language of the Roman liturgy, a certain distance existed right from the beginning: the Romans did not speak in the style of the canon or of the collects of the Mass. From a theological perspective the use of sacred language in the liturgy belongs to the "solemnity" (St Thomas Aquinas) that is observed in the celebration of the sacraments, especially of the Eucharist. The German philosopher, Josef Pieper, proposed a broad definition of "sacred language," which includes signs and gestures as well as the words used in public worship; this would cover more or less the same ground as Aquinas' idea of *solemnitas*. See: C. Mohrmann, *Liturgical Latin: Its Origins and Character. Three Lectures* (London: Burns & Oates, 1959); T.A. Becker, "The Role of *Solemnitas* in the Liturgy According to Saint Thomas Aquinas," M. Levering & M. Dauphinas (eds), *Rediscovering Aquinas and the Sacraments: Studies in Sacramental Theology* (Chicago: Hillenbrand, 2009), pp. 114–35; J. Pieper, B. Wald, (ed.) *Religionsphilosophische Schriften*, Werke 7 (Hamburg: Felix Meiner, 2000), pp. 477–536.

Sacred Triduum Sometimes also called the "Paschal Triduum," this term denotes the three days at the end of Holy Week beginning with the Mass of the Lord's Supper on Holy (or Maundy) Thursday, including Good Friday and Holy Saturday, and ending on Easter Sunday at Vespers. Marking, as they do, the central mysteries of the Christian faith their rites are ancient, particular and rich in meaning.

Sacrosanctum Concilium *see* Constitution on the Sacred Liturgy

Sanctoral The annual cycle of saints' feasts. These feasts can be universal (celebrated throughout the universal Church), local (celebrated in certain dioceses, regions or countries), or particular (pertaining to a given religious order or congregation). Liturgical history has seen the growth of the sanctoral and also its pruning at times, including following the Council of Trent and the Second Vatican Council. The latter attracted some controversy due not only to the pruning it enacted, but due to the changes made to the timing of many feasts which conflicted with local and cultural customs.

Sarum rite The principal late medieval English use of the Roman rite, often called "the use of Salisbury." Archdale King states that "the use of Sarum ... was the most important factor in the liturgy of the English Church from the 13th century until the change of religion in the 16th" (*Liturgies of the Past*, p. 292). Scholars differ on its origins. It is possible that it has developed from French, if not Norman, sources from an early form of the Gregorian sacramentary, as distinct from the *Hadrianum*. It seems that one can assert that "there existed a self-conscious Sarum liturgical tradition" by the end of the twelfth or beginning of the thirteenth century (Pfaff, *The Liturgy in Medieval England*, p. 364). The use spread far beyond the confines of Salisbury and even England, throughout the British Isles. The Sarum liturgy was displaced by the first prayer book of Edward VI in 1549, was restored briefly during the reign of Queen Mary—including the printing of a Sarum missal in 1557—but was proscribed following the accession of Elizabeth I in 1558. Priests coming to the "English mission" in subsequent decades brought with them the Roman liturgical books with which they were familiar. At the time of the restoration of the Catholic hierarchy to England and Wales in 1850 some discussion was held about the restoration of the Sarum rite, again when Westminster Cathedral was built, however in both cases the Roman rite was preferred. Sarum liturgical uses were popular with some nineteenth and twentieth century Anglicans. In modern times there have been very occasional celebrations of Mass according to the Sarum use. See: Archdale A. King, *Liturgies of the Past* (London, New York & Toronto: Longman's, Green & Co., 1959); Richard W. Pfaff, *The Liturgy in Medieval England: A History* (Cambridge: Cambridge University Press, 2009).

Scaenographia A type of drawing based on one-point perspective.

Schmemann, Alexander (1921–83) Russian by birth, Schmemann's family fled to Paris where he studied at the Orthodox Theological Institute of St Sergius before coming to St Vladimir's Orthodox Seminary in the USA in 1951 and served two decades as dean until his death in 1983. Producing works with a remarkably long shelf life, he has inspired many to re-examine the meaning of liturgical theology.

Schola (*schola cantorum*) The term for a Gregorian chant choir, from the Latin, 'school of chant'. Originally *schola cantorum* referred to clergy in the pope's retinue in Rome, this term has been expanded to include any formalized group of singers at the Mass, particularly those responsible for singing the liturgical chant. The term also originally had an architectural meaning, which is the area in front of the sanctuary where the choir sang for the liturgy in antiquity.

Schuster, Alfredo Ildefonso (1880–1954) As a Benedictine monk and, from 1918, abbot-ordinary of the abbey nullius of St Paul Outside the Walls in Rome, Schuster published the monumental work *The Sacramentary (Liber Sacramentorum) Historical & Liturgical Notes on the Roman Missal,* 5 vols (Burns, Oates & Washbourne: London, 1924–30). As cardinal archbishop of Milan from 1929 until his death, Schuster never failed to stress the centrality of the liturgical life of the Church by word or personal example. He was a zealous apostle of the Ambrosian rite and oversaw new editions of Ambrosian liturgical books. He was beatified in 1996. See: Alfredo Ildefonso Schuster, Inos Biffi (ed.), *La Sacra Liturgia: Il cuore della Chiesa orante* (Casale Monferato: Piemme, 1996).

Semiology The study of "signs" (from the Greek, "semeion"). As applied to Gregorian chant, it is the study of the ancient staffless neums. Dom Eugène Cardine (1905–88) was the first to attempt a closer reading of these manuscripts and to apply his theories to the performance of chant.

Sepulchrum In some late medieval liturgical texts of Spain, Portugal, Italy, and Hungary, this term when used in the context of Holy Thursday denotes the repository for the reservation of the Eucharist on this day (*see* Monumentum). Within the context of the *Depositio* rite of Good Friday, this term denotes the representation of the Tomb of Christ utilized for this ceremony (*see* Easter Sepulchre).

Sequence (prose) One of the proper chants for Mass, this hymn-like, poetic exposition of the subject of a particular Mass is sung immediately before the Gospel. Many medieval and neo-Gallican missals provided a wide variety of sequences for different occasions. The number of sequences in the 1570 missal of Pius V was reduced and these were reduced further still in the 1970 missal of Paul VI.

Sicard of Cremona (†1215) A gifted liturgist, historian and canonist, Sicard, Bishop of Cremona, Italy, authored one of the most important liturgical commentaries of the Middle Ages, the *Mitrale*, offering mystical interpretations of the ceremonies of Mass as well as other liturgical rites.

Society for Catholic Liturgy The Society for Catholic Liturgy was founded in the USA in 1995 by Msgr M. Francis Mannion, later founding director of the Liturgical Institute of St Mary of the Lake in Mundelein, Illinois. This multi-disciplinary association of Catholic scholars, teachers, pastors, and professionals (including musicians and architects) is committed to the scholarly study and practical renewal of the liturgy, with an emphasis on the intrinsically conservative and organic nature of the liturgy. The Society also advocates the importance of the aesthetic in liturgical renewal, especially in the areas of music, art, and architecture, so that artistic beauty and ceremonial dignity may be fostered. Its peer-reviewed journal, *Antiphon*, is published thrice yearly. Members meet annually in a general conference. Website: www.LiturgySociety.org

Square notation (*nota quadrata*) Square-shaped notation first used in twelfth-century French chant manuscripts. It became the quasi-official notation of Gregorian chant books, especially the modern books influenced by the researches of the monks of Solesmes.

Staffless neums Also known as nondiastematic or oratorical neums, in the sources they are *in campo aperto*, thus the exact pitches are not clearly represented.

Strophe The Greek word for a stanza; especially, in classical poetry, any of the irregular divisions of an ode, etc.; also stanza, verse.

Strophic Adjective used to refer to the form of a hymn, where each strophe, or stanza, is set to the same melody.

Style An expression to describe qualitative characteristics of appearance.

Summorum Pontificum The 7 July 2007 motu proprio of Benedict XVI legally establishing the right of all the faithful of the Western rite (clergy, religious, laity) to the celebration of the liturgical rites in use before the Second Vatican Council. The *mens legislatoris* of *Summorum Pontificum* may be discerned from Benedict XVI's accompanying "Letter to the Bishops" of the same date. A clarificatory Instruction, *Universae Ecclesiae*, was issued by the Pontifical Commission *Ecclesia Dei* on 30 April 2011. See: chapter 21 above.

Symmetria The method of using canons, or proportional systems, to relate the parts of a building to the whole.

Temporal The annual cycles of seasons of the liturgical year and its associated feasts (as distinct from the sanctoral). The temporal permits of less variation in the uses of the Roman rite, however there are differences between the Roman and Ambrosian temporal. Following the Second Vatican Council the observance of the pre-Lenten period that began with Septuagesima and the ancient octave of Pentecost were removed from the temporal.

Terminatio (final cadence) A distinctive melodic formula that signals the final resting place of the tone, much like the period in a sentence. Each tone has a distinctive termination, and some tones have more than one termination. The last note of the termination is not always the *finalis* of the mode. Since the psalm usually begins and ends with an antiphon, a termination is chosen which will make it possible to return smoothly to the first notes of the antiphon.

Theologia In the ascetical tradition, Evagrius identified this as the climax of three stages of growth: from *praktike* (ascetical discipline), to *physike* (a lower stage of contemplation, whose object is created things), to *theologia* (a higher stage of contemplation, whose object is the Trinity). More than "thinking about God," *theologia* involves "praying to God:" i.e. union with God in deification.

Theologia prima "Primary theology." The theology that is transacted by the Christian community in the matrix of liturgical worship.

Theologia secunda "Secondary theology," meant to be contrasted with *theologia prima*. Secondary theology is academic reflection on liturgy.

Theophoric procession An expression meaning "the transporting of God," this term in a Portuguese context denotes a solemn eucharistic procession of late medieval origin carried out on Good Friday in Braga, Portugal, to symbolize the burial of Christ, during which the Blessed Sacrament is carried on a veiled bier.

Tommasi, Giuseppe (1649–1713) Tommasi was a consulter to the Sacred Congregation of Rites who worked for the foundation of a Roman academic institute for the Liturgy and promoted good liturgical practice including the introduction of Gregorian chant into his titular church of S. Martino ai Monti during his fewer than six months as a cardinal. In his fourteen page *Breve istruzione del modo di assistere fruttuosamente al santo sacrificio della Messa, secondo lo spirito della Chiesa per le persone che non intendono la lingua latina,* first published in 1710, Tommasi set out for the simple faithful the rudiments of liturgical participation, giving a simplified vernacular version of the *Ordo Missæ* to be followed at the corresponding part of the Mass. He intended "to facilitate the most fruitful manner of assisting at Holy Mass," and encouraged responding verbally to the priest (in Latin) where this was possible. Tommasi worked towards an antiquarian breviary reform which was never promulgated. See: Alcuin Reid, *The Organic Development of the Liturgy*, 2nd edn (San Francisco: Ignatius Press, 2005), pp. 48–9.

Tonic accent The main stressed syllable of a Latin word, usually printed as a slanted line above a vowel in words of three or more syllables.

Trabeation A general term for post-and-lintel construction; the root *trabes* refers to a wooden beam.

Tra le sollecitudine *see* Pius X

Tract A proper chant in Lent, sung before the Gospel. Frequently, this is a long chant with several verses (sung by the cantor) which are generally set according to one of a pair of tonal formulae.

Transubstantiation The theological explanation given to the Catholic teaching stating that the substance of the eucharistic bread and wine is changed into Christ's Body and Blood after being consecrated by the priest, even though the qualities of the eucharistic elements perceptible to the senses remain unchanged. In 1215, the Fourth Lateran Council declared that Christ's "Body and Blood are truly contained under the appearance of bread and wine," because the elements were "transubstantiated." Using Aristotelian metaphysics, Aquinas developed the doctrine further by explaining that the elements' substance is replaced by the substance of Christ's Body and Blood at the consecratory words, while the elements' accidents, or qualities perceptible to the senses, are unaltered. In 1551, the Council of Trent responded to challenges to this doctrine as "inventions devised by impious men," and reaffirmed the doctrine of transubstantiation: "The holy council teaches and openly and plainly professes that after the consecration of bread and wine, our Lord Jesus Christ . . . is truly, really and substantially contained in the august sacrament . . . under the appearance of those sensible things" (DZ 1636). The decree asserted that this change of the elements into Christ's Body and Blood is "properly and appropriately called transubstantiation" (DZ 1642).

Trent, Council of (1545–63) A general council of the Catholic Church that met from December 1545 to March 1547, May 1551 to April 1552, and January 1562 to December 1563. In addition to reforming abuses within the Church by strengthening the jurisdiction of bishops and setting up new clerical standards in education, morality, and residence, the council rejected Protestant theology and defined Catholic doctrine. The Council declared that unwritten Tradition was of as much authority as Scripture. The council stated that there were seven sacraments, and that the sacraments conferred grace upon a recipient. It reiterated that the Mass was a propitiatory sacrifice offered for the sins, satisfactions, and punishments of the living and the dead, and that the elements of bread and wine were transubstantiated into the Body and Blood of Christ in the Mass. Baptism and Penance (after the commission of any mortal sin) were declared necessary for salvation, and the practice of infant baptism and all three stages of penance (contrition, confession, and satisfaction) were upheld. The liturgical reform ordered by the Council of Trent is studied in chapter 6, above.

Tres Abhinc Annos The Second "Instruction for the Right Application of the Constitution on the Sacred Liturgy of the Second Vatican Council," *Tres Abhinc Annos*, was prepared by the *Consilium* and issued by the Sacred Congregation of Rites on May 4, 1967. This Instruction broadens the use of the vernacular to include even the recitation of the Divine Office and the canon of the Mass, permitting the latter to be said aloud. Among other adaptations to the Mass, the communion rite is significantly altered (the "private" communion of the priest before the people is abolished), ceremonial actions and gestures are further simplified (e.g., the number of genuflections, signs of the cross, and kisses of the altar are radically reduced), and vesture prescriptions are modified (e.g., the maniple is made optional, and the chasuble is permitted in some cases where the cope was hitherto required).

Triglyphs The vertical component of a Doric frieze; Vitruvius maintains these represent the ends of wooden crossbeams that rest on the architrave over the columns.

Trope A medieval liturgical composition that constitutes an interpolated addition to a standard liturgical text, often arranged in the form of a series of antiphonal responses to each verse or phrase of the original liturgical text it amplifies, meditatively expanding upon the contents of the original text. The reform following the Council of Trent eliminated tropes from the liturgical books. In modern times they have been employed by some composers without authorisation.

Universal Prayer (Prayer of the Faithful/General Intercessions) Prayers, often in the form of a litany, for various particular needs that had fallen into disuse in the West in the Middle Ages. The solemn prayers of Good Friday and the *Oremus* said by the priest before the *offertorium* were the remnants of this practice, which is probably a development of the ancient custom of the deacon reading the names of the living and the dead to be commemorated during the canon that had been inscribed on "diptychs" of wax. The Second Vatican Council asked that the Universal Prayer be restored.

Use A liturgical "use" is a ritual tradition proper to a given place or religious order within an overall liturgical "rite," where "rite" is understood as the overarching ritual family sharing common traits (such as the Roman canon in the West). Hence, in the West one may speak of the Roman rite and its different uses (those of the religious orders and some of the patriarchal sees). One must, however, distinguish those Western patriarchal sees whose liturgical tradition is as venerable as that of Rome, which is certainly the case with the Ambrosian liturgy, which is itself a "rite" properly so-called. Variant uses of the Roman rite are, however, more commonly called "rites."

Usus antiquior A neutral, descriptive term referring to the more ancient use of the Roman rite, as distinguished from its more modern form, the right to the celebration of which by all the faithful of the Western rite was established by the 2007 motu proprio of Benedict XVI, *Summorum Pontificum*. The term itself comes from the letter of Benedict XVI accompanying *Summorum Pontificum* and is adopted in the 2011 Instruction *Universae Ecclesiae* of the Pontifical Commission *Ecclesia Dei*.

Usus recentior Whilst not originating from a pontifical document, the term *usus recentior* has emerged as a corollary to the neutral term *usus antiquior* and designates the liturgical rites promulgated following the Second Vatican Council.

Vade Mecum A small book (of prayers) that can be carried around in a large pocket or small bag.

Varietates Legitimæ On January 25, 1994, the Congregation for Divine Worship and the Discipline of the Sacraments issued the Fourth "Instruction for the Right Application of the Constitution on the Sacred Liturgy of the Second Vatican Council," *Varietates Legitimæ*. This Instruction concerns the adaptation of the Roman liturgy to local cultures, insisting (as does *Sacrosanctum Concilium*) that the process of inculturation should respect the substantial unity of the Roman rite. National and regional episcopal conferences may advance proposals regarding inculturation, such as the creation of new texts or the inclusion of indigenous traditions, subject to the approval of the Holy See.

Vatican, Second Council of the (1962–5) A general council of the Church convoked by John XXIII (1881; 1958–63) and continued after his death by Paul VI. Its first session considered the reform of the liturgy and its Constitution on the Sacred Liturgy was promulgated by Paul VI at the end of its second session. See: *Sacrosanctum Concilium*.

Verheul, Ambroos (1916–68) A Benedictine monk of the abbey of Affligem, and later the abbot of Keizersberg near Leuven. Verheul was for some time professor of liturgical studies at KU Leuven and as a follower of the "Mystery Theology" of Dom Odo Casel, endeavoured to propagate a correct understanding of the Church's liturgy. His *Inleiding tot de liturgie. Haar theologische achtergrond* (Patmos: Antwerp, 1961) was translated into English as *Introduction to the Liturgy: Towards a Theology of Worship* (London: Burns & Oates, 1968) and also into German, Italian and Spanish.

Vernacular The common language of a given people.

Vestments The liturgical clothing prescribed by the liturgical books for the sacred ministers and their assistants when carrying out their liturgical roles. The vestments worn distinguish the liturgical function and rank of the minister. The tradition of wearing particular clothing for the celebration of the Sacred Liturgy dates from approximately the sixth century. See: E.A. Roulin, *Vestments and Vesture: A Manual of Liturgical Art* (Westminster, MD: Newman Press, 1950).

Visitatio sepulchri An Easter Sunday ceremony common across northern and central Europe in the Middle Ages, this rite, known as "The Visit of the Sepulchre," constituted a liturgical dramatization of the discovery of the empty tomb on the first Easter. The *visitatio sepulchri* has been esteemed as the supreme expression of medieval drama.

Vonier, Anscar (1875–1938) Martin Vonier was one of six German boys recruited in 1888 for the monastery of St Mary at Buckfast, for which the exiled monks of La Pierre-qui-Vire (Yonne) had acquired the property. Martin arrived at Buckfast in August 1889 and, after four years in the alumnate, entered the noviciate (May 12, 1893), being given the name Anscar. He became abbot in 1906, an office he held until his death. Responding to the promotion of frequent communion by Pius X, he published *A Key to the Doctrine of the Eucharist* (London: Burns, Oates & Washbourne, 1925) in which he affirmed that all the baptized share in the priesthood of Christ. Controversial in its time, this insight was affirmed by the Second Vatican Council. Dom Anscar's point of departure for his interpretation of Aquinas is the assertion of Aquinas that "this sacrament is called sacrifice." But how is the sacrament understood to be a sacrifice? Vonier interprets Aquinas' thought thus: First there is the general principle applicable to all sacraments: What is contained in the sacrament is known through the signs that constitute the sacrament. As applied to the Eucharist the sign signifies sacrifice, and the word of consecration works sacramentally according to the power of signification. But the eucharistic sacrament contains a representation of the broken Christ on Calvary. Since the phase of Christ dead on the cross is represented realistically, we have a memorial in the sense of the representation of the real death of Christ which took place in historical time. This does not mean that Christ is immolated anew. Rather the historical immolation on Calvary is rendered present through the eucharistic Body and Blood. There is one sacrifice of Christ of which the sacrament is the representation of the natural sacrifice. The act is new, not the sacrifice.

Further reference works

The following reference works may guide further study and assist with technical vocabulary. Their scholarly assumptions should be approached critically and with regard to those prevalent at the time they were published.

Bradshaw, Paul F. (ed.), *The New SCM Dictionary of Liturgy and Worship* (London: SCM Press, 2005).

Davies, J.G. (ed.) *A Dictionary of Liturgy and Worship* (London: SCM Press, 1972).

—— *A New Dictionary of Liturgy and Worship* (London: SCM Press, 1986).

De Marco, Angelus A., *A Key to the New Liturgical Constitution: An Alphabetical Analysis* (New York, Tournai, Paris & Rome: Desclee, 1964).

Fink, P.E., SJ (ed.), *A New Dictionary of Sacramental Worship* (Dublin: Gill & Macmillan, 1990).

Jones, C., G. Wainwright, E. Yarnold SJ, & P. Bradshaw (eds) *The Study of Liturgy*, revised edn. (London & New York: SPCK & Oxford University Press, 1992).

Lercaro, Giacomo, J.B. O'Connell (ed.), *A Small Liturgical Dictionary* (London: Burns & Oates, 1959).

Podhradsky, Gerhard, *New Dictionary of Liturgy* (London: Geoffrey Chapman, 1967).

Wainwright, G. & K.B. Westerfield Tucker (eds), *The Oxford History of Christian Worship* (Oxford: Oxford University Press, 2006).

Wuest, J., T. Mullaney (trans.) & W.T. Barry (ed.), *Matters Liturgical* (New York & Cincinnati: Frederick Pustet Co., 1956).

INDEX

CPSIA information can be obtained
at www.ICGtesting.com
Printed in the USA
LVHW021949210721
693314LV00004B/48